# THE

# POSTAL HISTORY

# OF

# TRINIDAD & TOBAGO

By
**Joe Chin Aleong**
&
**Edward B. Proud**

**PROUD-BAILEY CO. LTD.**
P.O. Box 74.
Heathfield.
East Sussex.
TN21 8PZ

© 1997 Edward B Proud

ISBN 1 872465 24 2

Typeset by Carla Skinner & Cherry Smith

# CONTENTS

## BRITISH COLONIAL SERIES

The Postal History of Aden
The Postal History of Basutoland &
  Bechuanaland Protectorate
The Postal History of British Borneo.
  (Brunei, Labuan, N.Borneo & Sarawak)
The Postal History of Cyprus
The Postal History of Gambia
The Postal History of Gold Coast
The Postal History of Hong Kong
  (+ First Supplement of Hong Kong)
The Postal History of Iraq
The Postal History of Kenya
The Postal History of Malaya Volume I
  (Malacca, Penang, Singapore)

The Postal History of Malaya Volume II
  (Negri Sembilan, Pahang, Perak, Selangor.)
The Postal History of Malaya Volume III
  (Johore, Kedah, Kelantan, Perlis Trengganu)
The Postal History of Nigeria
The Postal History of Northern Rhodesia
The Postal History of Nyasaland
The Postal History of British Palestine
The Postal History of Sierra Leone
The Postal History of Southern Rhodesia
The Postal History of Swaziland and Zululand
The Postal History of Tanganyika
The Postal History of Uganda and Zanzibar

## COMMONWEALTH MILITARY SERIES

Australian Army Postal Service
British Army Postal Service Volume I
British Army Postal Service Volume II
British Army Postal Service Volume III
Naval and R.A.F. Postal Services
Canadian Army Postal Service Volume I
Canadian Army Postal Service Volume II

Canadian Army Postal Service Volume III
East African Army Postal Service
Indian Army Postal Service Volume I
Indian Army Postal Service Volume II
Indian Army Postal Service Volume III
New Zealand Military Postal Services
South African Army Postal Service

## OTHER TITLES

British Post Offices in the Far East
Postmarks of Date Impression Book Post Office Records Section 1
Postmarks of Date Impression Book Post Office Records Section 2
Postmarks of Date Impression Book Post Office Records Section 3
British Maritime Postal History Volume I
British Maritime Postal History Volume II
British Maritime Postal History Volume III
Postal History of British Airmails
Postal History of German East Africa
Postal History of the Occupation of Malaya and British Borneo 1941 - 1945
Penny Black Plates
The Post Offices of the World (except Germany) 1888

## COPIES CAN BE OBTAINED FROM THE FOLLOWING AGENTS:

R. PERRY., 673 Bourke Street, Melbourne 3000, Australia.
G.S. WEGG LTD., 53 Adelaide Street East, Toronto, Canada, M5C 1K6.
JAMES BENDON LTD., P.O. Box 6484, 3307 Limassol, Cyprus.
S. BOULE, Monaco Collections, 10 rue de la Grange Bateliere, 75009 Paris, France.
B. SCHNEIDER, Postfach 1728, D-63557, Gelnhausen, Germany.
EDIZIONI VACCARI, Via M. Buonarroti, 4641058 Vignola (Mo), Italy.
WILLIAM CARSON, P.O. Box 1836, Auckland, New Zealand.
STEPHAN WELZ & CO., P.O. Box 52431, Saxonwold 2132, South Africa.
G.ALEVIZOS, 2800 28th Street, Suite 323, Santa Monica, Calif., USA.
LT. COL. J.T. JOHNSON, P.O. Box 2178, Burlington, N.C. 27216, USA.

# FOREWORD

I was fortunate when visiting Trinidad recently in meeting Joe Chin Aleong and viewing some of his extensive collections. We both agreed that it would be ideal to combine our resources to produce this book. My co-author would very much like to thank his wife, Carol, without whose help and understanding over many years, his collections and studies would not have been possible.

We would both like to acknowledge the considerable amount of information and assistance unselfishly provided by:-

        Mr G. Buchanan
        Mr D. Druett
        (the late) R. M. Leotard
        Mr M. Hamilton
        Mr D. Horry
        Sir J. Marriott
        Mr B. Walker
        Mr R. Wike

Also the help from the following organisations:-

        Post Office Records
        Public Records Office
        Royal Commonwealth Society Library
        Foreign Office Library

I would always like to hear from anyone having additional information.

Letters to:-

        Edward B. Proud,
        P.O. Box 74,
        Heathfield,
        East Sussex.
        TN21 8PY.

# PREFACE

This book uses standard "Proud" (copyrighted) system and nomenclature for Postmarks ie.,

## DATES & DATE STAMPS

Where dates have been taken from official sources they are given in bold type. Other dates obtained from actual correspondence, etc., are given in brackets and can probably be extended. The postmarks are listed in the following order, each section having an individual code number:

| | |
|------|-------------------------------------|
| P S | pre stamp |
| K | killer obliterator |
| KD | combined killer datestamp (duplex) |
| D | datestamp |
| HS | handstamped slogans |
| M | machine postmarks |
| R | registered |
| AR | advice of receipt (avis de reception) |
| IN | insured |
| PD | paid |
| OPD | official paid |
| PM | printed matter |
| PP | parcel post |
| A | accountancy |
| EXP | express |
| DP | departure & delivery |
| UP | unpaid, postage due |
| I | instructional marks |
| AM | airmail |
| PB | postmans beat |
| SL | ships letter, paquebot |

## STANDARD ABBREVIATIONS

| | |
|--------|----------------------|
| A.O. | Already open |
| S. O. | Still open |
| S. U. | Still used |
| G.P.O. | General Post Office |
| I.U. | In use |
| N.S. | Not Seen |
| P.O. | Post Office |
| P.A. | Postal Agency |
| R.A. | Rail Agency |
| T.P.O. | Travelling Post Office |

## STANDARD ABBREVIATIONS CONT.

**D.L.O.**      Dead Letter Office
**U.P.U.**      Universal Postal Union (initially the General Postal Union)
**Tr.**         Translation
**Recon.**      Reconstruction from a partial strike
*               Reported, but not seen by author -

## POST OFFICES

Post Offices are listed alphabetically, preceded by G.P.O., with any T.P.O.s listed separately  at the end.  These are in capitals or upper case,  postal agencies are lower case.

N.B. Military and foreign offices operating in the area are not included, nor any associated sea post offices which are not under the control of the postal administration.

An attempt has been made to describe all postal markings applied to letters etc., but not labels or censor marks.

## VALUATIONS

Refer to clear examples on piece or stamp
(at least ⅔ complete.)

Refer to clear examples on complete cover or postcard.

A system of one point equal to 10p. has been used.  This being the retail price of Proud-Bailey Co. Ltd., at the time of going to press.  A minimum valuation of 20p. reflects the handling cost and fifty examples of a common mark would probably not be worth ten pounds.  Registered covers with unusual frankings etc., are worth a premium.

## N.B

It  should be emphasised that many of the postage due, instructional and airmail marks were of a standard design and used by most of the main post offices, so that they can only be identified on cover.

# CAN YOU HELP ?

Our publishing programme for the series on the Postal History of the British Colonies, which is as follows:-

**1997:-** Burma, Malta, Cyprus, British Guiana, British Honduras, Bahamas & Turks & Caicos, and Bermuda.

**1998:-** Leeward Islands, Barbados & Grenada, St. Vincent & St. Lucia, Sudan, Seychelles, B.I.O.T. Maldives, and Hong Kong Vol. II.

**1999:-** Ceylon, British Solomon Islands and Tonga, Gilbert and Ellice Islands and New Hebrides, Jamaica and Cayman Islands, Falklands and Dependencies, Ascension, St. Helena and Tristan da Cunha.

**2000:-** Aden and British Somaliland.

We are interested in hearing from any individual, study circles or organisations who could co-operate on any book; also to loan, purchase relevant material, photographs, proofs, etc.

Letters to:-

c/o Edward B. Proud
P.O. Box 74,
Heathfield
East Sussex
TN21 8PZ

# CHAPTER 1

## GENERAL HISTORY

## TOBAGO

It is generally accepted that on 13 August, 1498, on leaving the Gulf of Paria, Columbus before sailing West, first sailed East and North and sighted two islands. The first he called Assumption and which we now know as Tobago and the other he named Conception, now known as Grenada. Early sixteenth century maps refer to Tobago as Madalena and it has been surmised that this name may have been given to Tobago by Ojeda and Juan de la Cosa in 1500.

It is not known who gave the island the name which has long survived - Tobago (originally Tabaco, said to be the name given by the Caribs to their long-stemmed pipe) but the earliest reference to it that we have been able to trace is in a Cedula dated 23 December, 1511, at Burgos, in which the King of Spain gives permission to "wage war against the Caribs of the Islands of Trinidad . . . and Cabaco". In 1627, a captain Joachim Gijsz, on his way home to Holland from Brazil, visited Tobago. He found it unoccupied by Europeans and does not appear to have met any of the native inhabitants. He reported so favourably on Tobago that Jan de Moor, the Burgomaster of Flushing and a member of the State Council of Holland, decided to settle the island and obtained the exclusive right to do so from the Dutch West India Company and organised an expedition under the command of Jacob Maersz.

They arrived in Tobago in April 1628 and settled on the northern side of the western end of the island, probably near what is now Plymouth, and gave the name New Walcheren to the settlement as well as to the whole island.

In March 1629 this settlement was strengthened by the arrival of more settlers from Flushing but in the same month, Don Luis de Monsalves, the Spanish Governor of Trinidad, having learned of New Walcheren, wrote to the council of the Indies, in Spain, requesting arms and men so that he might destroy it. Realising however that it might be a long time before he had a reply, he encouraged the Caribs of Grenada and St. Vincent to join with those of Tobago to harass the Dutch settlers at New Walcheren with the effect that by early 1630, they had become so dispirited that they abandoned their settlement and sought refuge at the Dutch settlement of Kykoveral in Guayana.

In 1632, Jan de Moor sent out another expedition which also settled at New Walcheren and there they built a fort as well as a smaller one at Rocky Point. In 1936, this settlement, by then under the command of Cornelis de Moor, the son of Jan de Moor, was captured by an expedition led by Don Lopez de Escobar, then the Governor of Trinidad. In retaliation the Dutch, in October 1637, sacked and burned San Jose de Oruna.

As news of the eviction of the Dutch from Tobago spread throughout the Caribbean, a group of Puritans, from Barbados, tried to settle there, near present-day Roxborough, but eventually they were killed by the Caribs and only three of them survived by swimming to a ship offshore.

**The Capture of Tobago in the West Indies**

In 1639, Duke Jacobus of Courland, sent an expedition which settled near the site of the former Dutch settlement of New Walcheren, but in less than a year this was abandoned after most of the settlers had died from disease.

In 1628, Charles I, of Britain, had granted to the Earl of Montgomery, later of Pembroke, Letters Patent that gave him the rights to four islands including Tobago. In early 1639, the Letters Patent passed into the hands of the Earl of Warwick who, later that year, sent out an expedition to Tobago. This, and another expedition sent by Warwick in 1642, were unsuccessful, both lasting only about a year.

Duke Jacobus, sent out, in 1642, a second expedition which again had to be abandoned by 1950. Having bought from the Earl of Warwick, the Letters Patent that included Tobago, Duke Jacobus sent out a third expedition in 1654 and the settlers built Fort Jacobus near Jacobus Bay (now Great Courland Bay). In the four following years, six ships carried out additional settlers and supplies, so that by 1655, produce was being shipped back to Europe. This was the first settlement that could be said to have achieved any success.

Also in 1654, an expedition sent out by the Brothers Adriaen and Cornelis Lampsius of Flushing, settled on the south at Roodklyp, now known as Rockly Bay.

After Sweden had invaded Courland in 1658 and captured Duke Jacobus, the Dutch at Roodklyp Bay, sowed dissension among the Courlanders at Fort Jacobus with the result that the soldiers mutineered and handed over Fort Jacobus to the Dutch. In effect this was the end of the Courland adventure in Tobago.

After a treaty with Sweden in 1664, Duke Jacobus tried to have his claim to Tobago recognised and made several attempts to resettle it. After his death in 1681, his son Fredrich Casimir, also tried to resettle Tobago, but finally in 1688, the remaining settlers returned to Europe.

After establishing a settlement at Roodklyp Bay in 1654 and gaining control of the Courland settlement at Jacobus Bay in 1654 and gaining control of the Courland settlement at Jacobus Bay in 1658, the Lampsius brothers obtained a grant of Tobago from Louis XIV in 1662 and Adriaen was made Baron of Tobago. They then developed their settlement, building Dutch Fort overlooking what is now lower Scarborough, and two other forts at Black Rock and Jacobus Bay.

Towards the end of 1665 however, privateers from Jamaica captured the Dutch settlement just before a fleet under Lord Willoughby, governor of Barbados arrived there Willoughby entered into an agreement with the Jamaican privateers who handed over what they had not destroyed of the settlement to him. Willoughby sailed to attack the Dutch settlements in Guayana leaving behind a garrison at Dutch Fort.

In 1666, the French with a small force dumped re-occupied Tobago with Pieter Constant as governor. Dutch Fort was rebuilt and a new township, Lampsiusburg, founded on the site of the present lower Scarborough.

In 1672, Britain and then France declared war on Holland and towards the end of 1672 the British captured Tobago and destroyed Lampsiusburg and the Fort.

Britain withdrew from the war at the peace of Westminster in 1674, and the Dutch again occupied Tobago and rebuilt the Fort and Lampsiusburg.

In February 1677 a French Fleet under Vice Admiral Comte Jean d'Estrees started to attack the Dutch Fleet which had made its base at Roodklyp Bay in Tobago. At the end of several days of almost incredible fighting, the entire Dutch fleet of thirteen vessels under the command of Vice Admiral Jacob Binckes and half of the French Fleet had been destroyed but the French did not capture Tobago then. In December that year d'Estrees again attacked Tobago and this time Binckes was killed when Dutch Fort was blown up. By the treaty of Nymwegen in 1678, Tobago was given to the French but from then until 1748, except for a few French settlers and native Caribs and Arawaks, it was largely occupied.

By the treaty of Aix-la-Chappelle in 1748, Tobago was declared neutral but by the treaty of Paris in 1763, it was given to Britain.

George the Third on 7 October, 1763, granted Letters Patent to erect the Government of Grenada which consisted of the islands of Grenada, the Grenadines, Dominica, St. Vincent and Tobago and on the following day General Robert Melville was appointed Governor General.

In November, 1763, Commissioners for the sale of lands were appointed with Sir William Young, Bart, as Chief Commissioner. A Chief Surveyor, James Simpson was sent out in 1764.

Alexander Brown had been commissioned as Lieutenant Governor of Tobago on 11 August, 1763 but did not arrive in Tobago until 22 November, 1764 at Petit Cochon Bay (now King's Bay).

Brown and Simpson decided that the country around Petit Cochon Bay was not suitable for the seat of Government and chose instead the area at Gros Cochon Bay (now Barbados Bay). Melville approved the area when he arrived in Tobago on 28 November, 1764.

On a further visit in January, 1765, Melville decided to divide the island into seven divisions and Parishes (the still existing ones of St. Patrick, St. Andrew, St. David, St. George, St. Mary, St. John, St. Paul). It was also decided that the settlement was to be named George Town and the headland to the east of it was named Granby Point and to build there Granby Fort. Further, Rockly Bay and Courland Bay (Great Courland Bay) were to retain their names but the following were to be changed: Petit Cochon Bay to King's Bay, Carapuse to Queen's Bay, Gros Cochon Bay to Barbados Bay, Poyntz Bay to Hillsborough Bay.

In February, 1765 the land Commissioners made a tour of the island and approved the map drawn up by Simpson showing the boundaries of the Divisions and Parishes and the amount of land in each Division to be put up for auction. They again visited Tobago on 19 May, 1765, 12 May, 1766, in 1767, 1768 and 1771 and on each occasion lots of land were sold to various persons. By 1771 seventy-seven per cent of all the land in Tobago had been sold.

On a visit to Tobago in June, 1768, Melville agreed to a legislature of Tobago consisting of an upper chamber of appointed members and a lower chamber of elected members. The new legislature held its first meeting in George Town on 11 July, 1768.

Roderick Gwynne had been commissioned as Lieutenant Governor since 23 September 1767 but did not arrive in Tobago until 1769 and on 17 April, 1769, the legislature met for the first time in Scarborough and from that date replaced George Town as the principal town and capital of Tobago.

By 1770 the first shipment of sugar from Tobago was made and the Census for 1770 gave the population as 238 Whites and 3,090 Negroes with 5,084 acres of land cleared.

By 1775 the produce from Tobago was 3,700 tons of sugar, 206,052 gallons of rum, 258,031 pounds of cotton and 4,260 pounds of indigo while the population was 391 Europeans, 8,643 slaves with 17,514 acres cleared. This had been achieved in spite of slave rebellions in November 1770, 1771 and 1774.

Shortly after France signed a treaty with the United States of America on 6 February, 1778, war was declared between Britain and France.

In May 1781, the French attacked Tobago with a vastly superior force. The Lieutenant Governor George Ferguson at first refused to surrender and organised the best resistance he could with the resources at his disposal, retreating to the Cordia Hill, north of Scarborough and then to Calendonia, near the centre of the island. Only after the French started to burn the estates and threatened to burn four more every four hours, Major Henry Stanhope of the 86th Regiment refused to carry out an order and entreated by the inhabitants in the Militia, did Ferguson agree to consider terms of capitulation and the final articles of capitulation were signed on 2 June 1781.

By the Treaty of Versailles in September, 1783, Tobago remained French and gradually had to change from a captured British island to a French colony. On 5 October, 1786, Comte Dillon arrived in Tobago as Governor and Roume de St. Laurent as Ordonnateur. Scarborough was renamed Port Louis and the fortifications on Scarborough Hill became Fort Castries. On 25 February, 1788, over three hundred and fifty male inhabitants signed an Oath of Allegiance to France at Port Louis and in that same year a Colonial Assembly similar to the others in the French Antilles was instituted and the first steps were taken to introduce French laws. In the following year 1789, French coinage was introduced to replace the existing British coinage.

The French Revolution broke out on 14 July, 1789 and its repercussions did not leave Tobago untouched for Port Louis was practically destroyed by fire on 2 May, 1790. The Tricolour was raised in Port Louis on 24 February, 1791 but as an indication of the uncertain state of Tobago at this period, General Philipe de Maingot who had arrived in Tobago on 26 June, 1792 as Governor, fled to St. Vincent early in 1793.

Louis XVI was guillotined on 21 January, 1793 and France declared war on Britain on 1 February, 1793. By 12 April, 1793, acting on a letter from the Secretary of State, Henry Dundas, Major General Cornelius Cuyler and a squadron under Vice Admiral John Laforey sailed for Tobago. The troops landed at Great Courland Bay on 14 April, 1793 and marched to Mount Grace. At first, the French refused to surrender but did so after the British made a direct attack on Fort Castries. Losses were very light with eighteen killed on both sides. Cuyler immediately restored the island to its former status with a British constitution and British laws and appointed officers of the Government and members of the Council.

Tobago was formed into a separate Government with appointed Legislative Council and an elected General Assembly and on 4 January, 1794, George Rickettes arrived as Captain General and Governor in Chief.

Generally, the ten years from 1793 to 1802 under British rule were years of increasing prosperity for the planters and the merchants of Tobago with the quantity of sugar exported in 1802 almost double that in 1793. One of their greatest fears, however, came to pass when with the Treaty of Amiens on

27 March, 1802, Tobago was returned to France. Peace did not last for long for by May 1803 Britain and France were again at war and on 30 June, 1803, the British again captured Tobago.

In 1805 the "Limitation Act" was passed. The intent of this Act was to deny British capital to captured islands, like Tobago, until it was ascertained which were to be retained by Britain. Further, an Act abolishing the Slave Trade was passed in March, 1807. Finally the price of sugar had fallen by 1807 to less than half its peak in 1798 but the average yearly amount exported over the period 1803 to 1807 was practically the same as in 1799.

This combination of circumstances meant that despite all his efforts, Sir William Young, (the son of the Chief of Tobago on 18 February, 1807, could do little to improve conditions and when the Treaty of Paris was signed on 30 May, 1814, even though Tobago remained British, it was still desperately struggling to find its place in the sun.

In 1833, Major-General Henry Darling took office as Lieutenant-Governor for Tobago which then stopped being a separate government and became part of the Windward Islands Government with Barbados, Grenada and St. Vincent (and St. Lucia in 1838) and with Barbados as the seat of the Government. On 29 August, 1833 the Abolition of Slavery Act was passed and on 1 August, 1834, all slaves were emancipated and made apprentices to their former owners and stipendiary magistrates were appointed to ensure the provisions of the Act were carried out.

At Emancipation, there were 11,589 slaves in Tobago, for whom £233,875 compensation was paid. Contrary to what had been expected by many, the ex-slaves behaved with decency and restraint and many flocked to the churches in their best clothes to thank God for having delivered them from the evil that was slavery, as they did again, when, on 1 August , 1838, they obtained their complete freedom.

On the night of 11 October, 1847, a disastrous hurricane, preceded by an earthquake, struck Tobago. The last time this happened was on 10 August, 1790 and the inhabitants more or less considered themselves free from such occurrence, so that very little, if any, precautions were made. Fortunately the loss of life did not exceed seventeen, but damage was extensive and estimated at £100,000 to £150,000.

During the period of apprenticeship from 1834 to 1838 and more so after the final freeing of all slaves in 1838, there was a shortage of labour in all the British West Indies and immigration was generally believed to be the only, and certainly the most effective, way to meet the demands. Immigrants from Europe, Asia and Africa were tried in various West Indian territories but in the case of Tobago immigration was from Africa only. In 1851, Tobago received 292 liberated Africans and a further supply in 1862 of 225, both from the island of St. Helena.

In January, 1854, the garrison at Fort George or Fort King George (formerly Fort Castries) was withdrawn so that not only the troops were withdrawn from Tobago but also the large sum of money that was spent on the purchase of their wares and provisions. Immediately after, on 11 January, 1854, two Acts were passed, one to augment the Police Force and the other to form a military prison and cells into a convict prison and in 1861 the military hospital was converted into a public gaol.

On 9 February, 1855, "An Act for the Better Government of the Island" was passed. This provided for the establishment of a Privy Council and an Executive Committee. Their duties were to advise and assist the Lieutenant-Governor in the General administration of the island and in the preparation of all estimates of revenue and expenditure and they were the official means of communication between the Lieutenant-Governor and the Legislative Chambers.

On 8 June, 1860 an Act "to extend the franchise and otherwise provide for the representation of the people" was passed and on 3 July, 1871 the franchise was extended to all 5 holders.

On 14 September, 1874, the "Single Chamber Act" was passed by which the two Legislative Houses then in existence were done away with and replaced by a single Legislative Assembly consisting of six nominated members and eight elected members. The Constitution Act of 6 December, 1876 changed the constitution of the government by abolishing the Legislative Assembly and Tobago was from then on administered as a Crown Colony.

In April, 1884, the failure of one of the largest sugar estate companies, Messrs Gillepsie & Co. of London, brought about the financial collapse of the island. The firm owned at least thirteen of the operating estates and held mortgages on many of the others, and it was estimated that it controlled about eighty per cent of the produce and exports of the island.

In 1885, Barbados was made a separate colony and the other four islands formed the Windward Islands government with Grenada as seat of government and each island had its own Legislature and Administrator.

On 1 January, 1889, Tobago was united with Trinidad into the united colony of Trinidad and Tobago and Loraine G. Hay became its first Resident Commissioner.

Regrettably, union with Trinidad did not bring any improvement in the grave economic conditions of Tobago and on 1 January, 1899, Tobago became a ward of the colony of Trinidad and Tobago.

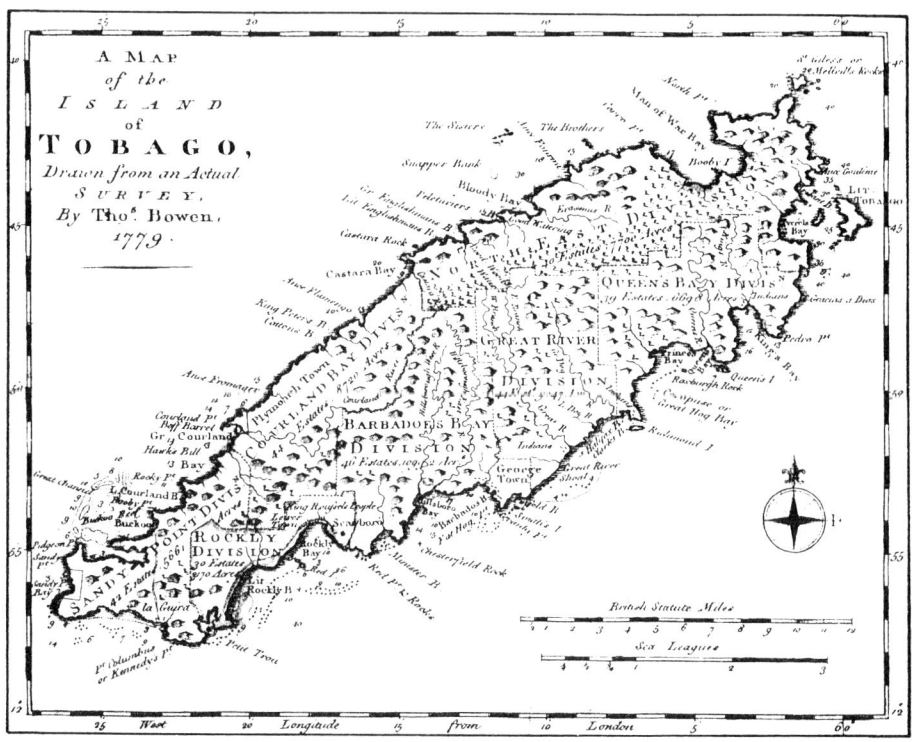

# TRINIDAD

In May, 1498, the southern half of an island known as Kairi - the Arawak word for island, was inhabited by the Arawaks with their main centre at Naparima, while the northern third was occupied by the Caribs with their main settlement at Cumucurapo. Unlike the Caribs, the Arawaks were inclined to a peaceful way of life and as they were good fishermen and hunters, they were also good swimmers and canoe builders.

On 30 May, 1498, Columbus left Spain on his third voyage having decided to set a course much further south than on his first two voyages. On 31 July, with not more than one cask of water left on each ship and most of the provisions spoilt, the personal servant of Columbus, Alonzo Perez Nizzardo, saw the summits of three hills, and in thanksgiving Columbus gave the name la Trinidad to the island of Kairi. The three hills are still known as the Trinity Hills.

The next day, the ships anchored at present-day Erin, where boats went ashore and found abundant water to fill the casks. Continuing west along the south coast, Columbus saw land away to the south-west and presuming it to be another island, named it Isla Sancta, not knowing that he was beholding for the first time the continent of which he had dreamed so much and which by one of those quirks of history is known as America.

On 3 August, a large canoe with several of the islanders approached the ships but they could not be enticed aboard with trinkets, and music and dancing had the opposite effect to that intended, for the islanders let fly a flight of arrows and paddled away.

The islanders, all young men, were light in colour and had long straight hair, wore a coarse cotton about their loins and a cotton band round their foreheads.

Columbus continued to explore the Gulf of Paria, leaving it on 13 August, 1498.

On 12 July, 1530, Antonio Sedeno was appointed Governor of Trinidad by the Queen of Spain. He left Spain on 18 September, 1530 and landed in Trinidad on 8 November, 1530. Maruana, the Cacique of the southern half of the island, helped Sedeno to build a fort, probably around present-day Erin, where they had landed, and initially, gave them supplies of food as long as he had to spare. Eventually, Sedeno had to withdraw from Trinidad to the mainland where he left some of his men while he went to Puerto Rico for help and supplies. Sedeno, in 1532, and again in 1533, tried to settle on the northern part of Trinidad, near Cumucurapo, but both attempts proved unsuccessful. Sedeno died in 1538 with the island still uncolonized.

In 1569, Juan Trejo Ponce de Leon, the son of the conquistador of Puerto Rico, also made an unsuccessful attempt to settle Trinidad.

In 1582, Antonio de Berrio was granted the right by the King of Spain to be governor of the lands he might conquer and made three attempts in 1584, 1587 and 1590 to find the fabled El Dorado starting eastward from the kingdom of new Granada. He then decided to try by going west using Trinidad as his base.

In 1952 he sent Domingo de Vera to settle Trinidad. Vera landed in Trinidad on 15 May, 1592, at Cumucurapo. He proceeded up the Caroni river and met the Cacique who gave him an area for the church, the Governor's house, the Cabildo and the prison.

Walter Raleigh reached Trinidad on 22 March, 1595, tried out the pitch at Piche or Tierra de Brea in the caulking of his ships, then went on to anchor at Peurto de los Hispanioles. He sent ashore Whiddon (who had visited Trinidad the year before) under a flag of truce. Breaking the truce, Raleigh later captured San Josephe de Oruna, freed five caciques that were imprisoned there, then sacked and burnt the fledgeling town. He also took Berrio prisoner but later released him at Comana.

Berrio, then seventy-five years old, decided to make one last attempt to find El Dorado. He sent word to his son, Fernando, in New Granada, to meet him with what men and supplies he could gather, at San Thorne de Guayana, and he, himself, with a few followers, went up the Orinoco to wait there for his son. It was not till June, 1597 that Fernando was able to reach San Thorne, just before the death of his father. The ever faithful Vera, who had heard of Berrio's ill health, reached there after his death. Vera decided to resign any claim he might have to the governorship of Trinidad and Guavana and to support Fernando's claim.

Vera, himself, died later that year at San Josephe de Oruna and Fernando de Berrio was appointed Governor of El Dorado, Guayana, Manoa and Trinidad.

Obsessed, like his father before him, with El Dorado, Fernando made several attempts to conquer Guayana and it was not until he decided to live at San Josephe de Oruna.

By then, Spain was spending what resources it could spare mainly on Mexico and Peru and Fernando found himself more or less on his own. Mainly by becoming one of the main sources of supply of tobacco for Europe, he was able to rebuild and extend San Josephe de Oruna and in 1606 purchase four hundred African slaves from the Dutch, this probably being the first significant arrival of Africans in Trinidad. The Council of the Indies could not allow Fernando to continue defying them by growing tobacco and trading with the enemy and by 1611, acting on their advice, the King of Spain ordered a residencia (enquiry) on Fernando de Berrio. As a result of the residencia, Fernando was removed as governor, initially for life, but he was re-appointed in 1618 and this was confirmed in 1620 by the King of Spain his nephew Martin de Mendoza y Berrio then was captured and taken to the slave-market at Algiers. He died before he could be ransomed, but his nephew was ransomed in 1626. Mendoza was later appointed Governor of Trinidad and Guayana in 1640, arrived in Trinidad on 30 August, 1642 and died in 1656.

On 22 May, 1624, Don Luis de Monsalves arrived in Trinidad as Governor. At that time, San Josef had only about forty or fifty Spaniards and Puerto de los Hispanioles was a collection of fishing and trading huts. He was succeeded by Cristoval de Aranda in 1632. Also in 1632, Sir Henry Colt formed a settlement at Toco, but this was destroyed by an Expedition from Margarita and Colt was captured and taken to Margarita where he and ten of his companions were tried and executed.

By June 1636 when Don Diego Lopez de Escobar arrived in Trinidad as Governor, it was the sole Spanish Colony in the Lesser Antilles.

Soon after his arrival, Escobar learned that the Dutch had established a trading post at Punta Galera and were waiting on a ship with additional men and supplies before attacking San Josef. He immediately sent to San Thorne on the Mainland and to Margarita for help.

After receiving reinforcements, Escobar divided his forces into two groups, one was to proceed to Punta Galera overland and the other, under his command, by sea, along the north coast of the island. The two groups met as planned, and the small Dutch fort was overwhelmed and ten Dutchmen were captured. The Spaniards were about to return to San Josef when a Dutch Ship appeared offshore, but realising the post had been destroyed they sailed off and headed down the east coast of the island.

Escobar followed the Dutch Ship and eventually found it anchored off a second Dutch post that had been established near the centre of the south coast (possibly near what is now Moruga). Escobar attacked and captured this second Dutch fort and took nine Dutchmen and William Gayner, until recently the Governor of Tobago, prisoners. One group of Spaniards with all prisoners was sent overland to San Josef, while a second, under Escobar and his four pirogues, followed the Dutch ship until it sailed away through one of the Bocas. Escobar then went up the Caroni and St. Joseph rivers, back to San Josef. In less than two months, Escobar had taken his men right around Trinidad in open pirogues, in three stages, destroyed two Dutch trading posts and braved the presence of an armed vessel.

In November, 1636, Escobar decided to attack the Dutch settlement in Tobago and set out with a force of ninety men in eight pirogues. They captured a small fort at Rockly point and then later obtained the surrender of the main fort. The Dutch Governor, Cornelis de Moor (who had recently replaced William Gayner) surrendered his commission from the Prince of Orange. All prisoners were promised help in going to St. Christopher or returning to Holland. After destroying the fort and all other buildings, Escobar returned to Trinidad with the prisoners and spoils of war.

Unable to keep all the prisoners in Trinidad, he sent fifty-three of them and nineteen Dutch boys to Margarita. In spite of the promise made to them by Escobar, the fifty-three prisoners were executed.

On 22 July, 1637, the Dutch attacked and burnt San Thome. Escobar managed to escape and Cornelis de Moor regained his freedom. Later, on 14 October, 1637, the Dutch, with the help of Hyarima, the Chieftain of the Nepuyos, captured and burnt San Josef. Escobar was replaced as Governor by Mendoza in 1640.

On 29 April, 1687, a Royal Cedula established a new Mission of Capuchins in Trinidad and Guayana and ten Capuchin Fathers and Brothers left Spain on 20 June, 1687 with Don Sebastian de Roteta as Governor. They were joined by two other Capuchins from Cumana.

Initially, three "encomiendas" (plantations where converted Indians lived and worked) were established at Aricagua (San Juan), Tacarigua and Arauca (Arouca). Later in 1687, Missions were established at Savanna Grande (Princes Town), Naparima (San Fernando), Savaneta (Couva) and Monserrat. In 1688 a fifth Mission was established at Arena and later others at Mayaro, Guayaguayare and Moruga.

The Missions were, in fact, agricultural colonies. Cocoa had been found in the island in 1617 and became the staple crop but provisions and other short crops were also cultivated.

On 1 December, 1699, the Indians massacred two Capuchin Fathers and one Brother and then killed the Governor Don Jose de Leon y Echales and his party who were on their way to visit the Mission at Arena. One member of the party managed to escape and raised the alarm. The Indians fled to The Cocal but were followed and about twenty were killed, the rest dispersed but finally eighty-four were captured and taken to San Josef where their trial began on 6 January, 1700. Twenty-two of the men above the age of fourteen years were condemned to death and hanged. The women and children were given to Spanish inhabitants as servants.

A Royal Edict of 15 August, 1708, converted the Missions in Trinidad into missions of doctrine and the Indians were allowed to work for the planters. The Edict also declared the work of the Capuchins in Trinidad to be completed and called on them to go to Guayana and found new missions there.

By 1716, Trinidad was prospering due to its agricultural produce, especially its cocoa as its quality was considered to be superior to that produced elsewhere, and there was no regular trading with Spain. But in 1725, the prosperity of the planters vanished when the cocoa industry was destroyed by a "blast" and the commerce of the Island was crippled. Complete ruin soon followed and many of the colonists fled to the Mainland. San Josef was abandoned by most of its inhabitants except for a few officials.

In 1739 just when the island was improving with the revival of its agriculture, small pox decimated the population, especially the Indians. Also, 1743 saw the start of a long dispute between the Cabildo and successive Governors so that by 1751 the prosperity of the Island was at its lowest ebb. In 1757, the new Governor, Colonel Don Pedro de la Moneda was unable to find suitable accommodation in San Josef and established his residence at Puerto de Espana, then a village of about four hundred inhabitants.

The rebirth of the cultivation of cocoa again became the principal crop of the island.

On September, 1776, Charles III issued a Cedula de Poblacion (Decree of Population) granting not only Spaniards, but also foreigners, the right to settle in Spanish Colonies and to receive grants of lands on easy terms. On 30 December 1776, Don Manuel Falquez assumed duties as Governor. In 1777, Charles III ordered that an infantry regiment be stationed at Puerta de Espana and he placed the troops under Falquez as Military Governor, while Don Martin de Salaverria was appointed Civil Governor. On 8 September, 1777 he decreed that Trinidad should be placed under the Vice-Royalty of Caracas.

Soon after his arrival in Trinidad, Falquez had the Decree of Population translated into French and English and circulated throughout the Caribbean. As a result, in May 1777, a French planter of Grenada, Phillipe-Rose Roume de Saint-Laurent, visited Trinidad and was very impressed by its agricultural possibilities and its excellent geographical position for the development of trade. St. Laurent acquired in his wife's name Ariapita Estate on the western outskirts of Puerta de Espana an in 1779, visited Caracas and submitted to the Spanish authorities there a scheme for the colonisation of Trinidad. His proposals met with approval and he was authorised to visit neighbouring islands and invite qualified persons to migrate to Trinidad. As a result a number of French and a few Irish settled in Trinidad.

In 1783, St. Laurent went to Madrid and so convinced the authorities there that his scheme of colonisation would work that on 24 November, 1783, a new Decree of Population was issued.

As well as other benefits, the new decree granted 32 acres of land to each member of a white family and an additional 16 acres for each slave they possessed. People of colour and free negroes were allowed 16 acres for each person and 8 acres for each slave. The sole restrictions were that the immigrants were to profess the Roman Catholic Faith and to take the oath of allegiance to the King of Spain.

In 1784, the Cabildo decided to move to Puerto de Espana and held its first meeting there on 20 August. Also in 1784, Don Jose Maria Chacon took up his appointment as Governor of Trinidad.

The Cedula of 24 November, 1783, gave the first real impetus to the development of Trinidad. In a very short time there was a great influx of foreigners settling in the Island, mainly French but also some Irish and English. By 1789, six years after the publishing of the Cedula, the total population was 18,918, of which 2,151 were Europeans, 4,467 free coloured people, 2,200 Indians and 10,100 African slaves. The majority of the new settlers had come from Grenada which was in French occupation from 1779 to 1783 when it reverted to Britain by the treaty of Versailles. Trinidad was then a Spanish colony but the society was dominated by the French.

The Cedula of 1783 also resulted in the development of the sugar industry as the majority of the new settlers were already familiar with the growing of sugar cane and by 1793 sugar had become the staple product and remained so for more than a century.

On 3 January, 1787, Chacon made public his policy for the control and development of Trinidad. He divided the Island into three divisions, each consisting of a number of quarters, and each under a Commissary. Among his many improvements, he diverted the Rio Santa Ana (Dry River), established the village of San Juan, founded the town of San Fernando, reorganised the Cabildo. Generally, the people of the Island came to admire him and appreciate his sterling qualities so that on 13 April, 1788, a universal petition was sent to Spain requesting that his term of office be extended for a further five years.

Spain declared war on Britain on 5 October, 1796. In February 1797, a Spanish squadron of five ships under Admiral Don Sebastian Ruiz de Apodaca, was at Trinidad, anchored in Chaguaramas Bay, under the protection of guns and mortars at the eastern end of Gaspar Grande Island. But a fever (malaria) had swept through the crews so that their strength was greatly reduced. The British Fleet had assembled at Carriacou in the Grenadines and sailed for Trinidad on 15 February, 1797.

The British Fleet consisted of 9 Ships of War, 3 Frigates, 7 Corvettes, 1 Bomb Ketch and 40 Transports with a total land force of 6,750. Chacon had the five ships of Apodaca's squadron and a total land force of 634.

Early in the morning of 17 February, 1797, the western sky was lit up by flames and explosion after explosion was heard. Later that morning Apodaca arrived at Puerto de Espana and reported to Chacon that, after a Council of War of his senior officers, they had unanimously agreed to burn ships after spiking their guns, rather than letting them fall into the hands of the invaders.

As soon as the British were satisfied that the Spanish squadron no longer existed, the troops were landed at a place still known today as Invaders Bay and except for a skirmish at St. James advanced and took up positions on spurs of the La Ventine Hills overlooking the town. Chacon had sent out messengers in all directions in an attempt to rally the people in a last stand against the British, but when he went to the place of rendevous, he found himself alone except for Apodaca and his personal staff.

Later that night, Chacon accepted the offer of Lt.-General Sir Ralph Abercromby to surrender and at a conference the next morning, the terms were agreed by Chacon, Abercromby and Rear Admiral Henry Harvey and Trinidad became a British possession. The casualties were one British officer and seven Spanish soldiers.

About two months after the Capitulation, Abercromby left Trinidad and appointed as Governor his Aide-de-Camp, Lt.-Colonel Thomas Picton. On 17 April, 1797, Chacon, Apodaca and officers were sent to Spain and on arrival they were placed under arrest. On 8

August, the King decided that a Council of War (Court Martial) should examine the conduct of Chacon and Apodaca. The Report of the Council was submitted on 26 May, 1798, and acquitted both Chacon and Apodaca. This angered the French Republicans in Trinidad and they drew up a memorial which was presented in Paris to Napoleon who was the First Counsul at a time when France had come to control the affairs of Spain. The result was that on 20 March, 1801, the acquittal by the Council of War, was reversed by the King of Spain and both were stripped of their posts and Chacon was banished. Apodaca received a pardon on 7 July, 1809 but Chacon went into exile in Portugal and lived there for many years in poverty. Long after the fall of Napoleon and with the return of Ferdinand VII to Spain, Chacon was pardoned but by then was on his death-bed.

In August, 1797, when all those who were willing to take the oath of allegiance to the King of Great Britain had left, the total population was 17,643 made up by 2,086 Europeans, 4,466 Free Coloured, 1,082 Indians and 10,009 African slaves. By 1802, the produce and commerce of the island had increased as well as improvements in the roads and internal communications.

By the treaty of Amiens of 26 March, 1802, Trinidad was ceded to Great Britain and by letter of 5 July, 1802, Picton was informed that the Government of the Island was to be placed in Commission.

The three Commissioners were Colonel Willliam Fullarton, Senior Commissioner and Chairman, Civil; Brigadier-General Thomas Picton, Junior Commissioner, Military and Commodore Samuel Hood, Junior Commissioner, Naval.

Fullarton arrived in Trinidad on 3 January, 1803 and before Hood did so on the 22 February, 1803, there had already been signs of friction between Fullarton and Picton. Picton, from 1797 to 1802, had been firm, unrelenting and at times, excessively harsh. Fullarton visited the gaol late in January, 1803 and saw, probably for the first time, the horror and evil of slavery, for then the gaol in Trinidad had the reputation of being the worst in the West Indies, Fullarton also found out about the widespread practice of "Jusqu'a nouvel ordre" by which free-coloureds and slaves were imprisoned and punished until further orders, without being charged or without any indication of the offence. On investigation, Fullarton found out that at least twenty-four persons had suffered death, torture or mutilation at the command of Picton and many more had been deported and exiled.

For some reason, Hood came to dislike Fullarton personally and sided with Picton almost without question, to oppose all that Fullarton was trying to do. Fortunately for Trinidad, the Commissioners were relieved of their duties by letter of 20 May, 1803 and on 20 July, 1803, Brigadier-General Thomas Hislop arrived to take over from Fullarton as Lieutenant-Governor.

Arriving back in England, Fullarton caused a list of charges against Picton to be referred to the Privy Council. On his arrival in England in October, 1803, Picton was arrested by order of the Privy Council. At his first trial in January, 1806, Picton was found guilty of ordering the torture of Louisa Calderon. A retrial was obtained but did not take place until June, 1808 after Fullarton had died in February, 1808. The final verdict was not given until 1910 and it neither condemned nor acquitted Picton.

In October, 1806, 192 Chinese immigrants arrived in Trinidad and most of them decided to work on plantations on Government terms while a few preferred to be independent and work on a small rented estate. By July 1807, about forty of them had applied to return home and eventually the experiment proved to be a failure.

By the Abolition Act, all trading in African slaves was abolished from 1 January, 1808.

On the night of 24 March, 1808, a disastrous fire spread through Port of Spain and twelve blocks were entirely burnt out and nine were partially destroyed. Damage was estimated at 3,500,000 dollars and the British Government voted £50,000 for immediate relief.

On 14 June, 1813, Sir Ralph James Woodford, became Governor of Trinidad in his 29th year and his powers as Governor were detailed in his Commission. Spanish Law would continue to be the law of Trinidad and all powers of the Executive were to be vested in the Governor.

In 1813, the large majority of the free inhabitants were Roman Catholic. Woodford, a Protestant, found himself Royal Vice-Patron of the Roman Catholic Church as well as head of the Established Church of England. In 1818, the Vatican made Trinidad and the other British West Indian territories into a separate Vicariate-apostolic. In 1819, Bishop James Buckley was appointed Vicar-Apostolic and decided to reside in Trinidad. Woodford, on learning this, provided him with a fitting residence and also had it furnished.

Previously, on 25 March, 1816, Woodford had laid the foundation stone of the still standing Roman Catholic Cathedral and on 18 March, 1815, he had laid the foundation stone of the present Catholic Church at St. Joseph, as the original one had fallen into a very bad state of disrepair. Woodford also laid the foundation stone of the Protestant Trinity Church (later Cathedral) on 30 May, 1816. The plans for both cathedrals were drawn up by Woodford's Secretary, Philip Reinagle who was also an architect.

Woodford also took steps to strengthen the Trinidad Militia and to improve and beautify Port of Spain. He had also been trying to find a suitable site for an official residence and in 1817, arranged for the purchase of Paradise Estate, now the Queen's Park Savannah. In 1819, land to the north was purchased and this became the site of the Botanic Gardens and Government House. Woodford was responsible for the laying out of the Botanic Gardens and appointed David Lockhart as curator. Lockhart, on several occasions, visited St. Vincent, where the first Botanic Gardens in the West Indies had been established in 1763, in order to obtain plants from there.

Woodford was also responsible for improvements in the education and health services and improving conditions of the Indians, most of whom then lived in Arima.

Woodford died on his way back to England in May, 1828 and he had done so much to improve social and economic conditions in Trinidad that a grateful population subscribed to the cost of erecting two memorials to him in both cathedrals in Port of Spain.

On 27 December, 1831 the Council was re-constituted into a Legislative Council with the Governor as President and six Official and six non-Official members. There were no elected representatives and Trinidad remained governed through the Colonial Office in London.

On 28 August, 1833, the Abolition of Slavery Act was passed by which, from 1 August, 1834, slavery was abolished and all former slaves were to be apprenticed, field hands for six years and all others for four years. Special justices (stipendary magistrates) were to be appointed to see that the provisions of the act were properly carried out. Apprenticeship was eventually reduced to four years for all, so that on 1 August, 1838, at long-last, absolute freedom was obtained by all slaves.

At Emancipation in Trinidad, there were 20,687 slaves for whom compensation of £1,033,992 was paid.

On 15 July, 1834, forty-four Portuguese from Fayal (Azores) arrived as indentured labourers and were put to work on an estate at Las Cuevas but this first attempt to solve the problem of the shortage of labour by indentured labourers was a dismal failure.

Colonel Sir Henry MacLeod was sworn in as Lieutenant-Governor of Trinidad on 13 April, 1840. Soon after, with the agreement of the Cabildo, he changed it to the Town Council of Port of Spain.

On 22 July, 1844, the Criminal Ordinance was proclaimed, finally bringing the criminal laws of England to Trinidad and on 10 December, 1844, the first trial by jury took place in Trinidad.

The foundation stone of the Government Offices (now known as the Red House) was laid by McLeod on 15 January, 1844. The building was designed by Richard Bridgens, the head of the Public Works Department.

The problem of the shortage of labour was not solved by attempts with European immigrants and free Africans from Sierra Leone. In 1838, the first hill coolies had been brought from India to Br. Guiana, but charges of ill-treatment caused the British Government to suspend such emigration. In 1884 the Government of India repealed the prohibition of emigration to the West Indies and on 30 May, 1845, 225 Indians arrived at Port of Spain as indentured labourers. This was the beginning of East Indian emigration to Trinidad which was to continue every year until 1917 except for 1849, 1850 and 1916 and over the period there were a total of 141,615 emigrants.

In an effort to arrest the decline in cocoa, permission was given to import labourers from Madeira to work on the cocoa estates. On 9 May, 1846, the first set of 219 Portuguese from Madeira arrived, followed by another group of 179, on 16 December, 1846.

The *Lady McLeod*, a three masted paddle steamer owned by John Lamont and then by David Bryce, arrived in Trinidad on 23 October, 1845, under her own power. On 18 April, 1847 the following notice appeared in the *Port of Spain Gazette*: The Subscriber experiencing difficulty in collecting money for letters of Non-Subscribers has procured Labels, which may be had of him or the Agents for the Steamer, at five cents each, or Four Dollars per hundred. No other Letters but of those subscribers who have paid in advance, or such as have labels attached, will be carried, from and after the 24th instant. Freight for parcels and small packages as heretofore. David Bryce, Proprietor.

On 29 April, 1846, Lord Harris was sworn in as Lieutenant-Governor and on 28 December, 1846 was commissioned Governor and Commander-in-Chief.

Late in 1846, Harris drew up a plan to change the division of the island from the old Spanish quarters and their Commandmants into North and South Divisions each consisting of eight counties. Each county, in turn, was to be divided into a number of wards under the charge of a Warden. The plan was finally implemented in 1849.

Due to many complaints, East Indian emigration was suspended in 1849, and the sugar planters began to urge Government to import Chinese workers. Finally, in 1853, a total of 998 Chinese workers arrived in Trinidad. They were under the same terms as the indentured East Indians but were not entitled to a free return passage. After three years, 250 of them were able to end their indentureship by saving and trading and successful gambling. One of the major cultural contributions made by them was the introduction of the gambling game known as "Play Whe" and operated by the Government National Lotteries Board.

Among the improvements for which Harris was responsible were those of the Police Force by the Police Ordinance of 1849, and the Education system by the Education Ordinance of 1851. He was also responsible for the Inland Post which was started on 14 August, 1851.

On 2 June, 1857, the Coolie Orphan House was opened at Tacarigua to care for those East Indian children whose parents had died on the journey to Trinidad. In November, 1876, the orphanage became an industrial school for children of all races and is still known as "The Tacarigua Orphanage".

On 11 April, 1859, the Queen's Collegiate School was opened and it was eventually replaced by Queen's Royal College on 3 June, 1870.

The College of the Immaculate Conception (St. Mary's College), staffed by Fathers of the Congregation of the Holy Ghost, was founded on 1 August, 1863.

The Marriage Ordinance passed on 1 August, 1863, contained many clauses that were offensive to the Roman Catholics and caused much protest. It was not until an amending ordinance was passed in June, 1865, when the Hon. J.H.T. Manners-Sutton was Governor, that the Catholics were satisfied and when Manners-Sutton left Trinidad on 20 April, 1866, after a short term as Governor, the Catholics and Protestants were in a reasonable state of compromise.

The Hon. Arthur Hamilton Gordon arrived in Trinidad on 7 November, 1866, to assume the office of Governor. Soon after his arrival he travelled extensively around the island and saw the deplorable condition of the roads. The first major work undertaken was the extension of the Eastern Main Road to Arima and beyond so that by 1870 it had reached Valencia and later Manzanilla. At the same time existing roads were being improved and iron bridges were replacing old wooden ones.

Gordon decided not to fix a lower limit on the size of lots of Crown Lands to be sold and also reduced the price by half to £1 an acre. This enabled many planters to own their own cocoa estates especially in the Montserrat area in the Central Range.

The Leper Asylum at Cocorite had been opened on 12 May, 1845 but had become run-down. On the suggestion of Gordon, Archbishop Gonin of Port of Spain persuaded Dominican Sisters from France to run the Leprosarium and the first five Sisters arrived on 26 March, 1868. Remarkably, a petition signed by 600 Protestants, including their Archdeacon, was submitted to Gordon, objecting to the Sisters. In 1922, the Leprosarium was transferred to Chacachacare and the Dominican Sisters continued to care for the patients there until October, 1950.

In 1867, Gordon recommended to the Colonial Office that a thorough examination of the education system in Trinidad should be carried out. As a result, Patrick Keenan, an Inspector of National Schools in Ireland, began his investigation in February, 1869, not without grumblings from the Protestants who complained that Keenan was a Catholic. As a result of the Keenan report, a new Education Ordinance was passed on 27 April, 1870.

On 17 May, 1870, construction began on the line from Port of Spain to Arima of the Trinidad Government Railways. The first trip was made on 31 August, 1876. In 1880 a line linked St. Joseph with Couva and the extension to San Fernando was opened on 17 April, 1882. An extension from Jerningham Junction to Tabaquite. On 14 November, 1913, the extension of the line from San Fernando to Siparia was opened and in 1914, the extension from Tabaquite to Rio Claro. The Railways were still running in 1962 but the decision was made in that year to abandon them.

In 1870, the Church of England was disestablished and gradually the grant to the Church of England was reduced and that of the Catholics increased until the grants were in proportion to the numbers in the two religions. Aid was granted to all denominational schools and gradually, there was a cessation of former religious quarrels.

The Princes Albert and George, sons of H.R.H. the Prince of Wales arrived on a visit to Trinidad on 7 January, 1880. Among other places, they visited the Mission at Savanna Grande, which was renamed Princes Town in their honour.

On 17 August, 1887, Arima was made a Royal Borough, the first and only town in the British West Indies to be so honoured.

From 1 January, 1899, Tobago became a ward of the colony of Trinidad and Tobago.

By 1884, sugar produced in the British Colonies faced severe competition from European beet sugar which was entitled to a bounty from European governments when exported. The result was that cane sugar could hardly compete with beet sugar in the British market. The situation worsened by 1895 when bounties were increased but fortunately the United States of America imposed countervailing duties on bounty beet sugar imports so that by 1900 nearly three-quarters of British West Indian sugar was sold in the U.S.A. In 1902 the bounty on beet sugar exports was stopped, enabling cane sugar to recover somewhat.

In 1900, cocoa and sugar still accounted for more than half of the total exports from agricultural Trinidad.

Cocoa and sugar continued to be the main agricultural products of the economy until the emergence of the oil industry. The cocoa industry continued to prosper till 1920 when there was a tremendous drop in prices. There was a recovery in 1924 but prices again began to fall and by 1933, had fallen to their lowest point. Cocoa never regained the prominence it held between 1890 to 1920 when it was the backbone of the prosperity of many French creole planters.

The sugar industry continued to prosper largely because of the indentured East Indians. Gradually, however, as their indentures expired and they were able to obtain ten acres of Crown lands in exchange for their right to a free return passage to India, they became small holders growing mainly cash food crops and began to establish themselves in society. Eventually, by hard work, saving and a frugal way of life, they were able to educate their children in professions and firmly establish themselves in Trinidad.

With the decline of sugar prices from 1920 to their lowest point in 1930 and a similar pattern in cocoa, labourers were laid off and wages reduced. This led to mass demonstrations by sugar workers in 1934, followed by oil workers in 1935 and eventually to strikes and riots in June 1937. One result of the 1937 riots was the emergence of a Trade Union movement on British lines.

The place where the Pitch Lake is located was called Piche and by the Spaniards Tierra de Brea. It was not until about 1850, however, that definite uses for the pitch were suggested by the Earl of Dundonald. In 1888, J. W. Previte and A. L. Barber obtained a lease for the whole lake for twenty-one years but in 1898, The New Trinidad Lake Asphalt Co., Ltd. was formed to operate the concession.

In 1949 a new company The Trinidad Lake Asphalt Co., Ltd. was incorporated and was granted a new lease of the Pitch Lake in 1950 for thirty years. The production of crude asphalt, in selected years, was as follows:

| | |
|---|---|
| 1918 | 71,233 tons |
| 1922 | 182,655 tons |
| 1929 | 219,603 tons |
| 1933 | 111,337 tons |

An attempt to obtain oil in Trinidad was made by the Merrimac Company between 1857 and 1859. Other attempts to find oil by drilling were made in 1866 in San Fernando and Aripero and in 1867 at La Brea. The well at Aripero, drilled by Walter Darwent, produced oil but not in commercial quantities. Around 1900, Randolph Rust and John Lee Lum joined forces to explore for oil. They brought Aripero Estate and had estates at Guayaguayare. The first well drilled at Guayaguayare produced oil in July 1902. What could be called the first commercial oil well was drilled at Guapo in 1907 by the Trinidad Petroleum Company and in 1909 the first exports of oil by tanker were made. By 1919, oil accounted for ten percent of Trinidad's exports, fifty percent by 1932 and eighty percent by 1943.

In 1924, a Bill was passed to allow a mixed Legislative Council of seven elected, six nominated, and twelve Official members and the Governor. On 31 December, 1924, the existing Legislative Council was dissolved and for the first time, elections (with a very limited franchise) were held on 17 January, and 7 February, 1925. The second elections were held on 21 January, 1928. Not until 1946 were elections held under universal adult suffrage.

The Second World War had a major impact on the development of Trinidad which then produced about sixty percent of the oil production of the Br. Empire and which was the convoy assembly point for tankers carrying oil across the Atlantic. The Government used it as an excuse to stifle labour protest and the labour leader, Tubal Uriah Buzz Butler was imprisoned from November 1939 to April, 1945. On the other hand, under the "bases for old U.S.A. destroyers" deal, the Americans were leased large areas at Chaguaramas for a naval base and at Wallerfield for an air base. Construction of these bases and other infrastructure works, gave employment to many at high wages.

In the 1956 elections, the newly formed People's National Movement led by Eric Williams, won thirteen out of all the twenty-four seats, with 39 per cent of the votes, but did not have a majority of all the thirty-one members when the nominated members were counted in. The then Governor Beetham persuaded the Colonial Office to let the P.N.M. form the government and Williams became the chief minister.

Various opposition groups formed the democratic Labour Party in 1957 and by early 1958, Badase Sagan Maraj was elected its leader. The D.L.P. won the Federation of the West Indies elections later in 1958 and this set the stage for the general elections of 1961 and full internal self-government. This was a bitterly fought election, mainly on racial lines, and then the P.N.M. was not well known, as it was to become later, for its corruption and nepotism. With some gerrymandering, the P.N.M. won the election and then led Trinidad to Independence on 31 August, 1962, with Solomon Hochoy as Governor-General, Eric William as Prime Minister, and Rudrinath Capildeo as Leader of the Opposition.

# CHAPTER 2

## POSTAL HISTORY

## TOBAGO

The Island was not mentioned as being served by the British Packet Services until its capture from the French in April 1793. Although there is a reference in the Walsingham Papers (1788) that mail for Tobago (then French) is forwarded via Barbados

After the occupation of Tobago a proposal was made for that Island to become the distributing centre for the West Indies instead of Barbados. The proposal was referred to a committee of Packet Captains who reported on 14 September 1793:-

"......We beg leave to observe that the Packets ought to Rendezvous at Barbados instead of Tobago, in as much as the Packet can always reach Tobago from Barbados with a common Trade Wind but cannot reach Barbados from Tobago in the Winter Months owing to the strong North West currents which prevail there in that Season of the year.

We are also of opinion that the Packet from England of the schooner should proceed from Barbados to Tobago, St. Vincent, Grenada and St. Kitts; and the other to Dominica, Antigua, Montserrat, Nevis and St. Kitts.

"From Barbadoes to Tobago is one days sail      Should remain there two days
Thence to St. Vincent one days sail      Should remain there two days
Thence to Grenada one days sail      Should remain there two days
Thence to St. Kitts or Nevis four days sail.
The Packet from England or Schooner should
remain at Barbados two days and thence
proceed to Dominica which is two days sail      Should remain there two days
Thence to Antigua two days sail      Should remain there two days
Thence to Montserrat 12 hours      Should remain there 24 hours
Thence to Nevis and St. Kitts 12 hours."

A letter from the Admiralty to the Postmaster General states on 24 September 1793, regarding Correspondence between this Country and the Island of Tobago:-

"I am to acquaint your Lordships that the best method of carrying that service into Execution appears to be that a Packet or Schooner of such Burthen only as shall be found necessary should be contracted for at an Expense within or at most not exceeding 550 per Annum, to convey the Government Dispatches and the general correspondence to and from Tobago and Barbados, and that in order the better to secure the collection of of the additional Revenue to arise from the Conveyance of all letters to and from Tobago it will be proper that the vessel be under the direction of the Postmaster General. I am therefore commanded to signify your Lordships His Majesty's pleasure that you do *cause a proper Vessel to be engaged to pass between Tobago and Barbados and to meet the homeward bound Leeward Island Packet at St. Kitts or elsewhere for the Performance of the beforementioned service, and that the additional Revenue from the Postage of letters together with any sums to be raised by the conveyance of passengers (both of which will be closely regulated by your Lordships) if not sufficient to defray the whole Expense of the intended Packet shall be applied towards the discharge thereof, and the deficiency be paid to the Postmaster General by the Lords of the Treasury.*

*Should your Lordships think it is proper to communicate with the Governor Ricketts on this subject previous to his departure you will of course desire his attendance for that purpose."*

In reply the Postmaster General (Mr Collins) stated:

*".....our Captains have suggested to us that the Leeward Island Schooner may take the Tobago Mail and yet be in time to meet the Packet at St. Kitts. We send you a copy of their letter to us on the occasion.*

*We have referred the letter to the Meeting of West India Merchants and Planters for their opinion that We may be adopting it too hastily hazzard any infringement upon the present excellent Plan of an exact Co-operation in point of Time, but if it can be done as our Captains suggest it will save the third Schooner which by your letter of September 24 you propose to us to engage. We will consult Governor Ricketts and other proper persons where the third Schooner which you propose for us, if it is taken, is to fall in with the Packet homeward bound.*

*The sums which may be received by Postage will of course go to this Revenue and the Lords of the Treasury shall be applied to authorise us to incur the additional Expense of 550 per Annum for the third additional Packet if it is employed."*

Actually a further schooner was put into service from Barbados to Tobago, from which Island it proceeded to St. Kitts to meet the homeward bound Leeward Island Packet.

On 27 March 1794 Charles A Francklyn was appointed Deputy Postmaster General. The packet service was not regular as can be seen from a letter that Joseph Robley (Tobago) wrote to Henry Dundas (11 September 1794):-

*"The first July mail for Tobago being still detained at Barbados, I have not had the honour to receive from you any letter of a later date than 11 June. The delay of the Tobago mail at Barbados is a very great grievance to the Colony, not only to individuals, but to the public service and the more especially in this turbulent times: it would afford the community of this Island great relief if you would be pleased to remedy this evil by placing this Colony on the same footing as His Majesty's other islands that it may receive the mails regularly twice a Month."*

The Governor of Barbados took up the question, and his unremitting efforts to procure for Tobago a fair and proportionate share of the advantage of Packets was successful, and in 1796 Tobago was provided with three vessels attached to the Post Office.

During the Napoleonic Wars many Post Office Packets were captured as shown in the following list:-

| Packet | Captured by | Date Captured |
|---|---|---|
| Arab | Insurgent French Frigate | 24. 12. 93 |
| King George | French Frigate | 14. 7. 94 |
| Expedition | French Frigate | 23. 4. 94 |
| Antelope | Squadron of French Frigates | 19. 9. 94 |
| Thynne | Squadron of French Frigates | 23. 9. 94 |
| Queen Charlotte | French Frigate | 19. 1. 95 |
| Tankerville | French Privateer | 10. 2. 95 |
| Prince William Henry | Vengence Privateer | 7. 4. 95 |
| Tartar | French Privateer | 10. 6. 95 |
| Princess Brunswick | French Privateer | 17. 8. 96 |
| Active | French Privateer | 30. 9. 96 |
| Duchess of York | Detained at Corunna | Oct. 1796 |
| Princess Elizabeth | French Privateer, "Actif" | 28. 2. 97 |
| Swallow | French Privateer | 28. 3. 97 |
| Sandwich (Was carrying the Mails of 15 February and 1 March). | French Privateer, "Dugay" | 10. 3. 97 |
| Countess of Leicester | French Frigate | Dec. 1797 |
| Grantham | French Privateer | 2. 7. 97 |
| Prince Ernest | French Privateer | 11. 1. 98 |
| Portland | French Privateer | 9. 2. 98 |
| Schooner "Start" | French Privateer "Democrat" | 30. 7. 98 |
| Prince Edward | French Privateer | 25. 10. 98 |
| Duke of York | French Privateer | 11. 12. 98 |
| Princess Royal | | Mar. 1795 |

| Packet | Captured by | Date Captured |
|---|---|---|
| Carteret | French Privateer "Bellona" | July 1797 |
| Countess of Leicester | | Dec. 1797 |
| Roebuck | French Privateer "La Liberale" | Mar. 1798 |
| Swallow | French Privateer "La Liberale" | Mar. 1798 |
| Prince Adolphus | | June 1798 |
| Carteret | | Mar. 1799 |
| Chesterfield | | Apr. 1799 |
| Halifax | "Vengeance" | Nov. 1799 |
| Lady Harriott | | Mar. 1799 |
| Westmoreland | Privateer | Dec. 1799 |
| Adelphi | French Privateer "Grande Buonaparte" | Dec. 1799 |
| Princess Royal | French Privateer "Courier" | Feb. 1800 |
| Princess Charlotte | | May. 1800 |
| Princess Amelia | | May. 1800 |
| Duke of Clarence | | Dec. 1800 |
| Earl Gower | French Privateer "Telegraphe" | June. 1801 |
| Lady Arabella | | July 1801 |

The treaty of Amiens (27 March 1802) restored Tobago to France but when the War broke out again in May 1803 it was reoccupied on 1 July 1803 so that it was included shortly afterwards in the Packet Service. A modification dated 20 July 1803 stated:-

*"You will please to be informed that notwithstanding there are three Mail Boats in the Service of the Post Office, it frequently happens that on arrival of the first Packet of the Month (from Casualty) there is only one Boat here. Tobago being now a British Island, I have named it in the Plan sent."*

The Plan for the Route of the Southern Mail Boat being:-

*With the First Month Mail*

*The Mail Boat to go first to Tobago and wait there 24 hours for the Answers. To proceed from there to St. Vincent and there land the Mail for that Island without anchoring, from thence to Grenada and land the Mail in like manner without anchoring, and then to Trinidad and wait there 24 hours, and receive the Mails to this Island.*

*With the Second Month Mail*

*The same Route, only instead of returning here to stop 24 Hours at each of the Islands, on going for the answers, and to proceed directly from Trinidad to St. Kitts there to meet the Packet.*

*N.B. It would be advisable for the Mail Boats instead of, as now, going into Scarborough Bay (Altho' the Capital) at Tobago, to go to Great Courland Bay and take the Mail across the Country, which is only three miles distant and which will bring the Boat back round the East end of the Island on their way from Tobago for St. Vincent, Scarborough Bay being to the Southward of the Island.*

*Distance from one Island to the other*

| | |
|---|---|
| *from Barbados to Tobago* | *one night* |
| *from Tobago to St. Vincent* | *one night* |
| *from St. Vincent to Grenada* | *one night* |
| *from Grenada to Trinidad* | *24 Hours."* |

Mr George Mackintosh succeeded Henry Franklyn (resigned) as Postmaster on 5 January, 1808. In lieu of salary Mr. Mackintosh was allowed by the General Post Office one-fifth of the net annual amount of postage received in his post office. This amounted to £108 pounds sterling or £216 currency.

Mr. Mackintosh issued the following Post Office notice:-

*"The Postmaster most respectfully informs the public that without distinction no credit can in future be given at the Post Office as it tends to a loss on his part, and by keeping accounts delays that delivery of letters: he therefore flatters himself that after this notice no umbrage will be taken at his declining to deliver letters until paid for."*

On 30 October 1809 William Milikens produced a report on the working of the local Mail Boat Service:-

*The first Packet of the Month from England takes bags for*

| | | |
|---|---|---|
| | *Jamaica, Barbados,* | *} Delivered by the Packet.* |
| | *Martinique, Bahamas* | *}* |
| | | |
| | *{Tobago* | *} landed at Barbados and sent from hence in a Mail* |
| *Windward Is.* | *{Grenada* | *} Boat which returns to Barbados.* |
| | *{St. Vincent* | *}* |

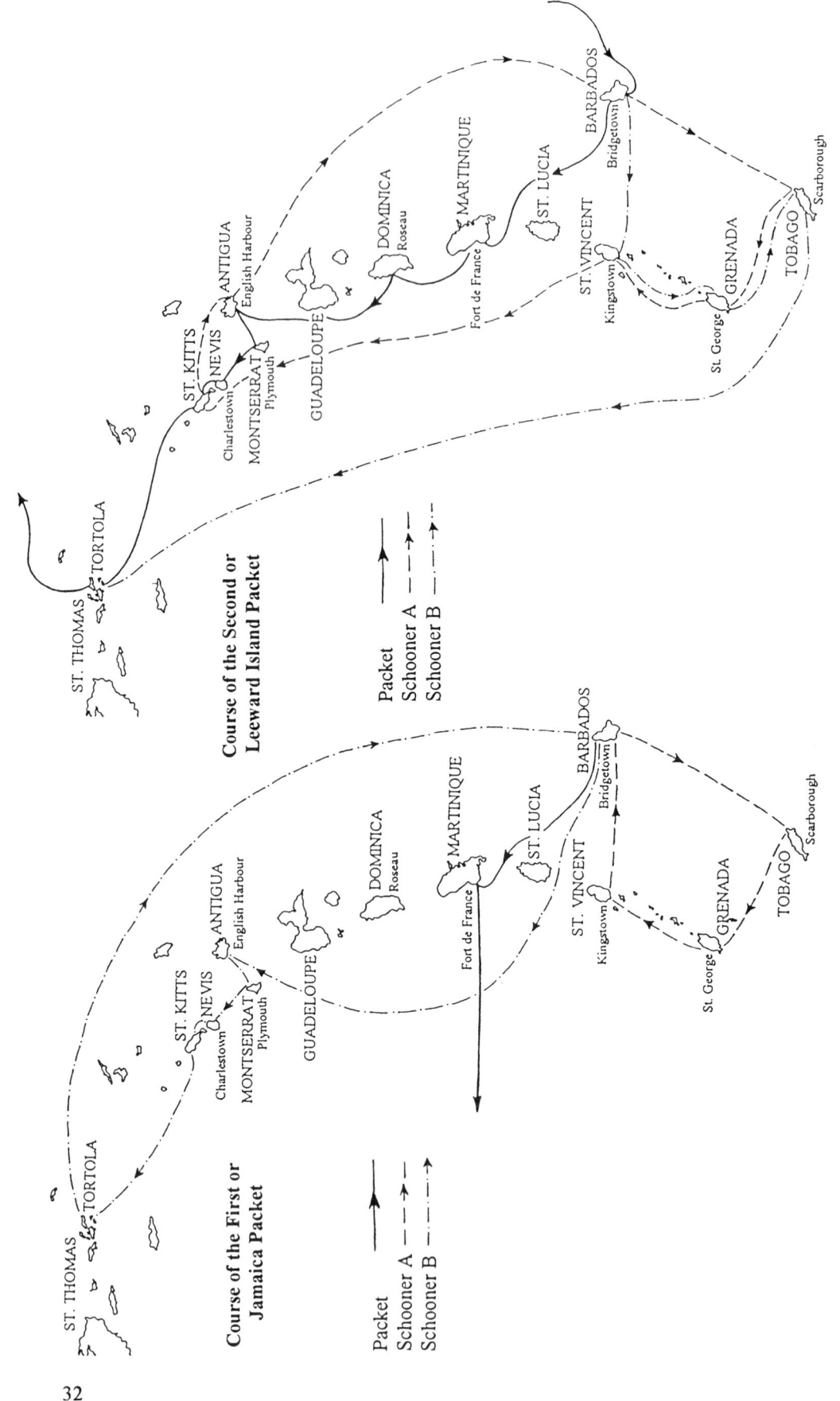

**Course of the Second or Leeward Island Packet**

Packet
Schooner A
Schooner B

**Course of the First or Jamaica Packet**

Packet
Schooner A
Schooner B

32

| Leeward Is. | {Dominica, Antigua | } landed at Barbados and sent from hence in |
| | {Montserrat, Nevis, | } a Mail Boat whcih returns to Barbados. |
| | {St. Kitts, Tortola, | } |
| | {St. Thomas .... .... .... | left at Tortola. |

| Trinidad, | } landed at Barbados and sent from hence in |
| Demerara, | } separate Mail Boats which return to Barbados. |
| Surinam | } |

*The Second Packet of the Month takes bags for*

| Barbados, Martinique, | } |
| Dominica, Antigua, | } |
| Montserrat, Nevis, | } *Delivered by the Packet.* |
| St. Kitts, Tortola, | } |
| St. Thomas | } |

| Tobago, | } landed at Barbados and sent from hence in a |
| Grenada, | } Mail Boat which meets the Packet at Tortola |
| St. Vincent, | } with Answers and returns to Barbados. |

| Trinidad, | } landed at Barbados and sent from hence in three |
| Demerara, | } Mail Boats which return to Barbados. |

Further details of the Packet Service will be found in the section on Trinidad.

At the death of Mr. Mackintosh, Mr. John Buchanan was appointed Postmaster on 7 March, 1810, pending the approval of the Lords Postmasters General. Mr. Buchanan was also Harbour Master, Pilot, and Marshall of the Court of Vice Admirality, and for his duties as a Postmaster he received £550 per annum, of which £210 was paid by the General Post Office, and £340 arose from postages, etc.

Mr. Buchanan wrote of his office thus:

*"No Office rent has been paid lately, the business being transacted in a room belonging to the Colony, but this indulgence may be discontinued at the pleasure of the Committee of Public Building. The duties of my Office are the receiving and delivering of letters."*

In June 1812 War broke out with the U.S.A.(peace was signed 24 December 1814), by 1813 the Caribbean swarmed with American privateers. The Treaty of Ghent was signed on 24 December.

Some of the Packets lost were:-

| Packet | Captured by | Date Captured |
| --- | --- | --- |
| Princess Amelia | Schooner "Rossee" | 15. 9. 12 |
| Swallow | U.S. Frigate "President" | 15. 10. 12 |
| Townsend | "Tom" and "Bona" | 23. 11. 12 |

| Packet | Captured by | Date Captured |
|---|---|---|
| Nocton | U.S. Frigate "Essex" | 11. 12. 12 |
| Mary Ann | "Governor Tomkin" | 8. 4. 13 |
| Express | | 14. 4. 13 |
| Anne | U.S. Frigate "York Town" | 21. 4. 13 |
| Duke of Montrose | U.S. Frigate "President" | 10. 6. 13 |
| Manchester | | 25. 6. 13 |
| Lapwing | "Rattle Snake" | 28. 6. 13 |

A new era commenced on 16 November, 1840, when Tobago passed an Act "To Encourage Steam Navigation between this Island and Great Britain for the conveyance of mails and passengers."

The British Government just entered into the first contract with the Royal Mail Steam Packet Company for a West Indian Service.

On behalf of the Royal Mail Packet, Mr McQueen inspected Tobago. He decided that a spot at Courland called Soldier's Hole was the place to land Tobago mails. He requested that a small store to place luggage and packages should be built, a small jetty erected, and a light maintained on the flag-staff.

But the inhabitants of Scarborough drew up a Memorial of protest and drew attention to the very inconvenient situation of Courland, which being six miles from the capital, with road impassable for carriages of any description, would prove highly injurious to the mercantile interests of the island. The memorialists also reverted to the danger of landing mails in an open bay, at the spot only marked by a rock off Plymouth, whilst Scarborough possessed a safer anchorage, as well as wharves.

The Mails however continued to be landed at Courland Bay, a Letter from the British Post returned to the local service:-

*The Conveyer of the Post Office in West Indies having commended that water-proof saddle bags should be supplied to your offices, for the purposes of enclosing the Mails conveyed between Courland Bay and Scarborough, I have caused to be transmitted to your offices, by the next mails, four saddle bags to be used for the protection of the mails in question.*

On 26 September 1850 the following notice was published:-

*Letters may in future be registered in this Island for the United Kingdom, or any British West India Colony.*

*The charge for the same will be six pence sterling, which together with the postage, must be paid in advance.*

*A printed receipt will be given to parties registering letters, and the Postmaster will be held responsible for the due delivery of the same.*

*This mode having been devised expressly with a view to the security of property, it may reasonably be expected, that all parties having occasion to transmit money &c., will avail themselves of the opportunity of securing it.*

Another correspondent wrote on 23 August 1852:-

*"The packet route steamer has by contract two days to remain at Tobago. The boat landing the English mails brings off the home ones which prevents the inhabitants acknowledging any letters for at least a fortnight. Thus our letters to England and elsewhere are received at the Scarborough Post Office about the same time that the steamer that brought them is more than half-way to Trinidad on her homeward voyage. Only in three instances out of fifteen has there been any opportunity of answering letters by the Packet that brought them, and by persons, as I can vouch, residing near the Post Office."*

Eighteen years later the conditions were not materially altered, as Gov. Rawson of Barbados reported on 2 August, 1870, after riding from Scarborough to Courland Bay, that carriages being uncommon, ladies and children had to be conveyed the six miles in open carts over very bad road. The Great River was often impassable, and the surf on the Beach at the Bay rendered embarkation and disembarkation dangerous. The Lieut.-Governor had to send his family over in a cart, whilst the Attorney General nearly lost his sister by the upsetting of a boat.

In 1858 the General Post Office made complaints about the accommodation for landing the mails at Courland Bay. The Governor cordially agreed (2 September, 1859) and stated that the obvious answer was "Scarborough" which having a lighthouse was infinitely superior. He therefore could entertain little hope of obtaining a grant of public money for the erection of a quay or jetty at Courland, where from the frequent heavy surfs it would in all probability be soon dashed to pieces. The Governor much regretted Mr. Trollope had not visited the Island during his Post Office inspection.

And in due course the Council uncompromisingly refused to be cornered in expending money on a jetty at Plymouth.

The British Government informed Tobago that no fresh mail contract would be made up after 1869 unless the Colony paid its due share (£1361) of the cost.

Robert Crooks, the Speaker of Legislative Assembly, forwarded the reply on (31 May, 1867) "The repeated refusals of the Royal Mail Co. to land mails at Scarboro' render the House indifferent to any arrangements the Imperial Government may make with that company."

Governor Knortright announced to the Council on 12 March, calling at Scarborough instead of Courland Bay. This change has been long sought for, and immediately the advantage will be great, but I am not in possession of such details as enable me to state whether the stay of the steamer at Tobago may not be very much curtailed." (The letter of the General Post Office authorising the change is dated 28 February, 1872.)

Tobago built at Scarborough with a new landing-stage, but were upset to find that under the new contract commencing 1 January, 1875, they were only to have one monthly visit from the R.M.S.P. Co.

The island had for some years no communication by Post Office conveyance, and consequently no charge was made upon letters beyond the usual Packet Rates. Persons residing in the more remote parts of the Island sent special messengers on the arrival of the mail, and in some instances a messenger was hired for a particular district for the purpose of carrying letters and parcels, and was paid by the public subscription.

A few years later an arrangement was made whereby Mr. Alleyne received 24s. for the carriage of each mail from Plymouth to Scarborough, and 16s. for the return mail, besides 4s. for the use of the office, and an allowance of 5s. for every twenty four hours the steamer was overdue. He was allowed an hour and a half for carrying the mails (after landing) to Scarborough.

The Colony had no written agreement with Mr. Alleyne, who consequently did much as he pleased, and dispatched the mails by foot runners whenever his mules were wanted for other employment.

This unsatisfactory arrangement was terminated by the General Post Office instructing that the service should be put up by tender to public competition, and on and after 1 January, 1864, the Contractor was more immediately under the control of the Department.

In the early days, a few parcels were delivered in Tobago by mail ships as the Governor would not appoint an agent on behalf of the British Customs to examine them at Courland.

"The directors," wrote Mr Chappell, on 14 January, 1847, "have issued instructions to Tobago from the R.M.S. Packets." This difficulty was overcome before the end of 1847.

The Post Office at Scarborough was kept at the Office of the Provost Marshal, Mr. Le Plastrier, who combined the duties at £600 a year.

During the Provost Marshal's absence on leave, his brother Mr. George Le Plastrier acted in his place. The Provost Marshal's post office was completely wrecked in a devastating hurricane on 11 October, 1847, and the post office had to be removed temporarily to "Mr. Charles Scobey's store, opposite the Doctor's shop."

Mr. Le Plastrier died on 25 December, 1868, and James Hamilton was provisionally appointed as Postmaster, until Arthur Kennedy arrived from England on 5 June, 1869. Mr. Kennedy's tenure was as short as Mr. Le Plastrier's had been long, for he failed to send in the monthly returns, and Messrs. Berkeley and Hamilton were empowered to visit the post office on 25 January, 1871. The Postmaster stated his readiness to lend them every assistance, but remarked that he did not understand the system and left the books entirely up to his clerk to keep. The examination showed discrepancies in the accounts, and very shortly afterwards the Postmaster absconded, escaping in an open boat from Plymouth, and landed on the north coast of Trinidad, and finally, it was believed, vanished somewhere in Porto Rico.

From a study of these Postal Accounts (1869-70), it would appear that the Tobago Post Office sold Money Orders to the value of £40 per month, and that the average monthly amount taken for postages was £15.

After this debacle, the office of Provost Marshal was altered to that of the inspector of Police, and Mr. James Hamilton on 13 February, 1871, was given sole charge of the Post Office, and a monthly audit was insisted upon.

At a Legislative Council held on 27 June, 1878, Mr. Moylan considered that Mr. Hamilton's contention, that he had the right to keep the Post Office closed for twenty-four days in the month, were preposterous. The Attorney General also remarked upon the great irregularities in the conducting of the Postal Business.

The following resolutions are recorded in the minutes:-

*"(1) That the Post Master or some duly qualified assistant shall attend every day at the Post Office from 11 a.m. to 3 p.m.; (2) That in view of the many robberies the Lt.-Governor should authorise and approve of the Post Master's assistant."*

As in other Colonies the police kept a foster paternal eye over the mails, and as the constables had to stand for re-election annually, when the inefficient were weeded cut, there were very few complaints. All went very smoothly until rumours of the transference of the Post Office were heard.

Lord Panmure's Circular Dispatch of 30 October, 1855, requesting information as to the views of the Colonies regarding the proposed postal transference to the local Governments, was answered by Lieut.-Governor Willoughby Shortland on 7 January 1856. He, having learnt that each colony would be entitled to one penny upon each sixpenny rate of postage on letters received from England, but nothing on Inter-Colonial letters, ascertained from his Postmaster that the sum to be expected from that source might be estimated at £30. "I also learn from that officer," continued the Governor, "that the expense at present incurred by the General Post Office for the maintenance of the office, amounts to £208 annually and that the revenue since March, 1854, has been insufficient to pay the disbursements of the office.

"It appears to me that the proposed change, as far as Tobago is concerned, would not prove beneficial either to the colony or to the public generally. The present establishment has reached a degree of effiency which would not be maintained under colonial managment. The rates of postage are now uniform and the careful supervision excercised by the Inspectors secures the public against fraud or gross mistakes. The Colony cannot maintain the present establishments and would not find the means for supporting an additional one without having recourse to increased taxation, probably an additional rate of postage might be imposed, which would doubtless be thought highly objectionable."

Governor Colebrook (Barbados, 12 Jan., 1856) in sending this report home took the opportunity of observing that although the local establishment in Barbados was appreciated for the convenience it afforded, yet it had not been found to defray its expenses even in a populous island like Barbados.

Tobago being a dependency of Barbados at this period, Governor Hincks (Barbados) wrote to Lieut.-Governor Drysdale (Tobago) late in 1859 acquainting him that the local authorities would have to take over their Post Office.

Governor Drysdale replied (6 Dec., 1859) that he had communicated with his Legislative Council and discovered that the cost of the present establishment was about £200 sterling per annum, whilst the revenue could not be estimated at more than £30 sterling. The expenditure included an annual charge of £50 for the transport overland of the mails from Courland Bay to Scarborough.

"From a conversation I have had with the Postmaster," continued Drysdale (*ibid.*), I am led to think that this latter amount although paid out by the Post Office Revenue in this Island, in the first instance, is subsequently refunded to the Postmaster General by the Royal Mail Steam Packet Company whose duty it is to bring the mails to Scarborough.

"On this point I can obtain no positive information and ...... trust I may be informed whether on the transfer of the Post Office to the local Government the resident Postmaster would be authorised to pay for the land transport of the mails out of the receipts of his office as it is at present done."

"In my opinion the retention of Courland Bay for landing the mails instead of the equally safe and more convenient port of Scarborough is a sufficient tax on the public without the Colony being required to pay for the cost it entails."

In addressing his Council the Tobago Governor proposed the Colony be entitled to one penny upon every sixpenny rate of postage on letters to and from England, and nothing on inter-Colonial letters.

On these points he was informed by Mr. F. Hill (G.P.O., London, 20 Feb., 1860) that the expense incurred in the conveyance of letters would be continued to be paid by the General Post Office Department and reclaimed from the Royal Mail Steam Packet Company. As regards inter-Colonial letters the Colony could charge its inland rates in addition to the British Packet rates upon all inter-Colonial letters despatched from or brought to Tobago.

At a meeting of the Legislative Council held on the 13 March, 1860, the Hon. Charles F. Cadiz laid on the table the following Circular Despatch from Governor-General Hincks relative to the transfer.

*Tobago.- Circular.*

*15 FEBRUARY, 1860.*

SIR,

*As the period is approaching when the several Post Offices in the West Indies will be transferred from Imperial to Colonial control, and as uniformity of legislation is desirable, I have deemed it expedient to transmit you a copy of an Ordinance which will shortly be submitted to the Legislative Council of St. Lucia, and which embraces all that is essential for the Colonies where it is not proposed to establish a local post. It is a requirement of the Imperial Government that no rate of postage shall be imposed by the local post authorities for transatlantic correspondence in excess of the 6d. per $\frac{1}{2}$oz. charged by the Imperial Post Office Department; 1d. of which is retained in the Colony, 1d. is the Imperial island rate, and 4d. the Atlantic rate. The Barbados Legislature has imposed a penny rate on all inter-colonial correspondence, and this example has been followed by British Guiana, and you will observe it is proposed to follow it into St. Lucia. I think that in the meantime it would be expedient that the legislation on this point should be uniform. If it should be deemed advisable hereafter to abandon the colonial charge of one penny it should be reciprocal throughout the Colonies. It seems to me very unadvisable to have separate Postmasters in those Colonies where no local post exists, and even with such an establishment my own opinion is the office should be combined with some other. In St. Lucia. I have arranged that the Treasurer shall perform the duty, but there is no reason why the office of Postmaster should not be conferred on some respectable merchant who would doubtless perform the duties for a commission of 10 to $12\frac{1}{2}$ per cent, which would be a much more economical arrangement for a small community than keeping up a separate establishment. In case the Treasurer or any other public officer should be required to perform the duties he might be compensated by a commission. Such a commission is sanctioned by the practice of the Imperial Post Office Department as well as by those in the principle Colonies. With regard to the penal clauses which may have been required, I have to observe that they were made the subject of a separate Act in Barbados,* *and I propose following a similar course in St. Lucia, but of course this is a point of little importance.*

(Sg.) F. HINCKS

*His Excellency Lieut.-Governor* DRYSDALE.

Tobago took over the Post Office on 1 May, 1860. Mr. Charles Issac Le Plastrier, the Provost Marshal, was appointed Colonial Postmaster, as he had over twenty years efficiently conducted and transacted the postal business of the island "in a mild, effective, and successful manner."

"The transfer of the Post Office to the local Government has been for some time completed, and under the new arrangement the department has been found to work economically and satisfactorily.

The system, however, is not fully developed and there are two points I would beg to draw your attention:

"In the first place it is recommended that the prepayment of postage on Transatlantic letters, be made compulsory. Uniformity of legislation on the subject is particularly desirable; and I have directed to be laid before you the Copy of an Ordinance recently introduced to Trinidad, the provisions of which, I consider, might be adopted with advantage."

"In most of the Colonies, the convenience of the public has been consulted, and provided for by the adoption of Colonial Postage Stamps, and I would invite your consideration of the question."

"I have prepared a memorandum of the cost of procuring an adequate supply of Postage Stamps - a Copy of this note will be laid before you, and should you be of the opinion that stamps should be furnished to the Postmaster, I will be happy to take the necessary steps to carry your wishes into execution."

The Governor laid upon the table a copy of the Trinidad Post Ordinance, and also the following memorandum:-

Memorandum of the Cost of Postage Stamps.

| | |
|---|---|
| The charge for engraving the original, dies, hardening and transferring that to a steel plate containing 60 Postage Stamps would be | £63 |
| For ditto, ditto, to a steel plate containing 120 stamps | £80 |
| For ditto, ditto, to a steel plate containing 240 stamps | £100 |
| Paper, printing, gumming and perforating 60 stamps on a sheet, per 1000 stamps | 2/3 |
| Ditto, ditto, 120 stamps on a sheet, per 1000 stamps | 1/9 |
| Ditto, ditto, 240 stamps on a sheet, per 1000 stamps | 1/- |

"Should more than one denomination be required and the Government are ready to leave out the denomination and let the colour of the stamp indicate its value, one plate would answer for as many stamps of all kinds as could be required."

"Government House, 12 March, 1861."

"On my arrival here a few months ago, I was struck by the want of any Inland Postal Communication. After consulting the Hon. Messrs. McCall and Yeates, I have prepared a scheme which I now submit to you for giving communication three times a week between Scarborough and the Windward and Leeward portion of the Colony. It is proposed that there should be four stations on the Windward route, namely,

| | |
|---|---|
| 1. Betsey's Hope. | 2. Roxborough. |
| 3. Richmond. | 4. Goldsborough. |

and three stations on the Leeward Line, namely,

| | |
|---|---|
| 1. Montgomery. | 2. Shirvan. |
| 3. Plymouth. | |

"The Deputy Postmaster should be paid a certain sum, probably about £6 per annum each for the use of an office and personal attendance. An Ordinance will therefore be wanted to impose a small rate on letters sent by the Island Post, which will be carried at first by the Police, who when employed on such extra service will be entitled to extra pay, say a shilling a day. The whole cost of the scheme ought not therefore to exceed at the outside
7 Stations and Deputy-Postmasters  ...   ...   ...   £42
308 Days Police Service (exclusive of 57 Sundays and Holidays)  ...   ...   ...   £30 16s.
Mail Bags  ...   ...   ...   £7  4s."

"I am also in communication with the Governor of Trinidad with a view to establishing a bi-monthly mail between this island and Port of Spain via Arima and Toco, - that such a communication is quite feasible was shown only last week when the Chief of Trinidad police (Capt. Baker) paid Tobago a visit, coming and going by the very route I have indicated. In the event of the Inland Postal Communication being established a portion of the Stamp Duty upon letters will have to be assigned to Mr. Hamilton. the Post Master, as he is paid by fees; a penny a letter I am sure would satisfy him."

The Legislative Council passed the Inland Postal Ordinance for establishing an Inland Post and to impose an uniform rate on Letters and newspapers transmitted by means thereof. on 27 April 1878.

It was ascertained that four post offices to Windward could be opened on the payment to the Deputy Postmasters of £6 per annum; arrangements were made for taking the first of the bi-monthly mails to and from Grenada by the sloop Encore at £150 per annum; and Mr. Gordon's tender for carrying the mails between Scarborough and Plymouth was accepted. The Clerk of the Council reported (3 July, 1878) that the delay of the Inland Postal Ordinance was due to the fact that the printer had kept it for nearly two months.

Unfortunately the Colony on the score of expense could not maintain its good postal intentions, as the estimated amount of £100 for the working of the Inland Post was struck off, the Legislative Council (22. Nov., 1878) agreeing to dispense with this service in 1879.

A year or two later it was attempted, the mails leaving Scarborough three days a week and reaching Roxborough at an early hour in the afternoon, but it was soon abandoned.

Stated The News on 16 February, 1884, *"In all the Windward Islands, Tobago is the only country in which there are no public facilities for internal communication. The absence of inland posts seem trifling at first, but on secondary consideration not so unimportant. There is little or no interchange of thought between people of one district or another in this island.....It costs a gentleman his servant's day's pay, together with his travelling expenses, to come to town for his letters, or a labourer his wages to receive a letter. The establishment of inland post offices is considered a great boon. About two years ago Mr. Laborde opened inland post offices in certain parts of the island to obviate the evils we have pointed out. The scheme was hailed with pleasure and advantage was taken of it, but twelve months had not passed before Mr. Laborde put a notice that as the island posts did not pay, they would be closed. The inland mail was conveyed by policemen and district post offices, with one or two exceptions, were kept at the police stations. We hope to see these offices revived at no distant date."*

After refusing to join the Post Union in 1878, Tobago eventually did so. The local paper "News" duly commented: *"Mr. Laborde, the Administrator, has plunged head over heels in the Postal Union. The labouring villager wakes in the morning and goes to his field, not returning till night; Packet day is a day entirely unknown to him. What benefit does he derive from the Union? Might not the money ill spent on the Union be appropriated to instructing the ignorant. Where is the wisdom of paying a large amount to the Union and £60 a year for the transmission of our bi-weekly mails in sailing vessels to and from Barbados."*

Tobago discovered that joining the Union was an expensive luxury as it was required to pay £100 towards the loss sustained by the imperial Government on its admission to the Union.

In spite of its name the sloop *"Encore"* as a mail carrier proved a fiasco, and a Company in the land procured from England a steamship of two tons, called *"The Dawn"*, in July, 1881. The activities of this vessel were limited, as the neighbours were all in quarantine, but she took the mails to Barbados and considerably opened up intercourse with Trinidad and Grenada. Her popularity was such, that the Administrator aboard had to forbid Captain Duncan receiving mail letters from the public:-

*Scarborough, 20 August, 1881.*

*The s.s. Dawn ,McGreen Master, will from time to time on leaving the Colony only take Consignees letters in her Bag. Other letters are recommended to be sent through the post.*

On 10 February, 1882, *"The Dawn"* struck a sunken rock at Castara Bay on the north side of the island. The attempt to refloat her proving futile, the wreck was sold in its entirety to Dr. R. B. Anderson, the Colonial Surgeon, as the vessel was lying at *his* bay. For weeks Dr. Anderson employed a number of men from Scarborough and all the labourers on his estate, and their united exertions proved successful, and to everyone's joy *"The Dawn"* steamed into Scarborough on 25 March, 1882. She was patched up, but proved so uncertain that mails were once again taken locally by sailing vessels until 1889, when Messrs. Turnbull, Steward & Co., of Trinidad, conveyed the mails by steamship fortnightly.

Occasionally a visiting steamer would take the mails, and a bellman was sent round the town to announce the fact.

On 1 July, 1885, a new contract commenced with the R.M.S.P. Co., whereby once in every four weeks the steamers after landing mails at St. Vincent, Grenada, Trinidad, and Barbados remained at Tobago for six days before returning. The naval officers and men amused themselves during the six days (August 1-5, 1885) with all manner of sports, but considered the lack of any hotel a great drawback, and that a few lamps about the streets of Scarborough would be an advantage.

This new contract was naturally vastly agreeable to the young maidens of Tobago, but the rest of the community realised the greatly desired fortnightly service was as far off as ever.

On 2 July, 1879, the current set of Fiscal Stamps were authorised for postal purposes, and after January 1, 1881, these were withdrawn in favour of the new *"Postage"* set. This resulted in the following being published:-

*Scarborough, 2nd July 1879*

*NOTICE is hereby given that from and after the 1st of August next all letters, newspapers, and other articles transmissible by Post must be pre-paid by having Postage Stamps of the proper value affixed to thereto.*

*Postage Stamps of the various values are on on sale at the Treasury and a supply will in future be kept at his office.*

*ROBT. W. MCEACHNIE,*
*Acting Postmaster.*

In 1887 the following notice was published:-

*Post Office,*
*25 March, 1887.*

*The Mails will be made up on FRIDAY 15th April next at 2 o'clock, p.m., punctually. After that hour correspondence will be received with an additional charge of 1d. until 3 p.m. the additional charge to be paid in Stamps affixed to the correspondence.*

*Letters will not be registered within the three hours previous to the time fixed for the closing of the Mails.*

*A. L. MARSHALL,*
*Postmaster*

The late fee was changed on 18 March 1890, *"the fee payable on late correspondence, will be equivalent to the single rate of postage, to which the correspondence is liable and not to the charge of four-pence, generally, as heretofore".*

The Royal Mail Steam Packet Company Time Table for the second half of 1890 and 1891 were:-

| Outward. | | Homeward. | |
| --- | --- | --- | --- |
| England. | Tobago. | England. | Tobago. |
| 9th July, 1890. | 24th July, 1890. | 30th July, 1890. | 13th Aug. 1890. |
| 23rd July, 1890. | 7th Aug. 1890. | 13th Aug. 1890. | 27th Aug. 1890. |
| 6th Aug. 1890. | 21st Aug. 1890. | 27th Aug. 1890. | 10th Sept. 1890. |
| 20th Aug. 1890. | 4th Sept. 1890. | 10th Sept. 1890. | 24th Sept. 1890. |
| 3rd Sept. 1890. | 18th Sept. 1890. | 24th Sept. 1890. | 8th Oct. 1890. |
| 17th Sept. 1890. | 2nd Oct. 1890. | 8th Oct. 1890. | 22nd Oct. 1890. |
| 1st Oct. 1890 | 16th Oct. 1890. | 22nd Oct. 1890. | 5th Nov. 1890. |
| 15th Oct. 1890. | 16th Oct. 1890. | 5th Nov. 1890. | 19th Nov. 1890. |
| 29th Nov. 1890. | 13th Nov. 1890. | 19th Nov. 1890. | 3rd Dec. 1890. |
| 12th Nov. 1890. | 27th Nov. 1890. | 3rd Dec. 1890. | 17th Dec. 1890. |
| 26th Nov. 1890. | 11th Nov. 1890. | 17th Dcc. 1890. | 31st Dec. 1890. |
| 10th Dec. 1890. | 25th Dec. 1890. | 31st Dec. 1890. | 14th Jan. 1891. |
| 24th Dec. 1890. | 8th Jan. 1891. | 14th January, 1891. | 28th Jan. 1890. |

The Steamers arrived on the morning of every alternate Thursday with the English and other Mails, and left on the following Wednesday, at 6 p.m.

On 16 May 1892 a Second Inland Postal Service was started with three routes:-

### ROUTE NO. 1 -
SCARBOROUGH TO ROXBOROUGH
On MONDAYS and WEDNESDAYS,

| Leave Scarborough ... ... ... ... | at 10 a.m. |
| do. Mt. St. George ... ... ... ... | at 12 noon. |
| do. Pembroke ... ... ... ... ... | at 1.30 p.m. |
| Arrive at Roxborough ... ... ... | at 3.30 p.m. |

Return on TUESDAYS and FRIDAYS

| Leave Roxborough ... ... ... ... | at 10 a.m. |
| do. Pembroke ... ... ... ... ... | at 12 noon. |
| do. Mt. St. George ... ... ... ... | at 1.30 p.m. |
| Arrive at Scarborough ... ... ... | at 3 p.m. |

### ROUTE NO. 2 -
SCARBOROUGH TO PLYMOUTH VIA MORIAH
On MONDAYS and THURSDAYS,

| Leave Scarborough ... ... ... ... | at 10 a.m. |
| do. Mason Hall ... ... ... ... | at 11.30 a.m. |
| do. Moriah ... ... ... ... ... | at 1 p.m. |
| do. Les Coteaux ... ... ... ... | at 2 p.m. |
| Arrive at Plymouth ... ... ... ... | at 3 p.m. |

Return on TUESDAYS and FRIDAYS

| Leave Plymouth ... ... ... ... ... | at 10 a.m. |
| do. Les Couteaux ... ... ... ... | at 11 a.m. |
| do. Moriah ... ... ... ... ... | at 1 p.m. |
| do. Mason Hall ... ... ... ... | at 2 p.m. |
| Arrive at Scarborough ... ... ... | at 3 p.m. |

**ROUTE NO. 3 -**

SCARBOROUGH TO SHIRVAN VIA MONTGOMERY,

On MONDAYS and THURSDAYS,

| | |
|---|---|
| Leave Scarborough  ...  ...  ...  ... | at 10 a.m. |
|    do.  Orange Hall  ...  ...  ...  ... | at 11 a.m. |
|    do.  Bethel (Montgomery) ...  ... | at 12.30 p.m. |
|    do.  Buccoo Point  ...  ...  ...  ... | at 2 p.m. |
|    do.  Canaan via Golden Grove ... | at 3 p.m. |
| Arrive at Shirvan  ...  ...  ...  ...  ... | at 3.30 p.m. |

Return on TUESDAYS and FRIDAYS

| | |
|---|---|
| Leave Shirvan  ...  ...  ...  ...  ... | at 10 a.m. |
|    do.  New Grange via Mt. Pleasant | at 11 a.m. |
|    do.  Bethel ...  ...  ...  ...  ... | at 12.30 p.m. |
|    do.  Orange Hill  ...  ...  ...  ... | at 1 p.m. |
| Arrive at Scarborough  ...  ...  ... | at 2.30 p.m. |

Three Letter Carriers were appointed:-

G. M. ANDREWS - To Route No. 1 - from Scarborough to Roxborough;
ALLEN ARMSTRONG - To Route No. 2 - from Scarborough to Plymouth via Moriah ;
G. W. HILLS - To Route No. 3 - from Scarborough to Shirvan via Montgomery.

A report on the Service was made on 5 January 1893:-

*I now have the honour to forward for the information of His Excellency the Governor, the following Report on the working etc.. of the Inland Postal Service since its commencement here on the 16th of May, to the 31st December last.*

*A committee composed of Messrs, S. J. Fraser, Chairman, Dr. J. P. Tulloch, William McCall Esqr. and myself, was appointed to make the necessary arrangements to put the service into operation - I enclose a copy of a placard issued, showing the number of Routes etc.. and asking for the Letter Carriers for the service. In answer to this a considerable number, to the amount of over fifty application were received, and the following applicants were appointed to the Routes set opposite to their respective names:-*

*Mr. G. M. Andrews to Route No. 1 - Scarborough to Roxborough - 17½ miles.*
*Mr. A. Armstrong to Route No. 2 - Scarborough to Plymouth, via Moriah - 12½ miles*
*Mr. C. Hills to Route No. 3 - Scarborough to Shirvan, via Montgomery - 9 miles.*

*These three Routes were fixed by the Committee being considered by it as the most convenient for the public - the postman passing along on the public roads through the most populous parts of the country, and within hail of nearly every resident in the districts through which the men pass.*

*The postmen are furnished with watches, and waterproof letterpouches, in which the mails are carried. They are met by the people at the stations en route where all letters etc.. applied for are delivered. As a rule, the whole of the letters etc.. are delivered en route, and at the stations by themselves, any undelivered correspondence being left in charge of the police at the termini of Routes Nos. 1 and 2, and in the charge of the postmaster at Shirvan, the terminus of Route No. 3. These remarks do not apply, either to the registered correspondence, or to the parcels post. A list of these articles is made out for every Route and handed to the*

*Postmen who inform the addressees accordingly, and to whom the articles are subsequently delivered direct from the Post Office at Scarborough.*

*There are two outward deliveries on each Route every week, on Mondays, and Thursdays - on the following days, Tuesdays, and Fridays, the men, before returning, clear the letter boxes at the termini of the Routes, and return the same way to the Post Office at Scarborough with all letters etc. for Inland as well as for Foreign delivery.*

*The following statement shows the Revenue derived from postage on letters, newspapers, etc. Inland as well as Foreign, dealt with by means of the Inland Post during the period from 16th May, to the 31st December last.*

*1. Posted in the Island for Inland delivery.*

**Letters.**
**Route No. 1**

| | | | | | | |
|---|---|---|---|---|---|---|
| *Outwards - 455 Rates @ 1d.* | £1 | 17 | 11 | | | |
| *Inwards - 290     do. @ 1d.* | 1 | 4 | 2 | | | |

**Route No. 2**

| | | | |
|---|---|---|---|
| *Outwards - 153 Rates at 1d.* | | 12 | 9 |
| *Inwards -   53   do.  at 1d.* | | 4 | 5 |

**Route No. 3**

| | | | |
|---|---|---|---|
| *Outwards - 97 Rates at 1d.* | | 8 | 1 |
| *Inwards -  51   do.  at 1d.* | | 4 | 3 |

------------------

| | | | |
|---|---|---|---|
| *Total 1099 Rates at 1d.* | £4 | 11 | 7 |

**Other Articles, Newspapers, Etc.**
**Route No. 1**

| | | | | | |
|---|---|---|---|---|---|
| *Outwards - 24 at ½d.* | £0 | 1 | 0 | | |
| *Inwards -     2 at ½d.* | | | 1 | | |

**Route No. 2**

| | | | |
|---|---|---|---|
| *Outwards - 16 at ½d.* | | 0 | 8 |
| *Inwards -           Nil.* | | | |

**Route No. 3**

| | | | |
|---|---|---|---|
| *Outwards - 7 at ½d.* | | 0 | 3½ |
| *Inwards -           Nil.* | | | |

------------------

| | | | | | |
|---|---|---|---|---|---|
| *Total 49 at ½d.* | £0 | 2 | 0½ | 2 | 0½ |

**Letters**
**2. Posted in the Island for Foreign delivery.**
**Route No. 1**

| | | | |
|---|---|---|---|
| *Inwards - 813 Rates at 1d.* | £3 | 7 | 9 |
| *Outwards - 28   do. at 2½d.* | | 5 | 10 |

**Route No. 2**

| | | | |
|---|---|---|---|
| *Inwards - 1104 Rates at 1d.* | 4 | 12 | 0 |
| *Outwards -  20   do.  at 2½d.* | | 4 | 2 |

**Route No. 3**

| | | | |
|---|---|---|---|
| *Inwards - 848 Rates at 1d.* | 3 | 10 | 0 |

### Route No. 3 Continued
Outwards - 25   do.   at 2½             5   2½

------------------

*Total 2838 Rates =*           £12   5   7½    4   13   7½

### Other Articles Newspapers, Etc.
### Route No. 1
*Inwards - 2 at 1d.*           £     0   2
   *do.*   *- 9 at ½d.*            0   4½
### Route No. 2
*Inwards - 1 at 1d.*            0   1
   *do.*   *- 1 at ½d.*              0½
### Route No. 3
*Inwards - Nil.*

-------------

*Total*            £0    0   8    12   6   3½

                               ---------------

                               £16   19   11½

*To this amount I would add the postage of the Inland official correspondence, which I estimate at £1 on letters, and £1. 2. 2. on papers, book packets, etc.............*      2   2   2

                               ---------------

*making a  total Revenue of*                 £ 19   2    1

*As against this, there was the following expenditure -*

| | | | |
|---|---|---|---|
| *For Salaries of three Letter Carriers for seven months and a half at £2. 10. 0 per month* | £56 | 5 | 0 |
| *For Salary of Postmaster at terminus of Route No. 3 at* $^{10}/_{-}$ *per month for seven months and a half* | 3 | 15 | 0 |
| *Cost of four letter boxes fixing them up etc., I at Scarborough and one at end of each Route* | 3 | 12 | 6 |
| *Three Watches for Postmen* | 3 | 0 | 0 |
| | ------------- | | |
| *Total* | £66 | 12 | 6 |

*showing a debit to the Inland Post of £47. 10. 5 to the 31st of December last.*

*This sum appears a large one, but I would point out that this is not due to extravagant expenditure on account of the inland service. The three postmen, paid at the rate of £2. 10. 0 each per month, use their own horses. They have travelled a distance of 5109 miles, have dealt with 10,452 postal articles, equal to 2.04 articles per mile, at a cost of 1.75 pence per mile to the public.*

*In conclusion, I would state that the inland post has worked so far, fairly well. The stations on the Routes have not been fitted up yet with tables, pigeon holes. etc.. as was intended, the expense to do so being too much at present, as soon as this can be done, the service will be more efficiently performed, greater facilities will be given, especially to the Country people for the posting, and receiving of their letters, etc.. and the service will be still more appreciated by them than it is at present.*

*I have the honour to be ,*
*Sir,*
*Your most obedient servant,*

*A. L. MARSHALL.*
*Postmaster.*

District Post Offices were opened at Moriah (Route 2) and Pembroke (Route 1) in January 1897, when it was stated that in future postage stamps would be sold at District Post Offices.

Tobago became a ward of Trinidad in 1899. The postal services started to be amalgamated in 1900, adhesives inscribed Trinidad and Tobago being issued.

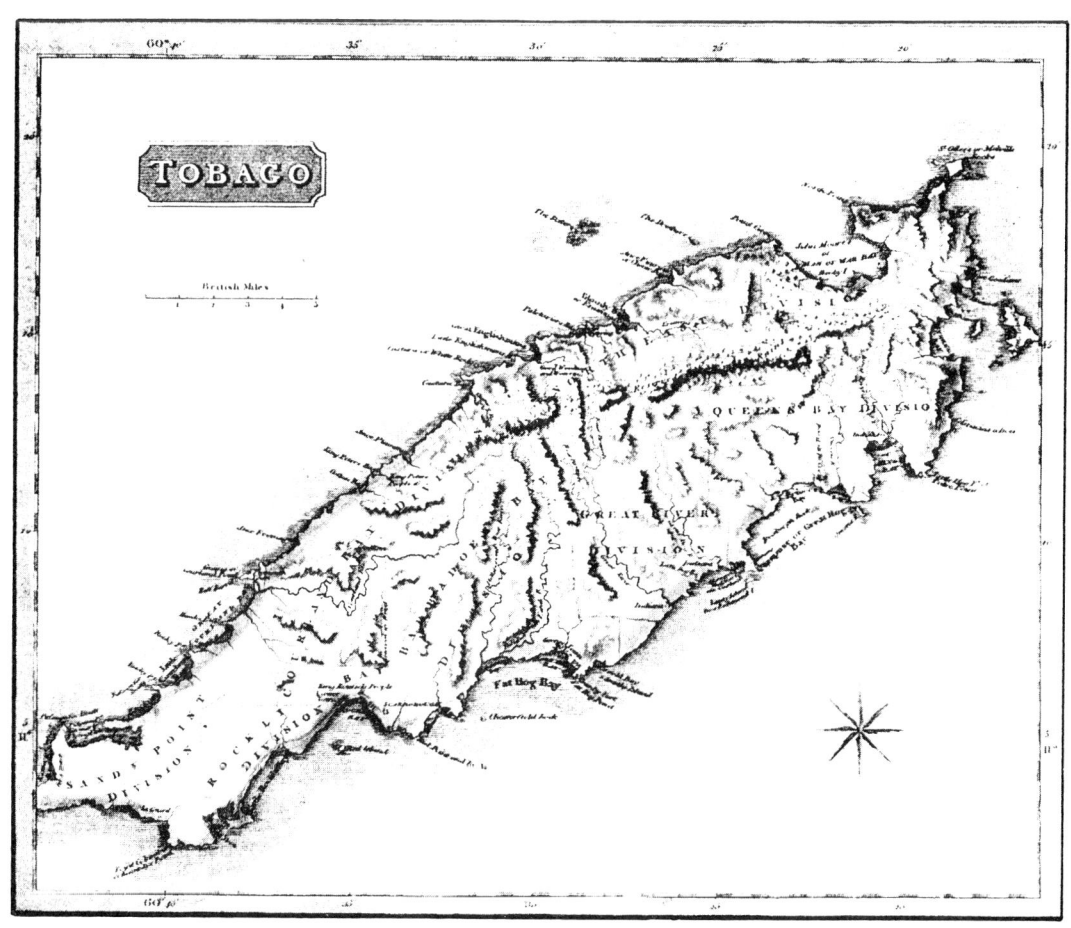

**1816 Map of Tobago**

Postmen of the British Empire:
Trinidad. West India Islands.

# TRINIDAD

After Trinidad was captured in 1797, there was no direct packet service and mail had to be collected from Grenada.

In 1800 arrangements were made for an additional mail boat to serve places to the south of Barbados. The route being:- "from Barbados to Surinam where the packet stayed 48 hours; on to Berbice (24 hours); to Demerara and Essequibo (48 hours); and to Trinidad where it stayed 48 hours; and then to St. Kitts to meet the Second Packet of the Month. Barbados to Surinam took about 6 days;4 days to Trinidad; and about 6 days from Trinidad to St. Kitts; The complete route taking 25 days including stops. The voyage from Barbados to Tobago, Grenada, St. Vincent and on to St. Kitts was about 10 days; there was ample time for the Colonies in question, to answer the Letters delivered by the First Packet as there were two or three days before the Packet with the Second Mail of the Month arrived.

By the Treaty of Amiens in 1802, however, the Settlements on the Guiana Coast were restored to the Dutch, and the Mail Boat Service to those places was discontinued by 1803.

When Lord Lovington, planned for improving the mail service to the West Indies he quoted the following;

*"The allowance to the three Antigua Boats for their present service would be fully equal to the services of the two Boats from Barbados to St. Vincent, Grenada, and Trinidad going once a month to Antigua to meet the Leeward Island Packet before her departure for England".*

The Committee of Captains reported against the proposed plan, and put forward another which Freeling passed on to the Postmaster General:-

*"Plan for the future employment of the two mail schooners from Barbados to the Southward, so as to accommodate the Island of Trinidad. On the arrival of the first monthly packet, one boat should proceed with the mail to St. Vincent, Grenada, and Trinidad and return to Barbados. On the arrival of the second or Leeward Island Packet one boat to sail to Trinidad direct, there remain 48 hours and return by Grenada, there to deliver the Trinidad Mail to the Boat which is to Sail from Barbados with the mails for St. Vincent and Grenada and then to follow the packet to St. Kitts. The Trinidad Boat may then return to Barbados, or occasionally, if she wants repairs she may take the mails from the Grenada Boat, and follow the packet to St. Kitts and call at Antigua on her return to her station at Barbados, and in that case the Grenada Boat should sail direct from that Island to Barbados to be in readiness for the next Voyage to St. Vincent, Grenada, and Trinidad."*

To this the Postmaster General added the following endorsement:

*"I do not hesitate to write this letter first because the plan does not inconvenience the Islands of St. Vincent and Grenada; second because it affords great facility to the correspondence with Trinidad; third because it saves nearly £500 per year paid for a Boat to and from Grenada and Trinidad; and fourthly it does not interfere with the plan proposed by Lord Lavington."*

On 2nd June 1803 Freeling sent the plan to C. Willoughby, the Postmaster at Barbados, with a covering letter:-

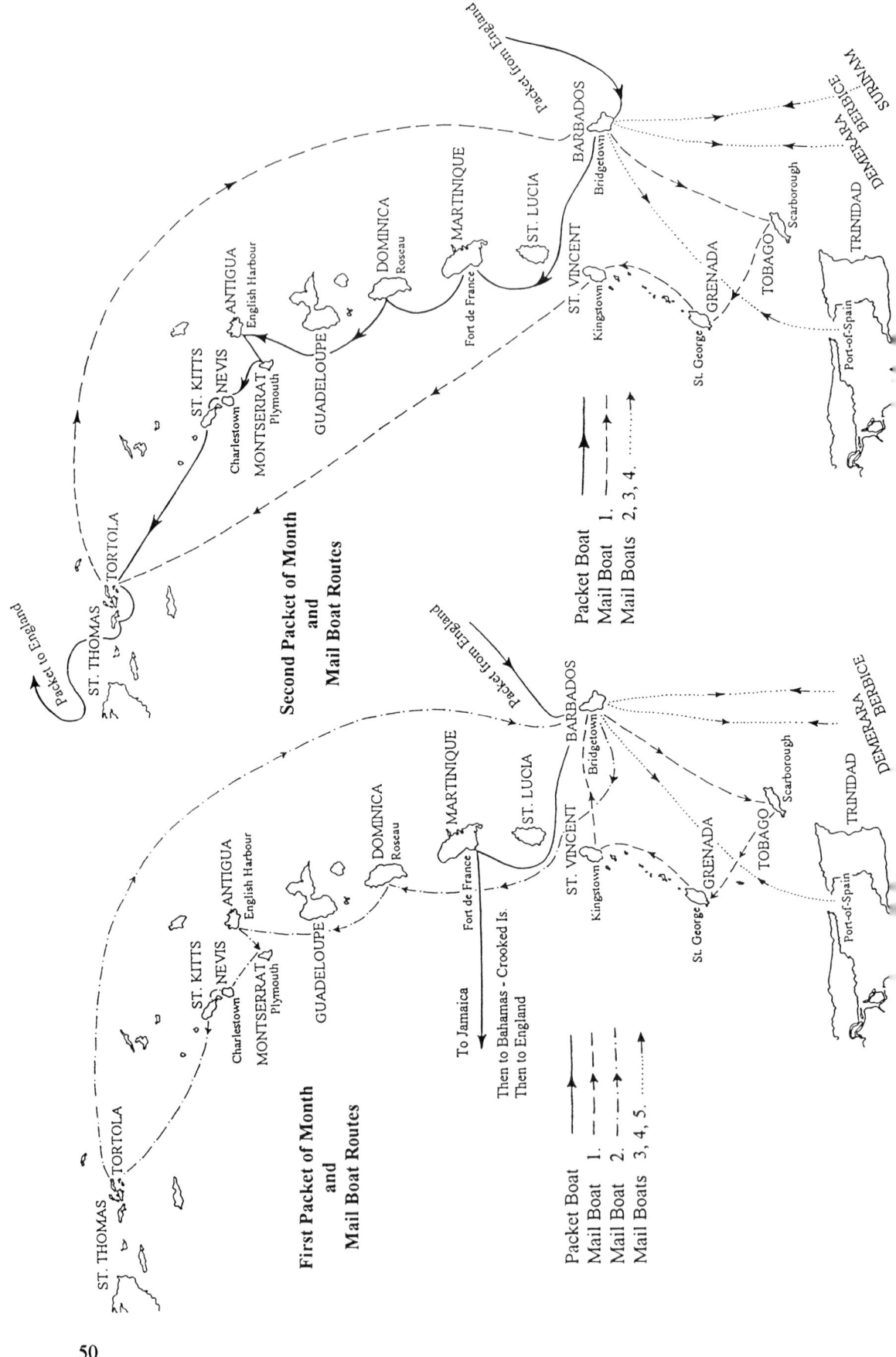

**Second Packet of Month and Mail Boat Routes**

Packet Boat ————▶
Mail Boat 1. — — —▶
Mail Boats 2, 3, 4. ·········▶

**First Packet of Month and Mail Boat Routes**

Packet Boat ————▶
Mail Boat 1. — — —▶
Mail Boat 2. —·—·—▶
Mail Boats 3, 4, 5. ·········▶

*"Enclosed I send you a plan for the future employment of the mail schooner from your island to the southward so as to accommodate the island of Trinidad which My Lords the Postmaster General very much approves of, particularly as it will save very heavy expenses to the revenue, which has hitherto been incurred for the conveyance of the letters to that Island from Grenada. You will therefore do well to submit it to the consideration of Lord Seaforth (Governor of Barbados, 1801-06), and if his Lordship should see no material objection to it you will give the necessary Orders for its being carried into execution accordingly."*

Willoughby consulted Lord Seaforth, and forwarded a further modification on 20 July 1803; and added:

*"You will please to be informed that notwithstanding there are three Mail Boats in the Service of the Post Office, it frequently happens that on the arrival of the first Packet of the Month (from Casualty) there is only one Boat here. Tobago being now a British Island, I have named it in the plan sent."*

Mr. Kentish (the Contractor for the Mail Boats) and other interested parties were consulted, and finally the following scheme emerged:

*"A Plan for the Route of the Southern Mail Boat -*

*With the first months mail*

*The Mail Boat to go first to Tobago and wait there 24 hours for the answers. To proceed from there to St. Vincent and there land the mail for that Island without anchoring, from thence to Grenada and land the mail in like manner without anchoring, and then to Trinidad and wait there 24 hours, and receive the mails to this Island.*

*With the second months mail*

*The same Route, only instead of returning here to stop 24 Hours at each of the Islands, on going for the answers, and to proceed directly from Trinidad to St. Kitts there to meet the Packet.*

*N.B. It would be advisable for the Mail Boats instead of, as now, going into Scarborough Bay (Altho' the Capital) at Tobago, to go to Great Courland Bay and take the mail across the country, which is only three miles distant and which will bring the Boat back round the east end of the Island on their way to Tobago for St. Vincent, Scarborough Bay being to the southward of the Island.*

*Distance from one Island to the other*

*from Barbados to Tobago.............. one night*
*from Tobago to St. Vincent ........... one night*
*from St. Vincent to Grenada...........one night*
*from Grenada to Trinidad...............24 Hours."*

On 30th October 1809 William Millikens produced a very clear report on the workings of the local Mail Service:

*"Cost of mail boats:*
*1 for Demerara at £1,296 per annum;*
*1 for Trinidad at £1,296 per annum;*
*1 for Surinam at £1,296 per annum".*

*The First Packet of the Month from England takes Bags for*

|  | Jamaica, Barbados,<br>Martinique, Bahamas, | }<br>} *Delivered by the Packet.* |
|---|---|---|
| Windward Is. | {Tobago<br>{Grenada<br>{St. Vincent | }<br>} *Landed at Barbados and sent from hence in*<br>} *a Mail Boat which returns to Barbados.* |
| Leeward Is. | {Dominica, Antigua<br>{Montserrat, Nevis<br>{St. Kitts, Tortola,<br>{St, Thomas...................left at Tortola. | } *Landed at Barbados and sent from hence in*<br>} *a Mail Boat which returns to Barbados.*<br>} |
|  | Trinidad,<br>Demerara,<br>Surinam | } *Landed at Barbados and sent from hence*<br>} *in separate Mail Boats which return to*<br>} *Barbados.* |

*The Second Packet of the Month takes Bags for*

|  |  |
|---|---|
| Barbados, Martinque,<br>Dominica, Antigua,<br>Montserrat, Nevis,<br>St. Kitts, Tortola,<br>St. Thomas | }<br>} *Delivered by the Packet.*<br>}<br>} |
| Tobago,<br>Grenada<br>St. Vincent | } *Landed at Barbados and sent from hence in a*<br>} *Mail Boat which meets the Packet at Tortola*<br>} *with Answers and returns to Barbados.* |
| Trinidad,<br>Demerara<br>Surinam | } *Landed at Barbados and sent from hence in*<br>} *three Mail Boats which return to Barbados.*<br>} |

The Plan pursued when possible has been, on the arrival of the first packet of the month from England to dispatch five boats from Barbados and four on the arrival of the second, giving at all times the preference to the Islands.

The Returns from the Postmaster of Barbados gives details for the Mail Boats for the last twelve months:

*Tobago, St. Vincent, Grenada,*    *21 regular, sailings*
*1 detained 6 days,*
*2 detained owing to sailing of Mail Boats 3 days*
*preceeding their arrival - forwarded with next mail.*

In 1818 the Postmistress of Trinidad, Mrs Galway, was instructed by the Governor to investigate the possibility of establishing a communication between Port of Spain and San Fernando. On 19 April 1819 she was able to report: *"On receipt of the Minute of the Council of 4 March I made necessary arrangement with the Secretary of the Steam Boat Company for the Master of the Steam Boat to call at this Office for Letters every day of Departure, and do the same at Mr. Huniston's, St. Fernando, which had regularly been done. Only two Letters have been forwarded, and very few from St. Fernando."*

An advertisement inserted in the Trinidad Newspapers on 9th June read:

*By Order of His Excellency the Governor and Honorable Board of Council. The following rates of Postage will be charged on all Letters sent to or from St. Fernando by the Steam Boat, viz.*

> *For every Letter under One Ounce, One Shilling Cy.*
> *For every Letter or Package exceeding One Ounce, Three Shillings Cy.*

*And the Public are informed that a Bag will be made up at this Office for St. Fernando a Quarter of an Hour before the time appointed by for the Departure of the Steam Boat; and the like will be done by Mr. William Huntiston at St. Fernando for Port of Spain.*

*E.R. Galway.*
*Postmistress."*

In 1820 G.H. Freeling, the Assistant Secretary to the Postmaster General and the son of Francis Freeling, was sent out to the West Indies to examine and report on all the aspects of the Postal Service which was submitted on 11 August 1820, he stated:-

*The Day after the arrival of the Packet, three mail boats are dispatched, one for Berbice and Demerara. Another carries the Mail for Tobago and Trinidad; and a third, those for St. Vincent and Grenada, remaining at each Island 48 hours; the two Boats meet at Grenada, whence one proceeds to overtake the Leeward Island Packet at St. Kitts, and the other returns to Barbados direct.*

*When I was at Trinidad, Sir R. Woodford urged the establishment of a boat direct from Barbados for that Island, which I felt it my duty to resist decidedly, both because there is no sort of pressure with regard to the correspondance, as the letters are received on the third day, and because if granted in one instance, every other island would have a right to demand a separate establishment for itself. As he appeared anxious that something should be done, I proposed to him to have the Trinidad letters dropt by the packet at Grenada and that the Colony should establish a Schooner to carry them over to Trinidad. This is the only other mode in which the Letters could be sent, and I did not hesitate to express my opinion, that the receipt would be later by this route than by Tobago. He however seemed pleased with the Idea, and I gave the necessary instructions to the Postmasters at Barbados and Grenada, to be acted upon when Sir R. Woodford should apprize them that the Colony had contracted for the schooner. I trust that he will abandon the intention and let the present arrangement stand, which is the best that can be made, and which ought to satisfy them. It is suggested that the mail boat with the letters from Tobago, Trinidad, Grenada, and St. Vincent would go on to St. Thomas instead of stopping as at present, at St. Kitts. Of the two Mail Boats which would thus proceed to St. Thomas, one would return direct to Barbados, and the other call at the various Islands in her way back to the pick up the return letters for those to Windward.*

The arrangements proposed by G. H. Freeling, with some slight modifications shown below, were approved by the Postmaster General on 28 August 1820, and commenced with the Leeward Island Packet of September. Instructions had been sent out by the Jamaica Packet at the beginning of that month.

# Routes of the Mail Boats

*On the arrival of the Jamaica Packet the mail boats to be dispatched:-*

*One Boat direct to Tobago and Trinidad;*
*    "      "      "      "  St. Vincent and Grenada;*
*    "      "      "      "  St. Lucia, Dominica, Antigua, Montserrat, Nevis, and St. Kitts;*
*    "      "      "      "  Berbice and Demerara.*

*These mail boats wait twelve hours at each place, and return direct to Barbados, bringing only the Island letters and to be in readiness for Duty.*

*On the arrival of the second packet at Barbados:-*

*One boat direct to Tobago and Trinidad, waiting 48 hours;*
*One boat direct to St. Vincent and Grenada, waiting at each 48 hours.*

*The Mail Boat to wait at Grenada the arrival of the boat from Trinidad, then to proceed to St. Kitts to meet the Packet on her return to England, the other boat to make the best of her way to Barbados.*

*One Mail Boat to Berbice and Demerara waiting 48 hours at each to receive the return letters and then to proceed without interruption to St. Kitts.*

*One boat is stationed at Antigua for the express purpose of conveying the Mails to Tortola, St. Thomas, and St. Croix.*

The Agent at Falmouth handed the following instructions to the Captain of the Leeward Island Packet on 6th September 1820:

*"The Postmaster General having determined upon a complete alteration in the arrangement of the Leeward Island Mail to commence with the Packet of the 3rd Wednesday in the present month, and your Ship being appointed to take out that Mail, and to sail from Falmouth on the 23rd Inst., You will be pleased to attend to the following directions as to the route and stay of the Packet in the printed list you will receive, that you are to remain 24 hours only at Barbados, and that at each of the other Islands you are not to anchor, but merely to land the Mail and proceed to St. Thomas, noting particularly your actual stay at each Island. Eight days after the Packet shall have sailed from Barbados, a mail boat will be dispatched to follow the same course touching at the various Islands without anchoring, and taking on the mails for this country, which the Master will deliver to you on board at St. Thomas. The boat from Grenada with the mails from that Island, Tobago, Trinidad, and St. Vincent, will also take them up to St. Thomas, instead of to St. Kitts as formerly, and it is calculated that both mail boats will reach St. Thomas within 8 days after the Packet; but be it more or less, so soon as they both shall have arrived and sent their mails on board, you will immediately make for Falmouth, of course bringing the bag from St. Thomas. To give this measure full effect, it is of particular moment that there should be no unnecessary delay, that you should strictly confine yourself to landing the Mails and proceeding on to your destination. You will further understand, that the Masters of the mail boats are to deliver the mails for this country on board your Packet at St. Thomas and you are to grant receipts to the Masters for the same. And on your arrival at Falmouth transmit with your journal, the abstract of the mail boats'*

*arrival and departure at the respective Islands, which the Masters have been desired to deliver with the mails."*

Originally it was decided in 1882 to transfer the Packet Service to the Admiralty to operate as from the 1 January 1823, but was postponed until the 5 April 1823.

A Treasury Minute of 6 December 1822 made the following points:

*"To avoid expense the changeover was to be gradual.*

*All Post Office Packets on the Falmouth Station were to be placed under the orders of the Lords of the Admiralty.*

*Contracts and agreements which the Postmaster General had entered into regarding the Packets to be transferred on the 5 April 1823 and made good by the Navy Board. At the expiration of these contracts the Admiralty to arrange for the conveyance of the mails from Falmouth.*

*The Packets to be refitted at Falmouth.*

*Temporary vessels to be put out of the Service at the end of their Term."*

*(On 4 January 1823 Musgrave, the Packet Agent at Falmouth, reported that the temporary Packets "Swiftsure" and "Fox" had already been discharged, and that the "Princess Elizabeth" would be discharged "on return from her present voyage.")*

*"Persons now employed to be continued in the service."*

For the guidance of the Admiralty the Post Office sent a copy of the Regulations in force for the Packets on the Falmouth Station:

*"**West Indies (including Jamaica) and America.***
*Mails are made up in London on the first wednesday in every month and are dispatched from Falmouth on the Saturday Morning following. The Senior Commander has his choice of these mails unless one of the Packets should have arrived from America in which case she is not to go twice following.*

***Leeward Island Mail**, is made up in London on the third Wednesday in every month and is dispatched from Falmouth on the Saturday following. It is taken out by the first packet in turn for Sailing. The Packets are fixed for the Mails they are to take out a fortnight before they sail, and reported in the daily return. The Packets go from the Inner Harbour, where they refit, into the Carrick Road the day previous to their sailing. Twentyone days are allowed for a refit; if they exceed that time their hire is stopped, except the wages of the crew. Packets are mustered weekly while in Harbour, and immediately before their sailing, and on their arrival, and the Captains mulcted the wages and victualling of any of the crew that may be short of complement. Commanders to have the appointment of their officers and crew; but are not allowed to introduce a new surgeon if a regular one is waiting for a vacancy. Officers or seamen rendered casualties while actually in service have their pay continued if there is hope of recovery. If the case is hopeless they are usually pensioned. If officers or seamen die in the service, pensions are granted to their families; pensions are also granted to worn-out seamen.*

*In the case of a commander on shore on leave of absence, one quarter of the mulct imposed is given to the officer appointed by him to command the Packet; the mulct is £30 for a voyage. Each commander is furnished with a proper set of charts for the voyage. He must furnish himself with a chronometre and all the necessary instruments.*

The Admiralty decided to replace the former Packets with ten-gun brigs, a fact which certainly did not please the Falmouth packetmen. They considered the naval vessels to be unstable and unsuitable for the service. Their fears were evidently fully justified, as up till 1830 no less than six of these ships had been lost at sea with all hands.

By 1827 there were 39 Packets on the Falmouth Station, including five on the Lisbon run. Of these 18 were still former Post Office Packets, and the remainder were Admiralty vessels.

A Minute in the Treasury Book, dated 13 March 1838, affords an interesting sidelight on one of the problems which presented itself under the new arrangement concerning allowances paid to persons employed in conveying the mail bags between the Packets and the different Post Offices; *"Previous to the transfer of the Packet Service to the Board of Admirality no expense was incurred for the conveyance of the mails to and from the waters edge, as that service was considered to be part of the packet duty, and was performed under the direction of the commander by parties employed in the vessels - generally the 2nd Officer or Steward, but the Lords of the Admiralty having declined to undertake any part of the land conveyance of the mails, it became necessary to employ persons specially for the purpose in question."*

The Packets on the Falmouth Station at the time of the Admirality assumed control on 3 February 1823 were:-

| Packet | Commander | Age of Packet | Tonnage | Remarks |
|---|---|---|---|---|
| Duke of Malborough | Bull | 17 | 190 | Considerable repairs in 1808, 1810 and 1814. |
| Duke ofKent | Colesworth | 21 | 188 | An established Packet, captured & recaptured & purchased by Capt. Colesworth had a general repair in 1816. |
| Lady Arabella | Porteous | 22 | 172 | |
| Duke of Kent | Lawrence | 16 | 189 | |
| Stanmer | Sutton | 5 | 212 | A general repair last voyage. |
| Sandwich | Schuyler | 12 | 194 | |
| Manchester | Elphinstone | 17 | 187 | Has had considerable repairs amounting to upwards of £2,000. |
| Lady Wellington | Procter | 9 | 191 | |
| Marquess of Sailsbury | Graham | 5 | 210 | |

| Packets | Commanders | Age of Packets | Tonnage | Remarks |
|---|---|---|---|---|
| Prince Regent | White | 1 | 233 | |
| Lord Hobart | James | 17 | 180 | Purchased on the resignation of Cpt. Gammage & had a general repair in 1821. |
| Walsingham | Bullock | 27 | 185 | Purchased on the resignation of Cpt. Roberts & had a general repair in 1821. |
| Queensberry | Hannah | 8 | 188 | |
| Osbornc | Hartney | 9 | 190 | |
| Montague | Watkins | 10 | 190 | |
| Duke of York | Price | 5 | 192 | |
| Blucher | Furse | | | |
| Lord Sidmouth | Pipon | 7 | 192 | |
| Francis Freeling | Cunningham | 15 | 191 | |
| Countess of Chichester | Kirkness | 13 | 193 | |
| Princess Elizabeth | Scott | 21 | 192 | |
| Marquis of Salisbury | Baldock | 2 | 236 | |
| Camden | Tilly | 3 | 191 | |
| Lady Mary Pelam | Cary | 5 | 201 | |
| Prince Ernest | Barron | 27 | 186 | |
| Lady Louisa | Figg | 9 | 190 | |
| Princess Elizabeth | Sleeman | 27 | 188 | |
| Nocton | Morphew | 15 | 191 | |

The itinerary of Mail Service in 1832 shows little alteration since 1820:

*"JAMAICA PACKET. First Wednesday in the Month; proceeds from Falmouth to Barbados, St. Vincent, Grenada, Jamaica, Crooked Island, and home to Falmouth.*

*On the arrival of the Jamaica Packet at Barbados, mail boats are dispatched on the following routes:-*

*One to Demerara, proceeds the next tide to Berbice where she remains three days and returns to Barbados, touching again at Demerara with the bags for England. A second boat proceeds to Tobago and Trinidad, remains at each 12 hours, and touches at Grenada and St. Vincents on her return to Barbados."*

*LEEWARD ISLAND PACKET. Third Wednesday in the Month; proceeds from Falmouth to Barbados, St. Lucia, Martinique, Dominica, Guadeloupe, Antigua, Montserrat, Nevis, St.Kitts, Tortola, St. Thomas, and home to Falmouth.*

*24 hours after the arrival of the Leeward Island Packet at Barbados a mail boat is dispatched to Demerara and Berbice, as in the case of the Jamaica Packet above a second boat goes to Tobago and Trinidad, remaining 72 hours at Tobago and then proceeds to Grenada. A third boat proceeds to St. Vincent, Grenada, Trinidad and Tobago. These two last-mentioned boats meeting at Grenada, one returns to Barbados, the other proceeds to St. Thomas, to deliver the mails for England. Eight days after this Packet has left Barbados another mail boat is dispatched to touch all the Islands where the Packet had previously landed Mails, and collects the bags for England, which she delivers to the Packet at St. Thomas.*

*One of the boats on the return to Barbados touches all the Islands to take up the bags; the other returns without stopping.*

Fresh vessels were supplied for the service as required, e.g. it was reported on 22 October 1832 that "Another fine Schooner, perfectly new, was being introduced for the Mail Boat Service", and on 14th January 1883, "Two fine new Bermuda Schooners, built purposely for the Mail Boat Service." The "Jane", however, was lost on 14 January 1833, and the "Emily"on 4 February 1839.

A new steamer service in the West Indies began in October 1840 but was only in operation in conjunction with the Sailing Packets for just over one year, when the Royal Mail Steam Packet Company began operating. The schedule being:-

*On the arrival of the Packet from England at Barbados, or as soon after the Governor or Senior Naval Officer may consider necessary for the preparation of correspondence, not however exceeding six hours, a Steam Packet is to be dispatched with the mails for Santa Cruz, St. Thomas, St. Juan Porta Rico, Cape Henri Haiti, St.jago de Cuba and Jamaica. The mails for the Spanish Main are to be landed at Port Royal, as at present, to be carried forward in the vessels appropriated for that service.*

*It is expected that the Packet will reach Jamaica on the seventh day from the arrival of the Sailing Packet from England at Barbados, in which case she is to remain eight days at Port Royal, but she is to leave as soon as possible after the expiration of the fifteenth day from such arrival from England, in order that the Homeward bound Sailing Packet, which in the mean time will have come up to Cape Henri, may not be delayed at that place. by the non-arrival of the Steamer from Jamaica at the appointed time.*

*On the arrival of the Packet from England at Barbados, a second steamer is to be dispatched with the mails for St. Vincent, Grenada, Trinidad and La Guayra.*

*A Third Steamer is to be dispatched from Barbados on the arrival of the Packet from England, to deliver mails at Tobago and proceed to Demerara, where the mails for Berbice are to be disembarked and forwarded overland to their destination. The Steamer will stop five days at Demerara, and then go on to Barbados, calling in at Tobago for the return mails. It is expected she will reach Barbados on the afternoon of the eleventh day from her departure from that island.*

*As soon as the sailing Packet from England has delivered the before mentioned mails to the several Steam Packets, she is to proceed to St. Thomas, dropping mails at St. Lucia, Martinique, Dominica, Guadaloupe, Antigua, Montserrrat, Nevis, St. Kitts, and Tortola; and on the morning of the twelfth day, from the arrival of the Packet at Barbados, the Steamer from Demerara, which had arrived on the previous evening, or one of the spare steamers which may have be in readiness at Barbados, is to proceed with the return mails to St. Vincent, there take in the return mails from that island, Grenada, Trinidad, and La Guayra, and then touch at St. Lucia, Martinique, Dominica, Guadaloupe, Antigua, Montserrat, Nevis, St. Kitts, Santa Cruz, and Tortola, for return mails, all of which she will deliver to the Falmouth Packet at St. Thomas. Then she is to return to Barbados, calling at all the intermediate Islands in her route.*

*As soon as the return mails from Guiana, La Guayra, and the Windward and Leeward Islands have been delivered to the sailing Packet at St. Thomas, she is to proceed to St. Juan Porta Rico, and Cape Henri, where she will receive the mails from Jamacia, Cuba, and the Spanish Main, and then proceed on her voyage back to England.*

With the development of steam power it was inevitable that the days of the Sailing Packets were numbered. In 1840 the Government signed a contract with the Royal Mail Steam Packet Co. for the conveyance of mails between the United Kingdom and the West Indies, and by the end of 1841 the Sailing Packet Service to the West Indies came to an end. On 1 January 1842 the R.M.S. "Thames" left Falmouth with the West India Mail. The Company continued to use Falmouth until 1843 when they transferred to Southampton.

In 1845 the steamer Lady McLeod arrived from Glasgow at Trinidad. On 3 November she made her first trip from Port of Spain to San Fernando.

A notice was published by the owners Turnbull & Stewart & Co. in the Port of Spain Gazette, announcing that letters, money and small parcels could be carried for subscribers at the rate of $1 per month. Letters of non-subscribers would be charged 10 cents each.

In November, 1846, the ship was sold to David Bryce who decided to issue a stamp, and on 16 April, 1847 the following was published in The Gazette:

*"The Subscriber experiencing inconvenience in collecting Money for Letters of Non-Subscribers, has procured Labels, which may be had of him or the Agents for the Steamer, at five cents each, Four Dollars per Hundred."*

*"No other Letters but those of subscribers who have paid in advance, or such as have these labels attached, will be carried, from and after the 24th instant."*

*"Freight for parcels and small packages as heretofore.*

*(signed) DAVID BRYCE,*
*Proprietor."*

The stamps probably remained on sale until Bryce sold the ship in 1849.

In 1847, a committee was appointed to inquire into and report on an Inland Postal Service. Their report included the following recommendations:

*(1) That a land service should be run three times a week between Port of Spain, St. Juan's, St. John's, Arouca and Arima, and a ship service five times weekly between the Port of Spain, Couva and San Fernando, with an extra service on Saturdays to La Brea and Cedros.*

*(2) Mail bags sent by ship should be put in charge of a police constable, who would be responsible for them while they are on board.*

*(3)Stamps should be ordered from England for use on letters, but newspapers should be delivered free. The stamps should be overprinted with the name "Trinidad."*

This resulted in stamps being ordered from Messers Perkins Bacon &Co. The stamps had no value indicated but were in different colours. This presumably was because the proposed Inland Postal Rates had not yet been settled.

The first supply was sent on 21 December 1848 (blue and lilac), the second in December1850 (blue and brown).

On 11 August 1852 the Inland Postal Service started, also delivering in the main towns of Port of Spain and San Fernando. Details as follows:-

*6 August, 1851.*

*Public Notice is hereby given, that His Excellency the Governor, under the authority of the Ordinance passed on 4 April last, "For establishing an Inland Post and rates of Postage within this Colony," has established a Postal communication between the Town of Port of Spain and the following places, viz:-*

| | |
|---|---|
| *Chacachacare, Monos,* | *Turture, Manzanilla, Nariva,* |
| *Carenage, Diego Martin,* | *Mayaro, Chaguanas, Couva,* |
| *Santa Cruz, San Juans,* | *San Fernando, Savanna Grande,* |
| *St. Joseph, Arouca, Arima* | *Oropouche, La Brea and Cedros.* |

*The new Postal arrangement is to commence on Thursday the 14th day of August instant.*

*Mails will be made up at the General Post Office in Port of Spain, for the undermentioned places viz:-*

| | |
|---|---|
| *Diego Martin and* | *} On Monday, Wednesday, and Friday,* |
| *Carenage* | *} in each week, at 8 o'clock, a.m.* |

*For Santa Cruz, San Juans, St. Josephs, Arouca, and Arima, every day in the week (Sunday excepted) at 7 o'clock, a.m.*

*For Turture, Manzanilla, Nariva and Mayaro, every Monday, at 7 o'clock, a.m.*

*For Chaguanas, on Tuesday, Thursday, and Saturday in each week, at three hours previous to high water of these days.*

*For Couva,* }
*San Fernando,* }
*Savanna Grande,* } *On Monday, Tuesday, Wednesday, and Thursday of each week, at half past*
*and Oropouche,* } *10 o'clock; and on Saturday at a quarter to 7 o'clock, a.m.*

*For La Brea and Cedros - Every Saturday at a quarter to 7 o'clock, a.m.*

*For Chacachacara and Monos - Every Saturday.*

*From San Fernando the Mails will be made up:-*

> *For Couva and Port of Spain, on Monday*
> > *Tuesday*
> > *Wednesday and*
> > *Thursday, at*
> > *1 o'clock, p.m.*
> > *Saturday, at 4 o'clock p.m.*

*For La Brea and Cedros, at 9 o'clock, a.m., on Saturday.*

*From Diego Martin for Port of Spain, on Monday, Wednesday and Friday.*
*From Santa Cruz for Port of Spain, on Monday, Wednesday and Friday.*
*From Arima and Arouca for Port of Spain, on Tuesday, Thursday and Saturday.*
*From St. Joseph's and San Juan's for Port of Spain, Daily, (Sunday excepted.)*
*From Chaguanas for Port of Spain, on Monday, Wednesday and Friday.*
*From Oropouche to San Fernando, Daily, (Sunday excepted.)*
*From Cedros and La Brea for Port of Spain every Saturday.*
*From Mayaro, Nariva, Manzanilla and Turture, for Arima and Port of Spain every Tuesday.*
*From Chacachacare to Monos every Saturday.*

*Stamps can be purchased upon application at the Colonial Treasury, the Custom House, the General Post Office in Port of Spain, and at the Post Office in San Fernando, and all the Branch Post Offices.*

> *By Command,*
> *THOMAS F. JOHNSTON*
> *Colonial Secretary.*

The following notice was also published in "The Gazette".

> *GENERAL POST OFFICE,*
> *PORT OF SPAIN,*
> *9th August, 1852.*

*"His Excellency the Governor having authorised A DAILY POSTAL DELIVERY (Sunday excepted) within the Towns of Port of Spain and San Fernando commencing this day, the undersigned hereby gives Notice thereof to the Public; and that in order to give greater facility to such delivery, it is*

*necessary that Parties should direct their correspondents to add to the usual address on their Letters, &c., the name of the Street, and also the number of the House in which they reside. In the case of Merchants' Letters, however, these particulars will be unnecessary."*

*"(Signed)*
*JAS. H. O'BRIEN,*
*General Postmaster."*

Mr James H. O'Brien was appointed General Postmaster on 13 August 1851 to administer the service. He was succeeded by Mr Ellys Layton (Colonial Postmaster) on 1 June 1853.

The Ordinance setting up the Inland Post was dated 4 April 1851 and proclaimed on 11 April. However the service only started on 14 August 1851, which was also the presumed date when stamps were issued. The regulations being:-

*AN ORDINANCE*
***For establishing an Inland Post and Rates of Postage within the Colony.***

*Whereas an Act was passed in the Session of Parliament held in the twelfth and thirteenth years of the Reign of Her present Majesty entitled "An Act for enabling Colonial Legislatures to establish Inland Posts"; And whereas it is expedient to establish an Inland Post and rates within this Colony: Be it enacted by His Excellency the Governor with the advice and consent of the Council of Government, that it shall be lawful for His Excellency the Governor from time to time to establish Post Office Communication between the Town of Port of Spain and such parts of the Colony as he may from time to time see fit: and when and so soon as such Post Communications shall have been established, the Governor and the officers appointed by him under this Ordinance and their respective agents and servants shall have the exclusive privilege of conveying from one place to another, between which such Post Communication may be established all letters except in the following cases, and shall also have the exclusive privilege of performing all the incidental services of receiving, collecting, sending, despatching and delivering all letters from any one place to another between such Post Communication may be established except in the following cases, that is to say:-*

*Letters sent by a private friend in his way, journey or travel so as such letters be delivered by such friend to the party to whom they will be directed:*

*Letters sent by messenger on purpose, concerning the private affairs of the sender or receiver thereof, and affidavits and writs, process or proceedings or returns thereof issuing out of a Court of Justice:*

*Letters sent out of the colony by a private vessel (not being a packet).*

*Letters of merchants, owners of vessels, of merchandise or the cargo or loading therein, sent by such vessels of merchandise, or by any person employed by such an owner for the carriage of letters, according to their respective directions and delivered to the respective persons to whom they shall be directed, without paying or receiving hire or reward, advantage or profit for the same in any wise:*

*Letters concerning goods or merchandise sent by Common known carriers to be delivered with the goods which such letters concern without hire or reward or other profit or advantage for receiving or delivering such letters:*

*But nothing herein contained shall authorise any person to make a collection of such excepted letters for the purpose of sending them in the manner hereby authorised.*

*And the following persons are expressly forbidden to carry a letter or to receive or collect or deliver a letter, although they shall not receive hire or reward for the same that is to say:-*

*Common known carriers, their servants or agents, except a letter concerning goods in their carts, wagons or carriages:*

*Owners, masters or commanders of ships, vessels steam boats or droghers sailing or passing coastwise or otherwise, between places within this colony or their servants or agents except in respect of letters of merchants, owners of ship or goods on board:*

*Passengers or other persons on board any such ships, vessels, steam boats or droghers.*

*II. And it be enacted, That there shall be one General Post Office in the Town of Port of Spain, where letters may be received from all places within the colony and parts out of the colony, and whence all letters may be despatched to all places within the colony and to parts out of the colony.*

*III. And be it enacted, That all letters transmitted by post to this Colony or from any place to any other place within this Colony shall, be delivered to the person to whom the same may be addressed at the post office nearest to the residence of such person.*

*IV. And be it enacted, That the Governor may appoint sufficient officers, agents and servants for the better carrying this Ordinance into execution.*

*V. And be it enacted, That no officer of the post office shall be compelled to serve in any corporate or other public office or employment or on any jury or inquest, any law or Ordinance to the contrary thereof, notwithstanding.*

*VI. And be it enacted, That the monies to arise by the several duties granted by this Ordinance shall be paid into the Colonial Treasury, and all charges outgoings and disbursements necessary for the receipt and management of the duties of postage and all other expenses attending the execution of this Ordinance shall be allowed and paid on the warrant of the Governor from the Colonial Treasury.*

*VII. And be it enacted, That half yearly accounts of all monies received by, and of all monies paid from the Colonial Treasury under this Ordinance shall be laid before the Council of Government on the first day of April and the first day of September in each year.*

*VIII. And it be enacted, That on every letter arriving in this colony from any place beyond the limits of the colony, if delivered from the General Post Office for the Port of Spain, and on every letter posted at the General Post Office in Port of Spain for transmission to any place beyond the limits of the colony, there shall be charged and shall be paid to Her Majesty for the use of the colony one uniform rate of one penny.*

*IX. And be it enacted, That the postage payable on all letters arriving in this Colony from any place beyond the limits of this Colony shall be paid by the person to whom the same may be addressed on the delivery of the same to him.*

*X. And it be enacted, That all letters arriving in the colony from any place beyond the limits of this colony, and delivered from any Post-office except the General Post-office in Port of Spain, for* transmission to any place beyond the limits of this colony, and all letters transmitted by the post from any one place to any other place within the limits of this colony, shall be charged by weight, according to the following scale, and the several numbers of rates of postage hereinafter set forth shall be charged, and shall be paid to Her Majesty for the use of the colony on all such letters, that is to say, on every letter not exceeding half ounce and not exceeding one ounce in weight, two rates of postage; on every letter exceeding two ounces and not exceeding three ounces in weight, six rates of postage; and on every letter exceeding three ounces and not exceeding four ounces in weight, eight rates of postage; and for every ounce in weight above the weight of four ounces there shall be charged and taken two additional rates of postage, and every fraction of an ounce above the weight or four ounces shall be charged as an additional ounce; and on all such letters there shall be paid the following rates of postage: that is to say, on every letter not exceeding half an ounce in weight one uniform rate of one penny, and on every letter exceeding half an ounce in weight, progressive and additional rates of postage (each additional rate being estimated at one penny) according to the scale of weight and number of rates herein before fixed and declared.

XI. Provided always, and be it enacted, That as regards all letters posted at any post office within this colony, all such letters when posted shall thereon or affixed thereto a stamp or stamps to the amount of the rates of postage payable on the same under this Ordinance, and in all cases in which any letter shall be posted at any post office within this colony without having thereon or affixed thereto such stamp or stamps or having thereon or affixed thereto any stamp or stamps, the value or amount of which shall be less than the rate of postage to which such letter would be liable under this Ordinance, such letter shall not in any case be forwarded by the post, but shall if posted at any other office other than the General Post Office be transmitted to such General Post Office and shall so far as may be practicable be returned to the sender thereof.

XII. And it be enacted, That the Governor shall from time to time provide proper and sufficient dies or other implements for expressing and denoting rates or duties of one penny and two pence, or rates or duties of any other value or amount as the Governor shall see fit for the purposes herein mentioned; and stamps shall be made or impressed from such dies or other implements as the Governor shall see fit from time to time by writing under his hand direct.

XIII. And it be enacted, That it shall be lawful for the Governor to appoint such persons as he shall see fit, to retail the stamps denoting the duties of postage on letters.

XIV. And be it enacted, That printed newspapers may be sent free of postage or liable to postage according to the rates and regulations hereinafter set forth, that is to say:

| | |
|---|---|
| Printed British or Foreign Newspapers brought to this colony by packet boats or private ships | } Free. } |
| Printed British or Foreign Newspapers or Island Newspapers transmitted by post from one place to any other place within this colony. | } Each One } Penny. |
| Island Newspapers sent by post from this colony. | } Free. |
| Printed votes and proceedings of the Imperial Parliament. Periodical Publications, Pamphlets, Magazines, Reviews and other Publications sent to this colony by Packet, if delivered at the General Post Office, in Port of Spain. | } } One } Penny. } |

| If delivered at any other Post Office, and if not exceeding one ounce. | } One |
| | } Penny. |

| If exceeding one ounce, for every ounce beyond that weight. | } One |
| | } Penny. |

PATTERNS:

| Packets or covers containing patterns or samples, being open at the sides, and not exceeding one ounce, and without any letter or writing in upon or within any such packet or cover, other than the name of the sender, his place of abode, the prices of the articles contained and the name and address of the person to whom the packet or cover shall be sent. | } |
| | } One |
| | } Penny. |
| | } |
| | } |

| Letters not open at the sides containing patterns or samples and not exceeding one ounce in weight. | } Two |
| | } Pence. |

*XV.* And be it enacted, That it shall not be compulsory to send newspapers by post.

*XVI.* And it be enacted, That no printed paper, whether newspaper or votes and proceedings in Parliament shall be sent by the post either free or at the aforesaid rates, unless the following conditions shall be observed;

*1st.* It shall be sent without a cover or in a cover open at the sides.
*2nd.* There shall be no words or communications written upon the paper or upon the cover thereof, except the name and address of the person to whom sent.
*3rd.* There shall be no paper or thing enclosed in or within any such paper.

*XVII.* And be it enacted, That the person having the chief charge of the Post Office in Port of Spain may examine any printed paper or any packet which shall be sent by the post without a cover open at the side, in order to discover whether it is contrary in any respect to the conditions hereby required to be observed, and in any case any one of the required conditions has not been fulfilled, the whole of every such paper or packet shall be charged with treble the duty of postage to which it would have been liable as a letter.

*XVIII.* And it be enacted, That the letters of the undermentioned persons transmitted either by post either to or from them shall be subject to the conditions hereinafter mentioned be exempt from postage; viz: the Governor, the Colonial Secretary, the Attorney General, the Registrar General, the Registrar of the Supreme Civil and Criminal Court and the Inspector and Sub Inspectors or the other Officers of Police: Provided always, that every letter shall be on the public business of the office or department from which the same shall be forwarded, or to which the same shall be addressed and shall be superscribed with the words "On Her Majesty's Service," and with the signature of the officer from whose office or department such letter shall be transmitted, or of the person transmitting such letter to such office or department.

*XIX.* And it be enacted, That no Inland postage shall be charged or payable under this Ordinance on any letter on his own private concerns sent or received by any private soldier or common seaman in this Island who will be actually employed on Her Majesty's Service.

*XX.* And it be enacted, That if any person shall forge or counterfeit or cause or procure to be forged or counterfeited any die, plate or other instrument or any part of any die, plate or other instrument which hath been, or shall or may be provided, made or used by or under the direction of the

Government for the purpose of expressing or denoting any of the rates or duties which are directed to be charged under or by virtue of this Ordinance; or if any person shall forge, counterfeit or imitate, or cause or procure to be forged, counterfeited or imitated the stamp, or mark or impression or any part of the stamp, mark or impression of any such die, plate or other instrument which shall or may be so provided, made or used as foresaid upon any paper or other substance or material whatever, or if any person shall knowingly and without lawful excuse (the proof whereof shall be on the person accused) have in his profession any false forged or counterfeit die, plate or other instrument or part of any such die, plate or other instrument which hath been or shall or may be so provided, made or used as foresaid; or if any person shall stamp or mark or cause or procure to be stamped or marked any paper or other substance of material whatsoever with any such false forged or counterfeit die, plate or other substance or material whatsoever with any such false forged or counterfeit die, plate or other instrument or part of any such die, plate or other instrument as foresaid; or if any person shall use, utter, sell, or expose to sale or shall cause or procure to be used, uttered, sold or exposed to sale or shall knowingly and without lawful excuse (the proof whereof shall lie on the person accused) have in his possession any paper or other substance or material, having thereon the impression or any part of the impression of any such false forged or counterfeit die, plate or other instrument or part of any such die, plate or other instrument, as foresaid or having thereon any false forged or counterfeit stamp or impression resembling or representing either wholly or in part or intended or liable to pass or be mistaken for the stamp, mark or impression of any such die, plate or other instrument which shall or may be so provided, made or used as aforesaid, knowing such false forged or counterfeit; or if any person shall with intent to defraud Her Majesty, Her Heirs or Successors privately or fraudulently use or cause or procure to be privately or fraudulently used any die, plate or other instrument so provided, made or used or hereafter to be provided, made or used as foresaid, or shall with such intent privately or fraudulently stamp or mark or cause or procure to be stamped or marked any paper or other substance or material whatsoever with any such die, plate or other instrument as last aforesaid; or if any person shall knowingly and without lawful excuse (the proof whereof shall lie on the person accused) have in his possession any paper or other substance or material so privately or fraudulently stamped or marked as aforesaid, then and in every such case, every person so offending, and every person knowingly and wilfully aiding, abetting or assisting any person in committing any such offence, and being thereof lawfully convicted, shall be adjudged guilty of felony and shall be liable at the discretion of the court to be imprisoned for any term not exceeding four years nor less than two years with or without hard labour during the whole or any part of the imprisonment as the court shall award.

*XXI. And be it enacted, That if any person shall fraudulently get off or remove or cause or procure to be gotten off or removed from any letter or cover, or any paper or other substance or material, the stamp or impression of any die, plate or other instrument so provided, made or used or hereafter to be provided, made up or used as foresaid with intent to use, join, fix or place such stamp or impression for with or upon any other letter, cover, paper or other substance or material; or if any person shall fraudulently use, join, fix or place for with or upon any letter or cover or any paper or other substance or material, any such stamp or impression as aforesaid which shall have been gotten off or removed from any other letter, cover, paper or other substance or material; or if any person shall fraudulently erase, cut, scrape, discharge or get out of or from or shall cause or procure to be so erased, cut, scraped, discharged or gotten out of or from any letter or cover of any paper or other substance or material, any name, date or other matter or thing thereon written, printed or expressed with intent to use any stamp or mark then impressed or being upon such letter or cover, paper or other substance or material, or that the same may be used for the purpose of defrauding Her*

*Majesty, Her Heirs and Successors of any of the rates or duties aforesaid; or if any person shall make, do or practise or be concerned in any other fraudulent act contrivance or device whatever, not specially provided for by this Ordinance with intent or design to defraud Her Majesty, Her Heirs and Successors of any rates or duties foresaid; every person so offending in any of the several cases in this clause mentioned shall forfeit and pay to Her Majesty, Her Heirs and Successors the sum of Twenty Pounds to be recovered with full costs of suit and all expenses attending the same.*

*XXII. And it be enacted, That every person employed in the execution of this Ordinance who shall contrary to his duty open or procure to be opened a post letter, or shall wilfully detain or delay, or procure or suffer to be detained or delayed a post letter, shall be guilty of a misdemeanor, and being convicted thereof before the Supreme Criminal Court shall suffer such punishment by fine or imprisonment, or by both as to the Court shall seem meet; Provided always that nothing herein contained shall extend to the opening or detaining or delaying of a post letter returned for want of a true direction, or of a post letter returned by reason that the person to whom the same shall be directed is dead or cannot be found, or shall have refused the same, or shall have refused or neglected to pay the postage thereof; or of a post letter returned by reason that the same at the time of posting the same had not thereto a stamp or stamps to the value or amount of the proper postage thereon, nor to the opening or detaining or delaying of a post letter in obedience to an express warrant in writing under the hand of the Governor.*

*XXIII. And be it enacted, That every person employed in the execution of this Ordinance who shall steal, or shall for any purpose whatever embezzle, secrete, or destroy a post letter shall be guilty of felony, and shall on conviction thereof before the Supreme Criminal Court be liable to be imprisoned for any time not exceeding two years; and if any such post letter so stolen or embezzled, secreted or destroyed, shall contain therein any chattel or money whatsoever, or any valuable security, every such offender shall be imprisoned for any term not exceeding four years.*

*XXIV. And be it enacted, That every person who shall steal from or out of a post letter any chattel or money or valuable security shall be guilty of felony, and shall be imprisoned with hard labour for any term not exceeding four years.*

*XXV. And be it enacted, That any person who shall steal a post letter bag or a post letter from a post letter bag, or shall steal a post letter from a post office or from an officer of the post office, or shall stop any person having the custody of any post letter bag with intent to rob or search the same shall be guilty of felony, and shall be imprisoned for any term not exceeding four years.*

*XXVI. And be it enacted with regard to receivers of any property sent by the post and stolen therefrom, That every person who shall receive any post letter or post letter bag, or any chattel or money or valuable security, the stealing or taking or embezzling or secreting whereof shall amount to a felony under this Ordinance, knowing the same to have been feloniously stolen, taken, embezzled or secreted, and to have been sent or have been intended to be sent by the post, shall be guilty of felony, and may be indicated and convicted either as an accessory after the fact or for a substantive felony, and in the latter case whether the principal felon shall or shall not have been previously convicted, or shall or shall not be amenable to justice; and every such receiver howsoever convicted shall be liable to be imprisoned for any term not exceeding four years.*

*XXVII. And be it enacted, That any person who shall fraudently retain or shall willfully secrete or keep or detain or being required to deliver up by an officer of the post office, shall neglect or refuse to deliver up a post letter which ought to have been delivered to any other person, or post letter bag or post letter which shall have been sent, whether the same shall have been found by the person secreting, keeping or detaining, or neglecting or refusing to deliver up the same, or by any other* person, shall be guilty of a misdemeanor, and being convicted thereof shall be liable to be imprisoned for any term not exceeding three years.

*XXVIII. And it be enacted. That every person employed in the execution of this Ordinance who shall steal or shall for any purpose embezzle, secrete or destroy, or shall wilfully detain or delay in course of conveyance of delivery thereof by the post, any printed votes or proceeedings in Parliament, or printed newspaper or other printed paper whatsoever sent by the post without covers or in covers open at the sides, shall be guilty of a misdemeanor, and being convicted thereof shall suffer such punishment by fine or imprisonment or by both as to the said Court shall seem meet.*

*XXIX. And be it enacted, That every person who shall solicit or endeavour to procure any other person to commit a felony or a misdemeanor punishable under this Ordinance shall be guilty of a misdemeanor, and being convicted thereof shall be liable to be imprisoned for any term not exceeding two years.*

*XXX. And be it enacted, That in every case where an offence shall be committed in respect of a post letter bag or a post letter, or any chattel, money, or valuable security sent by the post, it shall be lawful to lay in the indictment presented against the offender the property of the post letter bag or of the post letter, or any chattel or money or the valuable security sent by the post, in Her Majesty, and it shall not be neccessary in the indictment to alledge or to prove upon the trial or otherwise that the post letter bag or any such post letter or valuable security was of any value; and in any indictment to be preferred against any person employed under this Ordinance for any offence committed against this Ordinance it shall be lawful to state and alledge that such offender was employed under the post office of this colony at the time of the committing of such offence without stating further the nature or particulars of his employment.*

*XXXI. And be it enacted, That where a person shall be convicted of an offence punishable under this Ordinance for which imprisonment may be awarded, the Court may sentence the offender to be imprisoned with or without hard labour in the Royal Gaol, and may also direct that he shall be kept in solitary confinement for the whole or any portion of such imprisonment as to the Court shall seem meet.*

*XXXII. And be it enacted, That all duties of postage granted by this Ordinance may be sued for and recovered with full costs of suit in a summary manner by any Justice of the Peace on the complaint of any Post Master.*

*XXXIII. And be it enacted, That within the meaning of this Ordinance, all words and expressions importing the singular number only shall include several persons or things as well as one person or thing, and all words and expressions importing the masculine gender only shall include females as well as males.*

*Passed in Council this Fourth day of April, in the Year of our Lord One Thousand Eight Hundred and Fifty one.*

*RICHARD D. CADIZ, Clerk of Council.*

*The foregoing Ordinance was duly proclaimed by me, in Port of Spain, this 11th day of April, inthe year of our Lord one thousand eight hundred and fifty-one.*

*W. B. GOULD, Marshall.*

The "Port of Spain Gazette" of Friday 15 August 1851 described the event as follows:-

*"The working of the Inland Postal arrangements commenced on Thursday morning last (Lord Harris' birthday). Two mounted policemen left the General Post Office in Frederick Street at 8 o'clock in the morning with the letters for the eastern and western parts of the colony, and the mails for the southern portion were duly forwarded by the steamer. We sincerely wish this undertaking, which commenced so appropriately on the anniversary of the birth of its noble originator, every success; and trust that the advantages, which cannot but result from it, will again and again recall to the minds of the inhabitants of this Colony the deep debt of gratitude which they owe to his Excellency, Lord Harris, for his unceasing and energetic efforts for the improvement and prosperity of Trinidad". (Lord Harris was Governor of the Colony at this time).*

On 22 August 1851 the post office published the following:-

*"THE UNDERSIGNED begs to direct the attention of the public to the Ordinance now in force for "establishing an Inland Post and Rates of Postage within the Colony," by which it is enacted that on all letters received at this office from places beyond the limits of the Colony, and on those posted thereat for such places, there shall be paid one uniform rate of one penny - the penny postage stamp being affixed to every such letter when posted, and a penny being paid at the time of delivery at this Office.*

*It is also enacted, in the case of all such letters posted or received at any Inland Post Office, that the rates of postage shall be paid according to weight.*

*Newspapers are to be received at and dispatched from this Office from and to places beyond the limits of the Colony free of Inland postage, but are liable to a penny each when transmitted by Post from one place to another place within the Colony, which may either be on posting or on delivery.*

*(Signed.)*
*JAMES H. O'BRIEN,*
*Postmaster-General.*

On 9 October 1858 the following notice was published:-

*"IS HEREBY GIVEN, That from and after this date ALL LETTERS addressed to the UNITED KINGDOM must be PREPAID, in order to obviate the apprehended inconvenience of a large number of letters being detained, owing to the writers being ignorant of the new regulations, and thus posting them unpaid; the transmission of such letters for a further limited period, say, until 31st December next, has been sanctioned, but imposing on each a fine of Sixpence, in addition to the postage due upon them."*

*"(Signed)*
*ELLYS LAYTON, Colonial Postmaster."*

As only penny stamps where then available the following was published on 27 December 1858:-

*"FROM FIRST JANUARY NEXT all Letters addressed to the UNITED KINGDOM must be prepaid. Any Letters posted unpaid will not be forwarded to their destination, but will be opened and returned to the writers. The Colonial Penny Stamps now in use will answer the purpose of prepaying Letters, until such time as the requisite description shall have been received from England".*

*"ELLYS LAYTON, Colonial Postmaster."*

Higher denominations 4d, 6d & 1/= became available on 9 May 1859 and the public were reminded on 7 June 1859, that:-

*"All Letters posted for the United Kingdom must be prepaid by Stamps. The Postmaster General would beg to suggest to the public, that in the event of their wishing to pre-pay their Letters to those places where the pre-payment is not compulsory, they should use Stamps insteads of paying money at the Post Office."*

ELLYS LAYTON,
Postmaster General.

On 27 February 1860 the new steamer timetables were published:-

## NOTICE. General Post Office,

27th February, 1860.

THE following arrangements with regard to the Arrival and Departure of the R. M. S. PACKETS, in future, will commence on and after the 22nd March next, the day on which the first Steamer is due here, according to the New Regulations.

| Steamer leave England. | Due at Trinidad. | Leave for Tobago. | Due at Trinidad from Tobago. | Leave for England and the Colonies. | Mails close at G. P. O. | Latest hour at which Letters can be posted on payment of a fine. | Remarks. |
|---|---|---|---|---|---|---|---|
| 2d & 17th of each Month. | 6th & 22d at Noon. | 6 P. M. on 6th & 22d. Mails close at 4 P. M. | 5th & 24th at 1 A. M. | 8th & 24th at 8 A. M. | 7th & 23d at 7 P. M. | 8 P M. | When the preceding Month carries only 30 days, the Steamer will be due on the 7th instead of the 6th, and leave on the 9th instead of the 8th |

## TRINIDAD ROUTE.
### Twice a Month.

| Date. | | Places. | Distance in Miles. | Speed per Hour. | Steam-ings. | | Stoppages | | Coals. | From South-ampton. | |
|---|---|---|---|---|---|---|---|---|---|---|---|
| Arrival. | Departure. | | | | Days. | Hours. | Days. | Hours. | | Days. | Hours. |
| — | 20 & 5 8 p.m | From Barbados | | | — | — | ... | ... | — | 15 | 2 |
| 21 & 6, 6 a.m. | 21 & 6, 5 a.m. | To St. Vincent | 90 | 9 | ... | 10 | ... | 2 | ... | 18 | 12 |
| 21 & 6, 2 p.m | 21 & 6, 2 p.m. | " Carriacou | 50 | 9 | ... | 6 | ... | ... | ... | 18 | 20 |
| 21 & 6, 6 p.m. | 22 & 7, 2 a.m. | " Grenada | 32 | 9 | ... | 4 | ... | 8 | Coal. | 19 | — |
| 22 & 7, noon | 22 & 7, 6 p.m. | " Trinidad | 94 | 9 | ... | 10 | ... | 6 | ... | 19 | 18 |
| 23 & 8, 3 a.m. | 23 & 8, 1 p.m. | " Tobago | 85 | 9 | ... | 9 | ... | 13 | — | 20 | 9 |
| 24 & 9, 1 a.m. | 24 & 9, 8 a.m. | " Trinidad | 85 | 9 | ... | 9 | ... | 7 | ... | 21 | 7 |
| 24 & 9, 6 p.m. | 24 & 9, mid't. | " Grenada | 94 | 9 | ... | 10 | ... | 6 | Coal. | 22 | — |
| 25 & 10, 4 a.m. | 25 & 10, 4 a.m. | " Carriacou | 32 | 9 | ... | 4 | ... | ... | ... | 22 | 10 |
| 25 & 10, 10 a.m. | 25 & 10, noon | " St. Vincent | 50 | 9 | ... | 6 | ... | 2 | ... | 22 | 16 |
| 25 & 10, 10 p.m. | — | " Barbados | 90 | 9 | — | 10 | 9 | 22 | ... | 23 | 4 |
| ... | ... | | 702 | ... | 3 | 6 | 11 | 18 | | | |

|  |  |  |  |  |
|---|---|---|---|---|
| Time out to Trinidad | — | — | 19 | 18 |
| Do. Home from do. | ... | ... | 20 | 10 |
| Course of Post ... | — | ... | 42 | 00 |

Followed on 27 June 1860 by:-

*Antigua, 4th June, 1860.*

*Sir, - I beg to enclose for your information and guidance a copy of a Time Table of the arrivals and departures at the different Termini of the West India Packets.*

*As the trans-Atlantic Steamers sometimes perform the voyage to Saint Thomas in 13 days, it will be necessary that your Outward Mails for places on Routes No. 4 and 5 should be ready for dispatch at least 48 hours before the time laid down in the Table of Routes.*

*You will observe that no alteration is contemplated in the departure from Demerara and Barbados (excepting in the following cases), and the homeward Mails, must therefore, be made up as heretofore.*

*The Note 2 attached to the Time Table specially relates to occasions when the Outward Packets leave Southampton on the 3rd instead of the 2nd, and on the 18th instead of the 17th of the month, and you will see that in five instances the Branch Packets on Routes 4 and 5 are set down to leave Demerara and Tobago, on the return voyage, one day later than they would have left under ordinary circumstances.*

*A further exception is made when the Packets leaving on the 3rd or 18th shall arrive at Trinidad before time, in which case they are permitted to leave Demerara and Tobago the day previous to that laid down in the Time Table.*

*You will be good enough to give notice to the public of these alterations in the Packet Service; and I think you will do well to obtain from the Admiralty Agent in charge of the Outward Mails a notification in writing of the day and hour upon which the return Packet may be expected to arrive at Trinidad, as the Steamers cannot be detained by you for Mails under any plea whatsoever.*

*It is obvious that the earlier departure from Saint Thomas of the Packet proceeding to Windward is to facilitate as much as possible the arrival of the London Mails at Demerara and other important Colonies on Routes No.4 and 5.*

*I am, Sir, your obedient servant,*

*(Signed) CHAS. BENNETT.*

*To all the Postmasters and Packet Agents,*
*Routes No.4 and 5.*

The following table shows the outward and Homeward Routes of Barbados and Tobago:-

| Outward Route. | | Homeward Bout | |
|---|---|---|---|
| BRANCH No. 5. | | BRANCH No. 5. | |
| Barbados to Tobago. | | Tobago to Barbados. | |
| Leave Barbados | Arrive at Tobago. | Leave Tobago. | Arrive at Barbados. |
| 8 P.M. | 3 A.M. | 4 P.M. | 10 P.M. |
| April 20 | April 23 | April 23 | April 25 |
| May 5 | May 8 | May 8 | May 10 |
| May 20 | May 23 | May 23 | May 25 |
| June 4 | June 7 | June 7 | June 9 |
| June 20 | June 23 | June 23 | June 25 |
| July 6 | July 9 | July 9 | July 11 |
| July 20 | July 23 | July 23 | July 25 |
| August 4 | August 7 | August 7 | August 9 |
| August 20 | August 23 | August 23 | August 25 |
| Sept. 4 | Sept. 7 | Sept. 7 | Sept. 9 |
| Sept. 21 | Sept. 24 | Sept. 24 | Sept. 26 |
| Oct. 5 | Oct. 8 | Oct. 8 | Oct. 10 |
| Oct. 20 | Oct. 23 | Oct. 23 | Oct. 25 |
| Nov. 4 | Nov. 7 | Nov. 7 | Nov. 9 |
| Nov. 20 | Nov. 23 | Nov. 23 | Nov. 25 |
| Dec. 5 | Dec. 8 | Dec. 8 | Dec. 10 |
| Dec. 21 | Dec. 24 | Dec. 24 | Dec. 26 |
| 1861... Jan. 4 | Jan. 7 | Jan. 7 | Jan. 9 |
| Jan. 20 | Jan. 23 | Jan. 23 | Jan. 25 |
| Feb. 4 | Feb. 7 | Feb. 7 | Feb. 9 |
| Feb. 20 | Feb. 23 | Feb. 23 | Feb. 25 |
| March 8 | March 10 | March 10 | March 12 |
| March 20 | March 23 | March 23 | March 25 |
| April 5 | April 8 | April 8 | April 10 |

NOTE 1.—The Branch Packets, on the Outward Route, may start earlier than the time fixed if the Packets from Southampton or St. Thomas have arrived, and they are ready to proceed.

NOTE 2.—When the departure from England takes place on the 3rd instead of the 2nd, and the 18th instead of the 17th, of the Month, the Dates for Despatch of the corresponding Return Mails from the respective Termini are (except as regards Honduras) laid down in this Table one day later than they would have been under ordinary circumstances. In such cases, however, if the Branch Steamers have arrived before the time at which they are due according to this Table, and are ready to depart the day previous to the one therein mentioned, they may do so.

On 10 December 1860 a new Ordinance regarding Inter-Colonial letters was passed:-

*"Whereas it would tend to the public convenience if all Letters sent by the Post from or to this Colony to or from any other of Her Majesty's Colonies were prepaid, and the amount of Colonial Postage chargeable by the Colony, to which such Letters may be sent by Post, were*

paid to and collected by the Post Office Authorities of the Colony, from which such Letters may be sent: Be it enacted by His Excellency the Governor, by and with the advice and consent of the Council of Government, as follows:-

1. It shall be lawfull for the Governor from time to time to enter into an agreement with the Governor, or Lieutenant Governor, or the Post Office Authorities of any Colony belonging to Her Majesty for the mutual collection at the respective Post Offices of this Colony and of such other Colony, as well of the Postage chargeable by the Post Office of this Colony, as of the Postage chargeable by the Post Office of such other Colony, on Letters sent by Post from or to this Colony to or from such other Colony; and so long as such agreement shall remain in force the Postage on all Letters sent by the Post from this Colony to such other Colony chargeable by the Post Office of the Colony, to which the same shall be sent, as well as the Postage chargeable by the Post Office of this Colony shall be prepaid in one sum, and the Post Master General of this Colony shall account for and pay over to the Post Office Authorities of such other Colony the amount of the Postage, to which such Colony shall be entitled."

Due to the American Civil War the following notice was published by J. Scott Bushe, Colonial Secretary:-

Saint Thomas, 14th May, 1861.

SIR.- I beg to inform you that the communication by American Steamers between Havana and the States of North America has been suspended, in consequence of the disturbances in the latter country, and that the service has been, as a temporary relief, maintained by Spanish Vessels of War.

All Letters, &c., for the Federal Government of the United States which may have reached St. Thomas by the last Mail from your Office, will therefore be sent in a closed Bag to Halifax for conveyance, thence to Boston. The British Packet, upon this time, should leave St. Thomas on the 10th June next, and every fourth Monday subsequent to that date. The Packet which sails from Jamaica on the 5th of each month, will continue the communication as heretofore.

I beg to add that the Packet Service between the West Indies and the seceded States of America, is entirely interrupted by the blockade of the several Ports of the Confederacy, and the correspondance for those States, will, as a rule, be sent to Havana to await a favorable opportunity from that place.

In either case, however, the directions upon the face of the Letters, whether "via Jamaica, via Bermuda and Halifax, or, via Havana," will be considered as the route indicated by the Public for the transmission of correspondance to the Federal or seceded States of the Union.

I am, Sir,<br>
Your Obedient Servant,<br>
(S'd) CHAS. BENNETT.

To all Postmasters and Packet Agents in the West Indies.

Followed a few days later by a new Ordinance:-

18 May, 1861.

1. "The eighth clause of the said Ordinance (4th April, 1851) shall be and the same is hereby repealed."

2. "The postage on all the letters brought into this Colony from any place beyond this Colony, and

on all letters posted at any Post Office of this Colony for transmission to any other place within the limits of the Colony or beyond the limits of the Colony shall be charged by weight according to the following scale, and the several numbers of rates of postage hereinafter set forth shall be charged and shall be paid to Her Majesty for the use of the Colony on all such letters; that is to say: on every letter not exceeding half an ounce in weight, one rate of postage; on every letter exceeding half an ounce and not exceeding one ounce in weight, two rates or postage; on every letter exceeding one ounce and not exceeding two ounces in weight, four rates of postage; on every letter exceeding two ounces and not exceeding three ounces of weight, six rates of postage; and on every letter exceeding three ounces and not exceeding four ounces in weight, eight rates of postage; and for every ounce in weight above the weight of four ounces there shall be charged and taken two additional rates of postage and every fraction of an ounce above the weight of four ounces shall be charged as one additional ounce; and on all such letters there shall be paid the following rates of postage; that is to say: on every letter not exceeding half an ounce in weight, one uniform rate of one penny, and on every letter exceeding half an ounce in weight, progressive and additional rates of postage (each additional rate being estimated at on penny) according to the scale of weight and number of rates herein before fixed and charged."

Therefore letters brought into this Colony from any place beyond this Colony and letters posted at any Post Office of this Colony for transmission to any other place within the limits of the Colony or beyond the limits of the Colony will be charged an Inland Rate by weight in addition to the Imperial Postage, that is:-

A letter not exceeding $\frac{1}{2}$oz in weight - 1 penny, and on every letter exceeding half an ounce in weight progressive and additional rates of postage (each additional rate being estimated at one penny) according to the scale of weight and number of rates.

This notice refers to Inter-Colonial Postages only, as the same scale is already in existence in respect to letters to and from the United Kingdom, and to places the correspondance of which is transmitted through the United Kingdom.

WILLIAM EVERSLEY,
Postmaster General.
18th May, 1861.

Regulations regarding ship letters were published on 25th July 1862:-

1. The Postmaster General may allow to the Masters of Ships two pence for each letter which they shall deliver to the Post Office in this Island, and every Master of a Ship bound inward shall cause all Letters on board his Vessel, except those addressed to the owner of the Vessel or of the goods on board, to be collected and enclosed in some bag or other envelope, and shall deliver that same at the Port or Place in this Island, where the Vessel shall report, and shall at such a Port or Place sign a declaration in the presence of the Postmaster General or other Officer having charge of the Post Office at such Port or Place will also sign the same, and such declaration shall be in form and to the effect following:-

I. (A.B.) Master of the (state the name of the Ship or Vessel), arrived from (state the place) do, as required by Law, solemnly declare, that I have to the best of my knowledge and belief delivered or caused to be delivered to the Post Office every Letter, Bag, Package, or Parcel of Letters that were on board the (state the name of the Ship) except such Letters as are exempted by Law.

*And no Receiver General or Officer of the Customs shall permit any Vessel to report until such declaration shall be made and produced, and no Vessel shall be permitted by an Officer of Customs to break bulk or make entry until all Letters on board the same shall be delivered to the Post Office, except Letters addressed to the owners of the Vessel of goods on board, and also except all such Letters as shall be brought by a vehicle liable to the performance of Quarantine all which last mentioned Letters shall be delivered by the persons having the possession thereof to the persons appointed to superintend the Quarantine, that all proper precautions may be taken before the delivery thereof; and the Harbour Master and Officers of Customs shall search every Vessel for Letters which may be on board.*

*II. Every person being either the Master of a Vessel bound to this Island or one of the Officers or one of the Crew thereby who shall have knowingly have any Letter in his possession, after the Master shall have sent any part of his Ship's Letters to the Post Office, shall forfeit for every letter five pounds, and whether the Letter be in the luggage or on the person of the offender or otherwise in his custody, it shall be held to be in his possession, and every such person who shall detain any such Letter after demand made, either by any Officer of the Customs or by a person authorised by the Postmaster General to demand Ship Letters, shall forfeit for every Letter ten pounds.*

*III. All penalties imposed by this Ordinance may be sued for and recovered with full costs of suit in a summary manner before any Justice Of Peace on the complaint of any Officer of the Post Office.*

*IV. On every Ship Letter delivered from any Post Office in this Colony shall be charged and shall be paid to Her Majesty for the use of the Colony the sum of two pence, together with the same rates of postage as are chargeable on all Letters brought into this Colony under Ordinance No. 24 of 1860, entitled "An Ordinance for altering the Rates of Postage on Letters."*

At this time Unpaid Letters were opened and returned to the sender. When the postage was missing a list was published, examples being:-

> General Post Office,
> 10th December, 1862.

*The writers of the letters bearing the following addresses are hereby informed that they cannot be forwarded to their destination unless the postage chargeable thereon be prepaid - if they are not claimed within one month from date, they will be opened and returned by virtue of Ordinance No. 18, of 1859:-*

| | |
|---|---|
| *Madame Foheringham,* | *Southhampton* |
| *Monsieur Fongainville,* | *Martinique* |
| *Mlle. Hannah Febeuse,* | *Cayenne* |
| *Francais H. Moore, Esq,* | *Barbados* |
| *John B. Holder,* | *Barbados* |
| *Mrs James Sparrock,* | *Barbados* |
| *Mr. Emanuel Morris,* | *Demerara* |
| *Monsieur Vachier* | *Martinique* |
| *Monsieur Deriveire,* | *Martinique* |
| *Coursaoi Place Mouryage* | *Martinique* |
| *Aline* | *Martinique* |
| *Mrs Allsopp, London, W.* * | |
| *Mary Charles, England.* * | |

*\* Posted with Demerara stamps not available in this Colony.*

*WILLIAM EVERSLEY, Post Office General.*

The cost of various Mail Services were:-

|  | 1861. | 1862. |
|---|---|---|
| Subsidy Steamer | £2, 676 11 8 | £2, 578 0 0 |
| Sailing Vessels |  | 68 6 5½ |
| Oropouche | 30 0 0 | 30 0 0 |
| Chacachacare | 20 0 0 | 20 0 0 |
| Mayaro | 80 11 8 | 83 7 6 |
| Boats Landing Mails | 93 19 2 | 82 10 0 |
| Express | 12 8 11½ | 17 4 9½ |
| San Fernando Jetty |  | 12 0 0 |
| Arima and Port of Spain | 338 2 0 | 370 5 0 |
| Diego Martin | 93 6 0 | 64 2 6 |
| Sav. Grande, by Tram | 122 6 8 | 120 0 0 |
| Miscellaneous | 12 1 8 |  |
|  | £3, 479 7 9½ | £3, 446 6 3 |

The rules regarding official letters were strictly applied from 1 January 1863, letters not properly endorsed being returned.

A monthly service to Venezuela by the Steamer 'Toro' started on 10 February 1863.

From 7 September 1863 Mails could be sent to the U. K. by French Packet (if so endorsed) at the same rate as by British Packet.

In 1868 the following notices were published regarding packets:-

*2nd March, 1808.*

*LETTERS can be forwarded to the UNITED STATES by the AMERICO-BRAZILIAN STEAM-ERS which leave ST. THOMAS on the 14th of each month if specially directed "By United States Packet from St. Thomas." Letters can likewise be forwarded for the United States via Havana - if so directed - by the British Packets proceeding to this Port from St. Thomas about the 16th of every month, as well as by the Spanish Packets which have lately been subsidized by the British Government to ply twice a month between St. Thomas, Puerto Rico, Sto. Domingo, Puerto Plata, Sto. Jago de Cuba, and other Ports in the Island of Cuba.*

*Letters, &c. for the United States if not specially directed will be forwarded by the Cunard Packets proceeding to Halifax from St. Thomas every lunar month.*

*The Cunard Packets will leave St. Thomas on the following dates of the current year:*

*9th March,*
*6th April,*
*4th May,*
*1st June,*
*30th June.*

*H. CHIPCHASE,*
*Postmaster General.*

*It has been found expedient to make an alteration in the time for despatching the homeward mails from Demerara and Barbados, under which the Packets on route No. 3 will be due at St. Lucia on their way to St. Thomas, at 10 a.m. on the 20th and 11th of each month, instead of at 8 p.m., on those days.*

*This change renders necessary a corresponding alteration in the Sailing of the homeward Packets on the Trinidad route, and such Packets will leave TRINIDAD on the 24th and 9th of each month at 6 p.m. instead of on the 25th and 10th at 8 a.m.*

*H. CHIPCHASE.*
*Postmaster-General.*

The 1871 Quarantine Regulations stated:- *The Harbour Master may receive from the Officer in charge of Her Majesty's Mails, or from the Master of any vessel in Quarantine, Letters, Documents and other Papers, but the same must be forthwith properly fumigated, and all other precautions observed at such time and in such manner as shall be directed by the Health Officer of Shipping.*

Trinidad joined the Universal Postal Union with effect from 1 July 1884.

On July 1884 the Mail arrangements for the U. S. A. were changed:-

*General Post Office,*
*Trinidad, 26th July, 1884.*

*"In future the Mail which is made up for the United States of America for despatch by the Royal Mail Steamer on the 27th of each month will be sent to Barbados, to be forwarded from there by a Steamer of the Royal Mail Steam Packet Company's Service, Leaving Barbados on the 29th of every month."*

*J. A. BULMER,*
*Postmaster General.*

In September of that year the service did not operate owing to the loss of the Royal Mail Steamship "Dart" at Santos, Brazil, mail being forwarded via St. Thomas. The service was restored 29 November 1884. Another sailing was cancelled on 27 May 1885. On 17 April 1885 the timing of the local mail services was changed to:-

*Mails for Cedros, La Brea, Irois Forest, Cap de Ville, Erin and Oropouche will be closed at Chief Office, Port-of-Spain, at 7 a.m. on Thursdays and Sundays.*

*Carenage Mails will be closed at Chief Office, Port of Spain, at 7.30 a.m. on Mondays, Wednesdays and Saturdays.*

*Mails from Carenage will be delivered at 7 a.m. on Tuesdays, Thursdays and Saturdays.*

*Five Islands and Monos.- Mails will be closed at Chief Office, Port-of-Spain, at 7.30 a.m. on Wednesdays.*

*Mails from Five Islands and Monos will be delivered in Port-of-Spain at 7 a.m. on Thursdays.*

The timetable for the revised West Indies Packet Service being published a few weeks later:-

A Table of the West India Mail Packet Service - For the Second Half of the Year 1885.

## HOMEWARD ROUTE.

| TABLE No. 5. | | | TABLES No. 3 AND No 4. | | | | TABLE No. 2. | | | TABLE No. 1. | | | | | |
|---|---|---|---|---|---|---|---|---|---|---|---|---|---|---|---|
| ST. THOMAS TO BARBADOS. | | | TOBAGO AND TRINIDAD TO BARBADOS. | | | | DEMERARA TO BARBADOS. | | | COLON TO BARBADOS. | | | | BARBADOS TO PLYMOUTH. | |
| No. of Voyage. | Leave St. Thomas. | Arrive at Barbados. | No. of Voyage. | Leave Tobago | Leave Trinidad. | Arrive at Barbados. | No. of Voyage. | Leave Demerara. | Arrive at Barbados. | No. of Voyage. | Leave Colon. | Leave Jamaica. | Arrive at Barbados. | Leave Barbados. | Arrive at Plymouth |
| | 8 p. m. Thurs. | 7 a.m. Mon. | | 6 p.m. Fri. | 5 p.m. Sat. | 7 a.m. Mon. | | 10 a m. Sat. | Midn't Sun. | | 9 a.m. Sun. | 4 p.m. Wed. | 5 p.m. Sun. | 5 p.m. Mon. | 10 p.m. Sat. |
| | | | | | | | (c). | | | (a). | | | (b). | | |
| 2 | 23 July | 27 Jul. | 30 | ...... | 25 Jul. | 27 Jul. | 58 | 25 Jul. | 26 Jul. | 86 | 19 Jul | 22 Jul. | 26 Jul. | 27 Jul. | 8 Aug |
| 4 | 6 Aug. | 10 Aug | 32 | 7 Aug | 8 Aug | 10 Aug | 60 | 8 Aug | 9 Aug | 88 | 2 Aug | 5 Aug | 9 Aug | 10 Aug | 22 Aug |
| 6 | 20 Aug. | 24 Aug | 34 | ...... | 22 Aug | 24 Aug | 62 | 22 Aug | 23 Aug | 90 | 16 Aug | 19 Aug | 23 Aug | 24 Aug | 5 Sep. |
| 8 | 3 Sept | 7 Sep. | 36 | 4 Sep. | 5 Sep. | 7 Sep | 64 | 5 Sep | 6 Sep. | 92 | 30 Aug | 2 Sep. | 6 Sep. | 7 Sep. | 19 Sep. |
| 10 | 17 Sept. | 21 Sep. | 38 | ...... | 19 Sep. | 21 Sep. | 66 | 19 Sep. | 20 Sep | 94 | 13 Sep | 16 Sep | 20 Sep. | 21 Sep. | 3 Oct. |
| 12 | 1 Oct. | 5 Oct. | 40 | 2 Oct. | 3 Oct. | 5 Oct. | 68 | 3 Oct. | 4 Oct. | 96 | 27 Sep. | 30 Sep. | 4 Oct. | 5 Oct. | 17 Oct. |
| 14 | 15 Oct. | 19 Oct. | 42 | ...... | 17 Oct. | 19 Oct. | 70 | 17 Oct | 18 Oct. | 98 | 11 Oct. | 14 Oct. | 18 Oct. | 19 Oct. | 31 Oct. |
| 16 | 29 Oct. | 2 Nov | 44 | 30 Oct. | 31 Oct | 2 Nov | 72 | 31 Oct | 1 Nov | 100 | 25 Oct | 28 Oct. | 1 Nov | 2 Nov | 14 Nov |
| 18 | 12 Nov | 16 Nov | 46 | ...... | 14 Nov | 16 Nov | 74 | 14 Nov | 15 Nov | 102 | 8 Nov | 11 Nov | 15 Nov | 16 Nov | 28 Nov |
| 20 | 26 Nov | 30 Nov | 48 | 27 Nov | 28 Nov | 30 Nov | 76 | 28 Nov | 29 Nov | 104 | 22 Nov | 25 Nov | 29 Nov | 30 Nov | 12 Dec |
| 22 | 10 Dec. | 14 Dec | 50 | ...... | 12 Dec | 14 Dec | 78 | 12 Dec | 13 Dec | 106 | 6 Dec | 9 Dec | 13 Dec | 14 Dec | 26 Dec |
| | | | | | | | | | | | | | | | 1886 |
| 24 | 24 Dec. | 28 Dec | 52 | 25 Dec | 26 Dec | 28 Dec | 80 | 26 Dec | 27 Dec | 108 | 20 Dec | 23 Dec | 27 Dec | 28 Dec | 9 Jan. |
| | 1886 | 1886 | | | 1886 | 1886 | | 1886 | 1886 | | 1886 | 1886 | 1886 | 1886 | |
| 26 | 7 Jan. | 11 Jan. | 54 | ...... | 9 Jan. | 11 Jan. | 82 | 9 Jan. | 10 Jan. | 110 | 3 Jan. | 6 Jan. | 10 Jan. | 11 Jan. | 23 Jan. |
| | | | | 1886 | | | | | | | | | | | |
| 28 | 21 Jan. | 25 Jan | 56 | 22 Jan. | 23 Jan. | 25 Jan. | 84 | 23 Jan. | 24 Jan | 112 | 17 Jan. | 20 Jan. | 24 Jan. | 25 Jan | 6 Feb |

## OUTWARD ROUTE.

| | TABLE No. 1. | | | | | TABLE No. 2. | | TABLES No. 3 AND No. 4. | | | | TABLE No. 5. | | |
|---|---|---|---|---|---|---|---|---|---|---|---|---|---|---|---|
| | SOUTHAMPTON TO BARBADOS. | | BARBADOS TO COLON. | | | BARBADOS TO DEMERARA. | | BARBADOS TO TRINIDAD AND TOBAGO. | | | | BARBADOS TO ST. THOMAS. | | |
| No. of Voyage. | Leave Southampton. | Arrive at Barbados. | Leave Barbados. | Arrive at Jamaica. | Arrive at Colon. | No. of Voyage. | Leave Barbados. | Arrivo at Demerara | No. of Voyage. | Leave Barbados. | Arrive at Trinidad. | Arrive at Tobago | No. of Voyage. | Leave Barbados. | Arrive at St. Thomas. |
| | 6 P.M. Thurs. | 7 a.m. Wed. | 9 a m. Thurs. | 8 a.m. Mon. | 7 a.m. Thurs. | | 2 p m. Wed. | 6 a.m. Fri. | | 8 p m. Wed. | 7 a.m. Fri. | 3 a.m Sat. | | 5 p m Wed. | 4 p.m. Sun. |
| 1 | 2 Jul. | 15 Jul. | 16 Jul. | 20 Jul. | 23 Jul. | 29 | 15 Jul. | 17 Jul. | 57 | 15 Jul. | 17 Jul. | ... | 85 | 15 Jul. | 19 Jul. |
| 3 | 16 Jul. | 29 Jul. | 30 Jul. | 3 Aug | 6 Aug | 31 | 29 Jul. | 31 Jul. | 59 | 29 Jul | 31 Jul. | 1 Aug | 87 | 29 Jul. | 2 Aug. |
| 5 | 30 Jul. | 12 Aug | 13 Aug | 17 Aug | 20 Aug | 33 | 12 Aug | 14 Aug | 61 | 12 Aug | 14 Aug | ... | 89 | 12 Aug | 16 Aug |
| 7 | 13 Aug | 26 Aug | 27 Aug | 31 Aug | 3 Sep. | 35 | 26 Aug | 28 Aug | 63 | 26 Aug | 28 Aug | 29 Aug | 91 | 26 Aug | 30 Aug. |
| 9 | 27 Aug | 9 Sep. | 10 Sep. | 14 Sep. | 17 Sep. | 37 | 9 Sep. | 11 Sep | 65 | 9 Sep. | 11 Sep. | ... | 93 | 9 Sep | 13 Sep. |
| 11 | 10 Sep. | 23 Sep. | 24 Sep. | 28 Sep | 1 Oct. | 39 | 23 Sep. | 25 Sep. | 67 | 23 Sep. | 25 Sep. | 26 Sep | 95 | 23 Sep. | 27 Sep. |
| 13 | 24 Sep. | 7 Oct. | 8 Oct. | 12 Oct. | 15 Oct. | 41 | 7 Oct. | 9 Oct. | 69 | 7 Oct. | 9 Oct. | ... | 97 | 7 Oct. | 11 Oct. |
| 15 | 8 Oct. | 21 Oct. | 22 Oct. | 26 Oct. | 29 Oct. | 43 | 21 Oct. | 23 Oct. | 71 | 21 Oct. | 23 Oct. | 24 Oct | 99 | 21 Oct | 25 Oct. |
| 17 | 22 Oct. | 4 Nov | 5 Nov | 9 Nov | 12 Nov | 45 | 4 Nov | 6 Nov | 73 | 4 Nov | 6 Nov | ... | 101 | 4 Nov | 8 Nov. |
| 19 | 5 Nov | 18 Nov | 19 Nov | 23 Nov | 26 Nov | 47 | 18 Nov | 20 Nov | 75 | 18 Nov | 20 Nov | 21 Nov | 103 | 18 Nov | 22 Nov. |
| 21 | 19 Nov | 2 Dec. | 3 Dec. | 7 Dec. | 10 Dec. | 49 | 2 Dec. | 4 Dec | 77 | 2 Dec. | 4 Dec. | ... | 105 | 2 Dec. | 6 Dec. |
| 23 | 3 Dec. | 16 Dec. | 17 Dec. | 21 Dec. | 24 Dec. | 51 | 16 Dec. | 18 Dec. | 79 | 16 Dec. | 18 Dec | 19 Dec. | 107 | 16 Dec. | 20 Dec. |
| 25 | 17 Dec. | 30 Dec. | 31 Dec. | 1886 4 Jan. | 1886 7 Jan. | 53 | 30 Dec. | 1886 1 Jan. | 81 | 30 Dec. | 1886 1 Jan. | ... | 109 | 30 Dec. | 1886 3 Jan. |
| 27 | 31 Dec. | 1886 13 Jan. | 1886 14 Jan. | 18 Jan. | 21 Jan. | 55 | 1886 13 Jan | 15 Jan. | 83 | 1886 13 Jan. | 15 Jan. | 16 Jan. | 111 | 1886 13 Jan. | 17 Jan. |

In order that the Royal Mail Steam Packet Company may be enabled to work in the new West India Contract with the current one, the Postmaster General of the United Kingdom has Sanctioned the following arrangement for this and next month.

### INWARD.
Arrive Trinidad Tuesday, 30th June.
Do.   do.   Friday, 17th July, 7 a.m.
Do.   do.   Friday, 31st July, 7 a.m.
and every alternate Friday afterwards.

### OUTWARD.
Depart from Trinidad Saturday, 27th June.
Do.   do.   Friday, 10th July.
Do.   do.   Saturday, 25th July.
and every alternate Saturday afterwards.

The hours for closing the Outward Mails will remain as at present, viz.: Letters bearing ordinary postage, up to 1.30 p.m., with late Fee affixed up to 3 p.m.

The Agents of the Royal Mail Steam Packet Company give notice that there will be no Steamer of that line running from Barbados to New York on 29th July next.

On 1 September 1885 all Trinidad stamps issued before 1 September 1883 became invalid. A Letter Carrier, Joseph Flaveney was found embezzling and detaining letters, some of the latter were listed in the "Gazette":-

## PAID INLANDS.
### (LETTERS SENT OUT FOR DELIVERY.)

| Address. | Origin. | Destination. | Received at San Fernando. |
|---|---|---|---|
| Bideau, Miss Marie ... | ... Port-of-Spain ... | San Fernando ... | 8th August, 1885. |
| Eastman, Wm. ... | ... San Fernando ... | ,, | ... 13th June, 1885. |
| Edward, John ... | ... Port-of-Spain ... | ,, | ... 23rd June, 1885. |
| Ferryton, Miss Jane ... | ... | ,, | ... 27th June, 1885. |
| Gardean, Mrs. George ... | ... Chaguanas ... | ,, | ... 7th August, 1885. |
| Juppy ... | ... ,, | ,, | ... 8th August, 1885. |
| Kelaart, Josephine ... | ... Port-of-Spain ... | ,, | ... 10th August, 1885. |
| Monagus, John ... | ... Chaguanas ... | ,, | ... 4th August, 1885. |
| Smith, Richard ... | ... San Fernando ... | ,, | ... 1st July, 1885. |
| Taylor, Joseph ... | ... Port-of-Spain. ... | ,, | .. 8th August, 1885. |
| Wears, Miss E. ... | ... ,, | ,, | ... 24th June, 1885. |

## PAID SEAS.
### (LETTERS SENT OUT FOR DELIVERY.

| Bullock, Mrs. George P. ... | ... St. Vincent ... | San Fernando ... | 20th June, 1885. |
|---|---|---|---|
| Dorway, Job ... | ... British Guiana ... | ,, | .. 27th June, 1885. |
| Hunt, Mrs. Mary ... | ... St. Vincent ... | ,, | ... 8th August, 1885. |
| Mason, Miss Elizabeth ... | ... Barbados ... | ,, | ... 12th June, 1885. |
| Richards, Browne ... | ... St. Vincent ... | ,, | ... 8th August, 1885. |
| Ceipio, Charles ... | ... Tobago ... | ,, | ... 8th August, 1885. |
| Willock, John ... | ... Montserrat ... | ,, | ... 20th June, 1885. |
| Alex. Chollong (Newspaper) | ... London ... | ,, | ... |

## OFFICIALS.
### (SENT OUT FOR DELIVERY.)

Jno. T. Prince ...Returned Letter from G. P. O. ...Received at San Fernando, 4th July, 1885.

Ramdeen, Mr. ...Registered Letter, Notice issued...Received at San Fernando, 11th July, 1885.

Ramkatan Lohar...Registered Letter, Notice issued...Received at San Fernando, 1st July, 1885.

## UNPAID SEAS.
### (LETTERS HANDED TO FLAVENEY ON BOARD THE PELICAN AND ELSEWHERE.)

| Address. | Destination. |
|---|---|
| Budree, Tywarry ... ... | ... India. |
| Burt, A. Hamilton ... ... | ... England. |
| Burg, C. A. ... ... | ... Germany. |
| Farrel, James R. ... ... | ... Venezuela. |
| Hamilton, Madame Arthur ... | ... Grenada. |
| Smith & Co., Messrs. Geo. ... | ... Glasgow. |
| Volker, A. H. ... ... | ... Germany. |

J. A. BULMER,<br>Postmaster-General.

General Post Office,
    Trinidad,
        1st September, 1885.

# UNPAID INLANDS.

## (LETTERS HANDED TO FLAVENEY ON BOARD THE "PELICAN" AND ELSEWHERE.

| Address. | Destination. |
|---|---|
| Abraham, Miss Octavia ... ... ... | San Fernando. |
| Betholomen, Madame Elizabeth ... ... | ,, |
| Bowen, Miss Theresa ... ... ... | ,, |
| Caral ... ... ... | California. |
| Cazo, Madame Lubren ... ... ... | Moruga. |
| Copeman, Wm. A. ... ... ... | Port-of-Spain. |
| Dick, Robert ... ... ... | Princes Town. |
| Edward, Robert ... ... ... | Moruga. |
| Fodderingham, Miss Florence ... ... | Port-of-Spain. |
| Ford, Emanuel ... ... ... | ,, |
| Hewitt, Miss Jane ... ... ... | ,, |
| Isaac, Miss Mary ... ... ... | San Fernando. |
| Hobson, H. P. ... ... ... | Princes Town. |
| Lee, Madame ... ... ... | St. Madeleine. |
| Lee, Madame ... ... ... | ,, |
| Pemberton, Edward ... ... ... | San Fernando. |
| Pemberton, Mrs. Susanah ... ... | ,, |
| Pemberton, Mrs. Susanah ... ... | ,, |
| Pollonais, Mrs. ... . ... ... | ,, |
| Sarah ... ... ... | California. |
| Simpson, Robert Thomas ... ... | Port-of-Spain. |
| Soyer, E. M. ... ... ... | ,, |
| Thomaseau, Miss Ismen... ... ... | Cedros. |
| Wise, Mrs. Samuel ... ... ... | Arima. |

In September 1883 J. A. Bulmer took over as Postmaster General. He instituted many reforms as given in his report for 1885. Here are some extracts from his report:-

*"That Trinidad so far as concerned its postal arrangements was long suffering in the past cannot be doubted when it is remembered that in 1883 it lacked all modern postal facilities, such as a Returned Letter Branch, Post Cards, Registered Letter Envelopes and Newspaper Wrappers, and that Postage Stamps could not be purchased at the Public Counter of the Chief Office."*

*"In all countries of the world the Post Office is the one Department least able to defend itself from wilfully false charges or charges of irregularity over which that department has absolutely no control, as notably in cases of theft or loss of letters entrusted to messengers and servants to post. The charge against the Post Office is generally formulated thus:- A letter was posted, &c., &c., the honesty of the messenger to whom it was entrusted to post cannot be doubted, &c., &c., the letter contained $5, &c.. &c., what has become of it? Verdict (if letter not accounted for ) Guilty against the Post Office, and probably the real offender, the messenger, joins in the chorus of execration that "things should be as they are and not what they seem."*

*"It might be supposed that the persons who forward letters would guard themselves by having all important letters, especially those containing remittances, registered, the fee for registration being so small (2d.). that sum also covering the cost of a stout linen lined official envelope supplied on application at any Post Office," but notwithstanding the following Caution issued 1883, viz:-*

### CAUTION.

*"Neither money nor any other article of considerable value ought ever to be sent through the post except by means of a Money Order or in a Registered Letter. Any person who sends money in an unregistered letter not only runs a risk of losing his property, but exposes to temptation every one whose hands his letter passes."*

*"Whenever Bank notes are sent by post, even in Registered Letters, they should be cut in halves, and the second halves should not be posted till it has been ascertained that the first halves have been received, and further, in order to afford the means of identification, a memorandum should always be made of the number of each Bank note, &c., &c., the practise still continues of enclosing Bank notes in letters the sender is impressing upon the messenger the necessity of being careful with the letter because it contains money and then trusting to its reaching its destination as an ordinary unregistered letter."*

*"Another version of "a new way of paying old debts" was tried recently by which the Post Office was to be made the scape-goat. Fortunately for this Department the evidences of tampering were over-done and the victimizer became the victim of his own misdeeds. A man owing a sum of money being pressed for payment and living at a distance from his creditor wrote and posted a letter stating the money was enclosed. On arrival of the letter no money was found, but there were evident traces of the envelope having been opened and reclosed. An investigation by the police disclosed the fact that the writer of the letter had not in his possession at the time of posting the letter anything approaching the sum stated to have been enclosed. Being a Public Servant he begged to be allowed to resign. He confessed having intentionally soiled and mutilated the envelope before posting it, and was dismissed the Service.*

*Another case showing that messengers are not always to be trusted and that the knowledge that the letters they are conveying to post contain money is direct temptation to dishonesty was exemplified very recently. The Manager of an Estate directed a Coolie boy to take a letter to the Post Office cautioning him that it contained a $5 note, and telling him to register the letter. On being handed in at the Village Post Office, the Sub-Post-Master called the boys attention to the appearance of the envelope where it was gummed down and remarked to him that it had been opened. The boy said the master had opened and re-sealed it, so the letter was registered and forwarded. On its arrival in Port-of-Spain the addressee did not find the Bank note enclosed, and immediately handed in the envelope and made a complaint. An Officer of this Department was instructed to proceed to the Village and investigate the case. On his arrival at the Village, within a few hours of the posting of the letter, the Sub-Postmaster remembered the circumstance of the letter being handed in, The Coolie boy being confronted with his master, confessed that on his way to the Post Office he handed the letter to a Coolie woman who opened it, took out the note, and reclosed the envelope."*

*"In such cases this Department cannot prosecute because the letter does not become the property of the Postmaster-General until it is posted. In both the cases quoted, the letters were delivered in the condition in which they were received, the tampering having taken place prior to the posting. In the last case the sender prosecuted the Coolie woman and lad."*

*"Had the letter posted by the Coolie boy been addressed to a distant Colony from whence a reply could not have been received under three or four weeks, the probability is that the sender and the Sub-Postmaster would both have forgotten by whom the letter was posted and the guilt of the messenger would not have been established."*

*"Similarly in the case of a Registered Letter to Barbados in which the sender enclosed, to him, a considerable sum in Bank notes. The letter on arrival did not contain any notes and the information of the loss reaching me quickly, I communicated with the sender before he was aware anything had gone wrong with his letter. As in nearly all cases of this kind the envelope bore traces of having been opened and reclosed. The result of investigation showed that the letter was entrusted to a friend to post and although I am not at liberty to give the*

whole particulars brought to light, it may be stated that the sender convinced himself that the theft had occurred prior to the letter being posted; and he voluntarily came forward, and both verbally and by letter exonerated this Department from any blame. These are not by any means isolated cases, but are given as examples of the charges to which this Department is liable, and showing with what difficulty such charges can be satisfactorily cleared up unless immediate complaint be made and the fullest information afforded."

"It is with pleasure that I can now state that all the principle Post Offices in Trinidad have been placed on a thoroughly sound footing not only as regards appliances for carrying on the work, but also as to a trained Staff of Clerks who, having definite and fixed rules for their guidance, have no longer any excuse for not performing their duties with satisfaction to the public and credit to themselves."

"Of the work which has occupied my attention since September 1883, it may briefly be summed up by saying that it consisted principally in entirely demolishing the out-of-date system which obtained prior to my arrival, and the building up of a more modern and less cumbersome system, the remodelling of books and forms, the introduction of fittings better adapted to the constantly increasing work, the opening of the Public Counter at the Chief Office for the sale to the public of Postage Stamps, &c., the introduction of Post Cards, Registered Envelopes, Newspaper Wrappers and Surcharge Stamps, the extension of the Money Order System by "Through Orders" to all the principle Countries of the world (except France) and also the extension of the Inland Money Order System to Princes Town, the introduction of the Parcel Post, the refitting of certain Sub-Offices, the establishment of a Returned Letter Branch, a Private Box Delivery, and the placing on Incremental Scale of the Officers on the Fixed Establishment, the Letter-Carriers and Resident Porter of this Establishment."

"The carrying out of these changes has occupied a somewhat longer time than they would have done had it been found practicable to carry out the most important part of the recommendtion contained within my Report of 13th March, 1884, and sanctioned conditionally by the Secretary of State for the Colonies by which, without increasing the number of the Officers employed or the amount paid in salaries, the whole of the financial transactions of this Department would be placed under the control of an Accountant possessing a thorough knowledge of every detail connected with Money Order business and general control, leaving the Head of Department free to carry out much needed improvements in distant parts of the Colony. Circumstances have hitherto prevented the carrying out of this arrangement, but I trust it will be possible shortly to relieve me from much of the work which should properly be performed by an Accountant and thus enable me to devote more time to the extension of Postal communication throughout the distant parts of the Colony."

"I have received in my somewhat difficult task of reorganizing the Post Office of this Colony, the most cordial and able support from Mr. Lewis, the Postmaster of San Fernando, and my duties during the past ten months have been considerably lightened by the intelligent and energetic co-operation of Mr. Bowen, my Chief Clerk. The Staff, without almost an exception, may now be said to be thoroughly efficient and anxious to give satisfaction."

"Prior to my arrival in this Colony the system of bringing to account the Surcharges on unpaid and unsufficiently paid correspondance had led to constant complications with Sub-Postmasters, the letters, &c., bearing charges, forwarded daily to the Sub-Offices were to be debited by each Sub-Postmaster in a monthly balance sheet, and it was the duty of Sub-Postmasters to forward this sheet and to account to the Chief Office at the end of each month for the sums collected by them on such letters, &c., as had been delivered during the month. The sum forwarded, added to the item shown in the sheet as "undelivered unpaid letters remaining on hand" should have represented as *the total debit against each Office, but in practice, it was found that the statement forwarded rarely, if ever, agreed with the record at the Chief Office."*

*"The result can scarcely be wondered at when some of the causes are known, the chief cause was the constant change of Officers at Police and Railway Stations at which postal business was transacted. Not infrequently at Railway Stations two or more changes would occur during the month and as no proper written transfer, of letters remaining undelivered, was made by out-going Sub-Postmaster, the last comer declined any responsibility if the statement submitted by him did not agree with the Chief Office records."*

*"Another cause of complication was the transfer of letters, bearing charges, from one Post Office to another, the addressee having removed, the system did not provide for such a contingency."*

*"As soon as it was possible to have a plate prepared and Stamps printed, the present system was adopted, viz: on 1st January, 1885, Surcharge Stamps of the value of ½d., 1d., 2d., 3d., 4d., 5d., 6d., 8d., and 1s. were issued to every Post Office and formed, from that time, a part of the credit stock of Stamps, &c., advanced to each Sub-Postmaster."*

*"The principle of the present arrangement for bringing to account Surcharge Revenue is that at whatever Office in Trinidad the tax is raised a Surcharge Stamp or Stamps to the value of the unpaid charges shall be affixed to the cover of the postal article, and the Stamps obliterated before the artcle is delivered to the addressee or forwarded to another Office."*

*"As the Surcharge Stamps have been advanced to me from the Treasury and sold by me to the several Officers who deal with unpaid or insufficiently paid correspondance and as unobliterated Stamps are accepted as cash in all balances, it follows that immediately the Stamps have been cancelled the surcharge has been paid into Revenue and it only remains for the Officer holding such unpaid correspondance to collect the tax from the addressee before delivery."*

*"In the case of unpaid correspondance between any two offices the amount of such correspondance forwarded by each mail is entered on a special form and accompanies the surcharged correspondance, the Receiving Office on the receipt of this form verifies the correspondance and if found correct forwards the amount claimed together with the form to the Sending Office by next mail."*

*"Thus also the unpaid letters in the hands of any Sub-Postmaster represent cash to him as he has already paid the charges upon them. If he is unable to deliver any of the unpaid letters, they are returned at fixed periods to Chief Office and whatever sum they represent is forwarded in exchange for them."*

*"If finally any unpaid letters, &c., are to be destroyed, from inability to deliver, or be returned to the country of origin, such letters, &c., are verified by the Audit Office and the sum represented is authorised to be written off."*

*"The advantage of this system is that instead of the taxes raised on unpaid or insufficiently paid correspondence running on for an indefinite time before being brought to account as Revenue, the Revenue is now satisfied the moment the tax is raised, there is no necessity for accounts between Chief Office and Sub-Offices because the mail following that in which the unpaid letters are forwarded brings back the sum they represent, and in all changes of*

Sub-Postmasters the out-going Officer will, in his own interest, claim from the incoming Officer the sum he holds in undelivered unpaid letters, &c."

"The public is also protected from fraud or error by being able to see that the sum they pay in surcharges is represented by the necessary stamps on the postal article handed to them."

"The Revenue is protected by the cancellation of the Stamps and the impossibilty of their being used a second time without detection."

"Surcharge Stamps are not sold to the public."

"It is somewhat difficult to account for the large increase in the Revenue derived from unpaid correspondance since 1882, and more especially the increase of £164 8s. 1d. in 1885, (the first year of the introduction of Surcharge Stamps) as compared with the previous year, seeing that the number of such letters received by sailing vessels has decreased by one-half since 1882. Some portion of the increase may be attributable to a larger number of unpaid letters received by ordinary mails, but my experience has not led me to think so.

STATEMENT SHOWING THE AMOUNT PAID INTO REVENUE AS SURCHARGES
ON UNPAID AND INSUFFICIENTLY PAID LETTERS, &c., DURING
THE YEARS 1882–83–84–85.

| Year. | | | | Amount. | | |
|---|---|---|---|---|---|---|
| | | | | £. | s. | d. |
| 1882 | ... | ... | ... | ... | 217 | 9 | 9 |
| 1883 | ... | ... | ... | ... | 249 | 13 | 1 |
| 1884 | ... | ... | ... | ... | 262 | 1 | 11 |
| 1885 | ... | ... | ... | ... | 426 | 10 | 0 |

NOTE.—The amount collected in 1885, was affixed by Surcharge Stamps,—of this sum £40 18 9 was afterwards written off as value of Surcharge Stamps affixed to letters destroyed or returned to Country of origin.

"By Ordinance No.13 of 1862, it is enacted that masters of sailing vessels shall be entitled to the sum of twopence for each letter delivered at the Post Office from beyond sea. During 1885, 6,658 letters were delivered to the Post Office in Trinidad by masters of sailing vessels and it has been found that at least 50% of such letters are never delivered. This represents a loss to the Colony not only of £27 14s. 11d. paid to the masters for conveyance, but also half that sum, viz: one penny per letter as the local tax. None of these letter ever bear postage stamps when handed in."

"The greater part of such letters bear no specific address and the most careful enquiry fails to bring to light the whereabouts of many of the persons whose names are given."

"I should loath to think that there is any attempt to defraud the Revenue by obtaining the fee on presentation of fictitious letters, but the fact remains that such undelivered letters received loose by *sailing vessels bear no proportion to the number of letters remaining undelivered when received in ordinary mails."*

*"The remedy for this evil appears to be to reverse the order of things and insist on all the letters, collected by masters of vessels, being handed to the Post Office at the Port of departure where a special Mail would be made up and payment, at the same rate as at present, made to the master of the vessel, but only on such letters as are prepaid. Letters not prepaid would be accepted for transmission, but no payment would be made to the master for these letters. I purpose adding a clause to this effect in the new Postal Ordinance which is now being prepared. Such a course would guard the Revenue of each Colony and would not curtail the postal communication between any of the Islands."*

*"The great falling off in the number of letters received loose by sailing vessels during the last three years, (see below) is accounted for by the much greater facilities now afforded for forwarding mails from Steamers between this Port and Barbados, and also to the fact that a very large number of letters from Venezuela were, prior to that date, included in the figures shown."*

### LETTERS RECEIVED IN TRINIDAD BY SAILING VESSELS.

| MONTH. | 1882. | 1883. | 1884. | 1885. |
|---|---|---|---|---|
| January ... ... ... | 1,262 | 935 | 718 | 429 |
| February ... ... ... | 1,417 | 139 | 761 | 646 |
| March ... ... ... | 1,325 | 779 | 608 | 692 |
| April ... ... ... | 1,187 | 925 | 717 | 516 |
| May ... ... ... | 1,148 | 922 | 828 | 616 |
| June ... ... ... | 1,242 | 1,317 | 659 | 712 |
| July ... ... ... | 1,056 | 1,316 | 864 | 564 |
| August ... ... ... | 1,217 | 1,456 | 775 | 510 |
| September ... ... ... | 1,085 | 594 | 988 | 451 |
| October ... ... ... | 1,276 | 933 | 840 | 586 |
| November ... ... ... | 1,240 | 797 | 847 | 408 |
| December ... ... ... | 1,051 | 692 | 863 | 528 |
| Total ... ... ... | 14,506 | 10,805 | 9,468 | 6,658 |
| Letters on which no Fee was claimed ... | 6,463 | 5,378 | 3,703 | ... |
| Letters on which 2d. each was paid to Master of Vessel ... ... | 8,043 | 5,427· | 5,765 | 6,658 |

*"With a view to afford greater facilities to the Coolie Immigrants for communication with their friends in India, Envelopes, bearing an embossed Postage Stamp representing the single rate of postage between India and Trinidad, have been obtained from the Indian Government and are now being sold to the Coolie at their actual cost delivered here, viz: 5½d each. These envelopes are addressed in English by or for the sender, with his full name and address in Trinidad and enclosed in the letter going to India so that the postage is prepaid for the return letter and on its arrival in Trinidad the letter can be forwarded to its destination without referring it to an Interpreter for translation of address."*

*"Prior to September, 1883, the entire sale of Postage Stamps in Port-of-Spain was in the hands of Stamp Vendors, and at that period as at present 4% was being paid as commision.*

*Either the Stamp Vendors must have been exceedingly expert in dealing with the final rush for stamps just prior to the closing of the English Mail, or the public posted earlier than at present. It now takes four Officers at the Public Counter to issue stamps, &c., weigh and register letters for about an hour prior to the closing of the Mail for ordinary prepaid correspondance, and notwithstanding the enormous increase in letters, newspapers, and book packets following the reduction of rates for such postal articles, the sum paid in commission to Stamp Vendors was only £57 14s 4=d. in 1885 as against £229 3s. in 1882. I venture to hope that so far as the public is concerned the change has been a beneficial one in every respect."*

*"The chief impediments which hampered the work of sortation of mails before the Post Office was removed to the present building, were the confined space, the inadequate appliances and the want of a system by which certain persons were priviledged by having a separate pigeon-hole assigned for the reception of their correspondance without regard to any fixed rule as to how such priviledge should be regulated. Constant application was being made by persons equally well entitled to such priviledge, to be placed on the same footing as their more favoured neighbours, but as the system had nothing to recommend it and could never give satisfaction, the present system of private boxes for which an annual charge of One Guinea is made was introduced when the present Office was opened. It was inevitable that there would be some opposition to the introduction of this new tax, and also that in the change from one system to another there should be some friction before the Staff could become thoroughly acquainted with the new method and machinery, and free criticism was not wanting, Some censure was deserved and some was not. However to show how necessary was the change it is only required to contrast the two periods, viz: September 1883 with an unruly mob clamouring for admittance, and when admitted fighting for a position at the Counter for letters and afterwards at a side window outside the Office for newspapers, the noise and confusion lasting for nearly two hours after the doors were opened, and 1886 with two separate rooms, one for box-holders and another for the general public, both classes eager to receive their correspondance but conducting themselves in an orderly manner, the box-holder quietly calling out the number of his box, and immediately receiving its contents, the entire rush in this branch being over in ten minutes, and in the general delivery a somewhat noisy crowd, but orderly and well content to wait their turn to be attended to, plenty of Counter room and a sufficient number of Officers to hand out the correspondance."*

*"The time occupied in sortation is now just one-third less than prior to September 1883 and complaints of mis-sorts are almost nil."*

*"I have it in contemplation when the present depression shall not necessitate such rigid economy, to ask for certain additions to the present building as would enable me, to still further, very much reduce the time necessary for delivering, letters to box-holders and by inducing more people to rent boxes relieve to a great extent the pressure in the General Delivery and thus proportionately accelerate the delivery in that branch. There are 98 Private Boxes rented at One Guinea each, and 28 assigned without charge to Public Departments."*

*In my Report of 13th March, 1884, I said:- "The Sub-Offices are also in a most neglected and inefficient condition and it will meet the wishes of the Director of Public Works, the Inspector Commandant of Police and myself if eventually it can be arranged to relieve the Station Masters and Police Officers from the performance of postal duties. At Police Stations the disadvantage is that one Officer cannot always remain in charge and the Postage Stamps, Registered Letters, &c., are in some cases transferred several times each day from one to the other of the Officers."*

*Several causes have combined to prevent the transfers being made as quickly as could be desired, more especially at the smaller Offices where the payment as salary to the Sub-Postmaster is at present so small as not to induce any small shopkeeper to offer to undertake the duties.*

*At none of the Sub-Offices, except San Fernando, and those recently fitted up, is there what I consider a necessary part of the fittings of every Post Office, viz: an Iron Safe, and a sum of money will be asked for in the next Estimates to meet this requirement, as also a sufficient sum to enable me to refit and transfer to private houses or small shops, many of the Offices now located at Police and Railway Stations.*

*Two additional Pillar Letter Boxes have been erected in Port-of-Spain, viz: one in King-street and one opposite the General Post Office, another is sanctioned to be placed opposite the Medical Hall, one has also been erected near The Knoll, Princes Town.*

*The Post Cards introduced on 18 February, 1884, are of the following descriptions, viz:-*

> *Single, ½d., 1d., 1½d., 2d. Double, 1d. reply, 1½d. reply and 2d. reply.*

*The Newspaper Wrappers value ½d. for Inland use and 1d. for use either Inland or beyond sea were introduced 18 June, 1884.*

*The Registered Letter Envelopes were also introduced on 18 June, 1884, they are of two sizes and are sold to the public, as are also Post Cards and Newspaper Wrappers at their face value.*

*On 1 October, 1885, a Parcel Post was established between this Colony and the United Kingdom, and since that date arrangements have been made to exchange parcels through the intermediary of the United Kingdom with other Countries.*

*Steps are being taken to establish a direct exchange between this Colony, Barbados and other West Islands.*

*The average number of Parcels received has, up to the present, been about 45 per mail and 10 forwarded.*

*The following short extract from my Report of 13 March, 1884, will show the urgent necessity there was for the establishment of a Returned Letter Branch:- "Notwithstanding the incessant calls upon my time hitherto in dealing with the transfer to new Offices and remodelling the forms, books and the entire system of this Office, I have found it necessary to deal with, between four and five thousand undelivered letters dating back in some instances to the early part of 1882, letters which should have been returned within three months from the date of posting, either to the writers direct or to the Officers of origin."*

*The principle recognised in Trinidad prior to September 1883 was that all undelivered Inland Letters should be destroyed, that letters posted in Trinidad for beyond sea if undelivered should be returned to the writers, and that letters received from beyond sea if they could not be delivered were to be returned to the Country of origin.*

*Had that principle been acted upon the only grievance the public of Trinidad would have had to complain of would have been the summary manner in which the undelivered local correspondence was dealt with. That five thousand undelivered letters, many of them to or beyond sea, dating back in some cases more than two years had to be dealt with in 1884, shows that however much the principle of a Returned Letter Branch was recognised the putting of this principle into practice was defective.*

*It will be seen that a yearly average of 3,277 undelivered Inland Letters are returned to senders and that 1,551 are destroyed from inability to find the writers. Of the letters forwarded beyond sea and returned undelivered 772 per annum are returneed to the writers and 467 destroyed. A yearly average of 1,938 letters received in Trinidad from beyond sea, the addressees of which cannot be found, are returned to the Countries of origin.*

*The limits of time before letters are dealt with in the Returned Letter Branch are as follows:-*

| *Class Of Correspondence* | *How Disposed Of* |
|---|---|
| *Inland Correspondence - that is to say, all Letters, &c., posted in Trinidad for delivery within the Island.* | *If undelivered, are returned to writer at expiration of one month.* |
| *Correspondence for beyond sea (except India and East of Suez).* | *Returned to Country of origin at expiration of 2 months.* |
| *Correspondence for India and East of Suez.* | *Returned to Country of origin at expiration of 3 months.* |

*Letters refused by addressee are returned immediately to the writer.*

*It would be of very great assistance to this Department and enable me to return far more letters and render it unnecessary that such letters should be opened in the Returned Letter Branch if Merchants and others would have the name of the Firm printed on the covers of their business letters. Some few do this at present, but the practise is capable of considerable extension.*

*It is a source of great annoyance to the receivers of letters and is frequently the cause of very unjust suspicion being cast upon this Department that the covers of letters., &c., are often so damaged in transit as to permit the contents to escape. Whenever such letters are observed the covers are specially closed with an official printed label. There are two distinct causes for this damage, one, the remedy for which rests with the senders of letter, viz: the wretchedly flimsy envelopes used, many of them of soft paper quite unfit to withstand the rough usage to which Mail Bags are often subjected on board Mail Steamers, the other remedy being one which probably a representation to the Postmaster-General of the United Kingdom would effect, viz: the unnecessarilly rough usage to which bags are subjected on the board the Royal Mail Steamers, instead of sliding bags down into the mail-room or from one deck to another as is done on the P. and Q. and other Mail Steamers, they are thrown down from a distance of several feet and not withstanding that the leters are carefully tied up in bundles and afterwards made up in brown stout paper parcels the covers of many letters burst open.*

*The closing of the European Mails was extended by a half hour to 2pm from 3rd April 1886 the late fee (upto 3pm) was mentioned as being an extra single rate. The Inland Parcel Post was started on 1 August 1887.*

On 2 August 1887 there was an alteration in the mails:-

*On and from the 2nd August, 1887, the Mails for Oropouche, La Brea, Erin, Irois Forest, Chatham, Cedros and Hicacos, hitherto closed at 3.30 p.m. on Tuesdays, will be closed at 3.15 p.m.*

*The last collection for these Mails from Pillar Boxes (except King Street) will be at 10 a.m. The last clearance from King Street Pillar Box will be at 3.10 p.m.*

> J. A. BULMER,
> Postmaster-General.

Tenders for the Inland Mail Service in 1889 were asked for in December 1888 the details being:-

TENDERS are invited for the conveyance of Mails by Horse or Mule on the undermentioned Sections for a period of one year, from 1st January, to 31st December, 1889.

| Sections. | Distance. | Yearly Distance to be travelled. | Number of Journeys. |
|---|---|---|---|
| Arima to Mayaro ... | 41 Miles | 8,528 Miles ... | Twice a week in each direction. |
| Arima to Toco ... | 40 ,, | 8,320 ,, | Twice a week in each direction. |
| Arima to Blanchisseuse ... | 19 ,, | 1,976 ,, | Once a week in each direction. |
| Couva viâ Tortuga to Gran Couva and back. | 19 ,, | 5,947 ,, | Daily (Sundays excepted). |
| Princes Town to Moruga ... | 20 ,, | 2,080 ,, | Once a week in each direction. |
| Port-of-Spain to Diego Martin and back | 13 ,, | 4,069 ,, | Daily (Sundays excepted). |
| Port-of-Spain to Maraval and back | 8 ,, | 2,504 ,, | Do. do. |

A new contract with the Royal Mail Steam Packet Company came into effect on July 1890, the first time tables being:-

| INWARD. | | | | OUTWARD. | | | |
|---|---|---|---|---|---|---|---|
| Arrive Trinidad 7, a.m., Wednesday, July | | 23 | | Depart from Trinidad, Thursday, July | | | 17 |
| ,, | ,, | August | 6 | ,, | ,, | ,, | 31 |
| ,, | ,, | ,, | 20 | ,, | ,, | August | 14 |
| ,, | ,, | Sept. | 3 | ,, | ,, | ,, | 28 |
| ,, | ,, | ,, | 17 | ,, | ,, | Sept. | 11 |
| ,, | ,, | Octr. | 1 | ,, | ,, | ,, | 25 |
| ,, | ,, | ,, | 15 | ,, | ,, | Octr. | 9 |
| ,, | ,, | ,, | 29 | ,, | ,, | ,, | 23 |
| ,, | ,, | Novr. | 12 | ,, | ,, | Novr. | 6 |
| ,, | ,, | ,, | 26 | ,, | ,, | ,, | 20 |
| ,, | ,, | Decr. | 10 | ,, | ,, | Decr. | 4 |
| ,, | ,, | ,, | 24 | ,, | ,, | ,, | 18 |

A Timetable of the Direct Service between Trinidad and New York, and Vice Versa, to date from 1 July, 1890:-

| OUTWARD. | | INWARD. | |
|---|---|---|---|
| **Leave Trinidad.** | **Arrive New York.** | **Leave New York.** | **Arrive Trinidad.** |
| Saturday 12 July. | Sunday 20 July. | Saturday, June 28. | Monday, 7 July. |
| " 26 " | " 3 Aug. | " July 12. | " 21 " |
| " 9 Aug. | " 17 " | " " 26. | " 4 Aug. |
| " 23 " | " 31 " | " Aug. 9. | " 18 " |
| " 6 Sept. | " 14 Sept. | " " 23. | " 1 Sept. |
| " 20 " | " 28 " | " Sept. 6. | " 15 " |
| " 4 Oct. | " 12 Oct. | " " 20. | " 29 " |
| " 18 " | " 26 " | " Oct. 4. | " 13 Oct. |
| " 1 Nov. | " 9 Nov. | " " 18. | " 27 " |
| " 15 " | " 23 " | " Nov. 1. | " 10 Nov. |
| " 29 " | " 7 Dec. | " 15. | " 24 " |
| " 13 Dec. | " 21 " | " " 29. | " 8 Dec. |
| " 27 " | " 4 Jan. '91. | " Dec. 13. | " 22 " |
| | | " " 27. | |

Tenders were also called for regards the Local Steamship Services.

*1. A Service by Steam-boat twice a week in each direction between San Fernando and Icacos, calling at Oropouche, La Brea, Cap-de-Ville, Irois Forest and Cedros.*

*The Steamer to leave San Fernando every Tuesday and Friday after the arrival of the first train from Port-of-Spain (about 9.30 a.m.) and to reach Icacos not later than 5. p.m.*

*From Icacos the Steamer to leave at 7. a.m., on Wednesday and Saturday and reach San Fernando not later than 2.30. p.m.*

2. *A Service daily (Sundays excepted) between Port-of-Spain and Monos, calling at Caren-age, Five Islands, Careras (provided there be Mails or passengers for or from that Island) and Gaspril and making Chacachacare the terminus on two days in each week, by Steamers not less than 70 feet long and with proper and sufficient passenger accommodation for not fewer than thirty saloon and forty steerage passengers. The journey between Port-of-Spain or Monos or vice versa to be performed, including stoppages, in not more than two hours.*

*Contractors will be required at their own cost on both Services to land and embark all Mails conveyed, or intended to be conveyed, by them at all places at which such Mails are to be landed or embarked.*

*The Steamers employed on either of the before-named Services shall not (except with the special permission of His Excellency the Governor) convey passengers between the Port-of-Spain of San Fernando or vice versa.*

*There shall be conveyed free of charge, when travelling on duty, all officers of the Post Office, the Customs, the Police, Gaol Officials and Prisoners.*

*The Contract to be for a period of 5 years commencing from the 17th January, 1891.*

*The Government does not bind itself to accept the lowest or any tender.*

*Sealed Tenders which will be received either for one or both Services, marked "Gulf Mail Service," addressed to the Colonial Secretary, Government House, will be received up to 12 noon, on the 1st September, 1890.*

*The Contractor for each Service will be required to find security in the sum of one thousand pounds for the due performance of the Contract and to be liable to a penalty of £10 per diem whenever the Service is not performed according to the Contract.*

On 12 January 1891 the following alteration in times came into effect:-

*Mails for Carenage, Five Islands and Monos will be closed at this Office at 7. a.m., on Monday, Wednesday and Saturday.*

*The Mails from the abovenamed places will be delivered in Port-of-Spain at 7. a.m., on Tuesday, Thursday and Sunday.*

*Mails for Oropouche, La Brea, Cap-de-Ville, Erin, Irois Forest and Cedros will be closed at this Office at 6.30 a.m., on Monday, and at 3.15 p.m. on Tuesday and Friday.*

*Mails from the abovenamed places will be delivered in Port-of-Spain at 7. a.m., on Tuesday, Thursday and Sunday.*

*J. A. BULMER,*
*Postmaster-General.*

And on 2 February 1891:-

*Until further Notice the Mails from CEDROS, ERIN, CAP-DE-VILLE, LA BREA and OROPOUCHE, will be delivered in Port-of-Spain, at 10. a.m. on Tuesday and Thursday, and at 7. a.m. on Monday.*

The times Port-of-Spain pillar boxes were cleared, were altered as from 29 March 1892:-

|  |  | A.M |  | A.M |  | P.M. |
|---|---|---|---|---|---|---|
| Woodbrook | ... | 5.30 | ... | 9.30 | ... | 2.30 |
| All Saints | ... | 5.45 | ... | 9.45 | ... | 2.45 |
| Chancery Lane | ... | 5.50 | ... | 9.50 | ... | 2.50 |
| Richmond Street | ... | 6.00 | ... | 10.00 | ... | 3.00 |
| Medical Hall | ... | 6.05 | ... | 10.05 | ... | 3.05 |
|  |  |  |  |  |  |  |
| Court House | ... | 6.05 | ... | 10.05 | ... | 3.05 |
| Brunswick Square | ... | 6.05 | ... | 10.05 | ... | 3.05 |
| Duncan Street | ... | 5.45 | ... | 9.45 | ... | 2.45 |
| Railway | ... | 5.50 | ... | 9.50 | ... | 2.50 |
| King Street | ... | 6.00 | ... | 10.00 | 12 Noon | 2 p.m., 3 p.m. |
| St. Anns | ... | 5.45 | ... | 9.45 | ... | 2.45 |
| Wash House | ... | 6.00 | ... | 10.00 | ... | 3.00 |
| Park Street | ... | 6.05 | ... | 10.05 | ... | 3.05 |

On 1 August, 1892 1d and 2d single and reply cards were withdrawn from general sale (except at G.P.O.), being finally withdrawn on 30 November 1898, when the remainders were sent to the Crown Agents.

The following notice was published on 21 March 1893:-

*The Colonial Postmaster of Barbados advises that an interruption has taken place in the running of the Steamers of the U. S. and Brazil line, and that it is not known how long this interruption may continue. Until further Notice Correspondence for Brazil, the Argentine Republic, Paraguay, and Uruguay will be forwarded via London.*

A small mail for Trinidad (sent from London 7 January 1895) was lost on the wrecked French Packet "Amerique."

The 1895 Post Office report mentioned:-

*In accordance with instructions from His Excellency the Governor, dated February, 1885, a Committee composed of the Honorable Colonial Secretary (Chairman), the acting Collector of Customs (Mr. A. C. Ross), the Registrar of the Supreme Court, the Registrar-General, the Postmaster-General, the Stipendiary Magistrate of Port-of-Spain, considered the question of abolishing the present Fee Stamp and introducing a New design of Postage and Revenue Stamp. It was recommended that Fee Stamps should be abolished as soon as the New Design of Postage and Revenue Stamps were ready for issue.*

*The Commmitee also recommended that the New Stamps should be of value of ½d., 1d., 2½d., 4d., 5d., 6d., 1/-, 5/-, 10/-, and 20/-, and that the design of the values under 5/- should be somewhat similar to the old Britannia pattern of Stamp but that the stamps of 5/-, 10/-, and 20/- should be oblong and in size like the Stamps of South Australia.*

*Whilst in England I put myself in communication with Messers. De la Rue & Co. and obtained from them several designs for the New Stamps and eventually sent out these designs to this Colony for approval.*

The order to proceed with the preparation of the necessary dies was given to Messrs. De la Rue & Co. in December last, and the stamps may be expected about the end of the month.

It was also one of the recommendations of the Committee that the commission on the sale of Postage Stamps should be reduced from 4 to $2\frac{1}{2}$ per cent. on the introduction of the new Stamps as it is believed the sale of the higher value stamps for Fee purposes would more than repay Stamp Vendors for the reduction in the rate of commission. Postage Stamp Vendors not having hitherto been permitted to sell Fee Stamps.

As the new stamps could not be obtained at so early a date as was anticipated it was decided from 1 April, 1896, to reduce the rate of commission and to permit Postage Stamps to be used as Fee Stamps until the new issue arrives.

I may here state that during the last twelve years it has not been found necessary to Surcharge any Postage Stamps of this Colony but on two or three occasions spectators in Stamps have brought up the whole remaining stock of the higher values of Postage Stamps in the hope that the Department would be compelled to resort to Surcharges - some little temporary inconvenience to the general public was thus caused but the difficulty was met by telegraphing for further supplies and they usually reached me within six weeks.

For some years past this Department has imported, from the Indian Post Office, envelopes embossed with the postage stamp approximating to the single rate of postage then in force. The present envelope is of value of two annas, six pies being the equivalent of our $2\frac{1}{2}$ d. rate of postage and the envelopes are supplied to the coolies at face value.

In nearly all cases where Money Orders are being forwarded by coolies to India one of these envelopes, legibly addressed with the name of the sender, his official number and the estate on which he is employed is enclosed so that the person to whom the money is being forwarded may send an acknowledgement, the postage being prepaid from this side.

This system is of great benefit to the Post Office as no interpretation of address is necessary and the letters very rarely fail to reach addressee.

In 1883 there were 40 District Post Offices in this Colony, of these 25 were located in Police Stations and the duties were performed by Police Officers, 7 were located in Railway Offices, the duties being performed by the collectors, and 7 only were in buildings either belonging to, or rented by Government, these latter Offices being worked by Officers paid solely by this Department.

The allowance paid by this Department to the Police and Railway Officers was usually about $5 a month.

From the nature of the duties of the Police Officers in Country Districts and the frequency with which they were changed, it was impossible that they could devote that attention to Postal duties or become insufficiently proficient in those duties to warrant the system being continued. Somewhat similar disadvantages obtained as regards Officers at Railway Stations, and it was decided to gradually transfer all Post Offices from Railway and Police Stations.

*Since 1883 nine new Post Offices have been added, and these Offices are now located as follows:-*

| | | |
|---|---|---|
| *In the premises belonging to or rented by the Government* | . . . . . | *42* |
| *At Police Stations belonging to or rented by the Government* | . . . . . | *5* |
| *At Railway Stations belonging to or rented by the Government* | . . . . . | *2* |

*49*

*I hope to be able to transfer the 7 remaining Offices from the Police and Railway at an early date.*

*Of the District Post Offices, 30 are rented and 12 are Government Buildings 5 Police, and 2 Railway. In many Districts especially at Toco, Arima, Cedros, Mayaro and St. Joseph, great difficulty has been experienced in finding suitable accommodation for the Post Office, and it is my intention to ask for the current year's Estimates for provision to be made for building Post Offices at some of the places mentioned.*

*J. A. BULMER,*
*Postmaster-General*

On 20 August 1896 new arrangements were made regarding late fees at the G.P.O:-

*Late Fees on English Mail Day.*

*Letters and other postal matter with ordinary postage may be posted at any pillar box in Port-of-Spain and at the General Post Office up to 2.30 p.m.*

*Note:- Letters, &c., posted in pillar boxes in Port-of-Spain after 2.30 p.m. on English Mail day will not go forward that mail.*

*Letters and Postal articles with late fee of 1d, at General Post Office only, up to 3 p.m..*

*Letters (but not other postal articles) with late fee of 2½d., at General Post Office only, up to 3.30 p.m.*

*Letters (but not other postal articles) with the late fee of 5d., at General Post Office only, up to 4 p.m.*

*All posting boxes will be closed at the General Post Office at 2.30 p.m. on the Outward English Mail day and all late fee letters and local letters between that time and 4 p.m. should be handed to one of the counter clerks.*

*From 3.30 p.m. late fee letters will be received only at the stamp window, in private box department.*

*The delivery of letters, &c., at the master of the General Post Office on the arrival of the English Mail will be abolished and all letters, &c., except those private box holders and poste restante letters, will be delivered by Letter Carrier.*

*There will be three deliveries by Letter Carrier daily (Sundays and public holidays excepted) viz. at 7 a.m., 10 a.m. and 3 p.m. On Sunday the General Post Office will be open for the delivery of letters, &c., to the public from 7 to 8 a.m.*

*On public holidays there will be one delivery by Letter Carrier viz: at 7 a.m.*

*The main portion of the General Post Office will be closed to the public at 12.30 p.m. on Saturdays, but all mails will be despatched as usual on that day, and postage stamps, &c., may be obtained on application at the private box stamp window.*

The Post Office report for 1896 mentioned:-

*The new stamps of the denominations of ½d., 1d., 2½d., 4d., 5d., 6d., 1/-, 5/-, and including 6d., are printed in fugitive colours on a mauve ground, the value being printed in distinctive colours usually adopted, viz: ½d. green, 1d. red, 2½ d. blue, and so on. The denominations of 1/-, 5/10, 10/- and 20/- are printed on a green ground, the values also being denoted in different colours.*

*It was also expected that when the fact became known that the old pattern stamps were to be abolished there would be an increased demand for these stamps, but so abnormal was the demand that I found it necessary on three occasions to telegraph to England for further supplies, and all other orders received up to Saturday, 15 August were executed. The balance of old pattern stamps remaining were afterwards destroyed.*

*On the introduction of the new stamps there was also an unusually large demand for them, each mail bringing in orders from Stamp dealers and collectors beyond sea for supplies, and to this fact and not increased use of the stamps for postage and revenue purposes.*

*In the earlier days of the Royal Mail Company's contract the inward English Mail usually arrived in Trinidad after 8 p.m., and the delivery of the mail at the counter of the General Post Office frequently took place after 10 p.m. to the very great discomfort of the public generally and much more so to the postal staff working, as they had to do, in a cramped space and with very adequate fittings and appliances.*

*The system of delivery at the counter , however, had many serious drawbacks, and the worst of it being the insecurity as to the correct delivery owing to the similarity of names and the inability of the officers of this department to identify the persons applying or to satisfy themselves that the applicants had any right to the letters asked for.*

*Except when mails are conveyed from Barbados by the cargo steamer, the inward English Mail usually arrives in the early morning of Wednesday with the punctuality of an express train, and it was thought desirable that the delivery of letters at the counter should be abolished and that an extra staff of letter carriers should be employed for a special service on incoming mail days. The necessary funds for this service were voted in the Estimates for last year, and the alteration effected.*

*The result has been all I could desire. Letters are now delivered at specific times and in proportion to the quantity of postal matter dealt with, cases are very rare indeed where a complaint is made of error in delivery. If an error occurs someone is usually remembered of the letter, and it can be traced if complaint is made at a reasonable time.*

*There is much to be desired in the proper numbering of houses in Port-of-Spain, and it is only letter carriers of long experience who can be fully acquainted with all the peculiarities of the town in respect to the numbering of the houses.*

*The receipt of the English Mail once a month direct from Barbados by Cargo Steamer is of doubtful advantage to this Colony. The time of arrival on Tuesday is very uncertain, and occasionally the delivery of letters cannot be commenced before 4 p.m., when most of the stores are closed. On such occasions more work is caused to the Officers of this department.*

*At the end of 1895 there remained 7 sub-offices located in Police and Railway Stations; of that number 5 have since been transferred to specially appointed offices, and the remaining 2 will be transferred as early as possible during 1897. It is to be regretted that the money for the erection of new Post Offices at Mayaro, Moriga, Gran Couva, Tortuga was not voted in the Estimates for 1897. This difficulty is experienced in renting suitable premises in country districts, and this only prevents me from extending the Money Order system, but there is insecurity in the ordinary transaction of postal business where the space is cramped and the buildings are adapted for postal purposes.*

*During the past year the Post Offices at Claxton Bay, St. Joseph, Arima, Tortuga and Arouca have been removed to more suitable premises and fitted with modern appliances. The offices at Chaguanas and Carapichaima have also been refitted.*

*In consequence of the necessity for providing more accommodation in the General Post Office, a new wing was provided in which the Money Order, Accounting Correspondence and registration Branches are now located.*

*On 6 February, 1896, and for several days subsequently, the Government Railway was interrupted by floods and the mails between Port-of-Spain and the offices beyond Caroni were seriously delayed. Every advantage was taken to lessen as far as possible the inconvenience thus caused by the Gulf Steamers for special journeys to Couva and San Fernando. During the interruption I received every possible assistance from the General Manager of the Railway and from the Harbour Master.*

On 14 October 1897 there were the following alterations:-

*There will be a daily Mail between Port-of-Spain and Sangre Grande, Sundays and Public Holidays expected.*

*The Mails for Sangre Grande (and Tumpuna) will be closed at the General Post Office at 8 a.m.*

*Mails for Arima, Port-of-Spain, &c., will be closed at Sangre Grande and Tumpuna at 9 a.m.*

*Until further notice the Wednesday Mail for Mayaro will be closed at the General Post Office at 3.45 p.m., instead of 1 p.m., as at present.*

The 1897 Post Office report mentioned:-

*Since my last report the Sub-Offices at Williamsville, Erin, Blanchisseuse and Oropouche have been removed to more suitable premises and fitted with modern appliances.*

*I had the occasion in my last report, to call attention to the great inconvenience and additional expense caused by the conveyance by Cargo Steamer once a month of the English Mails between Barbados and this Colony. In consequence, I understand, of some extra Cargo Boats being employed, the English Mails on three successive occasions, viz.: March 22, Avon 11.40 a.m.; April 5, Essequibo, 4.50 p.m.: April 19, Larne, 7.45 p.m., have been forwarded from Barbados by Cargo Steamer.*

*If mails are delivered to the Post Office before noon on Tuesday, they can be in the hands of Merchants and others if they want to leave their places of business at 4 p.m., but as in the case of the Essequibo and Larne where the Mails did not reach this Office till after 4 p.m., several Merchants have assured me that no benefit accrues to them in such a case, and that they would much prefer to have the English Mail arrive at 6 a.m. on Wednesday, as formerly.*

*As far as this Department is concerned, the conveying by Cargo Steamer of the English Mail is very rarely of any advantage in expediting, to any considerable extent, the Mails for the country; and it frequently necessitates keeping the entire staff on duty till 10 p.m., besides doubling the cost of Extra Letter Carriers.*

*I shall be glad if something can be done to remedy this drawback to the otherwise punctual and satisfactory performance of the Royal Mail Contract.*

*It could easily be arranged that if the Cargo Steamer cannot leave Barbados on Monday in time to reach Trinidad by noon Tuesday, the Mails should come by the Inter-colonial Steamer as usual, and notice forwarded to the agents here to that effect. This would enable me to advise the local Newspapers, the Post Office at San Fernando, and my Sub-Offices, and also permit me to arrange the attendance of my staff so as to save the Colony considerable expense.*

The outbreak of the Spanish-American War meant the Cuban letters could not be sent via New York (notified 21 May 1898).

On 1 February 1898 Express Delivery letters were accepted for the U.K. The 3d. per mile fee being collected on delivery.

On 21 November 1898 the Mails were charged as follows:-

| | |
|---|---|
| *For San Fernando and Intermediate Offices* | *6.45 a.m.* |
| *For Arima and Intermediate Offices* | *8.09 a.m.* |
| *For San Fernando and Intermediate Offices* | *11.04 a.m.* |
| *For Arima and Intermediate Offices* | *12.37 p.m.* |
| *For San Fernando and Intermediate Offices* | *3.32 p.m.* |
| *For Arima and Intermediate Offices* | *4.00 p.m.* |

*In future there will be four deliveries by Letter Carriers on the day of the arrival of the English Mail, viz.:*

*At 7 a.m., 10 a.m., 12 (noon), and 2 p.m.*

and on March 1899:-

*The following alterations will be made in the receipt and dispatch of Overland Mails between Port-of-Spain and Moruga. Mails close at Port-of-Spain: MONDAY and THURSDAY, 6.45 a.m. Letters, &c., will reach Moruga, at 4 p.m., on those days. Mails close at Moruga: TUESDAY and FRIDAY, 8 a.m. Letters, &c., will reach Port-of-Spain, at 6 p.m. on those days.*

# TRINIDAD AND TOBAGO

The following notice was published to take effect 15 October 1899:-

## *INSURANCE OF LETTERS*

*On and from the 15 October, 1899, Letters will be accepted for Insurance up to £120 at the following Post Offices - General Post Office, San Fernando, Tobago, Arima, Arouca, Cedros, Chaguanas, Couva, La Brea, Mayaro, Princes Town, Saint Joseph, and Sangre Grande, for the undermentioned Countries, viz.:-*

*Argentine Republic.*
*Austria-Hungary.*
*Belgium.*
*Bulgaria.*
*Chili.*
*Denmark (including Iceland and the Faroe Islands).*

*DANISH COLONIES:*
*St. Thomas.*
*St. John.*
*St. Croix.*
*Greenland.*

*Egypt*
*France (including Corsica, Algeria and Monaco).*

*FRENCH COLONIES:*

*Guadeloupe.*
*Martinique.*
*French Office at Tripoli.*
*Germany.*
*German Protectorate of Cameroons.*
*Great Britain.*

*BRITISH COLONIES:*
*British Guiana.*
*Ceylon.*
*Falkland Islands.*
*Gambia.*
*Hong Kong.*
*India.*
*Jamaica.*
*Lagos.*
*St. Helena.*

*Holland.*
*Italy.*
*Italian Colony of Erythea.*
*Luxembourg.*

*Norway.*
*Portugal (including Azores).*

*Portuguese Colonies in East and West Africa.*

*Madeira.*
*Cape Verde Islands.*
*Roumania.*
*Russia (including Finland).*

*Servia.*
*Spain (including Canary Islands).*
*Sweden.*
*Switzerland.*
*Tunis.*
*Turkey.*

*1. Insured letters will not only have all the advantages of the registration system, but if they or their contents are lost in the Post, the senders will, subject to the following regulations, have a claim for compensation:-*

*2. Postcards, or packets of "Printed Papers," or "Commercial Papers," or Sample Packets cannot be insured. The letters to which the Insurance System is specially applicable are those which contain ink notes, bonds, coupons, securities, &c.*

*3. Letters intended for insurance must be presented at the counter of a Post Office.*

*4. Insured letters may not contain coins, anything made of gold or silver, precious stones, jewellery, any article liable to Customs duty in the country of destination.*

*5. Insured letters must not be addressed to initials, or in pencil.*

*6. Every letter packet tendered for insurance must be enclosed in a strong cover, which must be securely fastened and sealed with fine wax, in such a way that it cannot be opened without either breaking the seals or leaving obvious traces of violation. Envelopes with black or coloured borders must not be used. Seals must be placed over each flap or seam or the cover of a packet; and if the packet is tied round with string or tape, a seal must be placed on the ends where they are tied. The seals on an ordinary envelope should be placed as shown below:-*

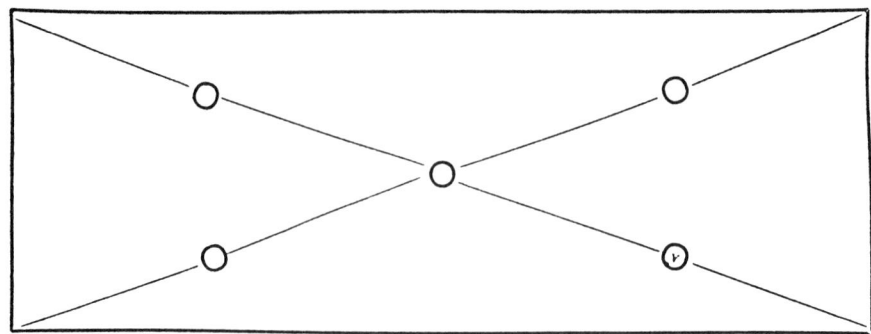

*7. All seals on a letter must be of the same kind of wax and must bear distinct impressions of the same private device. Coins must not be used for sealing; and the device must not consist purely of straight, crossed, or curved lines which could readily be imitated.*

*8. If a letter tendered for insurance does not, in the opinion of the Officer of the Post Office to whom it is tendered, fulfil the foregoing conditions as to packing and sealing, it is his duty to refuse to insure it. Nevertheless the onus of properly enclosing and sealing the letter lies upon the sender; and the Post Office assumes no liability for loss arising from defects of the cover or the seals which may not have been observed at the time of posting.*

*9. The amount for which the letter is insured (which must not exceed its actual value) must be written by the sender both in words and in figures at the top of the address side of the cover, thus:- "Insured for fifteen pounds (£15) 378 francs." No alteration or erasure of the inscription is allowed. If a mistake is made, the entry must be completely obliterated and an entirely new one made by the sender.*

*10. The sums payable for insurance are as follows:-*

| Fee | | Limit of Compensation. |
|---|---|---|
| *s.* | *d.* | *£.* |
| *0* | *8* | *12* |
| *1* | *0* | *24* |
| *1* | *4* | *36* |
| *1* | *8* | *48* |
| *2* | *0* | *60* |
| *2* | *4* | *72* |
| *2* | *8* | *84* |
| *3* | *0* | *96* |
| *3* | *4* | *108* |
| *3* | *8* | *120* |

*11. The fee (which includes the registration fee) must be prepaid, in addition to the full postage, by means of postage stamps, which the sender must affix to the cover of the letter.*

*12. As few stamps as possible should be used to prepay the postage and insurance fee. They must not be folded over the edge of the cover, and when more stamps than one are used, they must be affixed with spaces between them.*

13. *A certificate of posting must always be obtained by the sender of an insured letter. He may also obtain an acknowledgement of the delivery of the letter on paying a fee of 2½d.*

14. *Letters, which although have been addressed to a country or place to which the insurance system does not extend, have been irregularly insured, will be forwarded as registered letters; and if they or their contents are lost in the Post, the regulations as to the compensation payable in the case of registered letters will be applicable.*

15. *When an insured letter is re-directed from one country to another, a fresh insurance fee becomes payable for each transmission. If this fee is not prepaid, it is collected from the addressee on delivery. Insured letters can only be re-directed to countries which have adopted the insurance system.*

16. *Compensation for the loss in the Post of a letter or its contents will not exceed the amount of the actual loss, and will not be paid at all for a letter which has been delivered without an external trace of injury and has been accepted without remark by the addressee; nor does it follow as a matter of course that compensation will be given when loss arises from tempest, shipwreck, earthquake, war. or other causes beyond control. No claim for compensation will be admitted if made more than a year before the letter was posted.*

17. *No legal liability to give compensation in respect of any letter for which an insurance fee has been paid attaches to the Postmaster-General, either personally or in his official capacity. The final decision upon his questions of compensation rests with the Postal Administration of the country in which the loss has taken place.*

18. *Any insurance effected with the Post Office contrary to the foregoing regulations is invalid.*

The Packet Service timetable for 1900 was:-

## OUTWARD ROUTE.

### TABLE No. 1. — SOUTHAMPTON TO BARBADOS / BARBADOS TO COLON.

| No. of Voyage | Leave Southampton. 6 P.M. Wed. | Arrive at Barbados. 8 A.M. Monday. | Leave Barbados. 5 P.M. Monday. | Arrive at Jamaica. 7 A.M. Friday. | Arrive at Colon. 11 A.M. Monday. |
|---|---|---|---|---|---|
| 1 | 10 Jan. | 22 Jan. | 22 Jan. | 26 Jan. | 29 Jan. |
| 3 | 24 Jan. | 5 Feb. | 5 Feb. | 9 Feb. | 12 Feb. |
| 5 | 7 Feb. | 19 Feb. | 19 Feb. | 23 Feb. | 26 Feb. |
| 7 | 21 Feb. | 5 Mar. | 5 Mar. | 9 Mar. | 12 Mar. |
| 9 | 7 Mar. | 19 Mar. | 19 Mar. | 23 Mar. | 26 Mar. |
| 11 | 21 Mar. | 2 Apr. | 2 Apr. | 6 Apr. | 9 Apr. |
| 13 | 4 Apr. | 16 Apr. | 16 Apr. | 20 Apr. | 23 Apr. |
| 15 | 18 Apr. | 30 Apr. | 30 Apr. | 4 May | 7 May |
| 17 | 2 May | 14 May | 14 May | 18 May | 21 May |
| 19 | 16 May | 28 May | 28 May | 1 June | 4 June |
| 21 | 30 May | 11 June | 11 June | 15 June | 18 June |
| 23 | 13 June | 25 June | 25 June | 29 June | 2 July |
| 25 | 27 June | 9 July | 9 July | 13 July | 16 July |

### TABLE No. 2. — BARBADOS TO DEMERARA.

| No. of Voyage | Leave Barbados. 3 P.M. Monday. | Arrive at Demerara. 6 A.M. Wed. |
|---|---|---|
| 27 | 22 Jan. | 24 Jan. |
| 29 | 5 Feb. | 7 Feb. |
| 31 | 19 Feb. | 21 Feb. |
| 33 | 5 Mar. | 7 Mar. |
| 35 | 19 Mar. | 21 Mar. |
| 37 | 2 Apr. | 4 Apr. |
| 39 | 16 Apr. | 18 Apr. |
| 41 | 30 Apr. | 2 May |
| 43 | 14 May | 16 May |
| 45 | 28 May | 30 May |
| 47 | 11 June | 13 June |
| 49 | 25 June | 27 June |
| 51 | 9 July | 11 July |

### TABLE No. 3. — BARBADOS TO TRINIDAD AND TOBAGO.

| No. of Voyage | Leave Barbados. 8 P.M. Monday. | Arrive at Trinidad. 7 A.M. Wed. | Arrive at Tobago. 3 A.M. Thurs. |
|---|---|---|---|
| 53 | 22 Jan. | 24 Jan. | 25 Jan. |
| 55 | 5 Feb. | 7 Feb. | 8 Feb. |
| 57 | 19 Feb. | 21 Feb. | 22 Feb. |
| 59 | 5 Mar. | 7 Mar. | 8 Mar. |
| 61 | 19 Mar. | 21 Mar. | 22 Mar. |
| 63 | 2 Apr. | 4 Apr. | 5 Apr. |
| 65 | 16 Apr. | 18 Apr. | 19 Apr. |
| 67 | 30 Apr. | 2 May | 3 May |
| 69 | 14 May | 16 May | 17 May |
| 71 | 28 May | 30 May | 31 May |
| 73 | 11 June | 13 June | 14 June |
| 75 | 25 June | 27 June | 28 June |
| 77 | 9 July | 11 July | 12 July |

### TABLE No. 4. — BARBADOS TO ST. THOMAS.

| No. of Voyage | Leave Barbados. 5 P.M. Monday. | Arrive at S. Thomas. 1 P.M. Friday. |
|---|---|---|
| 79 | 22 Jan. | 26 Jan. |
| 81 | 5 Feb. | 9 Feb. |
| 83 | 19 Feb. | 23 Feb. |
| 85 | 5 Mar. | 9 Mar. |
| 87 | 19 Mar. | 23 Mar. |
| 89 | 2 Apr. | 6 Apr. |
| 91 | 16 Apr. | 20 Apr. |
| 93 | 30 Apr. | 4 May |
| 95 | 14 May | 18 May |
| 97 | 28 May | 1 June |
| 99 | 11 June | 15 June |
| 101 | 25 June | 29 June |
| 103 | 9 July | 13 July |

NOTE.—The Branch Packets on the Outward Route may start from Barbados, and on both Outward and Homeward Routes may leave intermediate Ports earlier than the time shown in this Table or in the detailed Tables of Routes, if they are in all respects ready to proceed. If the transfer of cargo at Barbados cannot be completed by the hour shown, the Branch Packets may remain to complete, on the understanding that the Company endeavours, by extra speed if necessary, to reach the various Ports according to the Table Time, and that the delay does not involve arrival at the final Port on any Branch after contract time.

## HOMEWARD ROUTE.

| TABLE No. 4. | | | TABLE No. 3. | | | | TABLE No. 2. | | | TABLE No. 1. | | | | | |
|---|---|---|---|---|---|---|---|---|---|---|---|---|---|---|---|
| ST. THOMAS TO BARBADOS. | | | TOBAGO AND TRINIDAD TO BARBADOS. | | | | DEMERARA TO BARBADOS. | | | COLON TO BARBADOS. | | | | BARBADOS TO PLYMOUTH. | |
| No. of Voyage. | Leave St. Thomas. | Arrive at Barbados. | No. of Voyage. | Leave Tobago. | Leave Trinidad. | Arrive at Barbados. | No. of Voyage. | Leave Demerara. | Arrive at Barbados. | No. of Voyage. | Leave Colon. | Leave Jamaica. | Arrive at Barbados. | Leave Barbados. | Arrive at Plymouth. |
| | 8 P.M. Tues. | 7 A.M. Sat. | | 6 P.M. Wed. | 5 P.M. Thurs. | 7 A.M. Sat. | | 10 A.M. Thurs. | 1 A.M. Sat. | | 10 A.M. Sat. | 2 P.M. Tues. | 4 A.M. Sat. | 5 P.M. Sat. | 9 P.M. Wed. |
| | | | | | | | | (c.) | | | (a) | | | (b) | |
| 2 | 30 Jan. | 3 Feb. | 28 | 31 Jan. | 1 Feb. | 3 Feb. | 54 | 1 Feb. | 3 Feb. | 80 | 27 Jan. | 30 Jan. | 3 Feb. | 3 Feb. | 14 Feb. |
| 4 | 13 Feb. | 17 Feb. | 30 | 14 Feb. | 15 Feb. | 17 Feb. | 56 | 15 Feb. | 17 Feb. | 82 | 10 Feb. | 13 Feb. | 17 Feb. | 17 Feb. | 28 Feb. |
| 6 | 27 Feb. | 3 Mar. | 32 | 28 Feb. | 1 Mar. | 3 Mar. | 58 | 1 Mar. | 3 Mar. | 84 | 24 Feb. | 27 Feb. | 3 Mar. | 3 Mar. | 14 Mar. |
| 8 | 13 Mar. | 17 Mar. | 34 | 14 Mar. | 15 Mar. | 17 Mar. | 60 | 15 Mar. | 17 Mar. | 86 | 10 Mar. | 13 Mar. | 17 Mar. | 17 Mar. | 28 Mar. |
| 10 | 27 Mar. | 31 Mar. | 36 | 28 Mar. | 29 Mar. | 31 Mar. | 62 | 29 Mar. | 31 Mar. | 88 | 24 Mar. | 27 Mar. | 31 Mar. | 31 Mar. | 11 Apr. |
| 12 | 10 Apr. | 14 Apr. | 38 | 11 Apr. | 12 Apr. | 14 Apr. | 64 | 12 Apr. | 14 Apr. | 90 | 7 Apr. | 10 Apr. | 14 Apr. | 14 Apr. | 25 Apr. |
| 14 | 24 Apr. | 28 Apr. | 40 | 25 Apr. | 26 Apr. | 28 Apr. | 66 | 26 Apr. | 28 Apr. | 92 | 21 Apr. | 24 Apr. | 28 Apr. | 28 Apr. | 9 May |
| 16 | 8 May | 12 May | 42 | 9 May | 10 May | 12 May | 68 | 10 May | 12 May | 94 | 5 May | 8 May | 12 May | 12 May | 23 May |
| 18 | 22 May | 26 May | 44 | 23 May | 24 May | 26 May | 70 | 24 May | 26 May | 96 | 19 May | 22 May | 26 May | 26 May | 6 June |
| 20 | 5 June | 9 June | 46 | 6 June | 7 June | 9 June | 72 | 7 June | 9 June | 98 | 2 June | 5 June | 9 June | 9 June | 20 June |
| 22 | 19 June | 23 June | 48 | 20 June | 21 June | 23 June | 74 | 21 June | 23 June | 100 | 16 June | 19 June | 23 June | 23 June | 4 July |
| 24 | 3 July | 7 July | 50 | 4 July | 5 July | 7 July | 76 | 5 July | 7 July | 102 | 30 June | 3 July | 7 July | 7 July | 18 July |
| 26 | 17 July | 21 July | 52 | 18 July | 19 July | 21 July | 78 | 19 July | 21 July | 104 | 14 July | 17 July | 21 July | 21 July | 1 Aug. |
| | | | | | | | | | | 106 | 28 July | 31 July | 4 Aug. | 4 Aug. | 15 Aug. |

NOTE (a).—If the Homeward Mails, &c. are embarked in time, and the Packet be in all other respects ready she may start from Colon the previous evening, but the departure from Jamaica homeward is not to be accelerated, unless from Quarantine or other causes the Packet may have to coal at another Port, in which case she may leave Jamaica as soon as she is ready.

NOTE (b).—If either of the Steamers on the Branch Routes has not reached Barbados, the Packet is to await the arrival of the missing Vessel two clear days, if necessary; otherwise the Packet is to start for England the moment the Mails, &c., from the several Branch Packets and from Barbados have been received on board.

The Mail Service to Tobago was then altered as per the notice dated 1 February 1900:-

*A Mail for Tobago leaves the Port-of-Spain every MONDAY AND THURSDAY, conveyed overland to Toco and thence by boat. Mails close at General Post Office at 8.09 a.m. Letters will only be forwarded by this Special Service. The mails will be despatched from Tobago at noon on WEDNESDAY and SATURDAY and should reach the General Post Office on FRIDAY and TUESDAY evening.*

On 22 July 1902 Royal Mail Steamers started to make direct calls at Port-of-Spain, the first vessel being the "Atroto". This resulted in the following notice being published, to take effect from 31 July 1902.

*Only mails for Grenada and St. Vincent will be made up for despatch by the Intercolonial Steamer.*

102

*The Mails for the above places will be closed at the General Post Office at 3.30 p.m. - No Late Fees. Money Orders will be issued on Grenada and St. Vincent up to 4 p.m. Wednesday. On Friday August 1 and every alternate Friday thereafter Mails for Europe and the Colonies (except Grenada and St. Vincent) will be made up at the General Post Office for despatch by the Royal Mail Ocean Steamer. Money Orders for this Mail will be issued up to 4 p.m. Thursday, and, for Europe only, with additional Commission from 8 a.m. to 10 a.m. on Friday. The Late Fees at present in force for the English and Colonial Mails will apply in future to the Mail made up on the Friday of the Outward Mail week, viz:-*

*Letters and other postal matter posted at the General Post Office or any Pillar Box in Port-of-Spain up to 2.30 p.m. will require ordinary postage only. Letters, etc., posted in Pillar Boxes in Port-of-Spain after 2.30 p.m. on English Mail Day will not go forward that Mail. Letters and Postal Articles with Late Fee of 1d. may be posted at the General Post Office only, up to 3 p.m. Letters (but not other Postal Articles) with Late Fee of 2½d. may be posted at General Post Office only, up to 3.30 p.m. Letters (but not other Postal Articles) with a Late Fee of 5d. may be posted at the General Post Office only, up to 4 p.m.*

*All posting boxes will be closed at the General Post Office at 2.30 p.m. on Friday the English Mail day, and all Late Fee letters and local letters between that time and 4 p.m. should be handed to one of the Counter Clerks.*

*From 3.30 p.m. on the Friday Late Fee letters will be received only at the Stamp Window in the Private Box Department.*

On 1 October 1902 the following notice was published:-

*Until further orders, the letters prepaid at ordinary rates by the stamps of this Colony, may be posted in the Letter Box on board any outward bound Royal Mail subsidised Steamers from 2.30 p.m. on the date of sailing up to the time the vessel leaves the port. These letters will be taken on shore at the first port and handed to the Post Office there. No loose letters will in future be conveyed on board by the Royal Mail agents or the officers of the several ships.*

followed on 4 November 1902 by:-

*Mails for Barbados and Europe by R.M.S. "Trent" will be closed as usual on FRIDAY 7TH INSTANT.*

*Mails for Demerara by R.M.S. "Esk" will be closed at this office at 11 a.m. on MONDAY 10TH INSTANT.*

*Mails for Jamaica and Colon per R.M.S. "Para" will be closed at this Office at 3 p.m. on MONDAY, 10TH INSTANT.*

*Mails for Tobago, Grenada, St. Vincent and La Guayra per R.M.S. "Eden" will be closed at this Office at 3 p.m. on MONDAY 10TH INSTANT.*

*Mails for St. Lucia, Martinique, Dominica, Guadelopue, Antigua, Montserrat, Nevis, St Kitts, St. Thomas, St. Domingo, Puerto Rico, Vera Cruz and Port au Prince per R.M.S. "Solent" will be closed at this Office at 3 p.m. on MONDAY, 10TH INSTANT.*

*Intercolonial Money Orders and Parcel Post will close at 12.30 p.m. on SATURDAY 8TH INSTANT.*

On 19 December 1902 a proclamation was made regarding the Venezuela Blockade by the British and German warships.

*By Sir ARCHIBALD LUCIUS DOUGLAS, Knight Commander of the Most Honourable Order of the Bath, Vice-Admiral in His Britannic Majesty's Fleet, and Commander-in-Chief of His Britannic Majesty's Ships and Vessels employed and to be employed on the NORTH AMERICA AND WEST INDIES STATION.*

*IT is hereby notified that a blockade of the Ports of LA GUAIRA, CARENERO, GUANTA CUMANA, CARUPANO, and the Mouths of the ORINOCO is declared and will be effectively maintained from and after the twentieth day of December subject to an allowance of the following Days of Grace for Vessels sailing before the date of this notification;-from West Indian Ports and from Ports on the East Coast of the Continent of America,-ten days for Steamers and twenty days for Sailing Vessels. From all other Ports,-twenty days for Steamers and forty days for Sailing Vessels. For Vessels lying in Ports now declared to be Blockaded,-fifteen days. Vessels which attempt to violate the Blockade will render themselves liable to all measures authorised by the Law of the Nations, and the respective Treaties between His Majesty and the different Neutral Powers.*

*Given under my hand on Board His Majesty's Ship "Adiandne" at TRINIDAD.*

followed 3 days later by the British Declaration of War on the United States of Venezuela.

On 31 January 1903 the U.K. and European Mail arrangements were changed again:-

*ON SATURDAY, 31st JANUARY and every alternate Saturday thereafter, Mails for Europe and Barbados will be made up at the General Post Office for dispatch by the Royal Mail Ocean Steamer.*

*Money Orders and Parcels for this Mail will be received up to 4 p.m., Friday. Registered articles will be received up to 9 a.m., on Saturday. The Late Fees at present in force for the English and Colonial Mails will apply in future to the Mail made up on the Saturday of the Outward Mail Week, viz:-*

*Letters and other postal matter posted at the General Post Office or any Pillar Box in Port-of-Spain up to 9 a.m., will require ordinary postage only. Letters etc., posted in Pillar Boxes in Port-of-Spain after 9 a.m. on English Mail day will not go forward that Mail.*

*Letters and Postal Articles with Late Fee of 1d. may be posted at General Post Office only up to 9.30 a.m. Letters (but not other Postal Articles) with Late Fee of $2\frac{1}{2}$d. may be posted at the General Post Office only up to 10 a.m. Letters (but not other Postal Articles) with Late Fee of 5d. may be posted at General Post Office only, up to 10.30 a.m.*

*All posting boxes will be closed at the General Post Office, at 9 a.m., on Saturday, the English Mail day, and all the Late Fee letters and local letters between that time and 10 a.m. should be handed to one of the Counter Clerks.*

*From 10 a.m. on the Saturday, Late Fee Letters will be received only at the Stamp Window in the Private Box Department. Mails for Demerara will close at 11 a.m. Monday. Mails for Grenada and St. Vincent will close at 3 p.m. Monday. Mails for St. Lucia, Martinique, Dominica, Guadeloupe, Antigua, Montserrat, Nevis, St. Kitts, St. Thomas, San Domingo,*

*Porto Rico and Vera Cruz, 3 p.m. Monday. Mails for Jamaica and Colon and Port-o-Prince will close at 10 a,m, Tuesday. Registration closes half a hour before the time fixed for closing Intercolonial Mails. Intercolonial Money Orders and Parcel Post will close at 12.30 p.m. on Saturday.*

*J. A. BULMER,*
*Postmaster-General.*

The Mail arrangements were changed again in 1904 and 1905 as shown in the following notices:-

GENERAL POST OFFICE, TRINIDAD
*11th October, 1904.*

*Owing to the earlier dispatch of the Homeward Steamer of the Royal Mail Steam Packet Company, ON FRIDAY THE 18TH NOVEMBER NEXT, and every alternate Friday thereafter Mails for Europe and the Colonies will be made up at the General Post Office, Port-of-Spain, as follows:-*

*Mail Orders for this Mail will be issued up to 4 p.m. on the previous day (Thursday). Parcels for transmission by Parcels Post will be received up to 4 p.m. on Thursday. Registration closes at 12 o'clock on Friday, the English Mail day, at the General Post Office. The hours for closing the Mails, and the Late Fees will be as follows:-*

*Letters and other Postal matter posted at the General Post Office or any Pillar Box in Port-of-Spain up to 12.30 p.m. will require ordinary postage only. Letters, &c., posted in Pillar Boxes in Port-of-Spain up to 12.30 p.m. on English Mail day will not go forward that mail. Letters and postal articles with Late Fee of 1d, may be posted at the General Post Office only, up to 1 p.m. Letters (but not other Postal articles) with Late Fee of 2½d. may be posted at the General Post Office only, up to 1.30 p.m. Letters (but not other Postal articles) with Late Fee of 5d. may be posted at the General Post Office only, up to 2 p.m. As Posting Boxes will be closed at the General Post Office at 12.30 p.m. on Friday the English mail day, all Late Fee Letters, and local letters between that time and 2 p.m. should be handed to one of the Counter Clerks.*

*General Post Office,*
*30th August, 1905.*

*In future and until further notice, the Coastal Steamer "Spey" will leave Port-of-Spain, on Wednesday the Incoming English Mail day at 8 p.m. for Tobago, the Spey will leave Scarboro on Monday at Midnight, call at Toco and the North Coasts Ports on Tuesday, and arrive at Port-of-Spain with Mails for England on Wednesday.*

*The Steamer will again leave Port-of-Spain, the same day, Wednesday at 6 p.m. with Intercolonial mails, call at Toco, and arrive at Scarboro on Thursday morning, perform her route around the Island, and leave Scarboro at 10 o'clock p.m. on Saturday, and arrive at Port-of-Spain, At 6 a.m. on Sunday to await the English mail on the Wednesday following.*

On 2 October 1905 the following notice was published regarding placing stamps on picture postcards, as collecting these had become widespread and some collectors liked to have adhesive placed on the picture side!

*The General Post Office, London, has called attention to Article No. XVIII, paragraph VII, of the detailed Regulations of the Convention of Washington, which stipulates that postage stamps for the prepayment of Post Cards sent unenclosed should be affixed to the front of the Card, that is to say* on the side bearing the address. *Several Post Cards violating this regulation have recently been returned to this Colony, and it is notified for general information that Post Cards bearing postage stamps otherwise placed than in the manner mentioned above will not be forwarded from this office.*

On 1 September 1909 following the decision of the U.P.U. Congress Rome. International Reply Coupons were placed on sale as the following notice shows:-

*ON AND AFTER 1ST SEPTEMBER, 1909, International Reply Coupons will be sold and redeemed at the General Post Office, Port-of-Spain, and at the Post Offices at San Fernando and Scarboro, Tobago.*

*They can also be handed in to the Sub-Postmaster at any Post Office in Trinidad or Tobago, to be forwarded to the Head Office, to be redeemed.*

*Reply Coupons from other Countries will be exchanged for Trinidad Postage Stamps to the value of $2\frac{1}{2}d$.*

*The object of the International Reply Coupons Service is to enable the writer of a letter to prepay the postage of the reply by means of these Coupons. For example, a resident in Trinidad desires some information from some one in France. It would cost the person written to $2\frac{1}{2}d$. to send the required reply, and therefore probably no reply would be sent. But if the resident here purchases a Reply Coupon and encloses it in the letter, the addressee can take it to any Post Office of a country which has adopted the International Reply Coupon arrangement, and the Coupon will be exchanged for a stamp to the value of 25 centimes ($2\frac{1}{2}d$).*

The First World War brought censorship and alterations in the Steamer Services.

Special Red Cross Stamps were issued as shown by the following notice:-

*THE 19th October, 1916, having been appointed as Flag Day for the Red Cross Society, there will be a special issue of penny Red Cross Postage Stamps on that day.*

*These stamps will be for sale at all the Post Offices of the Colony and can be used on any subsequent date; the object of the issue being to raise special funds for the Red Cross Society.*

> CLARENCE ROSS,
> Postmaster-General.

On 3 March 1917 the Post Office published the following regulations regarding the use of War Tax Stamps:-

*1d. War Tax Stamps must be affixed to all Inland Letters and letters addressed to places within the British Empire - or they will be chargeable on delivery (if otherwise prepaid) with a tax of 2d.*

*The prepaid rate of postage for letter post is as follows:-*

| | | | |
|---|---|---|---|
| *Not exceeding one oz. in weight* | .... | .... | *1d.* |
| *For every additional oz.* | .... | .... | *1d.,* |

*and one penny War Tax stamp in addition to each letter regardless of its weight.*

*½d. War Tax stamps must be affixed to all Inland Post Cards, and Commercial papers - or they will be chargeable on delivery (if otherwise prepaid) with a tax of 1d.*

*The prepaid rate of postage on every Inland Postcard is a half penny, and in addition to this a ½d. War Tax stamp must now be affixed. A postcard posted unpaid is chargeable on delivery with a postage of one penny and a War Tax stamp of one penny.*

*The rate of postage for Commercial papers and are allowed to pass as such at the reduced postage viz:- all papers and documents whether writings or drawings, produced wholly or partly by hand not having the character of an actual and personal correspondence, such as open letters and postcards of ancient date which have already served their original purpose, papers of legal procedure, deeds of all kinds drawn up by public functionaries, waybills or bills of lading, invoices, receipts, the various kinds of documents of Insurance Companies, copies of extracts from acts under private signature, written on stamped or unstamped paper, musical scores or sheets of music in manuscript, the manuscript of works or of newspapers, forwarded separately, pupils' exercises in original or with corrections, but without any comment on the work and other papers of a similar for printed papers.*

*Commercial papers are subject, so far as regards form and conditions of transmission, to the regulations prescribed for printing papers.*

*Commercial papers must not exceed 4 lbs. in weight, or measure more in any direction than 18 inches.*

*In the form of a roll commercial papers 30 inches in length and 4 inches in diameter may be forwarded.*

*Commercial papers must be put in such a manner that they can be easily withdrawn for examination.*

*It must be borne in mind that War Tax stamps can only be used for prepayment of postage on local letters and to places within the British Empire, and they must on no account be used for prepayment of postage on letters addressed to Foreign Countries.*

*CLARENCE ROSS,*
*Postmaster-General.*

The use of War Tax stamp was discontinued on 31 December 1919 and the stamp (including Red Cross) invalidated on 15 March 1922.

In 1939, KLM (which had started operating in the Caribbean in 1935) extended its routes to include Port-of-Spain to Barbados, as detailed in letters from the Postmaster General on the 14 and 15 February 1939:-

*Sir,*
*I have the honour to inform you that an Air Mail Service has been inaugurated between Trinidad and Ciudad Bolivar (Venezuela) and vice versa by planes of the Royal Dutch Air Lines (K.L.M.).*

*The mails will be closed at the General Post Office Port of Spain, on Fridays at 11.30 a.m. They are due to arrive at Ciudad Bolivar 2.30 p.m. on the day of despatch. In the reverse direction the planes leave Ciudad 3.00 p.m. on the same day.*

*For correspondence conveyed is forwarded in open transit (a decouvert) the usual A. V.2 forms should be forwarded with the relative despatch.*

British West Indian Airways was founded later the same year and made its first flight on 26 November 1940 to Tobago and Barbados, extending its service to Jamaica on 16 December 1944, British Honduras 4 March 1945 and British Guiana on 6 September 1945.

*I have the honour to inform you that an Air Service has been inaugurated between Trinidad and Barbados and vice versa by planes of the Royal Dutch Air Lines.*

*2. The mails will be closed at the General Post Office, Port of Spain at 12.30 p.m. on Mondays and Thursdays, and 7.00 a.m. on Saturdays. They are due to arrive Barbados 3.20 p.m. on Mondays and Thursdays and 10.20 a.m. on Saturdays. In the reverse direction the planes will leave Barbados at 3.45 p.m. on Mondays and Thursdays and 10.45 a.m. on Saturdays, arriving Port of Spain. (Trinidad) approximately two hours later.*

*3. For correspondence conveyed by this Service this Administration will require payment at rate of Francs 16.90 (gold) per kilogram, if forwarded in closed mails. If sent in open transit (a decouvert) the usual A. V.2 Forms should be prepared and credit at rate of five pence per half ounce afforded to this Administration.*

From 1 January 1922 due to International Reply Coupons the Postal Union Convention of Madrid in 1922, a fifty centime International Reply Coupon could be exchanged at any Money Order Office in this Colony for a postage stamp or stamps of the total value of 3d., and a twenty-five centime coupon for stamps of the total value of $1\frac{1}{2}$d. Coupons had to be presented within six months of the date of issue. Twenty-five centime Coupons could be purchased for 3d. each at the Port-of-Spain, San Fernando and Scarboro (Tobago) Post Offices. Not more than ten could be sold to or exchanged for the same person on any one day.

On 6 June 1922 the following was published:-

*Letters and Parcels destined for places in the United Kingdom will be accepted for express delivery in that country.*

*2. In the case of parcels the fee of sixpence must be prepaid; and there will be no charge for delivery to be paid by the addressee unless he resides more than one mile from the Post Office of delivery.*

*3. As regards letters the express fee cannot be prepaid, but will be collected from the addressee; this fee will be at the rate of sixpence per mile of the distance from the Post Office of delivery to the residence of the addressee.*

*4. Letters and parcels for the express delivery should be handed in at a Post Office; they should not be dropped into a Letter Box. They should be clearly marked "Express".*

In 1925 tenders were requested for two years for the following routes etc:-

| Section. | Frequency of Service. | Conveyance. | REMARKS. |
|---|---|---|---|
| Sangre Grande Upper Guaico (Nestor Village.) | ... Six times weekly in each direction except Sundays | ... Motor ... | |
| Sangre Grande Matura-Toco | ... Three times weekly in each direction | ... Motor | ... Tenders will also be considered for a daily service on this route, i.e., six times weekly in each direction. |
| Arima Post Office Arima Railway Station | ... Three times daily in each direction except Sundays | ... Motor. cab or hand cart | |
| Arima–Valencia | ... Twice weekly in each direction | ... Motor, animal or foot | |
| Blanchisseuse– Arima<br>*or*<br>Blanchisseuse– Caura | ... Twice weekly in each direction<br><br>... Twice weekly in each direction | ... Horse or mule ...<br><br>... Horse, mule or foot | Only one of these two sections from Blanchisseuse will be arranged for. |
| Rio Claro–Mayaro | ... Once daily in each direction except Sundays | ... Motor | ... One day in each alternate week to convey mails to Mayaro Depôt to connect with Coastal Steamer. |
| Mayaro–Guayaguayare | ... Three times weekly in each direction | ... Motor, animal or foot | |
| Couva–Gran Couva– Tortuga | ... Once daily in each direction except Sundays | ... Motor | .. The mails for Tortuga may be conveyed from Gran Couva by foot, animal, or motor. |
| Princes Town–Moruga– La Lune | ... Three times weekly in each direction | ... Motor | ... Tenders will also be considered for a daily service on this route, i.e., six times weekly in each direction. |

109

Again tenders were invited for the conveyance of Mails on 1 September, 1927, for 5 years on the following routes etc:-

| SECTION. | FREQUENCY OF SERVICE. | CONVEYANCE. | REMARKS. |
|---|---|---|---|
| Arima Post Office—Arima Railway Station | Six times daily in each direction except Sundays | Motor, cab or hand cart. | |
| Arima-Valencia .. | Twice weekly in each direction | Motor-bus, animal or foot. | |
| Blanchisseuse-Caura .. | Twice weekly in each direction | Mule, horse or foot. | |
| Couva-Gran Couva-Tortuga .. | Once daily in each direction except Sundays | Motor .. .. | The Mails for Tortuga may be conveyed from Gran Couva by foot, bicycle or motor. The contractor is required to deliver correspondence to certain places on main route. |
| Cumuto-Four Roads Tamana | Three times weekly in each direction | Motor. | |
| Guanapo Railway Station–Talparo | Once daily in each direction except Sundays | Motor | |
| Mayaro-Rio Claro .. .. | Once daily in each direction except Sundays | Motor .. | One day in each alternate week to convey Mails to Mayaro Depot to connect with Coastal Steamer. |
| Mayaro-Guayaguayare .. | Three times weekly in each direction | Motor, animal or foot. | |
| Princes Town Post Office—Princes Town Railway Station. | Three times daily in each direction except Sundays | Motor, cab or hand cart. | |
| Princes Town–New Grant–Tableland | Once daily in each direction except Sundays. | Motor. | |
| Princes Town–Moruga–La Lune | Three times weekly in each direction | Motor .. | Tenders will also be considered for a daily service on this route, i.e., six times weekly in each direction. |
| Sangre Grande–Biche .. | Three times weekly in each direction | Motor car, or Motor and sidecar. | |
| Sangre Grande–Nestor Village (Upper Guaico) | Once daily in each direction except Sundays | Motor car or Motor and sidecar. | |
| Sangre Grande–Manzanilla.. | Twice daily in each direction except Sundays. | Motor | |
| Sangre Grande–Matura–Toco | Once daily in each direction except Sundays | Motor car, bus, or sidecar. | |

110

Mail Contracts for 1 September, 1927 Continued:-

Mail Contracts.— *Continued*.

| SECTION. | FREQUENCY OF SERVICE. | CONVEYANCE. | REMARKS. |
|---|---|---|---|
| San Fernando–Point Fortin, &c., to Cedros | Three times weekly in each direction between San Fernando and Cedros, but once daily in each direction between San Fernando and La Brea. | Motor. | |
| Siparia–Erin .. .. | Once daily in each direction except Sundays | Motor. | |
| Siparia–Fyzabad .. .. | Once daily in each direction except Sundays | Motor, cab or foot | |
| Tacarigua–Caura or Tunapuna–Caura | Four times weekly in each direction<br><br>Four times weekly in each direction | Motor, horse or foot<br><br>Motor, horse or foot | Only one of these two sections to Caura will be arranged for. |
| Toco–Matelot .. .. | Twice weekly in each direction | Horse, mule or foot | |

Pan American Airways under Juan Terry Trippe in 1928 started its expansion in to Latin America. It was awarded virtually all Foreign Airmail (F.A.M.) contracts by the U.S. Post Office, which included F.A.M. 6 Miami - San Juan - Santo Domingo on 13 July 1928, being extended to Port-of-Spain. The first flight being 22 September 1929. The route being mainly operated by Sikorsky S - 38 amphibians.

In 15 September 1930 Pan American brought out the NYRBA Airline which had opened the Miami - Santigo Service via Brazil and Trinidad etc., on 18 February 1930 but without a U.S. mail contract which was given to Pan American on 24 September 1930 (FAM10).

**At the Islands, Trinidad.**

Tenders from 1st September, 1932 for 5 years on the following:-

| SECTION. | FREQUENCY OF SERVICE. | CONVEYANCE. | REMARKS. |
|---|---|---|---|
| Arima Post Office—Arima Railway Station | Six times daily in each direction except Sundays | Motor, cab or hand cart | |
| Arima–Valencia .... | ....Twice weekly in each direction .... | Motor bus, animal or foot | |
| Arima–Blanchisseuse or | ....Twice weekly in each direction .... | Motor, horse or foot | The mails may be conveyed to the 12th mile by Motor, thence by horse or foot. |
| Blanchisseuse–Caura | ....Twice weekly in each direction .... | Mule, horse or foot. | |
| Cedros–Icacos .... | ....Three times weekly in each direction | Motor | ....Tenders will be considered for a daily service on this route, i.e., six times weekly in each direction. |
| Couva–Gran Couva–Tortuga | Once daily in each direction except Sundays | Motor | ....The mails for Tortuga may be conveyed from Gran Couva by foot, bicycle or motor. The Contractor is required to deliver correspondence to certain places on main route. |
| Cumuto-Four Roads, Tamana .... .... | Three times weekly in each direction | Motor. | |
| Guanapo Railway Station—Talparo | Once daily in each direction except Sundays | Motor | |
| Mayaro–Rio Claro | ....Once daily in each direction except Sundays | Motor | ....The Contractor will be required to convey mails to Mayaro Depot to connect with Coastal Steamer. |
| Mayaro–Guayaguayare | ....Three times weekly in each direction | Motor | |
| Princes Town Post Office—Princes Town Railway Station | Three times daily in each direction except Sundays | Motor, cab or cart | |
| Princes Town–New Grant–Tableland | Once daily in each direction except Sundays | Motor | |
| Princes Town–Moruga–La Lune | Three times weekly in each direction | Motor | ....Tenders will be considered for a daily service on this route, i.e., six times weekly in each direction. |
| Sangre Grande–Biche | ....Three times weekly in each direction | Motor | |
| Sangre Grande–Nestor Village (Upper Guaico) | Once daily in each direction except Sundays | Motor | |
| Sangre Grande–Manzanilla | Twice daily in each direction except Sundays | Motor | |
| Sangre Grande–Matura–Toco, or | Once daily in each direction except Sundays | Motor | ....To start from Sangre Grande. |
| Toco–Matura–Sangre Grande | Once daily in each direction except Sundays | Motor | ....To start from Toco. |
| San Fernando–Point Fortin, &c., to Cedros | Once daily in each direction except Sundays | Motor | |
| Siparia–Erin .... | ....Once daily in each direction except Sundays | Motor | |
| Siparia–Fyzabad | ....Once daily in each direction except Sundays | Motor, cab or foot | |
| Tacarigua–Caura | ....Four times weekly in each direction | Motor, horse or foot | Tenders will also be considered for a daily service on this route, i.e., six times weekly in each direction |
| Toco–Matelot .... or | ....Twice weekly in each direction | Motor, animal or foot | |
| Grande Riviere–Toco | ....Once daily in each direction except Sundays | Motor | |
| **TOBAGO.** | | | |
| Scarborough–Moriah–Les Coteaux–Plymouth–and return to Scarborough | Once daily in each direction except Sundays | Motor | ....This service to include Bethel, Canaan, Mason Hall, Mount Grace and Lambeau. |

Tenders from 1 June, 1934 for two years for:-

| Section. | Frequency of Service. | Conveyance. | Remarks. |
|---|---|---|---|
| Tobago:—<br> Scarborough-Speyside | Three times weekly in each direction | Motor  ... | ...Service to include the Post Offices of Mount St. George, Pembroke, Roxborough, Delaford, Speyside. |

Tenders from 1 November, 1934 for two years for:-

| Section. | Frequency of Service. | Conveyance. | Remarks. |
|---|---|---|---|
| Tobago:—<br> Scarborough<br> Moriah<br> Les Coteaux<br> Plymouth<br> and return to Scarborough | Three times weekly in each direction | Motor  ... | ...Service to include:—<br> Bethel<br> Canaan<br> Mason Hall<br> Mount Grace and<br> Lambeau |

Tenders were invited for making 125 suits of Khaki drill uniforms for Postmen. The uniforms consisted of Tunic and Trousers. The tunic had a certain amount of red facing to the cuffs, and red piping down the leg of the trousers.

113

Tenders from 1 September, 1937 for 5 years for:-

| Section. | Frequency of Service. | Conveyance. | Remarks. |
|---|---|---|---|
| Arima Post Office-Arima Railway Station | Six times daily in each direction except Sundays | Motor, cab or hand cart. | |
| Arima-Valencia .... .... | Twice weekly in each direction .... | Motor bus, animal or foot. | |
| Cedros-Icacos .... .... | Once daily in each direction except Sundays | Motor. | |
| Couva-Gran Couva-Tortuga | Once daily in each direction except Sundays | Motor. | The mails for Tortuga may be conveyed from Gran Couva by foot, bicycle or motor. The Contractor is required to deliver correspondence to certain places on main route. |
| Cumuto-Four Roads, Tamana | Three times weekly in each direction | Motor. | |
| Guanapo Railway Station-Talparo | Once daily in each direction except Sundays. | Motor | |
| Mayaro-Guayaguayare .... | Three times weekly in each direction | Motor. | |
| Princes Town Post Office Princes Town Railway Station | Three times daily in each direction except Sundays | Motor, cab or cart. | |
| Princes Town-New Grant Tableland | Once daily in each direction except Sundays | Motor | |
| Princes Town-Moruga-La Lune | Once daily in each direction except Sundays | Motor. | |
| Sangre-Grande-Biche .... | Three times weekly in each direction | Motor. | |
| Sangre Grande-Nestor Village (Upper Guaico) | Once daily in each direction except Sundays | Motor. | |
| Sangre Grande-Manzanilla .... | Twice daily in each direction except Sundays | Motor. | |
| San Fernando-Point Fortin, &c., to Cedros | Once daily in each direction except Sundays | Motor. | |
| Siparia-Erin .... .... | Once daily in each direction except Sundays | Motor. | |
| Siparia-Fyzabad .... .... | Once daily in each direction except Sundays | Motor. | |
| Tacarigua-Caura .... | Once daily in each direction except Sundays | Motor | |
| Toco-Matelot .... .... | Once daily in each direction except Sundays | Motor. | |
| **Tobago.** Scarborough-Moriah-Les Coteaux Plymouth and return to Scarborough | Thrice weekly in each direction except Sundays | Motor | This service to include Bethel, Canaan, Mason Hall, Mount Grace and Lambeau. |
| Scarborough-Roxborough and Speyside and return to Scarborough | Thrice weekly in each direction except Sundays | Motor | This service to include Mount St. George, Pembroke and Delaford. |

The outbreak of the Second World War on 3 September 1939 saw the introduction of censorship, Trinidad being an important censorship station. On 15 December 1942 the following notice was published:-

*On account of existing military demands upon air transportation facilities the United States Government has found it necessary to impose limitations on the transportation of air mail from the United States to countries outside the American Continent, the West Indies, and other islands in the Caribbean area.*

*Regulations are accordingly published below dealing with letters so stamped or marked that they would ordinarily be transmitted via the United States to destinations outside the American Continent, West Indies, and other Islands in the Caribbean area - transmission from the United States onwards being by air. The effect of the regulations will be that if the letter exceeds two ounces in weight or is not in the usual and ordinary form of a letter or in any other case where the efficient prosecution of the war so demands the Postmaster-General will be authorised to despatch the letter in a mail bag for transmission from the United States onwards by surface mail.*

*It should be noticed that the regulations do not affect the transmission of mail to a destination in the United States or the transmission of a letter otherwise than via the United States or the transmission of a letter via the United States for carriage onwards by surface mail.*

This was resumed after the war 8 October, 1945:-

### AIR MAIL SERVICE - NORTH ATLANTIC
*It is notified for general information that letters not exceeding 1 lb. in weight may now be accepted for transmission to Europe by the North Atlantic Air Mail Service.*

• By the end of 1957, there were 51 Departmental Offices in Trinidad and 5 in Tobago, and 101 Postal Agencies in Trinidad and 21 in Tobago, a total of 178.

A new Post Office Headquarters building at Wrightson Road, Port-of-Spain, was occupied at the end of January, 1957. The upper floor of this new building accommodated the Administrative Branches and the ground floor was used as a Mail Transit Centre and the Post Office Stores.

In 1957 mails between Trinidad and Tobago continued to be carried by British West Indian Airways and coastal steamers chartered by Government but, due to a strike by B.W.I.A. Pilots, emergency arrangements were made with the Light Aeroplane Club to convey airmails to and from Tobago during the period 16 to 31 October, 1957. As from 1 July, 1957, Departmental Road Services replaced those previously operated by Bus Conductors in Trinidad, but subsidiary and feeder services in Tobago continued to be operated on a contract basis.

In 1958 a faster delivery of mails in South Trinidad resulted from extra van services operated twice daily from Port-of-Spain to San Fernando.

The postal services continued to expand steadily until Independence on 31 August 1962.

Caroni River.  Trinidad, B. W. I.          Muir, Marshall & Co.

# CHAPTER 3

## POSTAL RATES

## TOBAGO

In 1765 the rate between London and the British West Indies was 1/= per single letter sent or 4/= for 1oz. and between any two ports in British America, 4d. per single letter sheet or 1s. 4d. per oz.

On 5 January 1797 the rates between London and the B.W.I. remained unchanged, but between any two ports in British America were increased to the same level, viz:-

                    1/= per single letter sheet.

Up to 1850 the Tobago rates were the same as those given for Trinidad in the next section.

On 26 September a registration fee of 6d. to the U.K. and any B.W.I. Colony was introduced.

On 23 March 1854 the packet letter rate to the U.K. was reduced to 6d. per $\frac{1}{2}$oz. up to 1 oz. and then 1/= per additional oz. until April 1863 when it reverted to 1/= per $\frac{1}{2}$ oz.

A short lived inland postal service started on 5 November 1880, the letter rate being 1d. per $\frac{1}{2}$ oz. and newspapers 2d. per 2 oz.

When Tobago joined the Universal Postal Union on 1 January 1881 the following rates were introduced:-

| | |
|---|---|
| Registration | 2d., |
| Advice of Arrival (A.R.) | $2\frac{1}{2}$d. |
| Letters | 4d. per $\frac{1}{2}$oz. |
| Postcards | $1\frac{1}{2}$d. each |
| Newspapers | 1d. per 4 oz. |
| Printed Papers | 1d. per 2 oz. |
| Commercial Papers | 1d. per 2 oz. but minimum of $2\frac{1}{2}$d. |

Evidently it was pointed out that this was not according to the U.P.U. Convention. For countries nearer than 300 miles, so on December 1881 the proper U.P.U. rates for these countries was introduced i.e.:-

Barbados, St. Vincent, Grenada, Trinidad, St. Lucia, Dominica, Martinique and Guadeloupe (300 miles limit).

| | |
|---|---|
| Letters | $2\frac{1}{2}$d. per $\frac{1}{2}$oz. |
| Postcards | 1d. each |
| Newspapers | $\frac{1}{2}$d. each. |

As Dominica was found to be over 300 miles distant the inaugural rate of 4d. per $\frac{1}{2}$oz. and 1$\frac{1}{2}$d. each for postcards was re introduced on 7 March 1882.

On 1 October 1885 a parcel post service to the U.K. was introduced at a rate of 8d. per lb. with a limit of 7 lbs. (increased to 11 lbs. on 27 July 1886).

On 1 January 1889 Tobago was subordinated to Trinidad which had the immediate effect of having the inland letter rate of 1d., extended to Tobago, presumably all other Trinidad postal rates were also applied.

Typical Street Tobago. B. W. I.                    Muir, Marshall & Co.

# TRINIDAD

In 1814 the rate between U.K. and the West Indies was 1/1d.

From 1 January 1817 to 4 December 1839 the packet letter rate was 1s. 3d., for a single letter.

From 23 June 1825 the rate between the British West Indies and Colombia or Mexico was 1/= for a single letter.

On 5 December 1839 the packet rate between the U.K. and the British West Indies was 1/= per ½oz. up to 1 oz. and then 2/= per oz.

Incoming ship letters from Trinidad were charged from 10 October 1814 8d. (including Masters gratuity of 2d.) a single letter. This was amended on 5 December 1839 to 8d. per ½oz. when posted or delivered at the Port of arrival and 1/= per ½oz. if delivered at another place in the U.K.

On 14 August 1851 the Inland Postal Service started, the following rates being applied:-

*Letters 1d. per ½oz.*

| | |
|---|---|
| *Printed British or Foreign Newspapers brought to this colony by packet boats or private ships.* | *} Free }* |
| *Printed British or Foreign Newspapers or Island Newspapers transmitted by post from one place to any other place within this colony.* | *} Each One } Penny* |
| *Island Newspapers sent by post from this colony.* | *} Free* |
| *Printed votes and proceedings of the Imperial Parliament. Periodical Publications, Pamphlets, Magazines, Reviews and other Publications sent to this colony by Packet, if delivered at the General Post Office, in Port-of-Spain.* | *} } One } Penny* |
| *If undelivered at any other Post Office, and if not exceeding one ounce.* | *} One } Penny* |
| *If exceeding one ounce, for every ounce beyond that weight.* | *} One } Penny* |
| *PATTERNS:* | |
| *Packets or covers containing patterns or samples, being open at the sides, and not exceeding one ounce, and without any letter or writing in upon or within any such packet or cover, other than the name of the sender, his place of abode, the prices of the articles contained and the name and address of the person to whom the packet or cover shall be sent.* | *} } One } Penny } }* |
| *Letter not open at the sides containing patterns or samples and not exceeding one ounce in weight.* | *} Two } pence* |

On 5 April 1854 the packet rate to U.K. was reduced to 6d. per ½oz. up to 1 oz., with 1/= per additional oz.

On 1 March 1858 Registration of a fee of 6d. was introduced for U.K. and Colonies, U.S.A. and the Inland Post.

Compulsory Prepayment on letters to the U.K. was effective from 1 January 1859 followed by the Introduction on 1 February 1859 of the Colonial book post as per the following notice:-

*General Post Office,*
*17th January, 1859.*

*From 1 February next Book Packets may be forwarded to the several British Colonies in the West Indies, (Turks' Island excepted) as well as to the British Possessions of Bermuda, Malta, Gibraltar, and Hong Kong, at the following rates:-*

| Addressed to | Not exceeding 4 oz. in weight. | | Exceeding 4 oz. and not exceeding ½lb. | | Exceeding ½lb. and not exceeding 1lb. | | Exceeding 1lb and not exceeding 1½lbs. | | Exceeding 1½lbs. & not exceeding 2lbs. | |
|---|---|---|---|---|---|---|---|---|---|---|
| | s. | d. | s. | d. | s. | d. | s. | d. | s. | d. |
| The several British Colonies in the West Indies without passing through the United Kingdom. | 0 | 3 | 0 | 6 | 1 | 0 | 1 | 6 | 2 | 0 |
| Malta and Gibraltar via the United Kingdom. | 0 | 6 | 1 | 0 | 2 | 0 | 3 | 0 | 4 | 0 |
| Hong Kong via the United Kingdom and Egypt. | 0 | 7 | 1 | 2 | 2 | 4 | 3 | 6 | 4 | 8 |

*and so on for heavier Packets.*

*A book Packet may consist of Printed Books, Magazines, Reviews, Pamphlets, and any description of paper, whether, printed, manuscript or plain - it must not exceed 2 feet in length, breadth, or width; it must be in a cover and open at the end or sides, and must not contain any letter, or any communication in the nature of a letter written or printed on the cover in every such respect. The postage must in all cases be paid in advance.*

*ELLYS LAYTON,*
*Colonial Postmaster.*

**Harts Cut, Trinidad.**

A new rate table for mail sent via London was gazetted on 13 June 1860 as shown:-

| | FOR A LETTER | | | | | For each Newspaper. | FOR A BOOK PACKET | | | | | |
|---|---|---|---|---|---|---|---|---|---|---|---|---|
| | Not exceeding ¼ oz. | Above ¼ oz. and not exceeding ½ oz. | Above ½ oz. and not exceeding ¾ oz. | Above ¾ oz. and not exceeding 1 oz. | Above 1 oz. and not exceeding 1½ oz. | | Not exceeding 2 ozs. | 2 ozs. to 4 ozs. | 4 ozs. to 8 ozs. | 8 ozs. to 1 lb. | 1 lb. to 1½ lb. | 1½ lb. to 2 lbs. |
| | s. d. | s. d. | s. d. | s. d. | s. d. | | s. d. | s. d. | s. d. | s. d. | s. d. | s. d. |
| Aden | 0 11 | 0 11 | 1 10 | 1 10 | 3 8 | 2d. | 0 7 | 0 7 | 1 2 | 2 4 | 3 6 | 4 8 |
| Africa, West Coast of | 0 11 | 0 11 | 1 10 | 1 10 | 3 8 | Letter Rate. | · | - | Letter rate. | | | |
| Algeria | 0 8 | 1 4 | 2 0 | 2 8 | 3 4 | Book rate | 0 2 | 0 4 | 0 8 | 1 4 | 2 0 | 2 8 |
| Ascension | 0 11 | 0 11 | 1 10 | 1 10 | 3 8 | 1d. | 0 6 | 0 6 | 0 2 | 0 3 | 0 4 | 0 |
| Australia, South | 0 11 | 0 11 | 1 10 | 1 10 | 3 8 | 2d. | 0 7 | 0 7 | 1 2 | 2 4 | 3 6 | 4 8 |
| Australia, Western | 0 11 | 0 11 | 1 10 | 1 10 | 3 8 | 2d. | 0 7 | 0 7 | 1 2 | 2 4 | 3 6 | 4 8 |
| Austria | 1 2 | 1 2 | 2 4 | 2 4 | 4 8 | Cannot be prepaid | 0 2* | 0 4 | 0 8 | 1 4 | 2 0 | 2 8 |
| Azores | 0 9 | 1 1 | 1 10 | 2 3 | 4 | 2d | 0 5 | 0 7 | 1 2 | 2 4 | 3 6 | 4 8 |
| Baden | 0 9 | 1 6 | 2 3 | 3 0 | 3 9 | Book rate | 0 2* | 0 4 | 0 8 | 1 4 | 2 0 | 2 8 |
| Bavaria | 0 9 | 1 6 | 2 3 | 3 0 | 3 9 | ditto | 0 2* | 0 4 | 0 8 | 1 4 | 2 0 | 2 8 |
| Belgium | 0 9 | 0 9 | 1 6 | 5 2 | | ditto | 0 2 | 0 4 | 0 8 | 1 4 | 2 0 | 2 8 |
| Borneo | | | | | | Letter rate. | - | · | Letter rate. | | | |
| Bourbon | 0 11 | 0 11 | 1 10 | 1 10 | 3 8 | ditto | - | · | ditto | | | |
| Brazil | 1 5 | 1 5 | 2 10 | 2 10 | 5 8 | ditto | - | · | ditto | | | |
| Bremen | 1 2 | 1 2 | 2 4 | 2 4 | 4 8 | Cannot be prepaid | 0 2* | 0 4 | 0 8 | 1 4 | 2 0 | 2 8 |
| Brunswick | 1 2 | 1 2 | 2 4 | 2 4 | 4 8 | ditto | 0 2* | 0 4 | 0 8 | 1 4 | 2 0 | 2 8 |
| Buenos Ayres | 0 11 | 0 11 | 1 10 | 1 10 | 3 8 | Letter rate | · | - | Letter rate | | | |
| Canada | 0 10 | 0 11 | 1 10 | 1 10 | 3 8 | 1d. | 0 6 | 0 6 | 1 0 | 2 0 | 3 0 | 4 0 |
| Cape de Verde | 0 9 | 1 1 | 1 10 | 2 3 | 4 | 2d. | 0 5 | 0 7 | 1 2 | 2 4 | 3 6 | 4 8 |
| Cape of Good Hope | 0 11 | 0 11 | 1 10 | 1 10 | 3 8 | 1d. | 0 6 | 0 6 | 1 0 | 2 0 | 3 0 | 4 0 |
| Canary Islands | 0 11 | 1 5 | 2 4 | 2 10 | 4 | Book rate | 0 3 | 0 6 | 1 0 | 1 6 | 2 0 | 2 6 |
| Ceylon | 0 11 | 0 11 | 1 10 | 1 10 | 3 8 | 2d. | 0 7 | 0 7 | 1 2 | 2 4 | 3 6 | 4 8 |
| China | 0 11 | 0 11 | 1 10 | 1 10 | 3 8 | Letter rate | · | - | Letter rate | | | |
| Constantinople | 0 10 | 1 8 | 2 6 | 4 4 | 2 | Book rate | 0 2 | 0 4 | 0 8 | 1 4 | 2 0 | 2 8 |
| Dardanelles | 0 10 | 1 8 | 2 6 | 4 4 | 2 | ditto | 0 2 | 0 4 | 0 8 | 1 4 | 2 0 | 2 8 |
| Denmark | 1 4½ | 1 4½ | 2 9 | 2 9 | 5 6 | Cannot be prepaid | 0 2 | 0 4 | 0 8 | 1 4 | 2 0 | 2 8 |
| Egypt | 0 11 | 0 11 | 1 10 | 1 10 | 3 8 | Letter rate | · | Letter rate | | | | |
| Falkland Islands | 0 11 | 0 11 | 1 10 | 1 10 | 3 8 | 1d. | 0 6 | 0 6 | 1 0 | 2 0 | 3 0 | 4 0 |
| Fernando Po | 0 11 | 0 11 | 1 10 | 1 10 | 3 8 | Letter rate | · | Letter rate | | | | |
| France | 0 8 | 1 4 | 2 0 | 2 8 | 3 4 | Book rate | 0 2 | 0 4 | 0 8 | 1 4 | 2 0 | 2 8 |
| Frankfort | 1 2 | 1 2 | 2 4 | 2 4 | 4 | Cannot be prepaid | 0 2* | 0 4 | 0 8 | 1 4 | 2 0 | 2 8 |
| Galatz | 0 10 | 1 8 | 2 6 | 4 4 | 2 | Book rate | 0 2 | 0 4 | 0 8 | 1 4 | 2 0 | 2 8 |
| Gallipoli | 0 10 | 1 8 | 2 6 | 4 4 | 2 | ditto | 0 2 | 0 4 | 0 8 | 1 4 | 2 0 | 2 8 |
| Gambia | 0 11 | 0 11 | 1 10 | 1 10 | 3 8 | 1d. | 0 6 | 0 6 | 1 0 | 2 0 | 3 0 | 4 0 |
| Gibraltar | 0 11 | 0 11 | 1 10 | 1 10 | 3 8 | 1d. | 0 6 | 0 6 | 1 0 | 2 0 | 3 0 | 4 0 |
| Gold Coast | 0 11 | 0 11 | 1 10 | 1 10 | 3 8 | 1d. | 0 6 | 0 6 | 1 0 | 2 0 | 3 0 | 4 0 |
| Greece | 1 2 | 2 4 | 3 6 | 5 8 | 10 | Book rate | 0 2* | 0 4 | 0 8 | 1 0 | 2 0 | 2 8 |
| Hamburg | 1 2 | 1 2 | 2 4 | 4 4 | 8 | Cannot be prepaid | 0 2* | 0 4 | 0 8 | 1 4 | 2 0 | 2 8 |
| Hanover | 1 2 | 1 2 | 2 4 | 4 4 | 8 | ditto | 0 2* | 0 4 | 0 8 | 1 4 | 2 0 | 2 8 |
| Hesse | 1 2 | 1 2 | 2 4 | 4 4 | 8 | Cannot be prepaid | 0 2* | 0 4 | 0 8 | 1 4 | 2 0 | 2 8 |
| Hesse Homburg | 1 2 | 1 2 | 2 4 | 4 4 | 8 | ditto | 0 2* | 0 4 | 0 8 | 1 4 | 2 0 | 2 8 |
| Holland | 0 9 | 0 9 | 1 6 | 6 3 | 0 | 1d. | 0 2* | 0 4 | 0 8 | 1 4 | 2 0 | 2 8 |
| Hong Kong | 0 11 | 0 11 | 1 10 | 1 10 | 3 8 | 2d. | 0 7 | 0 7 | 1 2 | 2 4 | 3 6 | 4 8 |
| India | 0 11 | 0 11 | 1 10 | 1 10 | 3 8 | 2d | 0 7 | 0 7 | 1 2 | 2 4 | 3 6 | 4 8 |
| Ionian Islands | 0 11 | 0 11 | 1 10 | 1 10 | 3 8 | 1d. | 0 6 | 0 6 | 1 0 | 2 0 | 3 0 | 4 0 |
| Larnaca | 1 7 | 1 7 | 2 3 | 2 6 | 4 | Cannot be prepaid | 0 2* | 0 4 | 0 8 | 1 4 | 2 0 | 2 8 |
| Lauenburg | 1 4 | 1 4 | 2 8 | 2 8 | 5 4 | ditto | 0 2* | 0 4 | 0 8 | 1 4 | 2 0 | 2 8 |
| Liberia | 0 11 | 0 11 | 1 10 | 1 10 | 3 8 | Letter rate | · | Letter rate. | | | | |
| Lippe Detmold | 1 2 | 1 2 | 2 4 | 2 4 | 4 8 | Cannot be prepaid | 0 2* | 0 4 | 0 8 | 1 4 | 2 0 | 2 8 |
| Lubeck | 1 2 | 1 2 | 2 4 | 4 4 | 8 | ditto | 0 2* | 0 4 | 0 8 | 1 4 | 2 0 | 2 8 |
| Madeira | 0 9 | 1 1 | 1 10 | 2 | | 2d. | 0 5 | 0 7 | 1 2 | 2 4 | 3 6 | 4 8 |
| Malta | 0 11 | 0 11 | 1 10 | 1 10 | 3 8 | 1d. | 0 6 | 0 6 | 1 0 | 2 0 | 3 0 | 4 0 |
| Mauritius | 0 11 | 0 11 | 1 10 | 1 10 | 3 8 | 2d. | 0 7 | 0 7 | 1 2 | 2 4 | 3 6 | 4 8 |
| Mecklenburg | 1 2 | 1 2 | 2 4 | 4 4 | 8 | Cannot be prepaid | 0 2* | 0 4 | 0 8 | 1 4 | 2 0 | 2 8 |
| Moldavia | 1 5 | 1 5 | 2 10 | 2 10 | 5 8 | ditto | 0 2* | 0 4 | 0 8 | 1 4 | 2 0 | 2 8 |
| Mytelene | 0 10 | 1 8 | 2 6 | 4 4 | 2 | Book rate | 0 2 | 0 4 | 0 8 | 1 4 | 2 0 | 2 8 |
| Monte Video | 0 11 | 0 11 | 1 10 | 1 10 | 3 8 | Letter rate | · | Letter rate. | | | | |
| Nassau, Duchy | 1 2 | 1 2 | 2 4 | 4 4 | 8 | Cannot be prepaid | 0 2* | 0 4 | 0 8 | 1 4 | 2 0 | 2 8 |
| Natal | 0 11 | 0 11 | 1 10 | 1 10 | 3 8 | 1d. | 0 6 | 0 6 | 1 0 | 2 0 | 3 0 | 4 0 |
| New Brunswick | 0 11 | 0 11 | 1 10 | 1 10 | 3 8 | 1d. | 0 6 | 0 6 | 1 0 | 2 0 | 3 0 | 4 0 |

| | FOR A LETTER | | | | | | FOR A BOOK PACKET | | | | | |
|---|---|---|---|---|---|---|---|---|---|---|---|---|
| | Not exceeding ¼ oz. | Above ¼ oz. and not exceeding ½ oz. | Above ½ oz. and not exceeding ¾ oz. | Above ¾ oz. and not exceeding 1 oz. | Above 1 oz. and not exceeding 1¼ oz. | For each Newspaper. | Not exceeding 2 ozs. | 2 ozs. to 4 ozs. | 4 ozs. to 8 ozs. | 8 ozs. to 1 lb. | 1 lb. to 1½ lb. | 1½ lb. to 2 lbs. |
| | s. d. | s. d. | s. d. | s. d. | s. d. | | s. d. | s. d. | s. d. | s. d. | s. d. | s. d. |
| New South Wales ... | 0 11 | 0 11 | 1 10 | 1 10 | 3 8 | 2d. | 0 7 | 0 7 | 1 2 | 2 4 | 3 6 | 4 8 |
| New Zealand ... | 0 11 | 0 11 | 1 10 | 1 10 | 3 8 | 2d. | 0 7 | 0 7 | 1 2 | 2 4 | 3 6 | 4 8 |
| Newfoundland ... | 0 11 | 0 11 | 1 10 | 1 10 | 3 8 | 1d. | 0 6 | 0 6 | 1 0 | 2 0 | 3 0 | 4 0 |
| Norway ... | 1 10 | 1 10 | 3 8 | 3 8 | 7 4 | Cannot be prepaid | 0 2* | 0 4 | 0 8 | 1 4 | 2 0 | 2 8 |
| Nova Scotia ... | 0 11 | 0 11 | 1 10 | 1 10 | 3 8 | 1d. | 0 6 | 0 6 | 1 0 | 2 0 | 3 0 | 4 0 |
| Oldenburgh ... | 1 2 | 1 2 | 2 4 | 2 4 | 4 8 | Cannot be prepaid | 0 2* | 0 4 | 0 8 | 1 4 | 2 0 | 2 8 |
| Papal States ... | 1 2 | 2 4 | 3 6 | 4 8 | 5 10 | Book rate | 0 2* | 0 4 | 0 8 | 1 4 | 2 0 | 2 8 |
| Penang ... | 0 11 | 0 11 | 1 10 | 1 10 | 3 8 | 2d. | 0 7 | 0 7 | 1 2 | 2 4 | 3 6 | 4 8 |
| Poland ... | 1 5½ | 1 5½ | 2 11 | 2 11 | 5 10 | Cannot be prepaid | 0 2* | 0 4 | 0 8 | 1 4 | 2 0 | 2 8 |
| Portugal ... | 0 9 | 1 9 | 1 10 | 2 2 | 3 4 | 2d. | 0 5 | 0 7 | 1 2 | 2 4 | 3 6 | 4 8 |
| Prince Edward Island | 0 11 | 0 11 | 1 10 | 1 10 | 3 8 | 1d. | 0 6 | 0 6 | 1 0 | 2 0 | 3 0 | 4 0 |
| Prussia ... | 1 2 | 1 2 | 2 4 | 3 4 | 4 8 | Cannot be prepaid | 0 2* | 0 4 | 0 8 | 1 4 | 2 0 | 2 8 |
| Reuss ... | 1 2 | 1 2 | 2 4 | 2 4 | 4 8 | | 0 2* | 0 4 | 0 8 | 1 4 | 2 0 | 2 8 |
| [illegible] ... | 0 10 | 1 8 | 2 6 | 3 4 | 4 2 | Book rate | 0 2 | 0 4 | 0 8 | 1 4 | 2 0 | 2 8 |
| Russia ... | 1 5½ | 1 5½ | 2 11 | 2 11 | 5 10 | Cannot be prepaid | 0 2* | 0 4 | 0 8 | 1 4 | 2 0 | 2 8 |
| St. Helena ... | 0 11 | 0 11 | 1 10 | 1 10 | 3 8 | 1d | 0 6 | 0 6 | 1 0 | 2 0 | 3 0 | 4 0 |
| Samsom ... | 0 10 | 1 8 | 2 6 | 3 4 | 4 2 | Book rate | 0 2 | 0 4 | 0 8 | 1 4 | 2 0 | 2 8 |
| Salonica ... | 0 10 | 1 8 | 2 6 | 3 4 | 4 2 | ditto | 0 2 | 0 4 | 0 8 | 1 4 | 2 0 | 2 8 |
| Sardinia ... | 0 10 | 1 3 | 2 1 | 2 6 | 3 9 | ditto | 0 3 | 0 6 | 1 0 | 1 6 | 2 0 | 2 6 |
| Saxe Altenburg ... | 1 2 | 1 2 | 2 4 | 2 4 | 4 8 | Cannot be prepaid | 0 2* | 0 4 | 0 8 | 1 4 | 2 0 | 2 8 |
| Saxe Coburg Gotha ... | 1 2 | 1 2 | 2 4 | 2 4 | 4 8 | ditto | 0 2* | 0 4 | 0 8 | 1 4 | 2 0 | 2 8 |
| Saxe Meiningen ... | 1 2 | 1 2 | 2 4 | 2 4 | 4 8 | ditto | 0 2* | 0 4 | 0 8 | 1 4 | 2 0 | 2 8 |
| Saxe Weimar.. ... | 1 2 | 1 2 | 2 4 | 2 4 | 4 8 | ditto | 0 2* | 0 0 | 0 8 | 1 4 | 2 0 | 2 8 |
| Saxony ... | 1 2 | 1 2 | 2 4 | 2 4 | 4 8 | ditto | 0 2* | 0 4 | 0 8 | 1 4 | 2 0 | 2 8 |
| Schaumburg Lippe ... | 1 2 | 1 2 | 2 4 | 2 4 | 4 8 | ditto | 0 2* | 0 4 | 0 8 | 1 4 | 2 0 | 2 8 |
| Schwartzburg Rudolstadt ... | 1 2 | 1 2 | 2 4 | 2 4 | 4 8 | ditto | 0 2* | 0 4 | 0 8 | 1 4 | 2 0 | 2 8 |
| Schwartzburg Sonderhausen ... | 1 2 | 1 2 | 2 4 | 2 4 | 4 8 | ditto | 0 2* | 0 4 | 0 8 | 1 4 | 2 0 | 2 8 |
| Scutari ... | 1 2 | 1 2 | 2 4 | 2 4 | 4 8 | ditto | 0 2* | 0 4 | 0 8 | 1 4 | 2 0 | 2 8 |
| Seres ... | 1 2 | 1 2 | 2 4 | 2 4 | 4 8 | ditto | 0 2* | 0 4 | 0 8 | 1 4 | 2 0 | 2 8 |
| Sicilies, Two ... | 1 2 | 2 4 | 3 6 | 4 8 | 5 10 | Book rate | 0 2* | 0 4 | 0 8 | 1 4 | 2 0 | 2 8 |
| Singapore ... | 0 11 | 0 11 | 1 10 | 1 10 | 3 8 | 2d. | 0 7 | 0 7 | 1 2 | 2 4 | 3 6 | 4 8 |
| Sierra Leone ... | 0 11 | 0 11 | 1 10 | 1 10 | 3 8 | 1d. | 0 6 | 0 6 | 1 0 | 2 0 | 3 0 | 4 0 |
| Smyrna ... | 0 10 | 1 8 | 2 6 | 3 4 | 4 2 | Book rate | 0 2 | 0 4 | 0 8 | 1 4 | 2 0 | 2 8 |
| Spain .. ... | 0 11 | 1 5 | 2 4 | 2 10 | 4 2 | ditto | 0 3 | 0 6 | 1 0 | 1 6 | 2 0 | 2 6 |
| Sweden ... | 0 8 | 1 9 | 3 4 | 3 4 | 6 8 | Cannot be prepaid | 0 2* | 0 4 | 0 8 | 1 4 | 2 0 | 2 8 |
| Switzerland ... | 1 9 | 1 6 | 2 3 | 3 0 | 3 9 | Book rate | 0 2* | 0 4 | 0 8 | 1 4 | 2 0 | 2 8 |
| Syria ... | 0 10 | 1 8 | 2 6 | 3 4 | 4 2 | ditto | 0 2 | 0 4 | 0 8 | 1 4 | 2 0 | 2 8 |
| Tasmania ... | 0 11 | 0 11 | 1 10 | 1 10 | 3 8 | 2d. | 0 7 | 0 7 | 1 2 | 2 4 | 3 6 | 4 8 |
| Tchesme ... | 1 7 | 1 7 | 3 2 | 3 2 | 6 4 | Cannot be prepaid | 0 2* | 0 4 | 0 8 | 1 4 | 2 0 | 2 8 |
| Tenedos ... | 1 7 | 1 7 | 3 2 | 3 2 | 6 4 | ditto | 0 2* | 0 4 | 0 8 | 1 4 | 2 0 | 2 8 |
| Trebizond ... | 0 10 | 1 8 | 2 6 | 3 4 | 4 2 | Book rate | 0 2 | 0 4 | 0 8 | 1 4 | 2 0 | 2 8 |
| Tultcha ... | 0 10 | 1 8 | 2 6 | 3 4 | 4 2 | ditto | 0 2 | 0 4 | 0 8 | 1 4 | 2 0 | 2 8 |
| Tunis ... | 0 9 | 1 6 | 2 3 | 3 0 | 3 9 | ditto | 0 2* | 0 4 | 0 8 | 1 4 | 2 0 | 2 8 |
| Turkey in Europe (except places specified) | 1 2 | 1 2 | 2 4 | 2 4 | 4 8 | Cannot be prepaid | 0 2* | 0 4 | 0 8 | 1 4 | 2 0 | 2 8 |
| United States... | 1 2 | 1 2 | 2 1 | 2 4 | 4 8 | 1d. | . . Letter rate. | | | | | |
| Varna ... | 0 10 | 1 8 | 2 6 | 3 4 | 4 2 | Book rate | 0 2 | 0 4 | 0 8 | 1 4 | 2 0 | 2 8 |
| Victoria ... | 0 11 | 0 11 | 1 10 | 1 10 | 3 8 | 2d. | 0 7 | 0 7 | 1 2 | 2 4 | 3 6 | 4 8 |

A post office notice dated 3 October 1860 quoted a new rate to New York via Jamaica of 5d. per ½oz.

On the 7 November 1860 it was notified that the book post was extended to the Danish West Indies, at 3d. per 4 oz.

On 10 December 1860 the following ordinance was passed:-

*Whereas an Ordinance was passed in Council on the fourth day of April in the year 1851, entitled "An Ordinance for establishing an Inland Post and Rates of Postage within the*

*Colony;" and whereas it is expedient to alter and amend the mode of charging the Postage on Letters under the said Ordinance; Be it Enacted by His Excellency the Governor, by and with the advice and consent of the Council of Government as follows:*

*1. The Eighth Clause of the said Ordinance shall be and the same is hereby repealed.*

*2. The Postage on all letters brought into this Colony from any place beyond this Colony, and on all the letters posted at any Post Office of this Colony for transmission to any other place within the limits of the Colony or beyond the limits of the Colony shall be charged by weight according to the following scale, and several Numbers of rates of postage hereinafter set forth shall be charged and shall be paid to Her Majesty for the use of the Colony on all such letters; that is to say, on every Letter not exceeding half an ounce in weight and not exceeding one ounce in weight two rates of postage; on every Letter exceeding one ounce and not exceeding two ounces in weight four rates of postage; on every letter exceeding two ounces and not exceeding three ounces in weight, six rates of postage; and on every Letter exceeding three ounces and not exceeding four ounces in weight, eight rates of postage; and for every ounce in weight above the weight of four ounces there shall be charged and taken two additional rates of postage, and every fraction of an ounce above the weight of four ounces shall be charged as one additional ounce; and on all such letters there shall be paid the following rates of postage; that is to say, on every Letter not exceeding half an ounce in weight, one uniform rate of one penny, and on every Letter exceeding half an ounce in weight, progressive and additional rates of postage (each additional rate being estimated at one penny) according to the scale of weight and number of rates herein before fixed and charged.*

This was changed on 18 May 1861 to:-

*On every letter not exceeding half an ounce in weight, one rate of postage; on every letter exceeding half an ounce and not exceeding one ounce in weight, two rates of postage; on every letter exceeding one ounce and not exceeding two ounces in weight, four rates of postage; on every letter exceeding two ounces and not exceeding three ounces of weight, six rates of postage; and on every letter exceeding three ounces and not exceeding four ounces in weight, eight rates of postage; and for every ounce in weight above the weight of four ounces there shall be charged and taken two rates of postage and every fraction of an ounce above the weight of four ounces shall be charged as one additional ounce; and all such letters there shall be paid the following rates of postage; that is to say: on every letter not exceeding half an ounce in weight, one uniform rate of one penny, and on every letter exceeding half an ounce in weight, progressive and additional rates of postage (each additional rate being estimated at one penny) according to the scale of weight and number of rates herein before fixed and charged.*

*Therefore letters brought into this Colony from any place beyond this Colony and letters posted at any Post Office of this Colony for transmission to any other place within the limits of the Colony or beyond the limits of the Colony will be charged an Inland Rate by weight in addition to the Imperial Postage, that is:-*

*A letter not exceeding ½oz. in weight - 1 penny, and on every letter exceeding half an ounce in weight progressive and additional rates of postage (each additional rate being estimated at one penny) according to the scale of weight and number of rates.*

*This notice refers to Inter-Colonial Postages only, as the same scale is already in existence of which is transmitted through the United Kingdom.*

*WILLIAM EVERSLEY,*
*Postmaster General.*

On 6 August 1862 a Ship Letter rate of 2d. was gazetted.

On 1 December 1862 a letter rate to Barbados was 6d. per ½oz. up to 1 oz. and 1/= per additional oz., this was introduced being extended to:-

| | |
|---|---|
| St. Lucia | 1 February 1863. |
| British Honduras, Grenada and Tobago | 1 March 1863. |
| Antigua, Montserrat, St. Kitts and British Guiana | 1 April 1863. |
| Jamaica | 1 June 1863. |
| British Virgin Islands | 1 October 1863. |
| St. Vincent | 1 November 1863. |
| Dominica and Turks and Caicos Islands | 1 January 1864. |

On 1 April 1863 the packet letter rate to U.K. was increased to 1/= per ½oz.

On 3 February a rate of 1d. per ½oz. up to 1 oz., with 2d. for each additional ounce to La Guira and Intermediate ports in Venezuela was introduced, the service being advertised as:-

## Notice.
### GENERAL POST OFFICE.
30th January, 1863.

MAILS will be made up at this Office for transmission by the Steamer " TORC" on the 10TH OF EACH MONTH FOR CARUPANO, PAMPATAR, CUMANA, BARCELONA and LA GUIRA (and erentua'ly for PUERTO CABELLO); and on the 25th of each month on her return from LA GUIRA, &c., for PUERTO LAS TABLAS, BARANCAS and BOLIVAR.

On TUESDAY NEXT, the 3rd of February, MAILS will be made up for LA GUIRA and intermediate Ports. The Bags will be closed at 3h 45m P M. on that day.

**Port of Spain.**

On 1863 the following revised rate table was published:-

| | FOR A LETTER | | | | | For each Newspaper | FOR A BOOK PACKET | | | | | |
|---|---|---|---|---|---|---|---|---|---|---|---|---|
| | Not exceeding ½ oz. | Above ½ oz. and not exceeding ¾ oz. | Above ¾ oz. and not exceeding ½ oz. | Above ½ oz. and not exceeding 1 oz. | Above 1 oz. and not exceeding 1½ oz. | | Not exceeding 2 ozs. | 2 ozs. to 4 ozs. | 4 ozs. to 8 ozs. | 8 ozs. to 1 lb. | 1 lb. to 1½ lb. | 1½ lb. to 2 lbs. |
| | s. d. | s. d. | s. d. | s. d. | s. d. | | s. d. | s. d. | s. d. | s. d. | s. d. | s. d. |
| Aden | 1 5 | 1 5 | 2 10 | 2 10 | 4 3 | 2d. | 0 6 | 0 6 | 1 0 | 2 0 | 3 0 | 4 0 |
| Africa, West Coast of | 1 5 | 1 5 | 2 10 | 2 10 | 4 3 | 1d. | Letter rate. | | | | | |
| Algeria | 0 8 | 1 4 | 2 0 | 2 8 | 3 4 | Book rate. | 0 2 | 0 4 | 0 8 | 1 4 | 2 0 | 2 8 |
| Ascension | 1 11 | 1 11 | 3 10 | 3 10 | 5 9 | 1d. | 0 5 | 0 5 | 0 10 | 1 8 | 2 6 | 3 4 |
| Australia, South | 1 5 | 1 5 | 2 10 | 2 10 | 4 3 | 2d. | 0 6 | 0 6 | 1 0 | 2 0 | 3 0 | 4 0 |
| Australia, Western | 1 5 | 1 5 | 2 10 | 2 10 | 4 3 | 2d. | 0 6 | 0 6 | 1 0 | 2 0 | 3 0 | 4 0 |
| Austria | 1 5 | 1 5 | 2 10 | 2 10 | 4 3 | Book rate. | 0 3 | 0 6 | 1 0 | 2 0 | 3 0 | 4 0 |
| Asores | 1 5 | 1 11 | 3 4 | 3 10 | 6 2 | 3d. | 0 5 | 0 7 | 1 2 | 2 4 | 3 6 | 4 8 |
| Baden | 0 9 | 1 6 | 2 3 | 3 0 | 3 9 | Book rate. | 0 3 | 0 6 | 1 0 | 2 0 | 3 0 | 4 0 |
| Bavaria | 0 9 | 1 6 | 2 3 | 3 0 | 3 9 | ditto | 0 3 | 0 6 | 1 0 | 2 0 | 3 0 | 4 0 |
| Belgium | 1 3 | 1 3 | 2 6 | 2 6 | 3 9 | ditto | 0 2 | 0 4 | 0 8 | 1 4 | 2 0 | 2 8 |
| Borneo | 1 11 | 1 11 | 3 10 | 3 10 | 5 9 | 2d. | Letter rate. | | | | | |
| Bourbon | 1 5 | 1 5 | 2 10 | 2 10 | 4 3 | 2d. | ditto | | | | | |
| Brazil | 1 11 | 1 11 | 3 10 | 3 10 | 5 9 | 1d. | ditto | | | | | |
| Bremen | 1 5 | 1 5 | 2 10 | 2 10 | 4 3 | Book rate. | 0 3 | 0 6 | 1 0 | 2 0 | 3 0 | 4 0 |
| Brunswick | 1 5 | 1 5 | 2 10 | 2 10 | 4 3 | ditto | 0 3 | 0 6 | 1 0 | 2 0 | 3 0 | 4 0 |
| Buenos Ayres | 1 11 | 1 11 | 3 10 | 3 10 | 5 9 | 1d. | Letter rate. | | | | | |
| Canada | 1 5 | 1 5 | 2 10 | 2 10 | 4 3 | 1d. | 0 5 | 0 6 | 0 10 | 1 8 | 2 6 | 3 4 |
| Cape de Verde | 1 3 | 1 7 | 2 10 | 3 2 | 5 4 | 1d. | 0 5 | 0 7 | 1 2 | 2 4 | 3 6 | 4 8 |
| Cape of Good Hope | 1 11 | 1 11 | 3 10 | 3 10 | 5 9 | 1d. | 0 5 | 0 5 | 0 10 | 1 8 | 2 6 | 3 4 |
| Canary Islands | 1 5 | 1 11 | 3 4 | 3 10 | 6 2 | Book rate. | 0 3 | 0 6 | 1 0 | 2 0 | 3 0 | 4 0 |
| Ceylon | 1 5 | 1 5 | 2 10 | 2 10 | 4 3 | 2d. | 0 6 | 0 6 | 1 0 | 2 0 | 3 0 | 4 0 |
| China | 1 11 | 1 11 | 3 10 | 3 10 | 5 9 | 2d. | Letter rate. | | | | | |
| Constantinople | 0 10 | | | | | Book rate. | 0 3 | 0 6 | 1 0 | 2 0 | 3 0 | 4 0 |
| Dardanelles | 0 10 | 1 8 | 2 6 | 3 4 | 4 2 | Book rate | 0 3 | 0 6 | 1 0 | 2 0 | 3 0 | 4 0 |
| Denmark | 1 8 | 1 8 | 3 4 | 3 4 | 5 0 | ditto | 0 3* | 0 6 | 1 0 | 2 0 | 3 0 | 4 0 |
| Egypt | 1 5 | 1 5 | 2 10 | 2 10 | 4 3 | 1d. | Letter rate. | | | | | |
| Falkland Islands | 1 5 | 1 5 | 2 10 | 2 10 | 4 3 | 1d.* | 0 5 | 0 5 | 0 10 | 1 8 | 2 6 | 3 4 |
| Fernando Po | 1 5 | 1 5 | 2 10 | 2 10 | 4 3 | 1d. | Letter rate. | | | | | |
| France | 0 8 | 1 4 | 2 8 | 2 8 | 3 4 | Book rate. | 0 2 | 0 4 | 0 8 | 1 4 | 2 0 | 2 8 |
| Frankfort | 1 5 | 1 5 | 2 10 | 2 10 | 4 3 | ditto | 0 3 | 0 6 | 1 0 | 2 0 | 3 0 | 4 0 |
| Galatz | 0 10 | 1 8 | 2 6 | 3 4 | | Book rate. | 0 3 | 0 6 | 1 0 | 2 0 | 3 0 | 4 0 |
| Gallipoli | 0 10 | 1 8 | 2 6 | 3 4 | 4 2 | ditto | 0 3 | 0 6 | 1 0 | 2 0 | 3 0 | 4 0 |
| Gambia | 1 5 | 1 5 | 2 10 | 2 10 | 4 3 | 1d. | 0 5 | 0 5 | 0 10 | 1 8 | 2 6 | 3 4 |
| Gibraltar | 1 5 | 1 5 | 2 10 | 2 10 | 4 3 | 1d. | 0 5 | 0 5 | 0 10 | 1 8 | 2 6 | 3 4 |
| Gold Coast | 1 5 | 1 5 | 2 10 | 2 10 | 4 3 | 1d. | 0 5 | 0 5 | 0 10 | 1 8 | 2 6 | 3 4 |
| Greece | 1 2 | 2 4 | 3 6 | 4 8 | 5 10 | Book rate. | 0 3* | 0 6 | 1 0 | 2 0 | 3 0 | 4 0 |
| Hamburg | 1 5 | 1 5 | 2 10 | 2 10 | 4 3 | Book rate. | 0 3 | 0 6 | 1 0 | 2 0 | 3 0 | 4 0 |
| Hanover | 1 5 | 1 5 | 2 10 | 2 10 | 4 3 | ditto | 0 3 | 0 6 | 1 0 | 2 0 | 3 0 | 4 0 |
| Hesse | 1 5 | 1 5 | 2 10 | 2 10 | 4 3 | ditto | 0 3 | 0 6 | 1 0 | 2 0 | 3 0 | 4 0 |
| Hesse Homburg | 1 5 | 1 5 | 2 10 | 2 10 | 4 3 | ditto | 0 3 | 0 6 | 1 0 | 2 0 | 3 0 | 4 0 |
| Holland | 1 2 | 1 2 | 2 6 | 2 6 | 3 9 | 1d. | 0 2* | 0 6 | 1 0 | 2 0 | 3 0 | 4 0 |
| Hong Kong | 1 11 | 1 11 | 3 10 | 3 10 | 5 9 | 2d. | 0 5 | 0 6 | 1 0 | 2 0 | 3 0 | 4 0 |
| India | 1 5 | 1 5 | 2 10 | 2 10 | 4 3 | 2d. | 0 6 | 0 6 | 1 0 | 2 0 | 3 0 | 4 0 |
| Ionian Islands | 1 9 | 1 9 | 3 6 | 3 6 | 5 3 | 1d. | 0 5 | 0 5 | 0 10 | 1 8 | 2 6 | 3 4 |
| Italy (except Papal States) | 1 4 | 1 9 | 3 1 | 3 6 | 5 9 | Book rate. | 0 3 | 0 6 | 1 0 | 2 0 | 3 0 | 4 0 |
| Labuan | 1 11 | 1 11 | 3 10 | 3 10 | 5 9 | 2d. | 0 6 | 0 6 | 1 0 | 2 0 | 3 0 | 4 0 |
| Larnaca | 1 10 | 1 10 | 3 8 | 3 8 | 5 6 | Book rate. | 0 3* | 0 6 | 1 0 | 2 0 | 3 0 | 4 0 |
| Lauenburg | 1 6 | 1 6 | 3 0 | 3 0 | 4 6 | ditto | 0 3* | 0 6 | 1 0 | 2 0 | 3 0 | 4 0 |
| Liberia | 1 5 | 1 5 | 2 10 | 2 10 | 4 3 | 1d. | Letter rate. | | | | | |
| Lippe Detmold | 1 5 | 1 5 | 2 10 | 2 10 | 4 3 | Book rate. | 0 3 | 0 6 | 1 0 | 2 0 | 3 0 | 4 0 |
| Lubeck | 1 5 | 1 5 | 2 10 | 2 10 | 4 3 | ditto | 0 3 | 0 6 | 1 0 | 2 0 | 3 0 | 4 0 |
| Madeira | 1 3 | 1 7 | 2 10 | 3 2 | 5 4 | 1d. | 0 5 | 0 7 | 1 2 | 2 4 | 3 6 | 4 8 |
| Malta | 1 5 | 1 5 | 2 10 | 2 10 | 4 3 | 1d. | 0 5 | 0 5 | 0 10 | 1 8 | 2 6 | 3 4 |
| Mauritius | 1 5 | 1 5 | 2 10 | 2 10 | 4 3 | 2 d. | 0 6 | 0 6 | 1 0 | 2 0 | 3 0 | 4 0 |
| Mecklenburg | 1 5 | 1 5 | 2 10 | 2 10 | 4 3 | Book rate. | 0 3 | 0 6 | 1 0 | 2 0 | 3 0 | 4 0 |
| Moldavia | 1 9 | 1 9 | 3 6 | 3 6 | 5 3 | ditto | 0 3* | 0 6 | 1 0 | 2 0 | 3 0 | 4 0 |
| Mytelene | 0 10 | 1 8 | 2 6 | 3 4 | 4 2 | ditto | 0 3 | 0 6 | 1 0 | 2 0 | 3 0 | 4 0 |
| Monte Video | 1 11 | 1 11 | 3 10 | 3 10 | 5 9 | 1d. | Letter rate. | | | | | |
| Nassau, Duchy of | 1 5 | 1 5 | 2 10 | 2 10 | 4 3 | Book rate. | 0 3 | 0 6 | 1 0 | 2 0 | 3 0 | 4 0 |
| Natal | 1 11 | 1 11 | 3 10 | 3 10 | 5 9 | 1d. | 0 5 | 0 5 | 0 10 | 1 8 | 2 6 | 3 4 |
| New Brunswick | 1 5 | 1 5 | 2 10 | 2 10 | 4 3 | 1d. | 0 5 | 0 5 | 0 10 | 1 8 | 2 6 | 3 4 |
| New South Wales | 1 5 | 1 5 | 2 10 | 2 10 | 4 3 | 2d. | 0 6 | 0 6 | 1 0 | 2 0 | 3 0 | 4 0 |
| New Zealand | 1 5 | 1 5 | 2 10 | 2 10 | 4 3 | 2d. | 0 6 | 0 6 | 1 0 | 2 0 | 3 0 | 4 0 |
| Newfoundland | 1 5 | 1 5 | 2 10 | 2 10 | 4 3 | 1d. | 0 5 | 0 5 | 0 10 | 1 8 | 2 6 | 3 4 |
| Norway | 2 1 | 2 1 | 4 2 | 4 2 | 6 3 | Book rate. | 0 3* | 0 6 | 1 0 | 2 0 | 3 0 | 4 0 |
| Nova Scotia | 1 5 | 1 5 | 2 10 | 2 10 | 4 3 | 1d. | 0 5 | 0 5 | 0 10 | 1 8 | 2 6 | 3 4 |
| Oldenburg | 1 5 | 1 5 | 2 10 | 2 10 | 4 3 | Book rate | 0 3 | 0 6 | 1 0 | 2 0 | 3 0 | 4 0 |
| Papal States | 1 2 | 2 4 | 3 6 | 4 8 | 5 10 | Book rate. | 0 2* | 0 4 | 0 8 | 1 4 | 2 0 | 2 8 |
| Penang | 1 11 | 1 11 | 3 10 | 3 10 | 5 9 | 2d | 0 6 | 0 6 | 1 0 | 2 0 | 3 0 | 4 0 |
| Poland | 1 9 | 1 9 | 3 6 | 3 6 | 5 3 | Book rate. | 0 3* | 0 6 | 1 0 | 2 0 | 3 0 | 4 0 |
| Portugal | 1 5 | 1 11 | 3 4 | 3 10 | 6 2 | 3d. | 0 5 | 0 7 | 1 2 | 2 4 | 3 6 | 4 8 |
| Prince Edward Island | 1 5 | 1 5 | 2 10 | 2 10 | 4 3 | 1d. | 0 5 | 0 5 | 0 10 | 1 8 | 2 6 | 3 4 |
| Prussia | 1 5 | 1 5 | 2 10 | 2 10 | 4 3 | Book rate. | 0 3 | 0 6 | 1 0 | 2 0 | 3 0 | 4 0 |
| Reuss | 1 5 | 1 5 | 2 10 | 2 10 | 4 3 | Book rate. | 0 3 | 0 6 | 1 0 | 2 0 | 3 0 | 4 0 |
| Rhodes | 0 10 | 1 8 | 2 6 | 3 4 | 4 2 | ditto | 0 3 | 0 6 | 1 0 | 2 0 | 3 0 | 4 0 |
| Russia | 1 9 | 1 9 | 3 6 | 3 6 | 5 3 | ditto | 0 3* | 0 6 | 1 0 | 2 0 | 3 0 | 4 0 |
| St Helena | 1 11 | 1 11 | 3 10 | 3 10 | 5 9 | 1d. | 0 5 | 0 5 | 0 10 | 1 8 | 2 6 | 3 4 |
| Samsoon | 0 10 | 1 8 | 2 6 | 3 4 | 4 2 | Book rate. | 0 3 | 0 6 | 1 0 | 2 0 | 3 0 | 4 0 |
| Salonica | 0 10 | 1 8 | 2 6 | 3 4 | 4 2 | ditto | 0 3 | 0 6 | 1 0 | 2 0 | 3 0 | 4 0 |
| Saxe Altenburg | | | | | | | | | | | | |
| Saxe Coburg Gotha | | | | | | | | | | | | |
| Saxe Meiningen | | | | | | | | | | | | |
| Saxe Weimar | 1 5 | 1 5 | 2 10 | 2 10 | 4 3 | Book rate. | 0 3 | 0 6 | 1 0 | 2 0 | 3 0 | 4 0 |
| Saxony | | | | | | | | | | | | |
| Schaumburg Lippe | | | | | | | | | | | | |
| Schwartzburg Rudolstadt | | | | | | | | | | | | |
| Schwartzburg Sonder- | | | | | | | | | | | | |

| | FOR A LETTER | | | | | For each Newspaper | FOR A BOOK PACKET | | | | | |
|---|---|---|---|---|---|---|---|---|---|---|---|---|
| | Not exceeding ½ oz. | Above ½ oz. and not exceeding ¾ oz. | Above ¾ oz. and not exceeding ½ oz. | Above ½ oz. and not exceeding 1 oz. | Above 1 oz. and not exceeding 1½ oz. | | Not exceeding 2 ozs. | 2 ozs. to 4 ozs. | 4 ozs. to 8 ozs. | 8 ozs. to 1 lb. | 1 lb. to 1½ lb. | 1½ lb. to 2 lbs. |
| | s. d. | s. d. | s. d. | s. d. | s. d. | | s. d. | s. d. | s. d. | s. d. | s. d. | s. d. |
| Scutari | 1 10 | 1 10 | 3 8 | 3 8 | 5 6 | Book rate. | 0 3* | 0 6 | 1 0 | 2 0 | 3 0 | 4 0 |
| Seres | 1 10 | 1 10 | 3 8 | 3 8 | 5 6 | ditto | 0 3* | 0 6 | 1 0 | 2 0 | 3 0 | 4 0 |
| Singapore | 1 11 | 1 11 | 3 10 | 3 10 | 5 9 | 2d. | 0 6 | 0 6 | 1 0 | 2 0 | 3 0 | 4 0 |
| Sierra Leone | 1 5 | 1 5 | 2 10 | 2 10 | 4 3 | 1d. | 0 5 | 0 5 | 0 10 | 1 8 | 2 6 | 3 4 |
| Smyrna | 0 10 | 1 8 | 2 6 | 3 4 | 4 2 | Book rate. | 0 3 | 0 6 | 1 0 | 2 0 | 3 0 | 4 0 |
| Spain | 1 5 | 1 11 | 3 4 | 3 10 | 6 2 | ditto | 0 3 | 0 6 | 1 0 | 2 0 | 3 0 | 4 0 |
| Sweden | 1 11 | 1 11 | 3 10 | 3 10 | 5 9 | ditto | 0 3* | 0 6 | 1 0 | 2 0 | 3 0 | 4 0 |
| Switzerland | 0 9 | 1 6 | 2 3 | 3 0 | 3 9 | ditto | 0 2* | 0 4 | 0 8 | 1 4 | 2 0 | 2 8 |
| Syria | 0 10 | 1 8 | 2 6 | 3 4 | 4 2 | ditto | 0 3 | 0 6 | 1 0 | 2 0 | 3 0 | 4 0 |
| Tasmania | 1 5 | 1 5 | 2 10 | 2 10 | 4 3 | 2d. | 0 6 | 0 6 | 1 0 | 2 0 | 3 0 | 4 0 |
| Tchesme | 1 10 | 1 10 | 3 8 | 3 8 | 5 6 | Book rate. | 0 3* | 0 6 | 1 0 | 2 0 | 3 0 | 4 0 |
| Tenedos | 1 10 | 1 10 | 3 8 | 3 8 | 5 6 | ditto | 0 3* | 0 6 | 1 0 | 2 0 | 3 0 | 4 0 |
| Trebizond | 0 10 | 1 8 | 2 6 | 3 4 | 4 2 | ditto | 0 3 | 0 6 | 1 0 | 2 0 | 3 0 | 4 0 |
| Tultcha | 0 10 | 1 8 | 2 6 | 3 4 | 4 2 | ditto | 0 3 | 0 6 | 1 0 | 2 0 | 3 0 | 4 0 |
| Tunis | 0 9 | 1 6 | 2 3 | 3 0 | 3 9 | ditto | 0 2* | 0 4 | 0 8 | 1 4 | 2 0 | 2 8 |
| United States | 1 8 | 1 8 | 3 4 | 3 4 | 5 0 | 1d. | Letter rate. | | | | | |
| Varna | 0 10 | 1 5 | 2 6 | 3 4 | 4 2 | Book rate. | 0 3 | 0 6 | 1 0 | 2 0 | 3 0 | 4 0 |
| Victoria | 1 5 | 1 5 | 2 10 | 2 10 | 4 3 | 2d | 0 6 | 0 6 | 1 0 | 2 0 | 3 0 | 4 0 |
| Wallachia | 1 9 | 1 9 | 3 6 | 3 6 | 5 3 | Book rate. | 0 2* | 0 6 | 1 0 | 2 0 | 3 0 | 4 0 |

From 1 October 1864 the weight scale was changed as follows:-

*General Post Office,*
*19th September, 1864.*

*Directions having been received by me from the Imperial Postmaster General, that the present notified scale of progression for charging letters between the United Kingdom and the West Indies, above one ounce in weight, shall be extended, on 1 October next, to letters conveyed by Packet between any two British Colonies in the West Indies, between those Colonies and any Foreign Ports in the West Indies and between British Colonies in the West Indies and any Ports or Places on the Western Coast of South America: NOTICE is therefore given, that, on and after the 1st October next, all letters posted at any Post Office within this Colony, addressed to any other place in the West Indies, (whether British or Foreign), or to any Port of Place on the Western Coast of South America, will be charged according to the new scale; viz:-*

| | | |
|---|---|---|
| *Not exceeding ½oz.* | . . . . . | *1 rate* |
| *Above ½oz., but not exceeding 1 oz.* | . . . . . | *2 rates* |
| *Above 1 oz., but not exceeding 1½oz.* | . . . . . | *3 rates* |

*and so on, one additional rate being charged for each additional half ounce.*

*WILLIAM EVERSLEY,*
*Postmaster General.*

On 1 November 1864 new rates per French packets came into force as per the following notice:-

| DESTINATION. | Limit to which Letters may be paid. | Not exceeding ¼ oz. | Above ¼ oz. and not exceeding ½ oz. | Above ½ oz. and not exceeding ¾ oz. | Above ¾ oz. and not exceeding 1 oz. |
|---|---|---|---|---|---|
| **I.** | | s. d. | s. d. | s. d. | s. d. |
| France or Algeria.................... | Destination ...... | 0 7 | 1 2 | 1 9 | 2 4 |
| **II.** | | | | | |
| Martinique.................... | } Destination ... | 0 4 | 0 8 | 1 0 | 1 4 |
| Guadeloupe .................... | | | | | |
| Cuba .................... | } Port of Disembarkation ... | 0 4 | 0 8 | 1 0 | 1 4 |
| Mexico .................... | | | | | |
| **III.** | | | | | |
| *Foreign Countries viá France.* | | | | | |
| Spain.................... | } Through France...... | 0 7 | 1 2 | 1 9 | 2 4 |
| Portugal .................... | | | | | |
| Gibraltar ...... | | | | | |
| Cape-de-Verds .................... | } Port of Disembarkation ... | 0 7 | 1 2 | 1 9 | 2 4 |
| Uruguay .................... | | | | | |
| Argentine Confederation .................... | | | | | |
| Luxemburg .................... | | | | | |
| Baden .................... | | | | | |
| The Netherlands .................... | | | | | |
| Belgium .................... | | | | | |
| Rhenish Prussia .................... | | | | | |
| Bavaria .................... | | | | | |
| Wurtemburg .................... | | | | | |
| German States : viz., Hohenzollern, Birkenfeld, Hesse Hombnrg, Lippe Detmold, Schwartzburg-Rudolstadt, Reuss, Nassau, Saxe Coburg Gotha, Saxe Meiningen-Hildburghausen, Hesse Electoral, Hesse Darmstadt, Saxe Weimar-Eisenach, Frankfort-on-the-Maine, Hamburgh, Bremen, and Lubeck .................... | } Destination ... | 0 8 | 1 4 | 2 0 | 2 8 |
| Switzerland .................... | | | | | |
| Italy .................... | | | | | |
| Tunis .................... | } Port of Disembarkation... | 0 8 | 1 4 | 2 0 | 2 8 |
| Tangiers .................... | | | | | |
| Prussia (the Rhenish Provinces excepted)... | | | | | |
| Hanover .................... | | | | | |
| Saxony .................... | | | | | |
| Mecklenburg-Schwerin .................... | | | | | |
| Mecklenburg-Strelitz .................... | | | | | |
| Brunswick .................... | | | | | |
| Oldenburg (the Principality of Birkenfeld excepted) .................... | } Destination ... | 0·10 | 1 8 | 2 6 | 3 4 |
| Anhalt .................... | | | | | |
| Austrian Dominions and Belgrade.................... | | | | | |
| Senegal .................... | | | | | |
| Pondicherry .................... | | | | | |
| Saigon .................... | | | | | |
| Shanghai .................... | | | | | |
| Servia (Belgrade excepted).................... | } Extreme frontier of Austria | 0 10 | 1 8 | 2 6 | 3 4 |
| Montenegro .................... | | | | | |
| Denmark .................... | } Destination ... | 0 11 | 1 10 | 2 9 | 3 8 |
| Brazil.................... | | | | | |
| Papal States .................... | } Destination ... | 1 1 | 2 2 | 3 3 | 4 4 |
| Greece .................... | | | | | |

| DESTINATION. | Limit to which Letters may be paid. | Not exceeding 1/4 oz. | Above 1/4 oz. and not exceeding 1/2 oz. | Above 1/2 oz. and not exceeding 3/4 oz. | Above 3/4 oz. and not exceeding 1 oz. |
|---|---|---|---|---|---|
| Alexandria, Jaffa, Beyrout, Tripoli in Syria, Latakia, Alexandretta, Messina, Rhodes, Smyrna, Mitylene, Dardanelles, Gallipoli, Constantinople, Ineboli, Kerassun, Salonica, Samsoun, Sinope, Sulina, Trebizond, Tultcha, Varna, Volo, Galatz, and Ibraila | Destination ... | 0 9 | 1 6 | 2 3 | 3 0 |
| Moldavia ............... Wallachia ............... Turkey in Europe (the places at which France maintains Post Offices excepted) viâ Austria Sweden ............ Norway ............ Poland ............ Russia ............ | Destination ... | 1 4 | 2 6 | 4 0 | 5 4 |
| Any Foreign Country beyond Sea, to which Letters may be despatched from a Port in France, by Private Ship ............ | Port of Disembarkation ... | 0 8 | 1 4 | 2 0 | 2 8 |

The Postage upon Letters for Cuba, Mexico, Spain, Gibraltar, Cape-de-Verds, Uruguay, Argentine Confederation, Tunis, Tangiers, Servia, (Belgrade excepted,) and Montenegro, or for Foreign Countries beyond Sea, must be paid in advance. Letters for the other Countries specified may either be paid in advance or forwarded unpaid at the option of the Sender.

## Registered Letters.

Letters addressed to all those Countries and Places to which, according to the foregoing Table, the entire postage to destination can be paid in advance, may be registered at the desire of the Senders, and in such case the postage *may be so prepaid*, and at double the rates of postage chargeable for ordinary Letters.

A reduction in the registration fee to 4d. for the U.K. was gazetted on 21 February 1866.

An alteration in the book post to U.K. rate from 3d. per 4 oz. to 3d. per 1 lb. was gazetted on 9 May 1866. The following overseas rates were gazetted on the dates shown:-

27 June 1866     letters to New Zealand, via Panama, 6d. per ½oz., plus postage to Panama (discontinued 17 March 1868).

15 Aug. 1866     letters to Portugal and Madeira 1s. 5d. per ¼oz., 1/11d. per ½oz., 3s. 4d. per ¾oz.

14 Aug. 1867     letters to Honduras. 22s. 2d. per ½oz., newspapers 3d. each.

7 Oct. 1868     letters to Honduras via St. Thomas 5d. per ½oz., books 3d. per 4 oz., Newspapers 1d. each.

10 Nov. 1869     Book packets Mauritius to India 7d. per 4 oz. and others east of Suez 5d. per 4 oz., other British Colonies 4d. per 4 oz.

From 25 May 1875 the postage rates by Royal Mail freight steamers were the same as by Royal Mail Packets.

Trinidad joined the General Postal Union (renamed later Universal Postal Union) on 1 April 1877, the rates being:-

TABLE OF THE RATES OF POSTAGE PER ROYAL MAIL STEAMERS, FRENCH PACKETS, AND PRIVATE SHIPS, SHOWING THE AMOUNT OF POSTAGE TO BE COLLECTED UPON LETTERS, NEWSPAPERS, BOOK PACKETS AND PATERNS, ADDRESSED TO THE UNDERMENTIONED COLONIES AND FOREIGN COUNTRIES.

MEM.—1. Letters cannot be sent unpaid to the Countries the names of which are printed in Italics.
2. No Letter or other Article can be registered to the Countries marked (a); to all other Countries any Article may be registered.
3. An additional postage of 2d. per ½ ounce must be collected on Letters; 1d. on each Newspaper, and 1d. per 2 ounces on Book Packets and Patterns, for the Countries marked thus (*) when addressed to be sent *via Brindisi*.
4. No Book Packet, or Packet of Newspapers, addressed to the Countries marked (†) must exceed 2 lbs. in weight; and the weight of a packet of patterns for these Countries is limited to 8 ounces. The weight of a Book Packet, or Packet of Patterns, addressed to New South Wales or Queensland, is limited to 3 lbs. In all other cases the weight of a packet is limited to 5 lbs.
5. In addition to all kinds of Printed, Engraved, or Lithographed Matter, Legal and Commercial Documents and Music in manuscript may be sent as a Book Packet. Proofs of Printing, or of Music may bear corrections with a pen, and may have manuscript annexed to them. Circulars, &c., may bear the signature of the sender, his Trade or Profession, place of Residence, and a Date. A Book may have a dedication or complimentary Inscription in Manuscript and Printed or Lithographed Stock or Share Lists, Prices Current, and Market Reports, may have the Prices added in writing.

| COUNTRIES. | For a Letter. Every ½ ounce or fraction of ½ ounce. | | For each Newspaper. Prepayment compulsory. | | For a Book Packet or Packet of Patterns. See Mem. 4. | Registration Fee. | |
|---|---|---|---|---|---|---|---|
| | s. | d. | s. | d. | d. | s. | d. |
| *Aden | | | | | | | |
| †Algeria | 0 | 6 | 0 | 1 | 2 per 2 ozs. | 0 | 4 |
| †Austria | | | | | | | |
| †Azores | | | | | | | |
| (a) Africa, West Coast of | 0 | 11 | 0 | 1 | 5 per 4 ozs. | None | |
| (a) Ascension | | | | | | | |
| *Australia, South and West | 0 | 11 | 0 | 1 | 6 per 4 ozs. | 0 | 6 |
| †Belgium | | | | | | | |
| †Beyrout | 0 | 6 | 0 | 1 | 2 per 2 ozs. | 0 | 4 |
| †Bourbon | | | | | | | |
| Bolivia | 1 | 1 | 0 | 2 | 4 per 4 ozs. | 0 | 6 |
| (a) Buenos Ayres | 1 | 5 | 0 | 1 | 5 per 4 ozs. | None | |
| (a) Argentine Confederation | | | | | | | |
| (a)*Borneo | 1 | 5 | 0 | 2 | 6 per 4 ozs. | None | |
| †Brazil | 1 | 2 | 0 | 1 | 5 per 4 ozs. | 0 | 4 |
| California | | | | | 3 per 4 ozs. | See United States. | |
| Canada | 0 | 6 | 0 | 1 | | 0 | 6 |
| †Canary Islands | | | | | 2 per 2 ozs. | 0 | 4 |
| †Cape de Verds | 0 | 11 | 0 | 1 | 5 per 4 ozs. | 0 | 4 |
| Cape of Good Hope | | | | | | 0 | 8 |
| *China | 0 | 11 | 0 | 1 | 7 per 4 ozs. | 0 | 6 |
| *Ceylon | 0 | 6 | 0 | 1 | 2 per 2 ozs. | 0 | 4 |
| Chili | 1 | 1 | 0 | 2 | 4 per 4 ozs. | 0 | 6 |
| Chagres | | | | | | | |
| Carthagena, South America | | | | | | | |
| Colon | | | | | | | |
| Columbia, United States of | 0 | 6 | 0 | 1 | 3 per 4 ozs. | 0 | 6 |
| Columbia, British | | | | | | | |
| Costa Rica | | | | | | | |
| †Constantinople | 0 | 6 | 0 | 1 | 2 per 2 ozs. | 0 | 4 |

| COUNTRIES. | For a Letter. Every ½ ounce or fraction of ½ ounce. | | For each Newspaper. Prepayment compulsory. | | For a Book Packet or Packet of Patterns. See Mem. 4. | Registration Fee. | |
|---|---|---|---|---|---|---|---|
| | s. | d. | s. | d. | d. | s. | d. |
| †Dardanelles...... <br> †Denmark......... } | 0 | 6 | 0 | 1 | } 2 per 2 ozs. | } 0 | 4 |
| Ecuador ......... | 1 | 1 | 0 | 2 | 4 per 4 ozs. | 0 | 6 |
| †Egypt ......... | 0 | 6 | 0 | 1 | 2 per 2 ozs. | 0 | 4 |
| Falkland Islands......... } <br> (a) Fernando Po... } | 0 | 11 | 0 | 1 | 5 per 4 ozs. | 0 <br> None | 6 |
| Fiji Islands......... } <br> †France......... } | 0 | 6 | 0 | 1 | 3 per 4 ozs. <br> 2 per 2 ozs. | 0 <br> 0 | 6 <br> 4 |
| †Galatz......... ⎫ <br> †Gallipoli......... ⎪ <br> †Germany......... ⎬ <br> †Gibraltar......... ⎪ <br> †Greece ......... ⎭ | 0 | 6 | 0 | 1 | } 2 per 2 ozs. | } 0 | 4 |
| Gambia......... } <br> Gold Coast... } | 0 | 11 | 0 | 1 | } 5 per 4 ozs. | } 0 | 6 |
| Grey Town, St. Jn. de Nicaragua..... } <br> Guatemala......... } | 0 | 6 | 0 | 1 | } 3 per 4 ozs. | } 0 | 6 |
| †Holland......... ⎫ <br> *Hong Kong } | 0 | 6 | 0 | 1 | } 2 per 2 ozs. | } 0 | 4 |
| Honduras, British } <br> Honduras, Republic of } | 0 | 6 | 0 | 1 | } 3 per 4 ozs. | } 0 | 6 |
| *India......... ⎫ <br> †Ionian Islands......... ⎬ <br> †Italy......... ⎭ | 0 | 6 | 0 | 1 | } 2 per 2 ozs. | } 0 | 4 |
| †Japan......... } <br> †Java......... } | 0 | 6 | 0 | 1 | } 2 per 2 ozs. | } 0 | 4 |
| *Labuan......... } <br> †Larnica— } | 0 | 6 | 0 | 1 | } 2 per 2 ozs. | } 0 | 4 |
| Liberia......... | 0 | 11 | 0 | 1 | 5 per 4 ozs. | 0 | 4 |
| Madagascar ......... | 0 | 11 | 0 | 1 | 5 per 4 ozs. | 0 | 4 |
| †Madeira......... ⎫ <br> †Malta......... ⎬ <br> Mauritius ......... ⎭ | 0 | 6 | 0 | 1 | } 2 per 2 ozs. | } 0 | 4 |
| Mexico ......... | 0 | 6 | 0 | 1 | Letter Rate | 0 | 6 |
| †Moldavia......... | 0 | 6 | 0 | 1 | 2 per 2 ozs. | 0 | 4 |
| (a) Monte Video......... | 1 | 5 | 0 | 1 | 5 per 4 ozs. | None | |
| †Mytelene......... } <br> †Montenegro......... } | 0 | 6 | 0 | 1 | } 2 per 2 ozs. | } 0 | 4 |
| Natal......... | 0 | 11 | 0 | 1 | 5 per 4 ozs. | 0 | 6 |
| New South Wales......... ⎫ <br> New Zealand... ⎪ <br> New Brunswick......... ⎪ <br> Newfoundland......... ⎬ <br> Nicaragua ⎪ <br> Nova Scotia ⎭ | 0 | 6 | 0 | 1 | } 3 per 4 ozs. | } 0 | 6 |
| †Norway......... | | | | | 2 per 2 ozs. | 0 | 4 |
| †Netherlands......... | | | | | 2 per 2 ozs. | 0 | 4 |
| Oregon ......... | 0 | 6 | 0 | 1 | 3 per 4 ozs. | See United States. | |
| Panama......... ⎫ | | | | | 3 per 4 ozs. | 0 | 6 |
| Prince Edward Island......... ⎪ | | | | | 3 per 4 ozs. | 0 | 6 |
| *Penang......... ⎬ | 0 | 6 | 0 | 1 | 2 per 2 ozs. | 0 | 4 |
| †Poland......... ⎪ | | | | | 2 per 2 ozs. | 0 | 4 |
| †Portugal ......... ⎭ | | | | | 2 per 2 ozs. | 0 | 4 |
| Paraguay ......... } <br> Philippine Islands......... } | 1 | 5 | 0 | 2 | } 5 per 4 ozs. | 0 | 6 |

| COUNTRIES. | For a Letter. Every ½ ounce or fraction of ½ ounce. | | For each Newspaper. Prepayment compulsory. | | For a Book Packet or Packet of Patterns. See Mem. 4. | Registration Fee. | |
|---|---|---|---|---|---|---|---|
| | s. | d. | s. | d. | d. | s. | d. |
| Peru .................................... | 1 | 1 | 0 | 2 | 4 per 4 ozs. | 0 | 6 |
| *Queensland.................................. | 0 | 11 | 0 | 1 | 6 per 4 ozs. | 0 | 6 |
| †Reunion ......................................<br>†Rhodes..........................................<br>†Russia ...........................................<br>†Roumania ....................................... | 0 | 6 | 0 | 1 | — per 2 ozs. | 0 | 4 |
| St. Helena....................................<br>Sierra Leone.................................. | 0 | 11 | 0 | 1 | 5 per 4 ozs. | 0 | 6 |
| †Salonica ......................................<br>†Samsoun ......................................<br>†Scutari ..........................................<br>†Seres ...........................................<br>†Servia ...........................................<br>*Singapore .....................................<br>†Smyrna .........................................<br>†Spain ..........................................<br>†*Suez............................................<br>†Sweden ........................................<br>†Switzerland... ................................. | 0 | 6 | 0 | 1 | 2 per 2 ozs. | 0 | 4 |
| †(a) Syria ....................................... | 0 | 6 | 0 | 1 | 2 per 2 ozs. | None. | |
| (a) *Sumatra ................................... | 1 | 5 | 0 | 2 | 5 per 4 ozs. | None. | |
| Sandwich Islands............................<br>San Salvador, Republic of...............<br>Santa Martha ................................. | 0 | 6 | 0 | 1 | 3 per 4 ozs. | 0 | 6 |
| Tahiti .......................................... | | | | | 3 per 4 ozs. | 0 | 6 |
| Tangier........................................ | | | | | 2 per 2 ozs. | 0 | 4 |
| †Tchesme...................................... | 0 | 6 | 0 | 1 | 2 per 2 ozs. | 0 | 4 |
| †Tenedos....................................... | | | | | 2 per 2 ozs. | 0 | 4 |
| †Trebizond..................................... | | | | | 2 per 2 ozs. | 0 | 4 |
| †Tultcha ....................................... | | | | | 2 per 2 ozs. | 0 | 4 |
| *Tasmania .................................... | 0 | 11 | 0 | 1 | 6 per 4 ozs. | 0 | 6 |
| †Tunis ......................................... | 0 | 7 | 0 | 1 | 5 per 4 ozs. | 0 | 6 |
| United Kingdom............................. | 0 | 6 | If by R.M.S. Free, if otherwise 1d. | | 2 per 2 ozs. | 0 | 4 |
| United States of America................. | 0 | 6 | 0 | 1 | 3 per 4 ozs. | See next line. | |
| United States of America, Registered Letters ...................................<br>(Letters only may be registered.) | 1 | 0 | None | | None | 0 | 6 |
| Vancouver's Island.......................... | | | | | 3 per 4 ozs | 0 | 6 |
| Venezuela (See note below.)............. | 0 | 6 | 0 | 1 | 3 per 4 ozs | 0 | 6 |
| Vera Cruz...................................... | | | | | | 0 | 6 |
| †Varna ......................................... | | | | | 2 per 2 ozs. | 0 | 6 |
| * Victoria, Australia......................... | 0 | 11 | 0 | 1 | 6 per 4 ozs. | 0 | 6 |
| .†Wallachia................... ................. | | | | | 2 per 2 ozs. | 0 | 4 |
| West Indies (British)........................ | 0 | 6 | 0 | 1 | 3 per 4 ozs. | 0 | 6 |
| West Indies (Foreign)....................... | | | | | 3 per 4 ozs. | 0 | 6 |

NOTE.—Letters can be registered for La Guayra and Caracas only.

On 24 March 1879 the following was published:-

# ALTERATION IN RATES OF POSTAGE.

In consequence of the new Postal Convention signed at Paris on the 1st June, 1878, for the revision of the Treaty of Berne constituting the General Postal Union, the following alterations in the rates of Postage and conditions of transmission of correspondence of various kinds between the United Kingdom and the British Colonies mentioned in the margin will be made on 1st April, 1879 — Bermuda, British Guiana, British Honduras, Jamaica, Trinidad, Mauritius and its dependencies. The Gold Coast, Sierra Leone, Gambia, Lagos, Falkland Islands.

LETTERS.—The rate of postage will be reduced from 6d. to 4d. per fifteen grammes, when prepaid. Unpaid letters will be charged double, viz., 8d. per fifteen grammes. Insufficiently prepaid letters will be charged on delivery with double the amount of the deficiency of the prepaid rate, instead of, as at present, with the unpaid rate less the value of the stamps affixed.

POST CARDS.—The issue of Post Cards will no longer be optional as heretofore. The postage for each card will be 1½d., instead of 3d. Prepayment is compulsory. Post Cards must not exceed the following dimensions —

|  |  | inches. |
|---|---|---|
| Length, 14 Centimetres | = | 5½ |
| Width, 9 " | = | 3½ |

They must bear the superscription "*Universal Postal Union*" followed by the name of the Colony (to be repeated in the French language).

OTHER ARTICLES.—Commercial Papers, of which a definition will be found in Article XVI. of the detailed Regulations appended to the Postal Convention,* must be prepaid 2½d. for a packet of any weight not exceeding 4 ounces, and for a packet exceeding the weight of 4 ounces, a further postage of 1d. must be paid for every additional 2 oz.

The postage for Books and all other Printed Papers † and Patterns, will be reduced from 2d. to 1d. per two ounces. Any of the above articles may be sent together in one packet, but if Commercial Documents are included, the postage applicable to such documents must be paid for the whole packet.

REGISTRATION.—The Union Registration Fee may not exceed 50 centimes in countries beyond the limits of Europe.

The Registration Fee levied in the United Kingdom will be maintained at the uniform rate of 2d. for each letter or other postal packet.

The sender of a registered article may obtain an acknowledgement of its delivery by paying in advance a fixed fee of 2½d. at the maximum, in addition to the ordinary registration fee and postage.

The obligation to pay an indemnity of 50 francs to the sender, or at his request, to the addressee, in case of the loss of a Registered article (Article 6 of the Convention). will not be binding upon any Colony until such period as the measure may have been authorized by the Legislature of the Colony.

LIMIT OF WEIGHT AND SIZE.—The maximum weight allowed for a packet of Commercial Documents or Printed Papers is to be two kilogrammes, or about 4 pounds avoirdupois, instead of one kilogramme.

A limit has been fixed to the dimensions of a Packet of Patterns. No packet must exceed 20 centimetres in length, 10 in breadth, and 5 in depth.

| Centimetres. |  | Inches. |
|---|---|---|
| 20 | = | 8 |
| 10 | = | 4 |
| 5 | = | 2 |

* 1. The following are considered as commercial papers, and admitted as such to the reduced postage specified in Article V. of the Convention.—All papers or documents written or drawn wholly or partly by hand which have not the character of an *actual and personal correspondence*, such as papers of legal procedure, deeds of all kinds drawn up by public functionaries, way bills or bills of lading, invoices, the various documents of insurance companies, copies or extracts of deeds under private seal, written on stamped or unstamped paper, scores or sheets of manuscript music, manuscripts of works forwarded separately, &c.
2. Commercial papers must be forwarded under band or in an open envelope.

† 1. The following are considered as printed papers and admitted as such to the reduced postage sanctioned by Article V. of the Convention, viz: newspapers and periodical works, books, stitched or bound, pamphlets, sheets of music, visiting cards, address cards, proofs of printing, with or without the manuscript relating thereto, engravings, photographs, drawings, plans, maps, catalogues, prospectuses, announcements, and notices of various kinds, whether printed, engraved or lithographed, and, in general, all impressions or copies obtained upon paper, parchment or cardboard, by means of printing, lithographing, or any other mechanical process easy to recognize, except the copying press.

REDIRECTION.—As a rule, no supplementary postage is chargeable on a letter or other postal packet redirected to any place within the Union; but if a letter or packet, so directed, has previously been sent by the post from one part to another of the Country or Colony in which it is posted, it is liable, on redirection, to the rate of postage to which it would have been liable had it been in the first place addressed to the place of final destination.

A prepaid letter of this description must be charged according to the prepaid rate, deducting however any postage prepaid upon it, and an unpaid letter according to the unpaid rate.

PROHIBITED ARTICLES.—It is forbidden (as before) to send by post :—

1. Letters or packets containing gold or silver bullion, pieces of money, jewellery, or precious articles.

2. Any packets whatever containing articles liable to Customs Duty.

## PILLAR LETTER BOXES.

Pillar Letter Boxes have been erected at the upper corner of St. Ann's Road near Claytor's Causeway, at the corner of the Wash and Bath Houses, St. Ann's Road, and at the corner of Marli Street, All Saints Chapel of Ease, New Town, facing the Savanah.

These boxes will be cleared daily (Sundays excepted) at 6 o'Clock A.M., 10 o'Clock A.M., and at 3 o'Clock P.M. Postage Stamps may be purchased at the Shops immediately opposite the Pillar Boxes on the St. Ann's Road, and at the Police Station, Picton Street.

In connection with these Pillar Boxes, and for the accommodation of the Public generally, an additional Postal delivery in Port-of-Spain is now made about ¼ past 3 o'Clock P.M. daily (Sundays excepted.)

## POST CARDS.

Post Cards for Countries of the Postal Union will be issued on and after the first April next, from which date it is also intended to issue Inland Post Cards at the same rate as for Letters, viz., one penny each.

On 1 April 1882 the rates to Tobago, Grenada, St. Vincent and Barbados were reduced to:-

| | | |
|---|---|---|
| Letters | .... | 2½d. per ½oz. |
| Postcards | .... | 1d. each. |
| Printed Papers | .... | ½d. per 2oz. |
| Commercial Papers | .... | ½d. per 2oz. (minimum 2½d.) |

A notice gazetted 24 February 1883 pointed out that the front of a postcard was reserved for the address only and if anything is added it will be treated as a letter.

On 1 July 1884 a new rate table regulation came into effect:-

## FOREIGN AND COLONIAL.

| CLASS A. | | | |
|---|---|---|---|
| GRENADA. | BARBADOES. | ST. VINCENT. | TOBAGO. |

CLASS B.

| | | | |
|---|---|---|---|
| Algeria | Egypt | Liberia | Roumania |
| Argentine Republic | Falkland Islands | Leeward Islands | Savanilla |
| Austria | French Guiana | Luxembourg | San Domingo |
| Azores | France and French Co- | Madeira | Santa Martha' |
| Antigua | lonies and Estab'mts, | Marquesas Islands | Syria |
| Bahamas | including St. Mary's | Malta | St. Lucia |
| Belgium | and Tamatave (Mada- | Mauritius | Sierra Leone |
| Brazil | gascar) | Mexico | Servia |
| Bermuda | Germany | Montenegro | Spain and Spanish Co- |
| British Guiana | Gibraltar | Moldavia | lonies (except Phili- |
| British Honduras | Greece | Montserrat | pine) |
| Bulgaria | Gambia | Newfoundland | Sweden |
| Canada | Gold Coast | Nevis | Switzerland |
| Colon | Graytown, St. Juan de | Nicaragua | St. Pierre et Miquelon |
| Columbia, U. States of | Nicaragua | Norway | San Salvador, Repub. of |
| Cuba | Greenland | Netherlands and Nether- | St. Kitts |
| Curaçoa | Guatemala | land Colonies (except | St Thoma |
| Canary Islands | Guadaloupe | Java) | Tahita |
| Costa Rica | Hayti | Panama | Turkey |
| Cyprus | Holland | Porto Rico | Turks Island |
| Denmark and Danish | Honduras, Republic of | Persia (viâ) Russia | Tunis |
| Colonies | Italy | Portugal | United Kingdom |
| Dominica | Ionian Islands | Peru | U. States of America |
| Dutch Guiana | Jamaica | Prince Edward Island | Venezuela |
| Ecuador | Lagos | Russia | Virgin Islands |

The Rates of Postage, for Correspondence posted in Trinidad addressed to the above Countries of the Postal Union, are as follows: —

| | LETTERS. | | | POST CARDS. POST CARDS ARE ONLY SENT TO COUNTRIES IN THE POST'L UNION. | | NEWS-PAPERS. | | OTHER ARTICLES. PRINTED PAPERS & BOOKS. | COMMERCIAL PAPERS. | PATTERNS. |
|---|---|---|---|---|---|---|---|---|---|---|
| | Not exceeding ½ oz. | Every additional ½ oz. | REGISTRATION FEE. | Single. | Double or Reply. | Not exceeding 2 oz. and for every additional 2 oz. | Not exceeding 4 oz. and for every additional 4 oz. | For any weight not exceeding 2 oz. and for every additional 2 oz. | | |
| | d. | d. | d. | d. | d. | d. | d. | d. | Same as Printed Papers except that, the lowest charge for each packet is 2½d in all cases. | Same as Printed Papers except that, as regards those Countries where the postage is half penny per 2 oz. the lowest charge is 1d. |
| For Countries in Class A. | 2½ | 2½ | 2 | 1 | 2 | ½ | ... | ½ | | |
| For Countries in Class B. | 4 | 4 | 2 | 1½ | 3 | ... | 1 | 1 | | |

134

TO THE FOLLOWING COUNTRIES THE RATES OF POSTAGE ARE AS FOLLOWS:

Countries markd * are not in the Postal Union.—(a) denotes that an additional charge will be made on delivery.—(c) denotes that prepayment is compulsory.

| | LETTERS | | | POST CARDS | | NEWS-PAPERS | | OTHER ARTICLES | | |
| --- | --- | --- | --- | --- | --- | --- | --- | --- | --- | --- |
| | Not exceeding ½ oz. | Every additional ½ oz. | Registration Fee. | Post Cards are only sent to Countries in the Post'l Union. Single. | Double or Reply. | Not exceeding 2 oz. and for every additional 2 oz. | Not exceeding 4 oz. and for every additional 4 oz. | PRINTED PAPERS AND BOOKS. For any weight not exceeding 2 oz., and for every additional 2 oz. | COMMERCIAL PAPERS. | PATTERNS. |
| | s. d. | s. d. | d. | d. | d. | d. | d. | d. | | |
| Aden ... | 0 5 | 0 5 | 2 | 2 | 4 | ... | 1½ | 1½ | | |
| *Ascension ... | c.0 9 | 0 9 | in.2 | ... | ... | ... | 1 | 2 | | |
| Africa, W. Coast of, except native possessions | c.0 9 | 0 9 | 2 | 1½ | 3 | ... | 1 | 1 | | |
| *Australia, South and West | 0 9 | 0 9 | 2 | ... | ... | ... | 1 | 2 | | |
| Borneo ... | 0 5 | 0 5 | 2 | 1½ | 3 | ... | 1½ | 1½ | | |
| *Bolivia ... | c.a.1 1 | 1 1 | 1 in 2 | ... | ... | ... | a. 2 | 2 | | |
| *Cape Colony ... | 0 9 | 0 9 | 2 | ... | ... | ... | 1 | 2 | | |
| *China, except Hong Kong | 0 5 | 0 5 | 2 | ... | ... | ... | 1½ | 1½ | | |
| Ceylon ... | 0 5 | 0 5 | 2 | 2 | 4 | ... | 1½ | 1½ | | |
| Celebes ... | 0 5 | 0 5 | 2 | 2 | 4 | ... | 1½ | 1½ | | |
| Chili ... | 0 5 | 0 5 | 2 | 1½ | 3 | ... | 1 | 1 | | |
| *Fiji Islands ... | 0 6 | 0 6 | 2 | ... | ... | ... | 1† | 2† | | |
| Fernando Po. ... | 0 5 | 0 5 | 2 | 1½ | ... | ... | 1 | 1 | | |
| French Colonies East of Suez | 0 5 | 0 5 | 2 | 2 | 4 | ... | 1½ | 1½ | | |
| Hong Kong ... | 0 5 | 0 5 | 2 | 2 | 4 | ... | 1½ | 1½ | | |
| India ... | 0 5 | 0 5 | 2 | 2 | 4 | ... | 1½ | 1½ | | |
| Japan ... | 0 5 | 0 5 | 2 | 2 | 4 | ... | 1½ | 1½ | | |
| Java ... | 0 5 | 0 5 | 2 | 2 | 4 | ... | 1½ | 1½ | | |
| Labuan ... | 0 5 | 0 5 | 2 | 2 | 4 | ... | 1½ | 1½ | | |
| *Madagascar (ex. S. Mary and Tamatave) | c.1 1 | 1 1 | 1 none | ... | ... | ... | 2 | 3 | | |
| *Natal ... | 0 9 | 0 9 | 2 | ... | ... | ... | 1 | 2 | | |
| *New South Wales... | 0 9 | 0 9 | 2 | ... | ... | ... | 1† | 2† | | |
| *New Zealand ... | 0 9 | 0 9 | 2 | ... | ... | ... | 1 | 2 | | |
| Persia (via Brindisi and Bombay if specially addressed) | 0 5 | 0 5 | 2 | 2 | 4 | ... | 1½ | 1½ | | |
| Penang ... | 0 5 | 0 5 | 2 | 2 | 4 | ... | 1½ | 1½ | | |
| Philippine Islands ... | 0 5 | 0 5 | 2 | 2 | ... | ... | 1½ | 1½ | | |
| *Queensland ... | 0 9 | 0 9 | 2 | ... | ... | ... | 1† | 2† | | |
| *St. Helena ... | 0 9 | 0 9 | 2 | ... | ... | ... | 3 | ... | | |
| Sandwich Islands... | 0 6 | 0 6 | 2 | 1½ | ... | ... | 1 | 1 | | |
| Singapore ... | 0 5 | 0 5 | 2 | 2 | 4 | ... | 1½ | 1½ | | |
| Straits Settlements. | 0 5 | 0 5 | 2 | 1½ | 3 | ... | 2 | 1½ | | |
| Sumatra ... | 0 5 | 0 5 | 2 | 2 | 4 | ... | 1½ | 1½ | | |
| *Tasmania ... | 0 9 | 0 9 | 2 | ... | ... | ... | 1 | 2 | | |
| *Victoria (Australia). | 0 9 | 0 9 | 2 | ... | ... | ... | 1 | 2 | | |
| Zanzibar ... | 0 9 | 0 9 | 2 | 2 | 4 | ... | 1½ | 1½ | | |

COMMERCIAL PAPERS: The Rates of Postage for Commercial Papers are the same as for Printed Papers, except that the lowest charge for each packet is 2½d., even if the packet weigh less than 2 oz.

PATTERNS: The Rates for Patterns are the same as for Printed Papers, except that the lowest charge is 1d. for a Packet addressed to any of the Countries to which the Postage is 1d. per 2 oz., for Printed Papers.

† The weight of a Packet is limited to 3 lbs.—(in) denotes that registration is incomplete.

# LETTERS.

1. Prepayment is compulsory in those cases where the letter "c" is prefixed to the rates of postage. In some countries ("a") an additional postage (which cannot be prepaid) is charged on delivery.

2. Letters posted unpaid or insufficiently prepaid, to any country where prepayment is, compulsory, are returned to the writers.

3. Unpaid, or insufficiently paid, letters to or from Australia, New Zealand, Cape Colony or Natal are charged 6d. each in addition to the deficient postage; and those to or from St. Helena are charged double the amount of deficient postage.

4. Unpaid letters to or from Postal Union countries are charged double the prepaid rate. Partially prepaid letters are charged with double the deficiency.

5. No letter for a Colony or Foreign Country may exceed 2 feet in length or 1 foot in width or depth.

6. Letters not specially directed by a particular route are, as a rule, forwarded by the first Mail despatched.

7. The addresses of letters for Russia should be very plainly written; the name of the town and of the province in which it is situated should also be added in English, French or German.

## NEWSPAPERS.

1. The rates of postage *must be prepaid*.

2. Newspapers, whether posted in covers or without covers, must not be fastened so as to prevent easy withdrawal for examination.

3. Every Newspaper must be so folded as to admit of the title being readily inspected.

4. No Newspaper, whether posted singly or in a packet, may contain any enclosure except the supplement or supplements belonging to it.

5. There must be no writing or other mark on a Newspaper sent abroad but the name and address of the person to whom it is sent; nor anything on the cover but such name and address, the printed title of the publication, the printed name and address of the publisher or vendor who sends it, and words indicating the date on which the subscription to the newspaper will end.

6. No packet of Newspapers may exceed two feet in length or one foot in width or depth.

7. The weight of a packet of Newspapers, Commercial Papers, Printed Papers, or Books for Countries in the Postal Union is limited to 4 lbs., and the weight of a Pattern Packet for such Countries (except Belgium, France, Greece, Luxemburg, Portugal, Switzerland via France, and the United States) is limited to 8 oz. The limit of a Pattern Packet for Belgium, France, Greece, Luxemburg, Portugal, Switzerland via France, and the United States is 12 oz. In all other cases, except New South Wales, Queensland and Fiji (which see) the limit is 5 lbs.

## BOOK POST.

1. Articles which may be sent to places abroad under the Book Post Regulations consist of two classes, as follows:—

(a.) "Commercial Papers," under which are comprised all papers or documents written or drawn wholly or partly by hand (except letters or communications in the nature of letters, or other papers or documents having the character of an actual and personal correspondence), documents of legal procedure, Deeds drawn up by public functionaries, copies of or extracts from Deeds under private seal (and whether written or printed on stamped or unstamped paper), Way Bills, Bills of Lading, Invoices, and other documents of a mercantile character, documents of Insurance and other public Companies, all kinds of manuscript Music, the manuscript of Books and other literary works, and other papers of a similar description.

(b.) "Printed Papers," including periodical works, books (stitched or bound), pamphlets, sheets of music (printed), visiting cards, address cards, proofs of printing (with or without the manuscript relating thereto), engravings, photographs (when not on glass or in frames containing glass), drawings, plans, maps, catalogues, prospectuses, announcements, and notices of various kinds, whether printed, engraved, or lithographed, and in general all impressions or copies obtained on paper, parchment, or card-board by means of printing, lithographing, or any other mechanical process, easy to recognise, except the copying press, and anything usually attached or appurtenant to any of the before-mentioned articles in the way of binding, mounting, or otherwise, and anything convenient for their safe transmission by post which shall be contained in the same packet; also printed, engraved, or lithographed circulars, notwithstanding that such circulars may be letters or communications in the nature of a letter.

The two classes are subject to the same rates of postage, except that when addressed to countries in the Postal Union the minimum rate for Commercial Papers is higher than that for Printed Papers. If there be any mixture of the two in the same packet the whole packet is treated as Commercial Papers.

2. A book-packet may be posted either without a cover (in which case it must not be fastened, whether by means of gum, wafer, sealing wax, postage stamp, or otherwise) or in a cover entirely open at both ends. so as to admit of the contents being easily withdrawn for examination,* otherwise it is treated as a letter. For the greater security of the contents, however, it may be tied at the ends with string; Postmasters being authorised to cut the string in such cases, although if they do so they must again tie up the packet.

3. The limit of size for a packet addressed to any place abroad is 24 inches in length and 12 inches in width or depth. For limitation of weight see paragraph of Newspaper Regulations.

4. The rates of postage, *which must be prepaid*, on packets to places abroad are given in the Table of Foreign and Colonial Postage.

The following information respecting Books and Photographs for the United States has been received from the Post Office at Washington:—

"The only Books absolutely free from Customs Duty, under the United States laws, are "those which have been printed more than 20 years; and Pamphlets, Periodicals, and other "like Publications, for the personal use of the individual to whom they are addressed."

"Nevertheless any book valued at not more than one dollar is also considered as exempt "from Customs Duty; and so are Photographs, when sent in limited numbers, for the private "use of the person to whom they are addressed, or for distribution to relatives or friends."

## PATTERNS AND SAMPLES.

1. There is a Pattern and Sample Post to Foreign Countries and the Colonies generally; but it is restricted to *bonâ fide trade patterns or samples of merchandise*. Packets containing goods for sale, or in execution of an order (however small the quantity). or any articles from one private individual to another which are not actually patterns or samples, are treated as letters.

2. No article liable to Custom Duties can be sent as a sample or pattern.

3. The rates of postage, *which must be prepaid*, will be found above.

4. Patterns or Samples, when practicable. must be sent in covers open at the ends, and in such a manner as to be easy of examination. But samples of seeds, drugs, and such like articles, which cannot be sent in covers of this kind, may be posted closed in boxes or in bags of linen, or other material, fastened in such a manner that they may be readily opened.

5. There must be no writing or printing upon or in any sample packet except the address of the person for whom it is intended, the address of the sender, a trade mark or number, and the price of the articles. But a packet for any country in the Postal Union may have enclosed in it any of the articles designated as "Commercial Papers" if the rate applicable to Commercial Papers be paid for the whole packet.

6. Samples of saleable value must not be sent to any foreign country, or to any of the British Possessions which are comprised in the Postal Union. Samples of eider down, raw or thread silk, woollen or goats' hair thread, vanilla, saffron, or isinglass, are considered to fall under this rule, if they weigh more than three ounces.

7. Such articles as scissors, knives, razors, forks. steel pens. nails, keys, watch machinery, metal tubing, pieces of metal or ore, provided that they be packed and guarded in so secure a manner as to afford complete protection to the contents of the mail bags and to the officers of the Post Office, while at the same time they may be easily examined, may be sent as samples to places abroad. Liquids, indigo, and powders of all kinds are absolutely prohibited.

8. The limit of weight is not the same to all countries. For particulars see paragraph 7 of Newspaper Regulations.

9. A packet of patterns or samples sent to any place comprised in the Postal Union (except Belgium, France. Greece, Luxemburg, Portugal, Switzerland viâ France, and the United States) must not exceed 8 inches in length, 4 in width, or 2 in depth. The limit to Belgium, France, Greece, Luxemburg, Portugal, Switzerland viâ France, or the United States is 12 inches in length, 8 in width, and 4 in depth. The size of a packet for a non-Union country or colony is limited to 24 inches in length and 12 in width or depth.

---

* In order to secure the return of book packets which cannot be delivered, the names and addresses of the senders should be printed or written *outside*; thus, "From ——— —— of ——— ——"

### LETTERS.

| | | | | | | |
|---|---|---|---|---|---|---|
| Not exceeding ½ oz. | ... | ... | ... | ... | ... | 1d. |
| Every additional ½ oz. | .. | ... | ... | ... | | 1d. |

No Letter, unless it be sent to or from a Government Office, to exceed 2 lbs. in weight, 18 inches in length, and 9 inches in width or depth.

### NEWSPAPERS, CIRCULARS AND PRICES CURRENT.

For each Newspaper. Circular, or Prices Current, not exceeding 4 oz. ... ½d.

A Packet containing two or more Newspapers. Circulars, or Prices Current, not to be liable to to a higher rate than the Book Postage would be, viz.:—

| | | | | | | |
|---|---|---|---|---|---|---|
| Under | 4 oz. | ... | ... | ... | ... | ½d. |
| Every additional 4 oz. | | ... | ... | ... | ... | 1d. |

Prepayment of Newspapers, Circulars, and Prices Current compulsory.

No Packet of Newspapers, Circulars. or Prices Current to exceed 2 lbs. in weight, 2 feet in length, and 1 foot in width or depth.

### BOOK PACKETS.

| | | | | | |
|---|---|---|---|---|---|
| For any Book Packet not exceeding 4 oz. ... | | ... | ... | .. | ½d. |
| Every additional | 4 oz. ... | | ... | ... | 1d. |

No Book Packet, unless it be sent to or from a Government Office, to exceed 2 lbs. in weight, 18 inches in length, and 9 inches in width or depth.

### POST CARDS.

Official Post Cards impressed with a halfpenny Stamp may be transmitted between places in Trinidad with Letters printed or written upon the back.

Postage Stamps, Post Cards, Registered Letter Envelopes, and Newspaper Wrappers of the following denominations may now be obtained at the General Post Office. Port-of-Spain. and the Post Offices at San Fernando and Couva. At all other Post Offices in Trinidad all the undermentioned (except 1s. and 5s. Postage Stamps) may be obtained, viz:—

| POSTAGE STAMPS. | POST CARDS. | | REGISTERED LETTER ENVELOPES. | NEWSPAPER WRAPPERS. | |
|---|---|---|---|---|---|
| | Single. | Double or Reply. | | ½d. | 1d. |
| ½d. | ½d. | ... | ... | Available Inland, and for Grenada, Barbadoes. St. Vincent & Tobago. | Available outside the Colony. Where the Postage exceeds 1d. the additional sum should be affixed in Postage Stamps. |
| 1d. | 1d. | 2d. | Of two sizes. | | |
| 2½d. | 1½d. | 3d. | | | |
| 4d. | 2d. | 4d. | 2d. each. | | |
| 6d. | | | | | |
| 1s. | | | | | |
| 5s. | | | | | |

NOTE.—The Post Cards, Registered Letter Envelopes and Newspaper Wrappers are sold to the Public at their face value.

From 1 January 1885 St. Lucia was included in Class A, i.e. letters of 2½d. per ½oz. etc.

On 1 October 1885 a parcel post service to the U.K. being 8d. a lb. with a limit of 7 lbs. (increased on 1 May 1886 to 11 lbs.)

On 1 July 1886 an Intercolonial parcel post started and on 1 August 1887 an Inland parcel post, rates being 3d. up to 1 lb., 1½d. per add lb., with 11 lbs. maximum for class A offices and 4 lbs. maximum for class B offices.

On 5 July 1888 the following notices were published:-

*New Guinea and the German Post Office at Apia in the Samooan Islands, having joined the Postal Union, will be subject to the same rates of Postage (9d. per ½oz.) and conditions of transmission as are applicable to correspondence addressed to New Caledonia.*

*J. A. BULMER,*
*Postmaster-General.*

On 1 January 1889 Tobago was subordinated to Trinidad which had the immediate effect of having the Inland 1d. letter rate extended to Tobago, presumably all other Trinidad Postal Rates were also immediately applied. Later rates will therefore be found under Trinidad and Tobago.

Convict Depot Carrera Isle. Trinidad.                    Muir, Marshall & Co.

# TRINIDAD AND TOBAGO

On 1 January 1891 the letter rate to the U.K. and Empire was reduced to 2½d. per ½oz. as per:-

## FOREIGN AND COLONIAL

### CLASS A:

| | | | |
|---|---|---|---|
| Accra | Cyprus | Leeward Islands | *Queensland † |
| Antigua | Dominica | Malta | Sierra Leone |
| *Ascension (c) (in) | Falkland Islands | Maturin | Sarawak |
| *Australia, South & West. | *Fiji Islands † | Mauritius | Singapore |
| Bahamas | Gibraltar | Montserrat | Straits Settlements |
| Barbados | Gambia | *Natal | *St. Helena |
| Bechuanaland | Grenada | Newfoundland | St. Kitts |
| Bermuda | Gold Coast | Nevis | St. Lucia |
| British Columbia | Guiria | New Brunswick | St. Vincent |
| British Guiana | Hong Kong | *New South Wales † | *Tasmania |
| British Honduras | India | *New Zealand | Turks Island |
| Burmah | Jamaica | Norfolk Island | United Kingdom |
| Canada | Lubuan | Penang | *Victoria (Australia) |
| *Cape Colony | Lagos | Prince Edward Islands | Virgin Islands |
| Ceylon | | | |

\* Countries marked thus are not in the Postal Union - (c) denotes that prepayment is compulsory.

† The weight of a packet is limited to 3 lbs. - (in) denotes that registration is incomplete.

### CLASS B.

| | | | | |
|---|---|---|---|---|
| Algeria | Dutch Guiana | Hayti | Netherlands and Netherland Colonies (except Java) | Spain and Spanish Colonies (except Philipine) |
| Argentine Republic | Ecuador | Holland | Panama | Sweden |
| Austria | Egypt | Honduras, Republic of | Porto Rico | Switzerland |
| Azores | French Guiana | Italy | Persia (via) Russia | St. Pierre et Miquelon |
| Belgium | France and French Colonies and Establishments including St. Mary's, Tamatave (Madagascar) and Comoro Islands | Ionian Islands | Portugal | San Salvador, Republic of |
| Brazil | | Liberia | Peru | St. Thomas |
| Bulgaria | | Luxembourg | Russia | Tahiti |
| Colon | Germany | Madeira | Roumania | Tunis |
| Columbia, United States of | Greece | Marquesas Islands | Savanilla | Turkey |
| Cuba | Graytown, St. Juan de Nicaragua | Mexico | San Domingo | United States of America |
| Curaçoa | Greenland | Montenegro | Santa Martha | Venezuela |
| Canary Islands | Guatemala | Moldavia | Syria | |
| Costa Rica | Guadeloupa | Nicaragua | Servia | |
| Denmark and Danish Colonies | | Norway | | |

The Rates of Postage, for Correspondence posted in Trinidad addressed to the above Countries are as follows:—

| | LETTERS. | | | POST CARDS. | | NEWSPAPERS. | | OTHER ARTICLES. | | | |
|---|---|---|---|---|---|---|---|---|---|---|---|
| | Not exceeding ½ oz. | Every additional ½ oz. | Registration Fee. | POST CARDS ARE ONLY SENT TO COUNTRIES IN THE POSTAL UNION. | | Not exceeding 2 oz. and for every additional 2 oz. Within 300 miles | Not exceeding 4 oz. and for every additional 4 oz. Beyond 300 miles | Printed Papers and Books. | | COMMERCIAL PAPERS. | PATTERNS |
| | | | | Single. | Double or Reply. | | | For any weight not exceeding 2 oz. and for every additional 2 oz. Within 300 miles. | Not exceeding 2 oz. and for every additional 2 oz. Beyond 300 miles. | | |
| | d. | d. | d. | d. | d. | d. | d. | d. | d. | | |
| For Countries in Class A. ... ... | 2½ | 2½ | 2 | 1 | 2 | •½ | 1 | •½ | 1 | Same as Printed Papers except that the lowest charge for each packet is 3½d. in all cases. | Same as Printed Papers except that as regards those Countries where the postage is half-penny per 2 oz. the lowest charge is 1d. |
| For Countries in Class B. ... ... | 4 | 4 | 2 | 1½ | 3 | 1 | 1 | 1 | ... | | |

To the following Countries the rates of Postage are as follows :—

## CLASS C.

| | s. d. | s. d. | d. | d. | d. | d. | d. | d. | d. |
|---|---|---|---|---|---|---|---|---|---|
| Aden | 5 | 5 | 2 | 2 | 4 | … | 1½ | 1½ | … |
| Africa, West Coast of, except places mentioned in Class A. | 9 | 9 | 2 | 1½ | 3 | … | 1 | 1 | … |
| Borneo | 5 | 5 | 2 | 1½ | 3 | … | 1½ | 1½ | … |
| *Bolivia | c.a. 1 1 | 1 1 | in 2 | … | a. | … | 2 | 2 | … |
| *China, except Hong Kong | 5 | 5 | 2 | 2 | 4 | … | 1½ | 1½ | … |
| Celebes | 5 | 5 | 2 | 2 | 4 | … | 1½ | 1½ | … |
| Chili | 5 | 5 | 2 | 1½ | … | … | 1 | 1 | … |
| Fernando Po | 5 | 5 | 2 | 1½ | … | … | 1 | 1 | … |
| French Colonies East of Suez | 5 | 5 | 2 | 2 | 4 | … | 1½ | 1½ | … |
| Japan | 5 | 5 | 2 | 2 | 4 | … | 1½ | 1½ | … |
| Java | 5 | 5 | 2 | 2 | 4 | … | 1½ | 1½ | … |
| *Madagascar (except St. Mary's & Tamatave) | c. 1 1 | 1 1 | None | … | … | … | 2 | 3 | … |
| Persia (via Brindisi and Bombay if specially addressed | 5 | 5 | 2 | 2 | 4 | … | 1½ | 1½ | … |
| Philipine Islands | 5 | 5 | 2 | 2 | 4 | … | 1½ | 1½ | … |
| Sandwich Islands | 6 | 6 | 2 | 1½ | … | … | 1 | 1 | … |
| Sumatra | 5 | 5 | 2 | 2 | 4 | … | 1½ | 1½ | … |
| Zanzibar | 9 | 9 | 2 | 2 | 4 | … | 1½ | 1½ | … |

The rates of Postage for Commercial Papers are the same as for Printed Papers except that the lowest charge for each packet is 2½d. even if the packet weigh less than 2 oz.

The rates for Patterns are the same as for Printed Papers except that the lowest charge is 1d. for a packet addressed to any of the Countries to which the postage is ½d. per 2 oz. for Printed Papers.

Countries marked * are not in the Postal Union.—(a) denotes that an additional charge will be made on delivery.—(c) denotes that prepayment is compulsory.—(in) denotes that registration is incomplete.

# REGISTRATION.

1. The fee chargeable for registration to places beyond Sea is 2d. To some countries as shown thus *(in)*, an article can be registered only to the port of arrival ; it being left, in those cases, to the postal authorities of the country to which that port belongs to continue the registration or not as they may think proper. To Madagascar, as shown above, there is no arrangement whatever for registration.

2. Registration is applicable equally to letters, post-cards, newspapers, book packets, and patterns addressed to places abroad.

The sender of a registered article addressed to any Foreign Country or British Colony in the Postal Union may obtain an acknowledgment of its due receipt by the addressee on paying a fee of 2½d. as well as the registration fee, in advance, at the time of registration.

3. No article addressed to initials or to a fictitious name can be registered. The prohibition, however, does not extend to articles addressed to the care of a person or firm.

4. Every letter presented for registration must be enclosed in a strong envelope, securely fastened.

It is prohibited to send to a country of the Postal Union any registered article marked on the outside with the declared value of the contents ; and Postmasters will therefore refuse to receive articles which are so marked.

5. Registered articles must be prepaid as regards both postage and registration fee.

6. Articles to be registered must be given to an agent of the Post Office, and a receipt obtained for them ; they should on no account be dropped into a letter-box.

7. As it is forbidden to send coin, jewellery, or precious articles through the post to countries of the Postal Union, no letters or packets containing such articles can be accepted for registration.

8. The several Postal Administrations of the countries belonging to the Postal Union undertake to pay an indemnity of fifty francs in the event of its being proved to their satisfaction that a registered letter itself has been lost whilst in their custody, but no question of compensation is entertained by them for, or in respect of, the loss of the enclosure of any such letter.

## LETTERS.

1. Prepayment is compulsory in those cases where the letter "c" is prefixed to the rates of postage. In some countries ("a") an additional postage (which cannot be prepaid) is charged on delivery.

2. Letters posted unpaid, or insufficiently prepaid, to any country where prepayment is compulsory, are returned to the writers.

3. Unpaid letters to or from Postal Union countries are charged double the prepaid rate. Partially prepaid Letters are charged with double the deficiency.

4. No letter for a Colony or Foreign Country may exceed 2 feet in length or 1 foot in width or depth.

5. Letters not specially directed by a particular route are, as a rule, forwarded by the first Mail despatched.

6. The addresses of letters for Russia should be very plainly written ; the name of the town, and of the province in which it is situated, should also be added in English, French, or German.

## NEWSPAPERS.

1. The rates of postage *must be prepaid.*

2. Newspapers, whether posted in covers or without covers, must not be fastened so as to prevent easy withdrawal for examination.

3. Every newspaper must be so folded as to admit of the title being readily inspected.

4. No Newspaper, whether posted singly or in a packet, may contain any enclosure except the supplement or supplements belonging to it.

5. There must be no writing or other mark on a Newspaper sent abroad but the name and address of the person to whom it is sent ; nor anything on the cover but such name and address, the printed title of the publication, the printed name and address of the publisher or vendor who sends it, and words indicating the date on which the subscription to the newspaper will end.

6. No packet of Newspapers may exceed two feet in length or one foot in width or depth.

7. The weight of a packet of Newspapers, Commercial Papers, Printed Papers, or Books for countries in the Postal Union is limited to 4 lbs., and the weight of a Pattern packet for such countries (except Belgium, France, Greece, Luxemburg, Portugal, Switzerland viâ France, and the United States) is limited to 8 oz. The limit of a Pattern packet for Belgium, France, Greece, Luxemburg, Portugal, Switzerland viâ France, and the United States is 12 oz. In all other cases the limit is 5 lbs.

1. Articles which may be sent to places abroad under the Book Post Regulations consist of two classes, as follows :—

(a.) "Commercial Papers," under which are comprised all papers or documents written or drawn wholly or partly by hand, (except letters or communications in the nature of letters, or other papers or documents having the character of an actual and personal correspondence), documents of legal procedure. Deeds drawn up by public functionaries, copies of or extracts from Deeds under private seal (and whether written or printed on stamped or unstamped paper), Way Bills, Bills of Lading, Invoices, and other documents of a mercantile character, documents of Insurance and other public Companies, all kinds of manuscript Music, the manuscript of Books and other literary works, and other papers of a similar description.

(b.) "Printed Papers," including periodical works, books (stitched or bound), pamphlets sheets of music (printed), visiting cards, address cards, proofs of printing (with or without the manuscript relating thereto), engravings, photographs (when not on glass or in frames containing glass), drawings, plans, maps, catalogues, prospectuses, announcements, and notices of various kinds, whether printed, engraved or lithographed, and in general all impressions or copies obtained on paper, parchment, or card-board by means of printing, lithographing, or any other mechanical process easy to recognise, except the copying press, and anything usually attached or appurtenant to any of the before-mentioned articles in the way of binding, mounting, or otherwise, and anything convenient for their safe transmission by post which shall be contained in the same packet ; also printed, engraved, or lithographed circulars, notwithstanding that such circulars may be letters or communications in the nature of a letter.

The two classes are subject to the same rates of postage, except that when addressed to countries in the Postal Union the minimum rate for Commercial Papers is higher than that for Printed Papers. If there be any mixture of the two in the same packet the whole packet is treated as Commercial Papers.

2. A Book Packet may be posted either without a cover (in which case it must not be fastened, whether by means of gum, wafer, sealing-wax, postage stamps, or otherwise) or in a cover entirely open at both ends, so as to admit of the contents being easily withdrawn for examination.‡ otherwise it is treated as a letter. For the greater security of its contents, however, it may be tied at the ends with string ; Postmasters being authorised to cut the string in such cases, although if they do so they must again tie up the packet.

3. The limit of size for a packet addressed to any place abroad is 24 inches in length and 12 inches in width or depth. For limitation of weight see paragraph of Newspaper Regulations.

4. The rates of postage, *which must be prepaid*, on packets to places abroad are given in the Table of Foreign and Colonial Postage.

The following information respecting Books and Photogoaphs for the United States has been received from the Post Office at Washington :—

"The only Books absolutely free from Custom Duty, under the United States laws, are "those which have been printed more than 20 years ; and Pamphlets, Periodicals, and "other like Publications, for the personal use of the individual to whom they are "addressed."

"Nevertheless any Book valued at not more than one dollar is also considered as "exempt from Customs Duty ; and so are Photographs when sent in limited numbers, "for the private use of the person to whom they are addressed, or for distribution to "relatives or friends."

## PATTERNS AND SAMPLES.

1. There is a Pattern and Sample Post to Foreign Countries and the Colonies generally ; but it is restricted to *bonâ fide trade patterns or samples of merchandise*. Packets containing goods for sale, or in execution of an order (however small the quantity), or any articles from one private individual to another which are not actually patterns or samples, are treated as letters.

2. No article liable to Custom Duties can be sent as a sample or pattern.

3. The rates of postage, *which must be prepaid*, will be found above.

4. Patterns or Samples, when practicable, must be sent in covers open at the ends, and in such a manner as to be easy of examination. But samples of seeds, drugs, and such like articles, which cannot be sent in covers of this kind, may be posted enclosed in boxes, or in bags of linen, or other material, fastened in such a manner that they may be readily opened.

5. There must be no writing or printing upon or in any sample packet except the address of the person for whom it is intended, the address of the sender, a trade mark or number, and the price of the articles. But a packet for any country in the Postal Union may have enclosed in it any of the articles designated as "Commercial Papers" if the rate applicable to Commercial Papers be paid for the whole packet

---

‡ In order to secure the return of book-packets which cannot be delivered, the names and addresses of the senders should be printed or written *outside* ; thus, "From————of————."

6. Samples of saleable value must not be sent to any foreign country, or to any of the British Possessions which are comprised in the Postal Union. Samples of eider down, raw or thread silk, woollen or goats' hair thread, vanilla, saffron, or isinglass, are considered to fall under this rule, if they weigh more than three ounces.

7. Such articles as scissors, knives, razors, forks, steel pens, nails, keys, watch machinery, metal tubing, pieces of metal or ore, provided that they be packed and guarded in so secure a manner as to afford complete protection to the contents of the mail bags and to the Officers of the Post Office, while at the same time they may be easily examined, may be sent as samples to places abroad. Liquids, indigo, and powders of all kinds are absolutely prohibited.

8. The limit of weight is not the same to all countries. For particulars see paragraph 7 of Newspaper Regulations.

9. A packet of patterns or samples sent to any place comprised in the Postal Union (except Belgium, France, Greece, Luxemburg, Portugal, Switzerland viâ France, and the United States) must not exceed 8 inches in length, 4 in width, or 2 in depth. The limit to Belgium, France, Greece, Luxemburg, Portugal, Switzerland viâ France, or the United States is 12 inches in length, 8 in width, and 4 in depth. The size of a packet for a non-Union country or colony is limited to 24 inches in length and 12 in width or depth.

## PARCEL POST TO UNITED KINGDOM, BRITISH COLONIES AND FOREIGN COUNTRIES.

Parcels for dispatch by Outward English Mail must reach the General Post Office Port-of-Spain, not later than 4. P.M., on the day preceeding the departure of the Mail.

# INLAND.

## LETTERS.

| | | | | | |
|---|---|---|---|---|---|
| Not exceeding ½ oz. | ... | ... | ... | ... | 1d. |
| Every additional ½ oz. | ... | ... | ... | ... | 1d. |

No Letter, unless it be sent to or from a Government Office, to exceed 2 lbs. in weight, 18 inches in length, and 9 inches in width or depth.

## LETTERS, &c., "ON HER MAJESTY'S SERVICE."

Attention is drawn to Ordinance No. 6 of 4th April, 1851, which requires " That the " Letters of the undermentioned persons transmitted by Post either to or from them shall, " subject to the conditions hereinafter mentioned, be exempt from postage : viz.: the " Governor, the Colonial Secretary, the Attorney-General, the Registrar-General, the " Registrar of the Supreme Civil and Criminal Courts, and the Inspector and Sub- " Inspectors or other Officers of Police; Provided always that every letter shall be on the " public business of the Office or Department from which the same shall be forwarded or " to which the same shall be addressed, and shall be superscribed with the words 'On " 'Her Majesty's Service,' and with the signature of the Officer from whose Office or " Department such letter shall be transmitted or of the person transmitting such letter to " such Office or Department."

As the omission to superscribe on the envelope the signature of the Officer from whose Office or Department the letter is transmitted frequently causes considerable delay and necessitates the collection of a surcharge, His Excellency the Governor directs that in future no Inland Letters, &c., " On Her Majesty's Service," forwarded from any Public Office or Department in this Colony shall be transmitted through the Post unless bearing legibly inscribed in the bottom left hand corner of the envelope the designation of Office, or the official title or name of the sender, with the words " On Her Majesty's Service", either printed or written across the top of the envelope.

In order to prevent delay in transmission from Sub-Offices, owing to neglect of the above-mentioned precaution, all such correspondence should where practicable be handed to District Postmasters and not placed in the Letter Boxes.

For each Newspaper, Circular, or Prices Current, not exceeding 4 oz.   $\frac{1}{2}d$.

A Packet containing two or more Newspapers, Circulars, or Prices Current, not to be liable to a higher rate than the Book Postage would be, viz :—

| | | | | | | |
|---|---|---|---|---|---|---|
| Under | 4 oz. | ... | ... | ... | ... | $\frac{1}{2}d$. |
| Every additional 4 oz. | | ... | ... | ... | ... | 1$d$. |

Prepayment of Newspapers, Circulars, and Prices Current compulsory.

No Packet of Newspapers, Circulars or Prices Current to exceed 2 lbs. in weight, 2 feet in length, and 1 foot in width or depth.

## BOOK PACKETS.

| | | | | |
|---|---|---|---|---|
| For any Book Packet not exceeding 4 oz | ... | ... | $\frac{1}{2}d$. |
| Every additional | 4 oz | ... | ... | 1$d$. |

No Book Packet, unless it be sent to or from a Government Office, to exceed 2 lbs. in weight, 18 inches in length, and 9 inches in width or depth.

Book Packets from Government Offices are accepted under the Scales of Weights mentioned in Classes A and B of Inland Parcel Post Regulations below.

## POST CARDS.

Official Post Cards impressed with a half-penny Stamp may be transmitted between places in Trinidad with Letters printed or written upon the back.

Adhesive Stamps are not accepted in payment of Postage on Post Cards.   The front (or stamped) side is for the address only, in addition to the words printed thereon. Nothing else must be written, printed, or otherwise impressed on it or the Stamp.   On the reverse side any communication, whether of the nature of a letter or otherwise, may be written or printed.   Nothing whatever may be attached, nor may the Card be folded, cut, or otherwise altered.   If any one of these Rules be infringed the Card will be charged 1d. on delivery.

NOTE.—Postage Stamps, Post Cards, Registered Letter Envelopes, and Newspaper Wrappers of the following denominations may now be obtained at the General Post Office, Port-of-Spain, and the Post Offices at San Fernando and Couva.   At all other Post Offices in Trinidad all the undermentioned (except 1s. and 5s. Postage Stamps) may be obtained, viz :—

| POSTAGE STAMPS. | POST CARDS. | | REGISTERED LETTER ENVELOPES. | NEWSPAPER WRAPPERS. | |
|---|---|---|---|---|---|
| | Single. | Double or Reply. | | $\frac{1}{2}d$. | 1$d$. |
| $\frac{1}{2}d$.     ... | $\frac{1}{2}d$. | | ... | Available   Inland, | Available   outside |
| 1$d$.     ... | 1$d$. | 2$d$. | Of two sizes | and for Grenada, | the Colony. Where |
| 2$\frac{1}{2}$     ... | 1$\frac{1}{2}$ | 3$d$. | | Barbados,     St. | the   Postage   ex- |
| 4$d$     ... | 2$d$. | 1$d$. | 2$d$. each. | Vincent & Tobago | ceeds 1$d$. the addi- |
| 6$d$.     ... | | | | | tional sum should |
| 1s.     ... | | | | | be affixed in Pos- |
| 5s.     ... | | | | | tage Stamps. |

## INLAND MONEY ORDERS.

The following Offices now transact Money Order business :—

Arima.  
Arouca.  
Chaguanas.  
Cedros.

Couva.  
Princes Town.  
San Fernando.

It is not clear when or if the mistake was rectified or whether Trinidad elected to apply the U.P.U. rate (also 2½d.) to these countries, the Australian Colonies, New Zealand and Fiji however did not join until 1 October 1891. A new list of rates which came into effect 1 August 1892 was:-

## List of Countries which in addition to Trinidad and Tobago are comprised in the Postal Union.

| | | | | | |
|---|---|---|---|---|---|
| °Antigua | Cameroons | °Ecuador | Gambia | °Gold Coast | Jamaica |
| °Argentine Republic | °Canada (Dominion of) | °Egypt | Germany | °Greece | *Japan |
| Australia | Ceylon | °Falkland Islands | | Grenada | Labuan |
| °Austria-Hungary | °Chili | °Fiji Islands | German Colonies, viz.: Marshall Islands, New Guinea (portion of), Samoa (Apia), Togo Territory, including Bagcida, Little Popo, Lome and Porto Seguro and Territory in South-west Africa, viz.: Grand Nanqua, the Damaras Country, and Southern portion of Ovambo; also Bagamoyond Dar-es-Salaam, Lindi and Tanga in East Africa | Grenadines | Lagos |
| °Azores | °Columbia, Republic of | °France | | Guatemala | *Liberia |
| °Bahamas | °Congo, including Black Point, Majumba and Nyanza | °French Colonies, viz.: Martinique, Guadaloupe and dependencies, French Guiana (Cayenne), Senegal and dependencies, Gaboon and Grand Bassam (also Sette Cama and Assinie) Reunion, Comoro Islands, Mayotte and dependencies, Majunga, St. Mary and Tamatave (Madagascar), New Caledonia and dependencies, the French portion of the low Archipelago and the French Establishments in India (Pondicherry, Chandernagor, Karikal Mahé and Yanoon) and in Cochin China | | °Guiria | Luxembourg |
| °Barbados | °Costa Rica | | | °Hawaiian Islands | *Madeira |
| °Belgium | °Colon | | | °Hayti | Malta |
| Bermuda | Cyprus | | | °Honduras | *Marquesas Islands |
| °Bolivia | °Danish Colonies, viz.: Greenland, St. Croix, St. John and St. Thomas | | | Hong Kong | *Maturin |
| °Brazil | °Denmark (including Faroe Islands and Iceland, | | | °India | *Mauritius and dependencies |
| British Borneo | °Dominica | | Gibraltar, including the British Post Offices at Tangier, Laraiche, Rabat, Casablanca, Safi, Mazagan and Mogador | °Italy | *Mexico |
| °British Guiana | °Dominican (Republic) San Domingo | | | | *Montenegro |
| °British Honduras | | | | | Montserrat |
| British New Guinea | | | | | |
| °Bulgaria | | | | | |

146

| | | | | |
|---|---|---|---|---|
| °Netherlands | °Portugal | °St. Kitts | °Spain (including Balearic and Canary Islands) | °Tahiti |
| °Netherland Colonies, viz.: Dutch Guinea (Surinam), Curaçoa and dependencies, viz.: Bonaire, Aruba, the Netherlands portion of St. Martin, St. Eustache, Saba, Java, Madura, Sumatra, Celebes, Borneo (except Northwest part) Billiton, Archipelago of Riouw, Sunda Islands (Bali, Lombok, Sumbawa, Floris and the Southwest part of Timor) the Archipelago of Moluccas, and the North-west part of New Guinea (Papua) | °Portuguese Colonies, viz.: Goa and its dependencies (Damon and Diu), Macao, Timor, Cape Verd Islands and dependencies (Bissan and Cachen) Islands of St. Thomas and Prince (in Africa) with the Establishments of Ajuda, Angolo Delagoa Bay and Mozambique | °St. Lucia | °Spanish Colonies, viz.: Cuba, Porto Rico, Fernando Po, Annobon and dependencies, Philippine Islands, and Marian Islands | °Tortola |
| °Nevis | | °St. Pierre-et-Miquelon | | °Turkey |
| Newfoundland | | St. Vincent, West Indies | | °Turks Island |
| New Zealand | | | | °United Kingdom |
| °Nicaragua | | °Salvador | | |
| °Norway | °Roumania | °Servia | Straits Settlements | °United States |
| °Paraguay | °Russia | °Seychelles | | °Uruguay |
| *Patagonia | | °Siam | °Sweden | °Venezuela |
| °Persia | | Sierra Leone | °Switzerland | °Zanzibar |
| °Peru | | | | |

° *Prohibited Articles.*—The transmission by Letter Post of Gold, Silver, precious Stones, Jewellery, &c., is prohibited in those Countries of the Postal Union marked thus (°). Such articles however may be sent by Parcel Post, except in cases in which they are specially prohibited. (See Parcel Post Regulations.)

In Luxemburg the registration of such packets is compulsory, and everything of value, except Coin or bullion is liable to duty. In the undermentioned Colonies, viz.:—Bermuda, Ceylon, Falkland Islands, Gambia, Gibraltar, Hong Kong, Labuan, Lagos, Malta, Montserrat, Newfoundland, St. Vincent, Sierra Leone and Straits Settlements, articles of value are transmissible and with the exception of Jewellery addressed to Ceylon, Newfoundland and St. Vincent are exempt from Customs duty. Their transmission is also permitted in Cyprus, Grenada and Jamaica. In the Dutch East Indies articles of value are liable to Customs duty with the exception of Gold and Specie in Cyprus; Gold, Silver and Diamonds in Grenada; and Diamonds in Jamaica. In the Dutch East Indies articles of value are admissible except wrought Gold and Silver, but the packets containing them must be registered. Special prohibitions in Italy and United States of America, anything relating to foreign lotteries. In New Zealand Cuttings of Grape Vines. In the Cape of Good Hope and Queensland Jewellery and precious articles, if dutiable, are liable to detention until the duty is paid. In Spain and Victoria Jewellery is dutiable and liable to confiscation. Russia:—Printed matter in the Russian language is prohibited, and even such trifling articles as Photographs and Christmas Cards are liable to duty, though a single Photograph may be sent to Russia by Post. All letters or packets containing prohibited or dutiable articles of any kind, however small the value, are confiscated in that Country.

# Foreign and Colonial Mails.

## RATES OF POSTAGE.

| FOR | For a letter per ½ oz. | For single Post Card. | For a Reply Post Card. | For Newspapers or other printed papers per 2 oz. | Registration Fee. | For Commercial Papers. | For Patterns. |
|---|---|---|---|---|---|---|---|
| | d. | d. | d. | d. | d. | | |
| Countries and Colonies in the Postal Union | 2½ | 1 | 2 | ½ | 2 | | |
| Countries and Colonies not in the Postal Union, viz. :— | | | | | | | |
| Abyssinia ... ... ... | 2½ | ... | ... | ½ | in. 2 | | |
| Africa (West Coast Native possessions) | c.a. 2½ | ... | ... | ½ | in. 2 | | |
| Arabia ... ... ... | c. 2½ | ... | ... | ½ | in. 2 | | |
| Ascension ... ... ... | c. 2½ | ... | ... | ½ | in. 2 | | |
| Bechuanaland ... ... | 2½ | ... | ... | ½ | 2 | | |
| Do. Protectorate, including Kanye, Lake Ugami, Maclout-sie, Mashonaland, Matabeleland, Molepolole, Palacheve (Khamas Town), Shoshong, Tati River & Zambesi | a. 2½ | ... | ... | a. ½ | 2 | | |
| Cape Colony ... ... | 2½ | 1 | ... | ½ | 2 | | |
| Madagascar vid Marseilles (except St. Mary, Tamatave and Majunga, for which see French Colonies in Postal Union List, | c.a. 2½ | ... | ... | ½ | None. | Same as for Printed Papers, except that the lowest charge is 2½d. | Same as for Printed Papers, except that the lowest charge is 1d. |
| Do. vid Mauritius ... | c. 2½ | ... | ... | ½ | in. 2 | | |
| Morocco (except Tangier, Laraiche, Rabat, Casablanca, Saffi, Mazagan and Mogador, for which see Gibraltar in Postal Union List | ... | ... | ... | ... | ... | | |
| Prepayment to Morocco is compulsory, with the exception of Casablanca, Laraiche, Mazagan, Mogador, Rabat, Saffi, and Tangier, to which places only registration extends. To these places (at each of which the Gibraltar Post Office maintains an agency under the Postal Union Regulations) correspondence can be sent under the conditions applicable to Gibraltar. | | | | | | | |
| Natal ... ... ... | 2½ | 1 | ... | ½ | 2 | | |
| Orange Free State ... ... | 2½ | ... | ... | ½ | 2 | | |
| St. Helena ... ... ... | 2½ | ... | ... | ½ | ... | | |
| Sarawak ... ... ... | c.a. 2½ | ... | ... | a. ½ | in. 2 | | |
| Society Islands ... ... | c. 2½ | ... | ... | ½ | 2 | | |
| South African Republic (Transvaal)... | 2½ | ... | ... | ½ | 2 | | |
| Other Parts ... ... ... | c. 2½ | ... | ... | ½ | in. 2 | | |

(c) denotes that prepayment is compulsory, it being in all other cases optional ; (a) that an additional charge is made on delivery ; (in) that the registration is incomplete, not extending beyond Port of arrival ; and (None) that no registration can be effected.

# REGISTRATION.

1. The fee chargeable for registration to places beyond Sea is 2d. To some countries as shown thus *(in)*, an article can be registered only to the port of arrival; it being left, in those cases, to the postal authorities of the country to which that port belongs to continue the registration or not as they may think proper. To Madagascar, as shown above, there is no arrangement whatever for registration.

2. Registration is applicable equally to letters, post-cards, newspapers, book packets, and patterns addressed to places abroad.

The sender of a registered article addressed to any Foreign Country or British Colony in the Postal Union may obtain an acknowledgment of its due receipt by the addressee on paying a fee of 2½d. as well as the registration fee, in advance, at the time of registration.

3. No article addressed to initials or to a fictitious name can be registered. The prohibition, however, does not extend to articles addressed to the care of a person or firm.

4. Every letter presented for registration must be enclosed in a strong envelope, securely fastened.

It is prohibited to send to a country of the Postal Union any registered article marked on the outside with the declared value of the contents; and Postmasters will therefore refuse to receive articles which are so marked.

5. Registered articles must be prepaid as regards both postage and registration fee.

6. Articles to be registered must be given to an agent of the Post Office, and a receipt obtained for them; they should on no account be dropped into a letter-box.

7. As it is forbidden to send coin, jewellery, or precious articles through the post to certain countries of the Postal Union, no letters or packets containing such articles can be accepted for registration for places marked thus º

8. The several Postal Administrations of the countries belonging to the Postal Union undertake to pay an indemnity of fifty francs in the event of its being proved to their satisfaction that a registered letter itself has been lost whilst in their custody, but no question of compensation is entertained by them for, or in respect of, the loss of the enclosure of any such letter.

## LETTERS.

1. Prepayment is compulsory in those cases where the letter "c" is prefixed to the rates of postage. In some countries ("a") an additional postage (which cannot be prepaid) is charged on delivery.

2. Letters posted unpaid, or insufficiently prepaid, to any country where prepayment is compulsory, are returned to the writers.

3. Unpaid letters to or from Postal Union countries are charged double the prepaid rate. Partially prepaid Letters are charged with double the deficiency.

4. No letter for a Colony or Foreign Country may exceed 2 feet in length or 1 foot in width or depth.

5. Letters not specially directed by a particular route are, as a rule, forwarded by the first Mail despatched.

6. The addresses of letters for Russia should be very plainly written; the name of the town, and of the province in which it is situated, should also be added in English, French, or German.

## NEWSPAPERS, PRINTED PAPERS AND BOOKS.

1. The rates of postage *must be prepaid at least partly.*

2. Newspapers, whether posted in covers or without covers, must not be fastened so as to prevent easy withdrawal for examination.

3. Every newspaper must be so folded as to admit of the title being readily inspected.

4. No Newspaper, whether posted singly or in a packet, may contain any enclosure of the nature of a letter.

5. There must be no writing or other mark on a Newspaper sent abroad but the name and address of the person to whom it is sent; nor anything on the cover but such name and address, the printed title of the publication. the printed name and address of the publisher or vendor who sends it, and words indicating the date on which the subscription to the newspaper will end.

6. No packet of Newspapers, printed matter or Commercial papers for transmission to Countries of the Postal Union may exceed eighteen inches in length or one foot in width or depth.

7. The weight of a packet of Newspapers, Commercial Papers, Printed Papers. or Books for countries in the Postal Union is limited to 4 lbs., and the weight of a Pattern packet for such countries (except Belgium, France. Greece, Luxemburg. Portugal, Switzerland *riá* France, and the United States) is limited to 8 oz. The limit of a Pattern packet for Belgium, France, Greece, Luxemburg, Portugal, Switzerland *riá* France, and the United States is 12 oz. In all other cases the limit is 5 lbs.

8. "Printed Papers," including periodical works. books (stitched or bound), pamphlets, sheets of music (printed). visiting cards, address cards, proofs of printing (with or without the manuscript relating thereto), engravings, photographs (when not on glass or in frames containing glass), drawings, plans, maps, catalogues, prospectuses, announcements, and notices of various kinds. whether printed, engraved or lithographed, and in general all impressions or copies obtained on paper, parchment, or card-board by means of printing, lithographing, or any other mechanical process easy to recognise, except the copying press, and anything usually attached or appurtenant to any of the before-mentioned articles in the way of binding, mounting. or otherwise, and anything convenient for their safe transmission by post which shall be contained in the same packet; also printed, engraved, or lithographed circulars, notwithstanding that such circulars may be letters or communications in the nature of a letter.

9. A Book Packet may be posted either without a cover (in which case it must not be fastened, whether by means of gum, wafer, sealing-wax, postage stamps, or otherwise) or in a cover entirely open at both ends, so as to admit of the contents being easily withdrawn for examination,° otherwise it is treated as a letter. For the greater security of its contents, however, it may be tied at the ends with string; Postmasters being authorised to cut the string in such cases, although if they do so they must again tie up the packet.

The following information respecting Books and Photographs for the United States has been received from the Post Office at Washington :—

"The only Books absolutely free from Custom Duty, under the United States "laws, are those which have been printed more than 20 years; and Pamphlets, "Periodicals. and other like Publications, for the personal use of the individual to "whom they are addressed."

"Nevertheless any Book valued at not more than one dollar is also considered as "exempt from Customs Duty; and so are Photographs when sent in limited numbers, "for the private use of the person to whom they are addressed, or for distribution "to relatives or friends."

## COMMERCIAL PAPERS.

1. "Commercial Papers," under which are comprised all papers or documents written or drawn wholly or partly by hand, (except letters or communications in the nature of letters, or other papers or documents having the character of an actual and personal correspondence), documents of legal procedure, Deeds drawn up by public functionaries, copies of or extracts from Deeds under private seal (and whether written or printed on stamped or unstamped paper), Way Bills, Bills of Lading, Invoices, and other documents of a mercantile character, documents of Insurance and other public Companies, all kinds of manuscript Music. the manuscript of Books and other literary works, and other papers of a similar description.

## PATTERNS AND SAMPLES.

1. There is a Pattern and Sample Post to Foreign Countries and the Colonies generally; but it is restricted to *bonâ fide trade patterns or samples of merchandise*. Packets containing goods for sale, or in execution of an order (however small the quantity), or any articles from one private individual to another which are not actually patterns or samples, are treated as letters.

2. No article liable to Custom Duties can be sent as a sample or pattern.

3. The rates of postage, *which must be prepaid*, will be found above.

---

* In order to secure the return of book-packets which cannot be delivered, the names and addresses of the senders should be printed or written *outside*; thus, "From———of———."

150

4. Patterns of **Samples**, when practicable, must be sent in covers open at the ends, and in such a manner as to be easy of examination. But samples of seeds, drugs, and such like articles, which cannot be sent in covers of this kind, may be posted enclosed in boxes, or in bags of linen, or other material, fastened in such a manner that they may be readily opened.

5. There must be no writing or printing upon or in any sample packet except the address of the person for whom it is intended, the address of the sender, a trade mark or number, and the price of the articles. But a packet for any country in the Postal Union may have enclosed in it any of the articles designated as "Commercial Papers" if the rate applicable to Commercial Papers be paid for the whole packet.

6. Samples of saleable value must not be sent to any foreign country, or to any of the British Possessions which are comprised in the Postal Union. Samples of eider down, raw or thread silk, woollen or goats' hair thread, vanilla, saffron, or isinglass, are considered to fall under this rule, if they weigh more than three ounces.

7. Such articles as scissors, knives, razors, forks, steel pens, nails, keys, watch machinery, metal tubing, pieces of metal or ore, provided that they be packed and guarded in so secure a manner as to afford complete protection to the contents of the mail bags and to the Officers of the Post Office, while at the same time they may be easily examined, may be sent as samples to places abroad. Liquids, indigo, and powders of all kinds are absolutely prohibited.

8. The limit of weight is not the same to all countries. For particulars see paragraph 7 of Newspaper Regulations.

9. A packet of Patterns or Samples sent to any place comprised in the Postal Union (except Belgium, France, Greece, Italy, Japan, Luxemburg, Portugal, Switzerland *via* France, the Argentine Republic, and the United States) must not exceed 8 inches in length, 4 in width, or 2 in depth. The limit to the excepted places is 12 inches in length, 8 in width, and 4 in depth. The size of a packet for a non-Union country or colony is the same as for Book Post.

## PARCEL POST TO UNITED KINGDOM, BRITISH COLONIES AND FOREIGN COUNTRIES.

Parcels for dispatch by Outward English Mail must reach the General Post Office, Port-of-Spain, not later than 4 P.M. on the day preceding the departure of the Mail.

NOTE.—The Post Cards, Registered Letter Envelopes and Newspaper Wrappers are sold to the Public at face value.

From 1 January 1892 a uniform overseas rate of ½d. per 2 ozs. was applied for Newspapers, Books, Patterns (minimum 1d.) and Commercial Papers (minimum 2½d.) irrespective of whether the country was a member of the U.P.U.

On 20 August 1896 the late fees at the G.P.O. were changed:-

| | | |
|---|---|---|
| up to 3 p.m. | . . . . . . . . | 1d. |
| up to 3.30 p.m. | . . . . . . . . | 2½d. |
| up to 4 p.m. | . . . . . . . . | 5d. |

Trinidad joined the Empire Penny Post Scheme at it's inauguration on 25 December 1898 when it published a complete list of rates:-

# POST OFFICE NOTICE.

On and from December 25th, 1898, the following Rates of Postage will be charged on letters forwarded to the undermentioned places from Trinidad and Tobago :—

### 1d. per ½ oz. to—

| | | | |
|---|---|---|---|
| Antigua | Fiji | Lagos | St. Helena |
| Canada | Gambia | Montserrat | St. Lucia |
| Ceylon | Gibraltar | Nevis | St. Vincent |
| Cyprus | Gold Coast | Seychelles | St. Kitts |
| Dominica | Grenada | Sierra Leone | Turks Island |
| Falkland Islands | Hong Kong | Straits Settlements | United Kingdom |
| | | | Virgin Islands |

### 2½d. per ½ oz. to—

*Aden
*Argentine Republic
*Ascension
*Australia
*Austria-Hungary
*Azores
*Bahamas
*Barbados
*Belgium
*Bermuda
*Bolivia
*Bosnia
*Brazil
*British Borneo
British East Africa
*British Guiana
*British Honduras
*British New Guinea
*Bulgaria
Cape Colony (including Basutoland, British Bechuanaland, Pondoland, Griqualand East, Griqualand West, Namaqualand (Little), St. John's River Territory, Transkei, Tembuland, Walwich Bay)
*Cameroons
*Chili
*Colombia, Republic of
*Congo, including Black Point, Majumba and Nyanza
*Costa Rica
*Danish Colonies ; viz.— Greenland, St. Croix, Saint John, and Saint Thomas
*Denmark (including Faroe Islands and Iceland)
*Dominican Republic (San Domingo)
*Ecuador
*Egypt
*France
*French Colonies ; viz. Martinique, Guadeloupe and dependen-

cies, French Guiana (Cayenne), Senegal and dependencies, Ahgwey, Gaboon, Grand Bassam, Half Jack and Wydah (also Sette Cama and Assinie), Réunion, Comoro Islands, Mayotte & dependencies. French Establishments in Madagascar, viz. :—Ambosi-tra, Andevovante, Antananarivo, Diego Suarez, Fenerive, Fiaranantsoa, Foulpointe, Ivondro, Maevatanana, Mahambo, Mahanoro, Manoia, Maintirano, Majunga, Mananjary, Morandava, Morotsangana. Nossi-Vé, St. Mary, Tamatave, Vatomandry, Vohemar, New Caledonia and dependencies, the French portion of the Low Archipelago, and the French Establishments in India, Pondichéry, Chandernagor, Karikal, Mahé, and Yanoan), Annan, Cambodge, Tonkin, and in Cochin China. French Establishments in Morocco, viz. :—Casablanca, El-Ksar-el-Kbir, Fez Laraiche. Mazagan, Mogador, Rabat, Safii and Tangier
*Germany
German Colonies : viz. —Marshall Islands, New Guinea (portion of), Samoa (Apia). Togo Territory, including Bagei-da, Little Popo, Lome and Porto Seguro, and territory in South West Africa, viz. Grand Namaqua, the Damaras Country, and Southern

portion of Ovambo ; also Bagamoyo, and Dar-es-Salaam, Lindi and Tanga in East Africa
*Greece
*Guatemala
*Hawaiian (or Sandwich) Islands
*Hayti
*Herzegovina
*Honduras (Republic of)
Hong Kong
*India
*Italy
*Jamaica
*Japan
*Labuan
*Liberia
*Luxemburg
*Madeira
*Malta
*Marquesas Islands
*Mauritius and dependencies
*Mexico
*Montenegro
*Natal (including Zululand)
*Netherlands

*Netherlands Colonies, viz. — Dutch Guiana (Surinam), Curacao and dependencies, viz.— Bonaire, Aruba, the Netherlands portion of St. Martin, St. Eustache, Saba, Java, Madura, Sumatra, Celebes, Borneo, (except North-west part), Billiton, Archipelago of Banca, Archipelago of Riouw, Sunda Islands (Bali, Lombok, Sumbawa, Floris, and the South-west part of Timor), the Archipelago of the Moluccas, and the North-west part of New Guinea (Papua)
*Newfoundland

*New Zealand
*Nicaragua
*Norway
*Orange Free State
*Paraguay
*Patagonia
*Persia
*Peru
*Portugal
*Portuguese Colonies ; viz. Goa and its dependencies (Damoa and Diu), Mocao, Timor, Cape Verde Islands and dependencies (Bissau and Cacheu) Cabenda, Mucull a Mussera and islands or St. Thomas and Prince (in Africa) with the establishment of Ajuda, Angola, Delagoa Bay, and Mozambique
*Roumania
*Russia
*St. Pierre-et-Miquelon
*Salvador
*Sandwich (or Hawaiian) Islands
*Sarawak
*Servia
*Siam
*South African Republic (Transvaal)
*Spain (including Balearic and Canary Islands)
*Spanish Colonies, viz. :— Cuba, Porto Rico, Fernando Po, Annobon and dependencies, Philippine Islands and Marian Islands
*Sweden
*Switzerland
*Tahiti
*Tortola
*Turkey
*United States
*Uruguay
*Venezuela
*Zanzibar

## LETTERS.

Unpaid letters to or from Postal Union Countries are charged double the prepaid rate. Partially prepaid letters are charged with double the deficiency.

2. No letter for a Colony or Foreign Country may exceed two feet in length or one foot in width or depth.

---

* The transmission by Letter post of Coin, Gold, Silver, precious Stones or Jewellery, &c., is prohibited to those Countries marked thus*

3. Letters not specially directed by a particular route are, as a rule, forwarded by the first Mail dispatched.

4. The addresses of letters for Russia should be very plainly written ; the name of the Town, and of the Province in which it is situated, should also be added in English, French or German.

## POST CARDS.

1. Official Post Cards, single and reply, are transmissible to all parts of the World. Single cards are issued with impressed stamps of 1d., and Reply Cards bearing stamps of the value of 1d. on each half.

2. Inland Post Cards are also transmissible abroad if the additional postage required is supplied by means of postage stamps affixed to the cards.

## PRIVATE POST CARDS.

1. Private Post Cards bearing adhesive stamps of the value of one penny, and private reply cards with adhesive stamps of the value of one penny on each half, may be sent as post cards to places abroad, provided that they are in conformity with the official post cards. They must be of the same size and substance as the official cards, and must have the words " Post Card" printed or written on the address side, without the Royal arms.

2. The reply halves of private double cards must bear in print or writing the words " Post Card—Great Britain and Ireland" and " Reply."

3. *Plain cards without any printed or written inscription cannot be sent abroad as Single or Reply Post Cards.*

4. Engravings or advertisements may in future be printed on the face as well as on the back of a post card. They must not, however, interfere in any way with the clear indication of the address or with the stamping and marking of the postal service. Addresses of Post Cards may be written by hand or be shown upon a gummed label not exceeding two centimetres by five

5. Except stamps for prepayment and the labels mentioned above it is forbidden to join or attach to post cards any article whatsoever.

6. Post Cards may not exceed the following dimensions : length, 14 centimetres, width, 9 centimetres.

7. The sender of a post card with reply paid may indicate his name and address on the face of the "Reply" half, either in writing or by sticking a label on it.

## COMMERCIAL PAPERS.

1. The rate of postage for commercial papers is the same as for printed papers *except that the lowest charge is* 2½d.

2. The following are considered as commercial papers and allowed to pass as such at the reduced postage, viz.: ½d. for every two ounces—viz.: all papers and documents whether writings or drawings, produced wholly or partly by hand not having the character of an actual and personal correspondence, such as papers of legal procedure, deeds of all kinds drawn up by public functionaries, way-bills or bills of lading, invoices, the various documents of Insurance Companies, copies of or extracts from acts under private signature, written on stamped or unstamped paper, musical scores or sheets of music in manuscript, the manuscripts of works or of newspapers, forwarded separately, pupils exercises with corrections but without any comment on the work, &c.

3. Commercial papers are subject, so far as regards form and conditions of transmission, to the regulations, prescribed for printed papers.

Commercial papers must not exceed more than 4 lbs. in weight or measure more in any direction than 18 inches. In the form of a roll commercial papers 30 inches in length and 4 inches in diameter may be forwarded.

## SAMPLES.

1. Samples of merchandise are only allowed to pass at the reduced postage which is fixed for them under the following conditions.

2. They must be placed in bags, boxes, or removable envelopes, in such manner as to admit of easy inspection.

3. They must possess no saleable value nor bear any writing, except the name or the commercial style of the sender, the address of the person for whom they are intended, a manufacturer's or trade mark, numbers, prices, and indications relative to weight or measurement, and demensions or to the quantity to be disposed of, or such as are necessary to determine the origin and the nature of the goods. Articles of

glass, packets containing liquids, oils, fatty substances, dry powders, whether dyes or not, as well as packets of live bees, may be admitted to transmission as samples of merchandise, provided that they be packed in the following manner.:—

1. Articles of glass must be securely packed (boxes of metal, wood, leather or card board) in a way to prevent all danger to the correspondence and Postal Officers.

2. Liquids, oils, and fatty substances easily liquified must be enclosed in glass bottles hermetically sealed. Each bottle must be placed in a wooden box furnished with sawdust, cotton, or spongy material in sufficient quantity to absorb the liquid in case the bottle be broken. Finally, the box itself must be enclosed, in a case of metal, of wood with a screw top, or of strong and thick leather.

3. Fatty substances which are not easily liquified, such as ointments, soft soap, resin, &c., the transmission of which offers less inconvenience, must be enclosed in an inner cover (box, bag, of linen or parchment, &c.) which must itself be placed in a second box of wood, metal or strong and thick leather.

4. Dry powders, whether dyes or not, must be placed in cardboard boxes, which themselves are enclosed in a bag of linen or parchment.

5. Live bees must be enclosed in boxes so constructed as to avoid all danger and to allow the contents to be ascertained.

Transmission at the sample rate is likewise accorded to articles of natural history, dried or preserved animals and plants, geological specimens, &c., when sent for no commercial purpose and packed in accordance with the general regulations concerning samples of merchandise.

A packet of samples may not exceed 12 ounces in weight, 12 inches in length, 8 inches in breadth, and 4 inches in depth.

## SPECIAL EXCEPTIONS FOR THE UNITED KINGDOM.

The following articles specifically defined in the British Customs tariff as chargeable with duty either as being pure spirit or as containing spirits, or into the manufacture of which spirit has entered cannot be transmitted by sample post to the United Kingdom, viz.:—

### LIQUIDS.

| | | |
|---|---|---|
| Perfumed Spirits. | Ether Butyric. | Ethyl, Bromide. |
| Chloroform. | Ether Sulphuric. | Wine. |
| Collodion. | Ethyl, Sodide of. | Beer. |
| Ether, Acetic. | Ethyl, Chloride. | |

### OTHER THAN LIQUIDS.

Chlorate Hydrate.
Confectionery in the manufacture of which Spirit has been used.
Transparent Soap in the manufacture of which Spirit has been used.

## PRINTED PAPERS OF EVERY KIND—(½d for 2 ozs.)

1. The following are considered as printed papers and allowed to pass as such at the reduced postage: Newspapers and periodical works; books, stitched or bound; pamphlets; sheets of music; visiting cards; address cards; proofs of printing, with or without the manuscripts relating thereto; papers impressed with prints in relief for the use of the blind; engravings; photographs; and albums containing photographs, pictures, drawings, plans, maps, catalogues, prospectuses, announcements, and notices of various kinds; printed, engraved, lithographed or otographed, and in general, all impressions or copies obtained upon paper, parchment, or cardboard, by means of printing, engraving, lithography, orthography, or any other mechanical process, easy to recognise, except the copying press and the type writer. To printed papers are assimilated reproductions of a manuscript or type-written original when they are obtained by a mechanical process of polygraphy (chromography, &c.,) but, in order to pass at the reduced postage, these reproductions must be brought to the Post Office counter and must number at least twenty copies precisely identical.

2. Stamps for prepayment, whether obliterated or not, and all printed articles constituting the sign of a monetary value are excluded from transmission at the reduced postage.

3. Printed papers of which the text has been modified after printing, either by hand, or by means of a mechanical process, or bears any marks whatever, capable of constituting a conventional language, cannot be sent at the reduced rate.

4. By way of exception to the rule laid down by the preceding paragraph it is allowed—

(a.) To indicate on the outside of the missive the name, commercial style, and the address of the sender.

(b.) To add in manuscript on printed visiting cards, the address of the sender, his title as well as good wishes, congratulations, thanks, condolences or other formulas of courtesy, expressed in five words at most or by means of conventional initials (p. f. &c.).

(c.) To indicate or to alter in a printed paper in manuscript or by a mechanical process the date of despatch, the signature or the commercial style and the profession, as well as the address of the sender.

(d.) To enclose the "copy" with corrected proofs, and to make in those proofs alterations and additions which relate to accuracy, form, and printing. In case of want of space, these additions may be made on separate sheets.

(e.) To correct also errors in printing in printed documents other than proofs.

(f.) To erase certain parts of a printed text in order to render them illegible.

(g.) To make prominent by means of marks, and to underline words or passages of the text to which it is desired to draw attention.

(h.) To insert or correct in manuscript or by a mechanical process, figures in prices current, tenders for advertisements, stock and share lists, trades circulars, and prospectuses as well as the travellers name and the date and place of his intended visit, in travellers announcements.

(i.) To indicate in manuscript, in advices of the departures of ships, the dates of those departures :

(k.) To indicate in cards of invitation and notices of meetings, the names of persons invited, the date, the object, and the place of gathering ;

(l.) To add a dedication on books, sheets of music, newspapers, photographs and engravings, Christmas and New Year cards, as well as to enclose the relative invoice ;

(m.) In forms of order or subscription for books, newspapers, engravings, pieces of music ; to indicate in manuscript the works required or offered, and to erase or underline the whole or part of the printed communications ;

(n.) To paint fashion plates, maps, &c. ;

(o.) To add, in manuscript or by a mechanical process, to cuttings from newspapers and periodical publications, the title, date, number and address of the publication from which the article is extracted. Save the exceptions explicitly authorised herein, additions made in manuscript or by means of a mechanical process, which would deprive a printed paper of its general character and give it that of individual correspondence, are forbidden.

5. Printed papers must be either placed in wrappers, upon rollers, between boards, in cases open at both sides or at both ends, or in unclosed envelopes, or simply folded in such a manner as not to conceal the nature of the packet or lastly, tied with a string easy to unfasten. Address cards, and all printed matter of the form and substance of an unfolded card may be forwarded without wrapper, envelope, fastening, or fold. The face is reserved for postage stamps, for indications relating to the postal service, and for the address. The sender is allowed to indicate on it his name, calling, and address, by means of a stamp, autograph stamps, or other typographic process. Book orders may also bear the printed indication " Book Order Form " or " Order for Books." Cards, bearing the inscription " Post Card " are not allowed to go at the rate for printed matter.

The rate of postage for printed papers, Books of every kind is ½d. for any weight not exceeding 2 ounces, and ½d. for each additional 2 ounces.

No packet of printed papers or books may exceed 4 lbs. in weight, 18 inches in length, 12 inches in width or depth.

*Parcel Post.*—1. From the date mentioned above (25th December, 1898) the following rates of postage on parcels will come into operation upon all parcels forwarded to the undermentioned places, viz.:—

| | | | |
|---|---|---|---|
| Antigua | Gibraltar | Nevis | St. Vincent |
| Ceylon | Gold Coast | Seychelles | St. Kitts |
| Dominica | Grenada | Sierra Leone | Turks Island |
| Falkland Islands | Hong Kong | Straits Settlements | United Kingdom |
| Fiji | Lagos | St. Helena | Virgin Islands. |
| Gambia | Montserrat | St. Lucia | |

| | | | |
|---|---|---|---|
| A parcel weighing not over 3 lbs. | ... | ... | 1/- |
| Over 3 but not over 7 lbs. | ... | ... | 2/- |
| Over 7 but not over 11 lbs. | ... | ... | 3/- |

2. To all places not mentioned in the above list the present rates of postage on parcels will continue in force.

*Registration.*—1. The fee for registration is 2d. To some Countries an article can be registered only to the port of arrival; it being left in those cases, to the postal authorities of the Country to which that port belongs to continue the registration or not as they may think proper. To Madagascar there is no arrangement whatever for registration.

2. Registration is applicable equally to letters, post cards, newspapers, book packets and patterns addressed to places abroad.

3. The Sender of a registered article addressed to any Foreign Country or British Colony in the Postal Union may obtain an acknowledgment of its due receipt by the addressee on paying a fee of 2½d. as well as the registration fee in advance at the time of registration.

4. No article addressed to initials or a fictitious name can be registered. The prohibition, however, does not extend to articles addressed to the care of a person or firm.

5. Every letter presented for registration must be enclosed in a strong envelope securely fastened.

6. It is prohibited to send to a Country of the Postal Union any registered article marked on the outside with the declared value of the contents; and Postmasters will therefore refuse to receive articles which are so marked.

7. Registered articles must be prepaid as regards both postage and registration fee.

8. Articles to be registered must be given to an agent of the Post Office, and a receipt obtained for them; they should on no account be dropped into a Letter box.

9. It is forbidden to send coin, jewellery or precious articles through the Post to Countries of the Postal Union. No letters or packets containing such articles can be accepted for registration.

10. The several Postal Administrations of the Countries belonging to the Postal Union undertake to pay an indemnity of fifty francs in the event of its being proved to their satisfaction that a registered letter itself has been lost whilst in their custody, but no question of compensation is entertained by them for, or in respect of, the loss of the enclosure of any such letter.

## PARCEL POST TO UNITED KINGDOM, BRITISH COLONIES AND FOREIGN COUNTRIES.

Parcels for despatch by outward English Mail must reach the General Post Office, Port-of-Spain, not later than 4 p.m. on the day preceding the departure of the Mail.

NOTE.—The Post Cards, Registered Letter Envelopes and Newspaper Wrappers are sold to the public at face value.

J. A. BULMER,
Postmaster-General.

GENERAL POST OFFICE,
Trinidad, 11th October, 1898.

———

Laid before the Legislative Council at its Meeting on 31st October, 1898.

C. J. ROOKS,
Acting Clerk of Council.

This was shortly followed by another list of rates and regulations, effective 1 May 1899:-

# FOREIGN AND COLONIAL.

## LETTERS.

### At 1d. Per ½ oz. to—

Aden.
Antigua.
Ascension.
Bahama Islands.
Barbados.
Bermuda.
British Central Africa.
British East Africa.
British Guiana.
British Honduras.
British India.
Canada.
Ceylon.
Cyprus.
Dominica.
Falkland Islands.
Federated Malay States.
Fiji.
Gambia.
Gibraltar.
Gold Coast Colony.
Grenada.
Hong Kong.
Jahore.
Lagos.
Montserrat.
Natal.
Nevis.
Newfoundland.
Niger Coast Protectorate.
Niger Coast Territory.
Sarawak.
Seychelles.
Sierra Leone.
Straits Settlements.
St. Helena.
St. Kitts.
St. Lucia.
St. Vincent.
Turks Island.
Uganda.
United Kingdom.
Virgin Islands.
Zanzibar.

### At 2½d. per ½ oz. to—

Argentine Republic
*Australia*
Austria-Hungary
*Azores*
Belgium
Bolivia
Bosnia
Brazil
*British Borneo*
*British New Guinea*
Bulgaria
  *Cape Colony* (including Basutoland, British Bechuanaland, Pondoland, Griqualand East, Griqualand West, Namaqualand (Little), St. John's River Territory, Transkei, Tembuland, Walwick Bay)
Cameroons
Chili
Colombia, Republic of Congo, including Black Point, Majumba and Nyanza
Costa Rica
Danish Colonies; viz.—Greenland, St. Croix, St. John, and Saint Thomas
Denmark (including Faroe Islands and Iceland)
Dominican Republic (San Domingo)
Ecuador
Egypt
France
French Colonies: viz. Martinique, Guadeloupe and dependencies French Guiana (Cayenne), Senegal and dependencies, Aligwey, Gaboon, Grand Bassam, Half Jack and Wydah (also Sette Cama and Assinie), Rénnion, Comoro Islands, Mayotte and dependencies. French Establishments in Madagascar, viz.: Ambositra, Andevorante, Antananarivo, Diego Suarez, Feuerive, Fiaramntsoa, Foulpointe, Ivondro, Maevatanana, Mahatobo, Mahanoro, Mahela, Maintirano, Majunga, Mananjary, Morandava, Morotsangana Nossi-Vé, St. Mary, Tamatave, Vatomandry, Vohemar, New Caledonia and dependencies, the French portion of the Low Archipelago, and the French Establishments in India, Pondichéry, Chandernagor, Karikal, Mahe, and Yanaon Annan, Cambodge, Tonkin, and in Cochin China, French Establishments in Morocco, viz.:—Casablanca, El-Ksar-el-Kbir, Fez Laraiche Mazagan, Mogador, Rabat, Saffi and Tangier
Germany.
German Colonies: viz.—Marshall Islands, New Guinea (portion of), Samoa (Apia), Togo Territory, including Bageida, Little Popo, Lome and Porto Seguro, and territory in South West Africa, viz. Grand Namaqua, the Damaras Country, and Southern portion of Ovambo; also Bagamoyo, and Dar-es-Salaam, Lindi and Tanga in East Africa
Greece
Guatemala
Hawaiian (or Sandwich) Islands
Hayti
Herzegovina
Honduras (Republic of
Italy
*Jamaica*
Japan
*Labuan*
Liberia
Luxemburg
Madeira
*Malta*
Marquesas Islands
*Mauritius and Dependencies*
Mexico
Montenegro
Netherlands
Netherlands Colonies, viz.—Dutch Guiana (Surinam), Curacao and dependencies, viz.—Bonaire, Aruba, the Netherlands portion of St. Martin, St. Eustache, Saba, Java, Madura, Sumatra, Celebes, Borneo, (except North-west part), Billiton, Archipelago of Banca, Archipelago of Rhouw, Islands (Bali, Lombok, Sumbawa, Floris, and the South-west part of Timor), the Archipelago of the Moluccas, and the North-west part of New Guinea (Papua)
*New Zealand*
Nicaragua
Norway
Orange Free State
Paraguay
Patagonia
Persia
Peru
Portugal
Portuguese Colonies: viz.:—Goa and its dependencies (Damao and Diu), Macao, Timor. Cape Verde Islands and dependencies (Bissao & Cacheu) Cabenda, Muculla, Mussamdia Islands of St. Thomas & Prince (in Africa) with the establishment of Ajuda, Angola, Delagoa Bay, and Mozambique
Roumania
Russia
St. Pierre-et-Miquelon
Salvador
Sandwich (or Hawaii) Islands
Servia
Siam
South African Republic (Transvaal)
Spain (including Balearic Islands, Canary Islands)
Spanish Colonies
Porto Rico
Annobon
Philippine Islands and Islands
Sweden
Switzerland
Tahiti
Turkey
United States
Uruguay
Venezuela

## LETTERS.

Unpaid letters to or from Postal Union Countries are charged double the prepaid rate. Partially prepaid letters are charged with double the deficiency.

2. No letter for a Colony or Foreign Country may exceed two feet in length or one foot in width or depth.

3. Letters not specially directed by a particular route are, as a rule, forwarded by the first Mail dispatched.

4. The addresses of letters for Russia should be very plainly written ; the name of the Town, and of the Province in which it is situated, should also be added in English, French or German.

The transmission by Coin, Gold, Silver, precious Stones or Jewellery, &c., is prohibited.

## POST CARDS.

1. Official Post Cards, single and reply, are transmissible to all parts of the World. Single cards are issued with impressed stamps of 1d., and reply Cards bearing stamps of the value of 1d., on each half.

2. Inland Post Cards are also transmissible abroad if the additional postage required is supplied by means of postage stamps affixed to the cards.

## PRIVATE POST CARDS.

1. Private Post Cards bearing adhesive stamps of the value of one penny, and private reply cards with adhesive stamps of the value of one penny on each half, may be sent as post cards to places abroad, provided that they are in conformity with the official post cards. They must be of the same size and substance as the official cards, and must have the words " Post Card " printed or written on the address side, without the Royal arms.

2. The reply halves of private double cards must bear in print or writing the words " Post Card—Great Britain and Ireland " and " Reply."

3. *Plain cards without any printed or written inscription cannot be sent abroad as Single or Reply Post Cards.*

4. Engravings or advertisements may in future be printed on the face as well as on the back of a post card. They must not, however, interfere in any way with the clear indication of the address or with the stamping and marking of the postal service. Addresses of Post Cards may be written by hand or be shown upon a gummed label not exceeding two centimetres by five.

5. Except stamps for prepayment and the labels mentioned above it is forbidden to join or attach to post cards any article whatsoever.

6. Post Cards may not exceed the following dimensions : length, 14 centimetres, width, 9 centimetres.

7. The sender of a post card with reply paid may indicate his name and address on the face of the " Reply " half, either by writing or by sticking a label on it.

## COMMERCIAL PAPERS.

1. The rate of postage for commercial papers is the same as for printed papers *except that the lowest charge is* 2½d. for that sum however 10 oz. may be sent.

2. The following are considered as commercial papers and allowed to pass as such at the reduced postage, viz. : ½d. for every two ounces—viz. : all papers and documents whether writings or drawings, produced wholly or partly by hand not having the character of an actual and personal correspondence, such as papers of legal procedure, deeds of all kinds drawn up by public functionaries, way-bills or bills of lading, invoices, the various documents of Insurance Companies, copies of or extracts from acts under private signature, written on stamped or unstamped paper, musical scores or sheets of music in manuscript, the manuscripts of works or of newspapers, forwarded separately, pupils exercises with corrections but without any comment on the work, &c.

3. Commercial papers are subject, so far as regards form and conditions of transmission, to the regulations, prescribed for printed papers.

Commercial papers must not exceed more than 4 lbs. in weight, or measure more in any direction than 18 inches. In the form of a roll commercial papers 30 inches in length and 4 inches in diameter may be forwarded.

## SAMPLES.

1. Samples of merchandise are only allowed to pass at the reduced postage which is fixed for them under the following conditions.

2. They must be placed in bags, boxes, or removable envelopes, in such manner as to admit of easy inspection.

3. They must possess no saleable value nor bear any writing, except the name or the commercial style of the sender, the address of the person for whom they are intended, a manufacturer's or trade mark, numbers, prices, and indications relative to weight or measurement, and dimensions or to the quantity to be disposed of, or such as are necessary to determine the origin and the nature of the goods. Articles of glass, packets containing liquids, oils, fatty substances, dry powders, whether dyes or not, as well as packets of live bees, may be admitted to transmission as samples of merchandise, provided that they be packed in the following manner :—

1. Articles of glass must be securely packed (boxes of metal, wood, leather or card board) in a way to prevent all danger to the correspondence and Postal Officers.

2. Liquids, oils, and fatty substances easily liquified must be enclosed in glass bottles hermetically sealed. Each bottle must be placed in a wooden box furnished with sawdust, cotton, or spongy material in sufficient quantity to absorb the liquid in case the bottle be broken. Finally, the box itself must be enclosed, in a case of metal, of wood with a screw top, or of strong and thick leather.

3. Fatty substances which are not easily liquified, such as ointments, soft soap, resin, &c., the transmission of which offers less inconvenience, must be enclosed in an inner cover (box, bag, of linen or parchment, &c.) which must itself be placed in a second box of wood, metal or strong and thick leather.

4. Dry powders, whether dyes or not, must be placed in cardboard boxes, which themselves are enclosed in a bag of linen or parchment.

5. Live bees must be enclosed in boxes so constructed as to avoid all danger and to allow the contents to be ascertained.

Transmission at the sample rate is likewise accorded to articles of natural history, dried or preserved animals and plants, geological specimens, &c., when sent for no commercial purpose and packed in accordance with the general regulations concerning samples of merchandise.

A packet of samples may not exceed 12 ounces in weight, 12 inches in length, 8 inches in breadth, and 4 inches in depth.

## SPECIAL EXCEPTIONS FOR THE UNITED KINGDOM.

The following articles specifically defined in the British Customs tariff as chargeable with duty either as being pure spirit or as containing spirits, or into the manufacture of which spirit has entered cannot be transmitted by sample post to the United Kingdom, viz.:—

LIQUIDS.

Perfumed Spirits.
Chloroform.
Collodion.
Ether, Acetic

Ether Butyric.
Ether Sulphuric.
Ethyl, Sodide of
Ethyl, Chloride.

Ethyl, Bromide.
Wine.
Beer.

OTHER THAN LIQUIDS.

Chlorate Hydrate.
Confectionery in the manufacture of which Spirit has been used.
Transparent Soap in the manufacture of which Spirit has been used.

## PRINTED PAPERS OF EVERY KIND—(½d. for 2 ozs.)

1. The following are considered as printed papers and allowed to pass as such at the reduced postage : Newspapers and periodical works ; books, stitched or bound ; pamphlets ; sheets of music ; visiting cards ; address cards ; proofs of printing, with or without the manuscripts relating thereto ; papers impressed with prints in relief for the use of the blind ; engravings ; photographs ; and albums containing photographs, pictures, drawings, plans, maps, catalogues, prospectuses, announcements, and notices of various kinds ; printed, engraved, lithographed or otographed, and in general, all impressions or copies obtained upon paper, parchment, or cardboard, by means of printing, engraving, lithography, orthography, or any other mechanical process, easy to recognise, except the copying press and the type writer. To printed papers are assimilated reproductions of a manuscript or type-written original when they are obtained by a mechanical process of polygraphy (chromography, &c.,) but, in order to pass at the reduced postage, these reproductions must be brought to the Post Office counter and must number at least twenty copies precisely identical.

2. Stamps for prepayment, whether obliterated or not, and all printed articles constituting the sign of a monetary value are excluded from transmission at the reduced postage.

3. Printed papers of which the text has been modified after printing, either by hand, or by means of a mechanical process, or bears any marks whatever, capable of constituting a conventional language, cannot be sent at the reduced rate.

4. By way of exception to the rule laid down by the preceding paragraph it is allowed—

(a.) To indicate on the outside of the missive the name, commercial style, and the address of the sender.

(b.) To add in manuscript on printed visiting cards, the address of the sender, his title as well as good wishes, congratulations, thanks, condolences or other formulas of courtesy, expressed in five words at most or by means of conventional initials (p. f. &c.).

(c.) To indicate or to alter in a printed paper in manuscript or by a mechanical process the date of despatch, the signature or the commercial style and the profession, as well as the address of the sender.

(d.) To enclose the "copy" with corrected proofs, and to make in those proofs alterations and additions which relate to accuracy, form, and printing. In case of want of space, these additions may be made on separate sheets.

(e.) To correct also errors in printing in printed documents other than proofs.

(f.) To erase certain parts of a printed text in order to render them illegible.

(g.) To make prominent by means of marks, and to underline words or passages of the text to which it is desired to draw attention.

(*h.*) To insert or correct in manuscript or by a mechanical process, figures in prices current, tenders for advertisements, stock and share lists, trades circulars, and prospectuses as well as the travellers name and the date and place of his intended visit, in travellers announcements.

(*i.*) To indicate in manuscript, in advices of the departures of ships, the dates of those departures;

(*k.*) To indicate in cards of invitation and notices of meetings, the names of persons invited, the date, the object, and the place of gathering;

(*l.*) To add a dedication on books, sheets of music, newspapers, photographs and engravings, Christmas and New Year cards, as well as to enclose the relative invoice;

(*m.*) In forms of order or subscription for books, newspapers, engravings, pieces of music; to indicate in manuscript the works required or offered, and to erase or underline the whole or part of the printed communications;

(*n.*) To paint fashion plates, maps, &c.;

(*o.*) To add, in manuscript or by a mechanical process, to cuttings from newspapers and periodical publications, the title, date, number and address of the publication from which the article is extracted. Save the exceptions explicitly authorised herein, additions made in manuscript or by means of a mechanical process, which would deprive a printed paper of its general character and give it that of individual correspondence, are forbidden.

5. Printed papers must be either placed in wrappers, upon rollers, between boards, in cases open at both sides or at both ends, or in unclosed envelopes, or simply folded in such a manner as not to conceal the nature of the packet or lastly, tied with a string easy to unfasten. Address cards, and all printed matter of the form and substance of an unfolded card may be forwarded without wrapper, envelope, fastening, or fold. The face is reserved for postage stamps, for indications relating to the postal service, and for the address. The sender is allowed to indicate on it his name, calling, and address, by means of a stamp, autograph stamps, or other typographic process. Book orders may also bear the printed indication "Book Order Form" or "Order for Books." Cards, bearing the inscription "Post Card" are not allowed to go at the rate for printed matter.

The rate of postage for printed papers, Books of every kind is ½d. for any weight not exceeding 2 ounces, and ½d. for each additional 2 ounces.

No packet of printed papers or books may exceed 4 lbs. in weight, 18 inches in length, 12 inches in width or depth.

## PARCEL POST.

1. From the date mentioned above (1st May, 1899) the following rates of postage on parcels will come into operation upon all parcels forwarded to the undermentioned places, vizt.:—

| Antigua | Montserrat | Turks Island |
|---|---|---|
| Barbados | Nevis | United Kingdom |
| British Guiana | St. Lucia | Virgin Islands |
| Dominica | St. Vincent | |
| Grenada | St. Kitts | |

| | | | | | |
|---|---|---|---|---|---|
| A parcel weighing not over 3 lbs. | ... | ... | ... | 1/- |
| Over 3 but not over | 7 lbs. | ... | ... | .. 2/- |
| Over 7 but not over | 11 lbs. | ... | ... | ... 3/- |

2. To all places not mentioned in the above list the present rates of postage on parcels will continue in force.

*Registration.*—1. The fee for registration is 2d. To some countries an article can be registered only to the port of arrival; it being left in those cases, to the postal authorities of the Country to which that port belongs to continue the registration or not as they may think proper. To Madagascar there is no arrangement whatever for registration.

2. Registration is applicable equally to letters, post cards, newspapers, book packets and patterns addressed to places abroad.

3 The Sender of a registered article addressed to any Foreign Country or British Colony in the Postal Union may obtain an acknowledgment of its due receipt by the addressee on paying a fee of 2½d. as well as the registration fee in advance at the time of registration.

4. No article addressed to initials or a fictitious name can be registered. The prohibition, however, does not extend to articles addressed to the care of a person or firm.

5. Every letter presented for registration must be enclosed in a strong envelope securely fastened.

6. It is prohibited to send to a Country of the Postal Union any registered article marked on the outside with the declared value of the contents; and Postmasters will therefore refuse to receive articles which are so marked.

7. Registered articles must be prepaid as regards both postage and registration fee.

8. Articles to be registered must be given to an agent of the Post Office, and a receipt obtained for them; they should on no account be dropped into a Letter Box.

9. It is forbidden to send coin, jewellery or precious articles through the Post. No letters or packets containing such articles can be accepted for registration.

10. The several Postal Administrations of the Countries belonging to the Postal Union undertake to pay an indemnity of fifty francs in the event of its being proved to their satisfaction that a registered letter itself has been lost whilst in their custody, but no question of compensation is entertained by them for, or in respect of, the loss of the enclosure of any such letter.

## PARCEL POST TO UNITED KINGDOM, BRITISH COLONIES AND FOREIGN COUNTRIES.

Parcels for despatch by outward English Mail must reach the General Post Office, Port-of-Spain, not later than 4 p.m. on the day preceding the departure of the Mail.

---

The undermentioned Postage Stamps, Post Cards, Registered Envelopes, and Newspaper Wrappers are sold to the public viz. :—

| ½d. Postage Stamps. | | | Registered Envelopes F. |
|---|---|---|---|
| 1 | ,, | ,, | ,,      ,,      G. |
| 2 | ,, | ,, | ½d. Post Cards, Single. |
| 2½ | ,, | ,, | 1d. ,,    ,,    ,, |
| 4 | ,, | ,, | 1d. ,,    ,,    Double. |
| 5 | ,, | ,, | ½d. Newspaper Wrappers. |
| 6 | ,, | ,, | 1d. ,,        ,, |
| 1/- | ,, | ,, | |
| 5/- | ,, | ,, | |
| 10/- | ,, | ,, | |
| 20/- | ,, | ,, | |

All Post Cards, Registered Envelopes and Newspaper Wrappers are sold to the public at face value.

---

## INLAND.

There are house-to-house deliveries of letters in Port-of-Spain every day, except Sundays and Public Holidays, at 7 a.m., 10 a.m. and 2 p.m. On Public Holidays there is only 7 a.m. delivery.

Letters to or from public offices are exempt from postage if on the public business of the office, and bearing on the envelope the words "On Her Majesty's Service," and in the bottom left hand corner the signature of the writer, with the designation of the office from which sent.

### 2. INLAND RATES.

*Letters :* Not exceeding ½ oz., 1d. Every additional ½ oz., 1d. No letter, unless it be sent to or from a Government Office, to exceed 2 lbs. in weight, 18 inches in length, and 9 inches in width or depth.

*Newspapers, Circulars, and Prices Current :* For each, not exceeding 4 ozs., ½d. A packet containing two or more Newspapers, Circulars or Prices Current is not liable to a higher rate than the Book Postage would be, viz. :—Under 4 ozs., ½d. Every additional 4 ozs., 1d. No packet of Newspapers, Circulars, or Prices Current to exceed 2 lbs. in weight, 2 feet in length, and 1 foot in width or depth.

*Book Packets :* Not exceeding 4 oz., ½d. Every additional 4 oz., 1d. No Book packet, unless sent to or from a Government Office, to exceed 2 lbs. in weight, 18 inches in length, and 9 inches in width or depth.

*Official Postcards :* May be transmitted locally with letters printed or written upon the back. Nothing may be attached, nor may the card be folded, cut, or otherwise altered.

J. A. BULMER,
Postmaster-General.

General Post Office, Trinidad,
15th April, 1899.

Approved by the Legislative Council at its Meeting on the 1st of May, 1899.

C. J. BOOKS,
*Acting Clerk of the Council.*

On 9 December 1903 the Post Office published the following:-

General Post Office,
Trinidad
9 December, 1903.

*Instructions have been received from the General Post Office, London, that in future Pictorial Cards may be accepted with a ½d. stamp. provided that, in addition to the address, they have no written communication with the exception of the name and address of the sender and the date of despatch. If the cards bear the superscription "Post Card" it must be erased.*

*Clarence Ross,*
*Postmaster-General.*

On 18 July 1907 Insurance of Mail was introduced as detailed:-

ON AND FROM THE 18th JULY, 1907, Letters and Parcels will be accepted for Insurance at the following Post Offices—General Post Office, San Fernando, Arima, Arouca, Cedros, Chaguanas, Couva, Erin, Gran Couva, La Brea, Mayaro, Moruga, Princes Town, Roxborough, Saint Joseph, Sangre Grande, Scarborough, Tunapuna, Toco and Williamsville, for the undermentioned Countries, viz. :—

List of Countries for which Letters can be issued up to 10,000 francs (£400).

### UNITED KINGDOM.

### BRITISH COLONIES.

| | |
|---|---|
| Bermuda. | Leeward Islands. |
| British Guiana. | Malta. |
| Gambia. | Mauritius. |
| Jamaica. | Sierra Leone. |

### FOREIGN COUNTRIES.

| | |
|---|---|
| Argentine Republic. | German Offices in China and Morocco. |
| Austria and Austrian Agencies in the Levant. | Holland. |
| Belgium. | Hungary. |
| Bosnia-Herzigovina. | Italy. |
| Bulgaria. | Erithrea. |
| Chili. | Japan. |
| Denmark (with Faroe Islands, Iceland, and Greenland). | Luxemburg. |
| | Montenegro. |
| Danish West Indies. | Norway. |
| Dutch East Indies. | Portugal. |
| Egypt. | Portuguese Colonies. |
| France (also Agencies in Levant & Morocco). | Roumania. |
| French Colonies. | Russia (and Russian Agencies in China). |
| French Agencies in China. | Servia. |
| Germany (also Agencies in Levant). | Spain. |
| Cameroons. | Sweden. |
| German East Africa. | Switzerland. |
| Kiautchou. | Tunis. |
| Togo. | Turkey. |

List of Countries for which Parcels can be insured up to 10,000 francs (£400).

### UNITED KINGDOM.

### BRITISH COLONIES.

| | |
|---|---|
| Bahamas (Nassau only. For other places the limit is the same as at present). | Malta (Except in the case of parcels sent overland through France and Italy). |
| Bermuda. | Mauritius (Do. do. do.) |
| British Guiana. | New Zealand. |
| British Somaliland. | Sarawak. |
| Gambia. | Sierra Leone. |
| Leeward Islands. | Zanzibar. |

Austria (except for Parcels sent *viâ* Flushing.
Belgium.
Bosnia Herzigovina (Except *viâ* Flushing).
Cameroons.
Denmark (with Faroe Islands, Iceland and Greenland) Except *viâ* Flushing.

Egypt (Except *viâ* France and Italy).
Germany (Except *viâ* Flushing).
Hungary (Do.   do.)
Norway.
Russia.
Sweden (Except *viâ* Flushing).

## List of British Colonies for which Letters can be insured only up to £120.

Ceylon.
Hong Kong.
Lagos.

Falkland Islands.
India.
St. Helena.

1. Insured letters will not only have all the advantages of the registration system, but if they or their contents are lost in the Post, the senders will, subject to the following regulations, have a claim to compensation :—

2. Postcards, or packets of " Printed Papers," or " Commercial Papers," or Sample Packets cannot be insured. The letters to which the Insurance system is specially applicable are those which contain bank notes, bonds, coupons, securities, &c.

3. Letters intended for insurance must be presented at the counter of a Post Office

4. Insured letters may not contain coin, anything made of gold or silver, precious stones, jewellery, or any article liable to Customs duty in the country of destination.

5. Insured letters must not be addressed to initials, or in pencil.

6. Every letter packet tendered for insurance must be enclosed in a strong cover, which must be securely fastened and sealed with fine wax, in such a way that it cannot be opened without either breaking the seals or leaving obvious traces of violation. Envelopes with black or coloured borders must not be used. Seals must be placed over each flap or seam of the cover of a packet ; and if the packet is tied round with string or tape, a seal must be placed on the ends where they are tied. The seals on an ordinary envelope should be placed as shown below :—

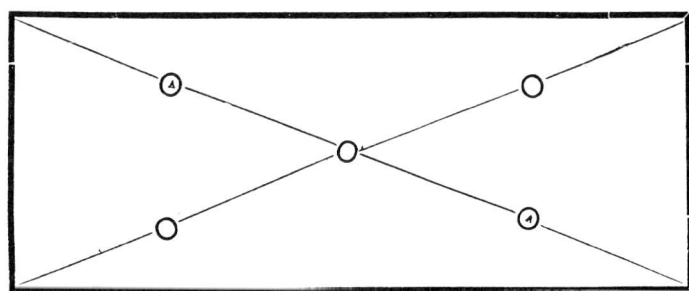

7. All the seals on a letter must be of the same kind of wax, and must bear distinct impressions of the same private device. Coins must not be used for sealing ; and the device must not consist merely of straight, crossed, or curved lines which could readily be imitated.

8. If a letter tendered for insurance does not, in the opinion of the Officer of the Post Office to whom it is tendered fulfil the foregoing conditions as to packing and sealing, it is his duty to refuse to insure it. Nevertheless the onus of properly enclosing and sealing the letter lies upon the sender ; and the Post Office assumes no liability for loss arising from defects of the cover or the seals which may not be observed at the time of posting.

9. The amount for which a letter is insured (which must not exceed its actual value) must be written by the sender both in words and in figures at the top of the address side of the cover, thus :—" Insured for fifteen pounds (£15) 378 francs." No alteration or erasure of the inscription is allowed. If a mistake is made the entry must be completely obliterated and an entirely new one made by the sender.

10. The sums payable for insurance are as follows :—

| Fee. | | Limit of Compensation. | Fee. | | Limit of Compensation |
|---|---|---|---|---|---|
| *s.* | *d.* | £ | *s.* | *d.* | £ |
| | 8 ... | ... 12 | 2 | 4 ... | ... 72 |
| 1 | 0 ... | .. 24 | 2 | 8 ... | ... 84 |
| 1 | 4 ... | ... 36 | 3 | 0 ... | ... 96 |
| 1 | 8 ... | ... 48 | 3 | 4 ... | ... 108 |
| 2 | 0 ... | ... 60 | 3 | 8 ... | ... 120 |

14. Letters which, although addressed to a country or place to which the insurance system does not extend, have been irregularly insured, will be forwarded as registered letters; and if they or their contents are lost in the Post, the regulations as to the compensation payable in the case of registered letters will be applicable.

15. When an insured letter is directed from one country to another, a fresh insurance fee becomes payable for each such transmission. If this fee is not prepaid, it is collected from the addressee on delivery. Insured letters can only be re-directed to countries which have adopted the insurance system.

16. Compensation for the loss in the Post of a letter or its contents will not exceed the amount of the actual loss, and will not be paid at all for a letter containing any prohibited article, or for any letter which has been delivered without external trace of injury and has been accepted without remark by the addressee; nor does it follow as a matter of course that compensation will be given when loss arises from tempest, shipwreck, earthquake, war, or other causes beyond control. No claim for compensation will be admitted if made more than a year after the letter was posted.

17. No legal liability to give compensation in respect of any letter for which an insurance fee has been paid attaches to the Postmaster-General, either personally or in his official capacity. The final decision upon all questions of compensation rests with the Postal Administration of the country in which the loss has taken place.

18. Any insurance effected with the Post Office contrary to the foregoing regulations is invalid.

CLARENCE ROSS,
Postmaster-General.

12th July, 1907.

---

On 17 October 1907 the Empire penny post unit was doubled to one ounce, the list of countries participating was:-

| | |
|---|---|
| Antigua | Jamaica |
| Ascension | Labuan |
| Australia | Malay States (Federated) |
| Bahamas | Malta |
| Barbados | Mauritius |
| Bermuda | Montserrat |
| British Central Africa | Natal |
| British East Africa and Uganda | Nevis |
| British Guiana | Newfoundland |
| British Honduras | New Zealand (with Cook's Island) |
| British North Borneo | Nigeria (Northern and Southern) |
| British Somaliland | Orange River Colony |
| Canada | Rhodesia |
| Cayman Islands | St. Helena |
| Ceylon | St. Kitts |
| Cape Colony | St. Lucia |
| Cyprus | St. Vincent |
| Dominica | Sarawak |
| Falkland Islands | Seychelles |
| Fanning Islands | Sierra Leone |
| Fiji | Straits Settlements |
| Gambia | Tobago |
| Gibraltar | Tortola |
| Gold Coast | Transvaal |
| Grenada | Trinidad |
| Hong Kong | Tristan D'Acunha |
| India (including Aden) | Turks and Caicos Islands |
| | Zanzibar |

On 1 July 1915:-

*The maximum limit of weight for a packet transmissible to the United Kingdom and the United States as "printed" papers was raised to 6 lbs. in the case of literature embossed for the blind, the postage will be at the rate of ½d. for every 2 ozs. up to 20 ozs. and above 20 ozs. and up to 6 lbs. 5d. irrespective of the weight.*

On 1 June 1918:-

*The rate of postage on letters for the United States of America (including the Virgin Islands of the U.S.A., Porto Rico, Alaska and Hawaii) was 1d. per ounce with the war tax stamp of 1d. affixed.*

At Independence the principal postal charges were:-

| | Inland (Trinidad and Tobago) | | British Isles, Dominions and British Possessions | | All Other Parts of the World | |
|---|---|---|---|---|---|---|
| Letters | Not exceeding 1 oz. | 5 | Not exceeding 1 oz. | 6 | Not exceeding 1 oz. | 12 |
| | For every additional oz. | 2 | For every additional oz. | 3 | For every additional oz. | 8 |
| Post Cards | For each card | 4 | For each card | 5 | For each card | 8 |
| Reply Post Cards | | | For each card | 10 | For each card | 16 |
| Printed Paper Packets | For every 2 oz. | 2 | For every 2 oz. | 5 | For every 2 oz. | 5 |
| | For every additional 2 oz. | 2 | For every additional 2 oz. | 2 | For every additional 2 oz. | 2 |
| Commercial | For every 2 oz. | 2 | Not exceeding 12 oz. | 15 | Not exceeding 12 oz. | 15 |
| Paper Packets | For every additional 2 oz. | 2 | For every additional 2 oz. | 2 | For every additional 2 oz. | 2 |
| Sample Packets | For every 2 oz. | 2 | Not exceeding 4 oz. | 5 | Not exceeding 4 oz. | 5 |
| | For every additional 2 oz. | 2 | For every additional 2 oz. | 2 | For every additional 2 oz. | 2 |
| Insured Boxes | No service | | Not exceeding 10 oz. | 50 | Not exceeding 10 oz. | 50 |
| | | | For every additional 2 oz. | 10 | For every additional 2 oz. | 10 |
| Registration Fee | For each article | 15 | For each article | 15 | For each article | 15 |
| Advice of delivery | For each article after | | For each article after | | For each article after | |
| (Registered or | posting | 10 | posting | 15 | posting | 20 |
| Insured Article) | Applied for on posting | | Applied for on posting | | | |
| Certificate of Posting | For each article | 2 | For each article | 2 | For each article | 2 |
| (Unregistered Article) | | | | | | |
| Blind Literature | FREE | | Not exceeding 2 lb. | 1 | Not exceeding 2 lb. | 1 |
| (Braille) | | | For every additional 3 lb. | 1 | For every additional 3 lb. | 1 |

## Inland Rates

| 1.7.84 - 1.12.05 | 2.12.05 - 1.4.17 | | | |
|---|---|---|---|---|
| 1d. per ½oz. | 1d. per ½oz. | | | |

| 2.4.17 - 31.12.19 | 1.1.20 - 30.6.22 | 1.7.22-31.12.27 | | |
|---|---|---|---|---|
| 1d. per oz + 1d. war tax. | 1d. per oz. | 1½d. to 1 oz., 1d. per add. oz. | | |

| 1.1.28 - 31.12.38 | 1.1.39 - 31.12.40 | 1.1.41 - 31.12.57 | 1.1.58 - | |
|---|---|---|---|---|
| 1d. per oz. | 2c. per oz. | 3c. to 1 oz. 2c. per add. oz. | 5c. to 1 oz. 2c. per add oz. | |

| 1.7.84 - 9.5.17 | 10.5.17 - 31.12.19 | 1.1.20 - 30.6.22 | | |
|---|---|---|---|---|
| ½d. | ½d. + ½d. war tax. | ½d. | | |

| 1.7.22 - 31.12.27 | 1.1.28 - 31.12.38 | 1.1.39 - 31.12.40 | 1.1.41 - 31.12.57 | 1.1.58 - |
|---|---|---|---|---|
| 1d. | ½d. | 1c. | 2c. | 4c. |

## Printed Matter

| 1.7.84 - 14.2.03 | 15.2.03 - 31.12.38 | 1.1.39 - 31.12.57 | 1.1.58 |
|---|---|---|---|
| ½d. to 4 oz. | ½d. per 4 oz. | 1c. per 4 oz. | 2c. per 2 oz. |
| 1d. per add. 4oz. | | | |

## Newspapers

| 14.8.51 - 30.6.84 | from 1.7.84 at printed matter rate. |
|---|---|
| 1d. each. | |

## Registration Fee [A.R. same from (1.1.20) until 31.12.57]

| 1.8.82 - 30.6.22 | 1.7.22 - 31.12.38 | |
|---|---|---|
| 2d. | 3d. | |

| 1.1.39 - 12.3.52 | 13.3.52 - 31.12.57 | 1.1.58 - |
|---|---|---|
| 6c. | 8c. | 15c. |
| | | (A.R. 10c.) |

## U.P.U. Letter Rates

| 1.4.77 - 30.9.07 | 1.10.07 - 30.11.21 | 1.12.21 - 31.12.38 |
|---|---|---|
| 2½d. per ½ oz. | 2½d. per oz., | 3d. per oz., |
| | 1½d. per add. oz. | 1½d. add oz. |

| 1.1.30 - 31.7.40 | 1.8.40 - 12.3.52 | 13.3.52 - 31.12.57 |
|---|---|---|
| 6c. per oz., | 6c. per oz., | 8c. per oz., |
| 3c. per add. oz. | 4c. per add. oz. | 5c. per add. oz. |

| 1.1.58 - S.U. |
|---|
| 12c. per oz., |
| 8c. per add. oz. |

## Postcards

| 16.9.14 - 30.11.21 | 1.12.21 - 31.12.38 | 1.1.29 - 31.7.40 |
|---|---|---|
| 1d. | 1½d. | 3c. |

| 1.8.40 - 12.3.52 | 13.3.52 - 31.12.57 | 1.1.58 - S.U. |
|---|---|---|
| 4c. | 5c. | 8c. |

## Imperial Letter Rates (including U.K.)

| 1.1.91 - 24.12.98 | 25.12.98* - 16.10.07 | 17.10.07 - 1.1.17 |
|---|---|---|
| 2½d. per ½oz. | 1d. per ½oz. | 1d. per oz. |

| 2.4.17 - 31.12.19 | 1.1.20 - 30.11.21 | 1.12.21 - 31.12.27 |
|---|---|---|
| 1d. per oz., | 2d. per oz., | 2d. per oz., |
| plus 1d. War Tax | ½d. per add. oz. | 1½d. per add. oz |

**Imperial Letter Rates** (including U.K.)

| | | |
|---|---|---|
| 1.1.28 - 31.12.28 | 1.1.29 - 31.12.31 | 1.1.32 - 31.12.38 |
| 1½d. per oz. | 1d. per oz. | 1½d. per oz. |
| 1d. per add. oz. | | 1d. per add. oz. |

| | | |
|---|---|---|
| 1.1.39 - 31.12.40 | 1.1.41 - 31.12.57 | 1.1.58 - |
| 3c. per oz., | 5c. per oz., | 6c. per oz., |
| 2c. per add oz. | 2c. per add. oz. | 3c. per add. oz. |

**Postcards**

| | | |
|---|---|---|
| 1.4.79 - 31.7.92 | 1.8.92 - 30.11.21 | 1.12.21 - 31.12.28 |
| 1½d. | 1d. | 1½d. |

| | | |
|---|---|---|
| 1.1.29 - 31.12.38 | 1.1.39 - 31.12.40 | 1.1.41 - 31.12.57 | 1.1.58 - |
| 1d. | 2c. | 4c. | 5c. |

**\* Empire Penny Post**

The following countries did not join initially but on the dates shown:-

| | |
|---|---|
| Gazetted on 25 May 1899 | Jamaica, Malta, Mauritius and British North Borneo. |
| 1 September 1899 | Cape of Good Hope. |
| 1 December 1900 | Transvaal and Orange River Colony. |
| 1 January 1901 | New Zealand. |
| P.O. Notice., 25 Sept. 1901 | New Zealand and Desperadoes. |
| 13 February 1902 | British Post Office in China (withdrew 1.10.16 except weihaienei). |
| P.O. Notice., 8 Sept. 1905 | Australia and British New Guinea. |
| 21 March 1906 | Egypt and Sudan |
| P.O. Notice., 24 March 1910 | Kelanton, Kedah, Perlis, Tregganu. |
| Gazetted on 23 February 1911 | British Post Offices in French India. |
| 1 April 1911 | Rhodesia |
| P.O. Notice 18 Sept. 1911 | Brunei. |
| P.O. Notice 7 December 1912 | Papua |
| 10 December 1912 | New Hebrides |

**Newspapers**

Initially free, but from 1 April 1877, 1d. each if not sent by the Royal Mail Steamship Co.

| | |
|---|---|
| 1.7.84 - 31.12.91 | 1.1.92 - |
| 1d. per 4 oz. | ½d. per 2 oz. |

**Imperial** (including U.K.)

| | | |
|---|---|---|
| 1.1.92 - 30.11.21 | 1.12.21 - 31.12.38 | 11.39 - 12.3.52 |
| 1½d. per 2 oz. | 3d. per 6 oz. | 6c. per 12 oz. |
| (minimum 2½d.) | 1d. per add 2 oz. | 1c. per add. oz. |

**Imperial** (including U.K.)

| | |
|---|---|
| 13.3.52 - 31.12.57 | 1.1.58 - |
| 8c. per 12c. | 15c. per 12c. |
| 1c. per add. oz. | 2c. per add 2 oz. |

**Registration Fee**

| | | |
|---|---|---|
| 1.12.21 - 31.12.38 | 1.1.39 - 12.3.52 | 13.3.52 - 31.12.57 |
| 3d. | 6c. | 8c. |

1.1.58 -
15c.

**A.R.**

| | | |
|---|---|---|
| 1.4.79 - 30.11.21 | 1.12.21 - 31.12.38 | 1.1.39 - 31.7.40 |
| 2½d. | 3d. | 6c. |
| 1.8.40 - 12.3.52 | 13.3.52 - 31.12.57 | 1.1.58 - |
| 9c. | 12c. | 15c. |

# CHAPTER 4

## AIR MAIL AND AIRMAIL RATES

The first flight in Trinidad and Tobago was in January 1913 when the American aviator Frank Boland was killed when he crashed on the Savannah, Port of Spain whilst making a trial flight. The first successful flight was made the following month when George Schmitt flew over the Port of Spain on 27 February. He planned to drop advertising cards the following day but was banned by the Governor of the colony for safety, following the previous crash and the erratic flight of the previous day. A few examples of the prepared "drop card" are known to exist.

The first official inward air mail was the arrival of mail from British Guiana on 28 March 1927, carried by the US Army airmen on the return leg of the "Round South America" flight. It was an unscheduled delivery of one bag of mail at the request of the Postmaster at Georgetown, British Guiana, none of this mail is thought to have survived. A further unscheduled airmail delivery was made by the same flight following its return from Venezuela on 4 April 1927, again no mail is known to have survived.

The same fliers carried the first official outward mail, taking one bag of mail for Grenada and one bag for St. Vincent when resuming their northbound flight on 7 April 1927,. A few items from this mail are known to have survived. Following this flight there was another unscheduled inward airmail when Captain W W Lancaster brought a bag of mail from Barbados at the request of that country's Postmaster, again no mail is known to have survived.

The US awarded Foreign Airmail Contract 6 (FAM 6) to Pan American Airways on 13 July 1928, this contract was for the carriage of mail by air from Miami - San Juan - Santo Domingo - Puerto Rico down through the Caribbean to Trinidad and thence to Suriname (Dutch Guiana). The service to Trinidad started at San Juan on 22 September 1929. Mail from US for the Caribbean was assembled at Puerto Rico, the original plan was for a single plane to be piloted by Charles Lindbergh but there was so much mail that a second plane was used as well as that of Lindbergh. Juan Trippe the founder of Pan American Airways accompanied Lindbergh together with their wives. The mail reached Port of Spain the same day carrying mail from the US and the intermediate stopping points.

The flight continued on to British Guiana and Surinam taking with it the first official scheduled airmail from the colony. The return flight brought mail from both countries. Mail was dispatched on the northbound flight on 26 September to all the stop-over points as well as to the US, Canada and the UK (air to US, then surface). Lindbergh did not fly the northbound leg but took one of the planes with his wife and the Trippes along the coast of South America on a survey flight, then up Central America on what was to become the FAM 5 Lindbergh Circle.

The next air line to arrive at Port of Spain was the New York, Rio and Buenos Aires Airline, (NYRBA), this was a planned air mail schedule from Chile to New York via the east coast of South America. It arrived with mail from Chile, Argentina and the various stop-overs on 25 February 1930 and carried mail from Trinidad north to the same destinations as FAM 6. On arrival at Miami, the mail for the US was seized by the US Post Office, as NYRBA did not have a contract to carry the mail onward to New York, its final destination. Again mail from the Caribbean was brought in on the southbound leg from Miami and mail was dispatched to South American destinations.

The airline also pioneered trial local feeder routes, including from Trinidad to Tobago and Grenada. Political manoeuvring within the United States ensured that NYRBA would not be awarded the US FAM 10 contract. As a result, the airline was bought out by Pan American Airways on 19 August 1930. The next day Pan American was awarded the FAM 10 contract. The final absorption of NYRBA was completed on 15 September 1930 with the transfer of the stock. As a result , Pan American did not pursue the local island feeder services.

Compagnie General Postale, a French airline was already operating a South Atlantic service as well as within Brazil. In 1930 it started up a Venezuelan subsidiary with the intention of expanding north and south to link up the French Caribbean colonies with the Brazilian operation. As part of this programme the airline commenced a service from Venezuela to Trinidad on 8 January 1931 which included airmail. This Airline used land-based planes and its Trinidad contracts had surveyed various locations for an airport before settling on the site of what is now Piarco International Airport. Unfortunately before the airline became fully established, the parent company was wound up and the service terminated in April 1931.

Meanwhile Pan America Airways had extended its FAM 5 route from Barranquilla, Columbia through Venezuela to Trinidad in February 1931, thereby completing the "Lindbergh Circle". This meant mail could be dispatched in either direction east or west to the United States, and brought 17 destinations into direct airmail service for the first time.

Three other events of aviation significance also occurred in the early 1930's. On 19 August 1931 the Dornier DoX called at Trinidad with the mail from South America and took the mail to onward destinations from Trinidad. Michael (Mikey) Cipriani, a local solicitor made a special mail carrying flight to Barbados and St. Vincent, on 29 July 1932. He was pioneering inter-island air routes. He died whilst flying to Tobago later the following year. Finally on 22 October 1933, the Graf Zeppelin flew over Trinidad on its journey from Brazil to the US, it did not stop or pickup or drop mail.

The French were very reluctant to allow Pan American Airways to land in their Caribbean possessions. It was not only until October 1931 that the very first dispatch was made to French Guiana. Martinique and Guadeloupe were not included until March and April 1935 respectively.

1935 and 1936 saw the first recorded crashes of aircraft carrying mail in Trinidad waters of Pan American Airways flights to South America. Covers survived from both crashes. The first was on 20 December 1935 and the second on 11 April 1936, some of the mail from this latter crash has an "ACCIDENT D'AVIATION" cachet applied.

The Dutch airline KLM had set up a West Indies Division in 1935 operating between the Dutch Islands of Aruba and Curacao extending to Maracaibo and Caracas in 1936 and 1937 respectively. The airline operated a mail carrying trial flight from Curacao to Trinidad and on to Barbados and return on 19 October 1938. A regular service commenced on 6 May 1939, later extended to Paramaribo, Surinam on 5 September 1939.

With the onset of war, communications within the Caribbean were severely disrupted and the Governor of Trinidad and Tobago sought to establish a regular air service to the neighbouring islands. A New Zealander, Lowell Yerex, then operating TACA, was persuaded to start an airline based in Trinidad, British West Indian Airways (BWIA), the first scheduled mail carrying flight to other West Indian Islands and eventually to the US and post war to the UK. In the 1950's it was part of the BSAA, later BOAC empire and carried mail at a reduced rate to the UK via Jamaica, as opposed to the route via the US Pan American Airlines.

During the war, Trinidad became a stop-over on the trans-Atlantic Pan American Winter route to Lisbon via Brazil and the Azores. Another war time route was the Pan American service to West Africa, linking up with the transcontinent route to Egypt.

The final expansion prior to Independence was the arrival of a direct service to London via Barbados and Bermuda operated by BOAC as part of its route to Venezuela on 27 October 1958. The route was extended to Bogotta, Columbia on 7 January 1960.

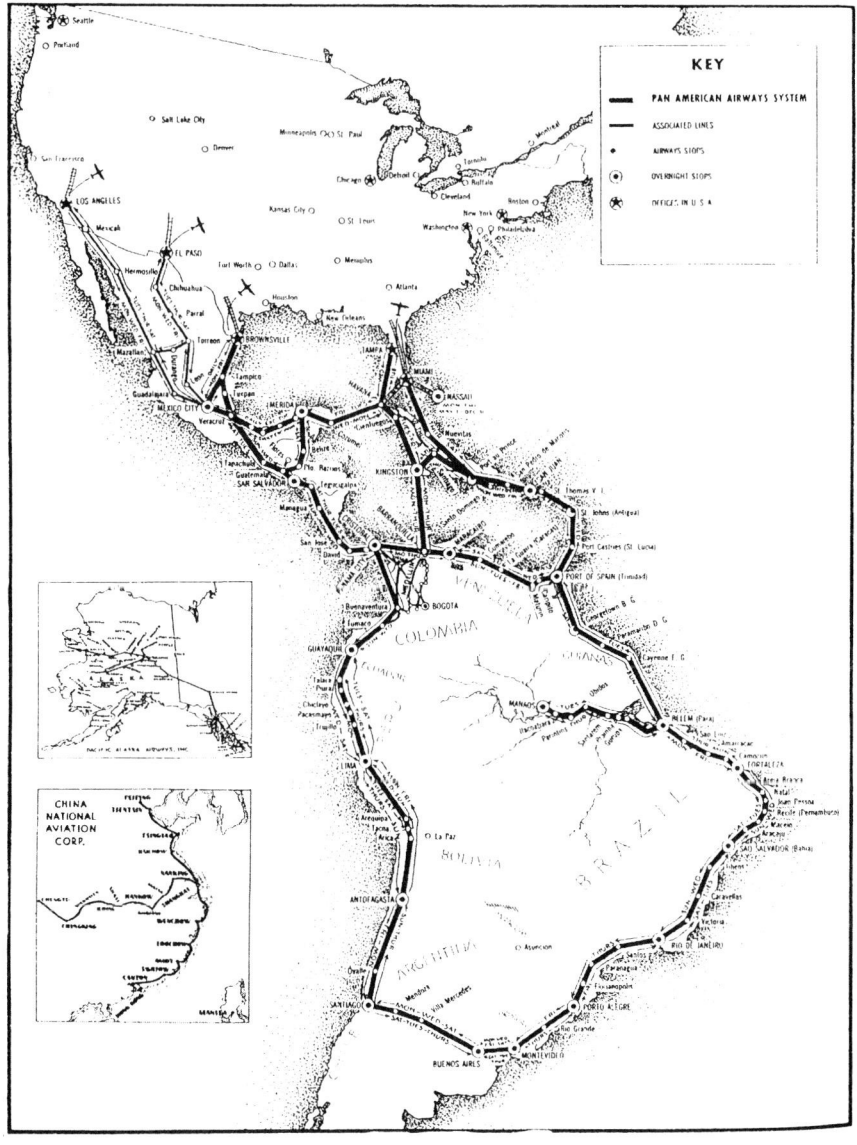

**1935 P.A.A. route map.**

## Airmail Rates

From 1 September 1929 mail could be sent to London for onward transmission by air if the appropriate air fee was paid. This facility was little used and would obviously not have been worthwhile for North and South America. The British rates at the time were:-

| Country of Destination | | Air Fee<br>(Additional to ordinary postage, express, late or registration fee). |
|---|---|---|
| Aden | | 2d. per oz. |
| Africa - NORTH | Algeria<br>Morocco<br>Tunis | Letters and Postcards: 4d. per half oz.<br>Printed Papers, Commercial Papers & Samples:<br> 4d. per oz. |
| Africa - EAST | Kenya, Uganda,<br>Tanganyika,<br>Zanzibar. | 2d. per oz. |
| Africa - WEST | French Guinea,<br>Senegal, Gambia,<br>Belgian Congo,<br>Sierra Leone. | Letters and Postcards: 1s. per half oz.<br>Printed Papers, Commercial Papers & Samples:<br>8d. per oz. |
| Africa - SOUTH | *See South Africa* | |
| AUSTRALIA | (except West<br>Australia) | (a) 3d. per half oz.<br>(b) 3d. per half oz. plus 2d, per oz.<br>(c) 8d. per half oz. |
| | (all parts) | (a) 5d. per half oz.<br>(b) 2d. per oz. |
| Austria | | 3d. per oz. |
| Belgium | | 2d. per half oz. |
| Bulgaria | | 4d. per oz. |
| Ceylon. Straits Settlements, Dutch<br>East Indies, Hong Kong etc.. | | (a) 5d. per half oz.<br>(b) 2d. per oz. |
| China (South) | | (a) 5d. per half oz.<br>(b) 2d. per oz. |
| Crete | | *Same as Greece* |
| Cyprus | | 2d. per oz. |
| Czecho-Slovakia | | 3d. per oz. |

| Country of Destination | Air Fee<br>(Additional to ordinary postage, express, late or Registration fee). |
| --- | --- |
| Danzig (Free City) | 2d. per oz. |
| Denmark | 3d. per oz. |
| Egypt & Sudan | (a) 2d. per half oz.<br>(b) 2d. per oz. |
| France | 2d. per oz. |
| Germany | 2d. per oz. |
| Greece | 4d. per oz. |
| Holland | 2d. per oz. |
| Hong Kong | *Same as China (South).* |
| India | (a) 5d. per half oz.<br>(b) 2d. per oz. |
| Iraq (including Kuwait) | (a) 3½d. per half oz.<br>(b) 3d. per oz.<br>(c) 5d. per oz. |
| Italy | 2d. per oz. |
| Jugo-Slavia | *See Serbs, Croats and Slovenes* |
| New Zealand | *Same as Australia* |
| Norway | 3d. per oz. |
| Palestine | (a) 2d. per half oz.<br>(b) 2d. per oz. |
| Persia (including Persian Gulf Ports). | 5d. per half oz. |
| Poland | 3d. per oz. |
| Roumania | 4d. per oz. |
| Serbs, Croats and Slovenes (Kingdom of) | 4d. per oz. |
| South Africa | 4d. per oz. |
| Spain | 2d. per oz. |

| Country of Destination | Air Fee |
| --- | --- |
| | Additional to ordinary postage, express, late or registration fee). |
| Sweden | 3d. per oz. |
| Switzerland | 2d. per oz. |
| Syria & Transjordan | *Same as Palestine* |
| Turkey | 4d. per oz. |

On 2 September 1929 the following notice was published:-

*INSTRUCTIONS.*

## AIR MAILS.

1. Any kind of Letter Packet may be sent by Air Mail, that is letters, postcards, printed papers and commercial papers and samples. An Air Mail packet may be posted at any Post Office in Trinidad and Tobago.

2. An Air Mail packet can be accepted for registration but it cannot be insured.

3. A special Air Mail label should be affixed to the top left hand corner of every Air Mail packet. These labels may be obtained free of charge on application.

If an Air Mail label is not available the packet should be clearly marked **" By Air Mail."**

4. All Air Mail correspondence must be prepaid in postage stamps. If the Air Mail fee is not fully prepaid, the packet will not go forward by Air Mail.

5. Air Mail packets posted at Sub-Offices are to be sent to Port-of-Spain in the ordinary mails tied in a separate bundle and labelled Air Mail, a note being made on the Letter Bill of the number of Air Mail packets forwarded.

6. **Make up and despatch of an Air Mail at General Post Office.**—An Air Mail must be made up and despatched in the same way as an ordinary mail, and an Air Mail label must be affixed at the head of the Letter Bill and Registered List as well as to the address label of the Bag.

7. A despatch by Air Mail is to be advertised in the same manner as is now done with regard to steamers.

### AIR MAILS INWARD.

1. The rules applicable to ordinary mails received from abroad apply generally to Air Mails, but steps must be taken to ensure that Air Mails are checked immediately on receipt and that the correspondence received in them secures the earliest possible delivery.

2. **Redirection and return of Undelivered Correspondence.**—Redirected Air Mail correspondence must be forwarded by the ordinary mail unless the postage for re-transmission by Air is prepaid.

Undeliverable Air Mail correspondence which is due to be returned to the country of origin must be returned by ordinary mail.

The Air Mail labels and all markings relative to Air Mail transmission borne by correspondence which is being redirected or returned undelivered by ordinary mail must be cancelled by means of two thick transverse strokes in red pencil.

B. B. LITTLEPAGE,
*Postmaster-General.*

## POST OFFICE NOTICE.

## AIR MAILS WITH U.S.A. AND INTERMEDIATE POINTS.

1. Arrangements have been made with the Postmaster-General of the United States of America whereby letters,

postcards,

printed papers,

commercial papers,

and samples

posted in the Colony will be received from and forwarded to the undermentioned places, viz. :

St. Lucia,

Antigua,

St. Thomas,

Porto Rico,

United States of America,

by Air Mail.

2. The prepaid rate of postage to the places mentioned above on any kind of letter packet, that is, letters, postcards, printed papers, commercial papers and samples is :—

|  | s. | d. |
|---|---|---|
| For the first half ounce or fraction thereof .. .. | 1 | 6 |
| For each additional half ounce or fraction thereof .. | 1 | 6 |

3. Air Mail correspondence must be fully prepaid in stamps with ordinary postage stamps. If the Air Mail fee is not fully prepaid the packet will not be forwarded by Air Mail.

4. An Air Mail packet can be accepted for registration but it cannot be insured.

5. A special Air Mail label should be affixed to the top left hand corner of every Air Mail packet. These labels can be obtained free of charge at any Money Order Post Office in the Colony. If an Air Mail label is not available the packet should be clearly marked by the sender : " **By Air Mail.**"

6. The above Air Mail Service is scheduled to start from :—

San Juan, Porto Rico to Trinidad on 22nd September, 1929.

Paramaribo to Trinidad and then on to :

St. Lucia,

Antigua,

St. Thomas,

Porto Rico and New York on 25th September, 1929.

B. B. LITTLEPAGE,
*Postmaster-General,*

General Post Office,
2nd September, 1929

## POST OFFICE NOTICE.

## AIR MAIL SERVICE.

Arrangements have been made whereby—
    Letters,
    Postcards,
    Printed Papers,
    Commercial Papers,
    Samples

posted in the Colony will be received from and forwarded to the undermentioned places :—
    British Guiana,
    Dutch Guiana,
by Air Mail.

2. The prepaid rate of postage to the places mentioned above on any kind of letter packet, that is, letters, postcards, printed papers, commercial papers and samples is :—

|  | s. | d. |
|---|---|---|
| For the first half ounce or fraction thereof .. .. | 0 | 9 |
| For each additional half ounce or fraction thereof .. | 0 | 9 |

3. Air Mail correspondence must be fully prepaid in stamps with ordinary postage stamps. If the Air Mail fee is not fully prepaid the packet will not be forwarded by Air Mail.

4. An Air Mail packet can be accepted for registration but it cannot be insured.

5. A special Air Mail label should be affixed to the top left hand corner of every Air Mail packet. These labels can be obtained free of charge at any Money Order Post Office in the Colony. If an Air Mail label is not available the packet should be clearly marked by the sender : " **By Air Mail.**"

       B. B. LITTLEPAGE,
         *Postmaster-General.*

General Post Office,
  Trinidad,
   16th September, 1929.

**Followed shortly afterwards on the 12 October 1929 extending the service to British and Dutch Guiana at a rate of:-**

      9d. per ½oz.

These rates were short lived as a new extensive list was published, dated 11 November 1929:-

| Country of Destination. | Approx. time to Destination. | Air Port. | Air Rate per half oz. or fraction of half oz. | | Route. |
|---|---|---|---|---|---|
| | | | s. | d. | |
| Antigua | 6 hours | St. Johns | 0 | 8 | Direct. |
| Bahamas | 4 days | Nassau | 2 | 3 | *via* Miami. |
| British Guiana | 4 hours | Georgetown | 0 | 8 | Direct. |
| British Honduras | 5 days | Belize | 2 | 3 | *via* Miami. |
| Canada | 6 days | Miami | 1 | 1 | *via* New York. |
| Canal Zone | 7 days | Christobal | 2 | 9 | *via* Miami. |
| Cuba | 3 days | Havana | 1 | 3 | Direct. |
| Do. | 3 days | Camaguey | 1 | 3 | Direct. |
| Do. | 2 days | Santiago | 1 | 3 | Direct. |
| Dominican Republic | 2 days | Santo Domingo | 1 | 3 | Direct. |
| Dutch Guiana | 7 hours | Paramaribo | 0 | 11 | Direct. |
| Guatemala | 5 days | Guatemala | 2 | 9 | *via* Miami. |
| Haiti | 2 days | Port-au-Prince | 1 | 3 | Direct. |
| Republic of Honduras | 6 days | Tela | 2 | 9 | *via* Miami. |
| Nicaragua | 6 days | Managua | 2 | 9 | *via* Miami. |
| Porto Rico | 1 day | San Juan | 0 | 9 | Direct. |
| St. Lucia | 3 hours | Castries | 0 | 8 | Direct. |
| United States of America | 4 days | Miami | 1 | 1 | Direct. |
| Virgin Islands of U.S.A. | 1 day | St. Thomas | 0 | 9 | Direct. |
| Great Britain | 4 days to New York | Miami | 1 | 1 | *via* New York and then by Steamer. |
| Europe | 4 days to New York | Miami | 1 | 3 | *via* New York and then by Steamer. |

Note.—If registered 3d. additional to be charged on each letter.

29 December 1929:-

| Country of destination. | Approximate time to destination. | Air Port. | Air Rate per half oz. or fraction of half oz. | | Route. |
|---|---|---|---|---|---|
| | | | s. | d. | |
| Venezuela | 1 day | Ciudad Bolivar | 1 | 1 | Direct. |
| Do. | 1 day | Caracas | 1 | 1 | Do. |
| Do. | 1 day | Maracay | 1 | 1 | Do. |
| Do. | 1 day | Tumeremo | 1 | 1 | Do. |
| Do | 1 day | Guasipati | 1 | 1 | Do. |
| Do. | 1 day | El Callao | 1 | 1 | Do. |
| Do. | 3 days | Coro | 1 | 1 | Do. |
| Do. | 3 days | Maracaibo | 1 | 1 | Do. |
| Jamaica | 5 days | Kingston | | 11 | Do. |

NOTE.—If registered 3d. additional to be charged on each letter.

18 February 1930:-

| Country of Destination. | Approx. time to Destination. | Air Port. | Air Rate per half oz. or fraction of half oz. | | Route. |
|---|---|---|---|---|---|
| | | | s. | d. | |
| Antigua | 6 hours | St. Johns | 0 | 7 | Direct. |
| Bahamas | 4 days | Nassau | 1 | 2 | via Miami. |
| British Guiana | 4 hours | Georgetown | 0 | 7 | Direct. |
| British Honduras | 5 days | Belize | 1 | 7 | via Miami. |
| Canada | 6 days | Miami | 1 | 2 | via New York. |
| Canal Zone | 7 days | Cristobal | 1 | 9 | via Miami. |
| Costa Rica | 7 days | Miami | 1 | 11 | via Miami. |
| Cuba | 3 days | Havana | 1 | 2 | Direct. |
| Do. | 3 days | Camaguey | 1 | 2 | Direct. |
| Do. | 2 days | Santiago | 1 | 2 | Direct. |
| Dominican Republic | 2 days | Santo Domingo | 1 | 2 | Direct. |
| Dutch Guiana | 7 hours | Paramaribo | 0 | 11 | Direct. |
| Guatemala | 5 days | Guatemala | 1 | 9 | via Miami. |
| Haiti | 2 days | Port-au-Prince | 1 | 2 | Direct. |
| Mexico | 5 days | Miami | 1 | 5 | via Miami. |
| Nicaragua | 6 days | Managua | 1 | 9 | via Miami. |
| Panama | 7 days | Miami | 1 | 11 | via Miami. |
| Porto Rico | 1 day | San Juan | 0 | 7 | Direct. |
| Republic of Honduras | 6 days | Tela | 1 | 9 | via Miami. |
| Salvador | 5 days | Miami | 1 | 9 | via Miami. |
| St. Lucia | 3 hours | Castries | 0 | 7 | Direct. |
| United States of America | 4 days | Miami | 0 | 11 | Direct. |
| Virgin Islands of U.S.A. | 1 day | St. Thomas | 0 | 7 | Direct. |
| Great Britain | 4 days to New York | Miami | 0 | 11 | via New York and then by Steamer. |
| Europe | 4 days to New York | Miami | 1 | 1 | via New York and then by Steamer. |

Note.—If registered 3d. additional to be charged on each letter.

**Mail was accepted for South America at the following rates published on 7 March 1930:-**

| Country of destination. | Approximate time to destination. | Air Port. | Air Rate per half oz. or fraction of half oz. | | Route. |
|---|---|---|---|---|---|
| | | | s. | d. | |
| Argentine | 6 days | Buenos Ayres | 1 | 9 | Direct. |
| Brazil | 1 day | Montenegro | 1 | 6 | do. |
| Do. | 1½ days | Para | 1 | 6 | do. |
| Do. | 2½ days | Natal | 1 | 6 | do. |
| Do. | 3½ days | Bahia | 1 | 6 | do. |
| Do. | 4 days | Rio de Janeiro | 1 | 6 | do. |
| Chile | 7 days | Santiago | 2 | 2 | via Buenos Ayres. |
| Uruguay | 6 days | Montevideo | 1 | 9 | Direct. |

NOTE :—If registered 3d. additional to be charged on each letter.

This was followed by a more extensive table on 2 February 1931:-

| Country of destination. | Air Port. | Air Rate per half oz. or fraction of half oz. | Route. |
|---|---|---|---|
| | | s. d. | |
| Venezuela .. .. | Maturin .. .. | 1 1 | Direct. |
| Do. .. .. | La Guaira .. .. | 1 1 | Do. |
| Do. .. .. | Maracaibo .. .. | 1 1 | Do. |
| Curacao .. .. | Curacao .. .. | 1 1 | Do. |
| Panama .. .. | Panama .. .. | 1 1 | Do. |
| Costa Rica .. .. | Costa Rica .. .. | 1 3 | Do. |
| Nicaragua .. .. | Nicaragua .. .. | 1 9 | Do. |
| Honduras .. .. | Honduras .. .. | 1 9 | Do. |
| El Salvador .. .. | El Salvador .. | 1 9 | Do. |
| Guatemala .. .. | Guatemala .. .. | 1 9 | Do. |
| Mexico .. .. | Mexico .. .. | 1 3 | Do. |
| British Honduras .. | British Honduras .. | 1 7 | Do. |
| Colombia .. .. | Baranquilla · .. | 1 1 | Do. |
| Do. .. .. | Cartagena .. .. | 1 1 | Do. |
| Ecuador .. .. | Ecuador .. .. | 1 1 | Do. |
| Peru .. .. | Peru .. .. | 1 6 | Do. |
| Chile .. .. | Chile .. .. | 2 0 | Do. |

NOTE.—If registered 3d. additional to be charged on each letter.

179

On 16 October 1931 a new rate table was published:-

| Country of Destination. | Air Port. | Air Rate per half oz. or fraction of half oz. | |
|---|---|---|---|
| | | s. | d. |
| Argentine .. .. .. | ..Buenos Ayres.. .. .. .. | 2 | 3 |
| Antigua .. .. .. | ..St. Johns .. .. .. | | 9 |
| Bahamas .. .. .. | ..Nassau .. .. .. .. | 1 | 6 |
| Brazil .. .. .. | ..Montenegro .. .. .. | 2 | 0 |
| Do. .. .. .. | ..Para .. .. .. | 2 | 0 |
| Do. .. .. .. | ..Natal .. .. .. | 2 | 0 |
| Do. .. .. .. | ..Bahia .. .. .. | 2 | 0 |
| Do. .. .. .. | ..Rio de Janeiro .. .. .. | 2 | 0 |
| Br. Guiana .. .. .. | ..Georgetown .. .. .. | | 9 |
| Br. Honduras .. .. | ..Belize .. .. .. | 2 | 1 |
| Canada .. .. .. | ..Miami .. .. .. | 1 | 6 |
| Chile .. .. .. | ..Chile .. .. .. | 2 | 7 |
| Do. .. .. .. | ..Santiago .. .. .. | 2 | 10 |
| Cuba .. .. .. | ..Havana .. .. .. | 1 | 6 |
| Do. .. .. .. | ..Camaguey .. .. .. | 1 | 6 |
| Do. .. .. .. | ..Santiago .. .. .. | 1 | 6 |
| Colombia .. .. | ..Baranquilla .. .. .. | 1 | 5 |
| Do. .. .. .. | ..Cartagena .. .. .. | 1 | 5 |
| Costa Rica .. .. | ..Costa Rica .. .. | 1 | 8 |
| Curacao .. .. | ..Maracaibo for Curacao .. .. | 1 | 5 |
| Dominican Republic .. .. | ..Santo Domingo .. .. | 1 | 6 |
| Dutch Guiana .. .. | ..Paramaribo .. .. .. | 1 | 3 |
| Ecuador .. .. | ..Ecuador .. .. .. | 1 | 5 |
| El Salvador .. .. | ..El Salvador .. .. .. | 2 | 3 |
| Europe .. .. .. | ..Miami .. .. .. | 1 | 5 |
| French Guiana .. .. | ..Cayenne .. .. .. | 1 | 3 |
| Great Britain .. .. | ..Miami .. .. . | 1 | 3 |
| Guatemala .. .. | ..Guatemala .. .. .. | 2 | 3 |
| Haiti .. .. .. | ..Port-au-Prince .. .. | 1 | 6 |
| Honduras .. .. | ..Honduras .. .. .. | 2 | 3 |
| Jamaica .. .. .. | ..Kingston .. .. .. | 1 | 3 |
| Mexico .. .. .. | ..Mexico .. .. .. | 1 | 8 |
| Nicaragua .. .. | ..Nicaragua .. .. .. | 2 | 3 |
| Panama .. .. .. | ..Panama .. .. .. | 1 | 5 |
| Peru .. .. .. | ..Peru .. .. .. | 2 | 0 |
| Porto Rico .. .. | ..San Juan .. .. .. | 1 | 0 |
| St. Lucia .. .. | ..Castries .. .. .. | | 9 |
| United States of America .. | ..Miami .. .. .. | 1 | 5 |
| Venezuela .. .. .. | ..La Guaira for Caracas .. .. | 1 | 5 |
| Do. .. .. .. | ..Maturin .. .. .. | 1 | 5 |
| Do. .. .. .. | ..La Guaira .. .. .. | 1 | 5 |
| Do. .. .. .. | ..Maracaibo .. .. .. | 1 | 5 |
| Virgin Islands of U. S. A. .. | ..St. Thomas .. .. .. | 1 | 0 |
| Uruguay .. .. .. | ..Montevideo .. .. .. | 2 | 3 |

Note.—If registered 3d. additional to be charged on each letter.

The Columbian rates were altered on 19 November 1931 as follows:-

| Country of Destination. | Town. | Air Port. | Air Rate per half oz. or fraction of half oz. | Route. |
|---|---|---|---|---|
| | | | s. d. | |
| Colombia .... | Barranquilla .... | Barranquilla .... | 1 9 | Direct. |
| Do. .... | Santa Marta .... | do. .... | 1 9 | do. |
| Do. .... | Calamar .... | do. .... | 1 9 | do. |
| Do. .... | Magangue .... | do. .... | 1 9 | do. |
| Do. .... | El Banco .... | do. .... | 1 9 | do. |
| Do. .... | Guamarra .... | do. .... | 1 9 | do. |
| Do. .... | Puerto Wilches .... | do. .... | 1 9 | do. |
| Do. .... | Barranca Bermeja.... | do. .... | 1 9 | do. |
| Do. .... | Pto. Berrio-Medellin | do. .... | 1 9 | do. |
| Do. .... | La Dorada .... | do. .... | 1 9 | do. |
| Do. .... | Giradot .... | do. .... | 1 9 | do. |
| Do. .... | Bogota .... | do. .... | 1 9 | do. |
| Do. .... | Cartagena .... | Buenaventura .... | 1 9 | do. |
| Do. .... | Sautata .... | do. .... | 1 9 | do. |
| Do. .... | Quibdo .... | do. .... | 1 9 | do. |
| Do. .... | Istmina .... | do. .... | 1 9 | do. |
| Do. .... | Buenaventura (Cali) | do. .... | 1 9 | do. |
| Do. .... | Guapi .... | do. .... | 1 9 | do. |
| Do. .... | Tumaco .... | do. .... | 1 9 | do. |

NOTE.—If registered 3d. additional to be charged on each letter.

On 19 November 1931 it was gazetted that the airmail rate to Colombia was increased to 1s. 9d. per ½oz.

On 1 December 1932 new rates were published:-

| Country of Destination. | Air Port. | Air Rate per half oz. or fraction of half oz. | |
|---|---|---|---|
| | | s. | d. |
| Argentine | Buenos Ayres | 2 | 5 |
| Antigua | St. Johns | | 11 |
| Bahamas | Nassau | 1 | 8 |
| Brazil | Montenegro | 2 | 2 |
| Do. | Para | 2 | 2 |
| Do. | Natal | 2 | 2 |
| Do. | Bahia | 2 | 2 |
| Do. | Rio de Janeiro | 2 | 2 |
| Br. Guiana | Georgetown | | 11 |
| Br. Honduras | Belize | 2 | 3 |
| Canada | Miami | 1 | 8 |
| Canal Zone | Cristobal | 1 | 7 |
| Chile | Chile | 2 | 9 |
| Do. | Santiago | 3 | 0 |
| Cuba | Havana | 1 | 8 |
| Do. | Camaguey | 1 | 8 |
| Do. | Santiago | 1 | 8 |
| Colombia | Baranquilla | 1 | 11 |
| Do. | Cartagena | 1 | 11 |
| Costa Rica | Costa Rica | 1 | 10 |
| Curacao | Maracaibo for Curacao | 1 | 7 |
| Dominican Republic | Santo Domingo | 1 | 8 |
| Dutch Guiana | Paramaribo | 1 | 5 |
| Ecuador | Ecuador | 1 | 7 |
| El Salvador | El Salvador | 2 | 5 |
| Europe | Miami | 1 | 7 |
| French Guiana | Cayenne | 1 | 5 |
| Great Britain | Miami | 1 | 5 |
| Guatemala | Guatemala | 2 | 5 |
| Haiti | Port-au-Prince | 1 | 8 |
| Honduras | Honduras | 2 | 5 |
| Jamaica | Kingston | 1 | 5 |
| Mexico | Mexico | 1 | 10 |
| Nicaragua | Nicaragua | 2 | 5 |
| Panama | Panama | 1 | 7 |
| Peru | Peru | 2 | 2 |
| Porto Rico | San Juan | 1 | 2 |
| St. Lucia | Castries | | 11 |
| United States of America | Miami | 1 | 7 |
| Venezuela | La Guaira for Caracas | 1 | 7 |
| Do. | Maturin | 1 | 7 |
| Do. | La Guaira | 1 | 7 |
| Do. | Maracaibo | 1 | 7 |
| Virgin Islands of U. S. A. | St. Thomas | 1 | 2 |
| Uruguay | Montevideo | 2 | 5 |

Note.—If registered 3d. additional to be charged on each letter.

Owing to reductions in the dollar exchange rate some of these were quickly amended by a notice published 19 December 1932 although dating them also from 1 December!

| Destination. | Weight not exceeding | | | Destination. | Weight not exceeding | | |
|---|---|---|---|---|---|---|---|
| | ½ oz. | 1 oz. | 1½ ozs. | | ½ oz. | 1 oz. | 1½ ozs. |
| Argentine .. | 2 7½ | 5. 0½ | 7. 7 | Europe, via Miami | | | |
| Antigua .. | 1. 0½ | 1.11½ | 2.11½ | ,, British .. | 1. 8½ | 3. 3½ | 4.11½ |
| Bahamas .. | 1. 9½ | 3. 5½ | 5. 2½ | ,, Foreign .. | 1. 9½ | 3. 4½ | 5. 1 |
| (via Miami) | | | | French Guiana .. | i. 7½ | 3. 0½ | 4. 7 |
| Brazil | 2. 4½ | 4. 6½ | 6.10 | Great Britain .. | 1. 6½ | 2.11½ | 4. 5½ |
| (Rio de Janeiro | | | | Guatemala .. | 2. 7½ | 5. 0½ | 7. 7 |
| Para, Bahia, etc. | | | | Haiti .. | 1.10½ | 3. 6½ | 5. 4 |
| British Guiana .. | 1. 0½ | 1.11½ | 2.11½ | Honduras .. | 2. 7½ | 5. 0½ | 7. 7 |
| British Honduras... | 2. 4½ | 4. 7½ | 6.11½ | Jamaica .. | 1. 6½ | 2.11½ | 4. 5½ |
| Canada .. | 1. 9½ | 3. 5½ | 5. 2½ | Mexico .. | 2. 0½ | 3.10½ | 5.10 |
| Canal Zone .. | 1. 9½ | 3. 4½ | 5. i | Nicaragua .. | 2. 7½ | 5. 0½ | 7. 7 |
| (Cristobal) | | | | Panama .. | 1. 9½ | 3. 4½ | 5. 1 |
| Chile .. | 2.11½ | 5. 8½ | 8. 7 | Peru .. | 2. 4½ | 4. 6½ | 6.10 |
| ,, Santiago .. | 3. 2½ | 6. 2½ | 9. 4 | Porto Rico .. | 1. 4½ | 2. 6½ | 3.10 |
| Cuba .. | 1.10½ | 3. 6½ | 5. 4 | (San Juan) | | | |
| Colombia .. | 2. 1½ | 4. 0½ | 6. i | St. Lucia .. | 1. 0½ | 1.11½ | 2.11½ |
| (Barranquilla, | | | | United States of | | | |
| Cartagena) | | | | America .. | 1. 9½ | 3. 4½ | 5. 1 |
| Costa Rica .. | 2. 0½ | 3.10½ | 5.10 | Venezuela .. | 1. 9½ | 3. 4½ | 5. 1 |
| Curacao .. | 1. 9½ | 3. 4½ | 5. 1 | Virgin Islands .. | 1. 4½ | 2. 6½ | 3.10 |
| (via Maracaibo) | | | | (St. Thomas) | | | |
| Dominican | | | | Uruguay .. | 2. 7½ | 5. 0½ | 7. 7 |
| Republic .. | 1.10½ | 3. 6½ | 5. 4 | | | | |
| Dutch Guiana .. | 1. 7½ | 3. 0½ | 4. 7 | | | | |
| Ecuador .. | 1. 9½ | 3. 4½ | 5. 1 | | | | |
| El Salvador .. | 2. 7½ | 5. 0½ | 7. 7 | | | | |

On 1 August 1933 new rates were published:-

| Country of Destination. | Air rate per ½ ounce or fraction of ½ ounce. | |
|---|---|---|
| | s. | d. |
| Argentine .. .. .. .. .. .. .. | 2 | 5 |
| Antigua .. .. .. .. .. .. .. | 0 | 8 |
| Bahamas .. .. .. .. .. .. .. | 1 | 6 |
| Bolivia .. .. .. .. .. .. .. | 2 | 2 |
| Brazil .. .. .. .. .. .. .. | 2 | 2 |
| British Guiana .. .. .. .. .. .. | 0 | 8 |
| British Honduras .. .. .. .. .. .. | 1 | 9 |
| Canada .. .. .. .. .. .. .. | 1 | 3 |
| Canal Zone .. .. .. .. .. .. | 1 | 1 |
| Chile .. .. .. .. .. .. .. | 2 | 2 |
| Colombia .. .. .. .. .. .. .. | 1 | 7 |
| Costa Rica .. .. .. .. .. .. | 1 | 4 |
| Cuba .. .. .. .. .. .. .. | 1 | 4 |
| Curacao .. .. .. .. .. .. .. | 1 | 1 |
| Dominican Republic .. .. .. .. .. | 1 | 4 |
| Dutch Guiana .. .. .. .. .. .. | 1 | 1 |
| Ecuador .. .. .. .. .. .. .. | 1 | 1 |
| Europe .. .. .. .. .. .. .. | 1 | 4 |
| French Guiana .. .. .. .. .. .. | 1 | 1 |
| Great Britain .. .. .. .. .. .. | 1 | 3 |
| Guatemala .. .. .. .. .. .. | 1 | 10 |
| Haiti .. .. .. .. .. .. .. | 1 | 4 |
| Honduras .. .. .. .. .. .. .. | 1 | 10 |
| Jamaica .. .. .. .. .. .. .. | 1 | 6 |
| Mexico .. .. .. .. .. .. .. | 1 | 4 |
| Nicaragua .. .. .. .. .. .. | 1 | 10 |
| Panama .. .. .. .. .. .. .. | 1 | 1 |
| Paraguay .. .. .. .. .. .. | 2 | 5 |
| Peru .. .. .. .. .. .. .. | 1 | 7 |
| Porto Rico .. .. .. .. .. .. | 0 | 10 |
| Salvador .. .. .. .. .. .. .. | 1 | 10 |
| St. Lucia .. .. .. .. .. .. | 0 | 8 |
| United States of America .. .. .. .. | 1 | 4 |
| Venezuela .. .. .. .. .. .. .. | 1 | 1 |
| Virgin Islands of the United States of America .. .. .. | 0 | 10 |
| Uruguay .. .. .. .. .. .. .. | 2 | 5 |

On 1 January 1934, a new tariff came into effect:-

| Country of Destination | Air rate per ½oz. or fraction of ½oz. | |
|---|---|---|
| | s. | d. |
| Argentina | 2 | 2 |
| Antigua | 0 | 8 |
| Bahamas | 1 | 4 |
| Bolivia | 1 | 11 |
| Brazil | 1 | 11 |
| British Guiana | 0 | 8 |
| British Honduras | 1 | 7 |
| Canada | 1 | 1 |
| Canal Zone | 1 | 0 |
| Chile | 1 | 11 |
| Colombia | 1 | 6 |
| Costa Rica | 1 | 3 |
| Cuba | 1 | 3 |
| Curacao | 1 | 0 |
| Dominican Republic | 1 | 3 |
| Dutch Guiana | 1 | 0 |
| Ecuador | 1 | 0 |
| Europe | 1 | 3 |
| French Guiana | 1 | 0 |
| Great Britain | 1 | 1 |
| Guatemala | 1 | 9 |
| Haiti | 1 | 3 |
| Honduras | 1 | 9 |
| Jamaica | 1 | 4 |
| Mexico | 1 | 3 |
| Nicaragua | 1 | 9 |
| Panama | 1 | 0 |
| Paraguay | 2 | 2 |
| Peru | 1 | 6 |
| Porto Rico | 0 | 9 |
| Salavador | 1 | 9 |
| St. Lucia | 0 | 8 |
| United States of America | 1 | 3 |
| Venezuela | 1 | 0 |
| Virgin Islands of the United States of America | 0 | 9 |
| Uruguay | 2 | 2 |

Note:- If registered 3d. additional to be charged on each letter.

On 14 January 1935 the following table was published:-

| COUNTRY OF DESTINATION. | To England by Steamer and Onward by Air. | | To New York by Air, Steamer to England and onward by Air. | |
|---|---|---|---|---|
| | First ½ oz. | Each additional ½ oz. | First ½ oz. | Each additional ½ oz. |
| | Cents. | Cents. | Cents. | Cents. |
| Palestine and Egypt .... .... .... .... | 9 | 8 | 32 | 31 |
| Iraq .... .... .... .... .... | 12 | 9 | 36 | 33 |
| India and Ceylon .... .... .... .... | 15 | 14 | 38 | 37 |
| Australia and New Zealand .... .... .... | 33 | 32 | 56 | 55 |
| Sudan .... .... .... .... .... | 9 | 8 | 32 | 8 |
| Kenya, Uganda, Tanganyika, Zanzibar, Nyasaland, Northern and Southern Rhodesia, South Africa.... | 15 | 14 | 38 | 37 |
| Syria and Trans-Jordan .... .... .... | 12 | 9 | 36 | 33 |
| Persia .... .... .... .... | 12 | 9 | 36 | 33 |
| Dutch East Indies .... .... .... .... | 30 | 27 | 54 | 51 |
| Mauritius .... .... .... .... | 15 | 14 | 38 | 37 |
| Siam .... .... .... .... .... | 28 | 25 | 52 | 49 |
| Hong Kong .... .... .... .... | 15 | 14 | 38 | 37 |
| Straits Settlements and Malay States .... .... | 15 | 14 | 38 | 37 |
| European Countries .... .... .... .... | 14 (1 oz.) | 9 (1 oz.) | 38 | 33 |

followed on 1 March 1935 by:-

| Country of Destination. | Air rate per ½ ounce or fraction of ½ ounce. |
|---|---|
| | Cents. |
| Argentine .... .. .... .... .... .... .... | 48 |
| Antigua .... .... .... .... .... .... .... | 15 |
| Bahamas ...,. .... .... .... .... .... .... | 30 |
| Bolivia .... .... .... .... .... .... .... | 42 |
| Brazil .... .... .... .... .... .... .... | 42 |
| British Guiana .... .... .... .... .... .... | 15 |
| British Honduras .... .... .... .... .... .... | 35 |
| Canada .... .... .... .... .... .... .... | 24 |
| Canal Zone .... .... .... .... .... .... | 22 |
| Chile .... .... . .... .... .... .... .... | 42 |
| Colombia .... .... .... .... .... .... | 32 |
| Costa Rica .... .... .... .... .... .... | 26 |
| Cuba .... .... .... .... .... .... .... | 26 |
| Curacao .... .... .... .... .... .... | 22 |
| Dominican Republic .... .... .... .... .... | 26 |
| Dutch Guiana .... .... .... .... .... .... | 22 |
| Ecuador .... .... .... .... .... .... | 22 |
| Europe .... .... .... .... .... .... | 26 |
| French Guiana .... .... .... .... .... .... | 22 |
| Great Britain .... .... .... .... .... .... | 24 |
| Guatemala .... .... .... .... .... .... | 37 |
| Haiti .... .... .... .... .... .... .... | 26 |
| Honduras .... .... .... .... .... .... | 37 |
| Jamaica .... .... .... .... .... .... | 30 |
| Mexico .... .... .... .... .... .... .... | 26 |
| Nicaragua .... .... .... .... .... .... | 37 |
| Panama .... .... .... .... .... .... | 22 |
| Paraguay .... .... .... .... .... .... | 48 |
| Peru .... .... .... .... .... .... .... | 32 |
| Porto Rico .... .... .... .... .... .... | 17 |
| Salvador .... .... .... .... .... .... | 37 |
| St. Lucia .... .... .... .... .... .... | 15 |
| United States of America .... .... .... .... | 26 |
| Venezuela .... .... .... .... .... | 22 |
| Virgin Islands of the United States of America .... .... | 17 |
| Uruguay .... .... .... .... .... .... .... | 48 |

Note.—If registered 6 cents additional to be charged on each letter.

On 5 March 1936 a new list was published:-

## AIR MAIL SERVICES.

Letters, postcards, printed papers, commercial papers and samples may be posted at any ℀ in the Colony for transmission by Air Mail.

An Air Mail packet can be accepted for registration but it cannot be insured.

Air Mail correspondence must be fully prepaid in stamps with ordinary postage stamps. If Mail fee is not fully prepaid the packet will not be forwarded by Air Mail. It will go forward ·ry mail.

A special Air Mail label should be affixed to the top left hand corner of every Air Mail packet. labels can be obtained free of charge at any Post Office in the Colony. If an Air Mail label available the packet should be clearly marked by the sender " BY AIR MAIL ".

The prepaid Air Rate on any kind of packet, that is, letters, postcards, printed papers, cial papers and samples is as follows :—

| Country of Destination. | Air rate per ½ ounce or fraction of ½ ounce. |
|---|---|
| | Cents. |
| Argentine .... .... .... .... .... .... | 48 |
| Antigua .... .... .... .... .... .... | 14 |
| Brazil .... .... .... .... .... ... | 43 |
| British Guiana .... .... .... .... .... | 14 |
| British Honduras .... .... .... .... .... | 35 |
| Canada .... .... .... .... .... .... | 24 |
| Canal Zone .... .... .... .... .... | 21 |
| Chile .... .... .... .... .... .... | 48 |
| Colombia .... .... .... .... .... .... | 32 |
| Costa Rica .... .... .... .... .... | 26 |
| Cuba .... .... .... .... .... | 26 |
| Dominican Republic .... .... .... .... | 26 |
| Dutch Guiana .... .... .... .... .... | 21 |
| Ecuador .... .... .... .... .... | 37 |
| Europe .... .... .... .... .... .... | 26 |
| French Guiana .... .... .... .... .... | 21 |
| Great Britain .... .... .... .... .... | 24 |
| Guadeloupe .... .... .... .... .... | 16 |
| Guatemala .... .... .... .... .... .... | 37 |
| Haiti .... .... .... .... ... . .... | 26 |
| Honduras .... .... .... .... .... | 37 |
| Jamaica .... .... .... .... .... .... | 24 |
| Martinique .... .... .... .... .... | 16 |
| Mexico .... .... .... .... .... .... | 37 |
| Nicaragua .... .... .... .... .... .... | 37 |
| Panama .... .... .... .... .... .... | 21 |
| Peru .... .... .... .... .... .... | 43 |
| Porto Rico .... .... .... .... .... | 16 |
| Salvador .... .... .... .... .... | 37 |
| United States of America .... .... .... .... | 26 |
| Venezuela .... .... .... .... .... | 21 |
| Virgin Islands of the United States of America .... .... | 16 |
| Uruguay .... .... .... .... .... .... | 48 |

—Registration fee 6 cents extra.

This cancels Air Mail Notice dated 1st March, 1935.

B. B. LITTLEPAGE,
*Postmaster-General.*

On 1 April 1937 rates were published as follows for the Trans-Pacific service:-

POST OFFICE NOTICE.

# TRANS-PACIFIC AIR MAIL SERVICE.

Effective with the Westbound flight leaving San Francisco on 21st April, 1937, the trans-Pacific Air Mail route will be available to Trinidad.

The Schedule will be :—

| | | | |
|---|---|---|---|
| San Francisco | .... | *dep.* | Wednesday |
| Honolulu .... | .... | *arr.* | Thursday |
| | | *dep.* | Friday |
| Guam | .... | *arr.* | Monday |
| | | *dep.* | Tuesday |
| Manila | .... | *arr.* | Tuesday |
| | | *dep.* | Wednesday |
| Macao | .... | *arr.* | Wednesday |
| Hong Kong .... | .... | *arr.* | Wednesday. |

To connect with this service, Mail Matter must be posted at Port-of-Spain by 6 p.m. on Fridays. (*Registration* 3.30 *p.m.*)

At Hong Kong connection will be made with the Chinese domestic Air-Mail system and with the British Air-Mail route for Malaya, Dutch East Indies, Australia, Siam and India.

Articles destined to all countries on this route should bear the Air-Mail Label and be marked (just over the address), " BY TRANS-PACIFIC ROUTE."

Short paid articles will not be despatched.

*Rates of Postage from Trinidad.*

| | | | | | | *Per ½ ounce.* |
|---|---|---|---|---|---|---|
| Honolulu (Hawaii) | .... | .... | .... | .... | | 52 cents |
| Guam | .... | .... | .... | .... | .... | 80 do. |
| Manila (Philippine Islands) .... | | .... | .... | .... | | 92 do. |
| Macao (Portuguese Colony) .... | | | .... | .... | | ....$ 1 00 |
| Hong Kong | .... | .... | .... | .... | | 1 00 |
| China | .... | .... | .... | .... | .... | 1 00 |
| Japan | .... | .... | .... | .... | .... | 1 00 |
| Indochina | .... | .... | .... | .... | | 1 00 |
| Malaya (Straits Settlements) | | | .... | .... | | 1 00 |
| Siam | .... | .... | .... | .... | .... | 1 00 |
| India | .... | .... | .... | .... | .... | 1 00 |
| Dutch East Indies .... | | .... | .... | .... | | 1 00 |
| Australia | .... | .... | .... | .... | | 1 00 |
| New Zealand | .... | .... | .... | .... | | 1 00 |

J. A. AYLES,
*Postmaster-General.*

General Post Office,
Trinidad, B.W.I.,
1st April, 1937.

On 1 July 1937 a new rate list was published:-

---

Post Office Notice.

---

## AIR MAIL SERVICES.

1. Letters, postcards, printed papers, commercial papers and samples may be posted at any post office in the Colony for transmission by Air Mail.

2. An Air Mail packet can be accepted for registration but it cannot be insured.

3. Air Mail correspondence must be fully prepaid in stamps with ordinary postage stamps. If the Air Mail fee is not fully prepaid the packet will not be forwarded by Air Mail. It will go forward by ordinary mail.

4. A special Air Mail label should be affixed to the top left hand corner of every Air Mail packet. These labels can be obtained free of charge at any Post Office in the Colony. If an Air Mail labe, is not available the packet should be clearly marked by the sender " BY AIR MAIL ".

5. The prepaid Air Rate on any kind of packet, that is, letters, postcards, printed papers commercial papers and samples is as follows :—

| Country of Destination. | Air rate per ½ ounce or fraction of ½ ounce. Cents. |
|---|---|
| Argentine | 56 |
| Antigua | 15 |
| Bahamas | 52 |
| Bolivia | 60 |
| Brazil | 50 |
| British Guiana | 15 |
| British Honduras | 41 |
| Canada | 25 |
| Canal Zone | 24 |
| Chile | 56 |
| Colombia | 37 |
| Costa Rica | 31 |
| Cuba | 31 |
| Dominican Republic | 31 |
| Dutch Guiana | 24 |
| Ecuador | 43 |
| Europe | 27 |
| French Guiana | 24 |
| Great Britain | 24 |
| Guadeloupe | 18 |
| Guatemala | 43 |
| Haiti | 31 |
| Honduras | 43 |
| Jamaica | 28 |
| Martinique | 18 |
| Mexico | 43 |
| Nicaragua | 43 |
| Panama | 24 |
| Peru | 50 |
| Porto Rico | 18 |
| Salvador | 43 |
| United States of America | 27 |
| Venezuela | 24 |
| Virgin Islands of the United States of America | 18 |
| Uruguay | 56 |

Note.—Registration fee 6 cents extra.

This cancels Air Mail Notice dated 1st March, 1936.

J. A. AYLES,
*Postmaster-General.*

General Post Office, Trinidad,
1st July, 1937.

On 5 May 1938 new rates some of which were affected by the second stage of the "all up" Empire air mail scheme, were published:-

| Destination | To London by steamer & air to destination. per ½oz. | Air to New York, steamer to London & air to destination. per ½oz. |
|---|---|---|
| AFRICA | | |
| Egypt; Sudan (Anglo Egyptian) | .09c. | .27c. |
| Basutoland; Bechuanaland; Gold Coast Colony; Kenya; Mauritius; N. Rhodesia; Nyasaland; Nigeria; Seychelles; S. W. Africa; S. Rhodesia; Swaziland; Tanganyika; Uganda; Union of S.Africa; Zanzibar. | .15c. | .33c. |
| Gambia; Sierra Leone | .21c. | .39c. |
| Algeria; Canary Islands; Morocco; Tunis | .14c. | .32c. |
| Libya | .16c. | .34c. |
| Belgian Congo; Portuguese East Africa, Portuguese West Africa | .22c. | .40c. |
| Madagascar | .26c. | .44c. |
| Dahomey; Eritrea; Ethiopia; French Cameroons; French Equatorial Africa; French Guinea: French Somali Coast; Italian Somaliland;Liberia; Senegal; Ivory Coast | .36c. | .54c. |
| ASIA | | |
| Palestine | .09c. | .27c. |
| Transjordan | .12c. | .30c. |
| Aden; Bahrein; Burma; Ceylon; Hong Kong; India; Malay States (Federated & Unfederated); North Borneo; Sarawak; Straits Settlements; Tibet | .15c. | .33c. |
| Iran; Iraq; Syria | .12c. | .30c. |
| Portuguese India | .18c. | .36c. |
| Siam | .28c. | .46c. |
| Union of Soviet Socialist Republics (Asia) | .30c. | .48c. |

| Destination | To London by steamer & air to destination. per ½oz. | Air to New York, steamer to London & air to destination. per ½oz. |
|---|---|---|
| ASIA Continued | | |
| Philippine Islands | .36c. | .54c. |
| French Indo China | .38c. | .56c. |
| China; Dutch East Indies | .42c. | .60c. |
| AUSTRALASIA | | |
| Australia; Fiji Islands; Norfolk Is. New Guinea; New Hebrides; New Zealand; Papua; Samoa; Solomon Islands | } } } } .33c. | .51c. |
| Dutch New Guinea | .30c. | .48c. |
| EUROPE | | |
| Albania; Belgium; Bulgaria; Danzig; Denmark; Estonia; Finland; France; Germany; Greece; Holland; Hungary; Italy; Latvia; Lithuania; Norway; Poland; Roumania; Sweden; Switzerland; Turkey; Union of Soviet Socialist Republics (Europe); Yugoslavia | } } } } } } } } } .11c. per 1oz. .06c. each add. oz. | .29c. |

| | Air to San Francisco & steamer to destination. per ½oz. | Air to destination. per ½oz. |
|---|---|---|
| TRANS-PACIFIC SERVICE* | | |
| Australia; New Zealand | .21c. | 1.38c. |
| Burma | .21c. | 1.20c. |
| Malaya (Straits Settlements) | .21c. | 1.22c. |
| Dutch East Indies | .24c. | 1.30c. |
| China; Indo China | .24c. | 1.00c. |
| Japan; Macao | .24c. | 1.00c. |
| Philippine Islands | .24c. | .92c. |
| Guam | .24c. | .80c. |
| Hawaii Islands | .24c. | .52c. |
| Hong Kong | .21c. | 1.00c. |
| India | .21c. | 1.30c. |
| Siam | .24c. | 1.22c. |

* This probably came into effect on 12 November 1937.

| Country of Destination. | Air rate per ½ ounce or fraction of ½ ounce. Cts. | Country of Destination. | Air rate per ½ ounce or fraction of ½ ounce. Cts. |
|---|---|---|---|
| Argentine .. .. | 48 | Great Britain .. | 21 |
| Antigua .. .. | 14 | Guadeloupe .. .. | 17 |
| Bahamas .. .. | 38 | Guatemala .. .. | 41 |
| Bolivia .. .. | 62 | Haiti .. .. | 28 |
| Brazil .. | 41 | Honduras .. .. | 41 |
| British Guiana .. | 14 | Jamaica .. .. | 27 |
| Bermuda .. .. | 38 | Martinique .. | 17 |
| Canada .. .. | 21 | Mexico .. .. | 41 |
| Canal Zone .. | 26 | Nicaragua .. .. | 41 |
| Chile .. .. | 62 | Panama .. .. | 26 |
| Colombia .. .. | 45 | Paraguay .. .. | 48 |
| Costa Rica .. | 41 | Peru .. .. | 48 |
| Cuba .. .. | 34 | Porto Rico .. .. | 20 |
| Dominican Republic .. | 28 | Salvador .. .. | 41 |
| Dutch Guiana .. | 17 | United States of America | 24 |
| Dutch West Indies .. | 34 | Venezuela .. .. | 22 |
| Ecuador .. .. | 48 | Virgin Islands of the | |
| Europe .. .. | 24 | United States of America | 20 |
| French Guiana .. | 17 | Uruguay .. .. | 48 |

Via BRAZIL, "AIR FRANCE" OR "LUFTHANSA" COMPANIES

| | | | | |
|---|---|---|---|---|
| (a) For Great Britain | .. | .. | .. | $1.00 per ½ oz. |
| (b) For Europe .. | .. | .. | ... | $1.02 do. |

Note.—Registration fee 6 cents extra.

On 31 May 1939 a notice was published regarding rates for the new North Atlantic service:-

## Air Mail Services.

It is notified for public information that an Air Mail Service has been inaugurated between New York and Europe *via* the Azores and Marseilles. Correspondence intended for conveyance by this route should be clearly marked **By Air to New York and onward by Air.** The postage rates which include Air Mail fees, are as follows :—

| Country of Destination. | Rate per half ounce. cents. | Country of Destination. | Rate per half ounce. cents. |
|---|---|---|---|
| Aden ... ... ... ... | 68 | Mauritius ... ... ... | 68 |
| Australia ... ... ... ... | 86 | New Zealand ... ... ... | 86 |
| Azores ... ... ... ... | 59 | Nigeria ... ... ... | 68 |
| Burma ... ... | 68 | Northern Rhodesia ... ... | 68 |
| Ceylon ... ... ... ... | 68 | Nyasaland ... ... ... | 68 |
| China ... ... ... | 95 | Palestine ... ... ... | 62 |
| Dutch East Indies ... ... ... | 83 | Persia ... ... ... | 65 |
| Egypt ... ... ... | 62 | Portuguese East Africa ... ... | 75 |
| European Countries (except Great | | Portuguese West Africa ... ... | 75 |
| Britain, Northern Ireland and Eire) | 59 | Siam ... ... .. | 81 |
| Fiji ... ... ... ... | 86 | Sierra Leone ... ... ... | 74 |
| Gambia ... ... ... ... | 74 | South Africa ... ... ... | 68 |
| Gold Coast ... ... ... | 68 | Southern Rhodesia ... ... | 68 |
| Great Britain, Northern Ireland and Eire | 56 | Straits Settlements ... ... | 68 |
| Hong Kong ... ... ... | 68 | Sudan (Anglo Egyptian) ... ... | 62 |
| India ... ... ... ... | 68 | Syria ... ... ... | 65 |
| Iraq ... ... ... ... | 65 | Tanganyika ... ... ... | 68 |
| Kenya ... ... ... ... | 68 | Trans-Jordan ... ... ... | 65 |
| Madagascar ... ... ... | 79 | Uganda ... ... ... | 68 |
| Malay States ... ... ... | 68 | Zanzibar ... ... ... | 68 |

Mails for despatch by this Service will be closed at the General Post Office, Port-of-Spain, on Thursdays at 6.00 p.m. They are due to arrive at Marseilles at 2.00 p.m. on the Monday following day of despatch.

D. M. FRASER,
*Acting Postmaster-General.*

New rates as follows became effective on 15 January 1940:-

| Country of Destination. | Direct. | To England by steamer and onward by Air | To New York by Air, to England by steamer, and onward by Air. | Via Natal and London | Via Trans-Pacific. | Via North Atlantic. | To New York by Air and onward by Steamer. |
|---|---|---|---|---|---|---|---|
| | $ c. | $ c. | $ c. | $ c. | $ c. | $ c. | $ c. |
| Aden | | 18 | 42 | 1 40 | .... | 84 | .... |
| Antigua | 18 | .... | .... | .... | .... | .... | .... |
| Argentine | 60 | .... | .... | .... | .... | .... | .... |
| Australia | .... | 42 | 64 | 1 62 | 1 72 | 1 08 | 26 |
| Azores | .... | .... | .... | .... | .... | 72 | .... |
| Bahamas | 48 | .... | .... | .... | .... | .... | .... |
| Barbados | 12 | .... | .... | .... | .... | .... | .... |
| Bermuda | 48 | .... | .... | .... | .... | .... | .... |
| Bolivia | 78 | .... | .... | .... | .... | .... | .... |
| Brazil | 52 | .... | .... | .... | .... | .... | .... |
| British Guiana | 18 | .... | .... | .... | .... | .... | .... |
| British Honduras | 52 | .... | .... | .... | .... | .... | .... |
| Burma | .... | 18 | 42 | 1 40 | 1 50 | 84 | .... |
| Canada | 26 | .... | .... | .... | .... | .... | .... |
| Canal Zone | 32 | .... | .... | .... | .... | .... | .... |
| Ceylon | .... | 18 | 42 | 1 40 | .... | 84 | .... |
| Chile | 78 | .... | .... | .... | .... | .... | .... |
| China | .... | 52 | 74 | 1 68 | 1 24 | 1 20 | 30 |
| Colombia | 56 | .... | .... | .... | .... | .... | .... |
| Costa Rica | 52 | .... | .... | .... | .... | .... | .... |
| Cuba | 42 | .... | .... | .... | .... | .... | .... |
| Dominican Republic | 36 | .... | .... | .... | .... | .... | .... |
| Dutch East Indies | .... | 38 | 60 | 1 56 | 1 62 | 1 04 | .... |
| Dutch Guiana | 20 | .... | .... | .... | .... | .... | .... |
| Dutch West Indies | 42 | .... | .... | .... | .... | .... | .... |
| Ecuador | 60 | .... | .... | .... | .... | .... | .... |
| Egypt | .... | 12 | 34 | 1 32 | 78 | .... | .... |
| European Countries (except Great Britain, Northern Ireland and Eire) | .... | 14 (1 oz.) | 36 | 1 28 | .... | 72 | 30 |
| Fiji | .... | 42 | 64 | 1 62 | .... | 1 08 | .... |
| French Guiana | 20 | .... | .... | .... | .... | .... | .... |
| Gambia | .... | 26 | 48 | 1 48 | .... | 92 | .... |
| Gold Coast | .... | 18 | 42 | 1 40 | .... | 84 | .... |
| Great Britain, Northern Ireland & Eire | .... | .... | .... | 1 24 | .... | 68 | 26 |
| Guadeloupe | 20 | .... | .... | .... | .... | .... | .... |
| Guam | .... | .... | .... | .... | 1 00 | .... | .... |
| Guatemala | 52 | ... | .... | .... | .... | .... | .... |
| Haiti | 36 | .... | .... | .... | .... | .... | .... |
| Honduras | 52 | .... | .... | .... | .... | .... | .... |
| Hong Kong | .... | 18 | 42 | 1 40 | 1 24 | 84 | 26 |
| Honolulu | .... | .... | .... | .... | 64 | .... | .... |
| India | .... | 18 | 42 | 1 40 | 1 62 | 84 | 26 |
| Indo-China | .... | .... | .... | .... | 1 24 | .... | 30 |
| Iraq | .... | 15 | 38 | 1 32 | .... | 80 | .... |
| Jamaica | 32 | .... | .... | .... | .... | .... | .... |
| Japan | .... | .... | .... | .... | 1 24 | .... | 30 |
| Kenya | .... | 18 | 42 | 1 40 | .... | 84 | ... |
| Macao | .... | .... | .... | .... | 1 24 | .... | 30 |
| Madagascar | .... | 32 | 56 | 1 50 | .... | 1 00 | .... |
| Madeira | .... | .... | .... | .... | .... | 72 | 30 |
| Malay States | .... | 18 | 42 | 1 40 | 1 52 | 84 | .... |
| Manila | .... | .... | .... | .... | 1 14 | .... | 30 |
| Martinique | 20 | .... | .... | .... | .... | .... | .... |
| Mauritius | .... | 18 | 42 | 1 40 | .... | 84 | .... |
| Mexico | 52 | .... | .... | .... | .... | .... | .... |
| New Zealand | .... | 42 | 64 | 1 62 | 1 72 | 1 08 | 26 |
| Nicaragua | 52 | .... | .... | .... | .... | .... | .... |
| Nigeria | .... | 18 | 42 | 1 40 | .... | 84 | .... |
| Northern Rhodesia | .... | 18 | 42 | 1 40 | .... | 84 | .... |
| Nyasaland | .... | 18 | 42 | 1 40 | .... | 84 | .... |
| Palestine | .... | 12 | 34 | 1 32 | .... | 78 | .... |
| Panama | 32 | .... | .... | .... | .... | .... | .... |
| Persia | .... | 15 | 38 | 1 32 | .... | 80 | .... |
| Peru | 60 | .... | .... | .... | .... | .... | .... |
| Porto Rico | 24 | .... | .... | .... | .... | .... | .... |
| Portuguese East and West Africa | .... | 27 | 50 | 1 44 | .... | 92 | .... |
| San Salvador | 52 | .... | .... | .... | .... | .... | .... |
| St. Thomas | 24 | .... | .... | .... | .... | .... | .... |
| Siam | .... | 36 | 58 | 1 52 | 1 52 | 1 00 | .... |
| Sierra Leone | .... | 26 | 48 | 1 48 | .... | 92 | .... |
| South Africa | .... | 18 | 42 | 1 40 | .... | 84 | .... |
| Southern Rhodesia | .... | 18 | 42 | 1 40 | .... | 84 | .... |
| Straits Settlements | .... | 18 | 42 | 1 40 | 1 52 | 84 | .... |
| Sudan (Anglo-Egyptian) | .... | 12 | 34 | 1 32 | .... | 78 | .... |
| Syria | .... | 15 | 38 | 1 32 | .... | 80 | .... |
| Tanganyika | .... | 18 | 42 | 1 40 | .... | 84 | .... |
| Trans-Jordan | .... | 15 | 38 | 1 32 | .... | 80 | .... |
| Uganda | .... | 18 | 42 | 1 40 | .... | 84 | .... |
| Uruguay | 60 | .... | .... | .... | .... | .... | .... |
| United States of America | 30 | .... | .... | .... | .... | .... | .... |
| Venezuela | 27 | .... | .... | .... | .... | .... | .... |
| Zanzibar | .... | 18 | 42 | 1 40 | .... | 84 | .... |

As the general British Empire Airmail rate had been fixed at 1s. 3d. per ½oz. on the outbreak of war many of the previous rates were obviously too low. This was rectified in a notice dated 15 May 1940:-

## AIR MAIL SERVICES.

1. It is notified for general information that rates of postage for correspondence by Air Mail addressed to :—

Aden. Australia, Burma, Ceylon, China, Dutch East Indies, Egypt, Fiji, Gambia, Gold Coast, Hong Kong, India, Iran, Iraq, Kenya, Madagascar, Malay States, Mauritius, New Zealand, Nigeria, Northern Rhodesia, Nyasaland, Palestine, Persia, Portuguese East and West Africa, Siam, Sierra Leone, South Africa, Southern Rhodesia, Straits Settlements, Sudan, Syria, Tanganyika, Thailand, Trans Jordan, Uganda and Zanzibar,

will, as from 1st June, 1940, be as follows :-

(a) To England by Steamer and onward by Air ... ...30 cents per half ounce.
(b) To New York by Air, to England by Steamer, and onward by Air ... ... .. 54 cents per half ounce.
(c) Via North Atlantic ... ... ... ...96 cents per half ounce.

2. Other rates of postage by Air Mail are as published in Post Office Notice, page 6 of the *Royal Gazette*, No. 1 of 4th January, 1940.

D. M. FRASER,
*Postmaster-General.*

On 2 December 1941 a post office notice was published regarding the new Pan-American Service to West Africa:-

## AIR MAIL SERVICE TO AFRICA.

It is notified for general information that an Air Mail Service will be inaugurated from Port-of-Spain *via* Belem (Brazil), Natal (Brazil), Bathurst (Gambia), and Lagos (Nigeria), to Leopoldville (Belgian Congo). The first flight is expected to leave Port-of-Spain on the 7th December, 1941, and mails will be closed at the General Post Office at 6 p.m. on Saturday, 6th December, 1941.

*Per half ounce.*

2. The rates of postage will be as follows:—

| | |
|---|---|
| Gambia, Liberia, Nigeria, French Equatorial Africa, Dahomey and Gold Coast ... ... ... | 48 cents. |
| Belgian Congo ... ... ... ... ... | 52 cents. |
| Kenya, Uganda, Tanganyika, Zanzibar, Northern and Southern Rhodesia ... ... ... ... | 54 cents. |
| Nyasaland and Union of South Africa ... ... | 56 cents. |
| Angola ... ... ... ... ... | 60 cents. |
| Sudan, Egypt and Palestine ... ... ... | 80 cents. |

3. *First flight Covers.*

Senders may address first flight covers to themselves or to persons at addresses other than on the route of flight so that they may be returned in the ordinary mails to the addressees after the first flight. The covers should be marked in the upper left hand corner to show the dispatch desired ; that is, "Port-of-Spain to Bathurst, Lagos, or Leopoldville" as the case may be. In order that covers may not be withdrawn from the flight by Censor at points on the route, no message should be contained in covers and they should not be sealed, the flap to be folded inside.

A cachet will be applied to all covers posted in Trinidad.

D. M. FRASER,
*Postmaster-General.*

On 20 March 1943:-

*"Air Mail for Antigua, Barbados, Grenada, St. Kitts and St. Lucia was five cents per half ounce".*

On 4 June 1943 St. Vincent was added at the same rate of 5c. per ½oz.

On 20 March 1943 a notice gave the air mail rate for Antigua, Barbados, St. Kitts and St. Lucia as 5 cents per ½oz.

On 25 March 1943 airmail rates to Africa were simplified as per the post office notice:-

*It is notified for general information that the postage by Air Mail for correspondence addressed to:-*

*Angola, Belgian Congo, Kenya, Mauritius, Mozambique, Nyasaland, Rhodesia (Northern and Southern), Tanganyika, Uganda, Union of South Africa and Zanzibar*

*is sixty cents per half ounce.*

On 1 January 1944 forces air letters were introduced:-

**AIR MAIL LETTERS FOR PERSONNEL OF HIS MAJESTY'S FORCES SERVING OVERSEAS**

*It is notified for general information that special Air Mail Letter Forms are available at all Post Offices in the Colony for communicating with members of the Armed Forces serving overseas.*
*The rate of postage is 12 cents, which must be prepaid.*

*This reduced rate of postage applies only to letters written on the special air letter forms, addressed to members of the Armed Forces overseas. The name and address of the sender must be written on the back of the form.*

*No enclosures of any kind are permitted. If anything is enclosed the letter will be sent by ordinary mail.*

*Air Mail Letter Forms cannot be accepted for Registration.*

On 5 October, 1944, special Air Letter Forms were available at 12 cents for the British Empire. This reduced rate of postage applied only to letters written on the special air letter forms. The name and address of the sender had to be written on the back of the form and no enclosures were permitted. Air Letter Forms could not be registered. The postage rate was five cents per half ounce. Correspondence posted for the first weekly despatch for the air service to Jamaica was closed at the General Office at 3.00 p.m. Thursday 11 December and were stamped by the Post Office with the impression "First Flight B. W. I. Airways Trinidad -- Jamaica".

New airmail rates became effective on 1 August 1945:-

LETTERS, postcards, printed papers, commercial papers and samples may be posted at any Post Office in the Colony for transmission by Air Mail.

An Air Mail packet can be accepted for registration but cannot be insured.

Air Mail correspondence must be fully prepaid by affixing postage stamps to the packet.

A special Air Mail Label should be affixed to the top left hand corner of every Air Mail packet. These labels can be obtained free of charge at any Post Office in the Colony. If an Air Mail Label is not available the packet should be clearly marked by the sender " BY AIR MAIL ".

*Special Air Letter Forms* are available at Post Offices in the Colony for communicating with countries in the British Empire. No enclosures of any kind are permitted. If anything is enclosed the letter will be sent by Ordinary Mail. Air Letter Forms cannot be registered.

The following rates of postage by Air Mail become effective on 1st August, 1945, and cancel all rates previously published :—

| Country of Destination. | Rate per half ounce. | Special Air Letter Form. | Country of Destination. | Rate per half ounce. | Special Air Letter Form. |
|---|---|---|---|---|---|
| | $ c. | $ c. | | $ c. | $ c. |
| Abyssinia | 72 | — | Haiti | 18 | — |
| Aden | 1 20 | 12 | Honduras Republic | 18 | — |
| Alaska | 20 | — | Hong Kong | 1 44 | 12 |
| Algeria | 72 | — | Honolulu | 1 44 | — |
| Angola | 72 | — | | | |
| Antigua | 05 | 05 | India | 1 20 | 12 |
| Argentina | 24 | — | Indo-China | 1 44 | — |
| Aruba | 18 | — | Iraq and Iran (Persia) | 1 20 | — |
| Ascension | 72 | 12 | Jamaica—*via* B.W.I.A. | 05 | 05 |
| Australia (to Panama by Air) | 18 | 12 | Jamaica—*via* P.A.A. | 18 | 12 |
| Azores | 72 | — | Japan | 1 44 | — |
| Bahamas | 36 | 12 | Kenya | 72 | 12 |
| Barbados | 05 | 05 | | | |
| Basutoland | 72 | 12 | Macao | 1 44 | — |
| Bechuanaland | 72 | 12 | Madagascar | 72 | — |
| Belgian Congo | 72 | — | Madeira | 60 | — |
| Bermuda | 36 | 12 | Malay States | 1 44 | 12 |
| Bolivia | 24 | — | Malta | 72 | 12 |
| Brazil | 24 | — | Manila | 1 44 | — |
| British Guiana | 18 | 12 | Martinique | 18 | — |
| British Honduras | 24 | 12 | Mauritius | 72 | 12 |
| British North Borneo | 1 44 | 12 | Mexico | 18 | — |
| Burma | 1 44 | 12 | Montserrat (*via* St. Kitts) | 05 | 05 |
| Cameroons | 72 | 12 | Newfoundland | 20 | 12 |
| Canada | 20 | 12 | New Zealand (to Panama by Air) | 18 | 12 |
| Canal Zone | 18 | — | Nicaragua | 18 | — |
| Canary Islands | 72 | — | Nigeria | 48 | 12 |
| Cape Verde Islands | 72 | — | Nyasaland | 72 | 12 |
| Ceylon | 1 20 | 12 | | | |
| Chile | 24 | — | Palestine | 72 | 12 |
| China | 1 44 | — | Panama | 18 | — |
| Colombia | 36 | — | Paraguay | 24 | — |
| Costa Rica | 18 | — | Persia | 1 20 | — |
| Cuba | 18 | — | Peru | 24 | — |
| Curacao | 18 | — | Puerto Rico | 18 | — |
| Cyprus | 72 | 12 | Portuguese East and West Africa | 72 | — |
| Dominica (B.W.I.) | 05 | 05 | Rhodesia (North and South) | 72 | 12 |
| Dominican Republic | 18 | — | | | |
| Dutch East Indies | 1 44 | — | San Domingo | 18 | — |
| Dutch Guiana | 18 | — | San Salvador | 18 | — |
| Dutch West Indies | 18 | — | St. Helena | 72 | 12 |
| | | | St. Kitts | 05 | 05 |
| Ecuador | 24 | — | St. Lucia | 05 | 05 |
| Eire (Ireland) | 60 | 12 | St. Thomas, V.I. | 18 | — |
| Eire—to New York by air and onward | | | St. Vincent | 05 | 05 |
| by steamer | 20 | — | Seychelles | 72 | 12 |
| Egypt | 72 | 12 | Siam | 1 44 | — |
| European countries (except Great | | | Sierra Leone | 72 | 12 |
| Britain and Ireland) | 72 | — | Solomon Islands | 1 44 | 12 |
| European countries (except Great | | | Somaliland | 72 | 12 |
| Britain and Ireland)—by air to New | | | South Africa | 72 | 12 |
| York and onward by steamer | 20 | — | South West Africa | 72 | 12 |
| | | | Straits Settlements | 1 44 | 12 |
| Falkland Islands | 24 | 12 | Sudan (Anglo-Egyptian) | 72 | 12 |
| Fiji | 1 44 | 12 | Swaziland | 72 | 12 |
| French Guiana | 18 | — | Syria | 72 | — |
| Gambia | 72 | 12 | Tanganyika | 72 | 12 |
| Gibraltar | 72 | 12 | Togoland | 72 | 12 |
| Gold Coast | 72 | 12 | Trans-Jordan | 72 | 12 |
| Great Britain and Ireland | 60 | 12 | | | |
| Great Britain and Ireland—by air to | | | Uganda | 72 | 12 |
| New York and onward by steamer | 20 | — | United States of America | 20 | — |
| Grenada | 05 | 05 | Uruguay | 24 | — |
| Guadeloupe | 18 | — | | | |
| Guam | 1 44 | — | Venezuela | 18 | — |
| Guatemala | 18 | — | Zanzibar | 72 | 12 |

General Post Office,
Trinidad,
25th July, 1945.

D. M. FRASER,
*Postmaster General*

195

Followed on 7 August 1945 by:-

|  | Rate per half ounce. | | Special Air Letter Form. | |
|---|---|---|---|---|
|  | $ | c. | $ | c. |
| Australia via San Francisco . . . . |  | 96 |  | 12 |
| Fiji via San Francisco     . . . . |  | 84 |  | 12 |
| New Zealand via San Francisco . |  | 96 |  | 12 |

*Packets must not exceed two ounces in weight.*

and on 22 October 1945:-

*Air Mail Rates to British Guiana are:-*

*via British West India Airways    05 cents per half ounce.*

*via Pan American Airways    18 cents per half ounce.*

On 26 October 1945 the rate to Columbia was reduced to 26 cents per half ounce.

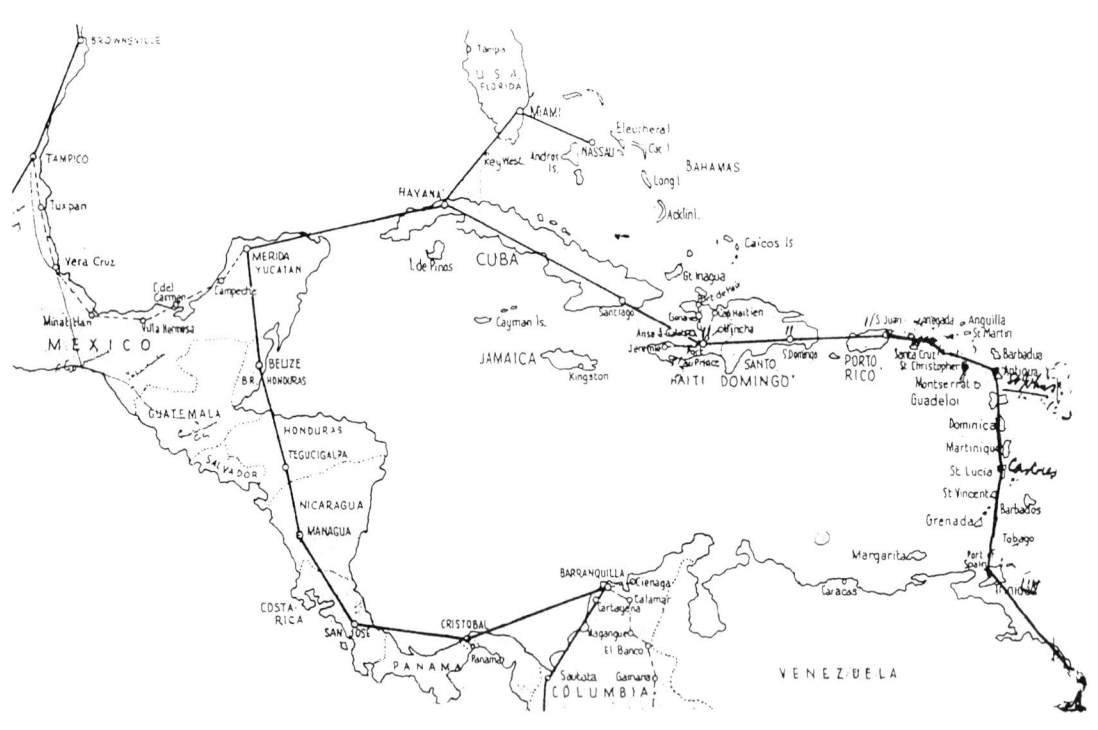

**The P.A.A. routes in 1929.**

# On 1 June 1947 new air mail rates became effective:-

## POST OFFICE—AIR MAIL SERVICES

LETTERS, postcards, printed papers, commercial papers and samples may be posted at any Post Office in the Colony for transmission by Air Mail.

An Air Mail packet can be accepted for registration but cannot be insured.

Air Mail correspondence must be fully prepaid by affixing postage stamps to the packet.

A special Air Mail label should be affixed to the top left hand corner of every Air Mail packet. These labels can be obtained free of charge at any Post Office in the Colony. If an Air Mail label is not available the packet should be clearly marked by the sender "BY AIR MAIL"

Special Air Letter Forms are available at Post Offices in the Colony for communicating with countries in the British Empire. No enclosures of any kind are permitted. If anything is enclosed the letter will be sent by Ordinary Mail. Air Letter Forms cannot be registered.

The following rates of postage by Air Mail become effective on 1st June, 1947, and cancel all rates previously published:—

| Country of Destination | Rate per half ounce | Post Cards | Air Forms |
|---|---|---|---|
| | c. | c. | c. |
| Abyssinia | 60 | 30 | — |
| Aden | 60 | 30 | 12 |
| Alaska | 18 | 09 | — |
| Algeria | 60 | 30 | — |
| Antigua via B.W.I.A. | 05 | 05 | 05 |
| Antigua via P.A.A. | 08 | 05 | 05 |
| Angola | 60 | 30 | — |
| Argentine | 24 | 12 | — |
| Aruba | 12 | 06 | — |
| Ascension | 60 | 30 | 12 |
| Australia | 60 | 30 | 12 |
| Azores | 36 | 18 | — |
| Bahamas | 18 | 09 | 12 |
| Barbados | 05 | 05 | 05 |
| Basutoland | 60 | 30 | 12 |
| Bechuanaland | 60 | 30 | 12 |
| Belgian Congo | 60 | 30 | — |
| Bermuda | 18 | 09 | 12 |
| Bolivia | 24 | 12 | — |
| Brazil | 24 | 12 | — |
| British Guiana | 06 | 05 | 05 |
| British Honduras | 24 | 12 | 12 |
| British North Borneo | 60 | 30 | 12 |
| Burma | 60 | 30 | 12 |
| Cameroons | 60 | 30 | 12 |
| Canada | 18 | 09 | 12 |
| Canal Zone | 24 | 12 | — |
| Canary Islands | 60 | 30 | — |
| Cape Verde Islands | 60 | 30 | — |
| Ceylon | 60 | 30 | 12 |
| China | 60 | 30 | — |
| Colombia | 24 | 12 | — |
| Costa Rica | 24 | 12 | — |
| Cuba | 18 | 09 | — |
| Curacao | 12 | 06 | — |
| Cyprus | 60 | 30 | 12 |
| Dominica (British West Indies) | 05 | 05 | 05 |
| Dominican Republic | 12 | 06 | — |
| Dutch East Indies | 60 | 30 | — |
| Dutch Guiana | 12 | 06 | — |
| Dutch West Indies | 12 | 06 | — |
| Ecuador | 24 | 12 | — |
| Eire (Ireland) | 36 | 18 | 12 |
| Eire—to New York by Air and onward by Steamer | 18 | 09 | — |
| Egypt | 60 | 30 | 12 |
| Europe (except Great Britain and Ireland) | 48 | 24 | — |
| Europe (except Great Britain and Ireland) by Air to New York and onward by Steamer | 24 | 12 | — |
| Falkland Islands | 24 | 12 | 12 |
| Fiji | 60 | 30 | 12 |
| French Guiana | 12 | 06 | — |
| Gambia | 60 | 30 | 12 |
| Gibraltar | 60 | 30 | 12 |
| Gold Coast | 60 | 30 | 12 |
| Great Britain and Ireland | 36 | 18 | 12 |
| Great Britain and Ireland—by Air to New York and onward by Steamer | 18 | 09 | — |
| Grenada | 05 | 05 | 05 |
| Guadeloupe | 08 | 05 | — |
| Guam | 60 | 30 | — |
| Guatemala | 24 | 12 | — |
| Haiti | 12 | 06 | — |

| Country of Destination | Rate per half ounce | Post Cards | Air Forms |
|---|---|---|---|
| | c. | c. | c. |
| Honduras Republic | 24 | 12 | — |
| Hong Kong | 60 | 30 | 12 |
| Honolulu | 60 | 30 | — |
| India | 60 | 30 | 12 |
| Indo-China | 60 | 30 | — |
| Iraq and Iran (Persia) | 60 | 30 | — |
| Jamaica—via B.W.I.A. | 05 | 05 | 05 |
| Jamaica—via P.A.A. | 12 | 06 | 05 |
| Japan | 60 | 30 | — |
| Kenya | 60 | 30 | 12 |
| Macao | 60 | 30 | — |
| Madagascar | 60 | 30 | — |
| Madeira | 48 | 24 | — |
| Malay States | 60 | 30 | 12 |
| Malta | 60 | 30 | 12 |
| Manila | 60 | 30 | — |
| Martinique | 08 | 05 | — |
| Mauritius | 60 | 30 | 12 |
| Mexico | 24 | 12 | — |
| Montserrat (via St. Kitts) | 05 | 05 | 05 |
| Newfoundland | 18 | 09 | 12 |
| New Zealand | 60 | 30 | 12 |
| Nicaragua | 24 | 12 | — |
| Nigeria | 60 | 30 | 12 |
| Nyasaland | 60 | 30 | 12 |
| Palestine | 60 | 30 | 12 |
| Panama | 24 | 12 | — |
| Paraguay | 24 | 12 | — |
| Persia | 60 | 30 | — |
| Peru | 24 | 12 | — |
| Puerto Rico | 12 | 06 | — |
| Portuguese East and West Africa | 60 | 30 | — |
| Rhodesia (North and South) | 60 | 30 | 12 |
| San Domingo | 12 | 06 | — |
| San Salvador | 24 | 12 | — |
| St. Helena | 60 | 30 | 12 |
| St. Kitts | 05 | 05 | 05 |
| St. Lucia | 05 | 05 | 05 |
| St. Thomas V. I. | 12 | 06 | — |
| St. Vincent | 05 | 05 | 05 |
| Seychelles | 60 | 30 | 12 |
| Siam | 60 | 30 | — |
| Sierra Leone | 60 | 30 | 12 |
| Solomon Islands | 60 | 30 | 12 |
| Somaliland | 60 | 30 | 12 |
| South Africa | 60 | 30 | 12 |
| South West Africa | 60 | 30 | 12 |
| Straits Settlements | 60 | 30 | 12 |
| Sudan (Anglo Egyptian) | 60 | 30 | 12 |
| Syria | 60 | 30 | — |
| Tanganyika | 60 | 30 | 12 |
| Togoland | 60 | 30 | 12 |
| Trans-Jordan | 60 | 30 | 12 |
| Uganda | 60 | 30 | 12 |
| United States of America | 18 | 09 | — |
| Uruguay | 24 | 12 | — |
| Venezuela | 08 | 05 | — |
| Zanzibar | 60 | 30 | 12 |

E. S. MOORE,
*Postmaster General.*

General Post Office,
Trinidad.
12th May, 1947.

On 2 August 1947 the following rates became effective:-

REGULATIONS MADE BY THE GOVERNOR IN COUNCIL UNDER
THE POST OFFICE ORDINANCE, Ch. 36. No. 1

1. THESE Regulations may be cited as the Post Office (Amendment) Regulations, 1950, and shall be read as one with the Post Office Regulations, 1938 as from time to time amended, which Regulations as so amended are hereinafter referred to as the Principal Regulations.

2. Sub-paragraph (XI) of paragraph (1) of regulation 12 of the Principal Regulations is hereby revoked and replaced by the following :—

"(XI) on all air mail packets the rates hereinafter respectively set out, that is to say :—

| Country of Destination | Route | Letter post per half ounce | Postcard | Special Air Letter Form |
|---|---|---|---|---|
| | | Cents | Cents | Cents |
| Abyssinia ... ... | ... | 66 | 33 | — |
| Aden ... ... | ... | 60 | 30 | 12 |
| Alaska ... ... | ... | 24 | 12 | — |
| Algeria ... ... | ... | 36 | 18 | — |
| Antigua ... ... | British ... | 05 | 05 | 05 |
| Antigua ... ... | Foreign ... | 08 | 05 | — |
| Angola ... ... | ... | 72 | 36 | — |
| Argentine ... ... | ... | 36 | 18 | 12 |
| Aruba ... ... | British ... | 10 | 05 | — |
| Aruba ... ... | Foreign ... | 12 | 06 | — |
| Australia ... ... | ... | 78 | 39 | 12 |
| Azores ... ... | ... | 30 | 15 | — |
| Bahamas ... ... | British ... | 16 | 08 | 12 |
| Bahamas ... ... | Foreign ... | 24 | 12 | — |
| Barbados ... ... | ... | 05 | 05 | 05 |
| Basutoland ... | ... | 72 | 36 | 12 |
| Bechuanaland ... | ... | 72 | 36 | 12 |
| Belgian Congo | ... | 72 | 36 | — |
| Bermuda ... ... | British ... | 18 | 09 | 12 |
| Bermuda ... ... | Foreign ... | 30 | 15 | — |
| Bolivia ... ... | ... | 32 | 16 | — |
| Brazil ... ... | ... | 24 | 12 | 12 |
| British Honduras ... | British ... | 05 | 05 | 05 |
| British Honduras ... | Foreign ... | 24 | 12 | — |
| British Guiana ... | British ... | 05 | 05 | 05 |
| British Guiana ... | Foreign ... | 08 | 05 | — |
| British North Borneo ... | ... | 84 | 42 | 12 |
| Burma ... | ... | 72 | 36 | 12 |
| Cameroons, British ... | ... | 54 | 27 | 12 |
| Cameroons, French ... | ... | 90 | 45 | — |
| Canada ... ... | ... | 24 | 12 | 12 |
| Canal Zone ... ... | ... | 16 | 08 | 12 |
| Canary Islands ... | ... | 36 | 18 | — |
| Cape Verde Islands ... | ... | 36 | 18 | — |
| Ceylon ... ... | ... | 72 | 36 | 12 |
| China ... ... | ... | $1.00 | 50 | — |
| Colombia ... ... | ... | 24 | 12 | — |
| Costa Rica ... ... | ... | 18 | 09 | — |
| Cuba ... ... | ... | 24 | 12 | 12 |
| Curacao ... ... | British ... | 10 | 05 | — |
| Curacao ... ... | Foreign ... | 12 | 06 | — |
| Cyprus ... ... | ... | 36 | 18 | — |
| Chile ... ... | ... | 36 | 18 | — |
| Dominica ... ... | ... | 05 | 05 | 05 |
| Dominican Republic ... | ... | 12 | 06 | — |
| Dutch East Indies ... | ... | 90 | 45 | — |
| Dutch Guiana ... ... | ... | 12 | 06 | — |
| Dutch West Indies ... | British ... | 10 | 05 | — |
| Dutch West Indies ... | Foreign ... | 12 | 06 | — |
| Ecuador ... ... | ... | 24 | 22 | — |
| Eire (Ireland) ... ... | British ... | 32 | 16 | 12 |
| Eire (Ireland) ... ... | Foreign ... | 48 | 24 | — |
| Eire (Ireland) ... ... | To New York by Air and onward by Steamer | 24 | 12 | — |

| Country of Destination | Route | Letter post per half ounce | Postcard | Special Air Letter Form |
|---|---|---|---|---|
| | | Cents | Cents | Cents |
| Egypt ... ... ... | | 48 | 24 | 12 |
| Europe ... ... | British ... | 36 | 18 | — |
| Europe ... ... | Foreign ... | 52 | 26 | — |
| Flakland Islands ... ... | | 36 | 18 | 12 |
| Fiji ... ... | | 60 | 30 | 12 |
| French Guiana | | 12 | 06 | — |
| Gambia ... ... ... | | 52 | 26 | 12 |
| Gibraltar ... ... | | 36 | 18 | 12 |
| Gold Coast ... ... | | 52 | 26 | 12 |
| Great Britain and Ireland ... | British ... 2nd Class Mail | 30 / 10 | 15 / — | 12 / — |
| Great Britain and Ireland | Foreign ... 2nd Class Mail | 48 / 16 | 24 / — | — / — |
| Great Britain and Ireland | To New York by Air only | 24 | 12 | — |
| Grenada ... ... | | 05 | 05 | 05 |
| Guadeloupe ... ... | | 10 | 05 | — |
| Guam ... ... | | 66 | 33 | — |
| Guatemala ... ... | | 24 | 12 | — |
| Haiti ... | | 15 | 08 | — |
| Honduras Republic ... | | 24 | 12 | — |
| Hong Kong ... ... | | 72 | 36 | 12 |
| Honolulu ... ... | | 40 | 20 | — |
| India ... ... | | 72 | 36 | 12 |
| Indo China ... ... | | 84 | 42 | — |
| Iraq and Iran ... ... | | 60 | 30 | — |
| Jamaica ... ... | British ... | 05 | 05 | 05 |
| Jamaica ... ... | Foreign ... | 12 | 06 | .— |
| Japan ... ... | | 60 | 30 | — |
| Kenya ... ... | | 66 | 33 | 12 |
| Liberia ... ... | | 52 | 26 | 12 |
| Libya ... ... | | 40 | 20 | — |
| Macao ... ... | | $1.00 | 50 | — |
| Madagascar ... ... | | 72 | 36 | — |
| Madeira ... ... | | 36 | 18 | — |
| Malaya ... ... | | 84 | 42 | 12 |
| Malta ... ... | | 36 | 18 | 12 |
| Manila ... ... | | 72 | 36 | 12 |
| Martinique ... ... | | 10 | 05 | — |
| Mauritius ... ... | | 80 | 40 | 05 |
| Mexico ... ... | | 26 | 13 | — |
| Montserrat ... ... | | 05 | 05 | 12 |
| Morocco ... ... | | 36 | 18 | — |
| Newfoundland ... | | 24 | 12 | 12 |
| New Guinea ... ... | | 60 | 30 | 12 |
| New Zealand ... | | 78 | 39 | 12 |
| Nicaragua ... ... | | 18 | 09 | — |
| Nigeria ... ... | | 52 | 26 | 12 |
| Nyasaland ... ... | | 78 | 39 | 12 |
| Pakistan ... ... | | 72 | 36 | 12 |
| Palestine ... ... | | 40 | 20 | 12 |
| Panama ... ... | | 16 | 08 | 12 |
| Paraguay ... ... | | 40 | 20 | — |
| Persia ... ... | | 54 | 27 | — |
| Peru ... ... | | 26 | 13 | — |
| Puerto Rico ... ... | | 12 | 06 | 12 |
| Portuguese East Africa | | 78 | 39 | — |
| Portuguese West Africa | | 72 | 36 | — |
| Rhodesia (North and South) | | 78 | 39 | — |
| San Domingo ... | | 15 | 08 | — |
| San Salvador ... | | 24 | 12 | — |
| St. Kitts ... ... | | 05 | 05 | 05 |
| St. Lucia ... ... | | 05 | 05 | 05 |
| St. Thomas (Virgin Islands) | | 12 | 06 | 12 |
| St. Vincent ... ... | | 05 | 05 | 05 |
| Senegal ... ... | | 52 | 26 | — |
| Seychelles ... ... | | 70 | 35 | 12 |
| Siam ... ... | | 78 | 39 | — |
| Sierra Leone ... | | 52 | 62 | 12 |
| Solomon Islands ... | | 60 | 30 | 12 |
| Somaliland ... ... | | 66 | 33 | 12 |
| South Africa ... ... | | 78 | 39 | 12 |
| South West Africa ... | | 78 | 39 | 12 |
| Strait Settlement ... | | 84 | 42 | 12 |
| Sudan (Anglo Egyptian) | | 60 | 30 | 12 |
| Syria ... ... | | 54 | 27 | — |

| Country of Destination | Route | Letter post per half ounce | Postcard | Special Air Letter Form |
|---|---|---|---|---|
| | | Cents | Cents | Cents |
| Tanganyika ... ... ... | | 66 | 33 | 12 |
| Togoland ... ... ... | | 54 | 27 | 12 |
| Tripolitania ... ... ... | | 40 | 20 | — |
| Trans-Jordan ... ... ... | | 48 | 24 | 12 |
| Tortola ... ... ... | | 12 | 06 | 05 |
| Tunisia ... ... ... | | 36 | 18 | — |
| Uganda ... ... ... | | 66 | 33 | 12 |
| United States of America | British ... | 20 | 10 | 12 |
| United States of America | Foreign ... | 24 | 12 | 12 |
| Uraguay ... ... ... | | 36 | 18 | — |
| Venezuela ... ... ... | | 12 | 06 | — |
| Zanzibar ... ... ... | | 66 | 33 | 12 |

Made by the Governor in Council this 14th day of March, 1950.

G. E. CHEN
*Clerk, Executive Council*

Approved by the Legislative Council this 17th day of March, 1950.

W. FUNG
*Clerk, Legislative Council*

## On 2 August 1949 the 12c. A.L.S. Service was extended to:-

*Argentina*  
*Brazil*  
*Cuba*  
*Germany (British Zone)*  
*Liberia*  

*Panama Canal Zone*  
*Panama, Republic of Phillipines*  
*Puerto Rico*  
*United States of America*  
*Virgin Islands (U.S.A.)*

New rates came into effect on 9 February 1953:-

AIR MAIL PACKET RATES

| Country of Destination | Letter Post per ½ oz. | Post Card | Special Air Letter Form | Printed papers, commercial papers, and small packets per ½ oz. |
|---|---|---|---|---|
| | cents | cents | cents | cents |
| Aden ... ... ... ... | 66 | 33 | 12 | 29 |
| Alaska ... ... ... ... | 30 | 15 | 12 | 17 |
| Algeria ... ... ... ... | 42 | 21 | 12 | 21 |
| Antigua ... ... ... ... | 06 | 05 | 05 | * |
| Angola ... ... ... ... | 66 | 33 | 12 | 29 |
| Argentine ... ... ... ... | 36 | 18 | 12 | 12 |
| | | | | |
| Aruba ... ... ... ... | 12 | 06 | 09 | 04 |
| Australia ... ... ... ... | 72 | 36 | 12 | 27 |
| Azores ... ... ... ... | 40 | 20 | 12 | 14 |
| | | | | |
| Bahamas ... ... ... ... | 16 | 08 | 12 | 05 |
| Barbados ... ... ... ... | 06 | 05 | 05 | * |
| Basutoland ... ... ... ... | 72 | 36 | 12 | 31 |
| Bechuanaland ... ... ... ... | 72 | 36 | 12 | 31 |
| Belgian Congo ... ... ... ... | 66 | 33 | 12 | 29 |
| Bermuda ... ... ... ... | 16 | 08 | 12 | 09 |
| Bolivia ... ... ... ... | 32 | 16 | 12 | 10 |
| Brazil ... ... ... .. | 30 | 15 | 12 | 10 |
| British Honduras ... ... ... | 06 | 05 | 05 | * |
| British Guiana ... ... ... ... | 06 | 05 | 05 | * |
| British North Borneo ... ... ... | 84 | 42 | 12 | 36 |
| Burma ... ... ... ... | 72 | 36 | 12 | 32 |
| | | | | |
| Cameroons (British) ... ... ... | 60 | 30 | 12 | 25 |
| Canada ... ... ... ... | 20 | 10 | 12 | 10 |
| Canal Zone ... ... ... ... | 16 | 08 | 12 | 06 |
| Canary Islands ... ... ... ... | 42 | 21 | 12 | 24 |
| Cape Verde Islands ... ... ... | 42 | 21 | 12 | 24 |
| Ceylon ... ... ... ... | 72 | 36 | 12 | 30 |
| China ... ... ... ... | 72 | 36 | 12 | 30 |
| Colombia ... ... ... ... | 24 | 12 | 12 | 16 |
| Costa Rica ... ... ... ... | 18 | 09 | 12 | 06 |
| Cuba ... ... ... ... | 18 | 09 | 12 | 07 |
| Curacao ... ... ... ... | 10 | 06 | 09 | 04 |
| Cyprus ... ... ... ... | 42 | 21 | 12 | 23 |
| Chile ... ... ... ... | 36 | 18 | 12 | 12 |
| | | | | |
| Dominica ... ... ... ... | 06 | 05 | 05 | * |
| Dominican Republic ... ... ... | 12 | 06 | 09 | 05 |
| Dutch Guiana ... ... ... ... | 10 | 06 | 09 | 04 |
| | | | | |
| Ecuador ... ... ... ... | 24 | 12 | 12 | 07 |
| Eire (Ireland) ... ... ... ... | 36 | 18 | 12 | 18 |
| Eire (Ireland) (to New York by Air and onward by Steamer) ... ... ... ... | 24 | — | — | — |
| Egypt ... ... ... ... | 48 | 24 | 12 | 25 |
| El Salvador ... ... ... ... | 20 | 10 | 12 | 07 |
| Ethiopia ... ... ... ... | 66 | 33 | 12 | 29 |
| Europe (except U.S.S.R.) ... ... ... | 42 | 21 | 12 | 20 |
| | | | | |
| Falkland Islands ... ... ... | 36 | 18 | 12 | 12 |
| Fiji ... ... ... ... | 60 | 30 | 12 | 21 |
| French Guiana ... ... ... ... | 12 | 06 | 09 | 05 |
| French West African Territories ... | 60 | 30 | 12 | 25 |
| | | | | |
| Gambia ... ... ... ... | 52 | 26 | 12 | 25 |
| Gibraltar ... ... ... ... | 42 | 21 | 12 | 23 |
| Gold Coast ... ... ... ... | 56 | 28 | 12 | 26 |
| Great Britain and Northern Ireland ... | 36 | 18 | 12 | 16 |
| Grenada ... ... ... ... | 06 | 05 | 05 | * |
| Guadeloupe ... ... ... ... | 10 | 06 | 09 | 04 |
| Guam ... ... ... ... | 66 | 33 | 12 | 22 |
| Guatemala ... ... ... ... | 24 | 12 | 12 | 08 |
| | | | | |
| Haiti ... ... ... ... | 15 | 08 | 12 | 05 |
| Hawaii ... ... ... ... | 40 | 20 | 12 | 14 |

| Country of Destination | Letter Post per ½ oz. | Post Card | Special Air Letter Form | Printed papers, commercial papers, and small packets per ½ oz. |
|---|---|---|---|---|
| | cents | cents | cents | cents |
| Honduras Republic ... ... ... | 24 | 12 | 12 | 07 |
| Hong Kong ... ... ... ... | 66 | 33 | 12 | 23 |
| India ... ... ... ... | 72 | 36 | 12 | 30 |
| Indo-China ... ... ... ... | 84 | 42 | 12 | 33 |
| Indonesia ... ... ... ... | 84 | 42 | 12 | 33 |
| Iran ... ... ... ... | 60 | 30 | 12 | 27 |
| Iraq ... ... ... ... | 60 | 30 | 12 | 27 |
| Israel ... ... ... ... | 45 | 23 | 12 | 23 |
| Jamaica ... ... ... ... | 06 | 05 | 05 | * |
| Japan ... ... ... ... | 56 | 28 | 12 | 19 |
| Kenya ... ... ... ... | 60 | 30 | 12 | 29 |
| Liberia ... ... ... ... | 60 | 30 | 12 | 25 |
| Macao ... ... ... ... | 68 | 34 | 12 | 24 |
| Madagascar ... ... ... ... | 72 | 36 | 12 | 31 |
| Madeira ... ... ... ... | 42 | 21 | 12 | 25 |
| Malaya ... ... ... ... | 84 | 42 | 12 | 33 |
| Malta ... ... ... ... | 40 | 20 | 12 | 23 |
| Manila ... ... ... ... | 68 | 34 | 12 | 19 |
| Martinique ... ... ... ... | 10 | 06 | 09 | 04 |
| Mauritius ... ... ... ... | 74 | 37 | 12 | 32 |
| Mexico ... ... ... ... | 26 | 13 | 12 | 09 |
| Montserrat ... ... ... ... | 06 | 05 | 05 | * |
| Morocco ... ... ... ... | 42 | 21 | 12 | 21 |
| Newfoundland ... ... ... ... | 20 | 10 | 12 | 10 |
| New Guinea ... ... ... ... | 90 | 45 | 12 | 30 |
| New Zealand ... ... ... ... | 68 | 34 | 12 | 25 |
| Nicaragua ... ... ... ... | 18 | 09 | 12 | 07 |
| Nigeria ... ... ... ... | 54 | 27 | 12 | 25 |
| Nyasaland ... ... ... ... | 68 | 34 | 12 | 30 |
| Pakistan ... ... ... ... | 66 | 33 | 12 | 29 |
| Panama ... ... ... ... | 16 | 08 | 12 | 06 |
| Paraguay ... ... ... ... | 40 | 21 | 12 | 10 |
| Peru ... ... ... ... | 26 | 13 | 12 | 09 |
| Puerto Rico ... ... ... ... | 12 | 06 | 09 | 04 |
| Portuguese East and West Africa ... ... | 68 | 34 | 12 | 31 |
| Rhodesia (North and South) ... ... | 68 | 34 | 12 | 30 |
| San Domingo ... ... ... ... | 12 | 06 | 09 | 04 |
| St. Kitts ... ... ... ... | 06 | 05 | 05 | * |
| St. Lucia ... ... ... ... | 06 | 05 | 05 | * |
| St. Thomas (Virgin Islands) ... ... | 12 | 06 | 09 | 04 |
| St. Vincent ... ... ... ... | 06 | 05 | 05 | * |
| Senegal ... ... ... ... | 56 | 28 | 12 | 25 |
| Seychelles ... ... ... ... | 60 | 30 | 12 | 27 |
| Sierra Leone ... ... ... ... | 52 | 26 | 12 | 25 |
| Singapore ... ... ... ... | 84 | 42 | 12 | 34 |
| Solomon Islands ... ... ... ... | 90 | 45 | 12 | 30 |
| Somaliland (British) ... ... ... | 60 | 30 | 12 | 27 |
| Somaliland (Italian) ... ... ... | 66 | 33 | 12 | 29 |
| South Africa ... ... ... ... | 72 | 36 | 12 | 31 |
| South West Africa ... ... ... | 72 | 36 | 12 | 31 |
| Sudan (Anglo Egyptian) ... ... ... | 56 | 28 | 12 | 25 |
| Syria ... ... ... ... | 48 | 24 | 12 | 24 |
| Tanganyika ... ... ... ... | 60 | 30 | 12 | 29 |
| Thailand ... ... ... ... | 78 | 39 | 12 | 31 |
| Togoland ... ... ... ... | 56 | 28 | 12 | 25 |
| Tortola ... ... ... ... | 12 | 06 | 09 | 04 |
| Tripolitania ... ... ... ... | 42 | 21 | 12 | 21 |
| Trans-Jordan ... ... ... ... | 52 | 26 | 12 | 23 |
| Tunisia ... ... ... ... | 42 | 21 | 12 | 20 |
| Uganda ... ... ... ... | 60 | 30 | 12 | 29 |
| United States of America ... ... ... | 20 | 15 | 12 | 10 |
| U.S.S.R. ... ... ... ... | 48 | 24 | 12 | 24 |
| Uruguay ... ... ... ... | 36 | 18 | 12 | 12 |
| Venezuela ... ... ... ... | 12 | 06 | 09 | 04 |
| Zanzibar ... ... ... ... | 66 | 33 | 12 | 29 |

| Country of Destination | For each first ½ lb., or part thereof | For each additional ½ lb., or fraction of a ½ lb., after the first |
|---|---|---|
| | $   c. | $   c. |
| Antigua ... ... ... .... | 24 | 14 |
| Barbados ... ... ... ... | 18 | 8 |
| Bermuda ... ... ... .... | 56 | 46 |
| British Guiana ... ... ... .... | 21 | 11 |
| Canada ... ... ... .... | 80 | 80 |
| Dutch West Indies ... ... .... | 30 | 20 |
| Grenada ... ... ... ... | 14 | 4 |
| Jamaica ... ... ... ... | 46 | 36 |
| St. Kitts ... ... ... .... | 26 | 16 |
| St. Lucia ... ... ... .... | 18 | 8 |
| United Kingdom ... ... ... .... | 2  16 | 2  00 |
| United States of America ... ... .... | 1  68 | 84 |

## and replaced on 1 April 1958 by:-

### Air Mail Packet Rates

| Country of Destination | Letter per ½ oz. | Postcards | Air letter Forms (Aero-grammes) | Printed Papers, Commercial Papers and Small Packets per ½ oz. |
|---|---|---|---|---|
| | Cents | Cents | Cents | Cents. |
| Aden ... ... ... ... | 30 | 25 | 15 | 20 |
| Afghanistan ... ... ... | 60 | 30 | 15 | 20 |
| Alaska ... ... ... ... | 25 | 12 | 15 | 8 |
| Algeria ... ... ... ... | 40 | 20 | 15 | 15 |
| *Antigua ... ... ... ... | 8 | 6 | 6 | 3 |
| Argentine ... ... ... ... | 35 | 18 | 15 | 12 |
| Aruba ... ... ... ... | 15 | 10 | 15 | 6 |
| Australia ... ... ... ... | 60 | 30 | 15 | 20 |
| Azores ... ... ... ... | 50 | 25 | 15 | 20 |
| Bahamas ... ... ... ... | 15 | 10 | 15 | 6 |
| Barbados ... ... ... ... | 8 | 6 | 6 | 3 |
| Belgian Congo ... ... ... | 60 | 30 | 15 | 20 |
| Bermuda ... ... ... ... | 15 | 10 | 15 | 6 |
| Bolivia ... ... ... ... | 25 | 12 | 15 | 8 |
| Brazil ... ... ... ... | 25 | 12 | 15 | 8 |
| *British Guiana ... ... ... | 3 | 6 | 6 | 3 |
| British Honduras ... ... ... | 15 | 10 | 15 | 6 |
| Brunei ... ... ... ... | 60 | 30 | 15 | 20 |
| Burma ... ... ... ... | 60 | 30 | 15 | 20 |
| Cambodia ... ... ... ... | 60 | 30 | 15 | 20 |
| Cameroons (British Sphere) ... ... | 50 | 25 | 15 | 20 |
| Cameroons (French Sphere) ... ... | 50 | 25 | 15 | 20 |
| Canada ... ... ... ... | 25 | 12 | 15 | 8 |
| Canary Islands ... ... ... | 40 | 20 | 15 | 15 |
| Cape Verde Islands ... ... ... | 40 | 20 | 15 | 15 |
| Ceylon ... ... ... ... | 60 | 30 | 15 | 20 |
| Chile ... ... ... ... | 35 | 18 | 15 | 12 |
| China ... ... ... ... | 60 | 30 | 15 | 20 |
| Colombia ... ... ... ... | 25 | 12 | 15 | 8 |
| Cook Islands ... ... ... | 50 | 25 | 15 | 20 |
| Costa Rica ... ... ... ... | 25 | 12 | 15 | 8 |
| Cuba ... ... ... ... | 25 | 12 | 15 | 8 |
| Curacao ... ... ... ... | 15 | 10 | 15 | 6 |
| Cyprus ... ... ... ... | 40 | 20 | 15 | 15 |
| Dahomey ... ... ... ... | 50 | 25 | 15 | 20 |
| *Dominica ... ... ... ... | 3 | 6 | 6 | 3 |
| Dominican Republic ... ... ... | 15 | 10 | 15 | 6 |
| Ecuador ... ... ... ... | 25 | 12 | 15 | 8 |
| Egypt ... ... ... ... | 40 | 20 | 15 | 15 |
| Eire ... ... ... ... | 35 | 18 | 15 | 12 |
| El Salvador ... ... ... | 25 | 12 | 15 | 8 |
| Eritrea ... ... ... ... | 50 | 25 | 15 | 20 |
| Ethiopia ... ... ... ... | 50 | 25 | 15 | 20 |
| Europe (except U.S.S.R.) ... ... | 40 | 20 | 15 | 12 |
| Falkland Islands (to Uruguay only by Air) | 35 | 18 | 15 | 12 |
| Fanning Island ... ... ... | 60 | 30 | 15 | 20 |
| Fiji ... ... ... ... | 40 | 20 | 15 | 15 |
| Formosa ... ... ... ... | 60 | 30 | 15 | 20 |
| French Equatorial Africa ... ... | 60 | 30 | 15 | 20 |
| French Guiana ... ... ... | 15 | 10 | 15 | 6 |

*Minimum of 6 cents.

| Country of Destination | Letters per ½ oz. | Postcards | Airletter Forms (Aero-grammes) | Printed Papers, Commercial Papers and Small Packets per ½ oz. |
|---|---|---|---|---|
| | Cents | Cents | Cents | Cents |
| French Guinea ... ... ... | 50 | 25 | 15 | 20 |
| French Settlements in Oceania ... | 60 | 30 | 15 | 20 |
| French Somali Coast ... ... ... | 60 | 30 | 15 | 20 |
| French West Indies ... ... ... | 15 | 10 | 15 | 6 |
| Gambia ... ... ... ... | 50 | 25 | 15 | 20 |
| Gaza and Khan Yunis ... ... | 50 | 25 | 15 | 20 |
| Ghana ... ... ... ... | 50 | 25 | 15 | 20 |
| Gibraltar ... ... ... | 40 | 20 | 15 | 15 |
| Gilbert and Ellice Islands ... | 60 | 30 | 15 | 20 |
| Great Britain and Northern Ireland ... | 35 | 18 | 15 | 12 |
| *Grenada ... ... ... | 8 | 6 | 6 | 3 |
| Guatemala ... ... ... | 25 | 12 | 15 | 8 |
| Haiti ... ... ... | 15 | 10 | 15 | 6 |
| Hawaii ... ... ... | 35 | 18 | 15 | 12 |
| Honduras Republic ... ... | 25 | 12 | 15 | 8 |
| Hong Kong ... ... ... | 50 | 25 | 15 | 20 |
| India ... ... ... | 60 | 30 | 15 | 20 |
| Indonesia ... ... ... | 60 | 30 | 15 | 20 |
| Iran ... ... ... | 50 | 25 | 15 | 20 |
| Iraq ... ... ... | 50 | 25 | 15 | 20 |
| Israel ... ... ... | 50 | 25 | 15 | 20 |
| Italian Somaliland ... ... | 60 | 30 | 15 | 20 |
| Ivory Coast ... ... | 50 | 25 | 15 | 20 |
| *Jamaica ... ... ... | 8 | 6 | 6 | 3 |
| Japan ... ... ... | 50 | 25 | 15 | 20 |
| Jordan ... ... ... | 40 | 20 | 15 | 15 |
| Kenya ... ... ... | 50 | 25 | 15 | 20 |
| Korea ... ... ... | 50 | 25 | 15 | 20 |
| Laos ... ... ... | 60 | 30 | 15 | 20 |
| *Leeward Islands ... ... | 8 | 6 | 6 | 3 |
| Lebanon ... ... ... | 50 | 25 | 15 | 20 |
| Liberia ... ... ... | 50 | 25 | 15 | 20 |
| Libya ... ... ... | 40 | 20 | 15 | 15 |
| Macao ... ... ... | 60 | 30 | 15 | 20 |
| Madagascar ... ... | 60 | 30 | 15 | 20 |
| Madeira ... ... ... | 40 | 20 | 15 | 15 |
| Malaya ... ... ... | 60 | 30 | 15 | 20 |
| Malta ... ... ... | 40 | 20 | 15 | 15 |
| Marian Islands ... ... | 60 | 30 | 15 | 20 |
| Marshall Islands ... ... | 60 | 30 | 15 | 20 |
| Mauritania ... ... | 50 | 25 | 15 | 20 |
| Mauritius ... ... ... | 60 | 30 | 15 | 20 |
| Mexico ... ... ... | 25 | 12 | 15 | 8 |
| Morocco ... ... ... | 40 | 20 | 15 | 15 |
| Nepal ... ... ... | 60 | 30 | 15 | 20 |
| New Caledonia ... ... | 60 | 30 | 15 | 20 |
| New Guinea ... ... | 60 | 30 | 15 | 20 |
| New Hebrides ... ... | 60 | 20 | 15 | 20 |
| New Zealand ... ... | 50 | 25 | 15 | 8 |
| Nicaragua ... ... ... | 25 | 12 | 15 | 8 |
| Niger ... ... ... | 50 | 25 | 15 | 20 |
| Nigeria ... ... ... | 50 | 25 | 15 | 20 |
| North Borneo ... ... | 60 | 30 | 15 | 20 |
| Northern Rhodesia ... ... | 60 | 30 | 15 | 20 |
| Nyasaland ... ... ... | 60 | 30 | 15 | 20 |
| Pakistan ... ... ... | 60 | 30 | 15 | 20 |
| Panama (Republic of) ... ... | 25 | 12 | 15 | 8 |
| Panama Canal Zone ... ... | 25 | 12 | 15 | 8 |
| Paraguay ... ... ... | 35 | 18 | 15 | 12 |
| Peru ... ... ... | 25 | 12 | 15 | 8 |
| Philippines ... ... | 60 | 30 | 15 | 20 |
| Pitcairn Island ... ... | 60 | 30 | 15 | 20 |
| Portuguese East Africa ... ... | 60 | 30 | 15 | 20 |
| Portuguese India ... ... | 60 | 30 | 15 | 20 |
| Portuguese Timor ... ... | 60 | 30 | 15 | 20 |
| Portuguese West Africa ... ... | 60 | 30 | 15 | 20 |
| Persian Gulf Ports ... ... | 50 | 25 | 15 | 20 |
| Puerto Rico ... ... ... | 15 | 10 | 15 | 6 |
| Reunion ... ... ... | 60 | 30 | 15 | 20 |
| St. Helena ... ... ... | 60 | 30 | 15 | 20 |
| *St. Kitts ... ... ... | 8 | 6 | 6 | 3 |
| *St. Lucia ... ... ... | 8 | 6 | 6 | 3 |
| *St. Vincent ... ... ... | 8 | 6 | 6 | 3 |
| Samoa ... ... ... | 60 | 30 | 15 | 20 |
| Sarawak ... ... ... | 60 | 30 | 15 | 20 |
| Saudi Arabia ... ... ... | 50 | 25 | 15 | 20 |

| Country of Destination | Letters per ½ oz. | Postcards | Airletter Forms (Aerogrammes) | Printed Papers, Commercial Papers and Small Packets per ½ oz. |
|---|---|---|---|---|
| | Cents | Cents | Cents | Cents |
| Senegal ... ... ... ... | 50 | 25 | 15 | 20 |
| Seychelles ... ... ... ... | 60 | 30 | 15 | 20 |
| Sierra Leone ... ... ... | 50 | 25 | 15 | 20 |
| Singapore ... ... ... ... | 60 | 30 | 15 | 20 |
| Solomon Islands ... ... ... | 60 | 30 | 15 | 20 |
| Somaliland Protectorate ... ... | 50 | 25 | 15 | 20 |
| South Africa ... ... ... | 60 | 30 | 15 | 20 |
| Southern Rhodesia ... ... | 60 | 30 | 15 | 20 |
| Spanish Guinea ... ... ... | 50 | 25 | 15 | 20 |
| Spanish West Africa ... ... ... | 50 | 25 | 15 | 20 |
| Sudan ... ... ... ... | 50 | 25 | 15 | 20 |
| Surinam ... ... ... ... | 15 | 10 | 15 | 6 |
| Syria ... ... ... ... | 50 | 25 | 15 | 20 |
| Tanganyika ... ... ... | 50 | 25 | 15 | 20 |
| Thailand ... ... ... ... | 60 | 30 | 15 | 20 |
| Tibet ... ... ... ... | 60 | 30 | 15 | 20 |
| Togo (French Sphere) ... | 50 | 25 | 15 | 20 |
| Tonga ... ... ... ... | 40 | 20 | 15 | 15 |
| Tortola ... ... ... ... | 15 | 10 | 15 | 6 |
| Tunisia ... ... ... ... | 40 | 20 | 15 | 15 |
| Uganda ... ... ... ... | 50 | 25 | 15 | 20 |
| United States of America ... | 25 | 12 | 15 | 8 |
| Upper Volta ... ... ... | 50 | 25 | 15 | 20 |
| Uruguay ... ... ... | 35 | 18 | 15 | 12 |
| Union of Soviet Socialist Republics ... | 50 | 25 | 15 | 20 |
| Venezuela ... ... ... ... | 15 | 10 | 15 | 6 |
| Viet Nam ... ... ... ... | 60 | 30 | 15 | 20 |
| Virgin Islands of U.S.A. ... ... | 15 | 10 | 15 | 6 |
| Wake Island ... ... ... | 50 | 25 | 15 | 20 |
| Zanzibar ... ... ... ... | 50 | 25 | 15 | 20 |
| Yemen ... ... ... ... | 60 | 30 | 15 | 20 |

## International Air Parcel Services

Air surcharge, to be added to appropriate surface parcel postage rates

| Destination | | | | | Air Surcharge |
|---|---|---|---|---|---|
| Antigua ... ... ... ... ... | | | | | 10 cents per ½ lb. |
| Barbados ... ... ... ... | | | | | 5 do. |
| Bermuda ... ... ... ... | | | | | 50 do. |
| British Guiana ... ... ... | | | | | 10 do. |
| Canada ... ... ... ... | | | | | 70 do. |
| Aruba and Curacao ... ... | | | | | 15 do. |
| Grenada ... ... ... ... | | | | | 5 do. |
| Jamaica ... ... ... ... | | | | | 30 do. |
| St. Kitts ... ... ... ... | | | | | 15 do. |
| St. Lucia ... ... ... ... | | | | | 10 do. |
| Great Britain ... ... ... | | | | | $1.30 do. |
| United States of America ... ... | | | | | 65 do. |

## Air Mail to U.K. letters for ½oz. to New York and on by sea.

| 11.11.29 - 17.2.30 | 18.2.30 - 15.10.31 | 16.10.31 - 30.11.32 | 1.12.32 - 31.7.33 |
|---|---|---|---|
| 1s. 1d. | 11d. | 1s. 3d. | 1s. 5d. |

| 1.8.33 - 31.12.33 | 1.1.34 - 28.2.35 | 1.3.35 - 9.5.38 | 10.5.38 - 14.1.40 |
|---|---|---|---|
| 1s. 3d. | 1s. 1d. | 21cts. | 21cts. |

| 15.1.40 - 31.7.45 | 1.8.45 - 31.5.47 | 1.6.47 - 22.3.50 | 23.3.50 - |
|---|---|---|---|
| 26cts. | 20cts. | 18cts. | 24cts. |

## By air via North Atlantic.

| 31.5.39 - 14.1.40 | 15.1.40 - 31.7.45 | 1.8.45 - 31.5.47 | 1.6.47 - 22.3.50 |
|---|---|---|---|
| 56cts. | 68cts. | 60cts. | 36cts. |

| 23.5.50 - 8.2.53 | 9.2.53 -31.3.58 | 1.4.58 - |
|---|---|---|
| 30cts. British Carrier. | | |
| 48cts. Foreign Carrier. | 36cts. | 35cts |

## By air via Brazil.

| 10.5.38 - 14.1.40 | 15.1.40 - June 40 |
|---|---|
| $1 | $1.24 |

## Air Mail to U.S.A., letters per ½oz.

| 2.9.29 - 10.11.29 | 11.11.29 - 17.2.30 | 18.2.30 - 15.10.31 |
|---|---|---|
| 1s. 6d. | 1s. 11d. | 11d. |

| 16.10.31 - 30.11.32 | 1.12.32 - 31.7.33 | 1.8.33 - 31.12.33 |
|---|---|---|
| 1s. 5d. | 1s. 7d. | 1s. 4d. |

| 1.1.34 - 28.2.35 | 1.3.35 - 30.6.37 | 1.7.37 - 9.5.38 |
|---|---|---|
| 1s. 3d. | 26cts. | 27cts. |

| 10.5.38 - 14.1.40 | 15.1.40 - 31.7.45 | 1.8.45 -31.5.47 |
|---|---|---|
| 24cts. | 30cts. | 20cts. |

| 1.6.47 - 22.3.50 | 23.3.50 - 8.2.53 | 9.2.53 - 31.3.58 | 1.4.58 - |
|---|---|---|---|
| 18 cts. | 20cts. British Carrier. | 20 cts. | 25cts. |
| | 24cts. Foreign Carrier. | | |

# CHAPTER 5

## POST OFFICES & POSTMARKS OF TRINIDAD & TOBAGO

### POSTMARK INDEX

K3

K4

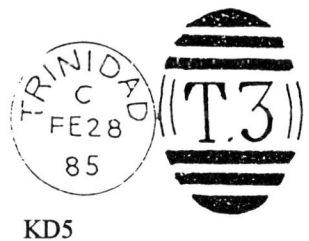

KD5

### TRINIDAD NUMERALS

| Number | Used upto 1886 at the following offices | After 1886 temporary cancellation at the following offices until the permanent date stamp arrived (or was being repaired) | Type & Period of use as temporary cancellation |
|---|---|---|---|
| 1 | Port of Spain | | circa 1925 (K4) |
| 2 | San Fernando | | |
| 3 | St. Joseph's | Unknown office | circa 1902/4 (K4) |
| 4 | St. Juan | Unknown office | circa 1907/9 (K4) |
| 5 | Santa Cruz | Todd's Road | 1905 (K3) |
| 6 | Arouca | | |
| 7 | Arima | | |
| 8 | Turure to (1861) Toco by (1869) | Four Roads | circa 1920 (K4) |
| 9 | Manzanilla | | |
| 10 | Mayaro | | |
| 11 | Nariya, Blanchisseuse & then Toco by (1861). Nariya again (1867-1869)? Tunapuna from 1878. | | |
| 12 | Carenage to (1861) then Blanchisseuse 1869 | Unknown office | circa 1919/20 (K4) |
| 13 | Diego Martin | Unknown office | circa 1919/20 (K4) |
| 14 | Monos to (1861) Moruga from 1869 | | |
| 15 | Chacachacare to (1861) Tacarigua (1867) | Belmont Unknown office | 1891/2 (KD5) (19.7.02)-(16.8.04) (KD5) |

| Number | Used up to 1886 at the following offices | After 1886 temporary cancellation at the following offices until the permanent date stamp arrived | Type & Period of use as temporary cancellation |
|---|---|---|---|
| 16 | Chaguanas | | |
| 17 | Couva | | |
| 18 | Princes Town (Savanna Grande) | Unknown office | (K3) |
| 19 | Oropouche | | |
| 20 | La Brea | | |
| 21 | Cedros | | |
| 22 | Claxton Bay | | |
| 23 | Cedros Steamer | Unknown office | circa 1901/4 (K4) |
| 24 | St. Madelaine | | |
| 25 | | Unknown office | circa 1896 (KD5) |
| 26 | Erin | | |
| 27 | Monos | Brothers Road | circa 1925? (K4) |
| 28 | Mucurapo | Unknown office | (1905/7) |
| | Chacachacare | | circa 1930/5 (K3) |
| 29 | N.R. (May have been issued to | Unknown office | circa 1907/14 (K4) |
| | Newtown, or Icacos) | Unknown office | circa 1918/20 (K4) |
| 30 | Carapichaima | Unknown office | circa 1915 (K3) |
| 31 | Caroni | | |
| 32 | St. Anns | Unknown office | (12.6.02) (KD5) |
| 33 | Maraval | | |
| 34 | Cunupia | | |
| 35 | California | Unknown office | (7.2.98)-(14.2.99) - 1900 (KD5 |
| 36 | Carenage | | |
| 37 | Not issued? | Unknown office | circa 1899/04 (K4) |
| 38 | Not issued | Unknown office | circa 1901/6 (K4) |
| 39 | Not issued | | |
| 40 | Not issued | Unknown office(s) | circa 1902/20 (K4) |
| 43 | Datestamp only - see Cunupia | | |

D14 (20.2.95)
Used at an unknown office

D15 Indian Walk (9.6.97)-(15.2.07)
Used at Port of Spain until 1892.

Temporary cancellations would have been used at the following offices during the following periods.

| | |
|---|---|
| Cumuto | 1.12.97 - circa March 98 |
| Five Islands | 1.9.98 - February 99 |
| Guaico | 1.12.97 - April 98 |
| Guanapo | 1.12.97 - March 98 |
| Matura | May 93 - July 93 |
| Rose Hill | July 97 - March 98 |
| St Juliens | 1.9.98 - December 98 |
| Siparia | (1906) - July 1907 |
| Tabaquite | 1.2.99 - July 99 |

## TOBAGO NUMERALS

| 14 | N°1 Mail Route | | See under Scarborough |
|---|---|---|---|
| 15 | N°2 Mail Route | Tentative Allocations | " |
| 16 | N°3 Mail Route | " | " |

A14      Scarborough

**Former G.P.O.**

Charlotteville

Speyside

Parlatuvier

Castara

Delaford

Des Vignes Road

Golden Lane

Moriah

Roxborough

Plymouth

Mason Hall

Belle Garden

Les Coteaux

Pembroke

Black Rock

Mount St George

Goodwood

Bethel

Hope

Buccoo Point

Scarborough

Mount

Patience Hill

Pleasant

Canaan

Carnbee

0 | 5 | 6 km
m

Grande Riviere

Toco

La Fillette

Sans Souci

Matelot

Cumana

Blanchisseuse

Maracas Road

Brasso Secco

Santa Cruz

Balandra

Maraval

Upper Santa Cruz

La Pastora

Diego Martin

Morne Coco

Matura

Monos

Carenage

St.Benedict

Lopinot

Chacachacare

Teteron

Four Roads

Vega d'Oropouche

Chaguaramus

Bay

Morvant

Tunapuna

Dabadie

Valencia

Five Islands

Port of Spain

San Juan

Arouca

Oropouche

Upper Guaico

Curepe

Arima

2nd Caledonian

Tacarigua

Sangre Grande

Caigual

## P.O.S.

St.Helena

Guanapo

Guaico

Fishing Pond

Point Cumana

Caroni

San Raphael

Cumuto

Dibe Road

Upper Belmont

Bejucal

Las Lomas

Cunapo Junction Road

Boissiere

Valley Road

Enterprise

Kelly

Talparo

Coryal

St.James

St. Anns

St.Fracois Valley Road

Felicity

Longdenville

Manzanilla

Newtown

Belmont

St.Barbs Road

Charlieville

Todds Road

Caratal

Gonzales

Woodb

Prizgar Lands

Chaguanas

Trou Macaque

Caparo

Tamana Four Roads

Fatima

Carapichaima

Plum Mitan

East Dry

Febeau

St.Andrew

Brasso Piedra

River

Blundell

Orange Valley

Freeport

Flanagin Town

California

Couva

Calcutta Settlement

## S.F.

Balmain

Brasso

Biche

Gasparillo

Gran Couva

Marabella

Claxton Bay

Tortuga

Navet

St.Madelaine

Bonne Aventure

Mayo

Tabaquite

Plaisance

Mon Repos

Cocoyea

Pointe-A-Pierre

Matilda

Piparo

Poole

Ecclesville

Pleasantville

Reform

Brothers Road

Rio Claro

Les Efforts

Williamsville Tableland

Fonrose

Mayaro

St. Johns

Bamboo

Jordan Hill

Village

San Fernando

Palmyra

Princes Town

La Brea

Cross

Indian Walk

Roussillac

St.Juliens

Vance River

La Romain

Hermitage

Lengua

New Settlement

Debe

Diamond

Point Fortin

Fyzabad

Timital

Barrackpore

Abyssinia

Newlands

Coromandel

Guapo

Delhi Road

Penal

Rock River

Granville

Cap de Ville

Siparia

Basseterre

Guayaguayare

Cedros

Forest Reserve

Santa Flora

Clark Rochard

Fullerton

Irois Forest

Los Bajos

Morne Diable

St.Marys

Quarry

Penal Rock Road

Moruga

Icacos

Palo Seco

La Lune

Erin

0 | 5 | 10 | 15 km
m | 5 | 10

**PORT OF SPAIN G.P.O.** (Or. from Port of the Spaniards) (Puerto de los Hispanioles).
In 1797 the population was 4,525. In 1808 it was almost completely destroyed by fire. Initially used time codes A to U by 1904 datestamps were set with time. In 1859 (1 January 1860?) the G.P.O. originally on Frederick Street moved to 13 Abercromby Street then to King Street. On 18 December 1883 Corner of St. Vincent and Queen's Street. On 24 October 1938 moved further along to St. Vincent Street and in January 1957 to Wrightson Road. The Postmaster General's were:-

| | | |
|---|---|---|
| 5 July 1800 | Joseph Galway | Deputy Postmaster General |
| 4 May 1816 | Mrs E. R. Galway | Packet Agent till 1858 |
| 1834-1851 | Mrs E. R. Galway | Deputy Post Master |
| 13 August 1851 | James H. O'Brien | General Postmaster |
| 1 June 1853 | Ellys Layton | Colonial Postmaster |
| 14 December 1860 | William Eversley | Postmaster General |
| 24 March 1865 | Charles Chipchase | |
| 12 October 1866 | Henry Chipchase | |
| 1 January 1879 | James W. O'Brien | |
| 1 September 1883 | J. A. Bulmer | |
| 1 September 1903 | Alfred Ernest Clarence Ross | |
| 10 September 1921 | George Perry Lewis | |
| 11 November 1922 | Edwin Eddington | |
| 18 January 1928 | Beverley Burnley Littlepage | |
| 17 April 1936 | James Arthur Ayles | |
| 7 June 1939 | Donald Mc Arthur Fraser | |
| 23 November 1946 | Ernest Stanley Moore | |
| 25 November 1950 | Cecil George Folwell | |
| 18 March 1955 | E. A. Driver | |

(20.2.04) - S.O. 31.8.62          **2**          **4**

**Prestamp (P.S.)**

PS1 (20.2.04)-(5.6.07)

PS2 (10.1.12)-(28.2.22)

PS3 (13.10.22)-(7.9.37)

Sent 13.1.40?
PS4 (25.4.40)- (25.12.53)

211

**Obilterators (K)**

K1 (21.8.51)-(24.11.52)          K2 (28.12.52)-(18.4.63)          K3 (1.11.58)- (23.5.65)

K4 (11.4.65)-(24.5.68)

K5 (7.11.71)-(7.4.81)
Recorded used as a duplex with D4 (1881)
Not confirmed, it seems probable that the
two marks were struck fortuitously.

K6 (27.6.81)-(1.8.83)                    K7

**Datestamp (D)**

Sent 31.10.51                 Sent 25.8.57
D1 (11.6.52)-(7.4.66)         D2 (9.7.58)-                 D3 (8.7.66)-(8.1.78)
Known set with 5 under date

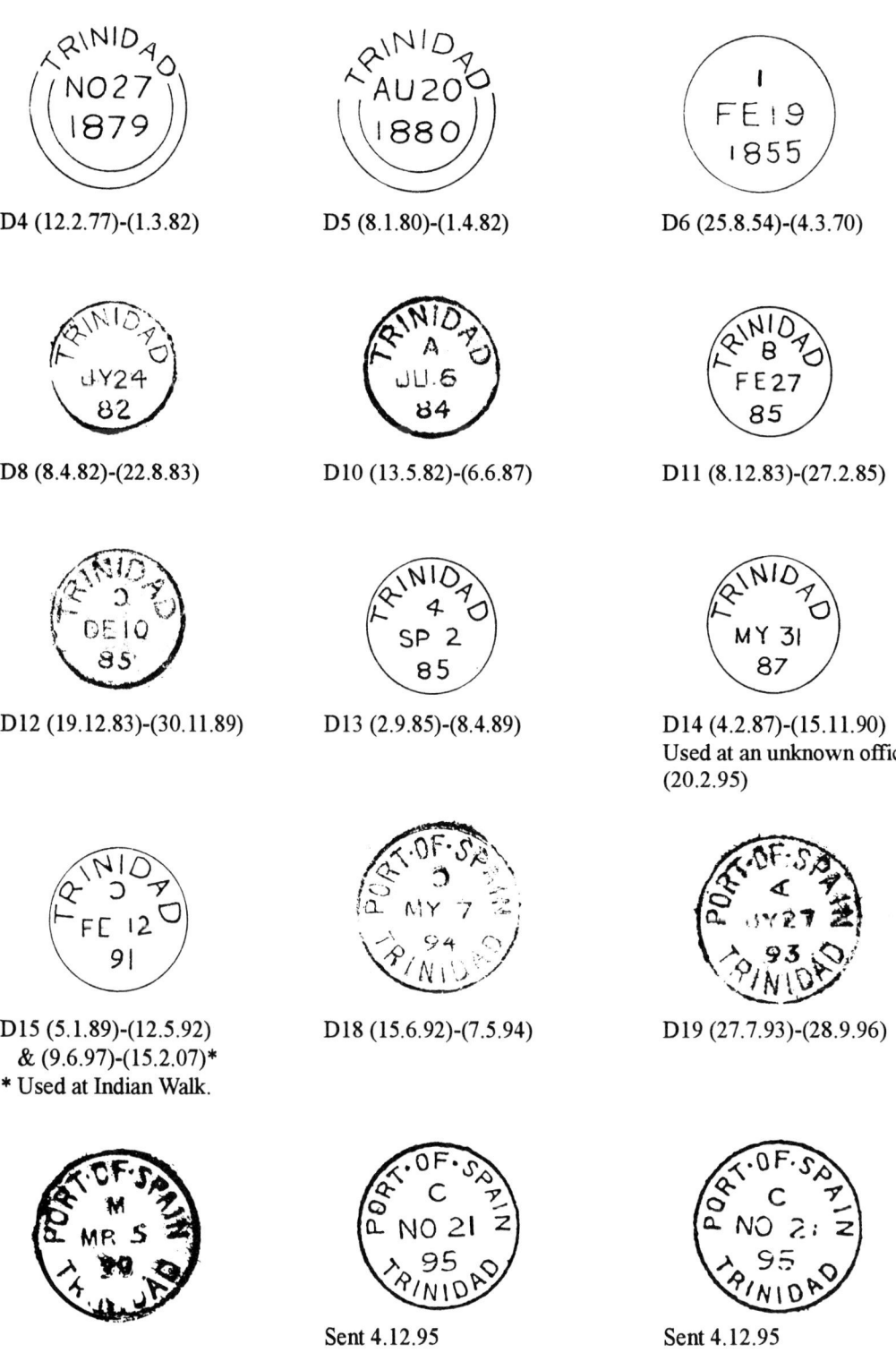

D4 (12.2.77)-(1.3.82)

D5 (8.1.80)-(1.4.82)

D6 (25.8.54)-(4.3.70)

D8 (8.4.82)-(22.8.83)

D10 (13.5.82)-(6.6.87)

D11 (8.12.83)-(27.2.85)

D12 (19.12.83)-(30.11.89)

D13 (2.9.85)-(8.4.89)

D14 (4.2.87)-(15.11.90)
Used at an unknown office
(20.2.95)

D15 (5.1.89)-(12.5.92)
 & (9.6.97)-(15.2.07)*
* Used at Indian Walk.

D18 (15.6.92)-(7.5.94)

D19 (27.7.93)-(28.9.96)

D20 (14.3.97)- (5.3.98)

Sent 4.12.95
D21 (25.11.96)-(7.6.02)

Sent 4.12.95
D22

To distinguish between the above datestamps easily, this sheet (or any other), may be ordered from the Publisher printed on clear plastic for £1 each (subject unsold).

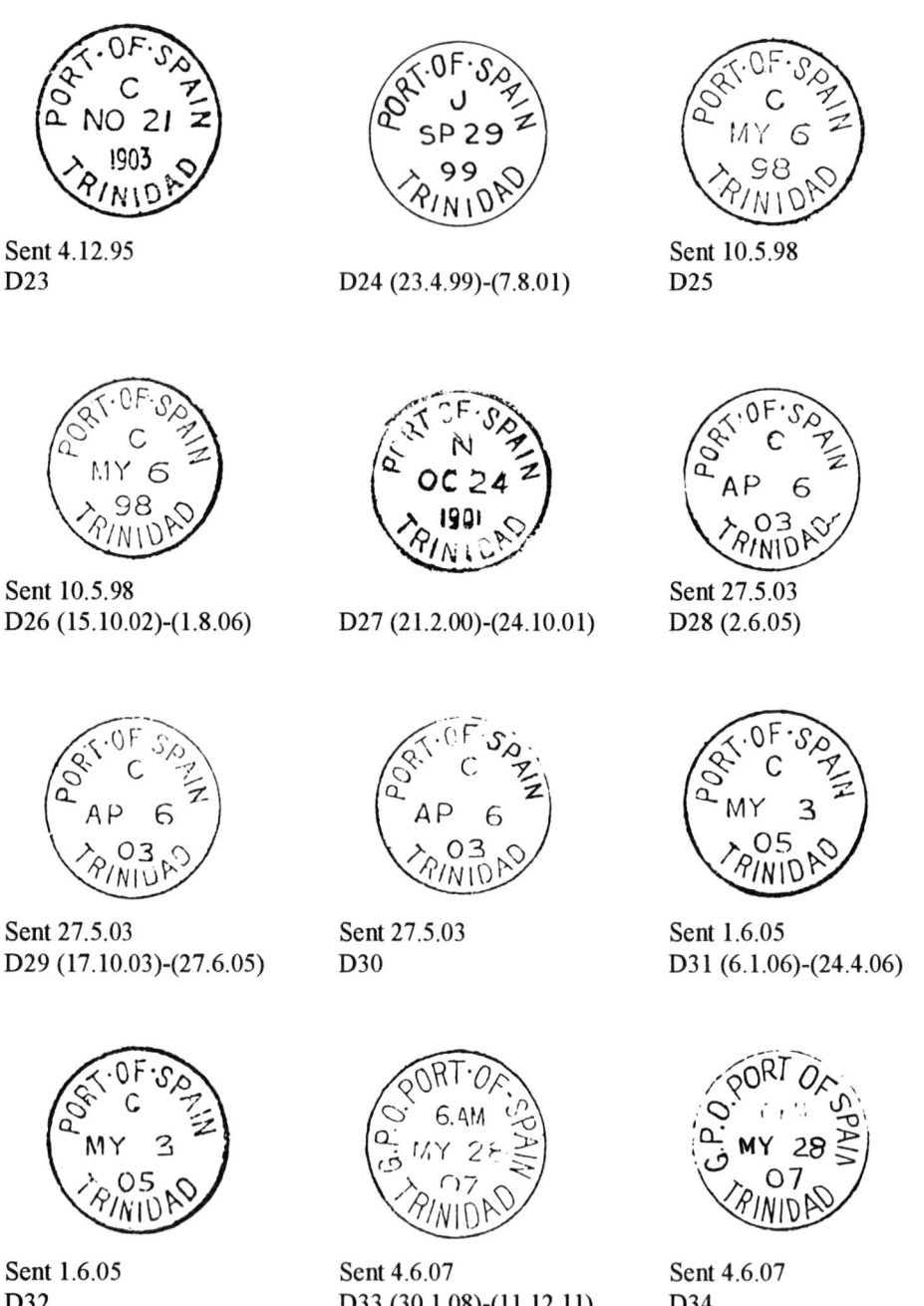

Sent 4.12.95
D23

D24 (23.4.99)-(7.8.01)

Sent 10.5.98
D25

Sent 10.5.98
D26 (15.10.02)-(1.8.06)

D27 (21.2.00)-(24.10.01)

Sent 27.5.03
D28 (2.6.05)

Sent 27.5.03
D29 (17.10.03)-(27.6.05)

Sent 27.5.03
D30

Sent 1.6.05
D31 (6.1.06)-(24.4.06)

Sent 1.6.05
D32

Sent 4.6.07
D33 (30.1.08)-(11.12.11)

Sent 4.6.07
D34

D20 to D32 used time codes (A to U), some date stamps have only been recorded using a few code letters however.

To distinguish between the above datestamps easily, this sheet (or any other), may be ordered from the Publisher printed on clear plastic for £1 each (subject unsold).

Sent 4.6.07
D35

Sent 29.6.08
D36 (6.4.12)-(16.1.15)

Sent 29.6.08
D37

Sent 29.6.09
D38

Sent 29.6.09
D39 (2.2.11)-(11.2.18)

D40 (23.8.10)-(17.11.10)

D41 (18.3.12)

D42 (4.3.13)-

D43 (6.9.15)-(2.2.18)

D44 (29.7.18)-(7.11.19)

D45 (7.12.14)-(21.9.18)

D46 (12.6.20)-(11.5.22)

D47 (1.2.21)-(1.5.30)

D49 (5.10.06)-(17.4.09)

D50 (22.8.06)-(25.7.11)

To distinguish between the above datestamps easily, this sheet (or any other), may be ordered from the Publisher printed on clear plastic for £1 each (subject unsold).

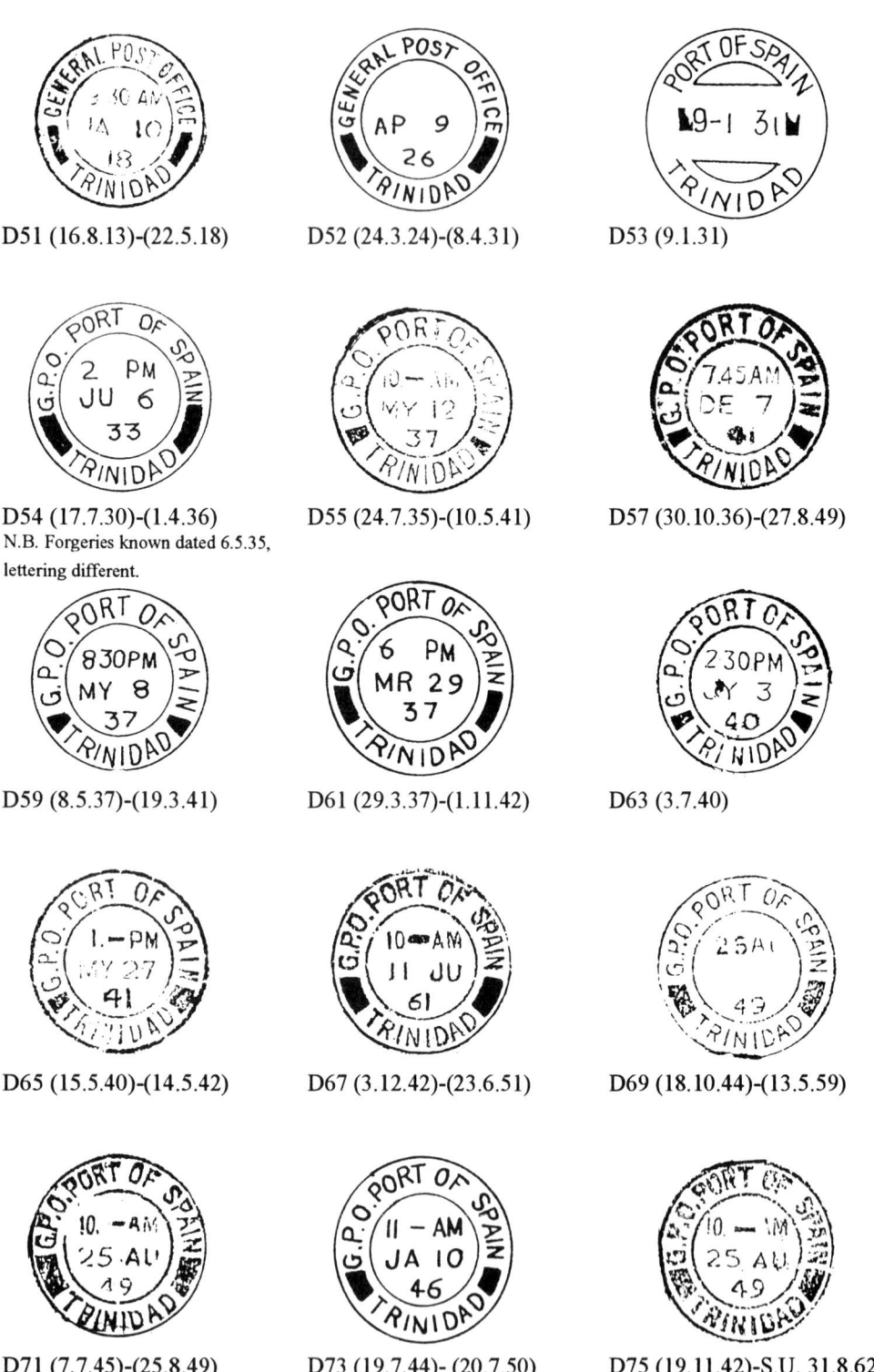

D51 (16.8.13)-(22.5.18)

D52 (24.3.24)-(8.4.31)

D53 (9.1.31)

D54 (17.7.30)-(1.4.36)
N.B. Forgeries known dated 6.5.35,
lettering different.

D55 (24.7.35)-(10.5.41)

D57 (30.10.36)-(27.8.49)

D59 (8.5.37)-(19.3.41)

D61 (29.3.37)-(1.11.42)

D63 (3.7.40)

D65 (15.5.40)-(14.5.42)

D67 (3.12.42)-(23.6.51)

D69 (18.10.44)-(13.5.59)

D71 (7.7.45)-(25.8.49)

D73 (19.7.44)- (20.7.50)

D75 (19.11.42)-S.U. 31.8.62

To distinguish between the above datestamps easily, this sheet (or any other), may be ordered from the Publisher printed on clear plastic for £1 each (subject unsold).

D77 (6.12.37)-S.U. 31.8.62

D79 (20.11.41)-(23..6.60)

D81 (20.12.38)-(29.7.60)

D83 (27.6.60)

D85 (25.8.49)-(6.12.50)

D87 (25.8.49)-S.U.31.8.62

D89 (26.1.51)-(17.12.53)

D91 (10.10.51)-(13.8.53)

D93 (23.10.51)-(8.11.55)

D95 (25.4.53)-(31.12.54)

D96 (9.4.54)-(24.11.54)

D97 (11.10.54)-(11.3.57)

D99 (20.3.57)-(1.7.60)

D101 (15.12.56)-(1.12.61)

D103 (24.6.58)-(1.12.61)

To distinguish between the above datestamps easily, this sheet (or any other), may be ordered from the Publisher printed on clear plastic for £1 each (subject unsold).

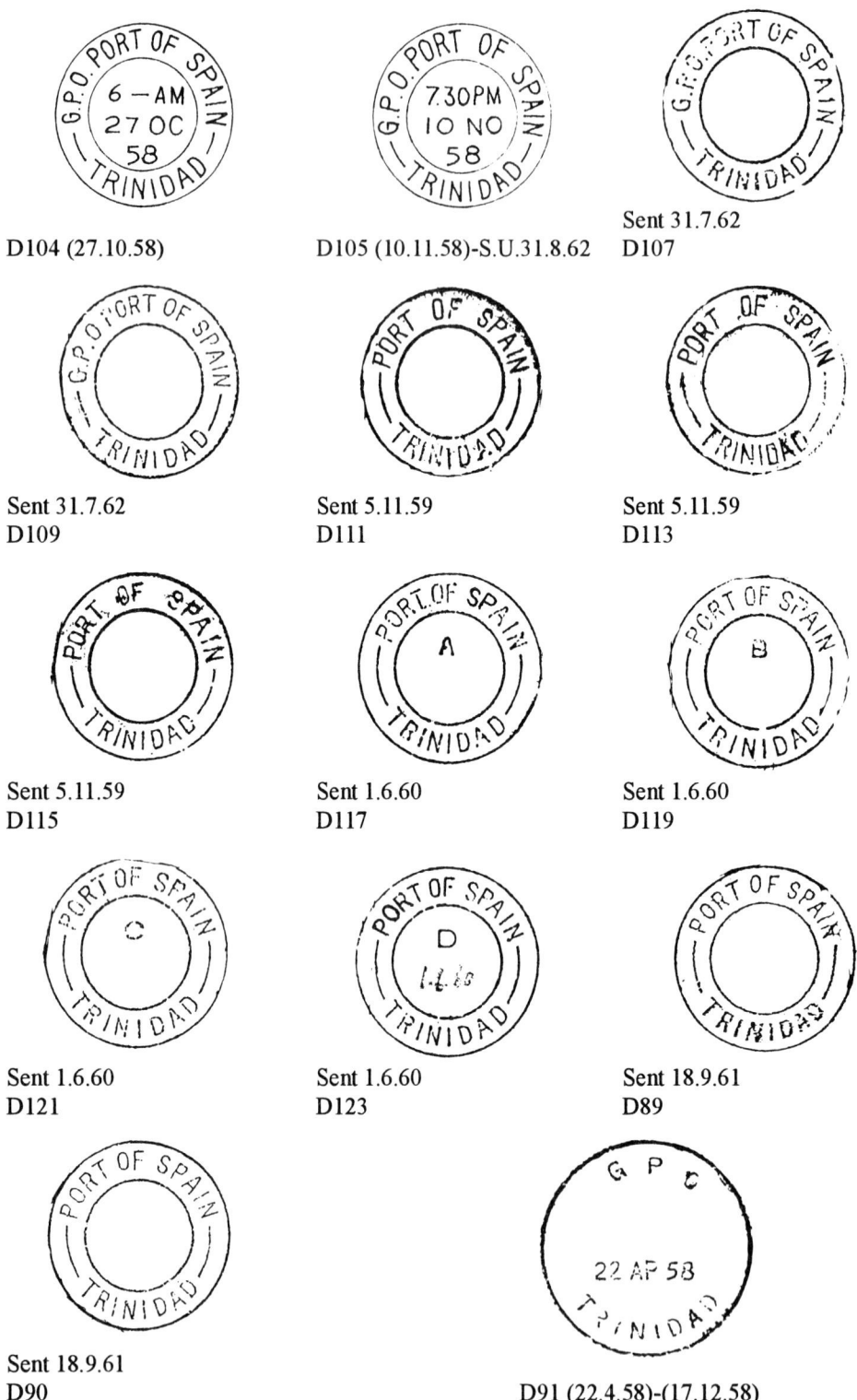

D104 (27.10.58)

D105 (10.11.58)-S.U.31.8.62

Sent 31.7.62
D107

Sent 31.7.62
D109

Sent 5.11.59
D111

Sent 5.11.59
D113

Sent 5.11.59
D115

Sent 1.6.60
D117

Sent 1.6.60
D119

Sent 1.6.60
D121

Sent 1.6.60
D123

Sent 18.9.61
D89

Sent 18.9.61
D90

D91 (22.4.58)-(17.12.58)

To distinguish between the above datestamps easily, this sheet (or any other), may be ordered from the Publisher printed on clear plastic for £1 each (subject unsold).

**PORT OF SPAIN G.P.O. Continued**

**Handstruck (HS)**

BRITAIN MUST WIN !
HELP THE BOMBER FUND

HS3 (24.9.41)-(4.10.41)

Slogans (except Red Cross?) were permanently withdrawn for the rest of the war at the request of the British P.M.G. (circular October 1941) due to problems with them being struck on mail to P.O.Ws etc..

**Machine Cancellation (M)**

M1 State 1 (28.6.23)-(13.7.23)

M2 State 1 (24.7.23)-(6.9.26)
  & (31.3.47)-(22.3.49)

M2 State 2 (22.12.41)-(22.12.47)

M2 State 3 (10.11.23)-(4.12.24)

M2 State 4 (15.10.26)-(15.7.32)

M2 State 5 (9.5.30)-(27.4.40)

**G.P.O. Wrightson Road**

## PORT OF SPAIN G.P.O. Continued

M2 State 6 (25.10.34)-(13.2.35)

M2 State 7 (15.11.34)-(16.11.34)

M2 State 8 (20.12.26)-(13.12.35)

M2 State 9 (1.3.36)-(6.5.38)

M2 State 10 (6.6.38)-(28.3.40)

Slogans (except Red Cross?) were permanently withdrawn for the rest of the war at the request of the British P.M.G. (circular October 1941?) due to problems with them being struck on mail to P.O.Ws etc..

M2 State 11 (28.11.40)-    12.47)

 GROW MORE FOOD DIG FOR VICTORY

M2 State 12 (17.7.40)-(1.11.40)

 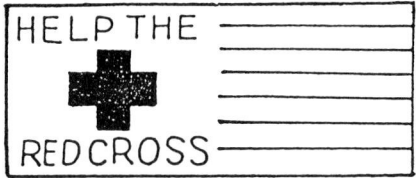

M2 State 13 (4.1.41)-(21.10.41)

M2 State 14 (24.1.42)-(12.9.45)          Later state-cross damaged (3.8.46)-(21.5.48).

M2 State 16 (31.12.48)-(31.1.49)

**PORT OF SPAIN G.P.O. Continued**

 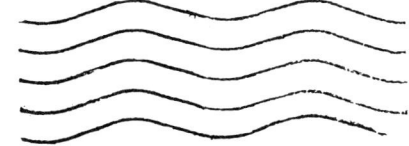

M3 State 1 (27.3.33)-(2.12.33)
 & (31.12.41)-(14.12.48)

M3 State 2 (11.7.47)-(14.12.48)

M3 State 3 (6.12.33)-(30.5.38)

M3 State 4 (25.11.34)-(9.5.40)

M3 State 5 (22.2.35)-(15.1.36)

M3 State 6 (13.2.36)-(2.10.36)

M3 State 7 (2.7.38)-(19.1.40)

 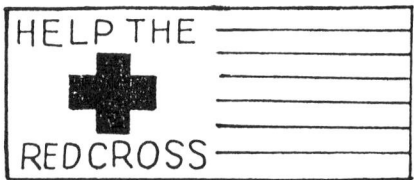

M3 State 8 (14.5.40)-(23.9.46)

GROW MORE FOOD

DIG FOR VICTORY

M3 State 9A (21.9.40)-(26.10.41)

Slogans (except Red Cross?) were permanently withdrawn for the rest of the war at the request of the British P.M.G. (circular October 1941) due to problems with them being struck on mail to P.O.Ws etc...

GROW MORE FOOD

M3 State 9B (1949)

M3 State 10 (19.12.41)-(12.12.45)

M3 State 11 (14.2.46)-(27.2.46)

 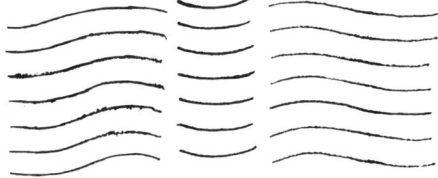

M4 State 1 (31.12.51)-(23.9.60)

 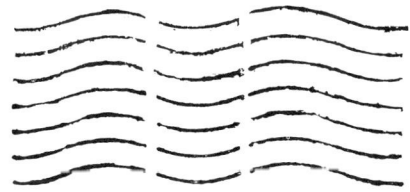

M4 State 2 (2.12.50)-(12.11.58)

 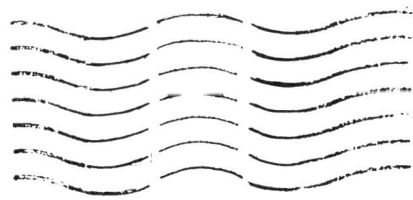

M4 State 3 (30.12.57)-(24.9.60)

M4 State 4 (27.2.46)-(14.3.46)

M4 State 5 (1.12.50)-(24.12.58)
N.B. See also State 22 for different style of letters.

M4 State 6 (16.12.50)-(29.2.56)

 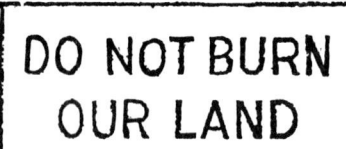

M4 State 7 (26.4.51)-(28.8.51)

M4 State 8 (10.5.51)-(15.12.60)

M4 State 9 (10.5.51)-(1.5.60)

M4 State 11 (14.2.53)-(16.10.53)

M4 State 12 (30.6.53)-(20.9.60)

M4 State 13 (20.7.53)-(1.7.61)

M4 State 14 (20.7.53)-(25.7.53)

M4 State 15 (20.7.53)-(21.5.59)

 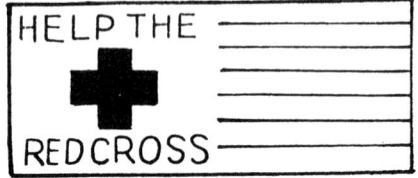

M4 State 16 (19.1.55)-(9.4.56)

M4 State 17 (16.3.55)

M4 State 18 (29.5.55)-(29.7.60)

M4 State 19 (2.12.56)-(14.12.56)

M4 State 20 (27.12.56)-(16.12.57)

M4 State 21 (21.6.58)-(25.6.58)

M4 State 22 (6.11.58)-(1.11.61)

M4 State 23 (18.2.59)-(17.10.60)

 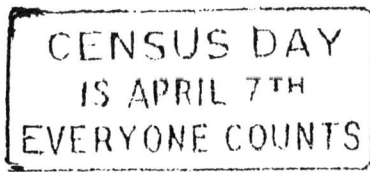

M4 State 24 (8.3.60)-(6.4.60)

VISIT
BOY SCOUT JAMBOREE
TRINIDAD
APRIL 4TH-14TH

M4 State 26 (3.2.61)-(12.4.61)

DO NOT BURN
OUR LAND

M4 State 27 (14.4.61)-(25.5.61)

SUPPORT
LOCAL
INDUSTRY

M4 State 28 (18.8.61)-S.U. 31.8.62

CORRECT ADDRESSING
IS A BLESSING
SAVES US GUESSING

M4 State 29 (6.12.60)-(17.12.61)

SAVE PRECIOUS WATER

M4 State 30 (13.7.60)

M4 State 31 (9.12.60)-(15.12.61)

M4 State 32 (12.3.62)-(10.4.62)

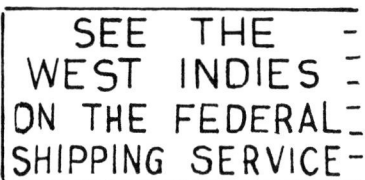 

M4 State 33 (1.8.61)-(2.2.62)

M4 State 34 (   2.62)

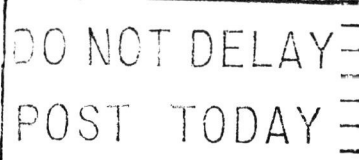 

M4 State 35 (21.12.61)

## PORT OF SPAIN G.P.O. Continued

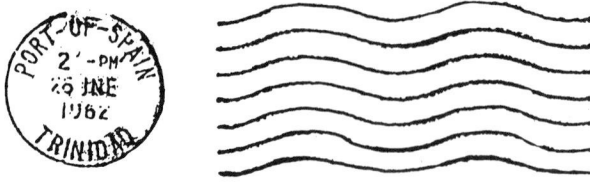

M5 State 1 (1.8.62)-S.U.31.8.62

M5 State 2 (25.2.60)

M5 State 3 (22.6.61)-(5.7.62)

M5 State 4 (23.7.61)-(28.7.62)

M5 State 5 (10.12.61)-S.U.31.8.62

SEE THE
WEST INDIES
ON THE FEDERAL
SHIPPING SERVICE

M5 State 6 (31.12.61)

≡ SAVE ≡
PRECIOUS
≡ WATER ≡

M6 State 2 (10.6.60)-S.U. 31.8.62

GO TO ST.CHRISTOPHER'S
SIPARIA
ON TRAVELLERS SUNDAY

M6 State 3 (13.7.62)-(10.8.62)

GO TO ST.CHRISTOPHER'S
SIPARIA.
ON TRAVELLERS SUNDAY.

M6 State 4 (27.6.62)-S.U.31.8.62

DO NOT BURN
OUR LAND

M6 State 5 (20.7.61)-S.U.31.8.62

**Registered (R)**

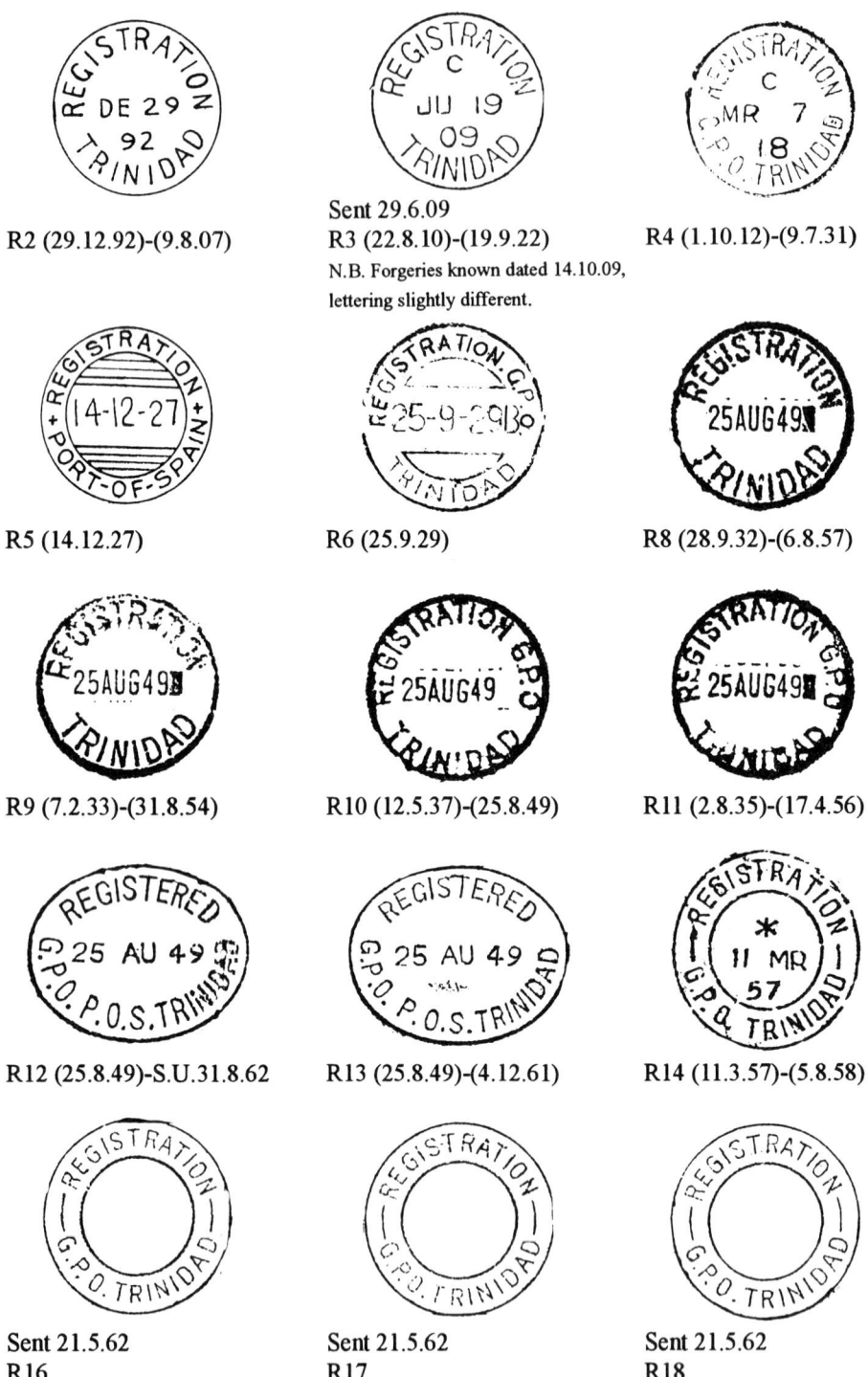

R2 (29.12.92)-(9.8.07)

Sent 29.6.09
R3 (22.8.10)-(19.9.22)
N.B. Forgeries known dated 14.10.09,
lettering slightly different.

R4 (1.10.12)-(9.7.31)

R5 (14.12.27)

R6 (25.9.29)

R8 (28.9.32)-(6.8.57)

R9 (7.2.33)-(31.8.54)

R10 (12.5.37)-(25.8.49)

R11 (2.8.35)-(17.4.56)

R12 (25.8.49)-S.U.31.8.62

R13 (25.8.49)-(4.12.61)

R14 (11.3.57)-(5.8.58)

Sent 21.5.62
R16

Sent 21.5.62
R17

Sent 21.5.62
R18

To distinguish between the above datestamps easily, this sheet (or any other), may be ordered from the Publisher printed on clear plastic for £1 each (subject unsold).

**PORT OF SPAIN G.P.O. Continued**

Sent 21.5.62
R19

R20 (9.12.71)-(8.9.74)

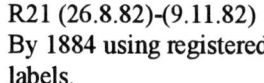

R21 (26.8.82)-(9.11.82)
By 1884 using registered
labels.

R22 (27.9.82)-(23.8.83)

R23 (21.3.84)-(25.12.10)

R24 (2.8.11)-(28.12.37)

R25 (1.2.35)

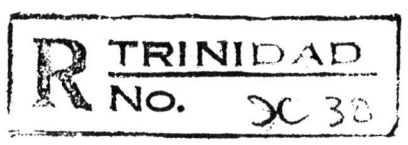

R26 (12.5.37)-(3.5.52)

R27 (12.5.37)

R29 (7.8.82)-(27.1.83)

Sent 29.6.09
R30 (27.12.94)

Sent 8.4.96
R31 (1.7.96)-(1.3.00)

Sent 8.4.96
R32 (4.1.00)

Sent 24.6.09
R33 (30.1.11)-(31.12.13)

**PORT OF SPAIN G.P.O. Continued**

R34 (5.9.46)

Sent 30.10.99
R36

**Advice of Arrival (A.R.)**

AR1 (3.12.97)

AR3 (26.5.24)-(25.11.43)

**Parcel Post (P.P.)**

PP2 (21.6.94)-(27.3.01)*

PP3 (20.4.07)

Sent 29.6.09
PP4 (15.5.11)-(9.1.33)

PP5 (15.8.39)-S.U. 31.8.62

PP6 (31.12.53)-(20.11.57)

PP7 (7.7.58)-S.U.31.8.62

## PORT OF SPAIN G.P.O. Continued

PP8 (14.5.57)

PP9 circa 1910-1913

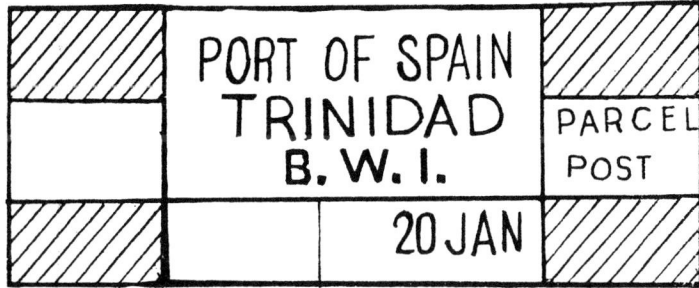

PP11 (25.4.35)-(2.12.35)
Recon

### Paid (P.D.)

Sent 1854
PD2
Used as a frank (9.2.58)-(25.1.59).
As a paid mark (10.3.59)-(7.4.66).

PD3 (9.12.66)-(1.1.67)

PD4 (24.5.67)-(20.5.68)

PD5 (9.2.69)-(12.3.82)
Sometimes used to cancel stamps.

PD7 (28.6.40)-(16.8.40)

## PORT OF SPAIN G.P.O. Continued

PD8 (16.4.41)- (24.11.54)
Known set with values between
1c & 26c also 30c in m/s.

Sent 4.10.61
PD9

POSTAGE PAID
2 CENTS

PD11 (M) (8.1.62)-S.U.31.8.62

### Official Paid (O.P.D.)

OPD12 (23.2.93)-(24.7.19)

OP13 (4.12.28)

OPD14 (11.3.24)

OPD16 (16.8.37)- (24.11.41)

**PORT OF SPAIN G.P.O. Continued**

**Unpaid (U.P.)**

UP3 (7.11.92)-(5.11.02)

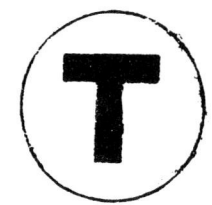

UP4 (24.1.95)-(18.9.14)

Sent 19.6.01
UP5 (3.4.06)-(21.6.47)

Sent 29.6.09
UP6 (1.2.21)-S.U. 31.8.62

UP7 (26.11.17)-(13.8.31)

UP8 (26.9.39)-(7.7.54)

UP9

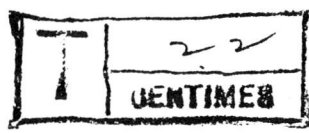

UP10 (31.8.48)-(7.6.54)

UP11 (19.2.55)-(24.2.56)

UP12 (20.6.56)-(7.11.58)

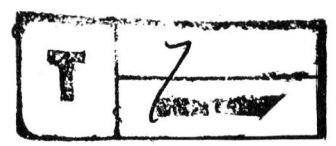

UP13 (30.12.60)-(5.4.62)

**Express Delivery (E.X.P.)**

## EXPRESS.

Sent 14.12.98
EXP1

**Forces (F)**

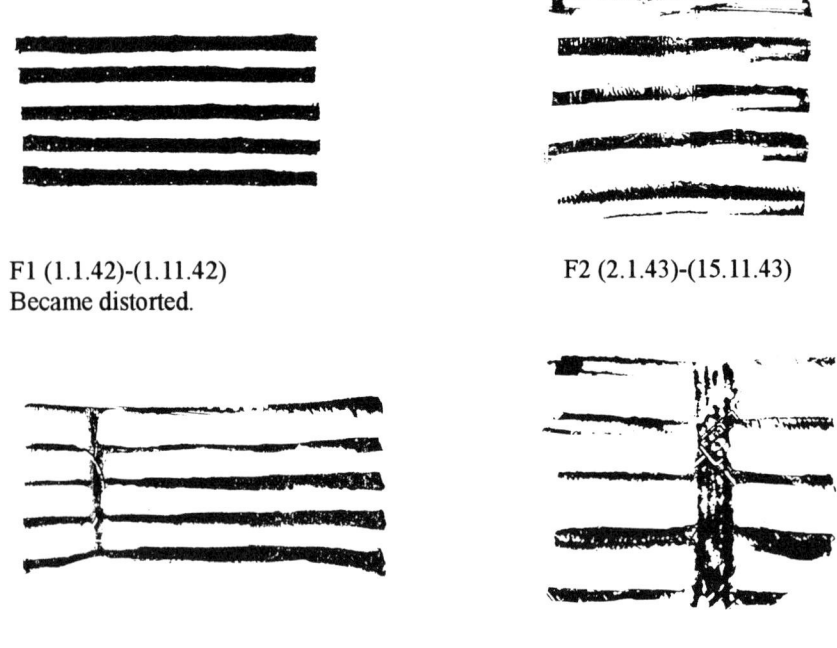

F1 (1.1.42)-(1.11.42)
Became distorted.

F2 (2.1.43)-(15.11.43)

F3 (   10.42)

F4

F1/4 were used as security marks usually on Forces or maritime mail.

F6 (1.1.44)-(1.11.44)

F7 (30.4.44)

F8

## PORT OF SPAIN G.P.O. Continued

**FROM H. M. SHIP POSTAGE PAID**

F10 (8.1.47)

F11 (7.12.42)-(8.1.47)

F12 (6.5.47)-(21.11.47)

**Air Mail (A.M.)**

```
FIRST  FLIGHT
B. W. I. AIRWAYS
TRINIDAD—JAMAICA
```

AM3 (14.12.44)

```
FIRST  FLIGHT
· PAN AMERICAN AIRWAYS
TRINIDAD — NEW  YORK
DIRECT
```

AM4 (18.7.46)

```
BY AIR MAIL
PAR AVION
```

AM5 (4.12.42)-(27.5.48)

**AIR MAIL**

AM7 (17.2.55)-(5.3.55)

AM8 (21.12.56)-(22.12.56)

**TO NEW YORK BY AIR AND ONWARD BY AIR**

AM9 (25.1.43)-(31.7.44)

**N. Y. AIR STEAMER ONWARD**

AM10 (10.10.44)-(11.11.49)

**BY AIR MAIL OVER U. S. Domestic Routes Only**

AM12 (15.2.46)

**TO U.S.A ONLY BY AIR**

AM13 (29.7.46)-(12.11.46)

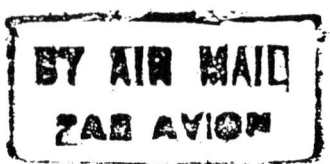

AM14 (12.4.41)-(10.10.46)

AM15 (7.1.47)-(25.1.49)

**BY AIR MAID**
PAR AVION

**BY AIR MAID**
ZAB AVION

AM16 (15.12.42)

AM17 (28.3.46)

AM20 (16.9.47)-(13.6.50)

AM21 (7.5.52)-(18.12.54)

AM22 (12.10.55)

**Instructional (I)**

*LATE FEE PAID*

TOO-LATE

LATE

I2 (22.1.32)-(3.7.40)

I3 (24.8.67)-(30.5.79)

I4 (24.9.82)-(7.11.82)

TOO LATE

TOOLATEFORBAC

UNCLAIMED

I5 (22.1.87)-(18.11.07)

I7 (16.1.31)

I8 (19.12.94)-(1.10.99)

UNCLAIMED          Unclaimed          UNCLAIMED

I9 (28.2.11)-(5.61)          I10 (20.5.31)- (29.5.46)          I11 (10.12.35)

UNCLAIMED          Unclaimed          Non Reclamé. Not called for.

I12 (20.12.41)          I13 (28.1.56)          I14 (19.12.94)-(27.5.95)

NOT CALLED FOR
NON RECLAMÉ.

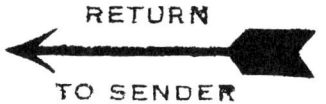

I15 (20.5.31)          I18 (15.7.42)

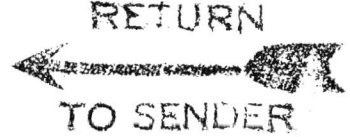          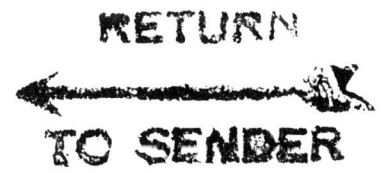

I20 (10.7.46)          I21 (25.7.53)-(17.8.55)

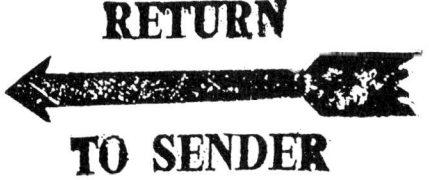          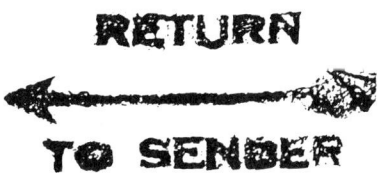

I22 (28.1.56)-S.U.31.8.60          I23 (28.4.57)-(16.1.58)

# RETOUR    RETOUR

I24 (5.7.39)-31.1.47)    I25 (11.11.49)

NOT KNOWN
INCONNU

INSUFFICIENTLY PAID

I26 (5.7.39)-(31.1.47)    I27 (2.12.07)

INSUFFICIENTLY PAID    Insufficiently Paid for
Transmission by Air Mail

I29 (8.4.30)-(17.8.37)    I32 (14.11.55)-(8.3.56)

Insufficiently Paid for
Transmission by Air Mail

DAMAGED
BY FIRE.

I33 (7.6.56)-S.U.31.8.62    I35 (10.6.21)

CLEARED FROM
LETTER BOX G. P. O.

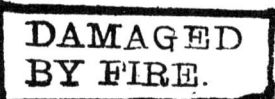
BY SURFACE MAIL
FROM
TRINIDAD, B.W.I.

I36 (1.8.42)-(1.9.55)    I38 (1.10.46)-(25.7.61)
Used on registered letters
"posted out of course".

REFUSED.
REFUSÉ

CANCELLED

CANCELLED

I39 (24.12.34)

I40 (28.2.11)

I41 (2.2.16)

CANCELLED

I43 (24.12.34)-(31.1.47)

I44
Held at G.P.O. in 1976

I42 and I43 were used on postage due labels when the charge was uncollected.

MISSENT
TO
TRINIDAD
B.W.I.

GONE AWAY
PARTI

I45 ( 9.41)

I49 (3.4.40)

I50 (7.7.55)-S.U.31.8.60

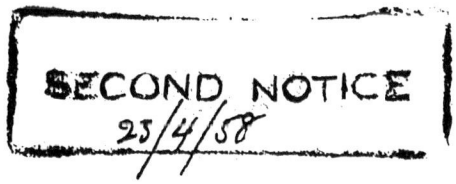

I51 (23.4.58)

SECOND NOTICE

RECEIVED IN DAMAGED CONDITION

I52

I55 (28.2.39)

SECOND POSTMAN

I72

**Ship Letters, Paquebot (S.L.)**

TRINICAD
SHIP LETTER

SL1 (20.5.48)-(31.5.48)

SHIP – LETTER
TRINIDAD

Sent 27.8.4]
SL2 (11.2.59)

SHIP-LETTER

SL3 (22.6.71)-(24.12.76)

SL4 (17.10.95)-(23.1.99)

PAQUEBOT

Sent 14.12.98
SL5 (27.9.00)-(16.5.07)

PAQUEBOT

SL6 (4.12.11)-(22.2.12)

SL7 (29.4.13)-(12.5.14)

SL9 (14.4.29)-(8.8.33)

SL10 (31.1.34)-(5.2.34)

PAQUEBOT
TRINIDAD

SL11 (26.2.34)- (7.3.36)

SL12 (2.2.37)-S.U. 31.8.62

Sent 18.9.61
SL13

**Port of Spain G.P.O.-Accountant Branch**

(10.10.18)-(17.11.50)     **30     300**

D2 (17.11.50)

Sent 29.6.09
R1 (10.10.18)-(20.5.42)                     R2 (23.10.46)
Used on Money order advice envelopes.

**Former G.P.O.**

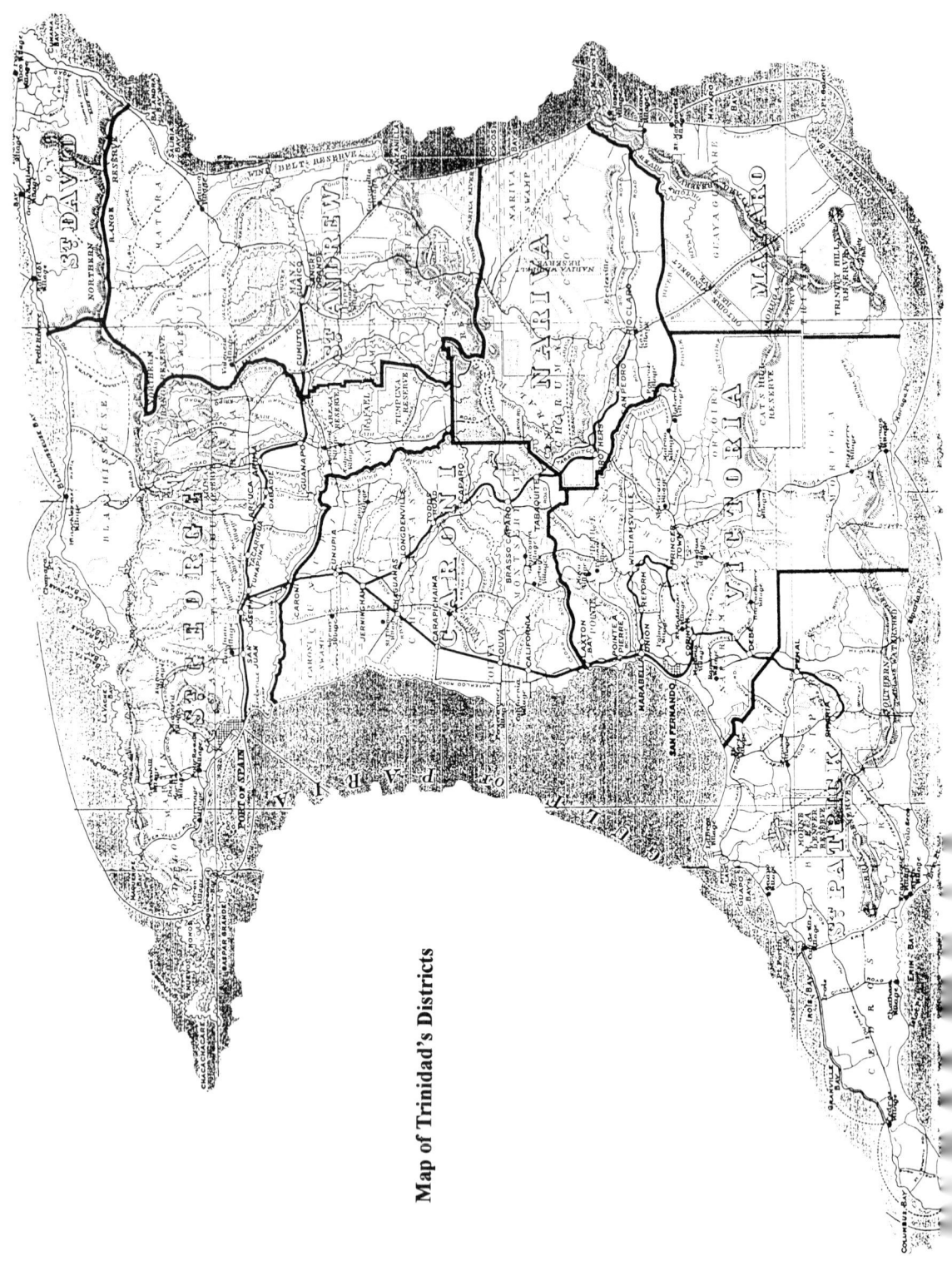

**Map of Trinidad's Districts**

**Port of Spain-Dead letter Office**

(20.5.31)-S.O. 31.8.62      -    **100**

D2 (20.5.31)-(27.2.35)                               D3 (10.12.35)-S.U. 31.8.62

**Abyssinia**

Postal agency under Guayaguayare. Situated on the Rio Claro-Guayaguayare Road, near Guayaguayare.

1.10.59-S.O. 31.8.62      **10**    **100**

Sent 1.10.59

D1 (  10.59)                                   D2 (20.9.60)-S.U. 31.8.62
Val x 20

**Abyssinia Post Office**

**Agricultural Show P.O. (Port of Spain)**
The post office was situated in the north east corner of the Princes Building. There were three collections daily. The total stamp sales were £3, 12s 9d.

(17.10.95)-(19.10.95)        **50**     **500**

```
┌─────────────────────────┐
│  AG. SHOW. P.O.         │
└─────────────────────────┘
```

D1 (18.10.95)-(19.10.95)

**ARIMA** (O. abb. of Hyarima, Chief of the Nepuyo Indians 1636).
Founded in1757 by Spanish Capuchin priests. Upto 1827 it was a restricted area for the people of Amerindian descent. On 31 August 1876 the railway was opened between Port of Spain and Arima. The population in 1881 was 1,973. This grew rapidly in 1942 to nearly 10,000 owing to the nearby U.S. base. In 1960 the population was 10,939.

The Post Office was moved from the police station to the registrars office, on 1 July 1860 moved in the gazette of 9 June 1860 but it was re-scribed on 29 June 1860. Eventually moved from the police station in February 1886. On 1 August 1891 it moved from 51 Queen Street to 42 Guanapo Street. In 1867 G. Cezair was postmaster. On 1 December 1890 Thomas A. John became Sub-Postmaster £70 p.a. until 1901 (Money Order Office). In 1902 J. A Samuel took over the position £70 p.a. In 1903 his salary was raised to £80 p.a. until 1906. In 1907 Miss M. Stanford became Sub-Postmistress £80 p.a. until 1925. On 1 July 1927 Miss L. Hamilton took over as Sub-Postmistress £100 p.a. until 1950. In 1951 Miss C. Owen-Henry became Sub-Postmistress till 1958/59. In 1962 situated on Broadway,in the county of St. George. Using time codes A to D.

On 20 April 1888 the following times were introduced for closing the mails:-

> For Dabadie, Arouca, Tacarigua, Tunapuna,   }
> St. Joseph, St. Juans, Port-of-Spain and   } 10.15 a.m.
> intermediate offices to San Fernando   }

For Port-of-Spain and San Fernando   ....    .... 3.05 p.m.
For Manzanilla and Mayaro ....   ....   ....   .... 6.00 p.m., Saturday & Wednesday.
For Toco    ....   ....   ....   ....   ....   ....   .... 6.00 p.m., Monday.
For Blanchisseuse ....   ....   ....   ....   ....   .... 10.00 a.m., Saturday.
For Tumpuna ....   ....   ....   ....   ....   ....   .... 3.00 p.m., Tuesday, Thursday & Saturday.

From 2 July 1888 there was an extra service to Toco on Thursday.

In 1930 a contract was signed for six daily services by Motor or hand cart between Arima Post Office and Arima Railway Station.

14.8.51-S.O. 31.8.62        **2**     **5**

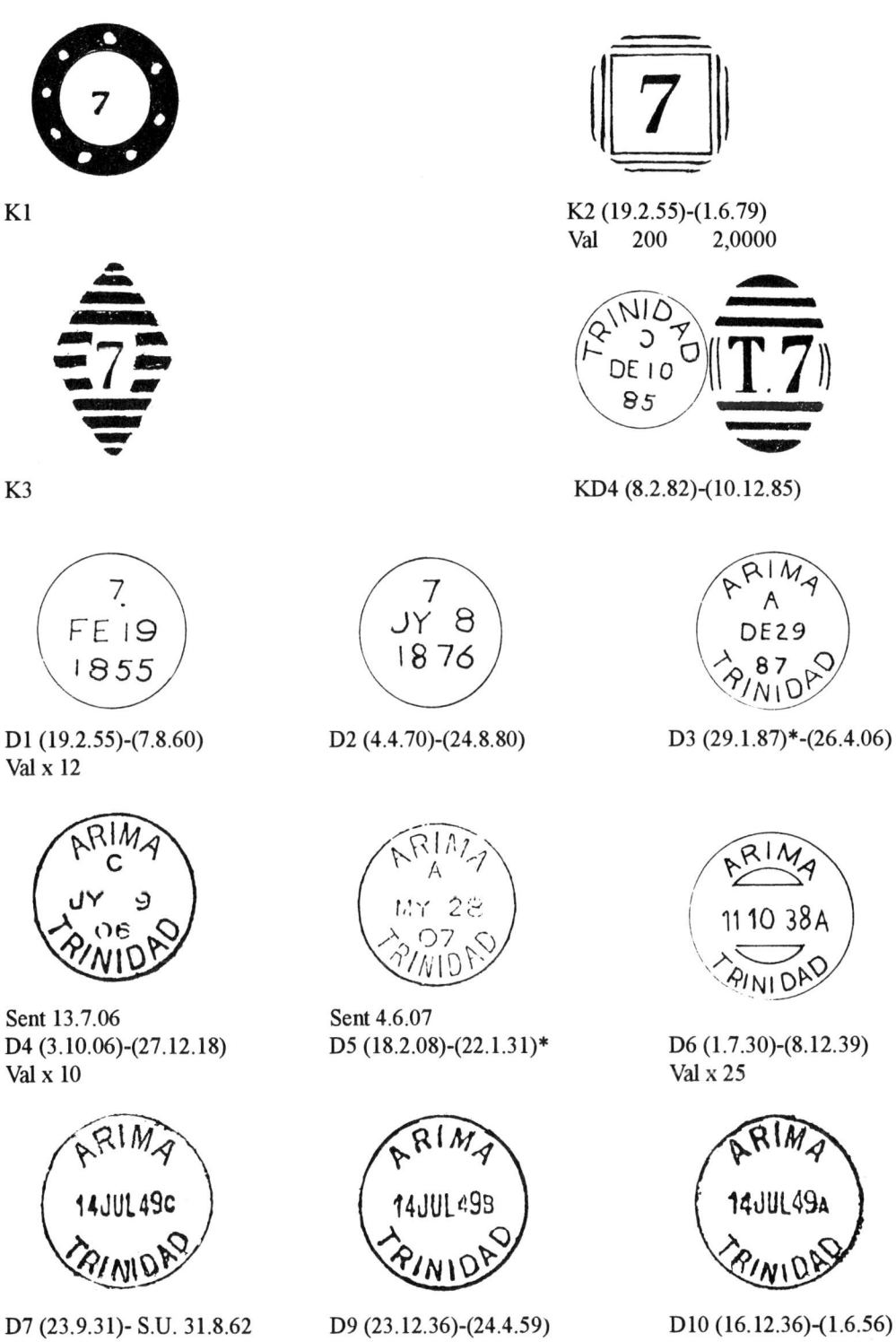

K1

K2 (19.2.55)-(1.6.79)
Val     200     2,0000

K3

KD4 (8.2.82)-(10.12.85)

D1 (19.2.55)-(7.8.60)
Val x 12

D2 (4.4.70)-(24.8.80)

D3 (29.1.87)*-(26.4.06)

Sent 13.7.06
D4 (3.10.06)-(27.12.18)
Val x 10

Sent 4.6.07
D5 (18.2.08)-(22.1.31)*

D6 (1.7.30)-(8.12.39)
Val x 25

D7 (23.9.31)- S.U. 31.8.62

D9 (23.12.36)-(24.4.59)

D10 (16.12.36)-(1.6.56)

To distinguish between the above datestamps easily, this sheet (or any other), may be ordered from the Publisher printed on clear plastic for £1 each (subject unsold).

D12 (23.6.59)
Val x 500

Sent 14.9.59
D13 (28.10.59)-S.U. 31.8.62

Sent 14.9.59
D14

UP2 (26.5.52)-(14.5.60)
Val x 10

UP3

**Arima Post Office**

**AROUCA** (Or. from Arquco (Arawak), tribe of Amerindians).

Situated between Tunapua and Arima, County St. George on the Eastern Main Road. On 30 April 1888 the post office was transferred from the police station to the house of Mr Gibbs (Postmaster in 1867). The Amerindians were resettled in 1897 to allow two estates to be established. Arouca was a station on the railway line in 1876 and in 1880 had a population of 2,847 dropping to 1,777 in 1900, and 1,231 in 1931. The last war brought on increase due to the nearby U.S. base at Cumuto and in 1946 the population was 3,661. In 1889 Mrs E. Woolford became Sub-Postmistress £40 p.a. until 1915 (Money Order Office). In 1916 Miss D. Chittenden took over the position £40 p.a. until 1923. In 1924 Miss M. Mason became Sub-Postmistress £67.10 p.a. until 1951. In 1952 (Miss) E. Gomez took over the position until 1958/59. Using time codes A B &C.

14.8.51- S.O. 31.8.62          **2          10**

K1
In 1851 probably issued with a mark similar
  to Arima K1.

K2 (1.1.65)-(1.6.79)
Val          200          2,0000

K3
Val          300          -

KD4 (18.9.82)-(5.3.86)
Val          50          1,000

D2 (5.3.60)-(26.6.74)

D3 (7.6.81)-(5.9.81)

D4 (11.1.88)-(26.4.07)

Sent 4.6.07
D5 (21.8.07)-(24.12.35)

D6 (11.1.36)-S.U. 31.8.62

Sent 30.7.58?
D7 (11.4.59)-S.U. 31.8.62

UP2 (14.4.08)  UP3  -S.U. 31.8.62

Unclaimed

I2 (14.4.08)-S.U. 31.8.62

**Arouca Post Office**

**Balandra**

Situated 6 miles south of Cumana, near Balandra Bay Road.  Postal Agency under Sangre Grande.

2.8.56-S.O. 31.8.62          **10      100**

D2 (4.6.58)-S.U. 31.8.62

UNCLAIMED

I2

**Balandra Post Office**

255

**Balmain (O. Spanish)**

Situated 3 miles east of Couva, fifty yards from Milton Road. Postal agency under Couva.

1.4.43-S.O. 31.8.62

**6    60**

D1 (28.12.44)

D2 (26.2.45)-S.U. 31.8.62
Only seen using time code A.

Val x 50

**Balmain Post Office**

**Bamboo Village**

Situated 2 miles south of San Fernando, at the junction of Southern Main Road and Dumfries Road. Postal agency under San Fernando.

6.7.61-S.O. 31.8.62

**30    300**

Sent 2.9.60
D2 (24.8.62)-S.U.31.8.62

**Bamboo Village Continued**

**Bamboo Village Post Office**

**Barrackpore**
Situated at the junction of Popoure Road and Rochard Road, 5 miles south of Princes Town.  Postal
agency under Princes Town.

1.7.46-S.O. 31.8.62         **10**      **100**

D1 (24.9.46)-(17.2.47)
Val x 50

D2 (24.1.49)*- S.U. 31.8.62

R1 (15.7.49)-S.U. 31.8.62
Val x 2

UP1 (15.7.49)-S.U. 31.8.62
Val x 2

Unclaimed

I1 (15.7.49)-S.U. 31.8.62
Val x 2

**Barrackpore Post Office**

## Basseterre

In 1962 situated in a Hardware store, 4 miles on Moruga Road.  Postal agency under Princes Town.
In 1910 J. W. Percival became Sub-Postmaster £12.10 p.a. until 1912.  In 1913 A. Thorpe took over
the position £12.10 p.a. until 1916.  Using time codes A, B & C.

1906*-S.O. 31.8.62 **2 20**

Sent 29.6.08
D2 (1.12.08)-(12.1.25)

Val x 4

D3 (26.1.27)-(25.3.39)
& (4.12.58)-(2.4.59)
Val x 5

D4 (25.3.39)*-S.U.31.8.62

UP2 (18.7.49)

**Basseterre Post Office**

# Unclaimed

I2 (18.7.49)

**Bejucal** (Or. Amerindian liane or vine)
Situated at the junction of Warren Road and Adjudah Road in Warren Village.  Postal agency
under Cunupia.

15.8.58-S.O. 31.8.62          **15      150**

D1 15.8.58-S.U. 31.8.62

**Bejucal Post Office**

**Belle Eau Road- Port of Spain**
Probably not opened.

Sent 2.9.60
D2

**Belle Garden-Tobago**
Situated south of Roxborough.  Postal agency under Scarborough   Using time codes A & B.

1.5.41*-S.O. 31.8.62      **10**     **100**

D2 (12.3.46)-S.U. 31.8.62

**Belle Garden Post Office**

## BELMONT

Suburb of Port of Spain, situated in county St. George. Daily house to house delivery started 1 February 1879. A post office opened on the Belmont Circular Road on 1 September 1891. On the 31 May 1895 it moved to the premises of Mrs Blandin. In 1889 the Sub-Postmistress was Mrs. L. Johnson £15 p.a. until 1904 (Money Order Office). In 1905 Miss Johnson took over the position £25 p.a. until 1912. In 1913 Miss L. Ovid became Sub-Postmistress with a raise in the yearly salary to £40. In 1932 Miss W. Donawa took over the position until 1936. On 1 July 1937 Miss C. Cottle became Sub-Postmistress until 1941when Miss I. Todd took over the position in 1942. In 1949 (Miss) E. B. Gill became Sub-Postmistress until 1958-59. Using time codes A, B & C.

1.9.91-S.O. 31.8.62                    **2**        **10**

KD3 (12.3.92)
Val x 100

D2 (14.6.92)*-(12.8.07)

Sent 4.6.07
D3 (24.8.07)-(20.6.27)

D4 (4.11.29)-(11.3.38)

D5 (13.6.38)-(25.7.58)

D6 (31.1.48)*-S.U. 31.8.62

D7 (1.7.58)-S.U. 31.8.62

R2 (5.5.59)

**BELMONT Continued**

UP3

UNCLAIMED                    UNCLAIMED

I2 (30.6.92)                 I3

**Belmont Post Office**

**Bethel-Tobogo**
Situated on the Orange Road 2 miles east of Buccoo Point. Postal agency under Scarborough.
Using time codes A B & C.

(1926)-S.O. 31.8.62 **10 10**

D2 (27.11.37)-S.U. 31.8.62

UNCLAIMED

I2 (23.6.55)
Val x 3

**Bethel Post Office**

## Biche

Situated on the Cunapo Southern Road, 1 mile south west of Poole, near the police station. Postal agency under Rio Claro. Miss B. Ablack became Sub-Postmistress at the Post Office in Biche during 1938 only.

(22.9.21)-S.O. 31.8.62      **10**     **100**

D2 (22.9.21)-(21.11.38)
(Known set with codes A, B, C, I & W).
Val x 4

D3 (28.10.40)-S.U. 31.8.62
Using time codes A & B.

R2 (5.5.59)
Val x 2

**Biche Post Office**

**Black Rock-Tobago**

Situated 1½ miles south of Plymouth. Postal agency under Scarborough.

1.7.52-S.O. 31.8.62         10     100

D1 (24.9.52)-(12.12.52)                      D2 (3.3.53)-S.U. 31.8.62
Val x 20

Black Rock Post Office

**Blanchisseuse** (Or. French, "washer women" were seen at the spot by the British surveying officer).

Opened as Blanchisseuse and Toco redesignated by 1869. Postal agency under Arima. In 1868 the mail was too received each Thursday by the boat going to Toco. In 1871 the population was 472. In 1946 it was 784. In 1888 the mails closed at the G.P.O. every Saturday at 8 a.m. and reached Blanchisseuse at 6.30 p.m. In the reverse direction they were closed every Monday at 10.30 a.m. and reached Port of Spain Tuesday morning. From 1937 there was a tri-weekly motor service from Arima. Upto 1928 communication was only by sea. In 1931 a road was opened to Arima, 12 miles away. In 1899 the Sub-Postmaster was R. N Davis £25 p.a. until 1914. In 1915 Miss V. Laveau took over the position £25 p.a. until 1916 In 1917 J. Brathwaite became Sub-Postmaster £25 p.a. until 1923. In 1924 N. Brathwaite took over the position until 1932 when S. A. Peters became Sub-Postmaster in 1933 until 1939. In 1940 R. L. Fields took over the position until 1942. Mr. Julien then became Sub-Postmaster for Blanchisseuse Post Office for the year 1943 only. Using time codes A, B & C.

(1861)-S.O. 31.8.62                5        50

K2
No. 11 from Tunapuna

K3
Used at Carenage until (1861)

KD3

D3 (24.6.89)-(19.8.12)
Val x 5

D4 (2.11.12)-(16.12.29)
Val x 4

D5 (3.9.30)- (19.9.45)
Val x 4

**Blanchisseuse Post Office**

**Blanchisseuse Continued**

D7 (22.11.48)-(5.11.49)
Val x 40

D8 (1.2.50)-(14.11.55)*

D9 (31.12.57)*-S.U. 31.8.62

UP1 (2.4.23)

**Blundell**
Situated in the Laventille area, on Laventille Road.  Postal agency under Port of Spain.
$\qquad$ 1.9.58-S.O. 31.8.62 $\qquad$ **10** $\qquad$ **100**

D1 1.9.58-S.U. 31.8.62

R1

UP1

UNCLAIMED

I1

**Blundell Post Office**

**Boissiere (Village)** (Or. Name of a French Settler).
Situated 1 mile north of Port of Spain.

(16.3.29)-1.10.60*　　　　　**10**　　**100**

D2 (16.3.29)-(1.9.35)

D3 (3.2.41)-(8.9.58)
Only seen with time code A.

Val x 10

**Bonne A Venture**
Situated 4 miles north east of San Fernando at 122 Elect Road. Postal agency under Couva.

1.6.45-S.O. 31.8.62　　　　　**5**　　**50**

D1 (24.7.45)-(14.1.46)

D2 (28.2.46)*-S.U. 31.8.62
Only seen with time code A & D.

Val x 50

**Bonne A Venture Post Office**

**Brasso (Brasso Caparo)** (Or. Spanish, brazo, meaning branch of a river).

Postal agency under Tabaquite. Initally opened at the railway station, when there were two mails daily in each direction. In 1900 the Sub-Postmaster for that year was James Black. In 1901 J. St Rose took over the position £12.10 p.a. until 1906 when J. Burns became Sub-Postmaster in 1907. In 1910 J. Bryan took over the position £12.10 p.a. until 1916. In 1918 Miss D. Archibald became Sub-Postmistress £25 p.a. until 1919. In 1920 Miss E. Tinto. took over the position £25 p.a. until 1924. Initially using time codes A & B later A, B & C.

1.2.99-S.O. 31.8.62        10    100

Sent 19.10.98
D1 (19.7.99)*-(6.11.05)
Val x 4

Sent 4.6.07
D2 (31.10.07)-(22.6.23)
Val x 3

D3 (3.10.27)-(10.7.28)
Val x 4

D4 (11.7.32)*-(28.7.59)

D5 (31.7.60)-(1.9.60)
Val x 5

Sent 1.6.60
D6 (14.6.60)-S.U. 31.8.62

**Brasso Post Office**

**Brasso (Brasso Caparo) Continued**

R2

UP2

UNCLAIMED

I2

**Brasso Piedra (Brasso Piedro)** (Or. Spanish meaning stone branch).
Situated in a shop 1 mile north east of Flanagin Town. Postal agency under Tabaquite. In 1910 T. Alexander became Sub-Postmaster for Brasso Piedra Post Office £12.10 until 1918. In 1919 Miss M. Mason took over the position £25 p.a. until 1921. In 1922 Miss N. Woodyear became Sub-Postmistress until 1923 when Mrs A. A. Nurse took over her position £40 p.a. in 1924. For the year 1925 only Miss A. Queeley became Sub-Postmistress £40 p.a.

(27.8.08)-S.O. 31.8.62          **10**     **100**

Sent 29.6.08
D2 (27.8.08)-(10.5.24)
Using time codes A, B & C.
Val x 4

D3 (28.12.25)-(13.12.38)

Val x 3

D4 (11.12.39)-(16.3.54)

D5 (5.8.54)-(20.5.57)
Val x 50

D6 (21.7.58)-S.U. 31.8.62

271

**Brasso Piedra Post Office**

# UNCLAIMED

I2 (22.9.14)

**Brasso Seco** (Or. Spanish meaning dry branch).
Situated in a shop on Mandomas Road in Paria, between Blanchisseuse and Arima.  Postal agency under Arima.

15.4.58-S.O. 31.8.62          **10      100**

D2 (27.6.58)-S.U. 31.8.62

**Brasso Seco Post Office**

## Brothers Road
Postal agency under Tabaquite.  Using time codes A, B & C.

1925-S.O. 31.8.62            **10**      **100**

K2
Held 1949, used in 1925?

Sent 25.11.57

D2 (30.1.29)-(12.5.30)       D3 (17.9.32)-(25.8.59)       D4 (21.1.60)-S.U. 31.8.62
Val x 20

R2 (14.7.49)
Val x 2

UP2 (14.7.49)-S.U. 31.8.62
Val x 3

UNCLAIMED

I2 (14.7.49)
Val x 4

**Brothers Road Post Office**

## Buccoo Point-Tobago
Coastal Village situated 5 miles south of Plymouth. Postal agency under Scarborough.

1.7.52-S.O. 31.8.62 **15** **150**

D1 (2.12.52)
Val x 10

D3 (23.3.53)-(24.10.53)
Val x 20

D3 (14.12.53)-S.U. 31.8.62

Sent 30.7.58
D4

Sent 30.7.58
D5

**Buccoo Post Office**

**Caigual** (Or. Amerindian name of a fruit).

Situated on the Caigual Road (branch off the Eastern Main Road) 5 ½ miles from Sangre Grande. The village grew from a Cocoa Estate and was initally cleared in 1894. Postal agency under Sangre Grande.

(1926)-S.O. 31.8.62          **10**     **100**

D2 (30.1.56)-S.U. 31.8.62
Date stamp issued 1 February 1953.

**Caigual Post Office**

**Calcutta Settlement**

Situated west of Couva. Postal agency under Carapichaima.

(11.10.06)-S.O. 31.8.62        **10**     **100**

Sent 25.9.09
D2 (8.11.09)-(30.12.48)
Using time codes A, B & C.
Val x 3

D3 (22.4.49)-S.U. 31.8.62
Only seen with time code A.

276

# UNCLAIMED

I2

**Calcutta Settlement Post Office**

**CALIFORNIA**
District office opened at the railway station. Situated 10 miles north of San Fernando. County Caroni, on Yallery Street. On 31 January 1889 moved from the station to a new office. In 1899 the Sub-Postmistress was Mrs A. Brown £25 p.a. until 1911. On 1 October 1912 Miss L. Hamilton took over the position for one year. In 1913 Miss Fergusson became Sub-Postmistress until 1915. In 1916 Miss W. Donawa took over the position £40 p.a. In 1917 her salary dropped from £40 to £25 p.a. In 1919 Miss I. Todd (Ag) became Sub-Postmistress £25 p.a. until 1924. In 1925 Mrs. A. A. Nurse took over the position for that year only £40 p.a. In 1938 Miss O. Sampson and in 1957 E. A. Clarke also became Sub-Postmistresses/masters for one year only. Using time codes A, B, C & D.

1.4.81-S.O. 31.8.62      **8    80**

KD1 (1.4.83)
Val x 20

D2 (2.6.86)*-(9.3.06)
Val x 7

Sent 4.6.07
D3 (16.1.08)-(22.6.26)
Val x 6

D4 (23.9.31)-S.U.31.8.62

Sent 30.7.58?
D5
Not used owing to spelling error?

Sent 29.1.59
D6 (16.3.59)-S.U. 31.8.62

UP2 (12.8.55)

**California Post Office**

**Canaan-Tobago**
Initially it probably operated as a receiving office only, without a datestamp. Later using time codes
A & B.

(1909)-S.O. 31.8.62 **10** **100**

D2 (22.3.43)-S.U. 31.8.62

**Canaan Post Office**

**Canaan Village-Trinidad**
Reduced from a post office to a postal agency in 1925.
(11.10.06)*-1926          **200** -
*listed as Canaan Village, Naparima.

To Cross in 1926

D2 (4.3.22)-(1.5.22)

## Caparo

Situated in a shop 2 miles north of Flanagin Town. Postal agency under Tabaquite originally opened at the railway station. In 1906 J. Burns became Sub-Postmaster £12.10s p.a. until 1907 when Blackman took over the position until 1908 £12.10s p.a. In 1910 J. Taylor became Sub-Postmaster for Caparo £12.10s until 1913. In 1914 C. Reefer took over the position for just one year £12.10s p.a. H. A. Atwell then became Sub-Postmaster in 1915 £12.10s p.a. until 1916. In 1920 Miss N. Woodyear became Sub-Postmistress until 1921 with a raise in salary to £25 p.a. In 1922 Miss O. Diaz took over the position until 1923. In 1924 E. Villafana took over the position for only one year. In 1925, for that year only, Miss C. Cottle became Sub-Postmistress with a raise in salary to £40 p.a. Using time codes A, B & C.

May 1905-S.O. 31.8.62        10     100

D2 (17.9.06)*-(5.6.30)       D3 (16.12.30)-(6.12.35)      D4 (3.2.34)*-S.U. 31.8.62
Val x 3                  Val x 4

Caparo Post Office

## Cap De Ville

Situated 2 miles south west of Point Fortin. Postal agency under Point Fortin. In 1899 the Sub-Postmaster was S. Allen (Police Sgt) until 1901. In 1902 G. Allen (Police Sgt) took over the position £12.10s p.a. until 1908. In 1910 P. Coker became Sub-Postmaster for the Cap De Ville Post Office £12.10s p.a. In 1911 E. Campbell took over the position for one year £12.10s p.a. until 1912 when C. Blades became Sub-Postmaster. In 1915 W. Woodley took over the position £12.10s p.a. until 1916. In 1921 the Post Office in Cap De Ville was vacant until 1922 when G. Bowen became Sub-Postmaster for two years.

| | | | |
|---|---|---|---|
| 9.10.91-31.10.37* | | 20 | 200 |
| 1.6.49-S.O. 31.8.62 | | 10 | 100 |

D2 (28.12.92)-(22.1.24)

D3 (12.7.37)
Val x 20

D4 (2.12.49)-(31.12.51)
Val x 10

D5 (30.3.52)-S.U. 31.8.62

**Cap De Ville Post Office**

# UNCLAIMED

12 (7.12.55)

**CARAPICHAIMA (Carapachaima)** (Or. Derived from a Carib tribe named Chayma).
Moved to a new departmental office from the railway station on 28 February 1889 . Situated in County Caroni, on Waterloo Road.  In 1899 the Sub-Postmistress was Mrs Caroline Giles (Money Order Office) £25 p.a. until 1900.  In 1901 Miss A. Archibald took over the position £25 p.a. until 1906.  In 1907 Miss R. E. Reid became Sub-Postmistress £25 p.a. until 1910.  In 1911 Miss L. Whitehead took over the position £40 p.a. until 1916.  In 1917 Miss C. Paredas became Sub-Postmistress £40 p.a.  In 1918 Miss L. Noguera took over the position £40 p.a.  In 1919 the Sub-Postmistress was Miss J. Smith (Ag) £40 p.a. until 1921.  In 1922 Miss C. Smith took over the position £40 p.a. until 1936.  In 1937 the Sub-Postmistress was Miss A. Smith until 1953.  In 1954 (Miss) M. Edwards took over the position until 1958/59.  Using time codes A, B & C.

(9.10.80)-S.O. 31.8.62          **3**          **30**

K1
Val x 40

KD3 (30.12.82)-(31.3.86)
Val x 50

D1 (9.10.80)-(27.3.82)
Val x 50

D2 (30.10.86)*-(22.8.07)
Val x 10

Sent 4.6.07
D3 (27.8.07)*-(11.7.12)*

D4 (3.11.14)*-(14.7.32)
Val x 6

D5 (11.11.32)-S.U.31.8.62

D6 (3.9.47)-S.U. 31.8.62

To distinguish between the above datestamps easily, this sheet (or any other), may be ordered from the Publisher printed on clear plastic for £1 each (subject unsold).

**CARAPICHAIMA (Carapachaima)**

RECISTERED

R1 (8.4.04)-(14.2.29)                    R2

UP2        -S.U.31.8.62

UNCLAIMED

I2

**Carapichaima Post Office**

**Caratal** (O. Spanish, Caratal Palm).
Situated south west of Manzanilla.  Postal agency under Sangre Grande.

22.9.48-S.O. 31.8.62

**10**     **100**

D1 (14.7.49)-(12.10.49)
Val x 20

D2 (22.3.50)-(5.9.55)
Val x 2

D3 (23.9.57)-S.U. 31.8.62

# UNCLAIMED

I1 (18.7.49)
Val x 4

**Caratal Post Office**

285

**Carenage** (Or. A bay, where ships were careened by tilting on their side for cleaning).
Postal Agency under St. James, served by the first inland postal service which started on 14
August 1851, with the post office being at the Police Station. Situated 5 miles north west of
Port of Spain in 1881 the area had a population of 1,239 served by a twice weekly service
from Port of Spain. In 1899 the Sub-Postmistress was Mrs J. Taylor with a salary of £25 p.a.,
she was the incumbent until 1923.

|  |  |  | N.S. |
|---|---|---|---|
| 14.8.51-(1861) |  |  |  |
| (1880)-S.O. 31.8.62 |  | 10 | 100 |

K1

K2

KD4

A mark probably was issued
in 1851 similar to La Brea K1

Val x 10

D2 (22.5.89)-(12.7.07)*

Sent 4.6.07

D3 (16.11.07)-(7.9.37)

D4 (30.12.40)-S.U. 31.8.62
Using time codes A, B, C & D.

Val x 5

Val x 3

**Carenage Post Office**

**Carnbee-Tobago**
Situated 5 miles west of Scarborough.  Postal agency under Scarborough.
8.6.55-S.U. 31.8.62          **10          100**

D1 (8.6.55)-(28.12.57)                    D2 (25.5.58)-S.U. 31.8.62
Val x 10

**Carnbee Post Office**

**CARONI** (O. Amerindian).
Situated 4 miles south of Tunapuna.  On 28 February 1889 moved from the railway station to a new office.  In 1962 situated in the Old Southern Main Road.  Using time codes A, B & C.  In 1899 the Sub-Postmistress was Miss R. E. Reid £25 p.a. (Money Order Office) until 1905.  In 1906 Mrs D. Ewing took over the position £25 p.a. until 1908.  In 1909 Miss L. Best became Sub-Postmistress for Caroni £25 p.a. until 1916.  In 1917 Miss E. Keith took over the position until 1918.  In 1919 the Sub-Postmistress was Miss W. Donawa (Ag) £40 p.a. until 1920.  In 1921 Miss P. C. Noguera took over the position £40 p.a. until 1925.  In 1926 Miss M. Bourgeois became Sub-Postmistress until

1927 when Miss I. Todd took over in 1928 until 1941. On 1 January 1942 Miss C. Cottle became Sub-Postmistress until 1943. In 1944 Miss C. Alcindor took over the position until 1953. In 1954 (Miss) S. Springer became Sub-Postmistress until 1958/59.

1880\*-S.O. 31.8.62          **8     80**

KD3 (31.3.86)

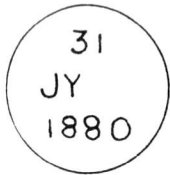

D1 (2.7.80)-(2.11.81)
Val x 10

D2 (1.6.86)-(19.2.24)
Val x 3

D3 (10.12.24)-(28.1.33)

Val x 4

D4 (30.7.33)-S.U. 31.8.62
Using time codes A to D

# Insured

R4

UP2

**Caroni Post Office**

### Castara-Tobago
Postal agency under Scarborough.  A license to deal in, or sell adhesive stamps was issued to Mr J. Dempster, Castara on 26 August 1902.

(18.5.04)-S.O. 31.8.62          **10**          **100**

Sent 12.11.02
D2 (18.5.04)-(17.8.04)

Val x 20

D4 (11.12.40)-S.U. 31.8.62
Using time codes Λ & B.

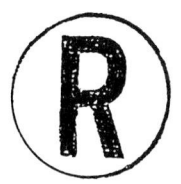

R2

UNCLAIMED                    **REFUSED**

12                                          13

**Castara Post Office**

**Caura** (Or. from the Arawak Cuara).
In 1871 the population was 989, in 1881, 1,467, the same year a road was opened from the
Eastern Main Road.    On 3 April 1888 a foot messenger service started between St. Mary's
and Caura.  In 1946 the village was cleared in order to build a dam (Abandoned April 1947).
In 1899 the Sub-Postmaster was J. L. Brown until 1900.  In 1901 A. J. Brown took over the
position £12.10s p.a. until 1904.  In 1905 S. Rodriguez became Sub-Postmaster £12.10s p.a.
until 1916.

(4.9.96)-30.4.48                              **25**      **250**

Sent 25.7.96
D2 (4.9.96)-(28.6.35)                    D4 (14.8.35)-(1.4.48)*
Initially set with code C, then asterisk from (8.5.01).

**CEDROS** (Or. Spanish for Cedars which originally grew in the area).

In 1871 the Ward of Cedros had a population of 3,500, in 1881 Cedros Village (orginally Bonasse) had a population 2,920 declining to 1,538 by 1960. Situated in County St. Patrick, on Cedros Main Road. Moved from the police station to Mr. Charles house on 8 February 1888. Stated to have moved in August 1885 in the "Annual Report". In 1899 the Sub-Postmistress was Mrs E. Matthew (Money Order Office) £40 p.a. until 1908. In 1909 Mrs L. Codrington took over the position £40 p.a. until 1926. In 1927 Mrs A. A. Nurse became Sub-Postmistress until 1928 when Miss C. Scott took over the position in 1929 until 1940. In 1941 Miss J. Scott became Sub-Postmistress until 1942. In 1943 Miss P. Francis took over the position until 1946. In 1947 Miss P. Francis-Bowen became Sub-Postmistress until 1949. In 1950 (Miss) A. Worrel took over the position until 1955. In 1956 (Miss) R. James became Sub-Postmistress. In 1957 S. Robinson took over the positfon until 1958/59. Using time codes A & B.

14.8.51-S.O. 31.8.62                 2        10

K1

K2 (19.9.57)-(25.5.67)

K3 (14.5.70)

KD5 (29.9.82)-(17.2.86)

D1 (19.9.57)-(25.5.67)

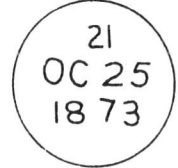

D2 (31.12.68)-(9.2:82)

D4 (19.6.86)-(27.7.12)

D5 (13.12.12)-(21.9.29)

D6 (12.10.29)-(12.12.33))

D7 (19.3.34)-S.U. 31.8.62

 REGISTERED

R2 (21.6.37)-S.U. 31.8.62

UP2 (23.2.39)-S.U. 31.8.62

UNCLAIMED

TOO LATE

I3

I4 (24.11.84)

**Cedros Post Office**

**Chacachacare** (O. Amerindian).

Postal agency under Port of Spain. Situated on Chacachare Island, north west point of Trinidad. In December 1861 the mails were made up in the house of Mr. J. Rush. In 1899 the Sub-Postmaster was J. B. Thomas until 1900. In 1901 A. Corke took over the position. In 1902 M. Bridgewater became Sub-Postmaster until 1903. In 1904 A. Bruce took over the position £12.10s p.a. until 1905. In 1906 Cecelia Walcott became Sub-Postmistress £12.10s p.a. until 1916.

|  |  |  |
|---|---|---|
| 14.8.51-(1861) |  | **N.S.** |
| (1899)-S.O. 31.8.62 | **10** | **100** |

K2

K3 (31.12.33)-(6.5.35)
Val x 3

Sent 15.5.00
D2 (29.8.00)-(22.2.28)
 & (15.6.35)-(9.8.39)
Val x 3
Seen with time codes B & C

D4 (18.2.41)-S.U. 31.8.62

REGISTERED

R1 (16.1.25)

**CHAGUANAS** (O. Amerindian tribe called Chaguanes).

Initally communcation was by coastal steamer. Mr. James Neilson was deputy postmaster on 20 February 1861 and the office was moved to his house. In 1880 it was reached by the railway. Situated in county Caroni on railway road. From 1868 to 1880 the postmaster was William Neilson. In 1899 the Sub-Postmistress was Miss M. Stanford (Money Order Office) £40 p.a. until 1900. In 1901 E. Cockerton took over the position £40 p.a. until 1902. In 1903 Miss L. Brown became Sub-Postmistress £40 p.a. until 1904. In 1905 Mrs L. Harris took over the position £40 p.a. until 1906. In 1907 the Sub-Postmistress was Miss A. Archibald £40 p.a. until 1908. In 1909 Miss E. Furlonge took over the position £40 p.a. until 1910. In 1911 Mrs E. Reid became Sub-Postmistress £40 p.a. until 1914. In 1915 Miss W. Hamilton took over the position £40 p.a. until 1916. Miss M. C. Corrie became Sub-Postmistress until Miss M. Paredes took over the position from 1 December 1916 £40 p.a. On 1 January 1919 Mrs L. A. Yates replaced her, but in 1920 the Sub-Postmistress was Miss L.

Greaves £40 p.a. until 1931. In 1932 Mrs L. Yates took over the position until 1935. On 1 April 1935 Mrs H. Winchester became Sub-Postmistress until 1938. In 1939 Miss O. Keith took over the position until 1942. In 1943 the Sub-Postmistress was Miss D. Chittenden until 1947. On 1 April 1947 Miss P. Dolabaille took over the position until 1953. In 1954 Miss C. Cottle became Sub-Postmistress until 1956. In 1957 C. Sandy took over the position until 1958/59. Using time codes A, B & C.

 14.8.51-S.O. 31.8.62          **6      60**

K1 In 1851 was probably issued with a mark similar to La Brea K1

K2 (26.10.65)-(25.1.76)

KD4 (23.5.82)-(29.5.85)

Val  100  1,500

Val  100  1,000

D1 (26.10.65)-(21.1.71)
Val x 30

D2 (26.8.76)-(27.3.82)
Val x 20

D3 (8.6.86)-(7.3.06)
Val x 5

Sent 4.6.07
D4 (30.1.08)-(22.7.25)
&   (8.4.29)-(22.12.31)
Val x 4

D5 (11.3.26)-(4.1.32)

Val x 8

D6 (3.2.32)-S.U. 31.8.62

Sent 5.11.59
D8 (11.1.60)-S.U. 31.8.62

D7 (12.12.39)-S.U. 31.8.62

UP2          -S.U. 31.8.62

**Chaguanas Post Office**

**Chaguaramas** (O. Amerindian)
Situated 10 miles west of Port of Spain.  It was closed in 1941 following the leasing of the area to
the United States under the "Bases for destroyers" agreement, so that the area around Chaguaramas
became a restricted area.

(1926) 13.6.41                                    **100     1,000**

D3 (23.5.41)-(13.6.41)

## Charlieville

Situated on the Perseverance Road, 2 miles north of Chaguanas, on the Old Chaguanas Road. Postal agency under Chagunas.

1.6.49-S.O. 31.8.62 **10** **100**

D1 (6.7.49)  
Val x 20

D2 (16.5.50)-(19.7.55)  
Val x 2

D3 (29.2.56)-S.U. 31.8.62

UP1  -S.U. 31.8.62

UNCLAIMED

I2

**Charlieville Post Office**

## CHARLOTTEVILLE-Tobago

Situated in the north of the island on Man of War Bay, county St. John. Settled in 1633 by the Dutch. In 1946 the population was 1,360. Initially probably only operated as a receiving office without a datestamp. In 1938 the Post Office in Charlotteville was vacant. In 1945 the Postmistress was (Miss) A. de Freitas until 1946. In 1947 (Miss) G. Davidson took over the position until 1958/59. Upgraded to a money order office 18 August 1940 and a money order and savings bank office 1 April 1944.

(1909)-S.O. 31.8.62 **10 100**

D2 (18.8.40)-S.U. 31.8.62
Using time codes A & B.

**Charlotteville Post Office**

## Chatham

Opened at the house of Mr Cadet. Mails being exchanged on Monday, Tuesday and Saturday with Port of Spain. In 1899 the Sub-Postmaster was C. Hypolite £12.10s p.a. until 1916.

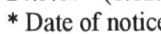

24.5.87*-(1.12.17)          **100    1,000**

\* Date of notice

D2 (22.10.88)-(1.12.17)
Using time codes A B & C.

## Clarke Rochard

Situated 2 ½ miles from Penal Rock, in a shop on Clarke Rochard Road. Postal agency under Princes Town.

16.11.48-S.O. 31.8.62          **10       100**

Sent 30.7.58

D2 (1.9.51)-(30.4.56)
Val x 3

D3 (22.6.56)?-S.U. 31.8.62

**Clarke Rochard Post Office**

## CLAXTON BAY

Situated 5 miles north of San Fernando, county Victoria on the Southern Main Road. The post office moved to the railway station 1 April 1881. Upgraded from a postal agency to district post office 21 October 1953. In 1899 the Sub-Postmistress was Miss A. Pinard £25 p.a. until 1902. In 1903 Miss S. Reid took over the position £25 p.a. until 1905. In 1906 Mrs B. Best became Sub-Postmistress £25 p.a. until 1911. In 1912 Mrs E. Ronalds took over the position £25 p.a. until 1923. For 1938 only, the Sub-Postmistress was Miss E. Bramble. In 1954 the Sub-Postmistress was (Miss) D. Reid until 1958/59. Using time codes A, B & C.

(23.1.76)-S.O. 31.8.62          **4          40**

K1
Val x 50

K2
Val x 50

K3
Val x 100

KD4
Val x 30

D2 (23.1.76)-(7.8.79)

Val x 30

D3 (10.6.86)-(15.1.07)

Val x 7

Sent 4.6.07
D4 (24.12.07)*- (15.3.28)
Known set with most letters
D to Y, possibly each mail
was lettered in sequence.
Val x 4

D5 (9.10.30)-(5.4.38)
Val x 15

D6 (31.1.36)-(14.12.59)

Sent 30.7.58
D7 (25.8.58)-S.U. 31.8.62

**CLAXTON BAY Continued**

Sent 30.7.58
D8 (4.3.60)-S.U. 31.8.62

R2 (17.5.40)-(2.8.44)
Val x 5

UP2 (14.4.24)-S.U. 31.8.62
Val x 5

**Claxton Bay Post Office**

**Cocoyea**

Situated on the Naparima Mayaro Road, 3 miles west of San Fernando. Postal agency under San Fernando.

1.5.51-S.O. 31.8.62        **15**        **150**

D2 (22.6.51)-(25.8.59)*

D3 (3.11.59)-S.U. 31.8.62

**Cocoyea Post Office**

UP2

UNCLAIMED

I1 (16.1.58)

## Coromandel

Situated 2 miles north east of Granville. Postal agency under Cedros.

15.11.52-S.O. 31.8.62

**10**    **100**

D2 (16.5.55)-S.U. 31.8.62
Using time codes A & B.

R1

T

UP1

**Coromandel Post Office**

**Coryal** (Or. Amerindian)
Situated south west of Sangre Grande, at 1 Cumuto Main Road. Postal agency under Sangre Grande.
(30.7.34)-S.O. 31.8.62        **10**     **100**

D2 (30.7.34)-S.U. 31.8.62
Using time codes B & C.

**Coryal Post Office**

**COUVA** (O. Amerindian)
Situated in county Caroni, on Railway Road. The railway reached Couva in 1880, when it was visited
by the royal princes Albert and George on 17 January . The population in 1921 was 2,667 in 1931,
1,895 at Independence it was about 4,000. In 1867 Mr Graham was postmaster. From 15 May 1883
the Sub-Postmaster was Robert Williams (Money Order Office) £60 p.a. until 1900. In 1901 Miss
M. Stanford took over the position £60 p.a. until 1903. In 1904 Mrs A. Corrie became Sub-Postmistress at Couva £60 p.a. until 1905. For 1906 only, Miss E. Cockerton took over the position. In
1907 Mrs L. Harris became Sub-Postmistress £60 p.a. until 1908. In 1909 Mrs A. Archibald took
over the position £60 p.a. until 1910. In 1911 the Sub-Postmistress was Miss E. Furlonge until 1914.
In 1915 Miss R. E. Reid took over the position £60 p.a. until 1916. In 1917 Miss M. J. Atkins became
Sub-Postmistress £60 p.a. until 1920. During 1921 the Post Office in Couva was vacant. In 1922
the Sub-Postmistress was Miss L. Best £60 p.a. until 1936. In 1937 Miss C. Smith took over the
position until 1943. On 1 August 1943 Mrs L. Yates became Sub-Postmistress until 23 October 1949

when (Miss) G. Lalla took over the position until 1955. In 1956 the Sub-Postmistress was (Miss) A. Callender until 1958/59. Using time codes A, B & C.

14.8.51-S.O. 31.8.62                    **2        20**

K1 In 1851 probably issued with a mark similar to La Brea K1.

K2 (5.7.53)-(11.8.76)

Val x 50

KD4 (26.8.84)

Val x 50

D1 (17.7.54)-(25.7.77)

Val x 30

D2 (17.8.77)-(29.3.82)
From (10.2.82) set with 17 at bottom and year at top.
Val x 20

D3 (22.5.85)- (18.4.06*)

Val x 10

D4 (15.9.06)*-(8.1.26)
 & (1.10.36)

Val x 5

D5 (8.3.26)-(2.10.29)

Val x 10

D6 (20.11.30)-(7.1.57)
(Known wrongly dated
22.6.22).

D7 (18.12.41)-S.U. 31.8.62

D8 (14.5.60)-S.U.31.8.62

**COUVA Continued**

R2 (19.8.08)-S.U.31.8.62

UP3

**Couva Post Office**

## Cross (The Cross)
Postal agency under San Fernando, situated at the railway station, one mile south east of San Fernando on the line to Princes Town.

1926-S.O. 31.8.62         **10**     **100**

D2 (24.4.28)-(1.1.33)*

Val x 10

D3 (23.2.34)-S.U. 31.8.62
Using time codes A, B & C.

**Cross Post Office**

## Cumana (O. Amerindian Tribal name).
Postal agency under Sangre Grande, situated in a shop. Using time codes A to D.

(22.2.32)-S.O. 31.8.62        **10**     **100**

D2 (22.2.32)-(1.6.40)
Val x 3

D3 (8.10.40)-S.U. 31.8.62

UNCLAIMED

I2

**Cumana Post Office**

**CUMUTO** (O. Amerindian)
Initially a Sub-Post Office at the Railway Station. Situated in county St. Andrews on Cumuto Main Road. In 1899 the Sub-Postmaster was R. H. Jones until 1900. In 1901 D. Pinard took over the position £12.10s p.a. until 1907. In 1908 L. Laguerande became Sub-Postmaster £12.10s p.a. until 1914. In 1915 J. Burns took over the position £12.10s p.a. until 1916. In 1920 Miss P. Noguera became Sub-Postmistress with a raise in salary to £25 p.a. until 1922. For 1923 only, Miss B. Da Costa became Sub-Postmistress. In 1924 Miss O. Diaz and in 1925 Miss E. Villafana both took over the position of Sub-Postmistress for a year only. In 1933 B. Greene took over the position until 1934. For 1938 only, Miss B. Volman became Sub-Postmistress. In 1949 (Miss) A. Worrel took over the position until 1950. For 1951 only, (Miss) P. Bowen became Sub-Postmistress. In 1952 (Miss) V. Hutchinson took over the position until 1958/59.

1.12.97-S.O. 31.8.62       **10**     **100**

## CUMUTO Continued

Sent 4.2.98
D2 (23.12.98)*-(25.12.07)         D3 (17.3.04)-(8.1.26)         D4 (8.2.26)-(26.9.35)
Val x 3                                                                                      Val x 3

D5 (7.1.36)*-S.U. 31.8.62
Set with time codes A, B & C.

UP3

**Cumuto Post Office**

**Cunapo Junction Road** (Or. Cunapo being Amerindian for Old Mangrove).
Situated 2 miles south of Sangre Grande.  Postal agency under Sangre Grande.
(1937)-S.U. 31.8.62                    **20**        **200**

D2 (31.8.38)*-S.U. 31.8.62
Using time codes A to D.

R1 (14.7.49)

UP1 (14.7.49)

**Cunapo Junction Post Office**

**CUNUPIA** (O. from Spanish Conupia meaning canopy).
Opened at the railway station. The village growing round Jerningham junction station. The offical village had been nearby, Alligator Village. In 1946 the population was 1,028. Situated 3 miles south of Caroni, in county Caroni or Chin Chin Road. In 1899 the Sub-Postmaster was E. Lewis £25 p.a. until 1902. In 1903 Mrs. E. Ronald took over the position £25 p.a. until 1906. In 1907 Miss B. Hamilton became Sub-Postmistress £25 p.a. until 1908. In 1909 Mrs R. Roach took over the position £25 p.a. until 1911. In 1912 the Sub-Postmistress was Mrs B. Best £25 p.a. until 1916. In 1917 Miss A. Chittenden took over the position £25 p.a. until 1918. In 1919 the Sub-Postmistress was Miss E. Chittenden £25 p.a. until 1923. For 1938 only, Miss M. Girod took over the position. In 1955 Mrs O. Alcindor-Logan became Sub-Postmistress until 1958/59. Using time codes A, B & C. Upgraded from a postal agency to a district post office on 15 January 1954.

24.8.80-S.O. 31.8.62        **10**     **100**

KD3
Val x 10

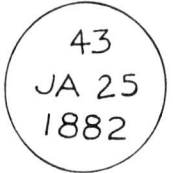

D1 (19.11.81)-(25.1.82)
Tentative allocation.
The digits are thought to
have been transposed.

D2 (16.1.88)-(4.1.01)

Val x 4

Sent 20.6.01
D3 (1.4.02)-(22.5.11)

Val x 3

D4 (28.6.15)- (28.10.30)
Val x 3

D6 (22.5.34)-(16.9.59)

Sent 14.9.59
D7 (12.2.60)-S.U. 31.8.62

REGISTERED

R2                                        R3

UNCLAIMED

I2

**Cunupia Post Office**

**CUREPE** (O. Amerindian).

Situated in county St. George on the Eastern Main Road. In 1950 Miss E. Cleveland became Sub-Postmistress until 1954. For 1955 only, (Miss) V. E. Dickie took over the position. For 1956 (Miss) F. Alcindor also became Sub-Postmistress for just one year. In 1957 C. Cottle took over the position until 1958/59.

2.8.49-S.O. 31.8.62          **4**     **40**

D1  2.8.49 - (31.12.51)
Initially date set in two lines until October 1949 when it was set in one line until (19.7.51), thereafter appears with both settings.
Val x 3

D2 (19.1.52)-S.U. 31.8.62
Set with time codes A to C & N° 1 to 3.

**Curepe Post Office**

**CUREPE Continued**

R1 (3.9.58)-S.U. 31.8.62
Val x 2

UP1 (5.9.57)-S.U. 31.8.62

I2 (22.7.60)-S.U.31.8.62

**Dabadie (D' Abadie)**
Situated between Arouca and Arima on the Mausica Road. Receiving office for stamped letters only opened at Mr Guy's Shop, D' Abadie's Village on 1 March 1860. Initially the post office was at the house of Mr. John Haynes (Schoolmaster), it moved to the railway station on 1 September 1886 where it was placed in charge of the station master. Upgraded to a post office in 1886. Postal agency under Port of Spain. For 1899 only, the Sub-Postmaster was J. H. Marshall. In 1900 J. Ferguson took over the position at £12.10s p.a. until 1910. From 1 June 1910 L. Hamilton and in 1913 F. Beckwith were both Sub-Postmasters at £12.10s p.a. for one year only. In 1913 D. Chittenden took over the position £12.10s p.a. until 1915. In 1916 the Sub-Postmaster was A. L. Rooks £12.10s p.a. until 1917. In 1918 Mrs A. L. Rooks took over the position with a rise in salary to £25 p.a. until 1923. Using time codes A, B & C.

|  |  |  |
|---|---|---|
| 30.4.86*-S.O. 31.8.62 | 10 | 100 |

\* Date of notice

D2 (14.7.87)-(9.3.27)     D3 (29.6.29)*-(2.4.30)     D4 (13.6.35)*-S.U. 31.8.62
Val x 5                            Val x 10

**Dabadie (D' Abadie) Continued**

UP2     -S.U.31.8.62

**Dabadie Post Office**

**Debe**
Situated in a petrol station 5 miles south of San Fernando on the Erin Road. Postal agency under San Fernando. Miss Eleanora White was confirmed as postmistress on 15 May 1920.

(15.5.20)-S.O. 31.8.62          **15     150**

D2 (3.7.22)*-(18.12.35)

Val x 3

D3 (10.11.36)-S.U. 31.8.62
Using time codes A, B, C & D.

# UNCLAIMED

I2 (19.8.53)

314

**Debe Continued**

**Debe Post Officc**

**Debe Road** see **Dibe Road?**

**Delaford-Tobago**
Situated 5 miles north of Roxborough.  Postal agency under Scarborough.

(1926)-S.O. 31.8.62      **10**  **100**

D2 (9.12.37)-S.U. 31.8.62
Using time codes A & B.

# UNCLAIMED

I2 (19.3.54)

**Delaford Post Office**

**Delhi Road**
Situated 1 mile north east of Fyzabad, on Delhi Settlement Road.  Postal agency under Fyzabad.

1.6.57-S.O. 31.8.62          **10**     **100**

D2 (26.2.58)-S.U. 31.8.62

**Delhi Road Post Office**

**Des Vignes Road-Tobago** (O. French Vineyard Road)
Situated at Runnemede 2 miles north of Moriah.  Postal agency under Scarborough.

1.2.61-S.O. 31.8.62          **30**     **300**

Sent 2.9.60
D1 (19.12.61)-S.U.31.8.62

**Des Vignes Road-Tobago Continued**

**Des Vignes Road-Tobago Post Office**

## Diamond (Diamond Village)
Postal agency under Princes Town, in a shop on Popourie Road.

6.11.48-S.O. 31.8.62  **10**  **100**

D1 (23.7.49)-(29.10.49)
Val x 20

D2 (16.11.51)-(24.6.55)
Val x 5

D3 (19.6.58)-S.U. 31.8.62

UP2

**Diamond Post Office**

**Dibe Road**
Situated on Dibe Road off Long Circular Road near Belle Vue, St. James.  Postal agency under St. James.

<table>
<tr><td>1.5.58-S.O. 31.8.62</td><td>**10**</td><td>**100**</td></tr>
</table>

|  | Sent 29.9.59 | Sent 30.7.58 |
|---|---|---|
| D1 (15.7.58) | D2 | D3 Error for Dibe Road |
|  |  | Not used? |

Val x 20

**Dibe Road Continued**

**Dibe Road Post Office**

**DIEGO MARTIN** (O. Named after the original Spanish discoverer of the river, Don Diego Martin).

The post moved from the police station to the school house on 12 November 1860. The village had a population of 764 in 1881 1,000 in1931, increased to 5,774 in 1946. Situated 8 miles north west of Port of Spain county St. George on the main road. The postmaster was Robert Roxburgh from 1867 to 1880. In 1899 A. J. Roxborough took over the position £15 p.a. until 1914. For 1915 only V. Atherton became Sub-Postmaster £15 p.a. In 1916 the Post Office in Diego Martin was vacant. In 1919 Miss A. Seales was Sub-Postmistress £25 p.a. until 1925. In 1952 (Miss) P. Bowen took over the position until 1956. In 1957 M. Jones became Sub-Postmaster until 1958/59.

| | | |
|---|---|---|
| 14.8.51-16.10.50 | 4 | 40 |
| 15.1.51-S.O. 31.8.62 | 2 | 20 |

K1 Similar to La Brea K1     K2                          K4

320

**DIEGO MARTIN Continued**

KD5

D3 (5.2.87)*-(18.9.26*)

D5 (5.12.29)*-(4.6.37)

D6 (3.10.37)-S.U. 31.8.62
Using time codes A, B & C.

REGISTERED

R2 (2.2.25)
Val x 2

UP2 (25.2.13)

UP3 (15.7.49)

UNCLAIMED

I2 (15.7.49)

UNCLAIMED

I3 (14.1.60)-(31.8.62)

321

**Diego Martin Post Office**

**East Dry River**
Postal agency under Port of Spain.  Situated at 41 Laventille Road, in the south district of Port of Spain.

1.9.48-S.O. 31.8.62            **10**     **100**

D1 (31.5.49)-(23.1.50)                 D2 (29.4.51)-S.U. 31.8.62
Val x 20

UNCLAIMED

I1 (14.7.49)-S.U. 31.8.62

**East Dry River Continued**

**East Dry River Post Office**

**Ecclesville**
Situated 3 miles north east of Rio Claro.  Postal agency under Rio Claro.
(20.7.37)-S.O. 31.8.62          10      100

**Ecclesville Post Office**

**Ecclesville Continued**

D2 (20.7.37)-S.U. 31.8.62

**Elswick**
Situated near Princes Town. On 16 June 1888 a foot messenger started a bi weekly service between Princes Town and Mr. Palmers house, Elswick Estate. In 1906 the Sub-Postmaster was A. R. Dickie £12.10s p.a. until 1910. In 1911 G. McLean took over the position £12.10s p.a. until 1916.

                      (20.4.92)-(10.7.34)        **100**    **1,000**

D2 (20.4.92)-(10.7.34)

**Enterprise**
Situated on the Southern Main Road, 2 ½ miles north of Longdenville. Postal agency under Chaguanas.

                      1.5.59-S.O. 31.8.62        **10**    **100**

D2 (19.6.59)-S.U. 31.8.62

UP1

**Enterprise Post Office**

**ERIN** (O. Spanish version of the original Amerindian name).
In 1871 the population was 175. In 1881 a road was opened to Cap de Ville, but the main communication was by coastal steamer. At Independence the population was about 1,000. Situated 1 mile east of San Francique county St. Patrick on Junction Road. On 1 August it became a Money Order Office. In 1899 the Sub-Postmistress was Mrs S. A. Punch £25 p.a. until 1902. In 1903 S. Matthews took over the position £25 p.a. until 1905. In 1906 Miss A. Laing became Sub-Postmistress £25 p.a. until 1908. In 1909 Miss B. Hamilton took over the position with a rise in salary to £40 p.a. For 1910 only, Miss A. Lang again became Sub-Postmistress. In 1911 Mrs A. Nurse took over the position £40 p.a. until 1912. In 1913 the Sub-Postmistress was Miss F. Peters £40 p.a. until 1932. In 1933 Miss C. Owen took over the position until 1939. In 1940 Miss B. Volman became Sub-Postmistress until 1947. In 1948 Miss A. Ceoline took over the position until 1952. In 1953 the Sub-Postmistress was Mrs C. Jordan-Spalding until 1956. In 1957 G. Khan took over the position until 1958/59. Using time codes A, B & C.

1868*-S.O. 31.8.62                    4        30

K1                              K2                              KD3 (25.9.82)
Held at Erin 1949

                                                        Val x 50

**ERIN Continued**

D2 (16.4.87)-(23.6.12)
Val x 10

D3 (28.9.12)-(6.5.31)
Val x 10

D5 (14.11.31)-S.U. 31.8.62

RECISTERED

R2 (5.3.97)-(15.7.49)

UP1 (17.3.26)

UP2 (15.7.49)-S.U. 31.8.62

UNCLAIMED

TOO LATE

I2 (15.7.49)

I3 (15.7.49)

**Erin Post Office**

## Fatima

Situated in the Laventille area, 4 miles south of Port of Spain at the junction of Laventille and Picton
Roads. Postal agency under Port of Spain.

1.9.58-S.O. 31.8.62 **10** **100**

D1 1.9.58-S.U. 31.8.62

R1

UP1

**Fatima Post Office**

# UNCLAIMED

I1

### Febeau
Situated in the southern district of Port of Spain in a shop, Laventille Road.  Postal agency under San Juan.

15.7.57-S.O. 31.8.62        10    100

D2 (8.9.58)-S.U. 31.8.62

**Febeau Post Office**

**Felicity**

Situated 3 miles north west of Chaguanas in a house on Nolan Street. Postal agency under Chaguanas.

2.7.51 -S.O. 31.8.62      **10**     **100**

D1 (6.7.51)-(21.7.51)
Val x 25

D2 (13.2.54)-S.U. 31.8.62

**Felicity Post Office**

**Fishing Pond**

Situated 8 miles east of Sangre Grande, in a shop on Fishing Pond Road. Postal agency under Sangre Grande.

16.6.51-S.O. 31.8.62 **10 100**

D1(16.6.52)
Val x 50

D2 (29.1.54)-S.U. 31.8.62

**Fishing Pond Post Office**

## Five Islands

Situated in the Gulf of Paria, 2 miles south of Carenage. In 1899 the Sub-Postmaster was L. S. Bynoe until 1901. In 1902 R. Gilkes took over the position £12.10s p.a. until 1906. In 1907 A. Warner became Sub-Postmaster £12.10s p.a. until 1916. After the post office closed there was a launch service listed under the "Harbour Master" serving the Five Islands (no date stamp but apparently using a cachet D4) which ceased on 30 November 1958.

1.9.98*-(13.12.)22         **100**    **1,000**

Sent 14.12.98
D2 (12.7.99)-(13.12.)22           D4

Stephens Ltd., Trinidad.        *Five Islands.*

**Five Islands**

## Flanagin Town

Situated in a house 1 mile north of Brasso. Named after Mr. Clifton Flanagin who became warden of the district in 1900 and arranged for a railway station to be opened in 1903. In 1931 the population was 423, in 1946, 733. Postal agency under Couva. In 1910 the Sub-Postmaster was J. Stapleton £12.10s p.a. until 1916. In 1919 Miss M. Branker took over the position £25 p.a. until 1920. For 1921 only, Miss O. Diaz became Sub-Postmistress £25 p.a. In 1922 Miss C. Cottle took over the position £40 p.a. until 1924. In 1925 Miss O. Diaz became Sub-Postmistress again for one year only £40 p.a. Using time codes A to C.

1908*-S.O. 31.8.62         **10**    **100**

**Flanagin Town Continued**

Sent 29.6.08
D2 (21.12.09)*-(20.5.34)
Val x 8

D4 (20.10.36)-S.U. 30.8.62

R2 (16.7.49)-S.U. 31.8.62
Val x 2

**Flanagin Town Post Office**

**Flanagin Town Continued**

UP2 (16.7.49)-S.U. 31.8.62

I2 (16.7.49)-S.U. 31.8.62

## FOREST RESERVE

Situated 5 miles south west of Fyzabad, county St. Patrick in Private Road. In 1931 the Sub-Post-mistress was Miss B. Greene until 1932. From 1 November 1932 Miss P. Dolabaille took over the position until 1935. In 1936 Miss A. Ceoline became Sub-Postmistress until 1947. In 1948 Miss B. Volman took over the position until 1949. In 1950 the Sub-Postmistress was Miss I. Dolabaille until 1955. In 1956 O. Thompson took over the position until 1958/59.

(30.7.25)-S.O. 31.8.62          6     60

D2 30.7.25)-(29.12.34)

D3 (24.3.36)-S.U. 31.8.62
Using time codes A to C.

Val x 5

R2 (13.9.48)-(4.5.61)

**Forest Reserve Post Office**

**Four Roads**
Situated near Diego Martin. Downgraded from a sub post office to a postal agency in 1926.
(9.10.23)-29.9.54 **20 200**

K2
(Held in 1949)

D2 (9.10.23)-(7.4.37)

Val x 5

D4 (25.5.38)-(20.9.54)
Using time codes A & B.

R2 (15.7.49)
Val x 2

UP2 (15.7.49)
Val x 2

UNCLAIMED

I2 (15.7.49)-(10.11.49)
Val x 2

## Freeport

Situated in a shop near the police station, three miles south of Chaguanas. Postal agency under Carapichaima.

15.9.47-S.O. 31.8.62       **10**    **100**

D1 (21.10.47)-(1.4.48)
Initially the date was set in one line.
Val x 20

D2 (30.11.48)-S.U. 31.8.62

R1 (16.7.49)-S.U.31.8.62
Val x 2

**Freeport Post Office**

UP1 (16.7.49)-S.U. 31.8.62

# UNCLAIMED

I1 (16.7.49)-S.U. 31.8.62

**Friendship**
Downgraded from a post office to a postal agency in 1925.

(1925)-1926                                                 **N.S.**

To St Johns

**Fullerton**
Situated in Cedros Bay, at the corner of Borel Street and Bush Road.  Postal agency under Cedros.

Nov. 1935                                                  **N.S.**
1.3.40- S.O. 31.8.62                          **10     100**

D2 (1.4.40)-S.U. 31.8.62
Using time codes A to D.

**Fullerton Post Office**

**FYZABAD** (Named after the town in India)

Situated 10 miles south west of San Fernando, county St. Patrick, on Gower's Well Road. A settlement founded in 1871 by K. Grant of the Canadian Mission to the Indians for East Indian workers who completed their indentures. Oil was dicovered in 1917 which caused the population to grow to 2,649 by 1921. For 1938 only the Sub-Postmistress was Miss V. Blaize. In 1949 (Miss) V. A. Blaize became Sub-Postmistress until 1950. In 1951 Miss C. Thompson took over the position until 1952. In 1953 (Miss) P. Jacob became Sub-Postmistress until 1958/59.

(9.12)11-S.O. 31.8.62          **8          80**

D2 (9.12)11-(24.6.40)
Val x 3

D3 (1.8.40)-(16.9.59)
Using time codes A, B & C.

Sent 25.11.57
D4 (30.5.58)-S.U. 31.8.62

Sent 4.2.58
D5 (16.9.59)-S.U. 31.8.62

**Fyzabad Post Office**

R2 (27.11.37)
Val x 3

R3 (15.7.49)-(14.1.57)
Val x 2

UP2 (12.3.34)

**Gasparillo** (Or. Spanish)
Foot messager service introduced on 2 May 1888. Situated 3 miles north east of San Fernando, on Gasparillo Road. Postal agency under Couva. In 1920 the Sub-Postmistress was Miss E. Bramble £25 p.a. until 1923. Using time codes A & B.

(27.11.89)-S.O. 31.8.62          **10          100**

D2 (27.11.89)-(9.9.33)
Val x 6

D4 (23.12.37)-S.U. 31.8.62

UP1 (21.8.30)-(3.4.43)

UP2

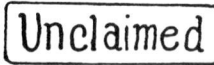

I2

**Gasparillo Continued**

**Gasparillo Post Office**

**Golden Lane-Tobago**
Situated 5 miles north east of Plymouth.  Postal agency under Scarborough.

1.7.52-S.O. 31.8.62 **15 150**

D1 (14.7.52)-(29.7.52)
Val x 20

D2 (8.4.53)-S.U. 31.8.62

R1

UP1

UNCLAIMED

I1

**Golden Lane Post Office**

### GONZALES (Gonzales Place)

Situated in the Gonzales Hills, 3½ miles from Port of Spain county St. George in Land Street. In 1956 the Sub-Postmistress was (Miss) I. Dolabaille until 1958/59.

13.9.55-S.O. 31.8.62      **10**     **100**

D1 (20.9.55)-(9.12.57)
Val x 3

D2 (16.1.58)-S.U. 31.8.62

UP1      -S.U.31.8.62

**Gonzales Post Office**

**Goodwood-Tobago**
Situated on the Windward Road south of Goldsborough Bay.  Postal agency under Scarborough.
1.3.40-S.O. 31.8.62          10     100

D2 (2.9.42)-S.U. 31.8.62
Using time codes A & B.

**Goodwood-Tobago Post Office**

### GRAN COUVA
Situated 5 miles east of Couva, county Caroni, on the main road. On 3 April 1888 a daily service started between Couva and Gran Couva. Became a Money Order Office on 1 June 1901. In 1899 The Sub-Postmistress was Mrs R. N. Tracey £25 p.a. until 1901. In 1902 Mrs M. Tracey took over the position with a rise in salary to £40 p.a. until 1917 (During this period of time, Mrs A. E. Tracey was also said to have worked with Mrs M. Tracey at the Post Office in 1903). In 1918 Mrs A. E. Tracey took over the position £40 p.a. until 1919. In 1920 Mrs M. L. Tracey and in 1921 Miss Archibald both became Sub-Postmistress £40 p.a. for one year only. In 1922 Miss A. B. Lang took over the position £40 p.a. until 1925. For 1926 only, Mrs A. B. Gonzalez became Sub-Postmistress. In 1927 Mrs B. Gonzalez took over the position until 1931. In 1932 the Sub-Postmistress was Miss H. Winchester 1935. In 1936 Mrs A. B. Gonzalez retook the position until 1938. In 1939 Miss L. Joseph became Sub-Postmistress until 1943. In 1944 Miss A. Colley took over the position until 1948. In 1949 the Sub-Postmistress was (Miss) D. Reid until 1953. In 1954 (Miss) D. Duff took over the position until 1958/59.

(2.6.86)-S.O. 31.8.62　　　　　　**10　　100**

D2 (31.3.87)-(21.1.27)

D3 (18.6.29)-(12.5.37)
   & (6.1.47)

D4 (7.6.38)-S.U. 31.8.62

Using time codes A, B & C.

Val x 3

Val x 6

UP1 (5.8.14)
Val x 2

UP2 (26.1.43)-(24.2.56)
Val x 2

**Gran Couva Post Office**

## Grande Riviere

Situated between Matelot and Sans Souci, on Toco main road. Opened at Mr Bristol's house (near the Police Station). Postal agency under Sangre Grande. In 1905 the Sub-Postmaster was J. M. Bristol £12.10s p.a. until 1916.

1.10.02*-S.O. 31.8.62      **10**    **100**

D2 (22.12.04)-(20.7.27)*
Using time codes A & B.
Val x 5

D4 (16.9.33)-S.U. 31.8.62

R2 (3.9.47)-S.U. 31.8.62
Val x 2

**Grande Riviere Post Office**

**Grande Riviere Continued**

UP2

I2

**Granville**
Situated 4 miles north of Bonasse.  Postal agency under Cedros.

(24.10.56)-S.O. 31.8.62          **10**     **100**

D2 (24.10.56)-S.U. 31.8.62

**Granville Post Office**

**GUAICO (Guiaco)** (Or. Amerindian for a type of reed).

Situated 1 mile west of Sangre Grande, county St. Andrew, on the eastern main road. Initially opened at the railway station. In 1899 the Sub-Postmaster was H. Lynch until 1901. In 1902 D. Blackman took over the position £12.10s p.a. until 1904. In 1905 W. Popewell became Sub-Postmaster for Guaico Post Office until 1910. In 1911 J. W. Ward took over the position £12.10s p.a. until 1914. In 1915 J. D. Richards became Sub-Postmaster £12.10s p.a. until 1916. For 1920 only, Miss V. Mitchell took over the position with a rise in salary to £25 p.a. In 1921 Miss M. Bourgeois became Sub-Postmistress £25 p.a. until 1925. For 1938 only Miss L. Owen took over the position. In 1956 (Miss) D. Guisseppi became Sub-Postmistress until 1958/59. A new post office was built in 1935.

1.12.97-S.O. 31.8.62 **10 100**

Sent 4.2.98
D2 (21.6.98)-(16.12.05)

Sent 4.6.07
D3 (20.9.09)-(12.8.35)
Using time codes A, B, M, N, O, R, S & Y.

D4 (16.5.36)-S.U. 31.8.62
Using time codes A, B, C, D & Y.

Val x 10

Val x 4

R2 (14.7.49)

UP1 (19.5.14)-S.U. 31.8.62
Val x 2

## UNCLAIMED

Sent 1.6.05
I1 (14.7.49)-S.U. 31.8.62

**GUAICO (Guiaco) Continued**

**GUAICO (Guiaco) Post Office**

**Guaico Tamana**

Postal agency under Sangre Grande.  Situated eight miles south of Guaico.

16.6.51-S.O. 31.8.62        **10**     **100**

D1 (25.9.51)-(3.9.52)
Val x 25

D2 (29.4.53)-S.U. 31.8.62

UNCLAIMED

I2 (11.5.55)-27.1.56
Val x 2

**Guaico Tamana Post Office**

**Guanapo** (Or. Amerindian).
Situated 2 miles south of Arima on the Tunapuna Road. Postal agency under Arima, initially opened at the railway station. In 1899 the Sub-Postmaster was J. L. Henry £12.10s p.a. until 1907. In 1908 D. Pinard took over the position £12.10s p.a. until 1914. For 1915 only S. Taylor became Sub-Postmaster £12.10s p.a. For 1916 only T. E. Martin took over the position £12.10s p.a.

1.12.97*-S.O. 31.8.62          **10     100**

Sent 4.2.98
D2 (1.3.98)-(4.9.16)
Became worn.

Val x 10

D3 (7.5.17)-(1.6.31)

Val x 6

D5 (17.7.34)-(S.U. 31.8.62)

Using time codes A, B & C.

**Guanapo Continued**

R2 (13.7.49)

UP1 (13.7.49)

UP2

UNCLAIMED

I2 (13.7.49)

**Guanapo Post Office**

**GUAPO** (O. Amerindian, Iguapo).
Situated 2 ½ miles east of Point Fortin, county St. Patrick on Young Street. In 1906 the Sub-Postmistress was Mrs R. Roach £25 p.a. until 1908. In 1909 Mrs E. Matthews took over the position £25 p.a. until 1919. In 1921 Miss M. Bowen became Sub-Postmistress £25 p.a. until 1923. In 1945 (Miss) M. E. Cox took over the position until 1958/59 (During this period of time (Miss) M. E. Cox got married in 1946 and became Mrs M. E. Cox-Raphael). Upgraded to a money order office 15 June 1944.

1.8.05*-S.O. 31.8.62          **10      100**

Sent 1.6.05
D1 (2.4.06)-(22.12.19)          D2 (26.7.26)-(15.7.35)          D3 (16.5.36)-S.U. 31.8.62
                                                                Using time codes A to D.

Val x 10

R2 (23.11.56)
Val x 2

UP1 (31.10.42)                    UP2
Val x 2

Unclaimed

I2 (11.11.55)-S.U.31.8.62

**Guapo Post Office**

**Guaracara Junction** (Or. Amerindian).
Situated at the junction of Guaracara Tabaquite Road and Guaracara Quarry road one mile north of Williamsville.  Postal agency under Couva.

1.11.58-S.O. 31.8.62                    **10**      **100**

D1 1.11.58-S.U. 31.8.62

UP1

**Guaracara Junction Post Office**

## GUAYAGUAYARE (O. Amerindian, from Arawak).

Situated in county Mayaro on the main road in the extreme south east of Trinidad. Site of first oil well in Trinidad, drilled by a Canadian, R. Rust. In 1912 the Sub-Postmaster was B. Small £40 p.a. until 1913. In 1914 A. Cuffie took over the position £40 p.a. until 1917. In 1918 Miss A. Cuffie became Sub-Postmistress £40 p.a. until 1921. In 1922 Miss M. Mason took over the position £40 p.a. until 1923. In 1924 the Sub-Postmistress was Miss C. Scott with a rise in pay to £67.10s p.a. until 1928. For 1929 only, Mrs A. A. Nurse took over the position. In 1930 Miss I. Bouis became Sub-Postmistress until 1934. On 16 March 1934 Miss C. Cottle took over the position until 1936. In 1937 the Sub-Postmistress was Miss F. Beckles 1940. In 1941Miss C. Alcindor took over the position until 1943. In 1944 A. Merrin became Sub-Postmaster until 1950. In 1951 (Miss) E. Phillip took over the position until 1958/59.

| | | |
|---|---|---|
| 1893* - (20.2.96) | **100** | **1,000** |
| (27.10.11)*-S.O. 31.8.62 | **10** | **100** |
| Closed (1900)-(1.10.06) | | |

Sent 21.6.93
D2 (11.2.95)-(20.2.96)

Val x 10

D3 (27.10.11)*-(8.11.33)
Using time codes A, B & C.
Val x 6

D4 (18.10.34)-S.U. 31.8.62
Only seen with time code A.

**Guayaguayare Post Office**

R2 (1.10.46)

UP3

**GUIACO** see **GUAICO**

**Hermitage**

Situated 1 mile east of Claxton Bay.  Postal agency under San Fernando.

1.4.55-S.O. 31.8.62 **10 100**

D2 (13.4.56)-S.U. 31.8.62
Using time codes A & B.

UNCLAIMED

I1 (3.11.56)
Val x 3

**Hermitage Post Office**

**Hicacos** see **Icacos**

**Hope-Tobago**
Situated near Mesopotamia.  Postal agency under Scarborough.

1.3.46-S.O. 31.8.62      10      100

D2 (28.5.48)-S.U. 31.8.62
Using time codes A & B.

Hope Post Office

**Icacos (Hicacos)** (Or. Amerindian from the Arawak name Icaco, a flowering tree).
Postal agency (from 1 September 1937) under Cedros.  Situated in the extreme south west tip of
Trinidad.  In 1881 the population was 502.  From 1878 to 1880 the postmaster was F. Albert.  In
1899 the Sub-Postmaster was J. B. Bhagan  until 1900.  For 1901 only, L. M. Currie took over the
position.  In 1902 M. Pollonais became Sub-Postmaster until 1903.  For 1904 only, A. Bonady took
over the position £15 p.a.  In 1905 A. Lucas became Sub-Postmaster £15 p.a. until 1908.  In 1910
N. Parsons and in 1911 A. Luces both took over the position of Sub-Postmaster £15 p.a. for one year.
In 1912 A. Leotaud took over the position £15 p.a. until 1916.

1874*-S.O. 31.8.62      15      150

355

**Icacos Continued**

Old Icacos Post Office

New Icacos Post Office

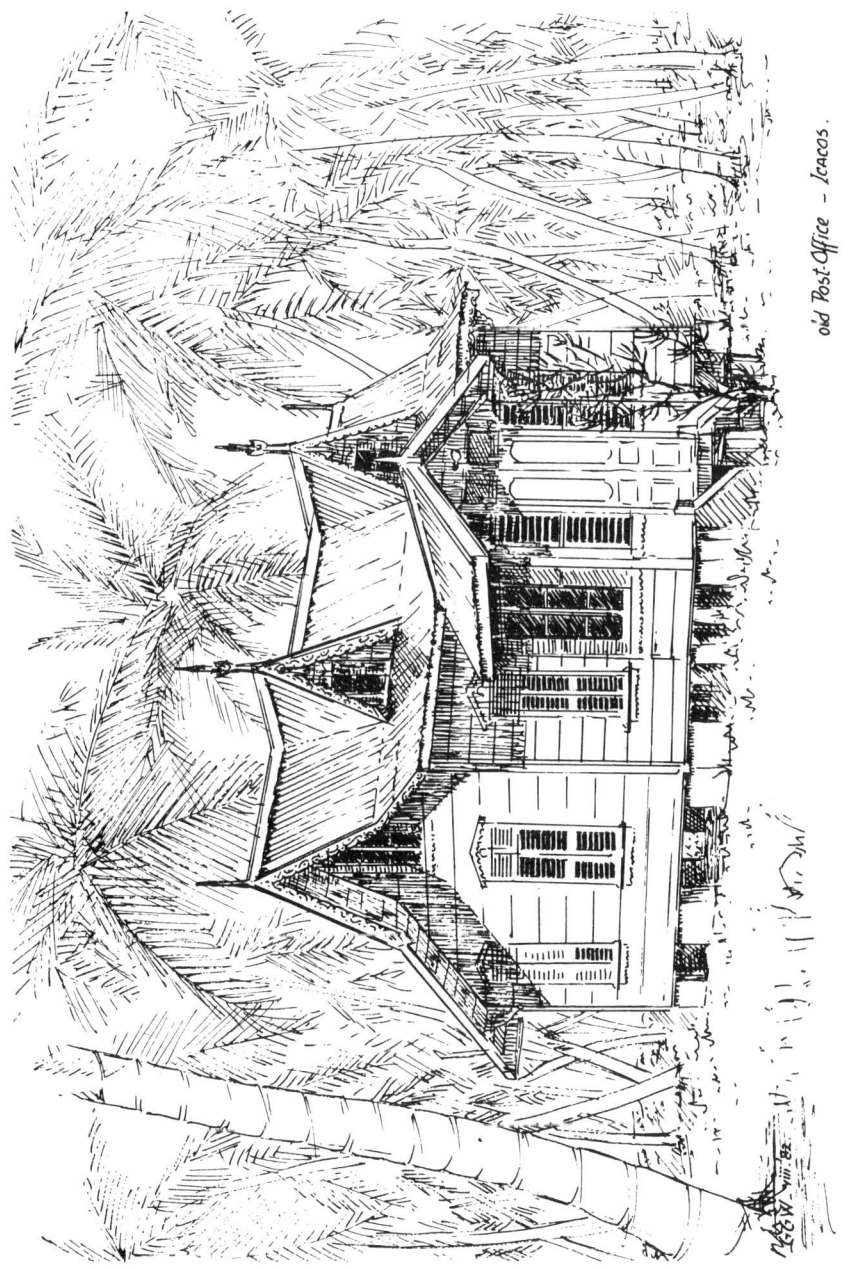

old Post-Office - Icacos.

**Old Post Office - Icacos**

Reproduced with permission of Gerald Watterson from his collection
of Trinidad drawings "This Old House".

**Icacos (Hicacos) Continued**

D2 (15.5.87)-(6.9.27)

Val x 5

D4 (7.6.35)-S.U. 31.8.62
Using time codes B & D.

**Indian Walk**

Situated 3 miles east of Princes Town. Postal agency under Princes Town. In 1899 the Sub-Postmaster was W. H. Stout (Pol. Sgt) £12.10s p.a. until 1904. For 1905 only, D. T. Seaton (Sgt) took over the position. In 1906 A. A. Wight became Sub-Postmaster £12.10s p.a. until 1916. In 1919 Miss A. Wright took over the position £12.10s p.a. until 1923. For 1924 only, Mrs A. A. Wright became Sub-Postmistress.

2.12.95*-S.O. 31.8.62          **10      100**

D2 (9.6.97)-(15.2.07)
Previously used at Port-of-Spain.
Val x 20

Sent 4.6.07
D3 (12.9.11)-(8.7.37)

Val x 6

D5 (2.3.38)*-S.U. 31.8.62
Using time codes A & B.

**Indian Walk Post Office**

**Indian Walk Continued**

Unclaimed

I2 (19.7.49)

UNCLAIMED

I3 (19.7.49)

### Irios Forest (Irois Forest)

Postal agency under San Fernando, situated 5 miles south west of Point Fortin. When closed in 1901 the mail was delivered by the Chatham Letter Carrier (Chas. St. Croix) either on application to him at the beach on arrival of Steamer or at his house Chatham Road. Postage Stamps &c., could be obtained from the Messenger on his journey to and from Chatham or at his house where a letter box was fixed. Postal agency under Princes Town. In 1899 the Sub-Postmaster was C. P. Griffith until 1901. In 1905 M. Fermin took over the position £12.10s p.a. until 1916. For 1938 only, Miss C. Celestine became Sub-Postmistress.

| | | |
|---|---|---|
| (1.2.88)-31.3.01 | 100 | 1,000 |
| (21.4.04)-S.O. 31.8.62 | 10 | 100 |

D2 (1.2.88)-(30.9.91)
& (21.4.04)-(26.2.07)

Sent 4.6.07
D3 (14.3.08)-(23.6.31)
Set with time codes A, B, C, H, O & V.
Val x 5

D5 (12.2.37)-S.U. 31.8.62
Only seen set with time codes A & C.

**Irios Forest Post Office**

## Jamboree B.O.

Boy Scouts Jamboree held at Valsayn.

|  | 4.4.61-14.4.61 | | 10 | 100 |

D1 4.4.61-14.4.61

## Jordan Hill

Situated on the Manahambre Road between St. Madeleine and Princes Town. Postal agency under San Fernando.

|  | 15.12.54-S.O. 31.8.62 | | 10 | 100 |

D2 (28.6.55)-S.U. 31.8.62
Only seen set with time code A.

**Jordan Hill Post Office**

**Kelly Village** see **Las Lomas No. 2**

**LA BREA** (Or French Derivation of the original Spanish "Tierra de Brea" meaning land of pitch). In 1595 Sir Walter Raliegh used the pitch to caulk his ships. It started to be commercially explored in 1850. On 30 April 1888 the office was transferred from the police station to the house of Mr Pawan. It became a money order office on 1 June 1895. The population in 1921 was 2,616 and 1960, 4,868. Situated 10 miles east of San Fernando county St. Patrick on Old Road. In 1899 the Sub-Postmaster was H. Belfield £60 p.a. until 1912. In 1913 Miss B. Small took over the position with a rise in salary to £70 p.a. until 1916. In 1917 Mrs R. E. Reid became Sub-Postmistress £70 p.a. until 1930. During 1931 the Post Office in La Brea was vacant. For 1932 only, A. Cuffie took over the position. In 1933 Miss F. Peter became Sub-Postmistress until 1943. On 1 August 1943 Miss C. Cottle took over the position until 1 September 1950 when Miss H. Winchester became Sub-Postmistress until 1955. For 1956 only, (Miss) A. Winn took over the position. In 1957 N. Winn became Sub-Postmaster 1958/59. Using time codes A & B until circa 1933 when the office used A, B & C.

14.8.51-S.O. 31.8.62          2      20

K1  14.8.51? -

K2 (9.4.63)-(7.7.76)
Val x 100

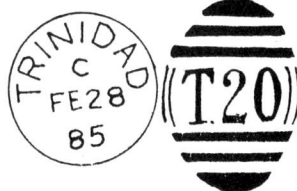

KD5 (26.10.82)
Val x 80

D1 (6.3.53)-(24.12.81)
Val x 100

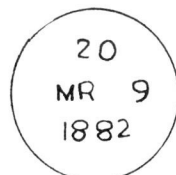

D2 (9.3.82)-(23.3.82)
Val x 80

D4 (28.3.88)*-(21.11.10)
Val x 12

D5 (26.7.10)-(3.11.31)
Val x 10

D6 (20.3.12)-(27.12.33)
Val x 10

D8 (6.8.30)*-(13.6.35)
Val x 15

**La Brea Post Office**

D9 (31.12.32)-(23.12.59)

D10 (8.1.37)-S.U. 31.8.62

D11 (12.5.37)-S.U. 31.8.62

D12 (5.9.58)-S.U. 31.8.62

R2 (29.8.21)-(30.10.34)

R3 (10.5.34)

UP2      -S.U. 31.8.62

**La Lune** (Or. French, the moon).
Postal agency under Princes Town.   Situated 3 miles north of Moruga. (not opened in 1906)   For 1938 only, the Sub-Postmistress was Miss W. Glodon.

(1.5.11)-S.O. 31.8.62          **10      100**

Sent 29.6.08
D2 (1.5.11)-(5.7.33)

Val x 10

D4 (31.8.34)-S.U. 31.8.62
Using time codes A, B, C & D.

**La Lune Post Office**

**Lambeau-Tobago** (Or. French for shred or scrap).

Situated 3 miles south west of Scarborough.  Postal agency under Scarborough.

(1926)-S.O. 31.8.62 **10** **100**

D2 (12.5.43)-S.U. 31.8.62
Using time codes A & B.

**Lambeau Post Office**

**Lance Noir (L'anse Noire)** (Or. French, black bay).

Situated on the north coast between Toco and Sans Souci.  Postal agency under Sangre Grande.

(28.10.34)-S.O. 31.8.62 **10** **100**

D2 (28.10.34)-S.U. 31.8.62

**Lance Noir Post Office**

**La Pastora Soscunosco** (Or. Spanish).
Situated 2 miles north from the junction of La Pastora Road and Saddle Road, Upper Santa Cruz.
Postal agency under San Juan.

$\qquad$ 1.10.58*-S.O. 31.8.62 $\qquad$ **15** $\qquad$ **150**

D1 1.10.58-S.U. 31.8.62

UP1

**La Pastora Soscunosco Post Office**

**La Romain**

Situated near Mosquito Creek, south of San Fernando. Postal agency under San Fernando.

2.2.42-S.O. 31.8.62 **10** **100**

D1 (21.6.44)-(16.5.45)

Val x 20

D2 (1.5.45)*-S.U. 31.8.62
* May be error 45 for 46 in which case the E.R.D. is (2.10.45).
Using time codes A, B & C.
Val x 3

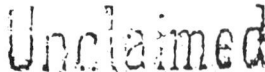

I2 (3.5.55)
Val x 2

**La Romain Post Office**

**Las Lomas No.1 (Las Lomas)** (Or. Spanish for "the hillocks").
Situated 5 miles south of Piarco Airport, next to the village school.  Postal agency under Cunupia.
(1948)-S.O. 31.8.62          **10      100**

No datestamp on (5.4.58)

D3
Val x 10

Sent 27.5.59
D4 (9.4.60)

**REGISTERED**

R1

**Las Lomas No.1 (Las Lomas) Continued**

**Las Lomas No.1 Post Office**

UP1

UNCLAIMED

I2

**Las Lomas No.2 (Kelly Village)**
Previouly known as Kelly Village, until 1 February 1960, when it was renamed Las Lomas
No. 2.  Postal agency under Arouca.

1.5.51*-S.O. 31.8.62     **10**     **100**

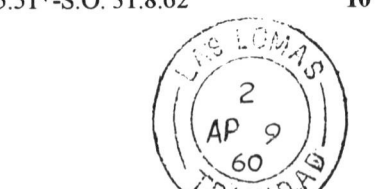

Sent 7.5.59

D2 (24.7.51)-(31.7.59)

D3 (8.4.60)-(21.3.61)
N.B. Set with 2 above date.

**Las Lomas No. 2 Post Office**

REGISTERED

R1

UP1

UNCLAIMED

I1

**LAVENTILLE**
Opened at Sucess Village Laventille next door to the police station. County St. George, there was one mail daily in each direction. Upgraded from a postal agency to post office 1 February 1950. In 1951 the Sub-Postmistress was Miss R. Hill-King until 1954. For 1955 only, Mrs H. Anthony-Winn took over the position. In 1956 (Miss) G. Jones became Sub-Postmistress until 1957. During 1958/59 E. Worrel took over the position. Using time codes A, B & C.

1.11.87-S.O. 31.8.62          4          40

D2 (31.7.88)-(29.8.32)

Val x 10

D4 (4.7.36)-(24.3.53)
& (22.10.54)*- S.U. 31.8.62
*- Recut.

D5 (6.3.50)-(4.5.51)

D6 (12.12.51)-S.U. 31.8.62

**Laventille Post Office**

**LAVENTILLE Continued**

R2 (4.1.52)-(4.6.52)

UP2

I4 (9.4.56)

**Lengua**

Situated 1 mile south of Princes Town on St. Croix Road.  Postal agency under Princes Town.

1.4.40-S.O. 31.8.62 **10 100**

D2 (12.2.46)-(7.9.57)                                              D3 (30.9.58)-S.U. 31.8.62
Only seen set with time code B.

**Lengua Post Office**

371

**Les Coteaux-Tobago** (Or. French, Hillsides).
Situated 3 miles east of Plymouth, at the junction of Arnos Vale Road and Providence Road.
Postal agency under Scarborough.

(1926)-S.O. 31.8.62 **10** **100**

D2 (26.9.40)-S.U. 31.8.62
Using time codes A & B.

**Les Coteaux Post Office**

**Les Efforts**
Situated 2 miles north of San Fernando post office at the corner of Drayton and Leotaud
Streets. Named after a sugar estate of the same name. Postal agency under San Fernando.

2.11.48-S.O. 31.8.62 **10** **100**

D1 State 1 (13.12.48)-(29.4.49)       D1 State 2 (23.6.49)-(1.12.49)
                                       Val x 5

## Les Efforts Continued

D2 (15.12.49)-(11.1.56)

D3 (16.1.56)-S.U. 31.8.62

**Les Efforts Post Office**

### Longdenville

Named in 1871 after Governor James Longden. It was started as a convict deport for felling timber. By 1899 the population was about 1,000, the railway having arrived in 1898. In 1936 a brick works opened . The population was 1,352 in 1946. Situated 2 miles east of Chaguanas. In 1906 the Sub-Postmaster was E. B. Huggins £12.10s p.a. until 1908. In 1910 J. B. Glasgow took over the position £12.10s p.a. until 1913. For 1914 only, S. Taylor became Sub-Postmaster £12.10s p.a. For 1915 H. A. Jarvis also took over the position £12.10s p.a. for one year only. For 1916 S. Taylor retook the position as Sub-Postmaster for a year £12.10s p.a. In 1918 the Sub-Postmistress was Miss M. Mason with a rise in salary to £25 p.a. until 1919. In 1920 Miss A. Mason took over the position £25 p.a. until 1925. Postal agency under Chaguanas.

1903*-S.O. 31.8.62            **10**      **100**

\* A receiving office was opened in the year ending 31 March 1904.

**Longdenville Continued**

Sent 1.6.05
D2 (6.10.05)-(15.5.29)          D3 (6.2.33)-(24.7.33)          D4 (9.3.37)-S.U. 31.8.62
Using time codes A, B & C                                      Using time codes A & B.
Val x 10                        Val x 20

**Longdenville Post Office**

R2

UP2 (28.7.59)-S.U. 31.8.62

# UNCLAIMED

Sent 1.6.05
I1          -S.U. 31.8.62

**Lopinot** (Or. Named after Charles Joseph Count de Lopinot, who settled in the area in 1805). In 1946 the area was settled by the disposed inhabitants of Caura. In 1960 the population was 411. Situated 5 miles north of Arima at Land Settlement Junction. Postal agency under Arouca.

12.3.56*-S.O. 31.8.62          **15     150**

D2 (27.11.56)-S.U. 31.8.62
Using time codes A & B.

UP1

**Lopinot Post Office**

**Los Bajos**

Situated 2 miles north east of Palo Seco at Los Bajos Junction. Postal agency under Siparia.

1.6.52*-S.O. 31.8.62 **10 100**

D2 (12.7.52)-S.U. 31.8.62

**MANZANILLA** (Or. Spanish "Little apples" after the Manchineel trees in the area).
Situated in county St. Andrew on Eastern Main Road. On the 31 March 1888 the office was moved from the police station to Mr. Grahams (Catechist) house. In March 1888 the mails were closed in the G.P.O. on Wednesday and Saturday at 3.45 p.m. arriving Thursday and Monday at 6 p.m. In the reverse direction mails were closed at 6 p.m. Tuesday and Friday arriving Port of Spain 12.15 p.m. the next day. In 1899 the Postmaster was J. M. Scobie £12.10s p.a. until 1916. In 1919 Miss C. Prescott took over the position with a rise in salary to £40 p.a. until 1923. In 1924 Miss D. Chittenden (District Postmistress) took over the position until 1940. In 1941 the Postmistress was Miss E. Cleveland until 1943. In 1944 Miss R. Hill took over the position until 1950 (During this period of time Miss R. Hill got married in 1946 and became Mrs R. Hill-King). In 1951 (Miss) H. Paul became Postmistress until 1958/59.

14.8.51-S.O. 31.8.62 **10 100**

K1
Similar to La Brea K1

K3 (2.5.72)

K4 (8.9.82)-(4.9.83)
Still held on 31 August 1962!

KD5 (8.9.82)-(1.9.86)

**MANZANILLA Continued**

D1 (10.3.71)*-(20.11.77)

D3 (26.7.87)-(24.5.06)

D4 (21.8.06)-(27.10.27)

D5 (8.5.31)*-(14.7.37)
Using time codes A & B.
Val x 5

D6 (11.11.37)-S.U. 31.8.62
Using time codes A to C.

**Manzanilla Post Office**

R2 (14.7.49)-S.U.31.8.62

UP2 (14.7.49)-S.U. 31.8.62

UNCLAIMED

I2 (14.7.49)

**MARABELLA** (Or. Spanish Mar Bella, beautiful sea view).
Became a resident area for oil workers at Pointe-a-Pierre refinery. Situated 1 mile   north of
San Fernando, county Victoria on the Southern Main Road.  Upgraded to a post office from
a postal agency on 7 August 1960.  Using time codes A to C.

1.3.37*-S.O. 31.8.62        8      80

D2 (20.4.38)-(20.7.60)

Sent 4.2.58?
D3

**Marabella Post Office**

**Marabella Continued**

Sent 14.9.59
D4 (12.8.60)-S.U. 31.8.62

Sent 14.9.59
D5 (14.9.60)-S.U. 31.8.62

R2

UP2

UNCLAIMED

I2 (23.10.61)

**Maracas Road**
Postal agency under Curepe. Site of the Carribbean Union College, situated north of St. Joseph.
16.4.51-S.O. 31.8.62          **10      100**

D2 (26.7.51)-S.U. 31.8.62

R2

# UNCLAIMED

I2

**Maracas Road Post Office**

**Maraval** (Or. Spanish, Valley of the Gris gris, a type of palm tree).

Postal agency under Port of Spain. Situated 3 miles north of Port of Spain in the Warden's office Maraval Road. A receiving office for stamps only was opened at the School House on 1 March 1860, it was opened as a branch post office in 1880 at the police station. On the 1 June 1888 it moved to Mr. Jackson's store. In 1899 the Postmaster was C. Carrera £12.10s p.a. until 1907. In 1908 G. Carrera took over the position £12.10s p.a. until 1916.

24.8.80*-S.O. 31.8.62       **10**    **100**

KD2
Val x 15

**Maraval Continued**

D2 (2.8.88)-(24.12.29)

Val x 5

D4 (11.2.31)-S.U.31.8.62
Using time codes A & D.

R1

UP2

## UNCLAIMED

I2 (19.9.14)-S.U. 31.8.62

**Maraval Post Office**

**Mason Hall-Tobago**

Situated 4 miles north of Scarborough. Postal agency under Scarborough. Using time codes A , B & C.

(1926)-S.O. 31.8.62       **10**    **100**

D2 (16.1.41)-S.U. 31.8.62

**Mason Hall Post Office**

**MATELOT** (Or. French Sailor).

Situated 5 miles west of Grande Riviere, county St. David, on the Paria Main Road. Upgraded from a postal agency to district post office on 3 May 1952. In 1899 the Postmaster was E. L. Ford until 1900. In 1901 M. Bovell took over the position until 1902. In 1903 J. Romain became Postmaster £12.10s p.a. until 1916. In 1953 (Miss) E. de Four took over the position until 1955. For 1956 only, Miss Roberts became Postmistress. In 1957 I. Polisher took over the position until 1958/59.

1896*-S.O. 31.8.62       **10**    **100**

**MATELOT Continued**

Sent 13.11.59

D3 (17.3.07)-(1.1.37)
Using time codes A to C.
Val x 5

D4 (11.1.38)-(16.1.60)*
Using time codes A & B.

D6 (22.1.60)-S.U. 31.8.62

R2

T

UP2 (10.4.61)-S.U. 31.8.62
Val x 2

**Matelot Post Office**

# UNCLAIMED

I2

# Insured

I3

**Matilda (Matilda Junction Road)** (Or. from Matilda Estate).
Postal agency under Princes Town. Situated 4 miles north of Princes Town, 25 yards from the junction at Matilda Road and Mayaro Road.

1.6.57-S.O. 31.8.62        **10**      **100**

D1 (21.10.57)
Val x 20

D2 (12.7.58)-S.U. 31.8.62

**Matura** (Or. Spanish "high woods") opened as a sub office.
Communcation was by sea until 1927 when a road was opened to Valencia. Situated 5 miles north east of Oropouche on Toco Main Road. Postal agency under Sangre Grande. In 1899 the Postmaster was Joseph Sorzano £12.10s p.a. until 1904. In 1905 W. Earl (Pol. Sgt) took over the position £12.10s p.a. until 1913. In 1914 M. La Croix became Postmaster £12.10s p.a. until 1917 (During 1917 M. La Croix gained a rise in salary to from £12.10s to £25 p.a.). In 1918 Mrs. M. La Croix took over the position £25 p.a. until 1923.

May 1893-S.O. 31.8.62        **10**      **100**

Sent 21.6.93
D2 (21.7.93)-(28.5.07)
    &       - (3.12.15)

Sent 4.6.07
D3 (22.1.08)-(12.7.12)

Val x 3

D4 (6.3.17)-(21.2.40)

D5 (10.8.42)-S.U. 31.8.62
Using time codes A & B.

**Matura Continued**

UP2 (16.7.49)-S.U. 31.8.62

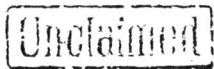

I2

**Matura Post Office**

**MAYARO** (Or. Amerindian, Arawak for "place of the Maya plant").
Situated on the coast 10 miles east of Rio Claro, county Mayaro on the Guayaguayare Road. Initially mails went by sea, from 1865 the service was on Mondays and Thursdays (Before 1865 on Thursdays only). On 28 March 1888 the mails at the G.P.O. were closed at 3.45 p.m. Wednesday and Saturday, arriving 6 p.m. on Thursday and Monday. In the reverse direction they closed noon on Tuesday and Friday arriving Port of Spain 12.15 p.m. the next day. When the railway was extended to Rio Claro in 1 September 1914 a daily overland mail service started using a donkey cart between Rio Claro and Mayaro.

The first post office was at Radix (Both Radix and Pierreville are localities in the general area known as Mayaro). On 1 May 1891 it became a money order office. On 1 September 1891 it moved from the Warden's office to Rev. S. F. Jardine's house. From 1898 to 1913 the Postmaster was S.F. Jardine, £40p.a. at St. Barthomers Church. In 1914 Miss J. Atkins took over a Post Office which had just been built until 1916. In 1917 Miss L. Best became Postmistress £40 p.a. until 1921. In 1922 Miss A. Cuffie took over the position and moved into a new Post Office 3 miles away at Pierreville or "Quarters" in 1931. Miss O. Cuffy became Postmistress until 1948 when another office was built. Miss I. Todd took over the position until 1950. In 1951 (Miss) C. Caliste became Postmistress until 1958/59.

14.8.51-S.O. 31.8.62          6      60

K1
In 1851 probably issued with
a mark similar to La Brea K1

K2

K3 (9.8.71)

Val x 30

Val x 30

K4 (10.1.82)
Val x 50

KD5 (10.11.82)-(16.1.85)
Val x 30

Sent 4.6.07

D3 (7.6.87)-(5.6.07)*
Val x 3

D4 (24.7.08)-(3.8.27)
Val x 3

D5 (1.10.27)-(28.12.33)
Val x 5

D6 (25.7.34)-S.U. 31.8.62
Using time codes A, B & C.

D7 (14.4.58)-(7.10.58)

Val x 4

# RECISTERED

R2 (27.2.14)-(9.9.47)
Val x 2

UP2 (20.5.46)-S.U. 31.8.62
Val x 2

**Mayaro Post Office**

**Mayo** (Or. Amerindian being the name of a plant, Bromelia Pinguin). Originally the site of a Jesuit mission, which was dispersed in 1824.

Situated 1 mile south east of Tortuga. Postal agency under Couva. In 1905 the Postmistress was Miss J. Atkins £25 p.a. until 1911. In 1912 Miss H. Donawa took over the position £25 p.a. until 1913. In 1914 Miss E. Lewis and in 1915 Miss Tronchin took over the position of Postmistress £25 p.a. for one year only. In 1916 Miss G. M. Farfan took over the position £25 p.a. until 1918. For 1919 only, Miss L. Joseph became Postmistress for Mayo £25 p.a. In 1920 Mrs. M. Blanchfield also took over the position for a year only £25 p.a. In 1921 Mrs. W. Charles (Aq) became Postmistress until 1923.

(19.9.04)-S.O. 31.8.62          **10      100**

**Mayo Continued**

Sent 21.3.04
D2 (19.9.04)-(21.4.27)
Using time codes A & B.
Val x 10

D4 (24.9.34)-S.U. 31.8.62
Using time codes A, B & C.

**Mayo Post Office**

**Monos (Island)** (Or. Spanish).
Situated west of Chaguaramus, from 20 December 1861 the mails were made up at the house
of Mr. Basanta. In 1899 the Postmaster was C. Morrison £12.10s p.a. until 1916.

| | | N.S. |
|---|---|---|
| 14.8.51-(1861) | | |
| (8.4.82)-(19.11.91) | 120 | 1,200 |
| 1.9.98*-1922 | 100 | 1,000 |
| (12.3.24)-(4.11.25) | 100 | 1,000 |

K1
In 1851 probably issued with
a mark similar to La Brea K1

K2
To Moruga by 1868

**Monos (Island) Continued**

K4 (8.4.82)

KD5 (8.4.82)

D3 (22.7.80)

D4 (13.2.89)-(19.11.91)
&  (11.1.07)-(14.12.08)*

Sent 14.12.98
D5 (12.3.24)-(4.11.25)

## REGISTERED

R2 (8.4.82)
Val x 2

## UNCLAIMED

I2 (8.4.82)
Val x 2

**Mon Repos**
Situated 2 miles due north from San Fernando on Smith Street, in the Mon Repos Housing Scheme
(started 1939) and ¾ mile from Cocoyea.  Named after the sugar estate of the same name.  Postal
agency under San Fernando.

|  |  |  |
|---|---|---|
| 6.12.41*-S.O. 31.8.62 | **10** | **100** |

D2 (17.1.44)-S.U. 31.8.62

**Mon Repos Continued**

R2 (28.2.55)-(7.4.56)

UP1        -S.U. 31.8.62

**MORIAH-Tobago**
Situated 7 miles north east of Plymouth, county St. David. Opened as a District Post Office at the house of Mr. J. B. Swalls. In 1932 the Postmaster was M. L. Jones until 1935. In 1936 Miss M. L. Jones took over the position until 1950. For 1951 only, (Miss) E. Gomez became Postmistress. In 1952 (Miss) O. Gibbs took over the position until 1953. In 1954 (Miss) F. R. Goindoo became Postmistress until 1958/59. Used time codes A & B.
1.1.97-S.O. 31.8.62                                **10      100**

D3 (21.2.29)-(26.5.38)
Val x 5

D4 (15.11.38)-S.U. 31.8.62

UP2

**Moriah Post Office**

**Morne Coco** (Or. French, coconut hill).
Situated west of Diego Martin on Morne Coco Road.  Postal agency under Diego Martin.

                    23.11.59*-S.O. 31.8.62        **15**      **150**

D2 (11.12.59)-S.U. 31.8.62

**Morne Diable** (Or. French, gloomy devil).
Situated 7 miles south of Penal on the Morne Diable-Quarry Road.   Postal agency under Princes Town

                    2.2.42-S.O. 31.8.62        **15**      **150**

D2 (19.9.44)-S.U. 31.8.62

**Morne Diable Continued**

**Morne Diable Post Office**

**MORUGA** (Or. Amerindian).
In 1861 the population was 304. At Independence it was 700. Upto 1928 communication was by sea. Situated on the coast 2 miles south of Basseterre, county Victoria on Moruga Road. On 2 December 1895 a district post office was opened at the rest home for the convenience of residents in Fifth Company Village and the neigbourhood. For 1899 only, the Postmaster was J. Carrington (Pol. Sgt). In 1900 S. Barnell (Sgt) and in 1901 C. Rawlins (Sgt) took over the position of Postmaster for one year only. In 1902 J. W. White (Cpl) became Postmaster £25 p.a. until 1905. In 1906 Mrs J. White took over the position until 1907. In 1908 Mrs M. White took over the position with a rise in salary to £40 p.a. until 1917. In 1918 Mrs J. White retook over the position as Postmistress £40 p.a. until 1923. A new office was built in 1912. In 1924 Mrs M. White became Postmistress until 1935. In 1936 Miss L. G. Carrington took over the position until 1950. For 1951 only, (Miss) V. Hutchinson became Postmistress. In 1952 (Miss) F. Alcindor took over the position until 1954. In 1955 (Miss) L. Francis-Alexander became Postmistress until 1958/59.

1868-S.O. 31.8.62      **10**     **100**

           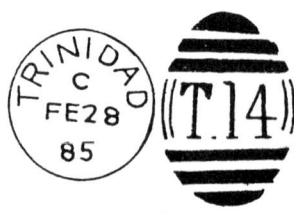

K2 (From Monos)      K3            KD4 (30.12.85)

                  Still held at post office on
                  31 August 1962.
                  Val x 10              Val x 10

**MORUGA Continued**

D3 (6.4.87)*-(31.10.24)

Val x 3

D4 (14.4.26)-(9.12.31)

Val x 5

D5 (30.5.34)-S.U. ·31.8.62
Using time codes A & B.

R2

REGISTERED

R3 (10.9.47)

UP2 (23.9.37)-S.U. 31.8.62
Val x 3

**Moruga Post Office**

REFUSED

I3

## MORVANT

In 1958 situated 2 miles north north east of Laventille post office and 50 yards off the Lady Young Road, 5 miles from Port of Spain, county St. George. Upgraded to a post office on 1 November 1960.

1.10.42-S.O. 31.8.62          **10    100**

D2 (14.11.44)-S.U. 31.8.62      Sent 28.11.61          Sent 28.11.61
Using time codes A to D.        D3                     D4

**Morvant Post Office**

R2

REFUSED          UNCLAIMED

I2                          I3 (25.9.56)

**Mount Grace-Tobago**
Situated 3 miles north of Scarborough.  Postal agency under Scarborough.  Using time codes A &
B.

| | | |
|---|---|---|
| (1937)-S.O. 31.8.62 | **10** | **100** |

D2 (12.2.40)-S.U. 31.8.62

**Mount Pleasant-Tobago**
Situated near the Shirvan Park race course.  Postal agency under Scarborough.  Using time codes A
& B.

| | | |
|---|---|---|
| 1.7.42-S.O. 31.8.62 | **20** | **200** |

D2 (23.9.44)-S.U. 31.8.62

**Mount Pleasant-Tobago Continued**

**Mount Pleasant Post Office**

**Mount St. George-Tobago**

Situated 1 mile east of Mesopotamia. Postal agency under Scarborough. Opened as a receiving house, it probably did not have a datestamp. Mrs. F. C. McEachrane being licensed to sell stamps.

(1909)-S.O. 31.8.62 **10 100**

D2 (12.1.46)-S.U. 31.8.62
Set with time code A, B & C.

**Mount St. George-Tobago Post Office**

**MUCURAPO** (Or. From Amerindian "Cumucupapo meaning "Place of the silk cotton trees"). Situated near St. James. On 31 March 1888 the office moved from the police station to Mr Camaron's house (next to the Warden's office.) In 1899 the Postmistress was Mrs. M. Peters £12.10s p.a. until 1916. In 1920 Mrs. F. Peters took over the position with a rise in salary to £25 p.a. until 1923. For 1938 only, Miss E. Miller became Postmistress. In 1945 (Miss) A. Semper took over the position until 1948 (During this period of time (Miss) A. Semper got married in 1946 and became Mrs A. Semper-Callender). On 16 August 1948 Miss C. Mason became Postmistress until 1954. Upgraded to a money order office 21 February 1944.

24.8.80-(11.7.53)           **10**    **100**
(To St. James in 1953? E.R.D. 15.7.53)

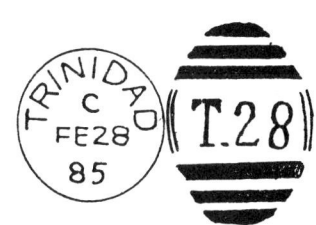

K1                                    K2                                KD3

**MUCURAPO Continued**

D2 (10.5.87)*-(13.6.32)
Used time codes A & B.

Val x 3

D3 (3.1.33)-(11.7.53)
Used with time codes A, B
& C.

D4 (20.12.49)-(14.3.51)

Val x 5

R2 (25.9.03)-(14.7.49)
Val x 2

UP2 (2.12.36)-(14.7,49)
Val x 2

I2 (4.7.17)-(14.7.49)

**Nariva** (Or. Amerindian).
Situated on the beach road, Mayaro to Manzanilla in the district of Nariva.

|  |  |  |
|---|---|---|
| 14.8.51-C1. by 1861 | | **N.S.** |
| (1.6.67)-(25.6.70) | **4,000** | - |

K1
In 1851 probably issued with a
mark similar to La Brea K1

K2
Used at Blanchisseuse and Toco early
1860's.  Tunapuna from 1878.

**Nariva Continued**

D2 (25.6.70)

**Navet**
Situated 3 miles north of the Rio Claro on Biche Road.  Postal agency under Rio Claro.

12.7.50*-S.O. 31.8.62      **10**    **100**

D1 (7.12.50)-(30.11.51)
Val x 5

D2 (6.3.52)-S.U. 31.8.62

UP1 (30.7.59)
Val x 2

**Navet Post Office**

## Newlands
Situated 2 miles north of Guayaguayare. Postal agency under Rio Claro.

                  16.5.61-S.O. 31.8.62                       **N.S.**

## New Settlement
Situated on the Egypt Road. Postal agency under Point Fortin.

                  1.5.58-S.O. 31.8.62              **10**      **100**

D2 (9.7.58)-S.U. 31.8.62

**New Settlement Post Office**

## NEWTOWN
Situated 3 miles from Port of Spain on the Maraval Road, county St. George. Initially opened on the south side of Tragarate Road between Picton and Woodford Streets. The pillar and letter boxes being cleared at 6 a.m., 10 a.m. and 3 p.m. daily except Sundays. The office moved to more commodious premises on 28 December 1937. In 1899 the Postmaster was E. Johnson £12.10s p.a. until 1906. In 1907 E. Rostant took over the position £12.10s p.a. until 1916. In 1920 Mrs E. Rostant became Postmistress with a rise in salary to £25 p.a. until 1923. In 1938 Miss C. Mason took over the position until 1948. In 1949 Mrs A. Semper-Callender became Postmistress until 1955. In 1956 (Miss) S. Burnett took over the position until 1958/59. Upgraded to a money order office 2 January 1938.

                  1.9.90-S.O. 31.8.62              **6**      **60**

## NEWTOWN Continued

D3 (29.5.08)-(30.1.24)
Still held at the post office in 1976.
Val x 6

D4 (22.3.30)-(1.5.39)

Val x 5

D5 (24.10.39)-S.U. 31.8.62
Using time codes A to D.

D6 (28.8.39)-S.U. 31.8.62

R2 (28.5.51)-(16.3.55)
Val x 2

REGISTERED

R3 (12.10.55)-S.U.31.8.62
Val x 2

UP2 (18.5.11)-S.U. 31.8.62
Val x 3

UNCLAIMED

I3

**Newtown Post Office**

**Orange Valley**
Situated at the corner of Orange Valley Bay Road and Waterloo Road in Couva Village. Postal
agency under Couva

15.9.58*-S.O. 31.8.62 **15** **150**

D1 15.9.58-S.U. 31.8.62

**Orange Valley Continued**

**Orange Valley Post Office**

**OROPOUCHE** (Or. Amerindian)

Situated about midway between San Fernando and Siparia, county Victoria on the Old Southern Main Road. On 8 February 1888 moved from the police station to Mr Culerhouse's store. In 1899 the Postmaster was P. R. Coker until 1901. In 1902 J. E. Coker took over the position £15 p.a. until 1916. In 1918 Mrs M. Glasgow became Postmistress with a rise in salary to £25 p.a. until 1925. For 1938 only, Miss D. Durham took over the position. In 1957 M. Prescod became Postmistress until 1958/59. Using time codes A & B.

                    14.8.51-S.O. 31.8.62                    **10**    **100**

K1                              K2                              KD5

In 1851 probably issued with
a mark similar to La Brea K1.

                                Val x 15                       Val x 15

**OROPOUCHE Continued**

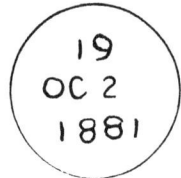

D2 (8.11.77)*-(12.11.81)
Val x 15

D3 (21.9.87)*-(5.5.20)
Val x 4

D5 (18.2.30)-(12.3.31)
Val x 5

D6 (2.1.35)-S.U. 31.8.62

**REGISTERED**

R2 (21.8.47)-(23.9.47)
Val x 2

**Oropouche Post Office**

**OROPOUCHE Continued**

UP2

**Palmyra (O. Syrian village, named after the town in Syria)**
Situated on the Naparima-Mayaro Road between San Fernando and Princes Town. Postal agency under San Fernando.

1.11.60-S.O. 31.8.62              **10      100**

Sent 2.9.60
D2 (28.3.61)-S.U. 31.8.62

**Palmyra Post Office**

**PALO SECO (Palo Secco)** O. Spanish for "Dry Tree".
Upgraded to a Post Office 1 May 1935. Situated between Santa Flora and Erin county St. Patrick on the Siparia Erin Road. During 1931 through to 1935 the Post Office in Palo Seco was vacant. In 1936 Miss E. Cameron and in 1937 Miss U. Smith both took over the position of Postmistress for only one year. In 1938 Miss J. Todd took over the position until 1939. In 1940 Miss C. Owen became Postmistress until 1950 (During this period of time Miss C. Owen got married in 1946 and became

Mrs C. Owen-Henry). In 1951 (Miss) O. Alcindor took over the position until 1954. In 1955 (Miss) E. L. Worrel became Postmistress until 1957. During 1958/59 G. Jones was Postmaster.

(21.4.31)-S.O. 31.8.62          **6**          **60**

D2 (21.4.31)
  & (15.4.35)-(30.7.36)
  & (9.8.45)-(11.8.45)

Val x 6

D3 (6.7.32)-(5.4.35)
  & (19.1.37)-(9.10.53)

Using time codes A, B & C.
Val x 2

D4 (30.10.53)*-S.U. 31.8.62

D5 (10.5.54)-S.U. 31.8.62

**Palo Seco Post Office**

**PALO SECO (Palo Secco) Continued**

R2 (6.8.49)-(30.6.54)
Val x 2

UP2 (1.12.39)-(6.8.49)
Val x 2

UNCLAIMED

I2 (6.8.49)

**Parlatuvier-Tobago**
Situated on the coast, 4 miles north east of Castara.  Postal agency under Scarborough.
(1926)-S.O. 31.8.62                                    **10**        **100**

D3 (18.12.43)-S.U. 31.8.62
Using time codes A to D.

**Parlatuvier-Tobago Continued**

**Parlatuvier Post Office**

**Patience Hill-Tobago**
Situated 5 miles west of Scarborough. Postal agency under Scarborgh.

|  |  |  |
|---|---|---|
| 1.3.46-S.O. 31.8.62 | **10** | **100** |

D1 (6.3.48)*
Similar to Penal D4

D2 (6.4.48)-S.U. 31.8.62
Set with time codes A & B.

R1 (3.4.58)

**Patience Hill Post Office**

## Pembroke-Tobago
Situated 7 miles south of Roxborough. Opened as a District Post Office in the residence of Miss. M. A. Murray. Postal agency under Scarborough. Using time codes A & B.

                      1.1.97*-S.O. 31.8.62          **10**     **100**

D4 (23.3.38)-S.U. 31.8.62

**Pembroke Post Office**

**PENAL (Penal Rock Junction until 1936)** (Or. Spanish meaning higher ground in a swampy area).

In 1946 the population was 1,204. Situated 3 miles north east of Siparia, county St. Patrick. Opened as a receiving office. In 1920 the Sub-Postmistress was Miss R. Deane £25 p.a. until 1922. For 1923 only, Miss A. Deane took over the position. In 1938 Miss C. Thompson became Postmistress until 1950. In 1951 (Miss) E. Merrin took over the position until 1953. For 1954 only, (Miss) L. Francis -Alexander became Postmistress. In 1955 also, Miss F. Alcindor took over the position for a year only. In 1956 the Postmistress was (Miss) E. Callender until 1958/59. Using time codes A & B. In 1949 the office was destroyed by fire as described in the "Trinidad Guardian" of 15 December:-

*SAN FERNANDO Dec. 14*

*Penal Post Office with staff quarters attached were completely destroyed by fire about noon today. Miss Cyrenia Thompson, postmistress and Miss Muriel Joseph, her assistant, lost all their personal belongings.*

A new building was occupied 7 November 1951. Using time codes A to C.

(11.12.11)-S.O. 31.8.62    6    60

**PENAL (Penal Rock Junction) Continued**

D2 (11.12.11)-(8.9.36)
Using time codes A, B & C.
Val x 10

D3 (6.12.36)-(7.12.49)
Probably lost in the fire 14.12.49.
Val x 2

D4 (16.12.49)-(5.12.51)

Val x 5

D5 (1.1.52)-S.U. 31.8.62

D6 (11.9.54)-S.U.31.8.62

R2 (20.11.51)
Val x 2

**Penal Post Office**

411

UP2 (6.12.33)
Val x 2

UP3 (23.9.39)-S.U.31.8.62

**Penal Rock Junction** see **Penal**

**Penal Rock Road**
Situated near Basseterre.  Postal agency under Princes Town.

1.10.38*-S.O. 31.8.62          **10**     **100**

D2 (2.6.48)-(19.3.53)
Using time codes A & B.
Val x 2

D3 (12.12.53)-S.U. 31.8.62

**Penal Rock Road Post Office**

**Piarco (Airport)**

An airmail transit centre was opened at Piarco on the 19 December 1955, it evidently did not accept mail from the public.

19.12.55*-S.O. 31.8.62          **N.S.**

**Piparo**

Situated 4 miles south west of Tabaquite, Pascual Road. Postal agency under Couva.

1.8.51-S.O. 31.8.62       **10**      **100**

D2 (25.9.51)-S.U. 31.8.62

**Piparo Post Office**

**Plaisance** (Or. French, Pleasure).

Situated on the Southern Main Road, 2 miles from Marabella. Postal agency under Marabella.

1.11.60-S.O. 31.8.62       **10**      **100**

Sent 2.9.60
D2 (29.3.61)-S.U. 30.9.62

**Plaisance Post Office**

**Plum Mitan**

Situated 2 miles south west of Manzanilla.  Postal agency under Sangre Grande.

16.6.51-S.O. 31.8.62 **10** **100**

D1 (21.3.52)
Val x 20

D2 (30.10.52)-S.U. 31.8.62

**Plum Mitan Post Office**

### Plymouth-Tobago

Situated on the coast 9 miles north west of Scarborough. Settled by the Dutch in 1628 it was called Niew Vlissingen. In 1763 it became the British capital of Tobago. In 1901 was a receiving office, Mrs. J.A. Gordon being licensed to sell stamps on 11 April 1901. In 1946 the population was 1,180. Postal agency under Scarborough.

(1908)-S.O. 31.8.62              10     100

D3 (12.10.40)-S.U. 31.8.62
Using time codes A, B & C.

**Plymouth Post Office**

## Point Cumana
Situated on the coast near Redhead north of Port of Spain at the corner of Rodney Street and Western Main Road. Postal agency under Port of Spain.

1.6.49-S.O. 31.8.62  **10**    **100**

D1 (11.6.49)-(30.11.49)*     D2 (14.7.50)-(9.9.55)     D3 (20.9.57)-S.U. 31.8.62
Val x 50     Val x 2

UP1

**Point Cumana Post Office**

**POINTE A PIERRE** (Or. French "Point of Stone").
The railway arrived in 1882, a station being built in 1885. Site of the main oil refinery in Trinidad. Situated on the coast. For 1939 only, the Postmistress was Miss V. Huskisson. On 1 December 1939 Miss E. Miranda took over the position until 1943. In 1944 Miss E. Mc Lean became Postmistress until 1947. In 1946 Miss M. Edwards took over the position until 1949. In 1950 Miss H. Winchester became Postmistress. On 1 September 1950 Miss C. Cottle took over the position until 1953. In 1954 Miss C. Alcindor became Postmistress until 1955. In 1956 (Miss) E. Callender took over the position until 1958/59. Using time codes A, B & C. Upgraded to a money order office 1 October 1938.

1.10.38*-S.O. 31.8.62          4          40

D2 (22.12.38)-S.U. 31.8.62

D3 (27.7.42)-S.U. 31.8.62

R2 (18.3.46)-(21.3.56)
Val x 2

UP2 (28.1.52)

**POINT FORTIN** (Or. after the estate belonging to a Frenchman Fortin, who came to Trinidad in 1783).

The harbour was developed in 1907 in connection with the oil fields which started producing in 1910. Situated 5 miles south west of La Brea, county St. Patrick on Frisco Road. A new Post Office which was more accessible to the public was opened in April 1935. Opened as a receiving office. For 1916 only, the Postmaster was N. Roberts £12.10s p.a. On 1 November 1919 Miss M. Cox took over the position with a rise in salary to £25 p.a. until 1924. In 1925 Miss M. Cox received another rise in her salary to £67.10s p.a.until 1 February 1938 when Miss R. Blakeley took over the position. On 1 May 1939 Miss I. Jordan became Postmistress until 1952. In 1953 Miss A. Ceoline took over the position until 1954. In 1955 Miss E. Cleveland became Postmistress until 1957. During 1958/59 the Postmaster was E. Cleveland.

|  |  |  |
|---|---|---|
| 1911-S.O. 31.8.62 | 3 | 30 |

D2 (19.3.12)-(30.8.28)
&  (18.10.30)-(8.7.31)*

Val x 5

D3 (15.10.29)-(2.6.30)*

Val x 30

D4 (11.11.31)-S.U. 31.8.62

Using time codes A, B & C.

**POINT FORTIN Continued**

D5 (16.9.39)-(23.1.56)
Using time codes A, B & C.
Val x 2

D6 (21.2.56)-S.U. 31.8.62
Using time codes A & B.

D7 (16.10.56)-(2.1.57)
Val x 30

D7 (24.7.58)- S.U. 31.8.62

**Point Fortin Post Office**

## POINT FORTIN Continued

R2 (6.7.26)-(1.7.50)
Val x 3

## CLEARED FROM LETTER BOX

I2 (4.4.61)

**Poole**
Postal agency under Tabaquite, situated on the San Pedro Road. In 1906 the Postmaster was
A. Lazzarri £25 p.a. until 1920. In 1921 M. Lazzarri took over the position £25 p.a. until
1923. In 1924 C. Lazzarri became Postmaster with a rise in salary to £40 p.a. until 1925.

(4.9.05)-S.O. 31.8.62          **10     100**

Sent 1.6.05
D2 (4.9.05)-(22.3.26)
Using time codes A & B
In 1906 year set as 1905?
(Seen dated 4.4.05 &15.6.05)
Val x 5

D4 (10.8.27)-(6.8.29)

Val x 10

D5 (20.2.31)-(1.4.60)
Using time codes A, B & C.

D6 (13.9.60)-(25.5.61)
Val x 25

Sent 2.9.61
D7          -S.U. 31.8.62

# UNCLAIMED

Sent 1.6.05
I1

**Poole Post Office**

**Port of Spain-Whitehall**
First Caribbean Intercolonial Stamp Exhibition.   Whitehall became the Prime Minister's Office.
6.5.48-9.5.48                              **8        80**

D1 6.5.48-9.5.48

**PRINCES TOWN** (Or. Spanish for "Great Plains").

Originally Savanna Grande renamed on 18 February 1880 in honour of the two royal princes visit, on 20 January 1880 (they were midshipmen on S.S. Bacchante). On 1 April 1885 it became a money order office. In 1921 the population was 4,983, in 1931 4,800. Situated 4 miles east of San Fernando county Victoria on Railway Road. In 1867 H. W. Sealy was postmaster, then A. Chisholm from 1868 to 1870, H. Marshall from 1878 to 1880 C. H. Culverhouse was appointed 1 May 1892 then the Postmaster was John T. Codrington £70 p.a. from 16 February 1894 until 1902. In 1903 Mrs B. T. Laing took over the position with a rise in salary to £80 until 1905. In 1906 Mrs M. A. Corrie became Postmistress £80 p.a. until 1922. In 1923 Miss I. Hamilton took over the position until 1942. In 1943 the Postmistress was Miss M. Cox until 1955. In 1956 (Miss ) G. Lalla took over the position until 1957.

14.8.51-S.O. 31.8.62 2 20

K1

K2    -(7.9.61)

Val x 50

K3 (8.5.76)-
Val x 50

KD5 (5.9.82)-(4.1.83)
Val x 50

D2 (7.9.61)-(26.3.77)
Val x 50

D3 (26.11.77)-(23.11.81)
Val x 50

D4 (10.6.85)-(22.9.98)
Val x 10

Sent 10.10.98
D5 (10.11.98)-(20.7.05)*
Val x 12

Sent 1.6.05
D6 (9.8.05)*-(14.5.28)
Val x 8

Sent 29.6.09
D7 (31.1.27)-(18.10.32)
Val x 8

# PRINCES TOWN Continued

D8 (24.11.24)-(19.12.32)    D9 (30.10.31)-(30.12.52)    D10 (25.5.37)-(9.10.61)

D11 (13.7.49)-S.U. 31.8.62    D12 (14.1.38)-(13.7.49)

D4 - D7 &D9 - D11 generally set with time codes A, B or C.

**Princes Town Post Office**

To distinguish between the above datestamps easily, this sheet (or any other), may be ordered from the Publisher printed on clear plastic for £1 each (subject unsold).

**RECISTERED**

R2 (8.12.00)-(16.12.08)

Sent 29.6.09
R3 (7.12.21)-(8.9.47)
Become distorted.
Val x 3

Sent 29.6.09
UP2

UP3 (21.10.03)-(10.12.38)
Val x 3

UP4

UNCLAIMED

Sent 1.6.05
I1

UNCLAIMED

I2 (6.10.56)

TOO-LATE

I3 (7.6.85)

**Prizgar Lands**
Situated 1 mile from Laventille post office, on Charton Circular Road.  Postal agency under
Port of Spain.

1.8.56*-S.O. 31.8.62          **10**     **100**

D2 (3.8.56)*-S.U. 31.8.62

UP1

UNCLAIMED

I1

**Prizgar Lands Post Office**

## Quarry

Situated between Siparia and Santa Flora on the Siparia-Erin Road. Postal agency under Siparia.

1.5.57-S.O. 31.8.62         **10**    **100**

D2 (13.6.57)-S.U. 31.8.62

UP2

**Quarry Post Office**

**Reform**

Situated 1 mile east of Marabella on Reform Road.  Postal agency under San Fernando.

(14.11.46)-S.O. 31.8.62          **10**     **100**

D2 (14.11.46)-S.U. 31.8.62
Set with time codes A, B & C.

R1

UP1 (3.1.57)-S.U. 31.8.62

**Reform Post Office**

UNCLAIMED

I1

**RIO CLARO** (Or. Spanish "Clear River").
Situated 3 miles south of Navet county Nariva on the Main Road. The village grew up round the half way house built 1850 on the Princestown (Savana Grande) to Mayaro Road. The railway arrived on 1 September 1914. In 1921 the population was 2,055 and was nearly 3,000 in 1946. For 1919 only, the Sub-Postmistress was Mrs M. Blanchfield £25 p.a. In 1920 Miss L. Joseph took over the position £40 p.a. until 1938 (Money Order Office). On 1 February 1939 Miss A. B. Gonzalez became Postmistress until 1946. On 1 July 1946 (Miss) R. Blakeley took over the position until 1954. In 1955 Miss R. Hill-King became Postmistress until 1956. In 1957 R. Cleveland took over the position until 1958/59.

1.10.14*-S.O. 31.8.62      4     40

D2 (14.4.15)-(16.7.27)
& (16.9.30)-(9.12.30)
D2, D4 & D5 used time codes A, B or C.
Val x 6

D3 (29.7.27)-(24.3.30)

Val x 12

**RIO CLARO Continued**

D4 (28.2.31)-S.U. 31.8.62
Val x 4

D5 (22.11.38)-S.U. 31.8.62

R1 (27.12.16)
Val x 2

R2 (27.11.40)-(25.2.59)
Val x 2

UP2 (20.10.34)-S.U. 31.8.62
Val x 2

**Rio Claro Post Office**

**Rochard Douglas**

Situated 3 miles from Preau on the Rochard Douglas Road.  Postal agency under Princes Town.

16.4.59*-S.O. 31.8.62          **10     100**

Sent 6.5.59

D1 (17.4.59)-(25.4.59)
Initially set with date slugs.
Val x 20

D2 (30.9.59)-S.U. 31.8.62

UP1

**Rochard Douglas Post Office**

**Rock River**
Situated 2 miles north of Basseterre.  Postal agency under Princes Town.
(1926)-S.O. 31.8.62          10     100

D2 (6.3.29)-(3.8.34)                    D3 (12.2.36)-S.U. 31.8.62
                                        Using time codes A, B & C.

Val x 20

Rock River Post Office

**Rose Hill**
Situated 1½ miles from Port of Spain at No. 27 Jackson Hill Road off Picadilly Street.
Opened as a Sub Office with two mails daily.  Downgraded from a Post Office to a postal
agency under Port of Spain on 1 October 1959.  In 1900 the Postmistress was Mrs E. Hall
until 1901.  In 1902 T. B. Gay took over the position £12.10s p.a. until 1905.  In 1906 F. Gage
became Postmaster £12.10s p.a. until 1907.  In 1908 F. Gay took over the position £12.10s
p.a. until 1912.  In 1913 E. Manning became Postmaster £12.10s p.a. until 1916.  In 1920
Mrs. E. Manning took over the position with a rise in salary to £25 p.a. until 1923.  For 1938
only, Miss W. Ronalds became Postmistress.  In 1949 (Miss) M. Prescod took over the
position until 1956.  In 1957 the Postmaster was C. Jordan-Spalding until 1958/59.  Using
time codes A, B & C.
12.7.97-S.O. 31.8.62          10     100

Sent 4.2.98
D2 (17.3.98)-(16.11.35)
Val x 3

D3 (12.2.36)-S.U. 31.8.62

R2 (17.1.59)
Val x 2

**Rousillac** (Or. Name of early French Settler).
Situated 2 miles south east of La Brea at the corner of Grants Trace. Postal agency under San Fernando.

1.6.57-S.O. 31.8.62          **10        100**

D2 (3.7.58)-S.U. 31.8.62

R1

UP1

# UNCLAIMED

I1

**Rousillac Post Office**

**ROXBOROUGH-Tobago** (Or. from the estate of the same name).
In 1876 the scene of severe rioting which lasted one week. In 1946 the population was 871.
Situated at Princes Bay on the Windward Road. Situated in county St. Paul. In 1917 the
Sub-Postmaster was A. Jones, £40 p.a. (Money Order Office) until 1 April 1933 when Miss
Maud Charity took over until 1953 when C. Sandy became postmaster being replaced by F.
Alcindor from 1957 to 1959. Used Time Codes A, B & C.

6.8.00-31.8.62 **8  80**

Sent 28.9.00
D2 (30.10.00)-(15.5.07)

Val x 8

Sent 4.6.07
D3 (14.12.07)-(3.7.38)
Known set with the letters A to Z.
Possibly the Postmaster changed the
letter code for each mail.
Val x 5

**Roxborough-Tobago Continued**

D5 (10.2.38)-S.U.31.8.62

D6 (6.6.41)-S.U. 31.8.62

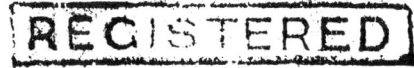

R2 (25.5.10)-(10.3.51)
Val x 2

UP2 (7.10.16)-S.U.31.8.62
Val x 2

**Roxborough-Tobago Post Office**

**St. Andrew (St. Andrew's)**

Situated ¾ mile west of St. Andrews Junction, Couva. Postal agency under Couva.

15.9.58-S.O. 31.8.62          **15**      **150**

D1 15.9.58-S.U. 31.8.62

**St. Anns**

Postal agency under Port of Spain. Initially a branch post office which opened at the police station. On 15 July 1891 it moved to the Warden's office. In 1899 the Postmistress was Mrs M. Tryhane £25 p.a. until 1906 (During 1905 Mrs. M. Tryhane salary became £12.10s p.a.). In 1907 Mrs M. Bouis took over the position £25 p.a. until 1923. Generally used time codes A & B.

24.8.80*-S.O. 31.8.62          **3**       **30**

KD2

**St. Anns Post Office**

**St Anns Continued**

Sent 4.6.07

D2 (10.11.87)-(29.7.07)
Val x 5

D3 (24.8.07)-(2.5.38)

D4 (15.6.38)-S.U. 31.8.62

R2

UP2

UNCLAIMED

I2

**St. Barb's Road Port of Spain**
Situated on St. Barb's Road half a mile from Belle Eau Road.  Postal agency under Port of Spain.
11.12.59-S.O. 31.8.62          **10     100**

Sent 20.10.59
D1 (17.12.59)-S.U. 30.8.62

R1

UP2

# UNCLAIMED

I1

**St Barbs Post Office**

## St. Benedict
Situated 8 miles from Port of Spain and 2 miles from Curepe post office on the St. John Road at the foot of Mount St. Benedict Hill. Postal agency under Tunapuna.

                         1.12.45-S.O. 31.8.62         **10**     **100**

D2 (4.5.48)-S.U. 31.8.62

R1 (16.3.51)
Val x 2

UP1 (15.7.49)
Val x 2

## St. Francois Valley Road

Situated at the junction of Upper St. Francois Valley Road and Upper Belmont Valley Road.  Postal
agency under Port of Spain.

23.11.59*-S.O. 31.8.62       **15**     **150**

Sent 20.10.59
D2 (17.2.60)-S.U. 31.8.62

**St. Francois Valley Road Post Office**

## St. Helena

Situated 1 mile south of Piaro Airport at the corner of Caroni and Golden Grove roads. Postal agency under Arouca.

1.5.57-S.O. 31.8.62          **15**     **150**

D2 (22.6.57)-S.U. 31.8.62

R1

# UNCLAIMED

I1

**St. Helena Post Office**

## ST. JAMES

Situated in the Western district of Port of Spain, county St. George on the Western Main Road. In 1955 the Postmistress was Miss C. Mason until 1957. In 1958/59 Miss E. Cleveland took over the position until 1960/61. Used time codes A, B & C.

From Mucurapo? L.R.D. 3.6.53

(15.7.).53-S.O. 31.8.62          **8     80**

D2 (15.7.53)-S.U. 31.8.62

D3 (1.9.53)-S.U. 31.8.62

R2 (11.2.55)-(1.2.58)

St James Post Office

**St. John's** (St. Johns Village near San Fernando).
Postal agency under Princes Town. Situated on the Cipero Road south west of Princes Town.
Used Time codes A, B & C.

(14.6.35)*-S.O. 31.8.62       **10**     **100**

**D2** (14.6.35)-(1.1.38)*              D3 (18.10.41)-S.U. 31.8.62
Val x 20

**St. John's Post Office**

**St. Joseph** (Or. from the orignal Spanish name San Jose de Oruna, given when the town was founded in 1592).
Shortly afterwards it was burnt by Sir Walter Raleigh and again in 1649 by the Dutch. It was the Spanish capital of Trinidad until 1784 when it moved to Port of Spain. On 18 June 1837 there was a short lived mutiny by part of the 3 West Indian Regiment. In 1881 the population was 1,814. Became a money order office on 1 September 1897. Downgraded to a postal agency under Curepe on 2 August 1949 being situated at the corner of Victoria and Abercromby streets. For 1899 only, the Postmistress was Miss C. Reid. In 1900 Miss L. Browne took over the position £40 p.a. until 1902. In 1903 Miss L. Ovid became Postmistress £40 p.a. until 1912. In 1913 Mrs B. Mootoo took over the position £40 p.a. until 1918. In 1919 Miss O. Keith (Ag) became Postmistress £40 p.a. until 1938. In 1939 Mrs H. Winchester

took over the position until 1943. In 1944 the Postmistress was Miss E. Cleveland until 1949. Used time codes A, B & C.

| | | | |
|---|---|---|---|
| 14.8.51-1.8.51 | | **10** | **100** |
| (12.12.54)-S.U. 31.8.62 | | **10** | **100** |

K1
Recon.

K2 (16.1.54)-(30.11.80)

Val x 15

K3

Val x 20

K4
Val x 20

KD5
Val x 10

D2 (25.2.54)-(7.8.60)

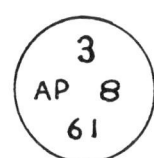

D3 (8.4.61)-(8.6.71)

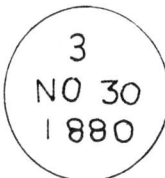

D4 (30.11.80)-(17.2.82)

D5 (26.6.86)-(17.6.07)

Val x 2

Sent 4.6.07
D6 (8.11.07)-(27.10.30)*

Val x 2

D8 (5.12.30)-(23.4.48)*
Still being held on 13 July
1949.

**St Joseph Continued**

D9 (5.8.47)-1.8.51
 & (12.12.54)-S.U. 31.8.62
Known dated 31.10.51, error for 31.10.54?

D10 (13.7.49)

Not used for postal purposes?

UP2 (16.3.43)

**St. Juan** see **San Juan**

**St. Juliens**
Situated 1 mile north on the Mayaro Road. Opened at St. Julien's Village , Moruga Junction.
Postal agency under Princes Town. For 1899 only, the Postmaster was A. Battersby. In 1900
E. Battersby took over the position £25 p.a. until 1923. Used time codes A & B.

1.9.98-S.O. 31.8.62      10      100

Sent 19.10.98
D2 (16.1.99)-(2.10.34)
Val x 4

D3 (27.10.35)-S.U. 31.8.62

UP2      -S.U.31.8.62

442

**St Juliens Continued**

**St. Juliens Post Office**

## St. Madeleine

Postal agency under San Fernando. Situated 2 miles east of San Fernando. The village took its name from a nearby sugar estate, which in time was named after the owner Marie Madelaine. In 1872 a sugar factory was built (Usine St. Madeleine) which was largely responsible for the development of the villages. On 8 February 1888 the office was transferred from the police station to Mr. Farfan's store. In 1899 the Postmaster was Pete Huggins £12.10s p.a. until 1916. For 1938 only, Miss V. Huggins took over the position. Used time codes A, B & C.

(26.5.76)-S.O. 31.8.62       **8**     **80**

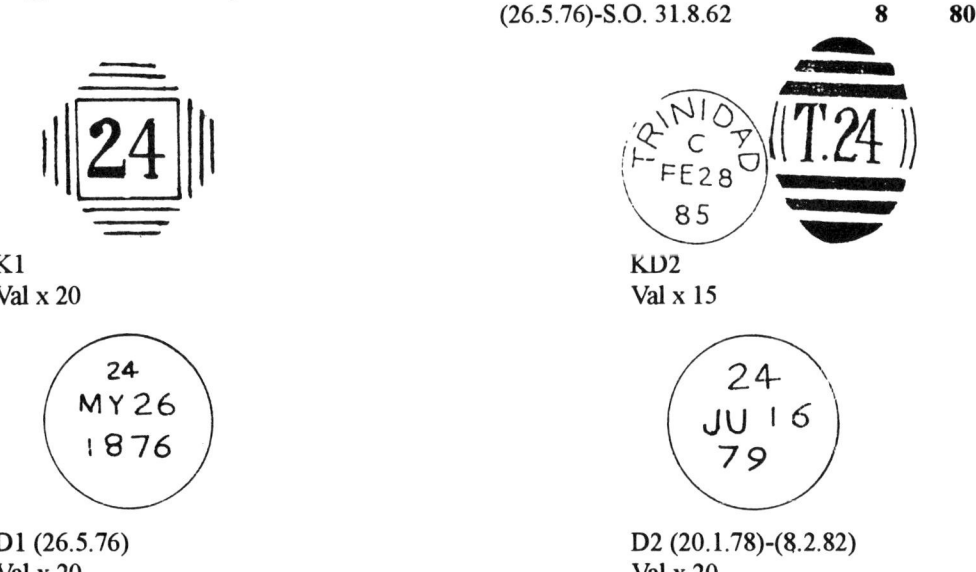

K1
Val x 20

KD2
Val x 15

D1 (26.5.76)
Val x 20

D2 (20.1.78)-(8.2.82)
Val x 20

D3 (14.5.87)-(22.1.30)
Val x 4

D5 (8.5.34)-S.U. 31.8.62

UP2

**St. Madeleine Post Office**

UNCLAIMED

I2 (31.8.53
Val x 3

**St. Mary's (St. Mary's Village Moruga)**
Postal agency under Princes Town. Situated 5 miles south west of Princes Town on the Moruga Road. In 1910 the Postmaster was J. L. Joseph £12.10s p.a. until 1911. For 1912 only, D. Williams took over the position £12.10s p.a. In 1913 E. Armour became Postmaster £12.10s p.a. until 1916.

(6.8.08)-S.O. 31.8.62          10      100

**St. Mary's (St. Mary's Village Moruga) Continued**

Sent 29.6.08
D2 (6.8.08)-(30.11.35)
Val x 4

D3 (15.5.36)-S.U. 31.8.62

**St Marys** before 1930 see Tacarigua

**St. Mary's Post Office**

**SAN FERNANDO** (Or. A Spanish mission was founded in 1680 which was renamed San Fernando de Naparima in 1784).

A receiving house for stamped letters only was opened at Hycorsbie & Co's Store, No. 2 Cipero Street on March 1860. On 1 April 1860 the office moved to 16 High Street. On 1 May 1818 the town was completely destroyed by fire. The railway to San Fernando was opened on 12 April 1882. The population at that time being over 6,000. John C. Lewis was postmaster from 6 September 1869 until W. E. Ross was appointed on 1 November 1909, on 1 January he was replaced by L. A. Vilain and on 17 July 1929 by John R. Rochford succeeded in turn by S. A. E. Ferreira, C. L. Gomez, G. A. Bobb and A. Hosein and on 14 July 1956 by G. Cumberbatch and then Miss R. Tree and S. Ishmael. A new office was built in 1885. Initially used time codes A, B & C later also D to G.

14.8.51-S.O. 31.8.62          2          5

## SAN FERNANDO Continued

K1  14.8.51(?)

K2 (9.10.51)-(26.12.51)

K3 (31.3.55)-(18.4.59)

K4 (23.4.60)-(22.11.67)

K5     -(5.3.83)

KD6 (6.2.82)-(21.4.85)

K7 (26.1.81)*-(10.3.97)

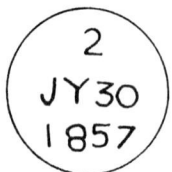

D2 (10.5.55)*-(30.7.57)

D3 (8.5.62)-(20.4.71)

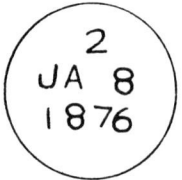

D4 (21.9.71)-(31.3.82)

D5 (5.5.85)-(5.3.96)
Known with codes A to C.

Sent 22.4.96
D6 (26.10.96)-(25.6.07)

Sent 14.12.98
D7 (5.1.07)-(17.12.29)
Known with codes A to D,
F & Y.

446

## SAN FERNANDO Continued

Sent 4.6.07
D9 (2.9.07)-(11.5.11)

D11 (29.3.11)-(7.10.24)

D12 (25.8.23)*-(19.9.29)
Known set possibly fortuitously
with codes A to K, M to O,
R, S, U, W, to Z.

D14 (27.12.24)-(17.6.38)

D15 (21.9.28)-(10.7.30)

D16 (17.6.30)-(31.11.30)
Val x 10

D15 & D16 known with time codes A to C.

D17 (6.12.30)-(3.1.50)
In 1949 being used in the
sorting office.

D18 (4.6.31)-(13.11.53)
In 1949 being used on the
counter.

D19 (28.7.38)-(12.10.53)
In 1949 being used in the
despatch office.

D20 (15.7.49)-(22.4.58)
Used in the parcel post section.

D21 (2.5.32)- (23.12.55)
In 1949 used by the cashier.

D23 (13.1.54)-(6.8.60)

To distinguish between the above datestamps easily, this sheet (or any other), may be ordered from
the Publisher printed on clear plastic for £1 each (subject unsold).

**San Fernando Post Office circa 1900**

Sent 5.11.59

D24 (17.9.54)-(22.5.62)    D25 (10.7.57)-(19.4.60)    D26

**SAN FERNANDO Continued**

HS1 (16.2.46)-(28.2.46)                     HS2 (16.2.41)-(28.2.46)

M1 State 1 (31.12.57)-(20.3.60)

M1 State 2 (10.3.59)-S.U.31.8.62

M1 State 3 (11.4.57)-(19.8.61)

SAVE FOR SECURITY WITH
THE POST OFFICE SAVING
BANK

M1 State 4 (22.5.57)-(20.10.57)

**San Fernando Post Office**

 POST EARLY FOR CHRISTMAS

M1 State 5 (7.12.57)-(17.12.57)

 POST EARLY FOR CHRISTMAS

M1 State 6 (27.11.57)-S.U.31.8.62

M1 State 8 (30.6.61)-(1.11.61)

M1 State 9 (7.2.62)-S.U.31.8.62

M1 State 10 (12.5.62)-(29.8.62)

R3 (16.1.12)-(19.11.46)

R5 (8.1.78)-(7.12.99)

Sent 3.11.03
R6

R8 (29.6.56-S.U. 31.8.62

## SAN FERNANDO Continued

PD4 (31.12.59)-S.U. 31.8.62

UP3 (25.6.18)-(3.4.51)

UP4 (26.9.55)-(25.2.56)

UP6

TOO-LATE

I4 (7.1.11)

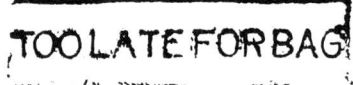

I6 (26.11.30)

CLEARED FROM
LETTER BOX

I9 (20.7.55)

REFUSED

I10

UNCLAIMED

I11

## SAN JUAN

Situated between Laventille and Tunapuna on the Eastern Main Road, county St. George. Established circa 1790. The railway arrived in 1876, in 1881 the population was 516, in 1946 nearly 6,500. In January 1889 moved from the police station to a new office. It moved again to a new building in December 1935. Became a money order office on 15 June 1915. In 1867 the postmaster was L. Eastman. In 1899 the Postmistress was Miss Eva Cockerton £25 p.a. until 1900. In 1901 Miss S. Reid took over the position £25 p.a. until 1902. In 1903 Miss A. Pinard became Postmistress until 1905. In 1906 Miss S. Reid retook over the position £25 p.a. until 1912. In 1913 Miss L. Agard and in 1914 Miss C. Reid both became Postmistresses for San Juan for one year only £25 p.a. In 1915 the Postmistress was Miss L. Greaves until 1919 (During 1918 Miss L. Greaves received a rise in salary to £40 p.a.). For 1920 only, Miss D. Archibald took over the position £40 p.a. In 1921 Miss L. Keith became Postmistress £40 p.a. until 1924. In 1925 Miss L. Keith received a rise in salary to £67.10s p.a. until 1932. From 16 May 1932, Miss P. de Lisle became Postmistress. On 1 November 1933 Miss R. Blakeley took over the position until 1938. In 1939 the Postmistress was Miss M. Cox until

1940. In 1941 Miss P. J. de Lisle took over the position until 1955. In 1956 A Merrin became Postmaster. In 1957 R. Hill-King took over the position for one year only. In 1958/59 Mrs A. B. Gonzales became Postmistress for San Juan. In 1960/61 Miss C. Cottle took over the position. Using time codes A, B & C.

14.8.51-S.O. 31.8.62 **3** **30**

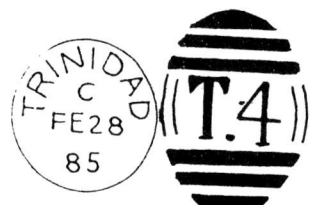

K1
In 1851 probably issued with
a mark similar to La Brea K1

K2

Val x 50

KD5

Val x 40

D4 (28.3.87)-(21.6.26)
Val x 10

D5 (30.7.27)-(1.2.29)
Val x 20

D6 (18.3.31)- (28.7.58)

**San Juan Post Office**

D7 (30.10.36)-(12.7.58)

D8 (12.12.56)-S.U. 31.8.62

D9 (21.12.56)-(18.10.58)

Sent 4.2.58
D10 (18.8.58)-S.U. 31.8.62

R2 (18.5.40)-(3.7.53)
Val x 2

UP2 (27.8.34)-(18.11.58)

UP3

I2 (24.3.51)-S.U. 31.8.62
Val x 3

**San Raphael** (Or. after the cocoa estate of the same name, originally called Tumpuna in 1903, it changed its name due to confusion with Tunapuna).
Opened at Mr. Borel's store when mails were exchanged on Monday, Wednesday and Satuarday with Port of Spain. On 1 February 1888 moved from Mr Borel's store to the house of Mr L. F. Oliver. Postal agency under Arima. Situated at the junction of the Cumuto and Tumpuna Road and Talparo Road. It became a money order office on 18 May 1900. For 1905 only, the Postmistress was Miss E. Cockerton. In 1906 Mrs R. E. Reid took over the position £25 p.a. until 1907. In 1908 Mrs B. Mootoo became Postmistress until 1912. In

1913 E. Beckwith took over the position £25 p.a. until 1919. In 1920 the Postmistress was Mrs W. Hermerlyn £25 p.a. until 1923. Used time codes A, B & C.

7.2.87-S.O. 31.8.62          **10     100**

D2 (1.7.90)-(21.6.06)
Val x 10

D3 (14.8.06)-(20.11.31)
Val x 3

D4 (13.12.33)-S.U. 31.8.62

R E C I S T F R E O

R1 (16.9.98)

U N C L A I M F O

I2

**San Raphael Post Office**

455

**SANGRE GRANDE** (Or. Spanish for Big Blood river for the largest of two tributaries of the Oropouche River, having reddish water).

The railway arrived in 1897 at Cunapo two miles away from Sangre Grande village. The station however was called Sangre Grande and officially became so! On 2 May 1897 moved from the rest house to a new office opposite the railway station. Situated in county St. Andrew on the Eastern Main Road. Became a Money Order Office on 1 February 1899. In 1921 the population was 1,999, in 1946, 3,762, in 1960, 5,147. In 1899 the Postmistress was Mrs B. J. Laing £25 p.a. until 1902. For 1903 only, I. E. Roberts took over the position £40 p.a. In 1904 Miss M. Stanford became Postmistress until 1906. In 1907 Miss E. Cockerton took over the position until 1908. In 1909 Mrs. E. Austin became Postmistress £80 p.a. until 1910. In 1911 the Postmistress was Miss A. Archibald until 1914. In 1915 Miss E. Furlonge took over the position £80 p.a. until 1919. In 1920 Miss M. Paredas became Postmistress for Sangre Grande Post Office £80 p.a. until 1950. In 1951 Miss E. Miranda took over the position until 1957. During 1958/59, R. Hill-King became Postmaster. Used time codes A, B & C. Post office opened at the house at Mr. James Murray Williams.

1.11.91-S.O. 31.8.62          2          20

D2 (7.11.93)-(11.6.06)

Val x 10

D3 (9.7.04)-(28.4.22)

Val x 8

D4 (11.8.06)-(30.4.31)
  & (22.1.36)

Val x 7

Sent 19.6.09
D5 (10.3.11)-(28.5.24)
  & (9.6.31)-(12.8.32)
Val x 15

D6 (25.4.33)

D7 (20.3.34)-S.U. 31.8.62

D8 (30.1.35)-S.U. 31.8.62

D9 (6.10.37)-(10.12.57)

To distinguish between the above datestamps easily, this sheet (or any other), may be ordered from the Publisher printed on clear plastic for £1 each (subject unsold).

Sent 29.9.06
R2

R3 (24.6.22)-(28.12.55)

Sent 29.9.06
UP2 (13.7.15)

UP3 (12.10.16)-S.U. 31.8.62

I4

UNCLAIMED

I5 (24.10.56)

**Sangre Grande Post Office**

**Sangre Grande-Oropouche Road (S. Gde. Oropouche Road)**
Postal agency under Sangre Grande, situated south east of the town.

1.7.61-S.O. 31.8.62                                   **N.S.**

Sent 28.11.61                          Sent 28.11.61
D2                                     D3

**Sangre Grande-Oropouche Road Post Office**

**Sans Souci** (Or. French "without care").
Postal agency under Sangre Grande being situated 3 miles east. In 1914 the Postmaster was
C. Mulcare £25 p.a. until 1916. In 1917 J. Ottley took over the position (Sub-Postmaster)
£25 p.a. until 1923.

(13.3.13)-S.O. 31.8.62                    **10        100**

                                                     Sent 6.5.59
D2 (4.3.13)-(7.1.29)    D4 (31.12.35)-(7.12.59)    D5 (8.2.60)-S.U. 31.8.62
Val x 4

458

**Sans Souci Continued**

R2

UP2

UNCLAIMED

I2

**Sans Souci Post Office**

**Santa Cruz** (Or. Village named after the church Santa Cruz de Buena Vista or Holy cross of the beautiful view).

On 30 April 1888 moved from the police station to the house of Mr. Layne (new Mr. Silverster's store). From that date the delivery of letter by Letter Carrier extended only as far as the Pillar Box opposite the residence of Carl De Verteuil Esq. The box being cleared daily (Sunday and Holidays excepted) at 11.30 a.m., residents beyond the Pillar Box instructed their messengers to meet the Letter Carrier at the Pillar Box between 11 and 11.30a.m. The letter Carrier was provided with stamps, and letters for dispatch could be handed to him. Two dispatches of mail daily from the Santa Cruz Post Office, viz., at 8 a.m. and 3.45p.m. Inward mails reaching the Post Office, Santa Cruz, at 9.30a.m., and 5p.m. Postal agency under San Juan. Situated 5 miles north. In 1867 the postmaster was G. Durham. In 1899 the Postmaster was J. Wilson £15 p.a. until 1916.

14.8.51-S.O. 31.8.62         **10**     **100**

K1              K2             K3
In 1851 probably issued with              Used at Todds Road by
a mark similar to La Brea K1             1905.

K4                         KD5

D5 (14.3.88)-(12.11.24)     D6 (6.10.26)-(20.7.35)     D7 (15.10.38)-S.U. 31.8.62
Using time codes A, B & C.
Val x 4

RE GISTE RE D

R2 (15.7.49)

460

**Santa Cruz Continued**

UP2

**U N C L A I M E D**

I2 (15.7.59)

**SANTA FLORA** (Or. Village named after the church at "Holy Flowers").
Situated on the Fyzabad Beach Road, 10 miles from Siparia, county St. Patrick. During 1958/59 the
Postmistress was Mrs B. Jurawan.

1.6.52*-S.O. 31.8.62          **10      100**

D1 (14.6.52)-(29.12.52)*    D2 (17.1.53)*-(14.12.59)    D3 (28.12.59)-S.U. 31.8.62
Val x 200

**Santa Flora Post Office**

## SCARBOROUGH (Tobago)

Established by the Dutch in 1654 and called Lampsiusburg. Renamed Scarborough by 1765, later it became the capital of Tobago. Under French control (1802-1803). In July 1900 the Post Office, Tobago, was refitted. The delivery of letters at the counter for residents in Scarborough, was discontinued on the arrival of the English Mail, and three special Letter Carriers delivered all postal matter on that day. This has had the effect of expediting the delivery of letters and relieve the lobbies of the Public Building in which the Court House, Post Office, and Wardens Office were located from the crowds of people blocking the passages during the sorting of the Mails. On 5 July 1878, R. M. McEachnie appointed Postmaster, 21 June 1880 Samuel Ferdinand Titzck appointed Postmaster, by March 1887 A. L. Marshall was Postmaster, 19 July 1895 A. L. Marshall was suspended and J. E. C. Sealy appointed Acting Postmaster, later confirmed, all ref. Tobago Gazette. In 1932 G. H. Frith was postmaster.

The following were also postmasters at Scarborough Post Office:-

| | | | |
|---|---|---|---|
| 21 Jan 1765 | | Alexander Middleton | (also D.M.P.G. Grenada) |
| 17 May 1770 | | William Rustat | (also D.M.P.G. Grenada) |
| 23 Sep 1772 | | George Kikup | (Deputy) |
| 1793 | | Mr. Collins | |
| 1 Nov 1793 | | Charles Alfred Francklyn | (Deputy) |
| 16 Sep 1803 | | Henry Francklyn | (Deputy) |
| 5 Jan 1808 | | George Mackintosh | |
| 7 Mar 1810 | | John Buchanan | |
| 25 Jun 1816 | 14 Mar 1827 | Charles Alfred Francklyn | |
| 25 Mar 1827 | 9 Aug 1834 | Duncan McKellar | |
| 10 Nov 1834 | | Charles Isaac Le Plastrier | |
| 1 May 1860 | 25 Dec 1868 | Charles Isaac Le Plastrier | (Colonial) |
| | 5 Jun 1869 | James Hamilton | |
| 5 Jun 1869 | 1871 | Arthur Kennedy | |
| 13 Feb 1871 | 1878 | James Hamilton | |
| | 31 May 1886 | S. F. Titzck | |
| 2 Jun 1886 | | A. L. Marshall | |
| 19 Dec 1895 | | James Ernest Cameron Sealy | |
| | | William Hamilton Gamble | |
| 1 Apr 1913 | | Leonardo Joseph Sorzano | |
| 16 Oct 1917 | | P. Lechmere Guppy | |
| 1 Dec 1928 | | James Ernest Cameron Sealy | |
| 29 Dec 1931 | | Geoffrey Hammond Frith | |
| 26 Oct 1933 | | Joseph Paul Raymond De La Bastide | |
| | | Joseph Henri Maingot | |
| | | T. Cambridge | |
| | | George Kelvin Lee | |
| | | F. R. Punnette | |
| | | Mrs R. A. Stephenson | |
| 14 Jul 1956 | | J. N. Kalloo | |

| | | | |
|---|---|---|---|
| (1.8.1787)-(4.10.1800) | | - | **2,000** |
| (16.3.1805)-S.O. 31.8.62 | | **2** | **10** |

PS2 (1.8.1787)

PS3 (31.12.1794)-(28.7.1800)

Val x 1,000

PS4 (4.10.1800)-(7.10.1801)
   & (1.8.1804)-(16.3.1805)
Val x 1,000

PS5 (12.4.1805)*-(18.10.1818)
Val x 50

PS6 (9.11.18)-(25.4.35)
Val x 30

Sent 26.5.35
PS7 (7.10.35)-(5.1.46)
Val x 25

Sent 14.4.58
K1 (22.5.58)-(27.9.83)
N.B. Forgeries known, figure
four, different type.

Val x 200

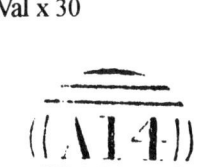

Sent 28.4.58
K2 (2.9.87)

K3 (2.11.92)-(8.12.95)
Used on inland post, route
1 mail (Scarborough to
Roxborough)
Val x 200

K4
Used on the inland post, route
2 mail (Scarborough to
Plymouth via Moriah).

K5
Used on inland post, route
3 (Scarborough to Shirvan
via Montgomery).
Val x 200

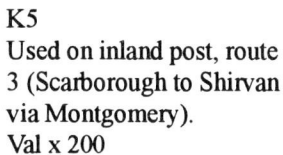

K6 (20.4.90)
Used to cancel stamps used
as postage dues.

Val x 5,000

K4 and K5 are tentative allocations for the inland post route 5 mail. The second inland post started on 16 May 1892. It is not certain whether the marks were applied to the mail when it arrived back in Scarborough or were applied by the Postman, who was equipped with a mark during his round and a waterproof letter pouch. Possibly the latter, as he probably was handed letters for delivery for villages en route. Presumably as A. 14 had been allocated previously to Scarborough, the Postmaster thought he should start a new series with this number.

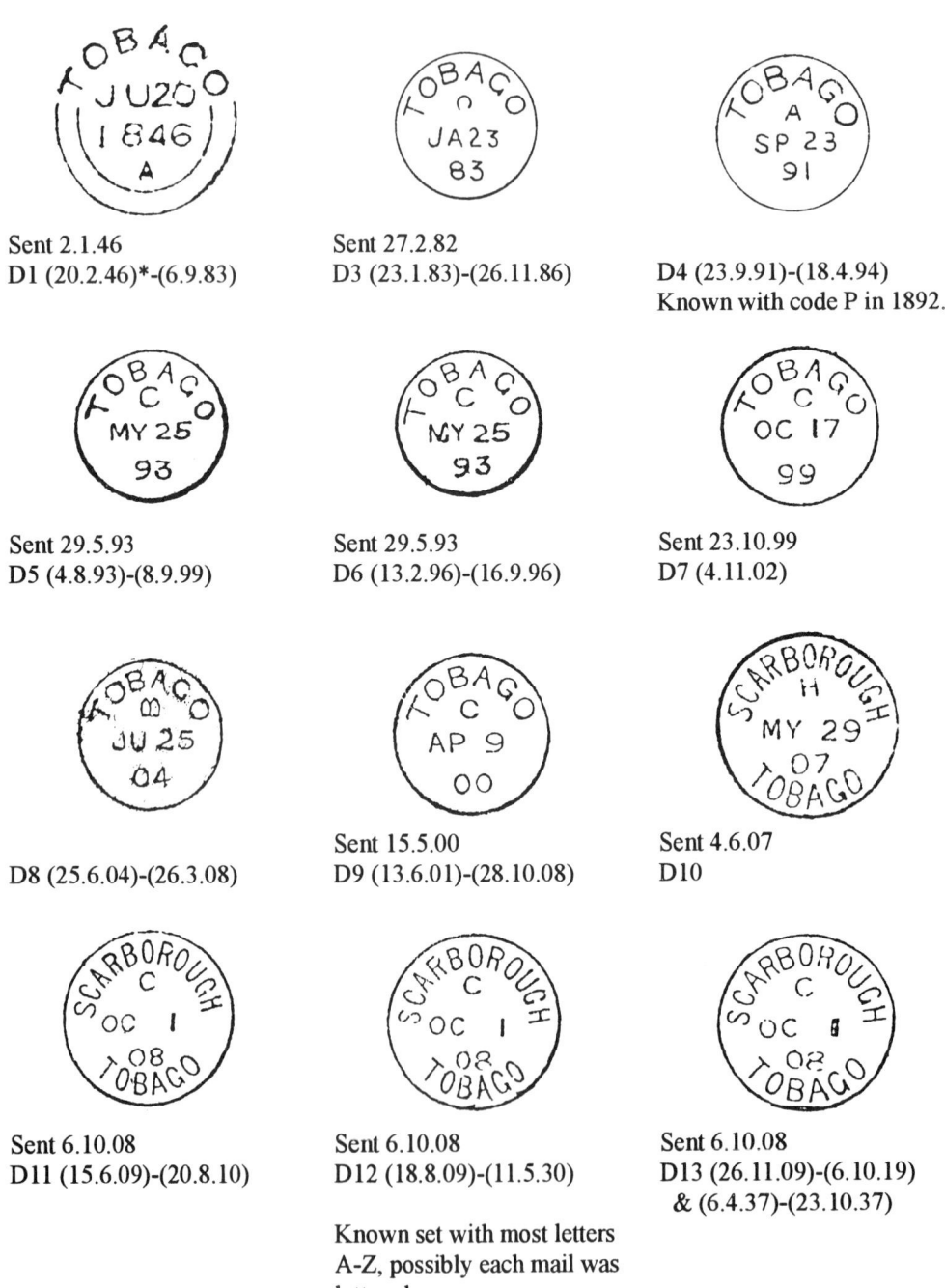

Sent 2.1.46
D1 (20.2.46)*-(6.9.83)

Sent 27.2.82
D3 (23.1.83)-(26.11.86)

D4 (23.9.91)-(18.4.94)
Known with code P in 1892.

Sent 29.5.93
D5 (4.8.93)-(8.9.99)

Sent 29.5.93
D6 (13.2.96)-(16.9.96)

Sent 23.10.99
D7 (4.11.02)

D8 (25.6.04)-(26.3.08)

Sent 15.5.00
D9 (13.6.01)-(28.10.08)

Sent 4.6.07
D10

Sent 6.10.08
D11 (15.6.09)-(20.8.10)

Sent 6.10.08
D12 (18.8.09)-(11.5.30)

Known set with most letters
A-Z, possibly each mail was
lettered.

Sent 6.10.08
D13 (26.11.09)-(6.10.19)
& (6.4.37)-(23.10.37)

To distinguish between the above datestamps easily, this sheet (or any other), may be ordered from the Publisher printed on clear plastic for £1 each (subject unsold).

## SCARBOROUGH (Tobago) Continued

D15 (10.1.24)-(17.9.39)

D16 (17.5.30)-(12.2.32)

D17 (13.10.31)-(11.6.59)
In 1949 used on the stamp
counter.

D18 (8.4.39)-(24.8.60)
In 1949 used on the money
order counter.

D19 (29.3.40)-S.U. 31.8.62
In 1949 used in the sorting
section.

D20 (22.11.48)-(14.7.49)
In 1949 used in the delivery
section.

D21 (14.7.49)-S.U. 31.8.62
In 1949 used by the cashier.

D22 (2.1.60)-S.U.31.8.62

Sent 10.2.73
R2 (1.12.76)-(2.9.88)

R4 (5.7.89)-(10.3.47)

PP2 (13.2.90)-(13.2.96)

Sent 30.7.58
PP5 (17.12.59)

Sent 30.7.58
PP6

To distinguish between the above datestamps easily, this sheet (or any other), may be ordered from
the Publisher printed on clear plastic for £1 each (subject unsold).

## SCARBOROUGH (Tobago) Continued

Sent 31.10.51
PD1 (8.8.52)-(1.1.71)*

PD2 (8.2.74)-(7.8.78)

UP1 (23.12.96)

UP2 (21.11.13)

UP3 (7.3.53)-(11.4.61)

MISSENT TO TOBAGO

Sent 27.2.82
I2

TOO LATE FOR BAG

Sent 27.2.82
I3 (1887)

**Scarborough Post Office**

UNCLAIMED

I6 (31.7.48)

UNCLAIMED

I7 (1.4.57)

# RETOUR

I10 (1.4.57)

## TOBAGO
## SHIP LETTER

Sent 27.8.1841
SL3 (4.5.05)-(1.1.39)

**SIPARIA**
Established circa 1758 was a Mission by Spanish Capuchin priest. On 14 November 1913 the railway from San Fernando was opened. The population at this time was nearly 4,000 recording 5,000 or more by 1962. Situated in county St. Patrick on the High Street. A receiving office was opened in the year ending 31 March 1904. On 17 August 1914 it became a Money Order Office. In 1904 the Postmaster was J. Alexander £7.10s p.a. until 1914 (During 1910, J. Alexander gained a rise in salary to £25 p.a.). In 1915 Miss C. Reid took over the position with a rise in salary to £40 p.a. until 1918. For 1919 only, Miss I. Noguera became Postmistress £40 p.a. In 1920 Miss M. Furlonge took over the position £40 p.a. until 1922. In 1923 Miss N. Donawa became Postmistress for Siparia for one year only. In 1924 Miss E. White took over the position £66.6s p.a. until 1954. In 1955 the Postmistress was Miss A. Ceoline until 1958/59. Using time codes A, B & C.

(11.10.06)-S.O. 31.8.62          2      20

Sent 4.6.07
D2 (8.6.08)-(7.2.36)        D3 (20.12.31)-(1.6.57)        D4 (16.11.37)-S.U. 31.8.62
Val x 8

**SIPARIA Continued**

Sent 25.11.57
D5 (19.3.58)-S.U. 31.8.62

D6 (7.12.59)
Val x 100

Sent 26.1.61
D7

R2 (18.8.19)-(25.2.59)
Val x 2

UP2 (21.4.25)-S.U. 31.8.62

**Siparia Post Office**

# UNCLAIMED

I2

**Siparia-Junction Road**
Postal agency under San Fernando.  Situated north of the town.
1.4.57-S.O. 31.8.62          **10     100**

D1 (24.4.57)-S.U. 31.8.62

**Siparia Junction Road Post Office**

## SPEYSIDE-Tobago

Situated in county St. John. In 1936 the Postmaster was C. Sandy until 1953. In 1954 (Miss) O. Gibbs took over the position until 1956. In 1957 Mrs C. O. Gibbes-Denoon became Postmistress until 1958/59.

| | | |
|---|---|---|
| (21.4.03)-(12.10.03) | 300 | - |
| (1.6.34)-S.O. 31.8.62 | 6 | 60 |

Sent 12.11.02
D2 (21.4.03)-(6.7.04)       D3 (1.6.34)-(28.6.34)       D4 (4.8.34)*-S.U. 31.8.62

**Speyside Post Office**

## TABAQUITE (Or. Amerindian)

Situated 2 miles south east of Brasso. The settlement started in the middle of cocoa estates which were planted in 1880s, a branch railway linking the town with the main line was completed 20 August 1898 at Jerningham Junction. Oil was discovered in 1911. Situated in county Caroni on Rio Claro Road. On 1 July 1919 it became a money order office. In 1900 the Postmaster was T. Gill £12.10s p.a. until 1908. In 1910 D. Blackman took over the position £12.10s p.a. until 1916. For 1918 only, Miss O. Keith became Postmistress with a rise in salary to £25 p.a. In 1919 Miss L. Keith took over the position until 1920 with a rise in salary to £40 p.a. In 1921 the Postmistress was Miss M. Branker until 1923. In 1924 Mrs M. Lopez took over the position until 1926. On 1 December 1926 Miss H. Winchester became Postmistress until 1931. In 1932 Mrs M. Andrews took over the position until 1944. In 1945 the Postmistress was (Miss) H. Anthony until 1954 (During this period of time (Miss) H. Anthony got married in 1949 and became Mrs H. Anthony-Winn). In 1955 (Miss) A. Guerin took over the position until 1956. In 1957 E. McIntosh became Postmaster for Tabaquite until 1958/59.

1.2.99*-S.O. 31.8.62       6     60

Sent 11.5.99
D2 (24.8.99)-(4.4.07)
Val x 6

Sent 4.6.07
D3 (3.9.07)-(27.11.26)
Val x 4

D4 (22.2.27)-(1.1.30)
Val x 10

**Tabaquite Post Office**

**TABAQUITE Continued**

D5 (9.7.31)-S.U. 31.8.62
Using time codes A to C.

D6 (20.1.40)-S.U. 31.8.62
& (2.12.37)

UP2 (15.11.13)
Val x 2

**TABLELAND**

Situated between New Grant and Fonrose, county Victoria on Naparima Mayaro Road. For 1910 only, the Postmaster was P. Blanchard £12.10s p.a. In 1911 H. Johnstone took over the position £12.10s p.a. until 1916. In 1920 J. N. Johnson became Sub-Postmaster with a rise in salary to £25 p.a. until 1923. In 1928 J. H. Johnson took over the position until 1929. In 1930 Miss L. Kelly then became Postmistress until 1932. On 1 November 1932 Miss I. Jordan Jordan took over the position until 1 April 1935, when the Postmistress was Miss G. Mitchell until 1950 (During this time Miss G. Mitchell got married in 1946 to become Mrs G. Mitchell-Lalla). In 1951 (Miss) M. Muural took over the position until 1953. In 1954 Miss R. Cleveland became Postmistress until 1956. In 1957 E. Nicholls took over the position until 1958/59.

(1909)*-S.O. 31.8.62                                  **8          80**

D2 (5.12.14)-(1.5.30)

Val x 4

D3 (18.5.30)*-(18.11.34)
& (2.12.37)-
Val x 6

D4 (15.2.35)-S.U. 31.8.62
Using time codes A & B.

D5 (20.12.39)-S.U.31.8.62

**TABLELAND Continued**

R2 (27.8.27)-S.U.31.8.62
Val x 2

UP2

UNCLAIMED

I2 (25.10.55)

**Tableland Post Office**

**TACARIGUA** (Originally St. Mary's renamed in 1923).

Situated in county St. George on the Eastern Main Road. A receiving house for stamped letters only was opened at the school house on 1 March 1860. From 1875 until (1880) the Postmistress was Miss MacDonald. For 1899 only, the Postmistress was Miss L. Brown. In 1900 Miss C. Reid took over the position £40 p.a. until 1913. In 1914 Miss K. Agard became Postmistress £40 p.a. until 1918. In 1919 Miss E. Keith took over the position £40 p.a. (Money Order Office) until 1931. In 1932 the Postmistress was Mrs E. Timothy until 1935. On 1 July 1935 Miss P. Dolabaille took over the position until 1947. In 1948 Miss R. Cleveland became Postmistress until 1953. In 1954 (Miss) M. Mural took over the position until 1958/59.

(1.6.67)-S.O. 31.8.62          8     80

K2 (24.5.70)          K3                    KD4 (27.11.82)-(1.12.86)
Previously used at                          Used later at Belmont
Chacachacare to (1861).                      (1891/2).
Val x 10                                     Val x 8

                      Sent 4.6.07
D3 (7.5.87)*-(12.4.06)    D4 (8.5.08)-(22.2.23)    D6 (3.10.23)-(12.12.35)
Val x 4                   Val x 4                  Val x 4

                                        Sent 25.11.57
D7 (14.2.36)*-(19.12.59)                D8 (23.12.59)-S.U. 31.8.62
Used time codes A, B & C.

RECISTERED

R2 (12.3.02)                             R3
Val x 2

UP2

UNCLAIMED

I2

**Tacarigua Post Office**

**Talparo (Talparro)** (Or. Amerindian).
Postal agency under Arima.  Situated 2 miles south of Brazil village, on Todds Road.

(1926)-S.O. 31.8.62       **10**    **100**

D2 (14.1.27)-(18.2.31)                   D3 (2.2.36)-S.U. 31.8.62
Val x 6                                  Used time codes A & B.

**Talparo (Talparro) Continued**

UP1 (18.2.31)                                    UP3
Val x 2

**Talparo Post Office**

**Tamana Four Roads** (Or. Tamana was an Amerindian tribal name).
Situated at the junction of Cumuto and Tamana roads, 4 miles south east of Talparo. Postal agency under Sangre Grande. From 5 May 1915, mails for Tamana Junction were sent from San Raphael on Mondays, Wednesdays and Fridays at 10 a.m.

|  |  |  |
|---|---|---|
| 5.5.15*-(cl by 1926?) |  | **N.S.** |
| (25.11.32)-S.O. 31.8.62 | **10** | **100** |

D3 (25.11.32)-S.U. 31.8.62

**Tamana Four Roads Continued**

R2

UP2

UNCLAIMED

I2

**Tamana Four Roads Post Office**

**Teteron Bay**
Situated between Chaguaramas and Carenage.

1.4.39-13.12.41                    **200**    -
The post office was closed on 13 December 1941 following the leasing of an area round the post office to the United States under the "Bases for destroyers" agreement. The whole of the Chaguaramas peninsula became U.S. controlled and a restricted area.

D2 (27.7.41)-(9.12..41)
Used time codes A & B.

**Timital** (Or. Timita Palm Tree).
Situated 5 miles south of San Fernando at the corner of San Francique and La Fortune Roads.
Postal agency under Penal.

2.7.51*-S.O. 31.8.62                    **10**    **100**

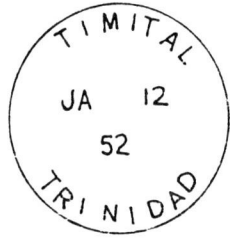

D1 (12.11.51)-(12.1.52)              D2 (7.1.53)*-S.U. 31.8.62
Val x 20

UP1 (14.8.56)
Val x 2

**TOCO** (Or. Amerindian name of plant).
Situated 3 miles east of Sans Souci, county St. David. Was the site of a short lived British settlement (1631-7) until they were expelled by the Dutch who in turn were evicted by the Spanish. It was a Port of Call on the Steam Service, started in 1818. The population remained at about 1,000. In 1888 the mail was closed at the G.P.O. every Monday at 3.45 p.m. and reached Toco 6 p.m. the next day. In the reverse direction it was closed at 6 p.m. every Wednesday reaching Port of Spain Friday morning. On 17 June 1901 it became a Money Order Office. In 1899 the Postmaster was Jas. Riley until 1900 when A. E. O'Riley took over for the remainder of that year (£40 p.a.). In 1901 P. R. Coker took over the position £40 p.a. until 1931 (During those years P. R. Coker gained two rises in salary. In 1916 it rose to £50 p.a. and in 1920 it went up again to £80 p.a.). From 1 April 1931 Miss A. B. Gonzalez became

Postmistress until 1935. On 1 April 1935 Miss L. Yates took over the position until 1943. From 1 October 1943 the Postmistress was Miss H. Winchester until 1 December 1948, Miss E. Miranda took over the position. On 1 January 1950 (Miss) M. Jones became Postmistress for Toco Post Office until 1956. In 1957 P. Bowen took over the position until 1958/59.

1869-S.O. 31.8.62          8     80

\* From (1861) operated as a joint office with Blanchisseuse

K2
Previously used at Turure.

K3

KD4 (15.2.87)

Val x 25

D2 (21.4.81)
Val x 15

D3 (7.11.87)-(3.2.98)
Val x 4

D4 (11.8.98)-(2.9.07)
Val x 4

**Toco Post Office**

**TOCO Continued**

Sent 4.6.07
D6 (4.10.07)-(9.5.31)*

Val x 3

D8 (22.12.31)-S.U. 31.8.62
Used time codes A, B & C.

Coastal Steamer, Toco. Trinidad. Nº 35

**TOCO Continued**

## REGISTERED

R2 (22.9.02)
Val x 2

UP2 (8.1.00)-S.U. 31.8.62
Val x 2

**Todd's Road**
Situated 1 mile north of Caparo. Postal agency under Tabaquite. Opened as a receiving office in the year ending 31 March 1904. In 1906 the Postmaster was J. Glasgow £12.10s p.a. until 1909. In 1910 E. B. Huggins took over the position £12.10s p.a. until 1917. In 1918 Miss C. Smith (Ag) became Postmistress £25 p.a. until 1921. In 1922 Miss C. Thompson took over the position until 1925. Initially used time codes A & B, later A, B & C.

                                           (10.5.05)-S.O. 31.8.62            **10**     **100**

K2 (10.5.05)

Sent 1.6.05
D2 (26.7.05)-(30.4.25)          D3 (11.6.35)-(2.5.38)          D4 (9.3.40)-S.U. 31.8.62
Val x 4                        Val x 6

R2

**Todd's Road Continued**

**Todd's Road Post Office**

UP2

UP3     -S.U.31.8.60

# UNCLAIMED

Sent 1.6.05
I2        -S.U. 31.8.62

**Tortuga** (Or. Spanish from Las Tortugas after the tortoises which roamed the area).
Founded in 1867.  Postal agency under Couva.  Situated 3 miles east of Claxton Bay, in the
Government buildings.  For 1899 only, the Postmistress was Miss Mary Green.  In 1900 Miss
A. Archibald also took over the position for one year only.  In 1901 Mrs C. Giles became
Postmistress £25 p.a. until 1920.  For 1921 only, Mrs A. Nurse took over the position.  In
1922 Miss W. Thomas became Postmistress until 1923.  Later used time codes A, B & C.
                        (7.4.87)*-S.O. 31.8.62              **10      100**

# Tortuga Post Office Continued

D2 (7.4.87)*-(4.5.11)

Val x 4

D3 (18.2.13)*-(31.5.39)
Known with codes A to E & N.
Val x 3

D4 (28.9.39)-S.U. 31.8.62

UP2

**Tortuga Post Office**

**Trou Macaque** (Or. Monkey hole).
Postal agency under Port of Spain, situated in the Laventille area.

1.9.58-S.O. 31.8.62      **15**     **150**

D1 1.9.58-S.U. 31.8.62

UP1

**Trou Macaque Post Office**

**Tumpuna** see **San Raphael**

484

**TUNAPUNA** (Or. Amerindian "on the river").

Founded in the late eighteenth century being centre of many sugar estates. The railway reached Streatham Lodge just south of the town on 31 August 1876. On 16 October 1878, mail for Tunapuna was forwarded to Streatham Lodge Station and a Post Office established there. In 1881 the population had grown to 3,948. On 31 January 1889 moved from the railway station to a new building. In 1931 6,838. Situated in county St. George on Railway Road. From 1878 to (1880) the Postmaster was J. Sorzano. In 1899 only, Miss L. Ovid was Postmistress £25 p.a. until 1902. In 1903 L. Codrington took over the position £40 p.a. until 1908. For 1909 only, Miss A. Laing became Postmistress £40 p.a. In 1910 Miss B. Hamilton took over the position £40 p.a. until l'914. On 1 October 1914 Miss L. Hamilton became Postmistress £40 p.a. until 1925. In 1926 Mrs B. Gooding took over the position until 1946. In 1947 the Postmistress was Miss A. B. Gonzalez until 1956. In 1957 A Merrin took over the position until 1958/59. Using time codes A, B & C. Upgraded to a money order office 18 May 1900.

16.10.78*-S.O. 31.8.62          2     20

| | | |
|---|---|---|
|  |  |  |
| K2 | K3 | KD4 (22.9.82)-(2.3.85) |

| | | |
|---|---|---|
|  |  |  |
| | | Sent 4.6.07 |
| D2 (5.4.81)-(3.3.82) | D3 (29.4.86)-(2.8.07) | D4 (9.8.07)-(24.9.30) |
| Val x 50 | Val x 15 | Val x 5 |

| | | |
|---|---|---|
|  |  |  |
| D5 (12.2.27)-(31.10.35) | D6 (31.3.31)-(19.12.59) | D7 (12.1.37)- (21.8.59) |
| Val x 10 | | |

D8 (10.9.59)-(16.9.59)
Val x 20

Sent 14.9.59
D9 (24.12.59)-S.U. 31.8.62

Sent 14.9.59
D10 (5.1.60)-S.U. 31.8.62

Sent 23.5.62
D11

**Tunapuna Post Office**

 R E C I S T E R E D

R2 (21.10.96)-(14.2.29)
Val x 3

R4 (21.8.50)-(24.1.57)
Val x 2

UP2 (17.2.38)-S.U. 31.8.62
Val x 3

UP3 (14.1.58)

U N C L A I M E D

I2 (5.7.17)-S.U. 31.8.62
Val x 5

**Turure**
Turure Settlement was formed in 1816, of disbanded soldiers from the First West India Regiment, along the banks of the Turure River (which joins the Oropouche River emptying into Matura Bay). In 1849 the lands of these settlers were surveyed and fifteen acres granted to each settler or his descendents.

6.8.51 - (25.3.61)<br>closed by 1867

**N.S.**

K1
Similar to K1 La Brea
Issued in 1851?

K2*
Used later at Toco.

\* Possibly not issued, or lost by August 1860 as an 1860 cover is known with manuscript paid 1d., the adhesive being affixed and cancelled at Arima.

## Upper Belmont Valley Road

Postal agency under Port of Spain. Reduced from a post office on 1 October 1960.

1.8.57-S.O. 31.8.62          **10**     **100**

D1 (2.8.57)-(17.6.58)
Val x 5

Sent 30.7.58
D2 (5.1.59)-(17.4.60)

Sent 30.7.58
D3

**Upper Belmont Valley Road Post Office**

## Upper Guaico

Postal agency under Sangre Grande. Situated 4 miles off the Eastern Main Road, North on the Guaico Tamana Road. A mail service, by foot messenger between Sangre Grande and Upper Guaico started on Thursday 1st May. The messenger performed three journeys in each direction each week:- From Upper Guaico, 9a.m., Tuesday, Thursday and Saturday. From Sangre Grande, 12 noon, Tuesday, Thursday and Saturday. Letters for Upper Guaico and district had to be addressed via Sangre Grande. In November 1951 the mail service to Guaico and Tamana was suspended due to the access road being damaged. Temporary mails being delivered to the Upper Guaico agency until the service resumed 3 December 1951.

1.5.02*-Closed by 1909*          **N.S.**
(3.3.14)-S.O. 31.8.62          **15**     **150**

*Not listed in October 1906.

**Upper Guaico Continued**

D3 (3.3.14)-(1.2.37)
Val x 5

D5 (8.2.38)-S.U. 31.8.62

**Upper Guaico Post Office**

## Upper Santa Cruz

In 1958 situated in Cantaro Village at the corner of Base and Mitchell streets, 1½ miles from La Pastoria. In 1926 reduced from a Post Office to a Postal Agency under San Juan. In 1910 the Postmaster was D. Lopez £12.10s p.a. until 1916.

1908*-S.O. 31.8.62          **10     100**

Sent 6.10.08
D2 (30.3.09)-(13.10.15)

Val x 5

Sent 29.6.09
D3 (7.3.33)-(6.7.37)

Val x 4

D4 (22.1.40)-S.U. 31.8.62
Used time codes A & C.

**Upper Santa Cruz Continued**

Sent 29.6.09
R1

Sent 29.6.09
UP1

UP2

I2 (7.2.56)-S.U.31.8.62

**Upper Santa Cruz Post Office**

## Valencia

Situated 5 miles east of Arima on Valencia Road.  Postal agency under Arima.  Using time codes A, B & C.

(11.8.32)-S.O. 31.8.62 **10** **100**

D2 (11.8.32)-(21.6.59)

Sent 25.11.57
D3 (4.1.60)-S.U. 31.8.62

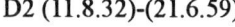

R2 (20.5.48)
Val x 2

UP2

**Valencia Post Office**

491

**Vance River**
Postal agency under La Brea.  Situated on the Southern Main Road between La Brea and Cochrane, Guapo.

1.12.61-S.O. 31.8.62

N.S.

Sent 18.9.61
D2

R1

UP1

Vance River Post Office

**Vance River Continued**

UNCLAIMED

I1

**Vega D'Oropouche**
Postal agency under Sangre Grande. Situated at the junction of Toco Main Road and Vega de Oropouche Road.

15.7.55-S.O. 31.8.62     **10**    **100**

D2 (30.4.56)-S.U. 31.8.62

**Vega D'Oropouche Post Office**

**T**

UP1

UNCLAIMED

I1

**Whitehall** see **Port of Spain-Whitehall.**

## WILLIAMSVILLE

Sub post office opened at the railway station, there being 3 mails daily in each direction.
Situated near San Fernando, county Victoria on the Guaracara Tabaquite Road. In 1899 the
Postmistress was Mrs A. V. Huggins £25 p.a. until 1911. In 1912 Miss I. Atkins took over
the position with a rise in salary to £40 p.a. until 1913. In 1914 Miss A. Carrington became
Sub-Postmistress (Money Order Office) £40 p.a. until 1930. In 1931 Miss M. Adams took
over the position until 1935. On 1 April 1935 Mrs I. Jordan became Postmistress until 1 April
1939 when Miss R. Blakeley took over the position until 1946. For 1947 only, the Postmistress was (Miss) R. Cleveland. In 1948 Miss E. Mc Lean took over the position until 1953.
In 1954 (Miss) R. James became Postmistress for Williamsville Post Office until 1955. In
1956 (Miss) A. Worrell took over the position until 1958/59. Using time codes A, B & C.

2.6.86-S.O. 31.8.62           6     60

D2 (7.4.87)-(8.7.07)*
Val x 5

Sent 4.6.07
D3 (8.10.07)*-(18.4.28)
Val x 4

**Williamsville Post Office**

WILLIAMSVILLE
18-1-30
TRINIDAD

D4 (18.1.30)
Val x 20

WILLIAMSVILLE
14JUL49
TRINIDAD

D5 (2.3.31)*-S.U. 31.8.62

R2 (18.9.31)-(20.4.53)
Val x 2

T

UP2

**WOODBROOK**

Situated in the Western District of Port of Spain, county St. George on Murray Street. In 1899 the Postmistress was Miss V. H. Graham £25 p.a. until 1901. In 1902 Mrs C. Phillips took over the position £25 p.a. until 1925. In 1926 Miss P. C. Noguera became Postmistress until 1933. In 1934 Miss P. De Lisle took over the position until 1940. In 1941 Miss D. Chittenden became Postmistress for Woodbrook Post Office until 1943. In 1944 Mrs E. Miranda took over the position until 1949. In 1950 Miss M. Edwards became Postmistress until 1953. In 1954 (Miss) A. E. Merrin took over the position until 1955. In 1956 the Postmistress was (Miss) V. E. Dickie until 1958/59. Using time codes A, B & C (later Daswell).

(31.12.90)-S.O. 31.8.62 **3** **30**

WOODBROOK
A
JU 23
96
TRINIDAD

D2 (31.12.90)-(2.11.05)*
& (1.11.26)-(11.12.31)
Val x 8

WOODBROOK
17 10 30

D3 (6.2.26)-(17.10.30)

Val x 20

**WOODBROOK Continued**

D4 (10.5.31)-S.U. 31.8.62

Sent 28.11.60
D5 (9.1.61)-S.U. 31.8.62

R2 (12.10.46)
Val x 2

**Woodbrook Post Office**

## 2nd Caledonia Road (Laventille East)

Postal agency under Port of Spain. Situated at the corner of 2nd Caledonia Road and Cipriani Avenue, near San Juan.

17.10.60-S.O. 31.8.62 **25** **250**

Sent 2.9.61
D2 (12.2.62)-S.U.31.8.62

R1

**2nd Caledonia Road Post Office**

**2nd Caledonia Road Continued**

UP1

UNCLAIMED

I1

# CHAPTER 6

## TRAVELLING POST OFFICES

### T.P.O. ARIMA SECTION
Used on the railway between Port of Spain and Arima. The line ran via San Juan, St. Joseph, Tunapuna, Tacarigua, Arouca and Dabadie, being completed on 31 August 1876.

1.1.99-29.4.99       500  -

Sent 8.2.99
D2 (23.3.99)*-(28.4.99)

The railway time table at about this time was:-

| DOWN. | | WEEK DAYS. | | | | | | | | SUNDAYS. | | | | | |
|---|---|---|---|---|---|---|---|---|---|---|---|---|---|---|---|
| Port-of-Spain —Departure... | ... | 7.10 A.M. | 8.30 A.M. | ... | 11.10 A.M. | 2.45 P.M. | ... | 4.00 P.M. | 5.19 P.M. | ... | 7.10 A.M. | 8.30 A.M. | ... | 4.00 P.M. | 5.19 P.M. |
| San Juan ,, | ... | 7.25 ,, | 8.44 ,, | ... | 11.25 ,, | 2.50 ,, | ... | 4.15 ,, | 5.33 ,, | ... | 7.25 ,, | 8.44 ,, | ... | 4.15 ,, | 5.33 ,, |
| St. Joseph ,, | ... | *7.34 ,, | *8.53 ,, | ... | *11.34 ,, | 3·07 ,, | ... | *4.24 ,, | *5.41 ,, | ... | *7.34 ,, | *8.53 ,, | ... | *4.24 ,, | *5.41 ,, |
| ARIMA LINE. { Tunapuna ,, | ... | ... | 8.59 ,, | ... | ... | 3.14 ,, | ... | ... | 5.48 ,, | ... | ... | 8.59 ,, | ... | ... | 5.48 ,, |
| Tacarigua ,, | ... | ... | 9.05 ,, | ... | ... | 3.20 ,, | ... | ... | 5.54 ,, | ... | ... | 9.05 ,, | ... | ... | 5.54 ,, |
| Arouca ,, | ... | ... | 9.11 ,, | ... | ... | 3.26 ,, | ... | ... | 6.00 ,, | ... | ... | 9.11 ,, | ... | ... | 6.00 ,, |
| Dabadie ,, | ... | ... | 9.19 ,, | ... | ... | 3.34 ,, | ... | ... | 6.08 ,, | ... | ... | 9.19 ,, | ... | ... | 6.08 ,, |
| Arima ,, | ... | ... | 9.25 ,, | ... | ... | 3.40 ,, | ... | ... | 6.14 ,, | ... | ... | 9.25 ,, | ... | ... | 6.14 ,, |
| Caroni ,, | ... | 7.47 ,, | ... | ... | 11.47 ,, | ... | ... | 4.37 ,, | ... | ... | 7.47 ,, | ... | ... | 4.37 ,, | ... |
| Cunupia ,, | ... | 7.59 ,, | ... | ... | 11.59 ,, | ... | ... | 4.49 ,, | ... | ... | 7.59 ,, | ... | ... | 4.49 ,, | ... |
| Chaguanas ,, | ... | 8.13 ,, | ... | ... | 12.13 P.M. | ... | ... | 5.03 ,, | ... | ... | 8.13 ,, | ... | ... | 5.03 ,, | ... |
| Carapichaima ,, | ... | 8.24 ,, | ... | ... | 12.24 ,, | ... | ... | 5.14 ,, | ... | ... | 8.24 ,, | ... | ... | 5.14 ,, | ... |
| Couva ,, | ... | 8.38 ,, | ... | ... | 12.35 ,, | ... | ... | 5.28 ,, | ... | ... | 8.38 ,, | ... | ... | 5.28 ,, | ... |
| California ,, | ... | 8.45 ,, | ... | ... | 12.45 ,, | ... | ... | 5.35 ,, | ... | ... | 8.45 ,, | ... | ... | 5.35 ,, | ... |
| Claxton Bay ,, | ... | 8.57 ,, | ... | ... | 12.57 ,, | ... | ... | 5.47 ,, | ... | ... | 8.57 ,, | ... | ... | 5.47 ,, | ... |
| GUARACARA LINE. { Princes Town ,, | 6.21 A.M. | ... | ... | 10.21 A.M. | ... | ... | 2.50 P.M. | ... | ... | 6.21 A.M. | ... | ... | 3.10 P.M. | ... | ... |
| Williamsville ,, | 6.41 ,, | ... | ... | 10.41 ,, | ... | ... | Pas. & Gds. | ... | ... | 6.41 ,, | ... | ... | 3.30 ,, | ... | ... |
| Union ,, | 7.06 ,, | ... | ... | 11.06 ,, | ... | ... | ... | ... | ... | 7.06 ,, | ... | ... | 3.55 ,, | ... | ... |
| Marabella Junction ,, | †... | †... | ... | †... | †... | ... | †... | ... | ... | †... | †... | ... | †... | †... | ... |
| San Fernando — Arrival... | 7.17 ,, | 9.18 ,, | ... | 11.17 ,, | 1.18 ,, | ... | 6.08 ,, | ... | ... | 7.17 ,, | 9.18 ,, | ... | 4.00 ,, | 6.08 ,, | ... |

| UP. | | WEEK DAYS. | | | | | | | | SUNDAYS. | | | | | |
|---|---|---|---|---|---|---|---|---|---|---|---|---|---|---|---|
| San Fernando —Departure... | ... | 7.06 A.M. | 9.07 A.M. | ... | 11.06 A.M. | 1.05 P.M. | ... | 3.55 P.M. | 5.57 P.M. | ... | 7.06 A.M. | 9.07 A.M. | ... | 3.55 P.M. | 5.57 P.M. |
| Marabella Junction ,, | ... | †... | †... | ... | †... | †... | ... | †... | †... | ... | †... | 9.19 ,, | ... | †... | 6.09 ,, |
| GUARACARA LINE. { Union ,, | ... | ... | 9.19 ,, | ... | ... | ... | ... | ... | 6.09 ,, | ... | ... | 9.19 ,, | ... | ... | 6.09 ,, |
| Williamsville ,, | ... | ... | 9.44 ,, | ... | ... | Pas. & Gds. | ... | ... | 6.34 ,, | ... | ... | 9.44 ,, | ... | ... | 6.31 ,, |
| Princes Town ,, | ... | ... | 10.03 ,, | ... | ... | for Guar'a. | ... | ... | 7.02 ,, | ... | ... | 10.03 ,, | ... | ... | 7.03 ,, |
| Claxton Bay ,, | ... | 7.29 ,, | ... | ... | 11.29 ,, | ... | ... | 4.18 ,, | ... | ... | 7.29 ,, | ... | ... | 4.18 ,, | ... |
| California ,, | ... | 7.41 ,, | ... | ... | 11.41 ,, | ... | ... | 4.30 ,, | ... | ... | 7.41 ,, | ... | ... | 4.30 ,, | ... |
| Couva ,, | ... | 7.48 ,, | ... | ... | 11.49 ,, | ... | ... | 4.37 ,, | ... | ... | 7.48 ,, | ... | ... | 4.37 ,, | ... |
| Carapichaima ,, | ... | 8.02 ,, | ... | ... | 12.02 P.M. | ... | ... | 4.51 ,, | ... | ... | 8.02 ,, | ... | ... | 4.51 ,, | ... |
| Chaguanas ,, | ... | 8.13 ,, | ... | ... | 12.13 ,, | ... | ... | 5.03 ,, | ... | ... | 8.13 ,, | ... | ... | 5.03 ,, | ... |
| Cunupia ,, | ... | 8.28 ,, | ... | ... | 12.28 ,, | ... | ... | 5.17 ,, | ... | ... | 8.28 ,, | ... | ... | 5.17 ,, | ... |
| Caroni ,, | ... | 8.39 ,, | ... | ... | 12.39 ,, | ... | ... | 5.28 ,, | ... | ... | 8.39 ,, | ... | ... | 5.28 ,, | ... |
| ARIMA LINE. { Arima ,, | 7.00 A.M. | ... | ... | 11.00 A.M. | ... | * | 3.50 P.M. | ... | ... | 7.00 A.M. | ... | ... | 3.50 P.M. | ... | ... |
| Dabadie ,, | 7.07 ,, | ... | ... | 11.07 ,, | ... | ... | 3.57 ,, | ... | ... | 7.07 ,, | ... | ... | 3.57 ,, | ... | ... |
| Arouca ,, | 7.15 ,, | ... | ... | 11.15 ,, | ... | ... | 4.05 ,, | ... | ... | 7.15 ,, | ... | ... | 4.05 ,, | ... | ... |
| Tacarigua ,, | 7.21 ,, | ... | ... | 11.21 ,, | ... | ... | 4.11 ,, | ... | ... | 7.21 ,, | ... | ... | 4.11 ,, | ... | ... |
| Tunapuna ,, | 7.27 ,, | ... | ... | 11.27 ,, | ... | ... | 4.17 ,, | ... | ... | 7.27 ,, | ... | ... | 4.17 ,, | ... | ... |
| St. Joseph ,, | *7.34 ,, | *8.52 ,, | ... | *11.34 ,, | 12.52 ,, | ... | *4.24 ,, | *5.41 ,, | ... | *7.34 ,, | *8.52 ,, | ... | *4.24 ,, | *5.41 ,, | ... |
| San Juan ,, | 7.43 ,, | 9.01 ,, | ... | 11.43 ,, | 1.01 ,, | ... | 4.33 ,, | 5.50 ,, | ... | 7.43 ,, | 9.01 ,, | ... | 4.33 ,, | 5.50 ,, | ... |
| Port-of-Spain — Arrival... | 7.55 ,, | 9.13 ,, | ... | 11.55 ,, | 1.13 ,, | ... | 4.45 ,, | 6.03 ,, | ... | 7.55 ,, | 9.13 ,, | ... | 4.45 ,, | 6.03 ,, | ... |

Trains marked thus * transfer Passengers at St. Joseph.    Trains marked thus † transfer Passengers at Marabella Junction.

On 26 October 1915 the following notice was published:-

*"Posting boxes have been fixed in all the 2nd Class brakevans of the passenger trains on the Trinidad Government Railways, are now ready for use, and late letters intended for the districts around and beyond Port-of-Spain, San Fernando, Princes Town, Sangre Grande and Rio Claro may be posted in the respective boxes of the brakevans assigned to those Districts to be collected for delivery on the arrival of the trains."*

*"The Public are particularly requested to enquire before posting which is the proper posting box to be used, and on no account should late letters intended to be posted be handed to the employees of the Railway, who are forbidden to receive them."*

### T.P.O. Cedros Line

On 1 October 1859 letter boxes were placed on the S.S. William Burnley (still in service 1868). These evidently were exchanged at each main port. In 1861 the report mentioned those in sevice as 1 at Port of Spain, 1 at Chaguanas, 2 at Couva, 1 at San Fernando, 1 at La Brea, and 1 at Cedros. In 1863 the S.S. Janet Tennant joined the service:- Port of Spain, Chaguanas, Couva, San Fernando, La Brea, Irois and Cedros. In 1871 the S.S. Alice was mentioned. In 1885 the service was twice weekly. The S.S. Alice was on the route from 1880 until it was replaced by S.S. Paria in June 1893 (Overhauled 1914).

The S.S. Iere and S.S. Paria shared two Routes - Cedros Route and the Monos Route until 4 September 1905 when the S.S. Naparima was put on the Cedros run. The Paria and Naparima then shared the Cedros Route and the Iere did the Monos Route and was later replaced by the S.S. St. Patrick.

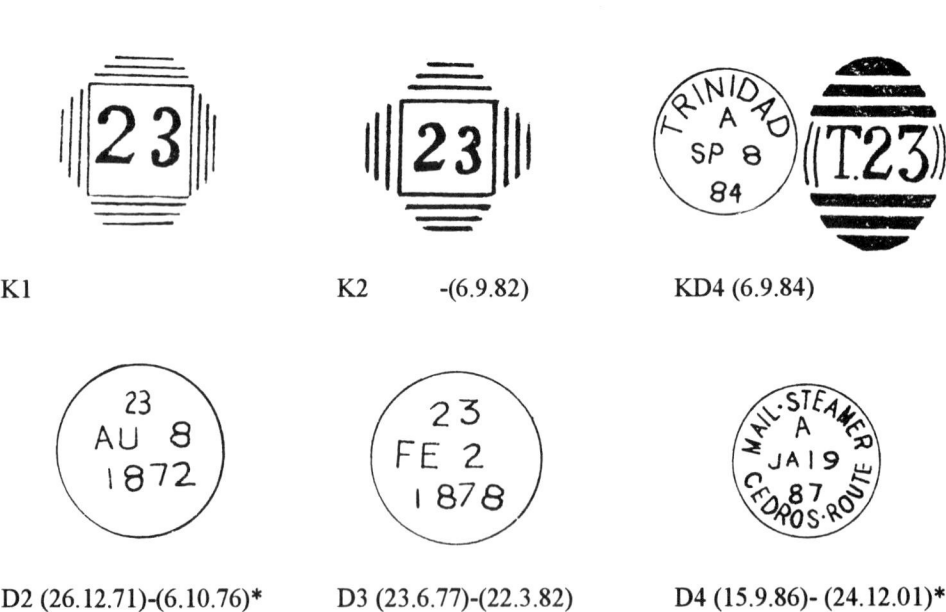

1.10.59-(13.5.22)                    **100    1000**

K1                          K2    -(6.9.82)         KD4 (6.9.84)

D2 (26.12.71)-(6.10.76)*    D3 (23.6.77)-(22.3.82)    D4 (15.9.86)- (24.12.01)*

500

**T.P.O. Cedros Line Continued**

D5 (16.8.05)-(4.7.06)
Probably used on S.S. Naparima, which came
into service in 1905. Later it was wrecked on
17 February 1926.

D6 (8.8.10)-(13.5.22)

**The S.S. Naparima.**

From 11 January 1886 the service was:-

*Mails will be closed at Port-of-Spain for Oropouche, La Brea, Cap-De-Ville, Irois Forest and Cedros,
as follows:-*

|  |  |
|---|---|
| *Monday ... ... ... ...* | *6.30 a.m.* |
| *Tuesday ... ... ... ...* | *3.30 p.m.* |
| *Saturday ... ... ... ...* | *6.30 a.m.* |

*The Mails in the reverse direction will be delivered in Port-of-Spain on Tuesday, Thursday, and
Sunday.*

On 12 June 1893 the service was listed as follows:-

### MAILS CLOSE

TUESDAY    ...   ...   ...    6.30 a.m. - For La Brea, Cap-de-Ville, Iros Forest and Cedros.
THURSDAY ...   ...   ...    6.30 a.m. - For La Brea, Cap-de-Ville, Iros Forest, Cedros and
Icacos.

*J. A. BULMER,*

The combined Cedros and Monos Services, known as Gulf Steamers from 31 July 1893.

Details being given in the following notice:-

*In addition to the places shown in the Time Tables the Steamers will stop off Pointe Gourde and off Grand Fond Bay, on the passages to and from Monos, to embark and dis-embark passengers, provided a boat is waiting.*

*The Steamers will also stop off Constance Estate, Icacos, for the same purpose and on the same condition.*

*Goods and Parcels for Stations between San Fernando and Cedros, will be received on board the Steamer at Port-of-Spain on Mondays between 1 and 3 p.m., and on Wednesdays on the arrival of the Steamer from Monos.*

*Arrangements are being made for running an extra Steamer from Port-of-Spain to Cedros and intermediate Stations, and back, leaving Port-of-Spain every Saturday at 6.40 a.m., and calling at all Stations going and returning as on Tuesday. Due notice will be given of the commencement of this service.*

### Timetable

Monday

| | | | |
|---|---|---|---|
| Leave | Port-of-Spain at | | 6.00 a.m. |
| Arrive | Monos | " | 7.20 a.m. |
| Leave | Monos | " | 7.30 a.m. |
| " | Gasprilla | " | 7.45 a.m. |
| " | Five Islands | " | 8.20 a.m. |
| " | Carenage | " | 8.35 a.m. |
| Arrive | Port-of-Spain at | | 9.20 a.m. |
| Leave | Port-of-Spain at | | 3.30 p.m. |
| " | Carenage | " | 4.15 p.m. |
| " | Five Islands | " | 4.30 p.m. |
| " | Gasparillo | " | 5.10 p.m. |
| Arrive | Monos | " | 5.20 p.m. |
| " | San Fernando | " | 8.20 p.m. |

Tuesday

| | | | |
|---|---|---|---|
| Leave | San Fernando at | | 9.25 a.m. |
| " | La Brea | " | 10.30 a.m. |
| " | Cap-de-Ville | " | 11.15 a.m. |
| " | Irois Forest | " | 11.35 a.m. |
| Arrive | Cedros | " | 12.25 p.m. |

Thursday

| | | | |
|---|---|---|---|
| Leave | San Fernando at | | 9.25 a.m. |
| " | Oropouche | " | 10.20 a.m. |
| " | La Brea | " | 10.50 a.m. |
| " | Cap-de-Ville | " | 11.40 a.m. |
| " | Irois Forest | " | 12.00 a.m. |
| " | Cedros | " | 1.00 p.m. |
| Arrive | Icacos | " | 1.40 p.m. |

Friday

| | | | |
|---|---|---|---|
| Leave | Icacos | at | 6.00 a.m. |
| " | Cedros | " | 7.00 a.m. |
| " | Irois Forest | " | 7.50 a.m |
| " | Cap-de-Ville | " | 8.10 a.m. |
| " | La Brea | " | 9.00 a.m. |
| " | Oropouche | " | 9.40 a.m. |
| Arrive | San Fernando at | | 10.30 a.m. |
| Leave | San Fernando at | | 12.00 a.m. |
| Arrive | Port-of-Spain at | | 2.30 p.m. |
| Leave | Port-of-Spain at | | 3.00 p.m. |
| " | Five Islands | " | 3.50 p.m. |

## Timetable

### Tuesday

| | | | |
|---|---|---|---|
| Leave | Cedros | " | 12.30 p.m. |
| " | Irois Forest | " | 1.20 p.m. |
| " | Cap-de-Ville | " | 1.40 p.m. |
| " | La Brea | " | 2.30 p.m. |
| Arrive | San Fernando at | | 3.40 p.m. |
| Leave | San Fernando at | | 4.00 p.m. |
| Arrive | Port-of-Spain at | | 6.30 p.m. |

### Friday

| | | | |
|---|---|---|---|
| " | Gasparillo | " | 4.20 p.m. |
| Arrive | Monos | " | 4.40 p.m. |
| Leave | Monos | " | 4.45 p.m. |
| " | Gasparillo | " | 5.00 p.m. |
| " | Five Islands | " | 5.30 p.m. |
| " | Carenage | " | 5.45 p.m. |
| Arrive | Port-of-Spain at | | 6.20 p.m. |

### Wednesday

| | | | |
|---|---|---|---|
| Leave | Port-of-Spain at | | 8.00 a.m. |
| " | Carenage | " | 8.50 a.m. |
| " | Five Islands | " | 9.10 a.m. |
| " | Gasparillo | " | 9.45 u.m. |
| " | Monos | " | 10.10 a.m. |
| Arrive | Chacachacare at | | 10.50 a.m. |
| Leave | Chacachacare at | | 3.30 p.m. |
| " | Monos | " | 4.10 p.m. |
| " | Gasparillo | " | 4.30 p.m. |
| " | Five Islands | " | 5.05 p.m. |
| " | Carenage | " | 5.20 p.m. |
| " | Port-of-Spain | " | 6.00 p.m. |
| Arrive | San Fernando at | | 9.00 p.m. |

### Saturday

| | | | |
|---|---|---|---|
| Leave | Port-of-Spain at | | 5.40 a.m. |
| " | Monos | " | 7.10 a.m. |
| " | Gasparillo | " | 7.30 a.m. |
| " | Five Islands | " | 8.00 a.m. |
| " | Carenage | " | 8.15 a.m. |
| Arrive | Port-of-Spain at | | 9.00 a.m. |
| Leave | Port-of-Spain at | | 1.30 p.m. |
| " | Carenage | " | 2.10 p.m. |
| " | Five Islands | " | 2.25 p.m. |
| " | Gasparillo | " | 2.45 p.m. |
| Arrive | Monos | " | 3.10 p.m. |
| Leave | Monos | " | 4.30 p.m. |
| " | Gasparillo | " | 5.00 p.m. |
| " | Five Islands | " | 5.25 p.m. |
| Arrive | Port-of-Spain at | | 6.00 p.m. |

From July 1895 the timetable was:-

## Timetable

### Monday

| | | | |
|---|---|---|---|
| Leave | Port-of-Spain at | | 6.00 a.m. |
| Arrive | Monos | " | 7.20 a.m. |
| Leave | Monos | " | 7.30 a.m. |
| " | Gasparillo | " | 7.45 a.m. |
| " | Five Islands | " | 8.15 a.m. |
| " | Carenage | " | 8.35 a.m. |
| Arrive | Port-of-Spain at | | 9.20 a.m. |
| Leave | Port-of-Spain at | | 3.00 p.m. |
| " | Carenage | " | 3.45 p.m. |
| " | Five Islands | " | 4.00 p.m. |
| " | Carenage | " | 4.30 p.m. |
| Arrive | Monos | " | 4.45 p.m. |
| Leave | Monos | " | 4.50 p.m. |
| " | Gasparillo | " | 5.00 p.m. |
| " | Five Islands | " | 5.30 p.m. |
| " | Carenage | " | 5.45 p.m. |
| Arrive | Port-of-Spain at | | 6.30 p.m. |

### Friday

| | | | |
|---|---|---|---|
| Leave | San Fernando at | | 6.30 a.m. |
| Arrive | Port-of-Spain at | | 9.00 a.m. |
| Leave | Port-of-Spain at | | 10.00 a.m. |
| " | Five Islands | " | 11.00 a.m. |
| Arrive | Port-of-Spain at | | 12.00 a.m. |
| Leave | Port-of-Spain at | | 1.00 p.m. |
| " | Five Islands | " | 1.50 p.m. |
| " | Gasparee | " | 2.20 p.m. |
| " | Monos | " | 2.45 p.m. |
| Arrive | Chacachacare at | | 3.30 p.m. |
| Leave | Chacachacare at | | 4.00 p.m. |
| " | Monos | " | 4.35 p.m. |
| " | Gasparee | " | 4.50 p.m. |
| " | Five Islands | " | 5.20 p.m. |
| " | Carenage | " | 5.40 p.m. |
| Arrive | Port-of-Spain at | | 6.20 p.m. |

|  | **Tuesday** |  |
|---|---|---|
| Leave | Port-of-Spain at | 6.40 a.m. |
| Arrive | San Fernando at | 9.10 a.m. |
| Leave | San Fernando at | *9.25 a.m. |
| " | La Brea " | 10.30 a.m. |
| " | Cap-de-Ville " | 11.10 a.m. |
| " | Irois Forest " | 11.25 a.m. |
| Arrive | Cedros " | 12.10 p.m. |
| Leave | Cedros " | 12.40 p.m. |
| " | Irois Forest " | 1.30 p.m. |
| " | Cap-de-Ville " | 1.50 p.m. |
| " | La Brea " | 2.40 p.m. |
| Arrive | San Fernando at | *3.50 p.m. |
| Leave | San Fernando at | 4.00 p.m. |
| Arrive | Port-of-Spain at | 6.30 p.m. |

|  | **Wednesday** |  |
|---|---|---|
| Leave | Port-of-Spain at | *8.15 a.m. |
| " | Carenage " | 8.55 a.m. |
| " | Five Islands " | 9.15 a.m. |
| " | Gasparillo " | 9.45 a.m. |
| " | Monos " | 10.15 a.m. |
| Arrive | Chacachacare at | 11.00 a.m. |
| Leave | Chacachacare at | 1.30 p.m. |
| " | Monos " | 2.10 p.m. |
| " | Gasparillo " | 2.30 p.m. |
| " | Five Islands " | 3.10 p.m. |
| " | Carenage " | 3.30 p.m. |
| Arrive | Port-of-Spain at | *4.20 p.m. |

|  | **Thursday** |  |
|---|---|---|
| Leave | Port-of-Spain at | 7.00 a.m. |
| " | San Fernando at | *9.30 a.m. |
| " | Oropouche " | 10.25 a.m. |
| " | La Brea " | 10.55 a.m. |
| " | Cap-de-Ville " | 11.40 a.m. |
| " | Irois Forest " | 12.00 a.m. |
| " | Cedros " | 12.50 p.m. |
| Arrive | Icacos " | 1.30 p.m. |
| Leave | Icacos " | 2.00 p.m. |
| " | Cedros " | 2.45 p.m. |
| " | Irois Forest " | 3.30 p.m. |
| " | Cap-de-Ville " | 3.50 p.m. |
| " | La Brea " | 4.40 p.m. |
| " | Oropouche " | 5.10 p.m. |
| Arrive | San Fernando at | 6.10 p.m. |

|  | **Saturday** |  |
|---|---|---|
|  | **Cedros Route** |  |
| Leave | Port-of-Spain at | 6.30 a.m. |
| " | San Fernando " | *9.25 a.m. |
| " | La Brea " | 10.30 a.m. |
| " | Cap-de-Ville " | 11.10 a.m. |
| " | Irois Forest " | 11.25 a.m. |
| Arrive | Cedros " | 12.10 p.m. |
| Leave | Cedros " | 12.40 p.m. |
| " | Irois Forest " | 1.30 p.m. |
| " | Cap-de-Ville " | 1.50 p.m. |
| " | La Brea " | 2.40 p.m. |
| Arrive | San Fernando at | *3.50 p.m. |
| Leave | San Fernando at | 4.00 p.m. |
| Arrive | Port-of-Spain at | 6.30 p.m. |

|  | **Saturday** |  |
|---|---|---|
|  | **Monos Route** |  |
| Leave | Port-of-Spain at | *8.15 a.m. |
| " | Carenage " | 8.55 a.m. |
| " | Five Islands " | 9.10 a.m. |
| " | Gasparee " | 9.30 a.m. |
| " | Monos " | 9.55 a.m. |
| " | Gasparee " | 10.25 a.m. |
| " | Five Islands " | 10.50 a.m. |
| " | Carenage " | 11.05 a.m. |
| Arrive | Port-of-Spain at | 11.45 a.m. |
| Leave | Port-of-Spain at | 1.00 p.m. |
| " | Five Islands " | 1.50 p.m. |
| " | Gasparee " | 2.10 p.m. |
| " | Monos " | 2.35 p.m. |
| Arrive | Chacachacare at | 3.15 p.m. |
| Leave | Chacachacare at | 3.30 p.m. |
| " | Monos " | 4.10 p.m. |
| " | Gasparee " | 4.30 p.m. |
| " | Five Islands " | 5.05 p.m. |
| Arrive | Port-of-Spain at | 6.00 p.m. |

*Steamers connect with the trains from and to Arima and San Fernando Lines. On Tuesdays and Saturdays, weather permitting, the steamer will connect with the Up afternoon train at San Fernando.

*From 6 July 1896 the timetable was:-*

### Monday

| | | |
|---|---|---|
| Leave | Port-of-Spain at | 5.00 a.m. |
| Arrive | Chacachacare at | 6.45 a.m. |
| Leave | Chacachacare at | 7.00 a.m. |
| " | Monos " | 7.40 a.m. |
| " | Gasparee " | 7.55 a.m. |
| " | Five Islands " | 8.25 a.m. |
| " | Carenage " | 8.45 a.m. |
| Arrive | Port-of-Spain at | 9.30 a.m. |
| Leave | Port of-Spain at | 2.00 p.m. |
| " | Carenage " | 2.45 p.m. |
| " | Five Islands " | 3.00 p.m. |
| " | Gasparillo " | 3.40 p.m. |
| " | Tetron's Bay " | 4.05 p.m. |
| Arrive | Monos " | 4.25 p.m. |
| Leave | Monos " | 4.30 p.m. |
| " | Gasparillo " | 4.55 p.m. |
| " | Five Islands " | 5.20 p.m. |
| Arrive | Port-of-Spain at | 6.00 p.m. |

### Tuesday

| | | |
|---|---|---|
| Leave | Port-of-Spain at | 7.00 a.m. |
| Arrive | San Fernando at | 9.30 a.m. |
| Leave | San Fernando at | 9.45 a.m. |
| " | La Brea " | 10.50 a.m. |
| " | Cap-de-Ville " | 11.30 a.m. |
| " | Irois Forest " | 11.55 a.m. |
| Arrive | Cedros " | 12.45 p.m. |
| Leave | Cedros " | 1.00 p.m. |
| " | Irois Forest " | 1.50 p.m. |
| " | Cap-de-Ville " | 2.10 p.m. |
| " | La Brea " | 3.00 p.m. |
| Arrive | San Fenando at | 4.10 p.m. |
| Leave | San Fernando at | 4.20 p.m. |
| Arrive | Port-of-Spain at | 7.00 p.m. |

### Wednesday

| | | |
|---|---|---|
| Leave | Port-of-Spain at | *8.15 a.m. |
| " | Carenage " | 8.55 a.m. |
| " | Five Islands " | 9.15 a.m. |
| " | Gasparillo " | 9.45 a.m. |
| " | Monos " | 10.15 a.m. |
| Arrive | Chacachacare at | 11.00 a.m. |
| Leave | Chacachacare at | 1.30 p.m. |
| " | Monos " | 2.10 p.m. |
| " | Gasparillo " | 2.30 p.m. |
| " | Five Islands " | 3.10 p.m. |
| " | Carenage " | 3.30 p.m. |

### Friday

| | | |
|---|---|---|
| Leave | Cedros at | 6.40 a.m. |
| " | Irois Forest " | 7.30 a.m. |
| " | Cap-de-Ville " | 7.50 a.m. |
| " | Brighton " | 8.30 a.m. |
| " | La Brea " | 8.40 a.m. |
| Arrive | San Fernando at | 10.00 a.m. |
| Leave | San Fernando at | 10.15 a.m. |
| Arrive | Port-of-Spain at | 1.00 p.m. |
| Leave | Port-of-Spain at | 2.00 p.m. |
| " | Five Islands " | 2.50 p.m. |
| " | Gasparillo " | 3.20 p.m. |
| " | Tetron's Bay " | 3.45 p.m. |
| Arrive | Monos " | 4.20 p.m. |
| Leave | Monos " | 4.35 p.m. |
| " | Gasparee " | 4.50 p.m. |
| " | Five Islands " | 5.20 p.m. |
| " | Carenage " | 5.40 p.m. |
| Arrive | Port-of-Spain at | 6.20 p.m. |

### Saturday
### Cedros Route

| | | |
|---|---|---|
| Leave | Port-of-Spain at | 7.00 a.m. |
| " | San Fernando " | 9.45 a.m. |
| " | La Brea " | 10.50. a.m. |
| " | Cap-de-Ville " | 11.30 a.m. |
| " | Irois Forest " | 11.55 a.m. |
| Arrive | Cedros " | 12.45 p.m. |
| Leave | Cedros " | 1.00 p.m. |
| " | Irois Forest " | 1.50 p.m. |
| " | Cap-de-Ville " | 2.10 p.m. |
| " | La Brea " | 3.00 p.m. |
| Arrive | San Fernando at | 4.10 p.m. |
| Leave | San Fernando at | 4.20 p.m. |
| Arrive | Port-of-Spain at | 7.00 p.m. |

### Saturday
### Monos Route

| | | |
|---|---|---|
| Leave | Port-of-Spain at | *8.15 a.m. |
| " | Carenage " | 8.55 a.m. |
| " | Five Islands " | 9.10 a.m. |
| " | Gasparee " | 9.30 a.m. |
| " | Monos " | 9.55 a.m. |
| " | Gasparee " | 10.25 a.m. |
| " | Five Islands " | 10.50 a.m. |
| " | Carenage " | 11.05 a.m. |
| Arrive | Port-of-Spain at | 11.45 a.m. |
| Leave | Port-of-Spain at | 1.00 p.m. |
| " | Five Islands " | 1.50 p.m. |

|  | **Wednesday** |  |  | **Saturday** |  |  |
|---|---|---|---|---|---|---|
| Arrive | Port-of-Spain at | *4.20 p.m. |  | **Monos Route** |  |  |

<table>
<tr><td colspan="3" align="center">Wednesday</td><td colspan="4" align="center">Saturday<br>Monos Route</td></tr>
<tr><td>Arrive</td><td>Port-of-Spain at</td><td>*4.20 p.m.</td><td>Leave</td><td>Gasparee</td><td>at</td><td>2.10 p.m.</td></tr>
<tr><td></td><td></td><td></td><td>"</td><td>Monos</td><td>"</td><td>2.35 p.m.</td></tr>
<tr><td colspan="3" align="center">Thursday</td><td>Arrive</td><td>Chacachacare at</td><td></td><td>3.15 p.m.</td></tr>
<tr><td>Leave</td><td>Port-of-Spain at</td><td>7.00 a.m.</td><td>Leave</td><td>Chacachacare at</td><td></td><td>3.30 p.m.</td></tr>
<tr><td>"</td><td>San Fernando "</td><td>*9.30 a.m.</td><td>"</td><td>Monos</td><td>"</td><td>4.10 p.m.</td></tr>
<tr><td>Leave</td><td>Oropouche "</td><td>10.25 a.m.</td><td>Leave</td><td>Gasparee</td><td>"</td><td>4.30 p.m.</td></tr>
<tr><td>"</td><td>La Brea "</td><td>10.55 a.m.</td><td>"</td><td>Five Islands</td><td>"</td><td>5.05 p.m.</td></tr>
<tr><td>"</td><td>Brighton "</td><td>11.10 a.m.</td><td>Arrive</td><td>Port-of-Spain at</td><td></td><td>6.00 p.m.</td></tr>
<tr><td>"</td><td>Cap-de-Ville "</td><td>noon</td><td></td><td></td><td></td><td></td></tr>
<tr><td>"</td><td>Irois Forest "</td><td>12.20 p.m.</td><td></td><td></td><td></td><td></td></tr>
<tr><td>"</td><td>Cedros "</td><td>1.20 p.m.</td><td></td><td></td><td></td><td></td></tr>
<tr><td>Arrive</td><td>Icacos "</td><td>2.00 p.m.</td><td></td><td></td><td></td><td></td></tr>
<tr><td>Leave</td><td>Icacos "</td><td>4.30 p.m.</td><td></td><td></td><td></td><td></td></tr>
<tr><td>Arrive</td><td>Cedros "</td><td>5.00 p.m.</td><td></td><td></td><td></td><td></td></tr>
</table>

*Steamers connect with the trains from and to Arima and San Fernando Lines. On Tuesdays and Saturdays, weather permitting, the steamer will connect with the Up afternoon Train at San Fernando.

## T.P.O.-MONOS LINE

In 1886 the service between Port of Spain, Carenage, Five Islands and Monos was four times a week. In 1886 the S.S. Ant was used on the Monos route. In June 1893 a new steamer the S.S. Iere arrived to replace the S.S. Ant. In 1912 the S.S. Iere was on the Monos route. (Taken out of service 1914) replaced by the S.S. Patrick.

(28.6.93)*-(24.10.21)                              **200**    -

D2 (28.6.93)*-(10.12.95)*                    D4 (17.10.17)-(24.10.21)

The time tables in 1892 being:-

*Wednesday.- Leave San Fernando at 9.30 a.m. for Cedros, calling at intermediate stations, and remaining at Cedros 45 minutes, then returning to Port-of-Spain, calling at all stations.*

*Friday.- Leave Port-of-Spain at 7 a.m. for Cedros, returning same day, calling at all stations.*

*The Government operates steamer services in the Gulf of Paria, as follows:-*

*(a) The southern service between Port-of-Spain and intermediate ports of call.*
*(b) The Islands and Bocas service between Port-of-Spain and the islands at the northern end of the Gulf, viz.: Five Islands, Gasparee, Teteron Bay, Monos, Huevos and Chacachacare.*

Each week a steamer leaves Port-of-Spain at 7 a.m. on Tuesday and Friday for Icacos, returning on the following day, and calling each way at San Fernando, La Brea (Brighton), Guapo, Point Fortin, Cap-de-ville, Irois Forrest, Granville and Cedros.

The steamer on the Islands and Bocas Service provides communications four times a week each way between Port-of-Spain and the islands.

From 11 January 1886 the service was:-

Carenage, Five Islands and Monos Mails will be closed at Port-of-Spain as folllows:-

| | |
|---|---|
| Monday ... ... ... ... | 1.30 p.m. |
| Wednesday ... ... ... ... | 7.30 a.m. |
| Friday ... ... ... ... | 2.30 p.m. |
| Saturday ... ... ... ... | 12.30 p.m. |

The Mails in the reverse direction will be delivered in Port-of-Spain on Tuesday, Thursday, Saturday and Sunday mornings.

In 1892:-

TIME TABLE—STEAMER "ANT."

MONDAY :

| | | | |
|---|---|---|---|
| LEAVE ...Port-of-Spain | at | 5 | A.M. |
| ,, ...Monos | ,, | 7 | ,, |
| ,, ...Gasparee | ,, | 7.45 | ,, |
| ,, ...Carreras | ,, | 8 | ,, |
| ,, ...Five Islands | ,, | 8.30 | ,, |
| ,, ...Carenage | ,, | 8.45 | ,, |
| ARRIVE Port-of-Spain | ,, | 9.30 | ,, |

| | | | |
|---|---|---|---|
| LEAVE ...Port-of-Spain | ,, | 2 | P.M. |
| ,, ...Carenage | ,, | 2.45 | ,, |
| ,, ...Five Islands | ,, | 3 | ,, |
| ,, ...Carreras | ,, | 3.30 | ,, |
| ,, ...Gasparee | ,, | 3.45 | ,, |
| ,, ...Monos | ,, | 4.30 | ,, |

THURSDAY :

| | | | |
|---|---|---|---|
| LEAVE ...Port-of-Spain | at | 8 | A.M. |
| ,, ...Carenage | ,, | 9 | ,, |
| ,, ...Five Islands | ,, | 9.30 | ,, |
| ,, ...Carreras | ,, | 10 | ,, |
| ,, ...Gasparee | ,, | 10.15 | ,, |
| ,, ...Monos | ,, | 11 | ,, |
| ARRIVE Chacachacare | ,, | 11.30 | ,, |

| | | | |
|---|---|---|---|
| LEAVE ...Chacachacare | ,, | 2.30 P.M |
| ,, ...Monos | ,, | 3 | ,, |
| ,, ...Gasparee | ,, | 3.45 | ,, |
| ,, ...Carreras | ,, | 4 | ,, |
| ,, ...Five Islands | ,, | 4.30 | ,, |
| ,, ...Carenage | ,, | 5 | ,, |
| ARRIVE Port-of-Spain | ,, | 6 | ,, |

SATURDAY.

| | | | |
|---|---|---|---|
| LEAVE ....Port-of-Spain | at | 5 | A.M. |
| ,, ...Monos | ,, | 7 | ,, |
| ,, ...Gasparee | ,, | 7.45 | ,, |
| ,, ...Carreras | ,, | 8 | ,, |
| ,, .. Five Islands | ,, | 8.30 | ,, |
| ,, ...Carenage | ,, | 8.45 | ,, |
| ARRIVE...Port-of-Spain | ,, | 9.30 | ,, |

| | | | |
|---|---|---|---|
| LEAVE ....Port-of-Spain | ,, | 1 | P.M. |
| ,, ...Carenage | ,, | 1.45 | ,, |
| ,, ...Five Islands | ,, | 2 | ,, |
| ,, ...Carreras | ,, | 2.30 | ,, |
| ,, ...Gasparee | ,, | 2.45 | ,, |
| ARRIVE...Monos | ,, | 3.30 | ,, |
| LEAVE ....Monos | ,, | 4 | ,, |
| ARRIVE...Port-of-Spain | ,, | 6 | ,, |

From June 1893 it was changed to:-

| | | |
|---|---|---|
| MONDAY .... .... .... | 3.00 p.m. | - For Carenage, Five Islands, Gasparilla and Monos. |
| WEDNESDAY .... .... | 7.30 p.m. | - For Carenage, Five Islands, Gasparilla, Monos and Chacachacare. |
| FRIDAY .... .... .... | 2.30 p.m. | - For Five Islands, Gasparilla, Monos and Chacachacare. |
| SATURDAY .... .... .... | 12.30 p.m. | - For Carenage, Five Islands, Gasparilla and Monos. |

## T.P.O.-COASTAL STEAMERS

(8.11.07)*-(22.7.13)          **200**   -

D2 (9.11.05)-(8.11.07)*          D3 (22.8.06)-(22.7.13)

As early as 1868 attempts were made to provide a coastal service. (hardly any roads, no railway). In 1874 the steamer Arthur provided a service. The First regular coastal service started on 6 October 1889 when S.S. Belair left on the Northern Route followed on 25 October 1889 by the S.S. Neptune on the Southern Route. In 1896 the S.S. Pioneer was carrying out the service but was wrecked in Tobago on 12 November 1897 and by 1898 the S.S. Manzanares was in service. On 18 March 1901, the contract started with the RMSP to carry out the service with the R.M.S. Kennet doing the service round Trinidad and the R.M.S. Spey round Tobago. The Coastal Steamer No. 1 and No. 2 cds were probably used on the Spey and Kennet.

The route etc in 1896 was published in the following notice:-

*The Southern Route shall be taken the week the Royal Mail arrives in Trinidad.*
*Time Table round the Island (Northern Route).*
*Leaves Port-of-Spain at 10 p.m., Wednesday, calling at -*

| | |
|---|---|
| Blanchisseuse | Manzanilla |
| Matelot | Mayaro |
| Toco | Galeota (Guayaguayare) |
| Tobago | Moruga |
| Saline (Matura) | Erin |

*Time Table round the Island (Southern Route).*
*Leaves Port-of-Spain 10 p.m., Wednesday, calling at -*

| | |
|---|---|
| Erin | Toco |
| Moruga | Tobago |
| Galiota (Guayaguayare) | Matelot |
| Mayaro | Blanchisseuse |
| Manzanilla | Port-of-Spain |
| Saline (Matura) | |

The five year contract with the Royal Mail Steam Packet Co which started on 10 February 1901 provided for steamers and included the following clauses.

*(a) A regular Steam Service round the Island of Trinidad of 42 weekly trips per year, going alternately by Northern and Southern routes.*
*(b) A regular Steam Service round the Island of Tobago of 42 weekly trips per year, going alternately by the Eastern and Western routes, proceeding to Port-of-Spain twice weekly and calling at Toco each way to and from Tobago once weekly, to connect with the service round Trinidad.*

*The Steamers to be employed in performing the services shall not be of less burthen than*
*(a) For the service round Trinidad. 500 tons gross register and shall steam at a rate of not less than nine knots per hour.*
*(b) For the service round Tobago, calling at Port-of-Spain and Toco, 300 tons gross register, and shall steam at a rate of not less than 9 Knots per hour.*

*Such Steamers shall be properly equipped and manned, and shall be subject to inspection by a qualified person to be appointed by the Government, whose recommendations "The Contractors" are to undertake to bind themselves to carry out if required by the Government. The Steamer shall be docked for cleaning and repairing at least twice a year.*

*The Service round the Islands, and to and from Tobago shall be according to the Time Table Schedule "C" attached to this agreement, in so far as dates and time of departures from Port-of-Spain and Scarborough are concerned.*

*All postal matter shall while on board be kept in a safe place under lock and key and shall be carried free, and duly taken from and delivered to the proper postal authorities at the ports visited by the steamers in Trinidad and Tobago under this agreement. Packages, plants and seeds from the Botanical Department shall also be conveyed free of charge.*

### SCHEDULE C
#### Time Table round Trinidad

| | |
|---|---|
| *Leaves Port-of-Spain at 10 p.m. calling at:-* | *Blanchisseuse* |
| | *Matelot* |
| | *Sans Souci* |
| | *Toco* |
| | *Saline (Matura)* |
| | *Manzanilla* |
| | *Mayaro* |
| | *Moruga* |
| | *Erin* |

*This route to be reversed on alternate weeks.*

### TOBAGO STEAM SERVICE
#### Proposed Time Table when Trinidad Steamer
#### proceeds Northwards.

*Leave Port-of-Spain 6 p.m. Wednesday.    (Takes English Mail).*
*Arrive Scarborough 6 a.m. Thursday.*
*Leave 2 p.m. Thursday.*
*Arrive Toco 6 p.m. Thursday.    (Connects with Trinidad Steamer).*
*Leave Toco 3 a.m. Friday.*
*Arrive Scarborough 7 a.m. Friday.*

## TOBAGO STEAM SERVICE
### Proposed Time Table when Trinidad Steamer
### proceeds Northwards.

*Proceeds round coast of Tobago and arrives at Scarborough Saturday at 6 p.m.*

*Leave Scarborough 10 p.m. Saturday.*
*Arrive Port-of-Spain 7 a.m. Sunday.*
*Leave Port-of-Spain 5 p.m. Monday.*
*Arrive Toco midnight.*
*Leave Toco 2 a.m. Tuesday.*
*Arrive Tobago 6 a.m. Tuesday.*
*Leave Tobago 6 p.m. Tuesday.    (Takes English Mail).*
*Arrive Port-of-Spain 6 a.m. Wednesday.*

### Proposed Time Table when Trinidad Steamer
### proceeds Southwards.

*Leave Port-of-Spain 6 p.m. Wednesday.*
*Arrive Scarborough 6 a.m. Thursday.*
*Proceed round coast of Tobago and arrive at Scarborough at 12 noon Saturday.*
*Leave Toco 8 p.m. Saturday.    (Connect with Trinidad Steamer).*
*Leave Toco midnight.*
*Arrive Port-of-Spain 6 a.m. Sunday.*
*Leave Port-of-Spain 5 p.m. Monday.*
*Arrive Toco 2 a.m. Tuesday.*
*Leave Toco 6 a.m. Tuesday.*
*Arrive Tobago 6 a.m. Tuesday.*
*Leave Tobago 6 p.m. Tuesday.*
*Arrive Port-of-Spain 6 a.m. Wednesday.*

### TIME TABLE ROUND TOBAGO
#### When Trinidad Steamer proceeds Northwards.

*Leave Scarborough 10 a.m. Friday.*
*Arrive Roxborough 1 p.m. Friday.*
*Leave Roxborough 4 p.m. Friday.*
*Arrive Man of War Bay 7 p.m. Friday.*
*Leave Man of War Bay 3 a.m. Saturday.*
*Arrive Plymouth 11 a.m. Saturday.*
*Leave Plymouth 2 p.m. Saturday.*
*Arrive Scarborough 6 p.m. Saturday.*

#### When Trinidad Steamer proceeds Southwards.

*Leave Scarborough 12 a.m. Thursday.*
*Arrive Plymouth 4 p.m. Thursday.*
*Leave Plymouth 8 a.m. Friday.*
*Arrive Man of War Bay noon Friday.*
*Leave Man of War Bay 2 p.m. Friday.*
*Arrive Roxborough 6 p.m. Friday.*
*Leave Roxborough 9 a.m. Saturday.*
*Arrive Scarborough 12 noon Saturday.*

*At the option of the Government, calling at such other Bays or stopping places around the coast of Tobago as may be found necessary and expedient.*

The Timetable for R.M.S. Kennet was:-

*The New Steam Coastal Service per R.M.S. "Kennet" will commence on Monday, 18 March 1901. The following is the revised Schedule of the Trinidad-Tobago Service viz:-*

### Inward English Mail Week - going South.

| Port | Arrival | Departure |
|------|---------|-----------|
| Port-of-Spain | - | Monday midnight. |
| Erin | Tuesday 6 a.m. | Tuesday 8 a.m. |
| Moruga | Tuesday 11 a.m. | Tuesday 1 p.m. |
| Mayaro | Tuesday 4 p.m. | Wednesday 4 a.m. |
| Manzanilla | Wednesday 6 a.m. | Wednesday 8 a.m. |
| Saline | Wednesday 10 a.m. | Wednesday noon. |
| Toco | Wednesday 2 p.m. | Wednesday 4 p.m. |
| Scarboro (Tobago) | Wednesday 6.30 p.m. | Thursday 8 a.m. |

### Connect with Inter-Colonial Mail Steamer from Trinidad.

| Port | Arrival | Departure |
|------|---------|-----------|
| Toco | Thursday 10 a.m. | Thursday 11 a.m. |
| San Souci | Thursday 11.30 a.m. | Thursday noon. |
| Matelot | Thursday 1 p.m. | Thursday 3 p.m. |
| Blanchisseuse | Thursday 4 p.m. | Thursday 6 p.m. |
| Port-of-Spain | Friday 6 a.m. | |

### Non-Mail Week - going South.

| Port | Arrival | Departure |
|------|---------|-----------|
| Port-of-Spain | - | Monday midnight. |
| Blanchisseuse | Tuesday 6 a.m. | Tuesday 8 a.m. |
| Matelot | Tuesday 9 a.m. | Tuesday 10 a.m. |
| San Souci | Tuesday 11 a.m. | Tuesday 1 p.m. |
| Toco | Tuesday 1.30 p.m. | Tuesday 3 p.m. |
| Scarboro (Tobago) | Tuesday 6 p.m. | Wednesday 8 a.m. |
| Toco | Wednesday 11 a.m. | Wednesday noon. |
| Saline | Wednesday 2 p.m. | Wednesday 3 p.m. |
| Manzanilla | Wednesday 4.30 p.m. | Thursday 4 a.m. |
| Mayaro | Thursday 6 a.m. | Thursday noon. |
| Moruga | Thursday 3 p.m. | Friday 4 a.m. |
| Erin | Friday 6 a.m. | Friday 8 a.m. |
| Port-of-Spain | Friday 4 p.m. | |

# BIBLIOGRAPHY

| | |
|---|---|
| Tobago Melancholy Isle Volume One.  Trinidad 1987. | R. D. Archibald |
| Tobago Melancholy Isle Volume Two.  Trinidad 1995 | R. D. Archibald |
| Tobago Melancholy Isle Volume Three. (In Manuscript). | R. D. Archibald |
| The Story of Trinidad.  Four Volumes (In Manuscript). | R. D. Archibald |
| A History of Modern Trinidad 1783 - 1962.  Jamaica 1981. | Bridget Brereton |
| The History of the West Indian Islands of Trinidad and Tobago. London 1961. | Gertrude Carmichael |
| The Mirror Almanack and General and Commercial Dictionary of Trinidad and Tobago.  1894 - 1916. | Gertrude Carmichael |
| Trinidad and Tobago Year Books 1897 - 1961. | Gertrude Carmichael |
| Trinidad Gazette | |
| London Illustrated News | |
| Graphic | |

## PHILATELIC

| | |
|---|---|
| The Philatelic History of Trinidad to 1862 | John B. Marriott F.R.P.S.L. |
| The Town Cancels of Trinidad and Tobago | E. F. Addiss |
| British Caribbean Philatelic Journal | |

# INDEX

# NOTES

# NOTES

# NOTES

# NOTES

# NOTES